REMAKING MODERNITY Politics, History, and Sociology

EDITED BY

JULIA ADAMS, ELISABETH S. CLEMENS, AND ANN SHOLA ORLOFF

DUKE UNIVERSITY PRESS   DURHAM AND LONDON 2005

© 2005 Duke University Press

All rights reserved

Printed in the United States of America on acid-free paper

Typeset in Minion by Keystone Typesetting, Inc.

Library of Congress Cataloging-in-Publication Data

appear on the last printed page of this book.

In memory of our friend,
ROGER V. GOULD

Contents

Acknowledgments

Many people, and some institutions, contributed to making this volume possible. Raphael Allen, our editor at Duke University Press who oversaw the Politics, History, and Culture series, was a tremendous source of support and constructive advice throughout what sometimes seemed like a very long process. We thank Erin Gould, Roger Gould's widow, for permitting us to publish Roger's essay, and Peter Bearman, Roger's literary executor, for graciously responding to our request for speedy completion of the editing. We are grateful to the *Archives Européennes de Sociologie* for permission to reprint a revised version of Rogers Brubaker's essay, which previously appeared there. We are also enormously appreciative of the help we got from Alan Czaplicki, Justin Faerber, Kari Hodges, Brady Muller, Pat Preston, and Kendra Schiffman, all of whom worked on disciplining aspects of the unruly text and bibliography. Our project was supported by the American Sociological Association/National Science Foundation Fund for the Advancement of the Discipline, which, along with the Weinberg College of Arts and Sciences and the Department of Sociology at Northwestern University, made possible the 2001 conference at which contributors presented their first drafts. The Department of Sociology at the University of Chicago and the International Institute of the University of Michigan provided generous subventions. Julia Adams also wishes to thank the American Council of Learned Societies and especially the Russell Sage Foundation, which provided a wonderful setting and practical support for work on the volume, including the final draft of the introduction. Ann Orloff is grateful to the Weinberg College of Arts and Sciences and the Department of Sociology at Northwestern University for supporting her research leave, during which she worked on revising her essay and the introduction.

We also owe thanks to those who read previous drafts of the introduction and generously offered responses. We were not able to address all the comments, but the essay is stronger because of the arguments they sparked. Our biggest thanks go to our fellow contributors and to Ivan Evans and Nicola Beisel, who participated in the conference organized around the volume but were not ultimately able to contribute essays. We are also grateful to those who responded in writing to an early version of the introduction: Andy Abbott, Gabi Abend, Raphael Allen, Ron Aminzade, Michael Burawoy, Craig Calhoun, Chas Camic, Geoff Eley, Ray Grew, Ira Katznelson, Meyer Kestenbaum, John Lie, Lyn Spillman, George Steinmetz, Art Stinchcombe, and two anonymous reviewers for Duke University Press. This early version was presented at the Sociology Department at Columbia University, Comparativist Day at UCLA, the European University Institute, and the Comparative and Historical Workshop at Northwestern University, and the essay benefited from those occasions as well. When the essay morphed into a Russell Sage Working Paper, we received helpful comments from Georgi Derluguian, Jack Goldstone, Heidi Gottfried, Alex Hicks, John Lie, James Mahoney, Jeff Manza, Steve Pfaff, Steve Pincus, Dietrich Rueschemeyer, Anne Showstack Sassoon, Robert Solow, Art Stinchcombe, Arland Thornton, Charles Tilly, and Viviana Zelizer.

The conversations and arguments we have had with these and other wonderful scholars have been intellectually delightful, as well as challenging and instructive—and testimony to the health and vibrancy of the field of historical sociology.

REMAKING MODERNITY

JULIA ADAMS, ELISABETH S. CLEMENS,
AND ANN SHOLA ORLOFF

Introduction: Social Theory, Modernity, and the
Three Waves of Historical Sociology

The spiral is a spiritualized circle. In the spiral form, the circle, uncoiled, unwound, has ceased
to be vicious; it has been set free.—Vladimir Nabokov

Sociology as a discipline is intimately entwined with modernity, both as
lived and as theorized. Sociologists have galvanized distinctive mechanisms
of social rationalization and technical regulation (not least statistics and
surveys) and authored ideas of the modern social space as a realm that we
denizens inhabit and control. Sociologists also have helped define modernity's significant Others, including the categories of tradition and post-
modernity. They have applied their intellectual energy to formulating what
might be called the "sociological modern": situating actors and institutions
in terms of these two categories, understanding the paths by which they
develop or change, and communicating these understandings to states, citizens, all manner of organizations, and social movements—as well as vast
armies of students. On this basis, sociologists have helped build and manage
today's sprawling, globally extended social edifice while simultaneously trying to diagnose and dismantle its disciplinary aspects and iron cages. The
discipline is itself a product of modernity, not simply in its institutions but
also, as we will argue, in its theoretical core.

The formation of modernity now figures as a place of disorder as well as
dynamism—troubled, fissured, perhaps even in civilizational crisis. This
is all the more ironic now that capitalism—surely a core constituent of
modernity—is thought by some to have arrived at a point of triumphant
stasis, the highest stage and culmination of history.[1] In this unsettled time,

1. See, for example, Fukuyama's (1993) neo-Hegelian meditation and Huntington (1996). Both books

the discipline of sociology finds itself in an interesting position. It is prey to heightened theoretical dispersion and home to a confused array of possible stances toward the place of the "modern" in ongoing global transitions, reconfigurations, and cataclysms. Many sociologists still embrace the familiar contrast between tradition and modernity and assume that a directional development from the former to the latter is under way.[2] They may celebrate or mourn the modernist rationalization and disenchantment of the social world against which romantic or neo-traditional energies are aimed and from which "we moderns" cannot turn back. Others, particularly of a more cultural studies bent, insist on the plasticity of all such distinctions or celebrate the viability of alternative modernities.[3] And so on. Yet what is often missing in the stew of sociological discussion, research, and political prescription is a sense of history as more than a vague preamble to the current moment.

Historical sociology is one place for reflection about theory in the broader discipline and its connections to other academic and intellectual formations and to the quandaries inherent in the "sociological modern" as it plays out in the social world. In part that is because historical sociologists have offered analyses and narratives of how people and societies became modern or not— what it was that changed in the series of "great transformations" and how these manifold processes are continuing to reshape the contemporary world (Polanyi 1957c [1944]). At times historical sociologists have done even more. "Doing justice to the reality of history is not a matter of noting the way in which the past provides a background to the present," as Philip Abrams eloquently put it; "it is a matter of treating what people do in the present as a struggle to create a future *out* of the past, of seeing the past not just as the womb of the present but the only raw material out of which the present can be constructed" (1982: 8).

---

have sparked much debate. For many in the human sciences, these worries have taken on fresh urgency in the wake of the terrorist attacks of September 11, 2001 (see Calhoun, Price, and Timmer, eds. 2002).

2. The stubborn persistence of modernization theory in demography and family sociology is critically discussed in Arland Thornton's (2001) presidential address to the Population Association of America. Roxborough finds modernization theory to be "alive and well" after a comeback in studies of development (1988: 753). These are but two of many possible examples. Wallerstein (1976), which begins with the words, "When a concept has died," was a tad premature. See also Bendix (1967). J. Alexander (1995a) analyzes the genealogy of modernization theory.

3. The notion that "modernity is not one, but many" is explored in Gaonkar "On Alternative Modernities," as well as the other essays in Gaonkar, ed. (2001). In historical sociology, Paul Gilroy's contribution to a vision of "alternative modernities" has been particularly influential, especially Gilroy (1993). See the section below on "World Systems, Post-Coloniality, and Remapping the World after the Second Wave."

In this introduction, we offer an archaeology and analysis of historical sociology as practiced by scholars in the United States. Reacting against the dominant ahistoricism of American sociology and to the dramatic political events of the 1960s, a number of sociologists both initiated a renaissance of historical research and reconstructed the discipline's theoretical canon as the foundation of their enterprise. These efforts, respectively, constituted the second and first waves of historical sociology. The second wave—with its tight framework of propositions and problems—generated both an impressive body of scholarship and a ramifying field of emendation and dissent. By tracing some of these diverse reactions—heightened attention to institutions, theorization of agents and signification, gendered analysis, and rejection of Eurocentrism—we identify sites of crystallization and momentum: promising swells but not yet a cresting third wave. What we find is a surprising convergence about historical process but a lack of consensus on theoretical frameworks, an openness that is both a virtue and a challenge. While one could just wait for the next dominant French philosopher to come along, this seems a poor strategy (Lamont 1987). Instead, we pursue lines of convergence across the dissents from the second wave's formulation of historical puzzles, themselves situated within second-wave readings of the sociological classics from a century ago. We must "remake modernity," by which we mean critique and reconstruct the modernist categories that have informed historical sociology to date. The past century has bequeathed contemporary historical sociologists new materials for making presents and thereby invites us to envision new pasts and possible futures.

it's also a very poor-authoritarian strategy, and one compatible with statism

Of History and Modernity

For much of its own history, sociological theory has evinced a deep concern for historical thinking. Attention to history has been tightly coupled to theoretical exploration as sociologists addressed the central questions of the discipline: How did societies come to be recognizably "modern"? How did selves come to be understood as individuated, coherently centered, and rationally acting human subjects? From Thomas Hobbes through Alexis de Tocqueville, Karl Marx, Emile Durkheim, Max Weber, Georg Simmel, and W. E. B. DuBois, various lines of theory developed as an effort to understand the processes by which social structures and social actors were created and transformed over the course of the transition from "traditional" or feudal societies to some distinctively modern social life.[4] How modernity was un-

*list
are
by
historical
sociology*

4. There are of course multiple lines of theory that can be identified in the sociological canon and multiple readings of theorists. And people change. The Durkheim of *The Division of Labor in Society*

I don't see how culture could be a factor of cohesion 4 the 3rd wave!

review and critique thesis...

derstood varied, of course: it might involve the rise of capitalism and class-structured actors, as in Marx; the formation of the disciplined bourgeois subject and his confinement in the iron cage of rationalized collective life, as in Weber; the twinned inventions of Enlightenment individualism and a new order of racial subordination, as in Du Bois; or still other broad evolutionary visions.[5] The proposed mechanisms of change were framed differently as well—in terms of political revolutions, the growth of the division of labor, colonialism and empire, pressures to manage the manifold anxieties of the self, opportunities for group cultural distinction, and so on. Yet within this diverse intellectual landscape, social theorists converged on a fundamentally historical project.

Sociological theory, however, has been marked by striking shifts in just how it has attended to history. As sociology was institutionalized in the twentieth century, particularly as it took shape in the United States, the historically informed theoretical vision gave way to more ahistorical models of social and cultural change.[6] If the sociologists of the first wave were obsessed with how their world (usually Europe) had become modern, many of their successors froze the distinction between tradition and modernity and concentrated their efforts almost exclusively on "modern society." Structural functionalism and other allied approaches invoked highly general and abstracted characteristics, processes, or sequences while claiming to explain change over time. These approaches paid little or no attention to the temporally bound logics of particular social and cultural configurations. Moreover, they lacked an emphasis on critical turning points and tended to assume that many constituent and possibly disjoint processes could be coherently collapsed or fused under one general and rather vague heading—"modernization." Ironically, these approaches either deployed the concepts of "modern," "modernity," and "modernization" in unreflective ways, with minimal explicit substantive content, or aligned the "modern" with a roster of associated static concepts.[7]

---

was closer to the stylized evolutionary models of Auguste Comte and Herbert Spencer than was the Durkheim of *Moral Education*, especially in his analysis of the reciprocal relationship between the modern state and the category of the individual.

5. While "modernism" generally designates an aesthetic movement, coined in 1890 by Nicaraguan poet Rubén Darío (P. Anderson 1998: 3), "modernity" is a messier congeries of categories with Wittgensteinian family resemblances. See below for further discussion of this point.

6. For the provenance of those ahistorical models, see George Steinmetz's essay in this volume.

7. See, for example, Parsons (1966). Parsons actually oscillated among different ways of melding history and sociology. In Parsons (1971: 139), for example, he is at times carefully historical in his claims, in what is a "directional" argument that explicitly seeks to update Weber. At other points the historical materials are awkwardly subordinated to an overly abstracted taxonomic impulse. See Zaret (1980).

By the 1970s and 1980s, these ahistorical approaches served as the foil for a resurgence of historical inquiry. Of course this arid, desert background is partly fictive. A certain reading of one master theorist, Talcott Parsons, came to stand for, to signify, a broader and more complicated intermediary epoch. Intellectual lineages are constructed out of many materials, including people's desire to claim forebears who will lend them academic credibility, the dynamics of disciplinary competition and collaboration, and authors' conscious and unconscious desires and identifications. We all interpret our predecessors, polishing some and vilifying others.[8] Nevertheless, we think the general point still stands. The mid-twentieth century the apex of presentism in U.S. sociology, as well as the moment of highest confidence in modernity.

Luckily, not all sociologists in the United States—and sociologists working in the United States were the most enthusiastically encamped in this presentist desert—were captured by modernization theory or its more sophisticated cousin, structural functionalism, even in their palmiest days. One immediately thinks of Barrington Moore Jr., Reinhard Bendix, Seymour Martin Lipset, or the early work of Charles Tilly, among others.[9] They were in dialogue with both like-minded scholars outside the United States and colleagues from more presentist persuasions.[10] Thus there were always a few engaged by fundamentally historical questions, particularly with respect to politics and political transformations. Their work nourished the next generation of historical sociologists—a "second wave" of the 1970s and 1980s[11]—

8. See J. C. Alexander and Sciortino (1996); Bloom (1997 [1973]); Camic (1992); Gieryn (1999); Latour and Woolgar (1986 [1979]). We may all stand "on the shoulders of giants" (Merton 1965), but it would be nice to have an occasional holiday from that lofty position. As Bloom noted, "Every forgotten precursor becomes a giant of the imagination. Total repression would be healthy, but only a god is capable of it" (1997 [1973]: 107). Too bad—it would save on footnotes.

9. See Lipset (1950, 1963); Moore (1966); C. Tilly (1964). Among his many writings, see, for example, Bendix (1964). Merton (1970) was originally published in Belgium in 1938.

10. In different ways, some of Lipset's work—as well as Bellah (1957b), Smelser (1959a), and Eisenstadt (1963)—attempted more or less successfully (opinion is still divided!) to bridge the perceived gap between the exigencies of doing justice to history and mapping structural-functionalist taxonomies. For a negative evaluation, consult M. Anderson (1971). Yet what is often forgotten is just how determinedly historical these works were in the context of prevailing sociological practice.

11. We are not the first to use the terminology of "waves" when describing the development of historical sociology. Dennis Smith (1991) discusses two (long) "waves" of historical sociology, the first comprising writers who now occupy the canon of the discipline (including Tocqueville, Marx, Durkheim, and Weber) and the second partially overlapping what we are calling the second wave. Smith divides the second wave into three "phases," encompassing the scholars who carried the torch of history in sociology during the ahistorical dominance of structural functionalism and those whom we identify as leading the resurgence of historical sociology in the late 1970s and 1980s; he also identifies a third phase ("partially overlapping" the second phase) that comprises scholars he sees as responding

and helped inspire programmatic calls for a return to historical inquiry.[12] The second wave was a "theory group" and a system of signs bound together by continuing engagement with questions inspired by Marxism.[13] It was also a social movement. (The sense of a movement was nourished both by interdisciplinary activity and by the spread of historical methods to a large number of core sociological topics and perhaps also by the influence of historians of, for example, the *Annales* school, who had earlier borrowed social scientific concepts and orientations.) This is not to say that everyone was then a Marxist but that even those who were not debated on largely Marxist terrain. Indeed, most of the best-known works of the comparative-historical renaissance of the 1970s and early 1980s—even those that did not explicitly embrace a Marxist theoretical stance—take off from puzzles within the Marxian tradition to which Marxism itself could not provide satisfactory answers. To resolve these puzzles, analysts had to draw on intuitions and concepts from other theoretical traditions.

Any such characterization necessarily simplifies along two lines. First, many of those who contributed to the consolidation of the initial resurgence of historical sociology have continued to grapple with the new intellectual currents that challenge contemporary work.[14] They have moved on after having created (and surfed) the second wave. For example, Charles Tilly

---

to the conservative political shifts of the 1980s and the decline of Marxism. We find it more useful to classify the latter two groups together, for they share theoretical and methodological proclivities that divide them from more recent scholars. Written in 1991, Smith's book could not have commented on more recent intellectual developments in historical sociology, such as the influence of rational choice theory or the cultural turns. Rather, his work describes the intellectual contributions of various key second-wave scholars. It does not address—as we do—the theoretical contradictions that helped to create challenges to this work. From the vantage point of 2003, the movement that was still young at Smith's writing has consolidated and begun to break up (as we discuss further below), producing rebellious intellectual progeny who may or may not come to share a single paradigm.

12. See, for example, Abrams (1982); Burke (1980); Grew (1980); Skocpol (1984a); Stinchcombe (1978); C. Tilly (1984, 1981).

13. We believe that the second wave was not primarily a generation of Young Turks engaged in the recurring ritual of overthrowing its academic predecessors (as, for example, Abbott [2001a: 23–25] wittily would have it), although surely Abbott is right to argue that the dynamic helped constitute it as an intellectual formation. He links this to a broader argument regarding the fractal patterns of sociological knowledge. See also Calhoun (1996: 306–307). The general concept of a "theory group" derives from Mullins (1973).

14. Most commentators on this era of scholarship underline the generational character of the movement. Yet age alone does not determine membership in any "wave." Senior scholars as well as precocious Ph.D.s in the making took part in the second wave resurgence, while we find among the *students* of the second wave "delayed" Ph.D.s (some of the contributors to the present volume included) who took time out from academia to participate in 1970s politics before completing their degrees. Thus someone's graduate school cohort might be one proxy for her or his "risk of participating" in various waves—but not a perfect one.

(1998a) has been engaged in the lively interdisciplinary work on social mechanisms; Theda Skocpol (1992) moved from revolutions to the emergence of the U.S. welfare state, in the process making a major contribution to the understanding of gendered politics and institutions; and Craig Calhoun (1995) has emerged as a leading voice of the cultural turn. The analytic contribution of a scholar in a field at one time does not exhaust her or his intellectual persona. Second, although the second wave was a broad, eclectic movement, sheltering a variety of actors who contributed to the resurgence of theoretically informed history in sociology and allied disciplines, it was quickly typecast in terms of some of its members and only some of their ideas. The canonical second wave was a system of signs as well as a movement of actors, and macroscopic, comparative scholars of revolution, state building, and class formation became the synecdochical representatives of the whole. Scholars associated with other vibrant subfields, notably historical demography, did not. Why should this have been so? First, the macro-political sociologists put forward programmatic statements and self-consciously forwarded historical approaches against the prevailing orthodoxy (see Abbott 2001b: ch. 4). Second, they had a well-defined theoretical agenda that put them in dialogue with thriving Marxist-inspired debates across history, anthropology, and to some extent political science. And third, let us not forget the *Zeitgeist* and the worldwide audience for radical politics and Marxist theory. Those who worked on key intellectual questions that intersected with that theoretical formation were most likely to be seen as central.

In what follows, we walk an analytic tightrope. We discuss the second wave in terms of its canonical version, which came to represent comparative historical sociology in the academic eye. But we will also insist that during the very period of this version's ascendancy in the 1970s and early 1980s, a number of historical sociologists were publishing important research that fell outside the hegemonic analytic framework. One might instance Andrew Abbott (1983), Charles Camic (1983), David Zaret (1985), and Viviana Zelizer (1979), among others. One of the nicer ironies of the present moment—reflected in many of the chapters that follow—resides in the ongoing rediscovery of some of the substantive contributions of these and other iconoclastic historical sociologists, some of whose work was marginalized during the moment of canonical second wave dominance, and some of which represented the leading wedge that helped shatter it.

As an emerging intellectual formation, then, second-wave historical sociology was defined by a shared set of commitments: a substantive interest in political economy centered on questions of class formation, industrialization, and revolution, along with a (usually implicit) utilitarian model of the actor. While motivating a forceful line of inquiry into the transformations associated with modernity, these core assumptions reproduced many of the exclusions and repressions of modernist social theory. Certain subjects—in the double sense of both topics and actors—tended to be marginalized or excluded: colonial peoples, women, and groups that we would now call people of color and gays or queers. The analytic dimensions of gender, sexuality, race, and nation were downplayed in parallel fashion. Moreover, culture, emotion, religion, the informal aspects of organization, and more were repressed by the powerful political-economic analytic framework undergirding the resurgence of historical sociology. And, in proper dialectic form, they returned. In the process, recent scholarship has greatly enriched historical sociology while shredding many of the core assumptions of second-wave scholarship.

Take, for example, the combination of structural determination and the utilitarian model of action that informs canonical second-wave analyses of the influence of economic position on political action. This double reductionism has been questioned as attention to culture and identity has unearthed the complex and contingent ways in which selves and discursive positions are formed. So what count as the key substantive elements of "structure" or psyche are analytically open and getting more open all the time.[15] The once robust combination of structural determination and comparative methods also is deeply contested. Thinking historically, it is increasingly acknowledged, undermines comparative strategies that isolate distinct events in an empty "experimental time."[16] Some see salvation for explanatory claims in terms of "mechanisms" that may be identified across diverse temporal and social settings.[17] Others pin their hopes on a more thoroughgoing reconstruction of sociology's own categories of analysis, now themselves under the historicizing microscope (Calhoun 1996: 306, 313). The latter approach owes something to post-structuralism and post-modernist critiques of Enlightenment universalism and the grand narratives of modern historical development, including those deployed by sociologists. Some sociologists have drawn on this post-modern repertoire to destabilize organiz-

15. We will have more to say about this below and about the vigorous rational-choice theoretic counter-attack, which replaces the implicit rational actor assumptions of earlier work with a much more explicit and sophisticated utilitarianism.

16. See, for example, Abbott (2001b); Burawoy (1980); McMichael (1990); Mahoney (1999); Roy (1987); Spillman (2002a).

17. McAdam, Tarrow, and Tilly offer one definition of "mechanism": "Mechanisms are a delimited class of events that alter relations among specified sets of elements in identical or closely similar ways over a variety of situations" (2001: 24). See also Hedström and Swedberg, eds. (1998); and Stinchcombe (1991). As a social science signifier, "mechanism" is fast becoming as messy and capacious as "modernity."

ing imageries of progress and modernity in productive ways. But because these organizing imageries are constitutive of our discipline, post-modernist and post-structuralist modes of thought are anathema to many sociologists, including the many historical sociologists who get twitchy when they see the very ideas of progressive social and cultural change being put into question. Thus a congeries of lively debates and oppositions—sometimes friendly, sometimes antagonistic—has replaced the relatively cohesive theory group that initially reestablished historical sociology in professional associations, streams of syllabi, and publications.

There is a great deal of legitimate uncertainty about what sort of claims can be made and sustained at this juncture. The open-endedness and fragmentation of the present academic moment evokes intellectual anxiety, overdetermined by recent epochal events. If, as Abrams argued, a fully historicized sociology explores the construction of futures out of pasts, recent events shift figure and ground in our understanding of trajectories of social change. The present problematizes the past in new and challenging ways. Yet we also see grounds for hope: a new intellectual openness associated with this unsettled moment, a willingness to forsake old antagonisms and to experiment with new ways of thinking sociologically and historically while drawing on the theoretical and analytical resources bequeathed by the sociological pioneers, our predecessors, and their critics. To this end, we gathered a diverse group of sociologists, first at a conference and then as contributors to this volume, to assess the accomplishments of the resurgence of historical inquiry and to peer into the future, delineating the challenges to come. We editors made certain choices among several possible strategies in assembling the group. All were students (or "grand-students") of contributors to the second wave; all shared an interest in politics. We chose to limit ourselves to sociologists currently working in the United States (although some in the group originally hail from other countries). This decision was not just a matter of money. Historical sociology, as international as it was and is, has clearly had its own history in the American academy; the concept of "historical sociology" itself was adopted most enthusiastically there, for reasons including the "brain drain" of historical sociologists to the United States from abroad.[18] We deliberately included people who comprise a wide range of theoretical orientations and a broad spectrum of understandings of what constitutes historical sociology. The intention was not to create or police new intellectual boundaries, but to take collective temperatures and

18. In J. A. Hall (1989), for example, the author describes the lineage of British historical sociology and laments the impact of the "brain drain" of historical sociologists from Britain to the United States (p. 564).

open further space for thought, discussion, and action. As should be obvious the scholars assembled in this book compose a loose and contingent coalition rather than a theory group.

All the contributors identify as historical sociologists, but what defines their common project? Some would sign on to what Craig Calhoun calls a minimalist list of inherent historical sociological objects: "rare but important sociological phenomena (e.g., revolutions); critical cases [for theory] . . . (e.g., Japanese capitalism); phenomena that occur over extended periods of time (e.g., industrialization, state formation, creation of modern family forms); phenomena for which changing historical context is a major set of explanatory variables (e.g., changing international trade opportunities)" (1996: 313–314). Other members of our group understand historical sociology as it was defined by Theda Skocpol in *Vision and Method:* works that "ask questions about social structures or processes understood to be concretely situated in time and space . . . address processes over time, and take temporal sequences seriously in accounting for outcomes . . . attend to the interplay of meaningful actions and structural contexts, in order to make sense of the unfolding of unintended as well as intended outcomes in individual lives and social transformations . . . [and] highlight the *particular* and *varying* features of specific kinds of social structures and patterns of change" (1984b: 1; author's emphasis). Still others would insist that even this is too limiting a frame and that the rightful province of historical sociology is the "problematic of structuring"—and therefore all of history and sociology. Here is Phillip Abrams again: "Sociology must be concerned with eventuation, because that is how structuring happens. History must be theoretical, because that is how structuring is apprehended" (1982: x).[19] The problem, we discovered collectively, is that the items on the minimalist list are rooted in the modernist frameworks of the first and second waves, while the process-oriented definitions provide few guides to problem selection. A sense of substantive fragmentation has replaced the intellectual cohesion—and constraint—of the second wave.

We editors also elected to bring together only sociologists, rather than a cross-disciplinary group. This may at first seem surprising. Historical sociologists are enthusiastically interdisciplinary. In examining any particular historical event or transformation, our own work—and that of all the contributors—has been deeply engaged in conversations with historians,

---

19. For these reasons, we editors invited members of our own midcareer and younger cohorts, rather than scholars who were originally the leading lights of the official or unofficial second wave. We expected this decision to create a conversation that was freer from people's (including our own) stock assumptions about representative figures and fixed intellectual positions.

so deeply engaged that a total of 1 Bloom book and 0 fish books are cited...

political scientists, literary theorists, economists, and anthropologists. And we recognize that the "historic turn," the move to historicize social inquiry, is decidedly a cross-disciplinary project (see esp. McDonald, ed. 1996). The contributors to this volume are joining with a broad range of scholars responding to the classics of social theory and to the problems of modernity, *sounds like 2nd wave... let it be more eclectic* post-modernity, or alternative modernities, however understood. Political theorists interrogate the classical canon for its textual silences or rhetorics; ethnographers in the "new ethnography" incorporate the situated nature of anthropology and sociology in the construction of the distinction, still alive and kicking, between modern selves and traditional Others, to cope with problems of power and modernity.[20] Sociologists have much in common with these categories or groups of scholars, but they also make distinctive contributions. Those of us who pursue a historicized sociology can tackle the processes conventionally grouped under the heading of "transitions to capitalist modernity" on empirical as well as theoretical grounds. Of course, historical sociology is about not only the past, but also the ways in which the past shapes the present and the future, inviting our remaking of modernist social analysis and the concept of modernity itself, which has significant disciplinary specificities. So perhaps we even have an intellectual responsibility, born of our middleman position, both to our own discipline and to others.

Disciplines—like any structure—provide both distinctive constraints and capacities embedded in theoretical and methodological orientations, transmitted through graduate education, hiring, the tenure process, and the gatekeeping of fellowship, research proposal, and manuscript review. We can illustrate this point with reference to the treatment of "race" in U.S. historical sociology versus historical political science.[21] Why is it that historical work foregrounding race and ethnicity has been less typically found among the most cited works of historical sociology while it has been central to studies of American political development, a core constituency in historical political science? In the historical study of American politics, the problems of race, slavery, and political freedom have loomed large, motivated both by the foundational position of liberalism in political theory and by the national crisis of the Civil War. Given these theoretical and empirical foci, work on race could not be so easily marginalized. Yet in historical sociology, race has been one of the areas of scholarship that had to be "brought back

(left margin handwritten): *it hunt for a claim to fame ... we don't need a tormented history*

(right margin handwritten): *truly colonial and fragmentation in intellectual history*

★

20. In political theory, see, for example, J. Landes (1988) and Zerilli (1994). On ethnography, see Tyler (1986). Post-modern ethnography converges in interesting ways with "the extended case method" forwarded in sociology by Burawoy and his students (Burawoy, ed. 1991, 2000).

21. We are grateful to Ira Katznelson and John Lie for helpful discussions on this issue.

ranging studies that can account for both capitalist development and peripheral poverty...

in" in the current period (although work on racial formations and identities was flourishing in other areas of sociology). Essential programmatic statements of historical sociology explicitly mention race as a keyword in the survey of current literature; for example, Skocpol (1984a: 358) includes in her survey, among others, Orlando Patterson's work on slavery. Yet the analysis of race was sidelined by the second wave's orientation to Marxian questions about the transition to capitalism, revolution, class conflict, and the state in modern Europe. The larger point is that disciplinary specificity still matters. Transdisciplinary intellectual projects—the historic, linguistic, or cultural turns; gender studies; Marxism; rational choice theory—attempt to reform or revolutionize knowledge and academic practices across these boundaries, yet their success will be reflected in their penetration of disciplinary canons and graduate training practices, and this requires engagement with the substantive, methodological, and theoretical particularities of each discipline.

Sociology is also a symptomatic site where people from a variety of disciplines can get a bird's-eye view of processes of paradigm formation, contention, and implosion. Historical sociology in particular lies at the crossroads of current intersecting trends in knowledges that touch all the social science disciplines—the rise of cultural analysis, neo-positivism, and the revival of the mechanism metaphor, to name but a few. Other disciplines have experienced some of these developments, of course, but not simultaneously; political science has witnessed the juggernaut of rational choice theory, while culturalist trends are almost entirely absent outside the subfields of political theory and constructionist international relations. Anthropology and history, on the other hand, have been most influenced by culturalist and poststructuralist trends and have proved inhospitable to rational choice approaches. But all of these orientations are well represented in sociology—and their representatives are fighting over claims to define the overall disciplinary field. Readers from many points in this range of contending perspectives, and from the other disciplines, should be interested in how these debates are progressing in the discipline where the alternative perspectives are most directly contending.

Finally, our group has given substantive pride of place to politics, broadly understood to include not simply forms of authoritative sovereign power, but also much of what, since Michel Foucault burst on the American academic scene, has come to be thought of as disciplinary power dispersed throughout the social landscape. The political focus has enabled participants to respond to a central legacy of historical sociology while at the same time broadening its concerns in light of the developments we signaled above. In their essays for *Remaking Modernity,* the authors have engaged a range of analytic strategies and/or theoretical models in light of more recent sociological research on a process or dimension of historical change. In some cases, there is an obvious continuity between classical theory and contemporary research. Given that secularization—including the changing institutional relations between church and state and the making of a "bourgeois" and secular self—was identified by Max Weber and others as an important aspect of modernity, for example, how do these claims and assumptions inform recent research? How is current work revealing the limits of these claims and theories? For other themes, the redefinition of key processes is critical. State formation, the transition to capitalism, and professionalization were originally theorized as European phenomena, so what happens when we widen our frame to take in post-socialist, colonial, or post-colonial states as well? Finally, for some topics, the absence of attention in classical theory is an important feature: how should we reconceptualize theories of social and cultural change in light of research on race, gender, sexuality, nation, and other concepts that were marginalized—or simply unknown—in earlier theoretical debates?

We think about these revisions and reformulations under the general heading of "remaking modernity." The *Oxford English Dictionary* defines "modern" as "of or pertaining to the present and recent times, as distinguished from the remote past." To be modern is to be in the now and (if the metaphor still has life in it) at the cutting edge of history. The concept is a moving index, pointing to everything—and nothing. Sociologists since the first wave have also understood that eternal present as the apex of a developmental lineage. They try to endow "modernity" with fixed referential content that can be defended as a platform for generalization and explanation, usually with "capitalism" or "industrialism" at the conceptual and causal core.[22] "As Max Weber observed," say Michael Löwy and Robert Sayre, "the principal characteristics of modernity—the calculating spirit (*Rechnenhaftigkeit*), the disenchantment of the world (*Entzauberung der Welt*), instrumental rationality (*Zweckrationalitat*), and bureaucratic domination—are inseparable from the advent of the 'spirit of capitalism'" (2001: 18). Others gesture toward Marx, whether modernity is taken to signal "the cultural articulations that accompany processes of capital accumulation" (Pred and Watts 1992: xiii) or, as Marshall Berman eloquently describes it, a "mode of vital experience—experience of space and time, of the self and others, of life's possibilities and perils—that is shared by men and women all over the world today. . . . To be modern is to be part of a universe in which, as Marx said, 'all that is solid melts into air' " (1976: 15).

---

22. At times this verges on the tautologous! "At its simplest, modernity is a shorthand term for modern society or industrial civilization" (Giddens and Pierson 1998: 94).

What is the relationship between these two understandings of the modern, as the present moment or as the distinctive social formation anatomized in the first and second waves of historical sociology? Most historical sociologists recognize that there are novel phenomena, that things have changed since the times of Marx and Weber. How to characterize this novelty is less clear. Debates over post-Fordism and post-modernism (as phenomena, not theories) turn on this issue.[23] While these debates are fascinating, we are more interested here in whether the concepts that sociologists associate with modernity help us understand the world (including historical sociology itself). Let's run through the typical list again: calculation; bureaucracy; rationality; capitalism; disenchantment; industrialization; secularization; individualism. To what extent do such concepts, whether singly or packaged together in what Jeffrey Alexander calls "the traditional/modern binary code" (1995a: 15), do the trick?

Some would argue that these concepts are basically fine as they are and that they remain central to understanding the world, even while venturing beyond the geographically restricted terrain upon which modernity was originally theorized. There are of course additions (the classical theorists, after all, largely ignored the question of war and failed to anticipate genocide as a distinctive feature of the twentieth century), but they supplement rather than undermine sociologists' favorite modernist signifiers.[24] Others would dispute this position and call for a more critical approach to the concept, but not for a univocal set of reasons.[25] The key difference turns on whether to reject or remake modernity. Some argue that the concept should just be jettisoned. They are convinced that it is either excessively vague or inalterably flawed by its implicit endorsement of conceptual repressions and exclusions mirroring existing relationships of domination. We vote for remaking it. We sympathize with the desire to raze conceptual foundations and start anew but are skeptical that it can or should be done. The concept does too much useful work—whether as an integrated ideal type or a separable cluster of signifiers—and it therefore systematically sneaks back into people's utter-

23. Some people are willing to be quite specific about the timing of this shift. Perry Anderson (1998) identifies the first use of "post-modern" in the work of Latin American expatriates in Europe in the 1930s, while Harvey (1989) declares that post-Fordism commenced in 1973. Steinmetz (this volume) treats the link between post-Fordism and historical sociology.

24. We understand signs as did Saussure (1959). Signs pair signifieds (concepts) with signifiers (for Saussure, who was a linguist, primarily sound or gestural patterns or written words). But anything can come to bear meaning—can function as a signifier—as our subsequent discussion will make clear.

25. See especially J. C. Alexander (1995a). Calhoun makes a persuasive case that historical sociology has an important role to play in unsticking the "canonical histories (and anthropologies) that have been incorporated into classical social theory and its successors" and that sociologists and social theorists have imbibed "from reading Weber and Durkheim rather than studying history directly" (1995: 314).

the concept of modernity is like language itself; it is indispensable for understanding the world...

ances even as they disavow it. And it now has an evolving history of its own. Part of the work of historical sociology, it seems to us, is historicizing modernity as an idea, capturing people's changing ideas of what is or is not modern, and assessing the valences of emotion and moral judgment that these mappings assume in varieties of discourse and institutions. Why, for example, has the idea of the modern (and its associated practices) been invested with such desires and hatreds? When has it been linked to pervasive repressions and elisions, when detached from them? What sort of work has it been doing in historical sociology itself?

The theme of "remaking modernity" is far too grand to approach as an integrated totality; we do not want to reinstate a grand narrative of the present day, a new Key To All Mythologies that the very terms "modernity" and its Others may seem to invite.[26] Our collective aim in this volume is more modest. We want to reflect on the key categories, theories that were built atop these categories, and substantive arguments that compose the edifice of macro-political historical sociology. That means in the first instance critically considering our own inherited categories—and so we turn back to the second wave.

[4:15] 6:30   15 → 135   expected × 9, but I did it right

The Second Wave and the Reappropriation of the Classics

In justifying their turn to history, the second-wave scholars latched onto the classics in a very particular way. The disciplinary canon with which they operated, filtered through Talcott Parsons, had enshrined Weber, Durkheim, and later Marx as the major scholars of reference.[27] Second-wave scholars wanted to bring to the fore class inequality, power, and the conflicts these engendered, and Marx became the most important figure for them as they antagonists cast themselves as the leading protagonists against modernization theory, of particularly the claim that all paths of development led from the "traditional" to the "modern."[28] From Marx they took their emphases on the importance of the "material" (understood as separate from and determinative of the "ideal") modes of production, class conflict as the basis of politics and the motor of history. The history that the second wavers drew out was

is huntington a neo-parsonian? what of struc funcism does he support?

26. Not least because the prospect of writing an analogous world-embracing, world-dominating text would give us the same terminal writer's block that darkened Casaubon's last days. See George Eliot's *Middlemarch* for a rendition of this, every academic's nightmare.

27. In Parsons (1937) Marx was classified as a utilitarian and therefore got short shrift.

28. For example, Charles Tilly, the editor of *The Formation of National States in Western Europe* (1975), the final volume in Princeton University Press's Studies in Political Development series (under the leadership of Lucien Pye), used the volume to critique the argument of the preceding seven volumes and of the whole "political development" project.

but is this claim false?   how does malinowski relate to parsons?

one of conflict, particularly of class conflict, expropriation, and bloody oppression. It was also one that was built around the tendential development of social structures and epochal transitions.[29] It is important to note that their Marx was leavened with an emphasis on elements of Weber's writings, as we will see below, and laced with a strong refusal of Durkheim, who was understood as the patron saint of the twin evils of cultural values and structural-functionalism (C. Tilly 1978).

The second wave—memorably described as an "uppity generation" by Theda Skocpol (1988b)—consigned modernization theory and structural-functionalism to the dustbin of intellectual history.[30] The radical political movements of the 1960s and 1970s had inspired many students to go on to graduate study, where they linked their political concerns to intellectual questions and found guidance from the historically inclined minority of senior scholars even as they rebelled against their more presentist colleagues. In sociology, Andrew Abbott notes that rebellious impulses helped to direct many younger sociologists to *historical* approaches, which allowed criticism of two then dominant tendencies: Parsonian functionalism and atheoretical and ahistorical empirical work: "Theoretically, historical sociology was for them a way to attack the Parsonian framework on its weakest front—its approach to social change—and a way to bring Marx into sociology. Methodologically, historical sociology damned the status attainment model for its micro focus, its antihistorical and antistructural character, its reifications, its scientism" (2001a: 94).[31]

Ensuing sociological debates arrayed second-wave scholars against more orthodox Marxists of various complexions. Second wavers, who tended to prefer an eclectic theoretical approach, were nevertheless powerfully pulled into the current of the Marxist problematic.[32] Modes of production were the

29. "Marxism is one of the theories most attuned to the need to specify clear breaks between epochs and to develop historically specific conceptual tools for understanding each" (Calhoun 1996: 322).

30. Unfortunately, this meant that some of the phenomena that modernization theorists had tried to explain—like totalitarianism or the relatively uniform rise of education, urbanization, or democracy— disappeared from second-wave scholarship. (We are grateful to Arthur Stinchcombe for helpful discussion of this point.) As we will see below, this disappearance set up opportunities for scholars— particularly John Meyer and his students—to retrieve these issues in the 1990s.

31. Calhoun sees the battle with the quantitative empiricists as having been thrust upon the historical sociologists when the "dominant quantitative, scientistic branch of the discipline dismissed their work as dangerously 'idiographic,' excessively political, and in any case somehow not quite 'real' sociology" (1996: 305). In any event, historicity split this intellectual movement from then dominant forces.

32. Structuralist Marxism of the 1970s engaged in attempts to understand contemporary class structures (e.g., the work of Erik Olin Wright), state forms (e.g., Nicos Poulantzas), and ideological structures (e.g., Louis Althusser, Goran Therborn). See Wright and Perrone (1977); Wright et al. (1982); Althusser (1972); Therborn (1980).

[handwritten top margin: major influence on sociology in the 50s and 60s ... shortcomings in marxs thought. but the more upsetting possibility is that of disregarding marx ... marx: sociology: kant: philosophy]

basic units of comparison, and transitions from one mode to another marked the significant historical transformations—that which was to be explained. Wallerstein's (1974) world systems theory, castigated as shockingly "circulationist" by many Marxists at the time, can in retrospect be seen as a close cousin and *Marxisant* variant.[33] Scholars of the second wave found this broad tradition of work useful but thought that it discouraged comparative work from explaining variation across regions, countries, cities, and other sites within the same mode of production or position within the world system. Even more problematically, it tended to consign history to the realm of the singular and idiographic, grist for the nomothetic mill of Marxist theory.[34] Still, while second-wave historical sociologists in the American academy appreciated Marx's *The Eighteenth Brumaire of Louis Bonaparte* (1963 [1852]) for the prominent role it awarded to politics in nineteenth-century France and excavated it as a meaty source of aphorisms on history as tragedy and farce, they had yet to appreciate its full potential as a source of anti-structuralist and cultural analysis.[35] The questions posed by the second wave derived from a Marxist theoretical agenda; its answers pushed beyond, informed by an engagement with Weber, to embrace "the relative autonomy of the political." In fact it is that impossibly cumbersome phrase that best characterizes both the promise and the limits of second-wave work.

The question of why revolutions did not happen how and where Marxists expected them animated exciting work by authors including Theda Skocpol (1979), who drew on the Weberian tradition in her discussion of the "great revolutions" of France, Russia, and China; Jack Goldstone (1991), who argued for the role of demography in revolution and rebellion in the early modern world; and Mark Gould (1987), who recruited Parsonian theory in his work on the English Revolution.[36] Immanuel Wallerstein (1974) worried about why socialism could not succeed in one country, and if his "one world system" answer was novel, it was certainly addressed to an ongoing preoccupation of the Marxian tradition. A different sort of revision that also deployed the idea of an interstate system emerged from the collaborative

33. By "circulationist," insiders of the day meant market-based rather than the more orthodox production-focused orientation.

34. In their now canonical second-wave article Skocpol and Somers (1980) argued that this was similar to the way in which Smelser (1959a) had deployed history to illustrate modernization theory. However, Smelser's choice of topic was itself a form of resistance to Parsons's mentoring.

35. Meanwhile, Stuart Hall (1977) was working through *The Eighteenth Brumaire* in exactly that kind of way. It took a long time for Hall's work to reach historical sociologists working in the United States—another index of the uneven and nationally specific rhythms of intellectual diffusion.

36. See also Trimberger (1978). Maurice Zeitlin (1984) crafted a perfect, and perfectly symptomatic, second-wave title: *The Civil Wars in Chile, or, the Bourgeois Revolutions that Never Were.*

[handwritten right margin: it isn't that either is right, but that both are indispensable ... but an ideological point, it also a point in which marx is fundamentally false]

[handwritten left margin: sociology without their children leave home ... but the truly upsetting possibility is that of the children never leaving at all]

[handwritten bottom margin: best sociology is politically motivated ... historical inquiry is a way to critique the present that transcends mere polemic ... it beats the prestigious present leaders at their own game of demonstrated benefits]

work of John Meyer and Michael Hannan, eds. (1970) and George Thomas et al. (1987). Ronald Aminzade (1981), Victoria Bonnell (1983), Craig Calhoun (1982), George Konrád and Iván Szelényi (1979), Jeffery Paige (1975), Sonya Rose (1988), William Sewell Jr. (1980), Charles Tilly, Louise Tilly, and Richard Tilly (1975), Mark Traugott (1980), and many others worked on the Marxian problem posed by the collective action of what were thought to be intermediary, transitional, or surprising groups such as artisans, counter-revolutionary peasants, women workers, intellectuals, and so on. Perry Anderson (1974a) studied absolutism—a state form emerging from within an economic context where it "should not have" appeared. This conundrum made sense within the space of Marxian theory, to which Anderson wedded fundamentally Weberian insights about state forms. Anthony Giddens (1985), J. A. Hall (1986), Michael Mann (1986), Gianfranco Poggi (1978), Theda Skocpol (1985a), and Charles Tilly (1990) (to name just a few) interrogated the sources of state formation and dissolution, highlighting the dynamics of war making and violence that were emphasized by Weber and Hintze but given short shrift in Marxian theory. Randall Collins (1986) staged a "confrontation" between Weberian and Marxian theories of capitalism. Michael Burawoy (1972) highlighted the "color of class" in a historical analysis of the Zambian copper mines; Michael Hechter (1975) studied the "Celtic fringe" and the puzzle of nation for issues of class formation; Judith Stacey's (1983) pioneering analysis tackled the role of gender in the Chinese revolution; and John Stephens (1979) and Walter Korpi (1978) sought to understand the socialist potential of social democracy and the welfare state in capitalist countries. This is, of course, just a partial list of contributors to what was an incredibly exciting moment of intellectual ferment. When we explore these individual works, we find that they differ on many important matters. They also have distinctive takes that relate to national and regional genealogies of intellectual debate. But in retrospect there is also an astonishing level of international conversation and convergence.

These trends extended across all the social sciences and history in the 1970s and early 1980s: one thinks of Louise Tilly and Joan Scott's (1978) groundbreaking research on women workers and family forms, David Abraham's (1981) class analysis of the breakdown of the Weimar Republic, Ira Katznelson's (1981) investigations of the ethnic and racial complications of working-class formation, or the interdisciplinary "Brenner Debate" on the transition from feudalism to capitalism (Aston and Philpin, eds. 1988). Indeed, this was also a period in which social scientists were avidly reading historians' work and forging interdisciplinary allegiances and ties—especially with the resurgent social history typified by the work of E. P. Thompson (1963), Sheila Rowbotham (1972), and the *History Workshop Journal*[37] and with the work of Fernand Braudel and the *Annales* school[38]—and with historians who were pondering the intersection between family and economic forms.[39] Consequently, the historical turn in sociology was linked to the erosion of the boundaries among social theory, scientific method, and historical research, exemplified by the changing contents of key journals such as *Comparative Studies in Society and History* and by the growth of the Social Science History Association (SSHA), incorporated in 1974. Reflecting the broader trends characterizing social science and history, the SSHA was at first a meeting place for historians wanting to learn "cliometric" methods from social *scientists;* then in the 1980s and 1990s it became the place for social scientists who wanted to do history with a second-wave twist, and later for both social scientists and historians who wanted to explore the cultural and linguistic turns, the uses of narrative, and network analyses, as well as substantive work that crossed the fields.[40]

7:30

320 min session!

37. Such work had a particular impact on some feminist historical sociologists, such as Rose (1986, 1992).

38. Many structuralist social scientists found particularly congenial the *Annales* school's broadly sociological approach and antagonism to an understanding of history as a "mere sequence" of events. See Dosse (1997). One could also include, by the 1980s—before the American appropriation of the cultural turn had hit full force—work on *mentalités* (e.g., N. Z. Davis [1983] and Ginzburg [1980]), which was beginning to deal with the cultural, but in the context of "total history" and still in a materialist framework. (See Eley 1996: 204–205.)

39. We are thinking, for example, of the debates over proto-industrialization, catalyzed by Kriedte, Medick, and Schlumbohm (1981), but one might think even more broadly about the nexus among family, economic experience, and historical memory (see, for example, Elder 1998 [1974]). One of the general virtues of the "Red Moment," quite evident in journals and at the Social Science History Association (SSHA) meetings of the time, was that it enabled conversations among historically minded scholars interested in macro-politics, economics, family, and demography. Discussions of the intersections among family strategies, modes of household production, and dynamics of proletarianization were common, for example. This convergence came undone as the second wave receded; it has yet to make a comeback.

40. See Kasakoff (1999). In an account originally published in 1991, Abbott (2001a) pointed out that sociologists and historians approached the task of melding "history" and "sociology" from very different disciplinary starting points and gravitated toward the SSHA for different reasons. He also argues that there was a sharp distinction between two groups of historical sociologists, only one of which—the quantitative historical sociologists (which he calls HS2)—was active in SSHA and, in his account, friendly to an essentially historical and narrative approach. The other group (HS1), the macro-political comparativists, dominated the American Sociological Association's section on Comparative and Historical Sociology (ASACHS). In the revised account of SSHA history in Abbott (2001a), the author indicates some ways in which the division between HS1 and HS2 has come undone. At this point, the two groups have pretty thoroughly comingled. In fact, by asking Ann Orloff to start the SSHA's States and Societies Network as a focus for HS1-type work, Abbott himself helped organize this process of dedifferentiation. The States and Societies Network is thriving, and there are more conver-

The Marxian heritage of the second wave functioned as an overall regime of knowledge. The second-wave comparative-historical sociologists varied in the extent to which they conceived of their project as revising Marxism or as combining diverse theoretical insights to create fresh understandings of important processes and events, but they consistently read and argued with each other. Even as they challenged this tradition, they leaned on its coherence, especially in terms of what Geoff Eley (1996: 194) calls "social determination," or the claims that collective action, subjectivities, politics, and culture rested on "material interests," themselves embedded in material life, however conceived. And while it raised hackles from the very beginning and continues to be controversial today, the work of these sociologists and others working in allied disciplines is in our view of lasting significance. Their attention to politics opened up a tremendously fruitful vein of analysis that gained force in the 1980s and early 1990s and continues today.[41]

It is also true that the appropriation of classical theory by second-wave scholars emphasized the political-economic and material, understood as opposed to the cultural and ideal, while the ironies and irrationalities of modernity hinted at by classical theorists disappeared from view. The enduring structuralist Marxist leanings of the second wave, emphasizing the necessary and sufficient conditions for transitions between modes of production, effaced the Marx who theorized the continuing cataclysm of capitalist development, including its contradictory impact on the individuals whom it continually reconstituted: "Constant revolutionizing of production, uninterrupted disturbance of all social conditions, everlasting uncertainty and agitation distinguish the bourgeois epoch from all earlier ones. All fixed, fast-frozen relations, with their train of ancient and venerable prejudices and opinions, are swept away, all new-formed ones become antiquated before they can ossify."[42] Where was *this* modernist Marx in the second wave? Similarly, the second-wave sociologists reached out to Weber's writings on the specificity of the organizational and political-economic,

sations between this group and political history scholars in SSHA. ASACHS now incorporates both HS1 and HS2 (e.g., prizes have gone to macro-comparative, quantitative, and narrative analysts and to people who mix these styles). ASACHS has now taken on questions of narrative—in various panels about analytic approach; in debates among section-affiliated authors such as Margaret Somers, Edgar Kiser, and Michael Hechter; and so on. The institutional differences between HS1 and HS2, if they were ever as sharp as Abbott argued (which we doubt), have eroded.

41. Note that the vast majority of historical work on social movements published in the *American Sociological Review* and the *American Journal of Sociology* (ASR and AJS) over the past two decades has been on the French Revolution or the U.S. Progressive Era and the New Deal period (Clemens and Hughes 2002).

42. Marx and Engels (1998 [1848]: 38–39); the citation is from M. Berman (1976).

drawing on his analyses of ideal types of organization, of relations between rulers and staffs, of power politics. Yet this resurgence of politics in a debate dominated by material determinism came at the cost of excising the Weber of *The Protestant Ethic* (1930), of complexes of meaning, the historical ironist who saw the personal losses and terrors instilled by processes of rationalization. The second-wave historical sociologists were by no means apologists for capitalism, and they clearly understood that the development of post-revolutionary states, democracy, social welfare, and so on was not linear and progressive—but they also viewed these matters and processes as neatly contained and often reducible to a single analytical principle. Certainly their own theoretical categories, and their position as analysts, remained serenely above the fray.

The legacy of the classical sociologists is more productive than the flattened 1950s version or the second-wave reappropriation would indicate—and also more troubling. Weber (1930, 1946c) offered a textured sense of the manifold ambiguities inscribed in elements of what came to be thought of as "the modern." He traced one long-run counter-intuitive result of people's rational conduct in pursuit of a calling: the emptying of the world of subjective meaning. The expansion of scientific rationality, he thought, would entrain "an ever more devastating senselessness . . . a senseless hustle in the service of worthless, moreover self-contradictory, and mutually antagonistic ends" (1946a: 357). Following Weber and Freud, Norbert Elias thought that the fruits of the "civilizing process" could be had only at the price of internalized regulation, discipline, and social repression. Marx and Engels wrote as apocalyptically (but with more hope for the future of humankind) when they celebrated the "most revolutionary part" played by the bourgeoisie in not only building the capitalist order, but also dialectically engendering the proletariat, "its own gravediggers" (1998 [1848]: 37, 50). "The development of modern industry, therefore, cuts from under its feet the very foundation on which the bourgeoisie produces and appropriates products" (p. 50). Durkheim (1961: chs. 4–6) saw the rise of the modern state as instrumental in creating the individuated selves that would in turn raise fundamental challenges for and to the state itself. The unintended consequences of human action could and did result in the opposite of what was desired or envisioned. The classical sociologists made passionate arguments for the historical genesis and limits of social formations and selves—and of their own foundational concepts. They described paradoxes and ironies that worked themselves out historically—and this infused their intellectual and practical encounters with "modernity" with lasting grandeur as well as pathos.

For all its complexity, however, this theoretical heritage inscribed a poten-

that's great, apart from the fact that it's totally false

tial conceptual dualism, assigning a whole series of subordinate concepts to the category of the "not modern." This continued to be the case in second-wave work and, as we will argue, still characterizes much contemporary historical sociology, particularly within the institutional and rational choice approaches. On one side were grouped capitalism, rationality, bureaucracy, and the public; on the other, feudalism, traditionalism, and so forth. And these oppositions took on strikingly gendered and racialized meanings. Men were aligned with the "rational" and women with the "irrational" and "traditional," while the "civilization of the metropole" was juxtaposed to "an Other whose main feature was its primitiveness" (Connell 1997; see also B. Marshall 1994, 2000). Of course this mode of dualistic and devaluative thought predated the classical sociologists, deriving from earlier lines of conservative and Enlightenment reasoning (Zerilli 1994) and from the properties of modernity itself—for example, the separation of home and work in the rise of industrial capitalism, the disembedding of family and state, and the impact on the metropole itself of the massive waves of European colonialism. These oversimplified oppositions embedded in core concepts of the classical sociological tradition functioned not only as a shared conceptual language, but also as a source of both theoretical closure and ideological consolation. It was all too tempting to juxtapose the supposed rationality of one's modernity to the irrationality of tradition—much more comfortable than analyzing the substantive irrationalities embedded in the process of rationalization itself. Herein lay the foundation for both the 1950s "pattern variable" version of what had been a great historical intellectual tradition and the second-wave appropriations of sanitized concepts of modernization, industrialization, bureaucracy, and so on.[43] Nonetheless, what was expelled from the idea of the modern could not be easily excised, even in theory. It continued to structure, in a subterranean way, the conscious text of social theory itself. We will return to this point below, in our discussion of the theoretical challenges that beset—and are remaking—historical sociology.

The Second Wave under Pressure

Like all significant intellectual innovations, the second wave courted its own upending. Theoretically, we claim, its hyper-structuralism invited assertions of agency and process. Its conceding to modes of production such a role in determining social formations and intellectual problems prompted counter-claims of the constitutive significance of culture.[44] The apotheosis of the

---

43. See, for example, Sewell's (1996b) comments on modernization.

44. The argument that the economic was determinate only in the last instance did not go far enough in

image of the coercive central state apparatus provoked counter-imageries of productive capillary power. Moreover, its repressions of key aspects of modernity—religion, emotion, habit, the arational core of war and state violence—virtually invited work that would bring all of those elements "back in."[45] The exclusion of various subaltern subjects has been challenged by those who would speak in their name. We will turn to these theoretical issues below.

Methodologically and epistemologically, the combination of a language of Humean constant conjunction (if complicated and conditional constant conjunction) with a research program that called for comparative histori-cal work was unstable at best.[46] Attempting to satisfy the requisites of posi-tivistically minded sociological gatekeepers did not (and perhaps cannot) mix easily with attention to history. Moreover, second-wave scholars ig-nored the textual foundations of their own practices at a time when dis-tinctions between literary and scientific argument were coming under increased questioning, both from mavens of science studies and from post-structuralists.[47] As we will see below, these characteristics of the approach itself articulated with pressures and pulls from other scholarly communities. Finally, second-wave historical sociology proved ill equipped to deal with key developments outside the academy, including new social movements, innovative forms of political action, identity politics, and the partial dis-placement of nation-states as the central organizing nodes of politics.

From the outset, second-wave historical sociology evolved methodologi-cal and epistemological practices that elicited challenges from both his-torians and more conventional social scientists. Early efforts to explain the distinctive methodological approaches and benefits of historical sociology usually began from the premise that this work was as scientific, or at least as systematic, as that of the positivist researchers. Second-wave scholars bran-dished John Stuart Mill's *A System of Logic* (1875) to show how analyses of substantively significant but relatively rare outcomes could still satisfy the

---

our view. For one influential attempt to spell out why, within a Marxian paradigm and inspired by some of Friedrich Engels's remarks, the "lonely hour of the last instance" never comes, see Althusser (1990 [1969]).

45. Two essays in this volume that frontally address this issue of repression are Gorski's (for religion) and Kestnbaum's (on war).

46. "If A, then B" is the simplest and most general form of a Humean statement of constant conjunc-tion. Hume (1975 [1748]).

47. Hayden White (1973) has been particularly influential in this turn toward ferreting out the literary tropes active in historical analysis. In Derrida (1987), the author questions our capacity to draw boundaries between texts and contexts. And in the other corner, those that object to the aestheticiza-tion of analysis include Megill (1985) and Habermas (1987). Lash (1985) tries to referee the fight.

requisites of conventional social science.[48] By insisting on historical sociology as a preeminently rigorous comparative method, practitioners sought and gained some tenuous legitimacy vis-à-vis the mainstream of sociology, a point that many have made but that Craig Calhoun (1996) captured best with his aphoristic reference to the "domestication" of historical sociology. However, second-wave scholars were also uncomfortable with what they took to be vague and general sociological concepts that had not been built up from the ground of historical particulars, and they were absolutely allergic to covering laws. None was willing to consign history to the merely idiographic.[49] Second wavers overall embraced historians' emphasis on sequence and timing.[50] Whether they conducted archival historical work or drew from secondary sources, in the context of 1970s and early 1980s sociology, they were unusually respectful of the histories of the countries, regions, and periods in which the processes at the center of their analyses unrolled.

Historical sociologists were attacking entrenched practices and violating disciplinary boundaries in sociology and history, and they stepped on some toes in the process. The response by mainstream sociologists has been heated, focusing on the supposed failure of comparative and historical sociologists to satisfy the requisites of social scientific method as conven-

48. For example, again, Skocpol and Somers (1980). The *comparative* dimension of historical sociological work has also generated a great deal of scholarly controversy and commentary, for it is here that some principal figures of what got defined as the official second wave staked their claims for the scientific standing of historical sociology and for their leadership of the burgeoning social movement that was bringing history back into sociology. Skocpol and Somers identified three major analytic strategies within comparative history (that is, "explicit juxtapositions of distinct histories"; 1980: 72): "comparative history as the *parallel demonstration of theory*," as "the *contrast of contexts*," or as "*macro-causal analysis*" (p. 73; authors' emphasis). It was in connection with the last of these that Skocpol and Somers invoked the enormously influential use of John Stuart Mill's methods of difference and agreement, a template that structured many an ensuing dissertation but that has since become a particular target of critics.

49. Smelser points out that "[Nomothetic and idiographic] approaches—insofar as both attempt to explain—do not necessarily differ substantively with respect to the nature of the causal forces invoked . . . do not call for different theoretical grounding points. The differences between them lie more in the mode of explanation, the mode of organizing variables, and the techniques of research employed" (1976: 204–205). Of course it is now the case that some historical sociologists (particularly those influenced by Foucauldian genealogical methods) would not see themselves as engaged in any version of an explanatory project.

50. Historical sociologists are collectively thinking through the implications of the interventions that seek to displace comparative method in favor of narrative or couple the two in some way. This task is made still more challenging by lack of agreement over what might be entailed in that move, already under way in some areas of our field (see special issues on narrative in the fall and winter 1992 numbers of *Social Science History* [vol. 16]). Are some forms of historical narrative more analytically acceptable, perhaps more "sociological" than others, and more easily integrated into accepted canons of social science research? (See Griffin 1993.) Or is that too narrow a way to contemplate this important problem and opportunity? Franzosi (1998) provides a recent overview.

tionally, positivistically understood.[51] These critics have argued that the choice of a "small-n" research design is inherently flawed because it suffers from too few degrees of freedom to cope with large numbers of potential causal factors; that "selecting on the dependent variable" introduces unacceptable bias into conclusions; that the failure to seek universal knowledge in the form of covering laws means that comparative-historical researchers are really no better than hopelessly idiographic historians—in short, they are not real social *scientists*. But the critics have no good answer to how we should better study relatively rare, overdetermined, but significant phenomena or processes unfolding over the *longue durée*, with which so many historical sociologists are concerned.[52] Nor can they help us with dimensions of social processes that function more like a language and less like a set of billiard balls. To the extent that historical sociologists underline the fundamental historicity of the categories and concepts of social life, in any case, they will inevitably be at odds with social scientists seeking universal covering laws.

Comparative-historical researchers have in time grown less fond of Mill, and some claim to have found firmer ground for claiming methodological advantages—even if it is often unclear whether they are claiming to escape positivist methodological prescriptions or to better satisfy them. Some have moved into a less defensive position, arguing that conventional statistical analysis rarely satisfies the methodological requisites of its own favored quantitative techniques.[53] Historical sociologists have long insisted on the significance of the temporal dimensions of analysis.[54] Some, like Andrew Abbott and Roberto Franzosi, are also developing formal methods for analyzing sequences.[55] Charles Ragin (1987, 2000) makes a strong case for a holistic, case-based logic of comparative research that addresses situations of

---

51. See especially Lieberson (1991) and Goldthorpe (1997). One recent response is Steinmetz (forthcoming c). Espeland and Stevens (1998) remind us to be sensitive to the socio-psychological conditions under which claims to commensuration—including our own!—are made or refused. See also Emigh (1997a).

52. Indeed, it is partly on these grounds that contemporary defenses of comparative and historical analyses are based. For example, see Lieberson's (1991) critique of Orloff and Skocpol (1984), in which he uses traffic incidents to illustrate his criticism of their analysis of the initiation of modern welfare programs in Britain and the United States. For the concept of the longue durée, see Braudel (1980: 25–34).

53. Ragin (2000). "In Ragin's view," James Mahoney comments, "the challenge is for statistical researchers to adapt their research to the more demanding standards of qualitative analysis rather than the reverse" (2001a: 584).

54. For example, Aminzade (1992); Skocpol (1984a); Zerubavel (2003).

55. Abbott (2001b) and Abbott and Tsay (2000). (Also see Wu 2000). *Theory and Society* ran a special issue (26 [2/3], 1997) on "New Directions in Formalization and Historical Analysis," edited by Roberto Franzosi and John Mohr.

multiple, conjunctural causation—the majority of "cases" that interest us—
better than does the array of standard quantitative techniques. Some call our
attention to the need for more systematic methods of discourse analysis.[56]
Others emphasize "biography as historical sociology."[57] Still others point to
the ongoing debates among representatives of various post-positivist perspectives that have appeared across the human sciences.[58] The participants
in all these debates and discussions certainly differ among themselves, but
together they have revealed that the positivist empiricism that characterizes
much mainstream sociology rests on shaky ground. These debates take on
additional urgency because they are occurring in virtually every discipline
with any scientific aspirations, at a time when the growing sophistication of
science studies illuminates the unsteady foundations for unreflective claims
to the scientific. Some science studies work in historical sociology questions quite basic assumptions of positivist social science, such as concept-
independence or the assumption of temporal invariability that underlies
scientific laws.[59] Defenders of positivism are under assault themselves, in
other words, and the critical arrows have penetrated multiple chinks in their
defenses. New attempts to please positivistically minded social scientists—
whether by invoking sociology as physics-in-the-making or by policing the
practices of historical sociologists with invocations against "unscientific
interpretation"—are just as likely to fail as earlier efforts and will keep
us from bringing to bear our combined forces on important aspects of
social life.

While mainstream social scientists attacked historical sociologists based
on the premise that we should be more general, abstract, and "scientific,"
historians often criticized historical sociology for its lack of engagement
with the particularities of each case, its failure to plumb relevant primary
documents, its condescending treatment of historians' theoretical debates,
its reduction of historiographical debate to fate, and its tendency to lose
itself in ungrounded, compounded abstractions—to create what Lawrence
Stone memorably called "sociological unicorns."[60] Ironically, these stinging

56. Adams and Padamsee (2001); J. Mohr (1998); Padamsee and Adams (2002).

57. Derluguian (forthcoming); B. Laslett (1991); Mary Jo Maynes, Barbara Laslett, and Jennifer Pierce,
"Agency, Personal Narratives, and Social Science History," Presidential Session, Social Science History
Association, November 2001 (available upon request from the authors). Steedman (1986) has been a
particularly influential model for the use of autobiography as a method of analysis.

58. See, for example, Somers (1998) and the response from Kiser and Hechter (1998); also see Abbott
(1998) and Ragin (1987, 2000).

59. Historical sociological works in this vein include Breslau (1998); Gieryn (1999); Shapin (1994);
Schweber (2001). See also Latour (1999).

60. Lawrence Stone seems remarkably blind to the beauty and allure of these sociological animals. Cf.

and, one must admit, sometimes just accusations stem from the very legacy of interdisciplinarity that historical sociologists have fostered and prized. As historical sociologists are increasingly evaluated from within the disciplinary canons of history as well as their home discipline, they are expected to do the kind of high-quality, original, archival, primary source research expected of historians without sacrificing the impulse toward sociological generalization. Meeting this expectation has made the work inherently more difficult and, some argue, less doable—at least by the lonely artisanal scholar who is still the norm in this corner of our discipline. And if the call to "Go to the archives, young woman" was not sufficiently challenging, historical sociologists are now pulled by the cultural turn in history and the humanities, which underlines a whole series of symbolic mediations: that archival documents are problematic texts, themselves in need of discursive deciphering; that explanatory accounts of history-writ-large must be understood as narratives with their own rhetorical devices and plots; and that every observation and utterance makes sense only in the context of a symbolic order.[61]

The methodological pulls of history and "proper" social science are powerful forces in creating cleavages among historical sociologists. In conjunction with the whip hand of tenure, academic review, and gatekeeping more generally, these have pulled what was once a more unitary body of historical sociologists in wildly different methodological directions.[62] Within departments, universities, and subfields, the local balance of forces between neo-positivist and various post-positivist approaches helps explain why particular individuals have taken certain scholarly paths. Thus, some are attuned to problems raised from the interpretive disciplines about texts, sources, and systems of meaning, and many have become more suspicious of claims that studies of the social can be scientific in the conventional sense. Others, however, are still attempting to speak to the critiques from the mainstream of social science—we think of James Mahoney and Dietrich Rueschemeyer's (2003) edited volume, which in many ways continues the second wave's project of seeking scholarly legitimacy through emphasizing the ways in which comparative-historical sociology fulfills the requisites of

Stone's (1992) review of Jack Goldstone's *Revolution and Rebellion in the Early Modern World*. Historians were divided in their response to Goldstone's book—an American Sociological Association "best book of the year" prizewinner—and in a way symptomatic of their general reception of big second-wave texts.

61. Some exemplary texts include Derrida (1996), Steedman (2002), and Hayden White (1973).

62. Certain aspects of the infrastructure of the discipline affect us in distinctive ways: research funding is still geared to more positivist approaches to social analysis (see Steinmetz, this volume), while the press system—more important to us than some of our colleagues because we are still, preeminently, "book people"—faces increasing difficulty in publishing monographs not geared to popular audiences (see Clemens et al. 1997).

social *science*. Those who attend to history—especially if they make use of narrative forms or appeal to textuality, rhetoric, and semiotics—are too often set up as straw men, spinners of Just-So stories. We editors see historically minded sociologists using a variety of ways to discipline their inquiries. All these strategies are both legitimate and at least potentially productive.

These methodological debates are obviously fascinating, thoroughly contested terrain. The contributors to this volume do touch on them, but our main brief is theory: the theoretical issues associated with understanding social and cultural change in the light of the intellectual challenges that beset and entice the present generation of historical sociologists. In that context, and before we delve into these challenges, we wish to signal some general, and paradigmatically related, theoretical problems of the analyses of the second wave. As more than one commentator has noted, most are relentlessly structural—and the structures are those of the political economy—and the work remains curiously dissociated from human experience and aspirations (Katznelson 2003). Since these features actually lent their work legitimacy in the academy and helped make the organizational case for historical sociology, they have proven notoriously hard to shake. But perhaps it is the attempt to shake them that best characterizes the theoretical impulses that motivate extremely diverse approaches within historical sociology today.

The problem is not with "structure" as a sociological category. It is certainly useful—nay, indispensable—if it is conceptualized as relatively enduring relations among bounded units of some kind. But the second wavers interpreted "structure" in a particular way, one that authorized certain sorts of intellectual advances yet ultimately proved too limiting. They wanted to rescue sociology from what they saw as overly individualistic or voluntaristic accounts of human action and complex social outcomes; "structures" were held up as the mediating feature that constrained human action but also crystallized its emergent properties. The analytic recourse to "structures" as a binarized sign in opposition to "culture" should be situated in the political and intellectual landscape of the time. Culture was often invoked to "blame the victim" (e.g., in so-called "culture of poverty" arguments) or to rationalize the persistence of repressive political regimes by pointing to values that legitimized the status quo.[63] Unfortunately, "structures" as a particular power term also authorized a naive structure/culture opposition—and that in spite

---

63. It seems obvious—now—that we cannot understand people's making revolutions without looking at what they thought they were doing. Yet recall that at that time, "culture" did not mean the sophisticated analytics of a Clifford Geertz or a William Sewell Jr. but was often deployed in rather simplistic ways, understood as homogenous and nationally unified (e.g., arguments that the United States lacked a proper welfare state because of its individualist national culture).

of the fact that social life is unthinkable without cultural structures, such as language and other systems of representation in which the bounded units in relationship are signs. In their responses to simplistic notions of culture and individual action, moreover, the second-wave analysts also shied away from analyzing properties of modernity that were not formal-organizational, and as a result their writings often seem strangely one-sided.[64]

It was not just the internal weaknesses of their particular understanding of structure that undermined the approach that characterized the classics of the second wave. The paradigm that guided second-wave work proved unable to deal with a whole series of epochal transformations, summed up in the events, or rather signs, of "1968" and "1989." The former is shorthand for a welter of things, but among them it stands for the genesis of "new" movements[65]—feminism, gay liberation, ongoing rebellions among post-colonials and racial and ethnic minorities within the metropole, "post-materialism"—that challenged Marxist-based organizations politically and opened the way for feminist theory, post-colonial theory, queer theory, and critical race studies to pull apart Marxism in the decades after (Laclau and Mouffe 1985). Of course, these challenges to modernist principles also applied to modernist and universalizing liberalism. The latter ("1989") signals the subsequent revival of liberalism, the vagaries of globalization, fundamental challenges to the order of nation-states, and the collapse of Marxism as a mode of imagining a future beyond capitalist modernity.[66] These signs, and the processes and events they reference, triggered the rethinking of the landscape of modernity that is currently in process.[67] The place of the state as a privileged unit of analysis is being eroded by globalization and transnationalism and the proliferation of parastatal and other ambiguous bodies.[68] Moreover, historical work in the vein of post-coloniality and other

64. Thus it is no accident that theoretical work on "structuration," which helped dispose of the second-wave use of structure, became a critical inspiration for today's historical sociologists. See, for example, Bourdieu (1977), Sewell (1992), and Giddens (1984).

65. We will not be the first to point out that most of these movements are not in fact "new" to the post–World War II world, yet they were and are understood as such by many analysts. Note that it is also true that "1968" is often cited as a sign for a series of explosive events fueling Marxist understandings.

66. Few social analysts predicted the events of 1989, and those who did probably did so accidentally. Thus one can hardly fault the second wave for unique theoretical lacunae. It was clear to many that structural Marxism was not equipped to deal with the forms of difference and power that were not reducible to class, yet second-wave scholarship, like modernist social science more generally, also obscured the workings of gender, race, and other forms of difference.

67. See, for example, P. Anderson (1998); Felski (2000); Hardt and Negri (2000); Harvey (1989); Jameson (1991); Pred and Watts (1992).

68. Appadurai (1996); Arrighi (1999); Deflem (2002); Jessop (2000); Lash and Urry (1987); McMichael (1990); Mitchell (1991); Sassen (1991).

approaches has stressed the ways in which metropoles have been formed by events and processes in the periphery (see Magubane, this volume). Current events, or rather signifiers of events—"9/11" above all for American scholars—have underlined global interdependency, sometimes cruelly. At this historical moment, the conjuncture of events both in the world and in the academy calls for rethinking certain premises of historical sociology.

Where Historical Sociology Stands Today

It is fair to say that the second-wave scholars' calls for reinfusing sociology with history have had a hearing and have indeed inspired new generations of scholars pursuing historical research—the contributors to the present volume included (J. R. Hall 1999a). Historical sociologists now enjoy a hard-won although partial acceptance within the discipline of sociology. The American Sociological Association section on Comparative and Historical Sociology (ASACHS) is well established. Historical articles appear in the pages of *American Sociological Review* and *American Journal of Sociology.* Sociologists identify themselves as specialists in "comparative/historical sociology" in the ASA *Guide to Graduate Departments,* and graduate departments are ranked by *U.S. News and World Report* in the specialty of historical sociology, along with economic sociology, stratification, cultural sociology, and social psychology. However, we are very far from having convinced mainstream sociologists that social inquiry demands a fundamentally historical approach that attends to the cultural and historical specificity of concepts and categories—if indeed that is a desirable goal. Indeed, some argue that our acceptance has come at the price of our compartmentalization. We tend to be located at major research institutions, in part because these institutions have had the resources to hire from among a subdiscipline that is still regarded—in spite of its classical legacy—as being at odds with the mainstream of sociological concerns. By the standards of mainstream sociology and despite diverse substantive foci, historical sociologists are all part of a subdiscipline that is regarded as something of a luxury good—the sociological equivalent of a Panerai watch or a Prada bag. On the one hand, our pursuits are considered arcane; on the other, pursuing them requires markers of cultural capital (e.g., theory, multiple languages, art appreciation), which may be useful in the quest for departmental "distinction" in the university setting. But any potentially serious disruption to the mainstream has been neutralized by our categorization and segregation as *historical* sociologists—rather than as sociologists who take seriously the claims of historicity implicit in elaborating explanations rooted in, and limited by, time and place. This segregation authorizes conventional work on contemporary—and by any seriously historicized standards, parochial—U.S. concerns without the need to specify historical and geographical context or limits.

Historical sociologists are often seen by outsiders as united in our focus on "history"—that is, on what is *not* the (U.S.) present. "History" is no unitary subject, however, and even if we historical sociologists were to surrender to the urge to define ourselves solely in terms of method, larger intellectual debates over positivism, interpretation, and textuality divide us. Theoretically, we find ourselves without the unifying analytic framework that undergirded second-wave efforts. This should not occasion regret or nostalgia. We know that some of the advances of the second-wave scholars came burdened with troubling repressions and exclusions attendant on that regime of knowledge. This is rather an opportunity for historical sociologists as they use new tools to re-ask the core questions that preoccupied the second wave, but also to ask new questions and identify and probe silences—particularly those to do with culture, agency, the character of modernity, gender, race, and the world beyond the West—in the earlier work.

Some contemporary historical sociology—notably the various institutionalisms—represents a series of friendly amendments to the second wave, while other work poses more fundamental challenges. The political-economic structuralism of the second wave is still present in institutionalist approaches but has developed away from comparative statics toward more processual accounts, often with improved methods (e.g., network analysis) that directly engage the assumed durability of different forms of structure. Moreover, there is a greater appreciation of the range of variation in the historical and political constitution of political actors, with some loosening of strictly political-economic understandings of identities and preferences, interests, or goals. Yet even so, institutionalism often operates with a utilitarian understanding of actors' goals, as well as a strictly goal-driven rather than practice-oriented understanding of action (see Biernacki, this volume). Among many institutionalists, many of the problematic exclusions and repressions of second-wave work continue, although the emergence of culturalist and gendered institutionalisms is a hopeful development.

We see important work going on in many directions. Our metaphorical model is not the superhighway from a past imperfect to an ever-improving future. We think rather of crooked and tangled side streets feeding into and radiating out of the broad avenues laid out by the second wave of the 1970s and 1980s. And "We'll always have Paris"—as Bogie said—with its high modernist Haussmann boulevards and its medieval and post-modern byways. So we refrain from organizing our discussion of the current state of historical sociology as a story of progress, with successive waves of scholarship getting closer and closer to the ideal theoretical and methodological approach. In what follows, we investigate strands of third-wave analysis that have developed in reaction to—and on the basis of—second-wave work. We identify five communities or foci of historical sociologists: (1) institutionalism, (2) rational choice, (3) the cultural turn, (4) feminist challenges, and (5) the scholarship on colonialism and the racial formations of empire, in which sociologists turn their eyes to the world beyond the second wave's favorite stomping grounds, Europe and the United States. Scholars pursuing these different challenges work within a range of intellectual frames, and we see no sign of the emergence of a dominant paradigm of the sort that commanded the second wave's allegiance. But we believe that the effort by historical sociologists to grasp their intellectual common roots, as well as their points of divergence, is a prerequisite to having more interesting and fruitful conversations, doing better theory, and making more effective alliances with potentially sympathetic groups in and outside of sociology. *Reculer pour mieux sauter.* A more active remembering of our own histories can spark thinking across the analytic divides around agency, signification, power, repression, and exclusion that have opened up in the last decade or two.

Institutionalism: Networks, Processes,
and the Institutional Opportunity

Much of the power of the second wave flowed from the invocation of structural determination. Yet this assertion of structure has been destabilized by a dialogue between Marx and Weber that echoes through much of the work described above. While questions of revolution and the transformation of economic regimes framed many of these projects, the explanations increasingly invoked Weberian themes of complex conjunctures, of the formation of social actors, and of the creation of rationalized structures of domination as specifically historical accomplishments. With this shift in emphasis, historical sociology was reoriented to intersect with important methodological and theoretical developments elsewhere in the discipline: network analysis and the various "new institutionalisms."[69] To a greater degree than other challenges, institutional analysis extends key projects of the second wave while opening familiar research questions to explorations of process, transformation, and agency.

The problematics of the second wave continued to inform important projects of historical research, particularly the questions of revolutions that should or should not have occurred or social classes that should or should

69. For example, see Emigh (1997b). More generally, see P. A. Hall and Taylor (1996).

see gould on 2e empire

not have been mobilized as political challengers. Armed with new technologies of network and organization analysis, researchers could address these anomalies in new and systematic detail. Working on nineteenth-century Paris, Roger Gould (1995) explored the complex ground of class formation: why was the uprising of 1848 organized around class lines and through rhetorics of class, whereas neighborhood solidarity served as the organizing framework for the insurrection of 1871? Peter Bearman's (1993) study of the English civil war mobilized fine-grained data on social ties to explain the emergence of new connections between court and country, as well as competing blocs within the bourgeoisie. Richard Lachmann (1987, 2000) examined the signal contribution of organizationally anchored elites—as distinct from classes—to the transition to capitalism and state formation in early modern Europe (see also Kimmel 1988). Addressing Sombart's classic query of "Why no socialism in America?," Kim Voss (1993) turned to an organizational analysis of locals of the Knights of Labor—a sweeping "producerist" organization of workers in the late nineteenth century—to identify the conditions under which local unions were formed, persisted, and engaged in active challenges to the economic order.[70] These works all share a project defined both theoretically and empirically: to move beyond explanations that rest on the presence or absence of a particular class actor, to develop theoretical explanations and methodologically sophisticated demonstrations of the processes through which class actors are mobilized.

While second-wave scholarship focused on breakdowns of and failed challenges to existing political orders (Goldstone 2003), more recent scholarship has moved to consider challenges that resulted in new political institutions. Some of this work engages now classic debates on state building in Europe, but the bulk deals with twentieth-century America.[71] Social science history has long given a central place to American politics.[72] But a key intellectual switching point may have been Skocpol's 1980 article on the New Deal and theories of the state,[73] which brought in its wake renewed interest in the United States as a case, in an at least implicitly comparative perspective.[74] (Structuralist Marxists also made a similar crossover; see, e.g. Block

70. On the politics of economic elites, see Kaufman (1999).

71. See, for example, Ertman (1997) and Downing (1992). These excellent books directly engage second-wave historical sociological debates, testifying to the interdisciplinarity of this particular space.

72. An important line of work deals with the historical sociology of educational institutions in America (e.g., R. Collins 1979; see also Emirbayer 1992; Rubinson 1986; Tolnay 1998; Walters and O'Connell 1988; Walters, James, and McCammon 1997).

73. For commentary, see Gilbert and Howe (1991); C.-J. Huang and Gottfried (1997); Manza (2000).

74. In sociology, see, for example, Amenta (1998); Amenta, Bonastia, and Caren (2001); Clemens (1993); Kleinman (1995); Weir (1992); Weir, Orloff, and Skocpol, eds. (1988). In political science,

1987.) Others have transposed analyses of competing class fractions and state autonomy to the development of welfare states.[75] As contemporary revolutionary openings seemed to close and revolutionary outcomes came to be viewed more sourly, a still modernist sensibility moved many scholars to consider a nonrevolutionary version of progress toward a more egalitarian future, the Progressive Era and New Deal origins of the U.S. welfare state.

With this renewed interest in U.S. social policy, historical institutionalists have been drawn into vibrant comparative debates over the origins and development of welfare states. Within this multifaceted intellectual community, scholars explore the conjunctural and multiple causation of a range of policy and political outcomes, even as interest has shifted from the origins and growth of welfare states to their contemporary character and uncertain future.[76] Of late, innovation has been especially notable in conceptualizing the qualitative dimensions of variation across cases and in formulating typologies of ideal types, or "welfare regimes" (at times incorporating gender), which have been linked to distinctive political coalitions and institutional configurations.[77] While some of this work, by focusing on presences and absences, tends toward a "comparative statics," much of it has opened toward processual analyses. Indeed, regime types have been understood as a way of thinking about distinctive political-institutional "opportunity structures," giving rise to varying sets of interests or preferences, identities and categories, coalitions, and administrative capacities that influence social politics in "path-dependent" ways.[78] The tempo of history shifts from the sharp alternation of system and contradiction-driven crisis to a more even cadence of contestation and consolidation.

The encounter of classic questions with new methodologies also generated new developments on the more Weberian pole of historical sociology.

---

this renewed interest grew under the banner of "American political development," including works by Stephen Skowronek, Karen Orren, Victoria Hattam, Martin Shefter, Christopher Howard, Sven Steinmo, and Paul Pierson.

75. Hooks (1990a); C. J. Jenkins and Brents (1989); Quadagno (1988). Stryker (1990) examines the role of economists in New Deal labor relations and American welfare policies.

76. Esping-Andersen (1985); Hicks (1999); Huber and Stephens (2001); Janoski and Hicks, eds. (1994); Orloff and Skocpol (1984); Skocpol (1992); Steinmetz (1993). Some of these scholars draw on T. H. Marshall (1950), Polanyi (1957c), and, of course, the social-democratic version of Marxism, in which socialism—or welfare states, the "next best thing"—can be achieved by peaceful, democratic means (see, e.g., Korpi 1978; Rueschemeyer, Stephens, and Stephens 1992; Stephens 1979).

77. Esping-Andersen (1990, 1999); Korpi (2000); Julia O'Connor, Orloff, and Shaver (1999); Orloff (1993a).

78. Pierson (2000). However, Katznelson (2003: 290–294) cautions us about institutionalism's potential neglect of the large-scale dynamics foregrounded by "macro-historical analysis," especially as this is expressed in the notion of "path dependency."

Just as studies of (non)revolutions generated more processual accounts of class formation, analyses of state formation also incorporated insights from new advances in the study of networks and identities. Influenced by the Simmelian heritage of positional network analysis (Harrison White 1963, 1992), John Padgett and Christopher Ansell (1993) take fifteenth-century Florence as a major case of the "political centralization [that] lies at the heart of state building." They analyze "the structure and the sequential emergence of the marriage, economic, and patronage networks that constituted the Medicean political party, used by Cosimo in 1434 to take over the budding Florentine Renaissance state" (pps. 1259, 1260; see also McLean 1998). This research explores how relatively strong states emerge out of webs of social relations. In *City of Capital*,[79] Bruce Carruthers extends this theoretical project and links it with the longstanding neo-Weberian concern with the "sinews of state power" (Brewer 1988)—war and money. Whether concerned with Renaissance Florence or early modern England, these studies harness the analysis of social ties and interactions to a processual account of state formation.

Although driven by network analysis and new interests in collective identities, these developments converged with broader trends in the social sciences that are grouped under the theoretical umbrella of "institutionalism." At the most general level, institutional theory draws attention to higher-order effects or emergent processes, rejecting the reductionism and methodological individualism that informed much of post–World War II social science.[80] In its initial formulations, institutionalism in historical analysis tended to invoke institutions as given, as opportunity structures within which strategic actors operate. The opportunities confronting mobilized groups with a particular interest, for example, will differ across centralized and decentralized political institutions. At some level, this style of analysis only loosens the combination of structural determinism and utilitarian actors characteristic of the second wave. To the extent that these assumptions inform institutional analysis, less attention is paid to both the emergent character and cultural dimensions of institutions.

More recent work, however, takes the institutional framework of states as both the outcome of historical processes and a factor that explains subsequent historical trajectories. Rather than selecting cases of revolution and

---

79. Carruthers (1996). Ertman (1997) argues that differences in constitutional institutions led to divergent trajectories of state formation.
80. The phrase "historical institutionalism" appears to have sprung from the collective conversations in a 1989 Boulder, Colorado, workshop organized by Sven Steinmo and appearing in Thelen and Steinmo (1992) (personal communication, Sven Steinmo). See also Clemens and Cook (1999); Thelen (1999).

insurrection, these studies focus on moments of institutional transformation or consolidation. For example, Ann Orloff's study of the initiation of modern pension programs in Britain, the United States, and Canada traces the political processes—as conditioned by institutional legacies—that produced the building of the new institutions of the modern welfare state (Orloff 1993b). Within American history, the Progressive Era has provided the classic case. Foundational works of institutional history used narrative history embedded in case comparisons to identify the common mechanisms and critical dimensions of variation in processes of state formation (Skocpol 1992; Skowronek 1982). As these studies foreground complex historical narratives—often through comparisons that highlight similarities and differences of process—they move away from the empty experimental time of second-wave historical sociology to a much deeper engagement with historicity and sequence.

In subsequent studies, these key insights into the dynamics of state transformation and consolidation have been coupled with the theoretical as well as methodological sensibilities that characterize the analysis of state building presented by Padgett and Carruthers. Theories of structuration—as opposed to simply structure—highlight the processual relationships of networks, resources, and cultural constructs.[81] Institutional consolidation is understood as a project of embedding the agencies in a complex supporting coalition, as well as in key experiments in service that enhanced the agencies' reputations (Carpenter 2000). The shift from a political system dominated by parties and centered on elections to one organized around interest groups and legislators was produced as political challengers transposed "organizational models" from nonpolitical activities to political mobilization (Clemens 1997). As with new work on early modern state formation, these accounts of institutional consolidation and transformation employ processual theories and methods to account for fundamentally Weberian questions of bureaucratization and rationalization.

With respect to the second wave, the emergence of institutionalism within historical sociology is essentially, as we said above, a friendly amendment. The substantive focus remains in the sphere of political economy, although the broadly Marxist terrain of the earlier theory group has been extended and crosscut by Weberian themes of state building and transformation. In the place of actors whose interests could be read directly from their economic position by invoking utilitarian assumptions, institutionalists have substituted actors who are boundedly rational, operating with repertoires— of collective action, of organization, of identity—that are culturally con-

81. See the references in note 63 above.

stituted in ways specific to time and place. But as historical sociology has encountered other intellectual trends, the challenges to basic assumptions have been much more fundamental.

Rational Choice Theory and the Cultural Turn

In very different ways, both rational choice theory and the ongoing cultural turn have given people languages with which to first criticize and then—if they follow these impulses—to depart from structuralist, Marxist-influenced historical work. Rational choice theory proceeds from rigorously worked out utilitarian assumptions about the properties of individual and group action. As a body of thought, it too descends from classical founding fathers Thomas Hobbes and Adam Smith. But just as twentieth-century versions of Marxian theory elaborated and relaxed some of Marx's core assumptions, so too has rational choice theory been reshaped, so much so that some practitioners believe that they have solved or transcended the famous Hobbesian problem of "explaining social order" on the basis of individualistic strategic-rational assumptions (Parsons 1937; Coleman 1990). Be that as it may, rational choice arguments have figured in some recent and historically relevant incarnations in sociology, such as Edgar Kiser and his collaborators' work on the fiscal aspects of state formation, which examined the longue durée development of different forms of fiscal extraction and administration in sites including China, Turkey, and western Europe (Kiser 1989; Kiser and Linton 2002; Kiser and Schneider 1994; Kiser and Tong 1992); William Brustein's (1996) analysis of the rise of Nazism; Rosemary Hopcroft's (1999) book on peasant communities and property relations in English history; Julia Adams's (1996) analysis of network mechanisms in the decay of Dutch colonialism; Arthur Stinchcombe's (1995) work on agency problems and slave societies in the eighteenth-century Caribbean; Paul Froese and Steven Pfaff's (2001) exploration of the "missing" religious revival in two of ten post-communist societies of East Central Europe; Abram De Swaan's (1988) tale of the introduction of state-provided education in the Netherlands; and Ivan Ermakoff's (1997) work joining game theoretic and interpretivist approaches to examine medieval European political marriages or crisis decision making in the Weimar Republic or Vichy France.

Except as whipping boy, rational choice theory is not a widespread presence in today's historical sociology—not yet. Our sense is that this theoretical tendency will become more influential for two reasons. First, like the cultural turn (with which it has some surprising if subterranean affiliations), rational choice theory is part of a powerful cross-disciplinary and inter-disciplinary intellectual movement, embracing historical work in political science, economics, psychology, and evolutionary biology as well as sociology.[82] The use of rational choice arguments in new institutionalism and in historical path-dependent reasoning will almost certainly increase as a fuller engagement occurs between historical institutionalism and political science and as a legacy of the explicit coupling of utilitarian and neo-evolutionary reasoning that is making dramatic headway all over the social sciences. Second, historical sociologists are groping for theoretical languages within which they can discuss strategic action, and rational choice theory is currently the most consistently developed paradigm.[83] We can expect to see more historical sociological analysis emerging under several rational choice rubrics, including game theory, which has been applied, inter alia, to the emergence of political actors, and coalitions and the creation and reproduction of political institutions, which have figured as the equilibrium outcomes of repeated games, linked together over time.[84] We can also expect strong resistance to these forms of analysis! Rational choice as an abstract theory has inspired hot and heavy reactions from other historical sociologists and will continue to do so.[85] But rational choicers' on-the-ground historical analyses, typically less orthodox than their self-conscious methodological pronouncements suggest, often wed utilitarian arguments to Weberian-style comparative institutional analysis or even (gasp) culture.

Historical sociologists with a rational choice bent have not had much to say about modernity per se. This is not just because such large and unruly concepts sit awkwardly with methodological individualism. Silence in this case also betrays the taken-for-granted quality of a very close relationship: the detached, individualistic modern self is the utilitarian's chief assumption and analytical building block (but see Kiser and Baer, this volume). Yet the genesis of the so-called modern rational actor is itself an outcome of historical developments, including some decidedly nonrational processes of psychic repression and restructuring described in the works of Norbert Elias (1994 [1939]), Sigmund Freud (Breuer and Freud 1937), and Franz Fanon (1991) (especially the latter) as foundational to the "civilizing process." Elias

82. See, for example, the recent collection by Bates et al. (1998). Rational choice theory has made very little headway in the discipline of history, although forms of utilitarian thinking are certainly to be found there (and therein lies another tale). Root (1987, 1994) is one of the few partisans.

83. Bourdieu's work—particularly as codified in Bourdieu (1984)—is often cited as an alternative. Taken as a whole, however, Bourdieu's arguments involving individual and group strategic action—developed as a relationship between "habitus" and "field"—have a conceptually incoherent relationship to utilitarian thinking.

84. An example of game theory applied to coalitions is Axelrod (1981). Historical sociologists interested in the analytic possibilities of game theory can consult Dixit and Skeath (1999).

85. See, for example, the responses to Kiser and Hechter (1991), including Somers (1998).

in particular argued that the capacity to think calculatively, linking ever-longer chains of means and ends, was necessarily bound up with increased self-discipline: the internalization of controls over socially inadmissable forms of anger, desire, and other emotions. Rational choice historical sociologists may well elect to ignore this, since culture is at best understood in an extremely limited and limiting way, as preferences, in utilitarian work (see Katznelson 2003), and emotions are excluded from the theory in its rigorous version. Tacitly, however, this growing body of work can help us arrive at a broader and more situated view, although it must be stressed that this view systematically departs from utilitarian frameworks. We believe that capturing the precise contours of conditional and idealized rational action can help illuminate its ascendancy as the dominant mode of action and characteristic trope in today's capitalist world.[86] Less can be said, as yet, about the post-modern causal conditions under which forms of strategic action and utilitarian self-understanding might be extended, undermined, or otherwise transformed. Certainly there is a great need for better description and analysis of the dispersion of the mode of detached utilitarian action into all sorts of surprising social spaces.[87]

If rational choice theory has a natural enemy within historical sociology, that appears to be the cultural turn, at least at first blush.[88] People's routes to and on "the turn" vary tremendously; we would be better off abandoning the highway metaphor and speaking of turns in the plural. The bottom line assumption, however, is that signification is a constitutive part of social life, with its own logic, that cannot be reduced to or "read off of" social position. In fact, those positions are themselves formed by processes of meaning-making. The cultural turn as a moniker covers an enormous intellectual field, part of the general shift toward linguistic modes of analysis in the twentieth century,[89] with ramifying roots in structural linguistics, philosophy, anthropology, history, literary theory, cultural studies, pragmatism, and feminist and post-colonial theory—and of course sociology itself. Here

86. See G. F. Davis and Useem (2002), for one example of the organizing power of this utilitarian language in economic institutions.

87. This point is adumbrated in U. Beck (1992). Orloff (this volume) discusses this issue with respect to risk management in welfare states. See also Zelizer (1985). The idea of measuring an agent's willingness to assume risk, found in Plato and Epicurus and reintroduced by Kant, became the core of von Neumann's and Morgenstern's expected utility theory. On this point see Charron (2000).

88. Things are not as simple as they seem. One of us (Julia Adams) has argued that rational choice theories of state formation from Hobbes to the present are built on tacit culturalist arguments (see Adams 1999).

89. Charles Taylor describes this epochal shift with great clarity in his "Language and Human Nature" and "Theories of Meaning" (in C. Taylor 1985a).

we want to signal the most important theoretical themes for historical sociology.[90]

The argument that all conceptual categories are fundamentally social, systemically organized, and historically mutable hails from Ferdinand de Saussure's *Course in General Linguistics* (1959) and Durkheim and Mauss's *Primitive Classification* (1963).[91] One could say that Saussure introduced the concepts of sign and system of signification, and Durkheim in particular underlined their sociality and emergent properties. No wonder Emile Durkheim was the founding father ritually abominated by the scholars of the canonical second wave: Durkheim's *The Elementary Forms of the Religious Life* (1995) could serve as a totem—whether worshipped overtly or not—for ways in which scholars foregrounding the historical transformation of classification systems and practices actively disrupted the second wave's social imaginary. Andrew Abbott's *The System of Professions,* to take one influential example, showed that jurisdictional claims—which revolve around "differences between archetypes" (1988: 61)—and struggles among actors over whether and how those archetypical arrangements would be recognized, and perhaps institutionalized, anchor an interdependent system of professions. The major dynamics of system-level change reside in a number of external and internal factors, including technologies and organizations, but the professional formations of valued knowledge, the attendant arguments for recognition, including rhetorics and the migration of metaphors, have their own cultural properties and tendencies of development (pp. 57–113).[92] Pierre Bourdieu's analyses of systems of taste and political language play out the relationship among objects of consumption or ways of speaking that function as signs of class difference in organized fields in which each element takes on its meaning in relationship to others. These elements are then available for actors' manipulation, accumulation, and so forth, but their relationships also constrain the possibilities for strategic action and thus of systemic transformation.[93]

Classification systems continue to generate wonderful historical sociological work. Their evolving modes of abstraction and application have been

90. For manifold other aspects, see the excellent review by Eley (1996). Suny (2002) considers the state of the cultural turn/rational choice face-off in political science.

91. Durkheim and Mauss were responding to Immanuel Kant.

92. While Abbott (1988) defines the archetypical units as "organized groups of individuals" (p. 117), in practice the argument is more complicated, recognizing two levels of archetypes—one a formation of signs, the other a concatenation of individuals and aggregates of individuals. Signs and relations among signs are treated as relatively fixed for purposes of the theory, however, thereby stabilizing and streamlining what is already a complex argument.

93. Bourdieu (1984, 1991b). Stanley Lieberson (1992) pokes a few holes in the empirical basis of Bourdieu's *Distinction*, while Jeffrey Alexander (1995b) takes apart the theoretical apparatus.

examined across a series of social fields, including double-entry bookkeeping and law.[94] As classification systems receive renewed attention, the construction and policing of boundaries necessarily comes to the fore, whether they be boundaries among institutionalized formations of knowledge, among perceived racial and class groupings, among medieval and early modern European status groups, or among categories of children, for example.[95] Some historical sociologists engaged by the disciplinary power residing in categorization also take Michel Foucault as one reference point.[96] Foucault's own unclassifiable work—which if not that of a standard *sociologue*, certainly flirts with historical sociology and is taught in many of our graduate theory courses—captures the historical emergence of normalizing discourses and "technologies of the self" and traces the processes by which they are embedded in and help create a range of disciplinary complexes, including the prison, the clinic, the confessional, and state apparatuses. These discourses contribute to creating the very individuals that they describe and regulate. These arguments have been an impetus for exciting sociological work detecting the fingerprints of power on shifting historical categories.[97]

Ironically, the state-centric heritage of the second wave actually has been helpful to historical sociologists working in the Foucauldian vein, helping them dodge two dangerous temptations. First, rather than displacing the central in favor of the capillary or washing out their analytical differences (as Foucault himself tended to do), historical sociologists have sought to reconnect them and trace the genealogies of their institutionalization in forms of rule and the formation of subjects. There Foucault meets Weber, one might say. Thus Ivan Evans analyzes the relationship between racialized forms of local vigilantism and state power in the twentieth-century United States and South Africa, while Philip Gorski traces the way in which capillary forms of Calvinist social discipline, forged in the crucible of the Reformation, are incorporated into state projects in early modern Europe.[98] The second temptation involves the reification of categories. We see this form of vulgar

---

94. See Carruthers and Espeland (1991). Stinchcombe (2001) modifies Max Weber's account of the relationship between formal and informal systems.

95. Lamont (1992, 2000) has explored the morality and historical development of perceived class and racial boundaries in the United States and France. Abbott (2001a) deals, inter alia, with boundaries among institutionalized formations of knowledge. See also Sutton (1988) and Clark (1995).

96. Foucault was not the first to examine the ways that categories come to be "transfer points" of power; his philosophical lineage rests on Nietzsche, Heidegger, Saussure, Derrida, and others, as well as the first wave of classical historical sociology. *Discipline and Punish* (1978) and the first volume of *The History of Sexuality* (1979) have been particularly influential in today's historical sociology.

97. See, for example, Torpey (2000) and Loveman (2001).

98. I. Evans (n. d.; working paper available from the author); Gorski (1993, 2003a). See also Biggs (1999).

Foucauldianism whenever categories are deemed coextensive with identities and subjectivities (and either celebrated or excoriated as such!) or when categories get treated as homogeneous, suffocating, instrumentally deployed weapons by which the powerful unfailingly repress the less powerful. The growing body of work on identities in historical sociology has by and large evaded this trap. A serious engagement with history makes it hard to ignore the complexity of actors or the unintended consequences of action for those on the top as well as on the bottom of the social heap.

The categories of politics—particularly with respect to nations and citizenship—attract the most scholarly attention in historical sociology. The power-political emphasis owes something to the second wave. But before that wave ebbed, politics was considered an arena of rational contestation, not aesthetic spectacle, and categories such as citizenship and nationhood were erased or "forgotten" (see Somers and Spillman/Faeges, this volume). No longer. There is now an analytical space for politics as the mobilization of desires and categories, not just interests.[99] Citizenship has been analytically reconstructed through the lens of the cultural turn, and a wealth of work engages the formation of nations and national identities in many forms of politics.[100] Benedict Anderson's influential concept of nations as "imagined communities" has been a touchstone and an inspiration.[101] Some of the new scholarship foregrounds Europe;[102] other scholarship looks beyond.[103] Many of these works on nations and national identities take conceptually hybrid forms as well, dovetailing with other foci. For example, Eiko Ikegami (1995) deploys the lens of collective identities in conjunction with institutionalism to locate the honorific culture of the samurai as the source of the nationally distinctive combination of collaboration and competition that characterizes the government institutions as well as corporations of modern Japan. Frank Dobbin (1994) weds cultural analysis to the national specifici-

99. Two quite different examples are Markoff (1996a), which analyzes shifting and emergent categories of political grievance in the French Revolution, and Falasca-Zamponi (1997).

100. Categories of citizenship and nation overlap, of course. See Brubaker (1992); Hanagan (1997); Somers (1993); Soysal (1994); Torpey (2000).

101. Anderson writes in keeping with the darker impulse behind some of the cultural turn (recall that his project began as an attempt to understand the wars among Vietnam, Cambodia, and China). "Who can be confident," he asked with depressing prescience in the 1983 first edition, "that Yugoslavia and Albania will not one day come to blows?" (p. 12).

102. A partial and telegraphic list of sociological works would include Berezin (1997); Brubaker (1996); Greenfield (2001); Joppke (1999); Kane (1997, 2000); Kennedy (1990a, 2002); Lie (2001); Olick and Levy (1997); Soysal (1994); Watkins (1991).

103. See, for example, Spillman (1997); Lo (2002); see also Lo (this volume); Charrad (2001); Shafir (1995). The contributors to Olick, ed. (2003) discuss collective memory, nation, and nationalism with respect to a wealth of European and non-European cases.

ties of industrial policy in his study of how policymakers' perceptions influenced the building of the railways in the nineteenth-century United States, Britain, and France. And John Meyer and his collaborators demonstrated that nation-state institutional forms and capacities for action have become a set of standardized, modular, and reproducible cultural templates in today's "world society" (see, e.g., J. W. Meyer 1999).

The making of modernity is central to the cultural turn in historical sociology in at least two ways. First, sociologists engage the substantive problems and questions associated with the formation of historically evolving cultural categories and practices. Often (but not always) these have an explicitly power-political focus.[104] How, Meyer Kestnbaum wonders in this volume, do we describe and explain the ways in which "the people" have become involved in war—as citizens or in the name of other identities—and the corresponding critical relationship between popular uprisings and military mobilization? Or to take another example—one that returns us to the root class-based concerns of the second wave but with a novel culturalist twist—how are class-based identities historically constructed and reconstructed, and what might that mean for politics, work, family life, community action, and so on? Howard Kimeldorf (1999) has examined such questions with special reference to the Wobblies in U.S. labor history.[105] Marc Steinberg's *Fighting Words* (1999a) examined the discursive construction of working-class boundaries in early-nineteenth-century English politics; Richard Biernacki (1995) analyzed the ways that distinctive conceptions of labor as a commodity shaped the practices of work in the textile industries of Germany and Britain. There are many other examples. In fact, this general genealogical project is almost definitive of the way that the cultural turn has played out in historical sociology.

Second, more generally, the very concept of identity, thought to inhere primarily in an authorized individual subject, is the result of a long historical process in which that authorizing power, originally socially located in God or Nature, descends to and is inherited by "the self."[106] Weber's *Protestant Ethic* (1930) marked out one significant moment of that embattled process. We are now located at an interesting intellectual and political moment at which this notion of the sovereign self and its associated practices are simultaneously being intellectually reinvigorated (for example, in rational choice theory)

104. For two delightful counter-examples, see Griswold (1986) and Silver (1989). We can expect the choice of analytic objects to broaden further as the second wave recedes.

105. See also Kalb (1998). Again, Lamont (2000) is an important work in this particular category. See also Aminzade (1993); the contributions to J. R. Hall, ed. (1997); and Gerteis (2002) on narratives of class and race in the Knights of Labor.

106. See J. W. Meyer and Jeppersen (2000). Also see Emirbayer and Mische (1998).

and quite thoroughly undermined. Powerful voices outside the academy are reasserting fantasized fundamentalist versions of tradition and person-hood.[107] But perhaps the strongest credible *intellectual* challenge to date emanates from the inroads of post-structuralism and post-modernism—currents that reached American sociology later than they did some of the other human sciences. The relevant critiques of the subject, Enlightenment universalism and the grand narratives of modern historical development, are by now familiar (Lyotard 1984; Benhabib 1990). Perhaps this shift has become so overriding, bringing with it a sense of meaning simultaneously crucial and fragile, because social processes associated with modernity and modernization are disenchanting the world.[108] No doubt the horrific political events of the twentieth and now twenty-first centuries are also an influence—including the total wars that ushered in Eric Hobsbawm's "age of catastrophe" and seem to "confirm what many have always suspected, that history—among many other and more important things—is the record of the crimes and follies of mankind" (1994: 584). Whereas the utilitarian vision aims for the crystalline clarity of a mathematical model, some of those who have taken "the turn" see through a glass darkly. But it must also be said that others find fundamental uncertainties exhilarating and take them as an invitation to playful resignification and cultural creativity.

Because modernist theoretical imageries are deeply constitutive of our discipline, however, post-modernist and post-structuralist modes of thought raise substantial problems for sociologists in general and historical sociologists in particular. Opinion is therefore divided within the sociological community with respect to the more avowedly "postie" versions of the cultural turn. Some historical sociologists are grappling with this repertoire, trying to destabilize organizing imageries of progress and modernity in constructive (rather than simply deconstructive) ways.[109] Others have responded by seeking to define these currents out of existence—or at least out of comparative historical sociology—in an attempt to make common cause with the more *soi-disant* scientific and soft-utilitarian subdiscipline of historical institutionalist political science. For James Mahoney and Dietrich Rueschemeyer,

107. "Cleric, rabbi, sadhi, and mullah mount the rostrum, occupy the public place, seeking to ordinate society according to a text originating outside of it." The quote is from Friedland (2001: 236).

108. The sense of progress, of progressive change, is one casualty. In her comparison of late-nineteenth- and late-twentieth-century commemorations, Spillman (1997) found that faith in progress had diminished in the twentieth century, even though there was more progress—by nineteenth-century criteria—in the twentieth.

109. Zald (1996). Things are complicated by the fact that "cultural sociology" has in part been constituted in reaction to cultural studies and "postie" thought—at the same time that it has been influenced by them and is itself a product of the same intellectual and historical moment. All the more reason to render the "turn" in "cultural turn" in the plural!

for example, "comparative historical analysis" should by definition exclude most interpretivists, whom they also call "cultural theorists." "The danger of not taking sides on this issue," they warn, "is that promising young researchers may be steered toward the theoretical nihilism embraced in the more extreme forms of postmodern theory" (Mahoney and Rueschemeyer 2003: 24). Since every prohibition is also an incitement, to paraphrase Foucault or (better) Oscar Wilde's Lord Henry Wotton, we would have thought that such finger wagging would only add to the temptations luring today's academic youth to their culturalist doom.

This latter strategy—*je refuse!*—seems as misconceived as it is to be expected. Work in the historical sociology of science—itself a wonderfully alive area in the cultural turn, as we noted above—would suggest that these efforts at boundary maintenance are characteristic of not only normal science, but also legitimatory moves emerging from within sociology. Think, for example, of the repressions that Charles Camic (1992) has shown were part and parcel of the Parsonian project of grand theorizing and institution building. Why should historical sociology be immune from this hegemonizing impulse? Nevertheless, we should resist it—and ironically there are good scientific grounds for doing so. Innovations in fundamental knowledge often emerge from the encounter with other fundamental knowledges, as Arthur Stinchcombe (2001: esp. 158–178) notes, and fundamental knowledge is not stratified along a single dimension. There is plenty to criticize about "the turn"—including some of its methods of analysis, which are as yet in their infancy—and criticism should be vigorously pursued. But given the rapid transformation of these knowledges and the world that they are seeking to map, who is to prophesy from whence will come the "cultural toolkit" for the historical sociologists of the third, fourth, or future waves?[110]

Feminist Challenges

Like their *compañeras* in other parts of the human sciences, feminists within historical sociology have contested the exclusions and repressions that have characterized social analysis and have revealed the promises and limits of both universalist modern categories and modern social structures themselves.[111] They are but one small wing of a set of multifaceted intellectual and political movements, emerging in the 1960s and continuing today, that have

110. Here we borrow Swidler's (1986) staunchly utilitarian metaphor.
111. The current renaissance of feminist intellectual work got under way in the late 1960s, concurrent with our second-wave historical sociologists; feminist academics in historical sociology and other disciplines have been allied with a social movement—the "second-wave" women's movement that peaked in the 1970s but continues in more institutionalized forms even today.

transformed social life and social theory across the globe. These movements, some of the most successful grassroots ventures in U.S. and, indeed, world history, have been dedicated to expressing what have been understood to be women's interests and identities and to reversing the exclusion of women from modernity's privileged intellectual spaces and fields of practice, including social theory and the university. Even with women's movements past their peak of popular mobilization, scholars in gender studies—including historical sociologists—often continue to be linked to feminist political activities outside academia. This differentiates them from some of the other challenges to second-wave work discussed above and gives the feminist challenges to historical sociology—usually, but not always, mounted by women— a stronger political charge than we find in most other areas.

Working against disciplinary resistance within both heterodox fields such as historical sociology and more orthodox areas such as stratification research, feminists have had real although uneven successes in bringing the insights of gender scholarship to bear on theory and research.[112] In so doing, they have upset many of the foundational concepts of modernist social theory; they continue to trouble sociological analysis. Social theorizing founders on the gendered divisions between rational and nonrational action and the evident unsuitability of practices such as mothering for theorizing agency in the rationalist mode of second-wave, rational choice, and institutionalist historical sociologists. Women and the work they do—care giving, housekeeping, sexual labor, varying modes of political activity—and gendered signification have been troublesome categories for sociological analyses of politics, capitalism, and modernity. Meanwhile, the gendered (masculine) character of the central sociological subjects of modernity—citizens, workers, soldiers—and what have been seen as core constituents of modernity—markets, public spheres, states—has also been revealed by feminist analysis, challenging the universalist modern on another front.[113] Feminist scholarly challenges raised difficulties for second-wave historical sociology, for they undermined taken-for-granted premises about who were the important political subjects and which were the critical events, upended periodization, and opened new arenas for political analysis—bodies, families, sexualities—while deepening the understanding of how gender structures even formal political spaces where women were excluded.

In the narrative of modernization theory, and in most varieties of Marx-

112. On the general issue of disciplines and feminism, see Stacey and Thorne (1985, 1996); Burawoy (1996).
113. Barbara Marshall (1994, 2000) argues that those aspects of feminism that challenge modernist premises have gone against the grain of sociology precisely because our discipline is a modernist project. See also Silverberg, ed. (1998).

ism, women have been seen to inhabit a "traditional," "private" world of family and home. As they move into the public sphere of the labor market, civil society, and the state—as did men before them in the transition from feudalism to modern capitalism—they too become modern subjects. We can now say that women's status and activities are important signs of what is understood to be modern or traditional, including by social scientists, even as the content and significance of these terms shift over time and place. "Women" represents a key category of modernity's Others, and liberal and autonomous individuals, citizens, workers, and soldiers—the categories of modern subjects—are defined in opposition to what is "woman," even when actual women are making decisions, working, or fighting. Their absence helped to constitute the modern bourgeois public sphere and citizenship. Later, their inclusion signifies that modernity has arrived, even if the structures themselves retain a masculine character. Once (in the nineteenth-century heyday of the "family wage") women's paid labor was taken as evidence of the barbaric (if not satanic) character of capitalism, which had to be civilized by protecting women from paid work.[114] Contemporary analysts often assume that modernizing developments will inevitably bring women out of what they see as traditional housewifery and into the paid labor force and that the exclusion of women from paid work demonstrates societal backwardness.[115] Feminists have shifted this narrative decisively, showing that women's expulsion from public social life and the erection of a public-private divide between domesticity, home, and family, on the one hand, and paid labor, democratic politics, and states, on the other, is very much a modern creation, not the residue of women's incomplete modernization.

Thanks to their cross-disciplinary ties through gender studies, feminist historical sociologists have been a conduit into the subdiscipline for a variety of intellectual trends, including women's history, feminist political theory, cultural studies, post-structuralism, and (post-)colonial studies. Women's politics and women's experiences, historical and contemporary—later to be subjected to deconstructive readings and political interventions—provided

114. Both men and women championed mothers' domesticity, although with different aims in mind; only a minority of women pursued the goals of gaining entry to paid labor, which today would be recognized as a "feminist" position. In many places (not simply the United States and Europe), women often struggled for resources and political recognition on the basis of gender "difference," in the instance of the late nineteenth and early twentieth centuries, on the basis of what were understood to be distinctively feminine virtues associated with mothering; see, for example, *Mothers of a New World: Maternalist Politics and the Origins of Welfare States*, edited by Seth Koven and Sonya Michel (1993).

115. International organizations use measures of women's status to construct a "gender-related development index," which can be compared to the general "human development index"; see, for example, United Nations Development Programme (2000). See also Berkovitch (1999).

the initial impetus for feminist work in the human sciences over thirty years ago. Within still second-wave historical sociology, feminists brought novel arguments and analyses about gender relations, previously understood only as "sexual difference" or marginalized as insignificant to the main action of modernization. Power and inequalities—core concerns of political and historical sociology—had a gendered face where they had been previously understood as principally about class and (sometimes) race. In this period, feminists in historical sociology—like their colleagues in the rest of the subfield and indeed throughout the human sciences—understood women and men to be natural groups, emerging from biological or social universals. They saw "women's interests" in the classical Marxian-Lukácsian fashion found throughout second-wave historical sociology: identifiable by social analysts (or feminist vanguards), who could read them off social-structural locations, even as their interpretations diverged on what provided the material basis for those interests—labor, citizenship, mothering, or sexuality. Sometimes these approaches construed women's interests and political demands in the same vaguely utilitarian mode as much mainstream institutionalist analysis. Yet at times feminist historical sociologists mounted an explicit challenge to utilitarianism and the concept of the atomized, rational individual pursuing his own interests. How, for example, could such premises accommodate the activities of mothers—and indeed fathers—caring and sacrificing for children? (The question remains a pertinent point of analytical vulnerability.)[116] An even more severe break with the fantasy of clear materialist determination was to come with the various culturalist and poststructuralist moves of the late 1980s and early 1990s.

Second-wave historical sociology experienced a series of challenges to its premises about power, the construction of agents, and signification with the cultural turns of the late 1980s and beyond (as we have outlined above). These challenges affected feminist historical sociologists from two directions—within the subdiscipline and within gender studies, where parallel contestations erupted, with scholars mounting devastating attacks on the concepts of a culturally or linguistically unmediated experience and a natural, presocial, and unified category of "women," heretofore the lodestars of women's movement politics and women's studies scholarship.[117] Joan Scott

116. Some rational choice thinkers are seeking to plug this analytical hole with a spot of evolutionary biology, but this analytic strategy has yet to make an appearance in historical sociology. No doubt it will—and soon.

117. Judith Butler, who became the iconic post-structuralist feminist theorist, conceived gender as performative. Yet her innovative work was less significant for historical sociologists than the others here cited, for her analyses are for the most part historically decontextualized. Moreover, to the dismay of sociologists, the now canonical (in gender studies) *Gender Trouble* (1990) did not explore the work

(1986, 1992) showed women's experience to be culturally mediated and variable, yet she argued, with wide influence in historical sociology, that a (changeable) gender is "a useful category of historical analysis," with two interrelated aspects: gender as "a constitutive element of social relationships based on perceived differences between the sexes" and as "a primary way of signifying relationships of power" (1986). Not all who embraced the turn to signification and culture took Scott's deconstructive path, but her formulation helped to establish cultural approaches for feminists doing historical work, including historical sociologists.

Another part of the culturalist challenge can be categorized as anti-essentialism, in which the category of "women" was exploded by consideration of multiple differences or post-structuralist decomposition. Analysts such as Evelyn Nakano Glenn (1992) mined the vein of difference beyond gender to unearth confounding dissimilarities and inequalities based on race and ethnicity, nationality, sexuality, and the like.[118] Much of the work around "multiple differences" or "intersecting inequalities" incorporates discursive and cultural issues, yet some of it has maintained the familiar materialist premises about groups and interests even as the possible bases of oppression multiply.[119] Denise Riley (1989)—an influential gender scholar hailing from the humanities—demonstrated that "women" were a fiction, "historically, discursively constructed . . . a volatile collectivity in which female persons can be very differently positioned . . . synchronically and diachronically erratic as a collectivity . . . inconstant [for the individual] and [unable to] . . . provide an ontological foundation" (pps. 1–2). The deconstruction of "women" also combined with concerns about multiple inequalities, raising difficult questions about what might be involved in relations *among* women. For example, Chandra Mohanty (1991) revealed the colonialist discursive moves embedded in the monolithic portrayal of "third world women" as Other to "Western feminism." These sorts of challenges raised particular difficulties for large-scale comparative or longue durée historical work; while historical case studies (or ethnography) may be well suited to unpacking the complex, cultural construction of identities at the intersection of multiple forms of difference, power, and inequality for small

of such obvious predecessors as Erving Goffman. Butler's work lost something by this refusal to engage both Goffman and Clio.

118. The critique of the idea of a unified category of woman was extremely widespread, and the literature on what has come to be called "multiple differences" or "intersectionality" is enormous. Bhavnani, ed. (2001) is an excellent collection on the debates around race, gender, colonialism, and sexuality. For an influential piece in history, see T. Liu (1991).

119. For "interlocking oppressions," see, for example, P. H. Collins (1990) and the critique of the limits on her "deconstructive zeal" by Gilroy (1993: 226–232).

groups of women (or men), undertaking studies of what Leslie McCall (2001) calls "complex inequality" on the vast terrain of the labor market, state, revolutions, and other collective political action is challenging indeed.

The intellectual shifts to representation and the multiplicity of identities and inequalities have been very powerful and open new understandings of modernity. Yet it is important to note that within historical sociology, as across the academy, feminism retains very diverse theoretical orientations and different attitudes about modernist analysis and its various "post" alternatives. And of course feminist theory and analysis continues to develop.[120] Feminism's increasing internal diversity is reflected among feminist historical sociologists, who run the gamut from deconstructionism—one end of culturalist work—to standpoint theory, which assumes a still robust social determinism. Historical sociologists, raised on earlier, largely materialist understandings of gender relations, were initially ambivalent about the deconstructionist and culturalist critiques. And, indeed, the materialist tendencies have not been extinguished, as much work continues in a still modernist vein, within an implicitly utilitarian institutionalist or power resources framework. Of late, however, with the spread of culturalist approaches throughout the discipline, historical sociologists have become friendlier to analyses featuring signification. Many feminist historical sociologists have been influenced by the cultural turn, but most have not taken what Geoff Eley (1996) calls "the escalator" all the way to post-structuralism, and only a few have ventured into post-structuralist archeologies of categories and concepts (especially the categories of "woman" and "man" themselves). Thus gender has entered (historical) sociology mainly as a dimension of analysis, to be incorporated into various theoretical frameworks rather than through the adoption of feminist theories. Feminist historical sociologists are trying to strike compromise positions. With respect to the analysis of collective political action and states, this is where we are today on this extremely unsettled ground.

Feminist historical sociology has had some impressive intellectual successes, yet we take note of a gendered patterning in the areas of scholarship where feminist analyses have, or have not, made headway and where they have found resistance. Gender analysis has faced resistance throughout the academy, echoing the opposition feminist politics have faced in the "real world." This resistance takes on a distinctive character in historical sociol-

---

120. The project of "gendering" sociology means different things for scholars in different subdisciplines and with different analytic and theoretical leanings. Sociologists of gender who identify with the historical wing of the discipline differ sharply from their rather presentist and too often positivist colleagues by their concern with the *explicitly* political institutions of modernity. See Julia O'Connor, Orloff, and Shaver (1999: 10–11).

ogy, with its center of gravity in the macro-political (Adams 1998; A. Baron 1998; Morawska 1998). R. W. Connell (1987) has argued that opposition to feminism grows stronger the closer one gets to what he calls the core institution of male power: the state apparatus, especially its military wing.[121] (He thinks feminists are capable of achieving "local reversals" in "peripheral" sites such as the family.) We do not sign on to Connell's overall analysis of patriarchy and state power—which is extremely bleak—but we do see a parallel relationship between resistance to feminism and feminist theory and proximity of an academic discipline or subdiscipline to the commanding heights of state power. Thus, it has been easier for gendered work to take hold in English than in economics or in the sociology of the family than in political sociology, including its historical wing. When we examine historical sociological research on the state, we find greater penetration by gender analysis in scholarship on welfare policy than in research on state formation and state building, including the symbolically masculine activities of war and coercion. The gender segregation of scholarship, ubiquitous in academia and intellectual life, disables historical sociologists from making convincing historicized accounts of modernity, capitalism, states, and politics. The recurring theoretical move of shunting "concerns of gender" to women scholars or to fields of scholarship marked as feminine prevents analysts of core political institutions and practices from understanding their gendered character—and thus results in fatally misunderstanding them. And gender scholarship is reciprocally impoverished by the lack of work on institutions and practices that are also central to the constitution of gender relations.

Feminists in the last two to three decades have built up a significant body of research on gendered processes of reproduction, understood broadly as encompassing biological, social, and cultural elements; on gendered processes of identity formation within classes, nations, and racial/ethnic formations; on gendered collective action and citizenship practices; and on gendered systems of social provision (welfare states). This research took off from the distinguished line of work among Marxist feminists on class reproduction, families, and gender but has evolved its own post-Marxist character (B. Laslett and Brenner 1989). Nicola Beisel's *Imperiled Innocents* (1997), for example, argues for the central role of the family, gender, and sexual politics in class formation and reproduction—including cultural aspects of these processes—and links these to the formation of Anthony Comstock's anti-vice movement in Victorian America.

Nevertheless, it must be said that the masculine preserves of states remain analytically off limits. There have been few if any historical analyses of the

---

121. A fascinating counter-argument is Jackson (1998).

gendered mechanics of war making itself—this in spite of the implicit invitation in Norbert Elias's *The Civilizing Process* (1994 [1939]), a text about, above all, the social disciplining and internalization of forms of *masculinized* coercion involved in the formation of "modern" states and male subjects.[122] And studies of state formation, one of the most significant and influential areas of scholarly activity by comparative-historical sociologists, have remained relatively untouched by gender analysis. For too many scholars in these areas, masculinity remains unmarked, and "gender" continues to signify "women" (Carver 1996). Yet recent work by historians and political theorists has revealed not only elements of women's role in state making, but also the ways in which masculine identities and men's gendered aims were implicated in the political activities that established modern states and democratic orders (J. Landes 1988; Pateman 1988b, 1989). Other analyses highlight the ways in which "woman" or particular women functioned as signs in sexualized political discourses and political culture.[123] Among historical sociologists, Pavla Miller (1998) has traced the making and unmaking of different forms of patriarchal governance across a number of Western sites, relating gender and family dynamics, technologies of the self, and larger processes of state making and capitalist industrialization. Gary Hamilton (1990) compares the intersection of families and states in China and Western Europe, reevaluating Weber's arguments about patriarchy and patrimonialism. Julia Adams's (1994, 2004) work on the Netherlands, England, and France uncovers the way in which representatives of family lineages mobilized signifiers of fatherhood and rule in the formation of patrimonial political structures and shows how the articulation of signs of paternity, elite family forms, and political structures contributed to the different fates of these three states. This general body of work has mostly concentrated on Europe—a limitation, to be sure, but also a rhetorical advantage, since Europe was often rendered as the premier site of rationalized state making, the site in which gender, associated with notions of traditionalism, was supposed to have been progressively extirpated (Steinmetz, ed. 1999).

While work on "the sinews of power"—war, bureaucratization, fiscal extraction—has not yet become a favored site for feminist historical sociology, it is not the case that feminist sociologists have neglected states altogether. Far from it. Gender analysts in historical sociology have thoroughly worked the ground of states and their critical role in social reproduction, particularly in systems of social provision and regulation—today's wel-

122. On the other hand, historical and political theoretical studies of representations of war abound. See, for example, the sections on masculinity and representations of war in Elshtain (1987).
123. Gregerson (1995); L. Hunt (1984, 1992); Maza (1993); Zerilli (1994).

fare states and their precursors (see Orloff, this volume). Feminist historical sociologists have changed the way welfare states or regimes are conceptualized. By beginning from feminist premises about women's (and men's) interests and focusing on different capacities to exercise citizenship rights, the distribution of paid and unpaid labor, employment opportunities, poverty levels, and support for caregiving, they have upended much of the common wisdom about the modern welfare state and citizenship, including the periodization of citizenship rights, the categorization of regimes, the import of key concepts such as de-commodification, and the prerequisites for state welfare. To take only one of these accomplishments: mainstream scholars of the early years of modern state welfare saw working men utilizing political rights to demand social rights, which in turn strengthened their collective political capacities. Feminists brought out the gendered content of these struggles, showing that trade unionists, employers, and others had gender and familial as well as occupational or class interests. In the struggles over protective legislation for women and for family provision, for example, many working men wanted women to be construed as wives, male employers wanted them to be (subordinate, cheap) workers, and women themselves often wanted recognition as mothers or as (equally paid and equal) workers (Pedersen 1993; Jenson 1986). Which group won out differed across countries and time periods. Furthermore, historical sociologists showed that for women, social rights preceded political rights—reversing the periodization handed down by T. H. Marshall to historical sociologists of welfare—and that women utilized distinctive political strategies and forms to win passage of legislation in the absence of the franchise (Skocpol 1992; Clemens 1997).

Gender analysts of welfare systems for the most part have followed the basic intellectual contours of institutionalism, including many of its utilitarian assumptions. But starting with women unravels many institutionalist premises. And considerations of gender often bleed into topics outside the normally dry parameters of institutionalist analysis, such as body rights or, even more commonly, unpaid care work (Julia O'Connor, Orloff, and Shaver 1999; Orloff 1993a). These subjects are difficult to assimilate to certain aspects of the utilitarian model of the actor, which depends on notions of an autonomous liberal individual whose gender is unmarked but masculine and is unburdened by care or other attachments. Moreover, opening up questions about care, women's exclusion, and bodies has troubled assumptions about the easy interpretability of "interests" apart from politics, culture, and signification. For example, many scholars have looked at different political struggles around the proper relationship of motherhood and paid labor, citizenship, and welfare benefits, finding that different groups of men and women take varying positions over time and across countries. Debates around the meanings of all these statuses are shifting and politically and culturally charged.[124] Within this research area, many are paying increased attention to the ways in which states create categories and subjects, leading some to consider the ways in which making claims on the state incorporates cultural or discursive dimensions, as in a host of studies on the ways in which discursive categories have been institutionalized in state agencies and professional-administrative practices at the local level, and either embraced or resisted by those to whom they have been applied.[125]

Scholars working on the broad topic of collective action—which has always been a contentious area with respect to gender—uncovered the contribution of women to class politics and social movements, then moved to consider the ways in which gendered identities and gender relations are politically and culturally created, sustained, or challenged by social movements and in the routines of institutionalized politics. Facile assumptions about working-class solidarity across gender lines or the content of political demands were undermined by the research of historical sociologists such as Ava Baron, Johanna Brenner, Elizabeth Faue, Ruth Milkman, Sonya Rose, and Carole Turbin, writing in the 1980s and early 1990s on the history of working-class or middle-class women, gender in the workplace, the gender politics of the labor movement, and the role of the state in creating sex segregation.[126] Others chronicled the rise of the different waves of women's movements (e.g., Ferree and Hess 1985; Freeman 1975). But their close ties to history also meant that they felt the pull of the cultural turn and the associated shift from the "history of women" (L. Tilly and Scott 1978) to the post-structuralist historical construction of sexual difference (e.g., J. W. Scott 1988; see also Eley 1996). The construction of distinctive masculinities and femininities in diverse contexts, and the sources of gendered political action, have been examined by many analysts, including, for example, Mary Ann Clawson (1989) in an analysis of nineteenth-century U.S. fraternal organizations and Raka Ray (1999) in a study of women's movements in two Indian

124. Adams and Padamsee (2001) and Padamsee and Adams (2002) draw on post-structuralism in their analysis of the deployment of the concept of "maternalism" in feminist histories of the U.S. welfare state; see also Orloff (2000).

125. See, for example, Bellingham and Mathis (1994); Gal and Kligman (2000); Haney (2002); Hobson and Lindholm (1997); see also Steinmetz (1993). Nancy Fraser has made several influential interventions to bring discursive approaches to gendered welfare scholarship; see Fraser (1989, 1997); Fraser and Gordon (1994b).

126. A. Baron, ed. (1991); J. Brenner and Ramos (1984); Cohn (1985); Deacon (1989); Faue (1991); Milkman (1987); Rose (1992); Turbin (1992).

cities, while Kathleen Blee (1991) incorporated the racialized dimensions of women's identities in a study of women's participation in the Ku Klux Klan. This focus on gendered mobilization extends to the formation of nations and states as well—for example, Gay Seidman's (1993) examination of post-apartheid South Africa and Daina Stukuls's (1999) study of processes of gendered normalization in post-Soviet Latvia. Theda Skocpol's (1992) analysis of the emergence and successes of "maternalist" movements in the first decades of the twentieth century challenged understandings of U.S. political and policy history and of the sources of collective action that had formed the basis for much political sociology. In all of these studies, we see not only better historical documentation of the varying forms and levels of gendered collective action (including armed struggle), but also interesting attempts to integrate culturalist preoccupations with political struggles and structures. Much of this work deals with the ways in which gender relations are interwoven with political struggles and gendered signs and symbols are constitutive of political discourse.

Feminists in historical sociology have conducted a spirited campaign to bring gender into the political and still masculinized core of modernity. The masculine redoubts of the working class (such as welfare states) have been revealed in exemplary historical sociological research as sites of gendered contestation and sources of gendering broader social orders, but we have been less successful in entering the corporate headquarters of modernity. We think this means less satisfying explanatory accounts of social transformation for all of us. Sociologists who want to incorporate gender analysis into their work will continue to find the road hard going, but we hope they will keep up their efforts. We editors also hope that they will resist certain intellectual tendencies within gender studies, particularly those that automatically reject any further congress between the liberal subject and womanhood. This rejection would be a grievous mistake at a moment when gendered meanings of "tradition" and "modernity," swirling around women's bodies and practices yet again, threaten to engulf whatever progress—situated and relative though it may be—women have achieved through a qualified embrace of modernity.

With respect to the wider community of historical sociologists and the discipline of sociology itself, la lucha continua (as we used to say). Linda Zerilli (1994) points out in her study of classical political theory and the signifier "woman" that political theory as an intellectual enterprise also participates in the construction of gender; the same point may be made of historical sociology (Adams 1998; A. Baron 1998). Witness how the areas of sociology in which gender analyses have scored some successes may be subject to redefinition by those who would prefer, consciously or not, to dispense with them.[127] The gendering encounters on intellectual territory are never finally fixed.

World Systems, Post-Coloniality, and Remapping
the World after the Second Wave

Historical sociology is built on theories of transitions to capitalist modernity, and those theories historically have been centered around versions of the European Experience. Both first- and second-wave sociologists overemphasized the originary importance of European historical lineages, as we have seen, and many simply assumed that the concepts and theories deriving from those lineages applied around the world. Certain key features of those lineages (such as their linkage to colonialism or Islam) were also deemed off the table. As people in and outside the academy reexamine this assumption, the process of academic soul searching in historical sociology is under way on three main fronts.

First, some scholars are critically reevaluating and extending second-wave work and debates. The filiation often is explicitly marked. Thus the reciprocal relationship between organized violence—including war making—and state centralization highlighted by Charles Tilly (among others) has been qualified and reformulated by Karen Barkey (1994), based on the case of the Ottoman Empire, and Miguel Centeno and Fernando Lopez-Alves, with respect to patterns of state formation in Latin America.[128] What role ideology might play in the genesis of revolutions, the topic of a well-known debate between Theda Skocpol and William Sewell Jr., spurred Mansoor Moaddel's (1992) study of the 1979 Iranian revolution.[129] Revolutionary processes and outcomes established in the state-centered tradition of second-wave research have been reexamined in non-European states by Jeff Goodwin (2001), Timothy Wickham-Crowley (1992), and others. Do certain class coalitions make particular paths of political development more likely? James Mahoney (2001b) and Jeffery Paige (1997) revisit Barrington Moore Jr.'s classic arguments in their respective studies of liberalism and the rise of democracy in Central America. Does a state's relative autonomy not simply from the bourgeoisie, but also from a colonial power, help secure the conditions of modernization? Fatma Müge Göçek (1996) reexamines the familiar

127. Some might wonder if the machine terminology attached to the intellectual move to "social mechanisms" is not at least partially an attempt to reclaim masculine intellectual space, for example! 128. Centeno (2002); Centeno and Lopez-Alves, eds. (2002). See also D. Davis (1994) and Parsa (2000). 129. For a quite different historical sociological interpretation, see Arjomand (1998, 2001). For the original debate, see Sewell (1985) and Skocpol (1985b).

second-wave question in her study of the Ottoman Empire.[130] This is only a sampling of recent scholarship in this genre. "While history may perhaps suffer less from this confusion than the social sciences," write Miguel Centeno and Fernando Lopez-Alves (2002: 5), "we are all used to assumptions that peasant means French, state means Germany, revolution means Russia, and democracy means Westminster." These and other excellent works disorganize these assumptions, tell us about Other Cases, and rewrite the empirical generalizations and sociological theories of state formation derived from internalist and nationally specific European histories.[131]

Another version of this approach, which we might call critical extensions of second-wave scholarship, follows in the path of Fernando Cardoso and Enzo Faletto (1979 [1971]), Andre Gunder Frank (1966b), Immanuel Wallerstein (1974), and other pioneers of dependency theory and world systems analysis.[132] This vision has been taken up in a variety of fruitful ways by Janet Abu-Lughod (1989), Giovanni Arrighi (1989), Beverly Silver (1999), Albert Bergesen and Ronald Schoenberg (1980), Terry Boswell (1989), Georgi Derluguian (2000), Peter Evans (1979), John Foran (1993a), Harriet Friedmann (1982), and David Strang (1996), among others. In the broadest sense, it has diffused beyond the boundaries of world systems analysis: the general world systems intuition is now quite widespread, with plenty of historical sociologists who do not sign on to the theory making free with some vague version of the concept. True, few historical sociologists have adopted Wallerstein's full argument that there is something one might call a "world system": a *single* network of core, peripheral, and semi-peripheral nodes sustained by the extraction of surplus based on economic specialization and rationalization rather than imperial force. Nevertheless, the impulse behind world systems analysis was remarkable, and it is still one that all of us might profitably take up, particularly when it comes to jettisoning the automatic identification of important social processes with the boundaries of contemporary sovereign states and nation-state borders.[133]

---

130. In the Marxian tradition, see also Chibber (1998, 1999).

131. Note that individual scholars with second-wave affiliations have followed the threads into other areas as well, such as historical institutionalism. Karen Barkey, for example, has since written on network organization in the Ottoman Empire in the manner of the "institutionalist challenge" described above. See Barkey and Van Rossem (1997). In general, this whole category of work overlaps substantially with similar moves in historical institutionalist political science.

132. An insightful contemporaneous discussion of this literature is Roxborough (1979). Foran (1992) examines the relationship among underdevelopment theory, dependency, and world systems theories.

133. See Wallerstein et al. (1996). The report of the Gulbenkian Commission, chaired by Wallerstein, includes an excellent section on the analytic problems associated with "state-centric thinking" (pp. 80–85). This does not mean that we should all analyze the world—a dubious project in any case, subject to all the objections that were raised about the vaulting ambition of Braudelian "total history."

In all this work, we continue to see the signs of the rending and tearing of the second-wave paradigm along several fault lines. Those who hold by its core dimensions, who try to explain what they are about in terms of expanding the reach and generalizability of second-wave models, are prey to increasingly sharp analytic tensions. Sometimes those tensions are explicitly thematized. Jeff Goodwin, for example, discusses the limitations of his "state-centered perspective" (2001: 55–58), including its failure to tackle associational networks and culture. These limits are reasonable trade-offs, he argues, when one is looking for a parsimonious rather than exhaustive explanation (p. 58). But the basic question—which Goodwin himself raises elsewhere in his work—is whether the omitted dimensions structure the state of affairs that sociologists are examining.[134] World systems analysts for their part want to incorporate dynamics of race, ethnicity, even religion into their analyses but find themselves corseted by the economistic propositions about what organizes the relationships among relevant network nodes.[135] The further insistence that there must exist a social totality, an integrated and in this case global regime, has blocked off valuable avenues of discussion with people of other theoretical inclinations.[136]

In general, the category of "race" is one symptomatic flashpoint at which these sorts of paradigmatic strains ignite. Race is easily digested within second-wave paradigms as long as it is taken to index fixed, underlying, and even biologically given attributes rather than shifting sets of signifiers that are not tethered to referents in any essential way. (The parallel developed in

---

(See especially Hexter's [1979] critical [and hilarious] comments on Braudel.) Note that Wallerstein also continues to make impassioned and inspiring arguments for not simply interdisciplinary but also de-disciplinary historical analysis. See Wallerstein (1999).

134. In Goodwin (1997) the author examines the absence of "sexual relationships and affectual ties" from social science analyses of collective action. Here's the memorable first sentence: "If the modern era is characterized by 'a veritable discursive explosion' (Foucault 1978: 17) about sexuality, then social-movement theory remains deeply embedded in the *ancien régime*" (p. 53).

135. A symptom of this problem is the widening distance between the theoretical propositions and the historical analyses or predictions that are adduced from them. See, for example, the five concluding propositions in Arrighi and Silver (1999: 271–289). The book is admirably historical; for example, it treats this era's hegemonic arrangements in relationship to previous hegemonic systems. But it is very difficult to see how propositions at this level of abstraction can be qualified by empirical evidence, much less gainsaid. The problem then is that historical materials take on a purely illustrative character. We would feel more confident of the overall argument if the authors also presented some materials that they felt were puzzling or less automatically incorporated into their theoretical system.

136. The versions of history featured in regulation-theoretic sociology share this totalizing feature as well. See, for example, Harvey (1989). Burawoy criticizes this tendency in "Grounding Globalization" in Burawoy, ed. (2000: 337–341). Steinmetz (this volume) offers a friendlier evaluation of regulation theory and its uses for historical sociology.

the previous section on feminist challenges to historical sociology is the reduction of gender to the category of biological sex.) Actors are assumed to have certain attributes and to fall into natural groups on this basis, groups that have one or another economic or political function within a social formation. Note that some superb second-wave work on the historical sociology of race, class, and states was conducted within this rubric.[137] But the analytical line in the sand drawn by the second wave precluded many of us historical sociologists from recognizing the plasticity and autonomy of systems of racial classification and their relationship to the structuring of societies and subjectivities. This has been problematic for the analysis of the entwined European, African, and American historical trajectories themselves because of the deep importance of chattel slavery and its unfolding impact on systems of racial classification and nationhood.

These trajectories and systems are precisely what are at issue in a second category of scholarship that problematizes the lines of connection between colonizer and colonized. This might mean explaining historical transitions among colonial formations that were basically bipolar at the outset of empire building but then sprouted more rival heads than a Hydra. Rulers might disagree among themselves, or the subject population may split into factions, or perhaps middlemen set up on their own accounts, having escaped the long arm of colonial and post-colonial control extended through principal-agent networks.[138] This relational research tradition dovetails with ongoing efforts in political science and historical economics to induct more well-known cases into more general utilitarian understandings of colonialism and post-colonialism (e.g., see Frieden 1994; Laitin 1998).

Much of this family of work on connections between colonizer and colonized, however, focuses on the circulation of discourses, categorization, and identification in colonial, imperial, and post-colonial settings. A number of the authors whose writings fall into this category are represented in this volume.[139] Nader Sohrabi, for example, analyzes the role of constitutionalist

137. See, for example, D. R. James (1988), who argues that institutional features of the local "racial state" were created and defended by white planters and farmers in order to forward their interests in maintaining certain features of labor-intensive cotton agriculture. A recent book on apartheid South Africa by Ivan Evans (1997) tackles just this issue—the racialization of bureaucracy—from a more culturalist angle. E. M. Beck and Tolnay's (1990) article on lynching in the South continues to generate responses and new applications. Two other pertinent works, excellent examples of third-wave historical sociology, are A. W. Marx (1998) and Seidman (1994).
138. On agency relations and empire, see Adams (1996); Kiser and Tong (1992); Spruyt (n.d.); Stinchcombe (1995).
139. See in particular works by Lo, Magubane, Sohrabi, Spillman, Faeges, and Steinmetz and the

discourses in key political conjunctures in the pre-revolutionary Ottoman Empire and revolutionary Iran. Zine Magubane charts the historical development of discourses about race, some of which were legally institutionalized, that circulate between Britain and South Africa. George Steinmetz deploys post-colonial theory to pinpoint and analyze shifts among colonialists'—and their indigenous inheritors'—"native policy models," racial discourses that categorize "natives" as civilizable or not. These discourses, he argues, are differentially implicated in genocidal state policies.[140] This style of historical sociology has some affinities with the broader field of post-colonial scholarship, which, Catherine Hall notes, argues that "the political and institutional histories of 'the centre' and its outer circles [are] more mutually constituted than we used to think" (1996: 70).[141] What is being constituted here is not typically economics, but the nexus of politics and culture. "Provincializing Europe"—to borrow Dipesh Chakrabarty's (2000) catchy phrase—is the overall intellectual project. This is a crucial but tricky business: it involves tacking back and forth between deconstructing and deploying European universalistic notions embedded in social theorizing and political practice. These notions were not developed in the isolated, modernizing, capitalist spaces of Europe—as second-wave historical sociology would have had it—but during centuries of colonial encounters that actors based in Europe organized and experienced.[142] That this formative process was mutual is clear, but its contours remain hazy and much detective work remains to be done, in historical sociology as well as elsewhere. On the purely theoretical level, as Zine Magubane discusses in this volume, historical sociologists are just beginning to ask how the particular colonialist optic of the classical theorists constitutes the terms of their concepts and theories and when that affects claims to universal applicability and reach.[143] This part

---

relevant essays in this volume. These and other historical sociological works do not take Eley's (1996) post-structuralist escalator all the way to complete concept-dependence. On the other hand, who does? (This was always a utopian—or dystopian, if you hail from other theoretical persuasions— formulation.) There are referents as well as signifiers and signifieds in their stories, and the problem of the relationship between signification and other mechanisms is also perennially on the table. For some of these authors, a theoretical touchstone is Sahlins's (1981) tale of how Captain Cook came, saw, and failed to conquer in Hawaii.

140. Magubane (2003); Sohrabi (1995, 2002); Steinmetz (2002, 2003a). See also Aminzade (2003); Go (2000); Jung (1999); Logan (2000); Raffin (2002a, 2002b).

141. Catherine Hall is quoted in Magubane (this volume). See also Ashcroft, Griffiths, and Tiffin, eds. (1995); Hansen and Stepputat (2001); Stoler (2002b); R. J. C. Young (2001).

142. C. L. R. James (1989 [1963]) has been a foundational text for those making this argument.

143. For one recent debate, see Connell (1997) and R. Collins (1997). The flip side of these discussions appears in Gilroy (1993), which argues, inter alia, that to "diaspora blacks," the "ambiguous intellectual traditions of the European Enlightenment" have served as both "a lifeline and a fetter" (p. 30).

of the provincialization project should also include scrutinizing the particular versions of world history embedded in classical theories that many sociologists still take as emblematic of—and sometimes a substitute for—history itself.

Finally, meta-narrative and synoptic grand theory are making a comeback as a third variety of the historical sociology that reaches beyond the second wave's internalist version of Europe and the United States. One major example is the work of S. N. Eisenstadt and others on the world's axial civilizations.[144] This move toward grand civilizational narratives is part of a more general intellectual impulse, we believe, and a thoroughly understandable reaction to academic dispersion and global religious resurgence.[145] We editors sympathize with the urge to reassemble the fragments—although we find the civilizational versions simultaneously nostalgic and premature—but not with what Jeffrey Alexander calls the "retrospective verifications of modernization theory" that accompany most "neo-modernist" visions (1995a: 42–43). There are far too many open questions of theory and method in historical sociology, many of them detailed in this volume, that cannot be readily folded into a new totalizing narrative. At least not yet!

Rather, historical sociologists need to ask, as concretely as possible, whether there are alternative practices conducted under the sign of modernity that have emerged from colonial and post-colonial encounters and, if so, what they look like.[146] How are categories and practices that are tagged by the actors themselves as "modern" or "Western" picked up, modified, rejected, recombined, transported, elaborated, and so on? Are dimensions of social and cultural life that historical sociologists in the United States and elsewhere take for granted as part of a modernist ensemble connected differently—or not at all—in different historical settings? There are many ways to approach these questions without falling back into simplistic polarities between the categories of "the West and the Rest" (S. Hall 1992). One strategy would analyze how notions of and practices associated with (say) property, economy, or civil society and the public sphere are appropriated and transformed in non-Western contexts—including Eastern Europe, which often

144. See especially Eisenstadt (2000, 2002). See also Arnason (2002); Goudsblom (1992, 1996); G. G. Hamilton (1994).

145. For samples of such engagements in other fields, see Huntington (1996); Mazlish and Buultjens (1993); Sherratt (1995).

146. Are they "the same but not quite," or are they radically different, and if so, how? At the core of colonial discourse, Bhabha argues, there is a fundamental ambivalence and "classificatory confusion": "colonial mimicry is the desire for a reformed, recognizable Other, *as a subject of difference that is almost the same, but not quite*" (1994: 86; emphasis in original). On alternative modernities, see for starters Gaonkar, ed. (2001); Gilroy (1993); Gole (1997); C. Taylor (1999).

gets lost in the binarizing shuffle.[147] A second strategy, which some are already pursuing, involves analyzing non-Western colonialisms—such as Japan's colonization of Taiwan (e.g., see Lo 2002). Yet another would engage in historicized ethnographies of the range of global connections emerging in today's "post-modern world."[148] There are of course further avenues of exploration, many quite promising. These are the kinds of new approaches that our reconstruction of concepts of modernity necessarily call for.

We live in a historical moment during which many U.S. academics and intellectuals assert that the Enlightenment notions of personhood, rights, and reason embedded in the "sociological modern" should be expunged as vestiges of classic forms of imperialism. Others (including Adams, Clemens, and Orloff) think that these notions—reclaimed, revised, retranslated—are essential to critical intellectual and political projects everywhere.[149] But no matter what the authors' preferred theory, values, or political position—no matter what their relationship to "modernity"—it is at least clear that such analyses are not antiquarian exercises. This is a thoroughly interdisciplinary arena of discussion, where sociologists have both plenty to learn and some distinctive theoretical and methodological tools for identifying social and cultural conditions for cosmopolitanism and other vaunted goals. It is also, in our experience, a very politically fraught space. We are convinced that we still stand to gain by struggling to keep "the prophet and the demogogue" off "the academic platform" and otherwise holding by Weber's injunctions to objectivity in "Science as a Vocation" (1946c).[150] And we have a collective shot at it. Having ignored the "colonial Other" for so long, sad to say, historical sociologists are at least relatively free of romantic visions of the "agency" of that Other or of its self-appointed academic representatives.[151]

147. See, for example, Calhoun, ed. (1993); Róna-Tás (1994); D. Stark (1996). How sociologists should deal theoretically and analytically with the end of communism is debated vociferously in a review symposium in the *American Journal of Sociology* (see Burawoy 2001; Eyal, Szelényi, and Townsley 2001; Kennedy 2001; D. Stark and Bruszt 2001). Goldstone (2002) is a fascinating analysis of efflorescences and economic growth in world history.
148. See the contributions in Burawoy, ed. (2000). See also Kleinman (2003).
149. There are clear parallels to the ongoing arguments about multiculturalism and history in the U.S. academy. Kymlicka (1998) advocates accommodations to "minority nationalism." Claims to cultural "authenticity" are fictive (if nonetheless deeply felt and historically institutionalized), argues David A. Hollinger (1995).
150. Note that Weber was by no means naive about the politics and symbolic violence present in cultural formations, including science itself. Here he is, for example, on the discovery of the concept: "In Greece, for the first time, appeared a handy means by which one could put the logical screws upon somebody so that he could not come out without admitting either that he knew nothing or that this and nothing else was truth, the eternal truth that never would vanish as the doings of the blind men vanish" (1946c: 141).
151. One controversial complaint is Dirlik (1997), delivered from a Marxist perspective, excoriating

Perhaps we can escape the trap of romanticizing the supposed collective *communitas* of the East as an antidote to the liberal individual, thus avoiding re-Orientalizing non-Western societies and selves (Said 1979). Let us hope so, for we will otherwise find ourselves flummoxed when professions of modernity and liberal individualism among political actors make an indigenous appearance in contexts far beyond the second wave's imagined European and North American spaces. As they do and will!

Conclusion: Remaking Modernity, Historicizing Sociology

As the careful reader will have noticed, the present moment lacks both the topical and theoretical coherence of the second wave. The second-wave framework identified important problems, such as rebellion and revolution; offered a dominant narrative of change fueled by class conflict; and tied contemporary concerns to past processes. The events of 1968 and imagined future upheavals were understood—both theoretically and viscerally—as part of a historical series that began with the English and French revolutions, with roots in the transitions to, and ongoing developments of, capitalism. For the core substantive topics of the second wave—transitions to democracy, the welfare state—past and present are linked in ongoing processes of social change.

But historical sociology will die if left solely to modify the second wave's answers to Marxist questions generated in the heat of the 1960s and 1970s. We (the editors) appreciate what came from the intense theoretical engagements that gave rise to and energized the second wave. It was fun to watch Marx and Weber duke it out via their second-wave proxies. Nonetheless, that moment is past, and we face different choices. Those who would counsel us simply to return to the so-called "big and important" questions of the second wave are leading us away from the springs of intellectual renewal. Historical sociologists can continue to take on new topics in an ad hoc fashion, but until and unless our inherited intellectual framework opens out, this path dooms us to academic involution. Others would simply celebrate the displacement of historical sociology, singular, by historical sociologies, plural. To be sure, the prospect of letting a thousand flowers bloom is more attractive than death by involution. But much of the vitality of historical sociology, and not simply the second wave, has come from the

---

post-colonial studies and its intellectual avatars. Some might argue that American sociologists have been busy romanticizing the agency of internal "Others" instead—particularly Black Americans. See Wacquant (2002), in which the author finds fault with the ethnographic work of Mitchell Dunier, Elijah Anderson, and Katherine Newman on just these grounds and is roundly criticized in return.

ambitious formulation of large-scale comparisons and far-flung "deep anal-ogies" (Stinchcombe 1978). Surrendering to centripetal forces kills conversa-tions about large-scale social change and relations across social domains. Luckily historical sociologists can embrace the topical differentiation and theoretical reformulations of recent work while endeavoring to reconstruct elements of a common intellectual project. This means, we argue, at least three things: first, recognizing and extending the theoretical debates that cross our substantive interests and undergird our inquiries; second, criticiz-ing and remaking our own concepts of modernity; and third, registering the subterranean shift in our basic imagery of historical change that has taken place since the heyday of the second wave.

From our discussion of third-wave challenges—institutionalist, rational choice, culturalist, feminist, and colonial/post-colonial studies—we have identified four main axes of theoretical descent and dissent from the second-wave framework. First, there are attempts to theorize agency against the second wave's structuralist approach, in which subjects' interests and ide-ologies were more or less automatically given by their social-structural loca-tion. Second, we have challenges to the exclusions of second wavers and their modernist forebears from scholars speaking on behalf of diverse subaltern groups and invoking the heretofore repressed dimensions of social life con-nected to relations between the unmarked, dominant subjects of modernity and these "Others" (gender, sexuality, "race," nation, etc.). Fueled in part by attention to the constitution of domination outside the formal polity, a third tendency has expanded the analysis of power to include capillary processes working through classification systems, therapeutic discourses, and other technologies of order. Finally, there are scholars investigating those ele-ments of the social that were repressed by the second wave's focus on the structures of the political economy. Here we find a whole variety of ap-proaches grouped under the rubric of the cultural turn or turns, efforts to "bring back in" religion, emotion, violence, habit, and all the nonrational elements of social life.

It will be a continuing struggle to discipline the dispersion that has come with all this theoretical experimentation. The kaleidoscopic quality of the substance of today's historical sociology—ranging from patrimonial states and their colonies to the origins of welfare politics and interest groups (to cite only our own concerns)—presents us with further daunting translation problems. But if what is wanted is a more unified intellectual formation than is implied by the option of historical sociologies (plural), we can but try. One essential ingredient is a common conceptual language into which our shared subdisciplinary dialects can be translated, so that we can debate theory and adjudicate empirical research. Our common language is relatively rudimentary, and this makes it hard for different varieties of historical sociologists to talk to each other, even given the emergent cross-cutting axes we described above. If culturalists working on agency cannot read institutionalist work on intersecting problems and vice versa, for example, we will all continue to gesture dumbly at one another, and sociology will be the poorer for it. Note that second-wave scholars *did* craft such an internal meta-language. Sometimes the go-rounds about the meanings of, say, "relative autonomy" or "potential autonomy" verged on navel-gazing scholasticism, but Marxists and Weberians managed to find common conceptual terrain on which to think about the changing historical relationships between politics and economics. A formation of concepts, like the Weber/Marx combinatory that defined the second wave, is looser than a paradigm and more internally contradictory but can be powerfully generative.[152] (The Weber/Marx formation was actually *especially* vibrant before it was normalized and institutionalized as a paradigm.) Happily such formations need not emerge fully blown from the mind of a dominant French philosopher but can take shape in the context of focused debate and even dustups. In any case, it is worth the collective effort and the gamble.

We will need to keep before our eyes the fissures in the concepts with which we conduct these inquiries and debates—particularly the modernist concepts that define our discipline and our restructured concepts of modernity itself. First, this means surrendering the correspondence theory of truth—in which concepts are taken to mirror referents—and, even beyond that, claims to some privileged paradigmatic access to "reality." All concepts are more or less productive translations; they do not mirror the real in any simple sense, even when they are far more straightforward than the multipronged and historically sedimented concepts that form the disciplinary foundation of sociology.[153] Second, as we have shown, the constitutive outsides and underbellies of these concepts were systematically repressed in second-wave scholarship. The historical sociologists who want all of us to stick with second-wave questions want to keep it this way. They continue to uncritically—and ahistorically—identify the "public/private distinction" with masculinity and femininity, for example. If the only way to arrive at a shared meta-language, much less a common paradigm, were on these terms, it really might be better to can the conversation altogether and to keep treading water.

152. We do not have the space to develop this distinction between paradigm and formation. This would involve discussions of both the relatively fuzzy concept of "paradigm" (which many have noted since the advent of Kuhn [1970]) and the historical sociology of relationships among conceptual formations, paradigms, and more general sign systems. Some other time perhaps!

153. See Quine (1960, 1987) on translation and the fundamental indeterminacy of concepts.

What we see is much more interesting and potentially productive, how-ever. Recomposing the concept(s) of modernity has already altered histor-ical sociologists' basic imagery of historical change from that which pre-vailed among second-wave scholars. We have come a long way from the stage-sequential thinking rife in the second wave. Rather than a sequence of coherent societal types, with modernity itself given pride of place, for exam-ple, we now see a more complex and layered flow of durable reproduction and episodes of transformation. In fact, the ideas of "durability and repro-duction," on the one hand, and their opposite numbers, "change and trans-formation," on the other, are themselves under reconstruction, especially since scholarship in all veins of historical sociology is questioning those accepted dichotomies. And in place of the once potent combination of structural determinism, a singular focus on political economy, and a tacit model of the rational actor, much recent work documents the multiplicity of structures, the under-determination of outcomes, and the complex consti-tution of human agency (for more on this, see Clemens, this volume). We can already discern some basic epistemic patterning in what we take to be a nascent third wave.

For historical sociologists, new directions of inquiry may also require—without being defined by—new research strategies. The repertoire of com-parative methods that complemented the political economy of the second wave tended to explore the unfolding of capitalism and modernity in an implicitly empty world in which "tradition" would be erased by the jugger-naut of a progressively modernizing social order.[154] In contrast to the imag-ery of clearly bounded, spatially separable cases existing in the empty "ex-perimental time" of comparative methods, today's historical sociologists define their objects as fully embedded in world historical time and explore sites and conjunctures in which legacies other than Western capitalism or democracy—post-colonialism, post-socialism, and aboriginality—resist or transform the allegedly homogenizing tendencies of globalization. As a practical matter, today's historical sociologists proceed from both extremes in order to understand the interpenetration of general processes and local settings as played out in world historical time. Some produce rich case studies that explore conjunctures and their consequences. In her study of Taiwanese doctors under Japanese colonialism, for example, Lo illuminates "the importance of the 'agents' of modernity by attending to how different social groups negotiate between the powerful narrative of the universality of

---

154. The exception in the second wave was world systems analysis, since its orthodox practitioners disavowed the disaggregative impulse behind comparision in favor of a more Hegelian analysis of the whole, the social totality.

science and the concrete political and social relationships through which science is delivered and developed" (2002: 10). Others harness the analytic power of comparison by tracking the inflection of a large-scale project— German colonialism for Steinmetz (2003a), the Marshall Plan for Djelic (1998)—across a series of spatial settings to exploit the analysis of variation deeply embedded in world historical time. For fundamental theoretical reasons, these comparative strategies reject the criterion of the independence of cases.

It must be said that the image of what historical sociologists do has yet to catch up with the range of new analytic practices. We are still closely identified with methods of archival research or systematic comparison based largely in secondary sources. These approaches might have been a necessary strategy for initially professionalizing a project with roots in political commitments. But they now limit the enterprise's scope, which we would take to be the whole canvas of social transformations, including those ongoing in the present. Sometimes we misunderstand ourselves! Take the widespread phenomenon of sociologists claiming that they "no longer do historical sociology" as they have taken up work on contemporary topics. The new subject matter is usually linked theoretically with their earlier work and reflects an extension of the analysis of social change to the present moment but simply does not demand use of sources, whether archival or not, that are conventionally defined as historical. More broadly, historical sociologists as a body should still be pushing to "historicize, always historicize!" the broader sociological project and to develop better translations of historicized inquiries for broader academic and nonacademic publics. These publics include not just other human science disciplines, of course, but those outside of the academy.[155]

Note that we emphasize "historicized" rather than simply "historical" sociology. We editors flatly reject the relegation of historical inquiry to a designated set of problems located securely in the past. Much of the "transitions" literature—the burgeoning body of research on post-socialist societies—illustrates this weird disconnect between "regular" and so-called historical sociology (Emigh, this volume). In these debates, the theoretical underpinnings of historical sociology are often rejected, both for their association with the collapsed political regimes and because the phenomena themselves—the creation of markets and civil societies, the reconfiguration of families and gender relations, the emergence of new racial/ethnic relations—appear to fall outside the empirical ambit of second-wave studies of revolution and class formation, especially when they were informed by a

155. We benefited from consulting Michael Burawoy et al. (n. d.).

loosely Marxist teleology. Instead an implicit imagery of modernization and convergence with the West now prevails. But just how are institutions of credit or property rights constructed? How might network ties rooted in party membership be transformed into resources for entrepreneurial endeavors? Out of which cultural materials and lineages do people assemble the alluring and aversive images of Western modernity that inform their political and other practices? It is hard to imagine that sociologists will make much headway in understanding these new social formations without linking past to present, without redescribing the past to inform our understanding of ongoing processes. But the fault lies not only in our more mainstream sociological interpreters! In fact the very label "historical sociology" may have occluded this possibility. What we need, as Martin Shaw puts it, is a "historical sociology of the present and future" (1998: 326).

Prediction is a dangerous game, particularly for historical sociologists. We are, after all, daughters and sons of Clio, as well as of sociology (which, being a creature of modernity, has no muse). But this vision of a more fully historicized sociology builds on the conviction that the study of the past illuminates both present and future. The current conversation among historical sociologists is symptomatic of a moment when world events, the reordering of signs and trajectories of social change, have confounded many people's expectations. Yet as new manifestations of the political, cultural, and religious past infuse the current moment, it is impossible to take this defeat of expectations as a signal of some sharp caesura between present and past. Perhaps different parts of the past demand our attention as we strive to understand processes of social change that have operated behind and beside those foregrounded by historical sociology's second wave. But we also want to avoid what Peter Baehr signals as the chief danger of arguments of continuity: "that they bring us back to where theoretically we started: normalizing a phenomenon in advance of rethinking it" (2002: 826). Perhaps this is also a genuinely unprecedented historical moment. We should consider these possibilities, carefully but urgently. Figure and ground have been disturbed; new figures are there to be found.

Many Americans in particular see their way of life as newly unsettled. For although the majority of the world's peoples have lived with this condition much longer than we have, this is a moment in which both world and theory have been shaken to the core. Historical sociologists, like other academics and intellectuals, have unconsciously depended on this sense of settlement, of achieved modernity, and are disoriented by its loss. So it is natural when they react with nostalgia for old totalities, a past of imagined theoretical stability, or with a sense of perceived threat—by policing the boundaries of intellectual inquiry to try to forcibly settle things anew or by simply refusing to debate or consider new ways of thinking. But unsettled times demand open minds. In a speech in Munich in 1918, at just such another troubling moment, Max Weber said that although "the ultimately possible attitudes toward life are irreconcilable, and hence their struggle can never be brought to a final conclusion, science"—which he meant in the broadest sense, as *Wissenschaft*—"offers us tools and training for thought, technologies for action, and the possibility of gaining some clarity about where we stand" (1946c: 150–151, 152). His vision of historical sociology still seems right to us—refusing ultimate guarantees or fundamental foundations; generous, not cramped; focused on "the demands of the day"; and wide open to the future.[156]

Overview of the Volume

The range and vitality of today's historical sociology—the burst of topical differentiation as well as theoretical reformulation—is certainly evident in this volume. As exemplified by the chapters that follow, the domain of the political has been stretched to include the interplay of politics and religion (e.g., Gorski) and the cultural constitution of nation and citizenship (e.g., Somers, Spillman and Faeges). Even within the domain of the economic, recent historical sociology extends the second wave's central interest in relations of production to include explorations in the creation of markets and relations of consumption (see the chapters by Carruthers and Emigh). In these lines of inquiry, as well as many others, both actors and the relationships among them are understood as profoundly constituted by culture and historical conjuncture, rather than as reflections of some underlying system of economic relations (see, for example, the chapters by Biernacki, Brubaker, Magubane, and Lo). Thus power relationships are reconceptualized in terms of classification systems, and formal political institutions are embedded within broader systems of capillary power that harness categories to projects of domination and contestation (Orloff, Sohrabi). With a recognition of the multiplicity of structures, new sites of agency are located where actors transgress and transpose the constraints of local but established interaction orders (see Gould).

These challenges and responses crosscut the various contributions to this volume. Here it is important to underline that we editors could have in-

---

156. Here is the full quote, the last sentences of Weber's "Science as a Vocation": "We shall set to work and meet the 'demands of the day,' in human relations as well as in our vocation. This, however, is plain and simple, if each finds and obeys the demon who holds the fibers of his very life" (M. Weber 1946c: 156).

cluded other topics as well so that we do not give the impression that we are making a claim to the canonical. That would be far from our project of forwarding rather than closing off debate. We did seek to include a chapter on the politics of family, for example, which would have detailed the peculiar history of convergence between macro-historical sociology and historical demography during the second wave, their subsequent divergence, and current hints of scholarly dissatisfaction with the split and possible reconvergence. Thesis; antithesis; synthesis? Perhaps we will read the answer in the later chronicles of the third wave.

Now on to what you *will* read here. The first section contains a trio of chapters that engage the development of sociology as a discipline. Richard Biernacki looks toward future theoretical possibilities in which assumptions of the goal-oriented actor, encoded in Parsonian sociology, are displaced by a developed theory of practice, attuned to the historical and cultural constitution of rationalities and other modes of action. Zine Magubane turns her eyes back toward the classical sociologists and to the ongoing debate over the shaping presence of particular visions of history, colonialism, and empire in their (and our) work. George Steinmetz explores the historical constitution of the midcentury discipline of sociology, against which a resurgent historical sociology defined itself.

In the next section, the Weberian imprint on historical sociology is most evident in the attention paid to state formation. Philip Gorski argues that historical analyses of both state formation and religious change have been hampered by the failure to address the deep mutual implication of these two processes. Drawing on rational choice arguments, Edgar Kiser and Justin Baer reconsider processes of bureaucratization. Close attention to the strategic choices confronting elites replaces a functional account of efficiency with analyses of the risks and benefits of domination by different means. But if the bureaucratic state developed as a mechanism for extracting resources, it now also delivers benefits, although with some hefty conditions. Ann Shola Orloff surveys the development of systems of social provision and regulation (including welfare states), a central topic for students of the second wave but now very much under reconstruction.

The next trio of chapters shifts perspective, examining politics from the vantage point of political contention, including the mobilization of violence. Meyer Kestnbaum turns to a topic that, with the hindsight of the twentieth century, is strangely absent from classical sociological theory: war. Long acknowledged as an exogenous shock that might catalyze economic or political contradictions, war making has only recently received sustained analysis in the context of state making and the changing relations between states and peoples. Nader Sohrabi addresses the flourishing research on revolutions, emphasizing how theorizing has been reshaped by attention to cases beyond Europe and to the intersecting politics of nations embedded in transnational relations and cultural conversations. And in an essay on contentious politics, the late Roger Gould (to whom this volume is dedicated) offers a bracing corrective to historicist tendencies, arguing that robust patterns have been identified across episodes and contexts of political conflict.

Just as historical sociologists have reconsidered the centrality of the tropes of the utilitarian and goal-oriented actor, so too has historical research transformed our understanding of the home turf of that actor: the economy. Rebecca Jean Emigh surveys responses to what was a central preoccupation of the first wave: the transition to capitalism. Historical research across a growing set of cases, both positive and negative, has redefined the puzzle as one of transitions to capitalisms, plural, just as the transformations signaled by "1989" have raised questions about the applicability and even generalizability of historical explanation. Bruce Carruthers then traces the path of another great question for classical theory—the development of markets—which after decades of exile in economic history now reemerges as a critical topic for historical sociology. The connections among race, ethnicity, class, and gender, along with colonial domination, anchor Ming-Cheng Lo's reconsideration of work on the history of the professions. As both a relic of guild society and a vehicle of rationalizing experts, these collectivities provide a powerful lens on the internal ambiguities of modernity.

The historical sociologies of both state building and political conflict have burst the bounds of institutional politics to address the formation of collective identities. Wars transform the relations between states and peoples; states are differentially embedded in religious communities and practices. Lyn Spillman and Russell Faeges directly explore these relationships in an essay on another of the surprising absences in classical theory: the nation. Margaret Somers's essay addresses the curiously checkered history of citizenship in historical sociology, in hopes that fresh approaches can help us think anew about citizens and subjects. Rogers Brubaker joins this general conversation, interrogating a concept both central and utterly taken for granted—the group—in the context of the politics of race and ethnicity.

Across a range of topics, the contributors to this volume explore how recent work in historical sociology has confronted the challenges and opportunities discussed throughout this introduction. Although these essays reveal few signs of an emergent theory group, patterns do emerge: key theoretical appropriations, persistent lines of division. In a concluding chapter, Elisabeth Clemens surveys these local maps of current historical sociology, arguing that recent research is at least partially organized around a set of theoretical puzzles—the articulation of practices, the embedding of institutional domains—rather than substantive questions such as which classes were or were not revolutionary.

Whereas many discussions of historical sociology have focused on questions of method, these chapters privilege the substantive and theoretical challenges presented by the making of modernity, by social change writ large. Many of the weightiest processes and events, both past and present, resist standard sociological methods, but our discipline is fundamentally weakened and trivialized if we ignore them for this reason. We hope that *Remaking Modernity* illuminates the possibilities of historicized sociology and the large-scale transformations that made and continue to make our worlds.

PART I Historical Sociology and Epistemological
Underpinnings

RICHARD BIERNACKI

The Action Turn? Comparative-Historical Inquiry
beyond the Classical Models of Conduct

The recent breakdown of the foundational assumptions about human action inherited from classical social theory is feeding some of the most creative efforts in comparative-historical inquiries today. Through much of the
1980s, historical sociologists, whether they were inspired by Marx, Weber, or
Parsons, called on a remarkably similar means-end model of conduct. In
this model, an action is explainable because individuals start from a standing end and then select the reasonable means that they control for pursuing
that end in the setting at hand. Ann Swidler once remarked that many
utilitarian and culturalist theories of conduct, although putative opposites,
actually "have a common explanatory logic, differing only in assuming
different ends of action" (Swidler 1986: 276). This common explanatory
logic is that of the means-end model. In the utilitarian theories of conduct,
the ends comprise economic and political payoffs for a class or individual. In
the culturalist theories, the ends are the fulfillment of values and normative
worldviews.

Weber insisted on the primacy of means-end reasoning for interpreting
human action even in his studies of religious culture. "In keeping with *the
law of marginal utility*," Weber wrote in his sociology of religion, "a certain
concern for one's own destiny after death generally arises when the most
essential earthly needs have been met, and thus this concern is limited
primarily to the circles of the elite and to the wealthy classes" (M. Weber
1963: 140; emphasis added).[1] In his defense of *The Protestant Ethic*, Weber

---

1. It is true that Weber's typologies include two kinds of action, affective and traditional, to which the
means-end model does not fully apply. As is widely recognized, however, Weber classifies the types of
action by their hierarchy within a means-end model, and he privileges instrumental rational action

said the inhumanly severe Calvinists did not display a unique psychology, merely a unique understanding of a goal, salvation, and of the means for pursuing it. It is enough to assume, Weber said, that "people of that past era possessed very concrete notions of what awaited them after their death and of the *means* to improve their luck in this respect, and that they directed their action thereby" (M. Weber 1982: 33). The convergence of Weber and Marx on the means-end model let Craig Calhoun put their perspectives on workers' collective action into easy dialogue in *The Question of Class Struggle* (1982: 218–219). From both perspectives, after all, *if* culture influences action, it does so principally by structuring the objectives that agents recognize and the costs of pursuing them.

Today investigators are dramatically upending these inherited models of action. In her research leading to *Talk of Love*, Ann Swidler (2001: 82–83) aimed to show how we are misled by the commonsense assumption that ends—the fundamentals for which action is undertaken—are the primary independent variable guiding action and preserving human autonomy. Her studies of the ethic of "individualist voluntarism" in the United States suggested that culture influences conduct primarily by crystallizing the problem-solving repertoires on which people draw, not by fixing final ends. The repertoires precede the choice of ends. They delimit the challenges that agents choose to deal with, and they lend actions similar styles of organization even when the ends of the action vary. Building from a critique of Weber's theory of action, Mustafa Emirbayer (forthcoming) has arrived at a similarly subversive agenda for research. Genuinely reasoned action, in his view, is organized not just as a rational adjustment of means to ends, but also as a process in which emotion and habit constitute an agent's appreciation of the environment and the openings through which he or she responds. Just as fundamentally, Hans Joas has tried to show how ends and means emerge together from the agent's ongoing appreciation of the situation at hand: "The concept of 'situation,'" Joas concluded, "is a suitable replacement for the means-ends schema as the primary basic category of a theory of action" (1996: 160). These innovators have not ruled out completely the contribution of autonomously chosen goals, as behaviorist psychologists once tried. They have instead delimited *how* goals fit compellingly into sociological explanation.

This widespread questioning has redirected comparative historical explanations of action in periods of epochal change. In his research about the

---

above others. His best-known case studies call upon means-end models to explain historical change; see Joas (1996: 39–40).

influence of the Protestant Reformation on state building, Philip Gorski (forthcoming a) focused on the templates for officeholding that Protestant-ism introduced rather than on the shifts in the inward goals of religious reverence. Likewise, through an extraordinary comparative study of the emergence of individuality in Russia across the caesura of the revolution, Oleg Kharkhordin uncovers the disguised continuities in religiously defined repertoires for recognizing personhood. Even the cutthroat deeds of Stalin, he shows, were structured by cultural formulas for the relation of self to the collectivity, not by the optimal pursuit of power (Kharkhordin 1999: 195, 230). In these signpost studies of reformation and revolution, culture influ-ences the course of change by reconfiguring the practices by which individ-uals coordinate their ties to each other and to the state, not by transforming meaningful life ends. The ferment in theories of action is reshaping the practice of historical explanation on the ground.

If it is premature to forecast the destinations that novel inquiries into action will reach, the intriguing question is how we assess their potentials in the current state of play. My thesis is that debates about the role of goals in action would benefit by evaluating the competing models as modes of *re-search practice*, not just as arguments about the real precedence of variables. The essay proceeds in three steps. The first is preparatory: I identify the features of the approach that offers the purest contrast case to the goals model because it inverts three founding premises. By taking a look at this alternative, in which action is analyzed as a problem-solving contrivance, we can discern how disparate historical investigations have actually followed the same path toward replacing the goals model. In the second part I offer an intensive illustration of the practices of explanation that follow the problem-solving model of action. I conclude by summarizing the returns to research from the two alternative models. Viewing action as a local contrivance offers profound methodological advantages in the use of evidence.

Reversing Three Premises of Action

The means-end model of classical social theory holds three premises that create a distinctive model of goal-directed action. The first premise that the problem-solving model of action reverses is that agents' goals are general, fixed prior to their encounter with the setting, but that the means of action are particular to the setting. Rather than treat goals as the general, transfer-able component of action that agents maintain across the particularities of diverse settings, the problem-solving model treats the goals of action as situationally specific, nontransposable elements of action. It focuses on the repertoires and schemas for practice as the constitutive elements of action about which we try to generalize. A pioneer study, Thomas Kuhn's *Structure of Scientific Revolutions*, powerfully illustrated the power of this reversal of the particular and the general. In his account of scientific conduct, Kuhn (1970: 37–38) bracketed goals that transcend the particularity of the moment, such as the discovery of truth or long-range professional rewards. The operative goals in his view are embedded within and inseparable from peculiar, concrete scientific puzzles at historical junctures of play. Kuhn opened up the intriguing possibility that it may prove adequate to abstract action's "means"—the know-how for identifying problems and heuristics for approaching their solution—for sociologists to characterize and explain conduct.[2] More radically, the means of action in Kuhn's histories of science subsume action's goals, because scientific paradigms inculcate techniques *both* for identifying puzzles and for attempting their solution (Kuhn 1970: 52–53).

The second tenet that the model of action as a problem-solving contrivance overturns is the premise that agents organize their action by integrating the proximate goals to be pursued in a particular setting within a system of more distant, final goals. In this goals model, agents organize their action rationally when the local arena of action is subordinated to an omnipresent hierarchy of goals. "It can be safely concluded," Parsons wrote in a preliminary sketch for the *Structure of Social Action*, "that precisely in so far as the action of an individual is guided by rational choice, its ultimate ends are to be thought of as constituting an integrated system. Rationality of action for an individual implies just as much the working-out of such a coherent system of ends as it does a rational selection of means" (1935: 295).[3] In *The Protestant Ethic*, Weber solved this problem of the ranking of goals by treating salvation as a supreme, sincerely held goal that did not have to be balanced against others. The necessities imposed by an encompassing architecture of means-end relations shift the agents' scope of freedom upward, away from local ingenuity and inventive construal of challenges toward the choice of only the highest, final ends. In *The Protestant Ethic*, the form taken by ascetic labor in a calling is fixed by the need to rationally adjust to the conditions of a functionally specialized setting, one in which purely capitalist institutions are already in place (M. Weber 1958: 67–68). In a striking illustration of the logic of the goals model of action, both Parsons and

---

2. "Though intrinsic value is no criterion for a puzzle," Kuhn wrote, as if to subvert the notion of action directed toward a good, "the assured existence of a solution is" (1970: 37).

3. Note: the two halves of my quote excise "then."

rational choice theorists started by assuming that the conditions of the environment are objectively observable or unambiguously fixed. Parsons (1949: 418) treated the environment of action as a kind of observable given so that the ultimate goals the agent pursues are the exclusive source of free self-determination.[4] Similarly, most rational choice theorists work from models of unambiguous game conditions in which the agents' identification of the conditions is taken for granted.

If we view action as a problem-solving contrivance, then the autonomy and ambiguity of the local setting, not its systematic integration into a hierarchy of objectives, sets up an arena for the agent to act with deliberation. The setting is a structure partially independent of prior goals and know-how because it is *never* automatically typifiable—never, say, unambiguously reducible to an instance of capitalist profit maximization, as it sometimes is for Weber (N. Z. Davis 1999: 73). The agent has to construe the features of the setting and the correspondingly appropriate problem-solving approach. For example, in his study of methods of geometrical proof in the seventeenth century, Amir Alexander (2002: 160–161, 186–187) has shown how the definition of a mathematical discovery and the criteria for appropriate solutions drew upon the transfer of cartographic and narrative repertoires already in use in the literal voyages of discovery. The setting of pure geometry nonetheless held its own autonomy, because the properties of points and lines carried their own suggestive challenges and opportunities for mathematicians. The extreme case of pure mathematics is an archetype for showing how a self-constituting game neither imposes its own problems on agents nor flows from the agents' choice of supervening goals. It shows how the rationality of action consists above all in how the agent typifies the setting, not just in calculation of means. The typification may consist of a new blend of characterizations when the dimensions of the setting activate diverse issues at once. For example, a recent blend, the label "same-sex marriage," calls up multiple repertoires for resolving the rights and roles of gays. The combination calls on the public, legitimizing repertoires of traditional marriage; the new technologies for conception and family reproduction; and templates for recognizing sex, love, and child rearing apart from gender (Fauconnier and Turner 2002: 269–270).

A third constituent of the goals model that an investigator using the problem-solving model of action turns upside down is the supposition that agents' rational action results from or is best represented as their internal

4. For a summary of how Parsons takes the environment of action as a scientifically verifiable, empirical condition, see Warner (1978).

reasoning to a logical conclusion. In the reasoning behind the agents' action, the goal given prior to the setting serves as the major premise, and the particularities of the means in the setting serve as minor premises. The conclusion about the optimal course of conduct that agents derive from these premises operates as the internal motor of acts. The issue is not that the goals model is obviously "unrealistic" or overly intellectual. Nor is my concern that of the relative empirical distribution in daily life of freshly calculated versus routinized actions. Instead, at the level of theory, the issue is the relation of the goals model to temporal process and the resulting necessity the goals model aims to establish between action and its causes in adequate explanations. If we view action as the consequence of the agents' conclusions once they relate means to ends, then we connect the reasons standing behind the action by placing them on a tableau within an analytically frozen instant. For instance, theorists assume that if we prefer A to B and B to C but the means used to reach A in a particular setting are more costly than the means for reaching C, the balance of reasons and the outcome can be frozen in a table or in a series of if-then premises. The "conclusion" is the motive of the act. The interrelations among the premises and the logical necessity leading from the premises to the conclusion are synchronic. As everyone knows, Weber in *The Protestant Ethic* inferred the inescapable consequences of Calvinism once he combined its novel theology with the economic institutions in place and with individuals' limited tolerance for anxiety. Weber saw neither the process of turning the motivation into action nor the orchestration of the acts as practices through time as problems requiring confirmatory evidence of their own.

With the alternative model of action as a problem-solving contrivance, investigators show only that the selected features of the action are apt, given the agents' characterizations of the setting. They do not dissect the act as if it resulted from a conclusion the agent drew prior to the act. They accept instead that since an agent's reflections flow through time, they are never unified in one instant. The temporal process of imagining first one course of action in its setting, then a second, then returning to the initial one may change the definition and valuation of the initial course.[5] Economists and rational choice theorists confront instances in which individuals prefer A to B and B to C but not, as the individuals' comparisons unfold and reshape the construals of the objects, A to C (M. Turner 2001: 94). Just as important, the

5. "Conception and systems of conceptions, ends in view and plans, are constantly making and remaking as fast as those already in use reveal their weaknesses, defects, and positive values," Dewey wrote (1929: 167).

agent often holds on to multiple, partially inconsistent typifications of the setting rather than encoding the setting univocally for solution of one preeminent problem.[6]

The differences between the two opposite approaches in method raise broader questions about our understandings of agency and rationality. In the goals model, the autonomy and priority of goals vis-à-vis the empirical features of the environment are key to preserving the autonomy of human agency. With action as a problem-solving contrivance, however, we discover agency in individuals' creative construal of puzzles and in their unforeseen transposition and modification of schemas. The felicitous interplay between a puzzle and its solution, not the free commitment to a transcendent goal, is agency's hallmark. In the goals model, a univocal reading of the setting and its constraints encourages rational deliberation among alternatives. In the problem-solving model, to the contrary, action is most reflective and rational when hybrid or ambiguous features of the setting provoke the agent to blend repertoires selectively and to cope with multiple challenges in a single process.[7]

A Case Example of the Problem-Solving Model

To illustrate the distinctive, interlocking features of research that result from so inverting the three founding premises of the goals model, let me revisit one of the celebrated art histories from Michael Baxandall's (1985) *Patterns of Intention*. In his marvelously detailed analysis of how the Renaissance artist Piero della Francesca composed the painting *Baptism of Christ*, Baxandall self-consciously adhered to a model of action as a problem-solving contrivance. In his portrayal, a great artist's chief task is to clarify the challenges of the assignment, taking in both the most immediate aesthetic challenges of the composition and the fragility of the generally available techniques of pictorial representation.

Baxandall set out to recover the puzzle that challenged the artist Piero: that of portraying for his contemporaries the major elements of Christ's baptism and to do so on the unusually narrow, vertical surface of an altarpiece (fig. 1). Piero and his middle-class contemporaries in business and the mechanical arts shared a refined, almost fetishized set of mathematical and geometrical techniques for measuring proportions, summed up by the ineffable word *commensurazione*. Artists of the time summoned these codified methods to break up a flat plane by using mathematically precise ratios and

6. For a counter-example to Weber's assumption that economic rationality requires the unambiguous delimitation of capitalist institutions, see N. Z. Davis (1999: 73).

7. See, illustratively, Katz (1999: 227).

Figure 1

to manipulate complex, three-dimensional objects as combinations of simpler geometrical shapes (Baxandall 1988: 95, 101). If the model of action as a problem-solving contrivance were merely a shorthand for summing up observable habits of artistic creation, we would predict that Piero's work would exhibit sensitivity to proportion and perspective—a pedestrian and blithery corollary that could be reframed after all as the conscious, overarching *goal* after which the artist strived. Instead, it is key to the problem-solving model that the schemas identified as the ingredients of the resulting action not merely harmonize by tautology with the action by restating the features of the action. They must also disclose new features of the action that would otherwise have remained unobservable and without which the action's production appears impossible. A schema does not consist merely of norms for how the action or its products should appear, but also comprises a method by which agents could not otherwise address the challenges of action they identify in their setting.

That necessity for revealing the internal constitution of the action requires Baxandall to retrace even more specifically the problems Piero had to solve in his art piece. For example, once Piero had set Christ as a tall, central figure in the middle panel—essential for any didactic illustration of the biblical story—he lacked room on the sides for the crowd of onlookers featured in the biblical narrative of the baptism. Piero persevered by organizing the severe perspectival recession of the background, and that contrivance enabled him to squeeze onlookers into a smaller patch of surface area. He faced a similar difficulty in placing a group of angels, who were needed for their choric function. He managed that challenge by putting them far to the side, partitioned from the main scene by a tree and arranged in poses that broke up their solidity as a group so they could not outweigh the visual magnitude of Christ's shape.[8] Piero used the principle of commensurazione to cope with this problem of crowding on his painting surface; if one dissects the whole surface area by halves, thirds, and quarters, one discovers that the regions for Christ, the angels, and John the Baptist, as well as the volumes of their limbs and the recessed objects in the background, are located with precision on the boundary lines of those proportions of space (fig. 1). The curious angle of John's upturned leg, the three directions in which the angels peer, the hovering position of the dove—all fall perfectly along these dividing lines. An amazing geometric formalism this may be; what matters is how

---

8. Piero played with the depth of the representation to deal not just with the complexity of shapes, but also with the complexity of the biblical narrative. Elements from each episode of the biblical narrative are arranged in chronological order from the rear of the painting to its foreground (Baxandall 1985: 127).

Piero resorted to it as a tool for the difficult job of fitting so many figures without congestion onto an exaggeratedly vertical plane.

Let us move to how Baxandall illustrated the second premise of the problem-solving mode, that of the autonomy of the puzzle from pre-given, ultimate goals. At no point does his deciphering of the picture's oddities resort to meanings or objectives extrinsic to the artist's challenge of performing well on the immediate work problem. For example, Baxandall comprehended the quirks in figures' posture and dress as solutions to problems of composition, not as attempts to convey a hidden message or as ties to the political context. The directive purpose of action is only our reconstruction of how the schemas on which the artist called happen to solve the problem.[9] With the goals mode, action is stylized as an exemplification of a general motive or point of concern for the agents. In *The Protestant Ethic* (M. Weber 1958), for example, it is that of doing business with a methodical, unrelenting spirit as a sign of salvation. Baxandall showed how the autonomy of the puzzle from goals outside the setting enables us to demonstrate how schemas compose action. For example, when Baxandall tried to explain how Piero in *The Baptism of Christ* came to lighten in bizarre ways the figures of the angels to make them less stolid and domineering, he did not search for parallels to other angels based on their biblical meanings:

> What we want is not something that looks like Piero's Angels but something that, having been transformed by Piero, would look like Piero's Angels. What we would enjoy most of all is something that looks very unlike Piero's Angels but reference to which, in the course of solving the larger problem of the picture, would have disturbed Piero's usual angel mode into something like the Angels here (Baxandall 1985: 131).

Detecting "easy" or obvious consistencies between Piero's picture and the larger cultural context in Italy trivializes or occludes the generative logic by which Piero actively manufactured a new cast of angels. Anthony Giddens articulated this principle by claiming that it is the logic in how agents transform a schema in a new context, not "empirical similarity of social items," that defines a schema for practice (1979: 64). The schema is not explanatory if it is merely the disposition to act in a routinized way. Invoking it pays only

---

9. "Intention," Baxandall summed up, "is not a reconstituted historical state of mind, then, but a relation between the object and its circumstances" (1985: 42). Baxandall accepts what he calls the minimal "intentiveness" of action as indispensable to the reconstruction of the steps artists take to innovate. By this somewhat affected term, Baxandall specifies the weaker import he would like to assign to "intent" when he is compelled, for simplicity of expression, to use this common term. "Intentiveness" is less errant, since it connotes a generic quality of the form of action that we as investigators impute when we set that form in relation to its circumstantial environment.

if the novelty of the situation to which it is applied confirms its nimble transposition.[10] Researchers who use the model of practice as a concretized schema do not merely illustrate principles of conduct with detail, but also require that uncanny findings be foregrounded, because it is in telltale features of the deed that the agent's improvised "transposition" of the structure of the original schemas can be discerned.[11]

Finally, let us consider the type of coupling Baxandall established between the problem and its solution, the action. Baxandall made the artists' deployment of schemas appear apt but not forced by deductive entailment. As Baxandall said upon finding the commonsense reasoning that propelled even such extravagant departures as Cubism, once the problems of the setting are specified fully, "There is often a curious impersonality about the [artist's] actual working out of a solution in the medium" (1985: 47).[12] Baxandall did not attempt to explicate Piero's commanding life goals or *why* Piero undertook the artistic assignment. He explained only the most striking features of how Piero carried out the assignment once he engaged in the play of art. The goals model, in keeping with the hypothetico-deductive style of explanation, tries to deduce the very occurrence of action from the antecedent goals and means. The problem-solving model, by contrast, starts from the historical record of action and uses comparison (with realized or counter-factual cases) to account for *variation* in the forms action assumes. Baxandall did not try to show that it was *necessary* for Piero in *Baptism of Christ* to switch from mirrorlike to transparent river water in the painting's

10. Greenblatt and Gallagher insist on the use of anecdote for revealing "the very condition for perception and action" (2000: 40). On the role of context for investigating agents' "tool kits," see M. Cole, Engeström, and Vasquez (1997: 10). The explanatory game built around the model of action as an embodied schema differs in two respects, then, from Carlo Ginzburg's evidentiary paradigm based on reading semiotic "clues" as symptoms. It does not take its object as that of developing a model of an encompassing worldview or personality structure, only that of establishing the practical reasoning at work in a case or discrete set of cases. It does not pursue hermeneutic associations on their own but invokes only the schemata that parsimoniously account for an act's pragmatic generation. See Ginzburg (1989: 123–124).

11. To risk an abstract elaboration, the form of explanation with the problem-solving model follows the study of "causal" processes laid out by the philosopher of science Wesley Salmon (1984: 139, 146, 155). We try to see how antecedent structures transmit some feature of themselves into the outcome by looking for the corresponding carry-through of signals or information. Salmon has termed this the basic criterion for the transmission of causal influence in the world. He has illustrated it by calling on examples so diverse as to include a radio's reception of sound (corresponding to the structure of the waves transmitted by the broadcasting station) and the body's ingestion, absorption, and response to a drug (corresponding to the chemical structure of the circulating drug).

12. Like Kuhn's scientists, therefore, Baxandall's artists assert the individuality of their goals primarily in deciding which of the equivalent problems within their niche they will take on. Baxandall refers to the making of art as the solving of puzzles in a "game" (1985: 63).

foreground. Baxandall compared the actual with concrete alternatives—having the water, say, mirror Christ's calves—to make Piero's execution appear the most appropriate use of the idioms of the day.

These three features of the problem-solving model—treating know-how, not goals, as general and transposable; preserving the novelty and ambiguity of settings; and recognizing the extemporaneous formation of action—interlock in other micro-level studies in historical sociology. In *The Fabrication of Labor*, I aimed to show how agents facing technically similar settings and the same pressures for commercial efficiency nonetheless drew upon consistently different templates for defining and managing the problem of the exchange of human labor. Similarly, in his analysis of the impact of the voyages of discovery upon pure mathematics, Amir Alexander (2002) focused on the transfer of problem-solving procedures, not cultural values or broader social imperatives.[13] He showed how imperfect, tentative, partially contradictory mathematical explorations were accepted as extemporaneous solutions because they advanced understanding of the inner structure of geometrical figures. Above all, the new studies focus on how agents typify the setting, not on whether they calculate optimal solutions given fixed conditions and transcendent goals.[14]

Methodological Returns of the Problem-Solving Model

The problem-solving model offers researchers three major advantages in the use of evidence: the observations needed to identify the operative variables are bounded and immediate; there is less distance between the antecedent ingredients of action and the action itself; and the concepts used in an explanation encourage progressively more insightful engagement with the evidence to specify the mechanisms of action.

Observation of Variables

We take it for granted that an investigator using the goals model can hypothesize the goal of an agent's conduct by referring to texts that are relevant

13. In *The Fabrication of Labor*, I endeavored to fulfill this new evidentiary game by showing how exceedingly minute features of managerial calculation in factory systems could find their way into practice only as the result of schemata for handling labor as an abstract ware. See Biernacki (1995: 51, 494 n. 45, 495 n. 46).

14. Other recent works consonant with the problem-solving model include Pickering (1995) and (as an illustration of the model's extensive affiliations), Hunt (1992). Rather than analyzing action after 1789 as if it were guided by final political goals, Hunt shows how it was improvised to deal with the immediate crises of organizing public and familial governance without resorting to patriarchal routines.

because they offer a "sign" of that conduct's meaning and motive. When we draw connections between the conduct and other signs in its historical context, how do we know what kinds of motives are deepest and most genuine? What are the criteria for assessing legitimate associations between conduct and contemporaneous symbols of conviction? For example, on what basis do we assume that theological assumptions operated, as Weber claimed in *The Protestant Ethic*, as a deep, sincere, psychic anchor for observed conduct? If we group social actions in master arenas such as the "religious," the "political," and the "economic," we may claim that motives belonging to the category of the religious are "deepest" and "most genuine." But the logic is circular: the evidence for the depth of one kind of motive depends on the relative depth of others, so we gain no starting point except by stipulation (as in Weber's special pleading about the depth of popular religiosity in "the era" of the Reformation). Whereas we may have the impression that we recognize the priority of motives after summoning the Western category of the "religious," in practice it is much the other way around: we invoke the "religious" to assign priority to motives. The ultimate conundrum is that if goals of action can be denoted by a symbolic frame that is superimposed to "interpret" that action and is not integral to action's efficient execution, we have no easy means for deciding which frame is most credible and therefore no evident and adjudicable way to designate agents' final goals.[15]

Unlike the goals model, the problem-solving model of action starts from the form of the action, from evidence, that is, immanent in the action's unfolding. The orienting puzzles, anomalies, and problems are defined from the pragmatics of the immediate field of play, independent of that play's terminal function or significance in an extrinsic frame of signs. For example, Baxandall restricts himself to the puzzles of creating three-dimensional representations on a flat surface. His interpretation of the schemas in use was anchored and delimited by the accessible evidence about the action itself.

---

15. To resolve this problem of assigning a framework of goals, no special authority can be granted to the agents themselves. When ethnographers collect the self-reports of goals from relatively sincere and self-aware respondents, such as laboratory scientists, they discover that the scientists' accounts vary among collaborators on the same experiment and evolve with the context of reporting in which the respondents find themselves (Heritage 1983: 118). Sociologists are increasingly aware of how people "use" cultural frameworks that impute purposes to action for the sake of accomplishing the business of social life. The agents may have a personally ironic and detached relation to the idioms of purpose they employ. This does not mean that action diverges or converges with its verbalizations: the verbal articulation is simply a different act, and we have no evidence that there is a fixed mental state outside action that both acts mirror (Mills 1940: 907).

Distance between Ingredients of Action and Action Itself

The goals model leads investigators into a circular and self-defeating procedure of explanation. First, to establish the precedence, generalizability, and transcendent quality of goals in relation to the empirical setting of action, investigators define the goal in abstraction from any particular setting. In consequence, since the goal is so distant from the proximate, situationally particular objectives of action, sociologists face the problem of showing that the general goal has any explanatory leverage in its own right. If the general goal is a shorthand for a collection of proximate motives, in what sense does it "guide" or explain those proximate motives? If we have information about the proximate goal specific to an act that explains the form of the act, why hypothesize that a more general goal or value is the independent "ultimate motive" and the more proximate goal is only the expression of this motive in the circumstances of action? The paradox is that the background, terminal goal of religious salvation appears supreme because it is so general. Once the terminal goal is removed from the immediate, efficient motives of action, however, its relevance to explanation is uncertain. Investigators expend their energies trying to undo the problem they created by having abstracted general, transcending goals in the first place.

As is well known, this distance between final goals and action bedevils the rational choice theorists when they postulate utility maximization as the supreme end and then try to derive its instantiation in proximate motives. But this causal distance also disables cultural analyses, such as Weber's *Protestant Ethic*. So distant is salvation theology from the logic of capitalist institutions that Weber (1982: 28, 47) acknowledged that Catholic entrepreneurs in Italy had practices with outward forms similar to those of Calvinist entrepreneurs despite divergent religious objectives. Conversely, the directives of Calvinist salvation theology could be satisfied through diverse forms of action, not just in ascetic labor in capitalist enterprise. To reestablish the relevance of the abstracted general goal of salvation for specific kinds of actions, Weber had to introduce subsidiary hypotheses about the testimonial value of business success and the closure of alternate venues for modest Protestants to find their livelihood. Once the subsidiary assumptions create proximate motives for more efficient business undertakings, however, the more distant motive of salvation no longer does any explanatory work in its own right. Precisely by this reasoning, in his dissection of the correlation between membership in Protestant sects and business success in the United States, Weber (1920) excised the supreme end of salvation altogether![16] It is simpler and more direct to build an explanation with the problem-solving model, since that model restricts itself to the publicly accessible schemas that are immediately implicated in the organization of the action itself.

Progressive Engagement with Evidence to Specify Mechanisms

In the goals model, the form of an action's artfully accomplished instantiation is emblematic of an underlying fit between means and ends, not an object of explanation in its own right. To be sure, the details of the form may be richly described, but that description has a relatively superficial role. The political scientist David Laitin's ethnographic accounts of religious services on the Yorubaland offered a well-known illustration. To examine the goals that are displayed in these religious services, Laitin attended to the devotees' manner of entry into places of worship and to the seating boundaries in Christian versus Muslim services. Laitin showed, for example, that Muslims toned down signs of inequality among worshipers by enforcing equalitarian greetings at the start of worship and by fluidly mixing worshipers on mats across the mosque's floor. Among the Christians, seating in pews, often priced, overtly accentuated social hierarchy (Laitin 1986: 68). As Laitin revealed how conduct exemplifies a value, he did not try to trace the telltale "how-to" that went into producing that conduct. No canny contrivance of observation was needed to register the church seating in the Yorubaland as stratificatory. Despite the astuteness of his observations, Laitin fell short of a lever by which to reveal details of the resultant action that would necessarily remain hidden to an observer who lacked his goals model. The goals model explains action as only a token, because it treats action as an emergent expression of more constant and substantial goals—"points of concern," in Laitin's phrasing—and therefore stylizes the action by means of those very general foundational forces.

By contrast, in the problem-solving model, analysts dissect "uncanny" features of the conduct that would have remained invisible. Invoking the schema is otherwise nothing but a circular redescription of the action. In *Baptism of Christ* Baxandall had to offer a wholly unexpected but eerily similar prototype of one of Piero's angels, for example. Kharkhordin had to uncover features of denunciation and penitence in Soviet political trials that no one else would have thought to consider without the precise analogies to

---

16. For an acute analysis of Weber's removal of ultimate goals from the explanation of the influence of Protestantism on capitalism, see Oakes (1993: 289).

Orthodox church rituals in hand. Amir Alexander (2002: 168–169) had to uncover miniscule features of Thomas Hariot's cartographic descriptions to show how his map-making procedures also enabled him to reanalyze the geometric paradoxes of spatial continuums. The problem-solving model sets up a richer dialogue with the evidence because it pushes investigators to isolate unsuspected novelties in action, not merely to categorize them.

An Agenda for Discovery

By presenting the problem-solving model as the purest reversal of three postulates in the goals model, I also have offered a framework for assessing other, intermediate theories of action. Pierre Bourdieu, for instance, modified but did not reverse the first postulate, the relative generality of goals and means. Rather than focusing on the independence of the general repertoires of action from the features of novel settings, Bourdieu supposed that agents' know-how is limited by and already congruent with the setting.[17] This "habitus" model, defensible in the abstract, has methodological disadvantages for historical research. If the schemas of action are harmoniously aligned with the setting rather than arduously, inventively transposed from dissimilar settings, we lack fruitful means of tracing their active use and permutations. The habitus becomes a circular restatement of the character of the action (Bourdieu and Wacquant 1992: 129), not an ingredient of a different order whose use is an object of study. It is telling that Bourdieu's model, after years of wide dissemination, is hardly the centerpiece of a corpus of comparative historical research into sequences of human events.

Of course this brief sketch lays out a program with unresolved questions. If it is methodologically awkward to explain action by general goals stretching across diverse problem settings, why do general goals prevail in our commonsense experience of what we and other individuals are doing? If action is an improvised adjustment to a stream of shifting challenges, how do we account for our personal experience of coherent life trajectories, as well as our belief in enduring, lifetime commitments to normative ideals? Finally, taking stock of the prior accomplishments of social inquiry, do we not vitiate analysis of power and economic interest if we forgo the goals model?

Each of these questions is based on dimensions of experience that are highlighted within the goals model, but each receives a more comprehensive and methodologically sound treatment within the problem-solving model.

---

17. Bourdieu grouped together normative and utilitarian traditions of action and declared, "I intend to break with the philosophy of action which haunts the unconscious of most sociologists" (1993: 273).

If we ask how the setting activates some normative principles and life interests rather than others—that is, how the agent comes to see the case at hand as an instance of a *kind* of case—the goals model resorts to unwarrantable dogma to edge the question off the table. Not only does it postulate that agents have a preset hierarchy of goals or values, it also supposes that agents classify the case unproblematically as a particular means in relation to that system of goals.[18] Those starting points are difficult to support with evidence, however. Market researchers, perhaps the most numerous and best-funded investigators of decision making in our day, find that consumers' goals are not fixed prior to the setting in which they make choices. Consumers' goals shift with the mix of affiliated products on display, because the features made salient by different mixes vary the problems of status display or social utility that the consumer tries to solve (Prelec, Wernerfelt, and Zettelmayer 1997: 118–125). Consider, too, the most accessible cases of controversy over normative issues: the politics of public policy. In the U.S. abortion debates, it does not seem that Americans weigh the relative finality of competing goals in the abstract to recommend a line of action. They neither establish nor consult general belief in the priority of protecting life versus the value of personal privacy, as the goals model would suppose. Instead, they debate what *kind* of case the instance of the abortion controversy represents—a problem of public morality, of the sacred in everyday life, of applicable U.S. statutes—and the corresponding repertoires of action and emotional scripts follow.[19]

Agents may articulate overarching life goals when they reflect upon the problem of organizing their life as a whole. But whether and how those normative formulas are deployed in particular sequences of action remains an empirical question that the problem-solving model addresses more satisfactorily. We have scant grounds for *assuming*, as does the goals model, that schemas for addressing the meaning of life as a comprehensive unit are pervasive in diverse moments of everyday life. Unless these meta-level formulas for action are required for an agent to improvise responses to ongoing challenges in the setting (Irvine 1999: 100), they are apt to remain sequestered in their own "special" setting, that of intellectual reflection upon action in the abstract.

18. When rational choice theorists take for granted that they know what game is in play, they assume agents have already typified the setting unambiguously in relation to standing goals. Parsons made the agents' classification of the setting unproblematic by supposing that the "means and conditions are action" comprised of "scientifically verifiable knowledge" (1949: 418).

19. On the irreality of supposing that people choose among competing courses of action with reference to hierarchical goals, see Herrnstein (1997: 311).

ZINE MAGUBANE

Overlapping Territories and Intertwined Histories: Historical Sociology's Global Imagination

Anyone who wishes to study the most terrible manifestations of human nature will find them in Africa. The earliest reports concerning the continent tell us precisely the same, and it has no history in the true sense of the word. We shall therefore leave Africa at this point, and it need not be mentioned again. For it is an unhistorical continent, with no movement or development of its own. . . . What we understand as Africa proper is that unhistorical and undeveloped land . . . which had to be mentioned before we cross the threshold of world history itself.—G. W. F. Hegel

Ethnology studies only barbaric and savage societies; sociology is interested, at least as much, in civilized societies. Ethnography can only be linked to the present, for one can only describe what one has seen; sociology also takes into account the past. . . . Today it may be that there is rather more to be gained by examining the great civilized societies of the West of the present day.—Emile Durkheim

In his *Lectures on the Philosophy of World History* (1975 [1822]) Hegel argued that from a philosophical perspective, non-European peoples—Native Americans, Africans, and Asians—were less human than Europeans because they were not fully cognizant of themselves as conscious, historical beings; nor had they contributed in any meaningful way to the historical development of the world. Thus history, as a disciplinary practice, could effectively proceed as if the inhabitants of these benighted areas of the world did not exist. Durkheim (1982 [1907]) can be seen as engaged in a similar project of delineating a "geographical basis" for the practice of sociology. He also distinguished the "unsociological and undeveloped" parts of the world, where, presumably, barbarism ruled, from those parts where individuals were aware of themselves as conscious, sociological agents. In the above excerpt, from an article entitled "Debate on the Relationship between Ethnology and Sociology," Durkheim, like Hegel, left no doubt as to which societies and peoples were the proper objects of historical sociological consciousness and inquiry. The dividing line between ethnography and sociology, according to Durkheim, lay primarily in the latter's ability to "take into account the past."

Although most historical sociologists would rush to distance themselves from the sentiments expressed by Hegel and Durkheim, a significant amount of work done in comparative-historical sociology—whether on states, revolutions, or democracy—devotes scant theoretical attention to happenings in the ex-colonial world (particularly Africa). Not only are there relatively fewer comparative-historical studies of industrialization, revolutions, or democracy in the formerly colonized world, but also studies of these events in the European context tend to proceed on the assumption that the natural direction of diffusion is from Europe and North America outward to the rest of the world. A significant strand within the Western historiographical and sociological tradition assumes that processes of class, state, and ideological deformation and reformation in Europe proceeded largely untouched by the realities of the colonial encounter.

In actuality, the idea that the West has remained sociologically "untouched" by the presence of Africans, Asians, and Native Americans is not only erroneous, but also theoretically limiting. It is this failure of what C. Wright Mills (1959) termed the "sociological imagination" that leads me to ask what past, present, and future efforts in historical sociology would look like if they were truly informed by Stuart Hall's idea that "colonization was never simply external to the societies of the imperial metropolis. . . . It was always inscribed deeply within them" (1996: 246). What, in other words, would be the intellectual, theoretical, and methodological consequences of, in the words of Catherine Hall, "remembering empire differently" (1996: 66). For, as she explains, "how the Empire is remembered" determines not only what kinds of historical questions are asked, but also influences what type of academic work is done (p. 69).

Research Agendas in Historical Sociology:
The Legacy of the Classics

In *Vision and Method in Historical Sociology*, one of the classic texts of the field, Theda Skocpol argued that "the classical questions and answers of Weber, Marx, Tocqueville, Durkheim, and others naturally live on in the ongoing enterprise of historical sociology" (Skocpol, ed. 1984: 5). When we consider the methodological blueprints and models historical sociologists inherited from the classics, we must remain cognizant of the fact that methodologies are not neutral sets of techniques. Instead we must see them as being profoundly influenced and inflected by set assumptions about society, history, and the purpose of scholarship. Indeed, it is in the classics that we can locate the roots of how and why macro-sociology, although methodologically comparative, was thoroughly Eurocentric when it came to the construction of theory.

The classical theorists devoted a considerable amount of time and attention to determining why certain social forms developed in some societies and not in others. The idea that the West has a special dynamism lacking in other societies is implicit in this form of questioning. Max Weber, whose central intellectual preoccupation was with the cultural significance and consequences of modern Western capitalism, is probably the foremost representative of this type of thinking. In order to explain the special dynamism of the West, Weber relied chiefly on comparisons—the analytic device that best allowed him to highlight the particular features of his chosen historical cases. In Weber's work, the visibility of structures in the so-called Occident is highlighted by means of contrast with the Orient, where they were lacking. As Thapar rightly observed, "the most frequently used word in Weber's analysis of . . . India is 'absence'—reflecting a sharp distinction in his mind between the characteristic features of the Occidental civilization and their absence in the Asiatic/Oriental" (1980: 110). Thus, it was primarily through the logical juxtaposition of aspects of Oriental and Occidental societies that Weber ultimately identified rationality as the primary motive in the development of European capitalism.

Durkheim was yet another classical scholar whose theories assumed a contrast between so-called primitive and modern societies. Indeed, it was Durkheim (1982 [1907]) who first postulated that comparative sociology was sociology itself and that if sociology was to advance from being purely descriptive and become a science, it had to embrace the comparative method. In Durkheim's work, however, the primitive exists not as a specter of what the West is not, but rather as a purified and simplified example of what the West once was. In his words, "the so-called lower societies have a very special interest for the sociologist: all the social forms which are observable as distinct and organized in more complex societies are to be found there in a state of inter-penetration which highlights better their unity. Moreover, the functioning of more advanced societies can only be understood when we are informed about the organization of the less developed societies" (p. 209).

The underlying assumption of the comparative work of both Weber and Durkheim is that the world consists of independent units that can be readily identified and used as the bases for comparisons. In other words, they both assumed that societies are essentially closed systems. Social change is thus viewed as a process that is internal to societies, and cultural differences among various peoples explain their different rates of development. Furthermore, societies are analyzed by using well-defined typologies, such as "rationalization" or the transition from mechanical to organic solidarity, which explain their past, present, and future progress. Thus, it is not important to know the specific history of a particular society in order to understand how it came to be what it is.

Sustaining this worldview required both Weber and Durkheim to assiduously avoid making any reference to the role of colonialism in the development of the West. Indeed, it was their studied avoidance of any mention of colonialism that allowed them to remain theoretically Eurocentric, despite their reliance on comparative methods. Although Weber, for example, asserted that "imperialist capitalism, especially colonial booty capitalism based on direct force and compulsory labor, has offered by far the greatest opportunities for profit," this understanding did not significantly impact his comparative studies of capitalist development (quoted in Gerth and Mills, eds. 1946: 168). Indeed, Weber attributed the development of capitalism in Western Europe and its failure to develop elsewhere to "the specific and peculiar rationalism of Western culture" (M. Weber 1998 [1920]: 26). His guiding assumption, therefore, was that the development of capitalism in the West and the development of its bastardized forms in the East proceeded largely independently of one another. In *The Protestant Ethic and the Spirit of Capitalism*, for example, there is not even the faintest suggestion that the economic development of the East and West proceeded together, albeit very differently, or that the development of the West and the underdevelopment of the East might be mutually implicated. Indeed, Weber's method of comparative-historical analysis is premised on the assumption that societies were independent units, endowed with the ability to change because of their internal dynamics. It was thus that he could posit that cultural differences among peoples explained their differing rates and paths of development.

Lucile Brockway has explained that it was under the auspices of the British East India Company that "the British succeeded in dismantling India's domestic industries and native handicrafts" (1979: 21). Thus, the deindustrialization of India occurred precisely because the country was forcibly transformed into a captive market for the cheap manufactured goods produced in England. Nowhere in Weber's work, however, do we find a sustained discussion of how the economies of Asia were disrupted by European colonialism or how their economies were subjected to the exigencies of first mercantile and later industrial capitalism. Such a discussion is lacking despite the fact that Weber's sources were Indologists and Orientalists whose knowledge was made possible by the colonial encounter (Said 1979).

Durkheim's theories about the transition from societies based on mechanical solidarity to those based on organic solidarity (in other words, the transition from pre-industrial to industrial society) were also premised on the idea that so-called primitive societies lay totally outside the influence of and were completely untouched by the economic machinations of European states in the form of imperialism and colonialism. Durkheim's texts, like Weber's, are marked by a curious elision whereby he must repeatedly deny any knowledge of precisely those colonial practices that make his work possible. In *The Elementary Forms of the Religious Life* (1965 [1915]), for example, Durkheim repeatedly pointed to Australian aboriginal and Native American religious practices as examples of primitive religions in their purest forms, utterly untouched by Western influence. However, much of the ethnological information extant about so-called primitive religious practices existed precisely because their practitioners were continually being dragooned into one colonial imbroglio after another. Indeed, as a "classic example of the armchair theorist," Durkheim relied extensively on the writings of district commissioners, colonial agents, missionaries, and other colonial officials (Fenton 1980: 163). In *The Elementary Forms of the Religious Life*, for example, he quoted extensively from the Bureau of American Ethnology and the work of Albert Gallatin (onetime secretary of the treasury under President Jefferson and founder of the American Ethnological Society). Durkheim's ethnographic sketches of "untouched" societies, based on information made available to him by colonial relationships, opened him up to rather severe criticism from his contemporaries. For example, H. Van Gennep, who reviewed *The Elementary Forms of the Religious Life* shortly after it was published, scoffed at the "abundance of references to documents provided by sundry informants, police agents, unspecified colonialists, obtuse missionaries, etc." (quoted in Lukes 1973: 525).

The fact that colonialism fell outside Durkheim's area of inquiry is significant not only from a methodological standpoint, but from a theoretical one as well. Ignoring the existence of colonialism allowed him to construct a theory of the transition from pre-industrial to industrial societies that focused exclusively on internal factors, such as the growing complexity of the division of labor and increased societal volume and density. As Fenton correctly observed, Durkheim's functionalism, which insisted on viewing societies as functioning wholes, was premised on the idea that so-called primitive societies were "integral units with an internal coherence and meaning system, rather than [parts] of a historically developing system of colonial relationships" (1980: 169).

Contemporary thinkers have carried forth the traditions of historical sociology launched by Weber and Durkheim in studies that rely on paired comparisons of social formations in the interest of either developing an explanation for a well-defined outcome or pattern in history (e.g., Bendix 1956; Moore 1969; Skocpol 1979) or making contrasts among cases in order to highlight features particular to each (e.g., Fredrickson 1981; Lipset 1963; Rueschemeyer 1973). There is nothing inherently Eurocentric about the use of comparisons per se. Rather, the Eurocentrism of comparative-historical sociology can be attributed in no small part to the manner in which some contemporary theorists, following the legacy of the founding fathers, have ignored key aspects of history (particularly colonialism) in their quest to depict societies, nations, and cultures as self-contained and thus independently comparable units. However, as Skocpol noted, this logic of comparison may not be applicable to "partial and variously situated units (such as nations) within a capitalist world economy" (Skocpol, ed. 1984: 384).

Despite the preponderance of studies that set up models of non-Western societies in order to prove a series of theses regarding modern European society, there have always been sociologists who have refused to treat the history of non-European peoples as a residual category useful only insofar as it enabled one to test hypotheses about the social evolution of the West. These theorists, whose work will be explored in more detail in the next section, have sought alternative organizing frameworks for macro-sociology that foreground issues of cultural conflict, exploitation, interpenetration, and exchange.

Constructing a "Counter-Canon": Alternative Visions
and Methods in Historical Sociology

Although he has never been recognized as one of our "founding fathers," George Washington Williams (the first major African American historian) inaugurated a critical, alternative strand in historical sociology. In 1882 he published *A History of the Negro Race in America from 1619–1880*, which, by placing African and diasporic history firmly within the history of the West, did much to refute the idea that Africa and Africans had played no part in the evolution of human history. More important, in arguing that "Western civilization" owed its immediate stimulus to Egyptian culture, Williams was among the first to challenge the idea that Europe rose to prominence solely due to the special dynamism of European peoples, a dynamism lacking in all other civilizations. Williams thus founded an intellectual movement that was carried forward by scholars such as Olaudah Equiano, W. E. B. Du Bois, Anna Julia Cooper, Edward Wilmot Blyden, C. L. R. James, Frantz Fanon, and Aimé Césaire, who, despite their varied methods and approaches, were in agreement that "African people in the Western hemisphere [had] been at the fulcrum of the most important social and political transformations in the modern world" (Kelley 1996: 104).

Much like the classical thinkers, the vision of these scholars was a product of their immediate historical and political context. As people of African descent, they had experienced firsthand the racism of Western society, which had produced a sociological practice "bent on demonstrating the inferiority of the Negro" (Charles 1980: 75). As Du Bois put it:

> Since the rise of the sugar empire and the resultant cotton kingdom, there has been a consistent effort to rationalize Negro slavery by omitting Africa from world history, so that today it is almost universally assumed that history can be truly written without reference to Negroid peoples. I believe this to be scientifically unsound and also dangerous for logical social conclusions. Therefore, I am seeking . . . to remind readers . . . of how critical a part Africa has played in human history, past and present, and how impossible it is to forget this and rightly explain the present plight of mankind (Du Bois 1965 [1946]: vii).

Du Bois observed that the types of questions posed under the general rubric of historical sociology—particularly questions about why certain social forms developed in some societies and not in others—were part of a larger racist framework that, although based in seemingly abstract theoretical principles, in actuality justified colonial domination. Thus, for him, the very act of posing an alternative set of questions and answers was an implicit challenge to racism. His rejection of the received sociological wisdom should not, however, be read as a rejection of positivism or the scientific method. As Robinson explained, Du Bois "realized the necessity of returning to the experience and training in historical research and writing he had gathered at Harvard University and the University of Berlin in the late 19th century. . . . His radical, and radically different interpretation[s] . . . would conform formally to the methodological canons of historiography so that he might subvert the substance of that tradition" (1983: 277).

The theories and methods developed by "New World" Africans like W. E. B. Du Bois involved important challenges to classically derived ideas about the role of cultural differences in societal change and evolution; the vaunted status of comparisons as the preferred analytical device for identifying the particularities of historical cases; and the objectivity of the concepts and typologies used to identify and explain the historical trajectories of different societies. These theoretical challenges continue to inform works in comparative-historical sociology that aim to place developments in the United States and Europe in a more comprehensive and complete comparative-historical perspective by using different types of evidence and methods of analysis.

It was in the context of analyses of slavery that West Indian and African American scholars began producing work that explicitly challenged the idea that cultural differences among peoples, rather than their distinct histories of interaction with global capitalism, explained their varied rates of development. Du Bois's magisterial study, *The Suppression of the African Slave-Trade lto the United States of America, 1638–1870*, originally published in 1896, was among the first to suggest that analyzing the European bourgeoisie's economic exploitation of Africa, Asia, and Latin America provided the necessary contextual basis for understanding the social origins and effects of the European industrial revolution. In writing the text, Du Bois was deeply influenced by Karl Marx's idea that England's industrial revolution owed its genesis to "the discovery of gold and silver in America, the extirpation, enslavement, and entombment in mines of the aboriginal population, the beginning of the conquest and looting of the East Indies, and the turning of Africa into a warren for the commercial hunting of dark skins" (1967 [1867]: 751). Hence, in *Black Reconstruction in America*, which more fully explicated many of the ideas first developed in *The Suppression of the African Slave-Trade*, Du Bois argued as follows:

> The dark and vast sea of human labor in China and India, the South Seas and all Africa; in the West Indies and Central America and in the United States—that great majority of mankind on whose bent and broken backs rest today the founding stones of modern industry— shares a common destiny; it is despised and rejected by race and color; paid a wage below the level of decent living; driven, beaten, imprisoned and enslaved in all but name; spawning the world's raw material and luxury. . . . All these are gathered up at prices lowest of the low, manufactured, transformed and transported at fabulous gain; and the resultant wealth is distributed and displayed and made the basis of world power and universal dominion and armed arrogance in London and Paris, Berlin and Rome, New York and Rio de Janeiro (1964 [1935]: 15).

Du Bois's analysis of the economic dynamics that lay behind the rise of the West critically informed the work of scholars such as Eric Williams (1964), Andre Gunder Frank (1971), and Walter Rodney (1981 [1972]), who developed pathbreaking analyses of the roles of slavery and colonialism in the emergence of capitalism in Western Europe. Echoes of Du Bois can also be discerned in Immanuel Wallerstein's (1974) analysis of the capitalist world system. Wallerstein, like Du Bois, argued that the West had not only impoverished the Third World, but had also forced it onto a path of social and political development that precluded any real technological or economic dynamism.

The desire of scholars such as Du Bois, Wallerstein, Gunder Frank, and Rodney to offer a vision of world history that would ultimately lead to the emancipation of Third World peoples led them to adopt a highly critical posture toward the favored analytical methods of classical sociology. A major methodological challenge to the classics came in their critique of the notion that comparisons are the best analytical device for highlighting the particular features of historical cases and, from there, developing coherent explanations for patterns in history. Wallerstein, for example, has questioned the utility of comparing individual capitalist nation-states, noting that the logic of such comparisons is inapplicable to the global capitalist economy, which is composed of partial and variously integrated nation-states. As Ragin and Chirot explained, focusing on a single social system has important methodological implications: "Because the capitalist world economy is defined as a single social system, its mechanisms cannot be discovered by comparing it to 'other' capitalist world economies. If only one case exists, there is no choice but to establish its nature by knowing its history" (1984: 286).

Yet another tradition of scholarship, emanating largely from radical Black thinkers based in the West Indies, focuses less on comparing the emergence of social phenomena (revolutions, social movements, democracy) in different societies with the purpose of showing the frequency with which the emergence of such phenomena in one society is critically impacted by happenings in another society. One of the founding fathers of this intellectual tradition is the Trinidadian scholar, C. L. R. James. His pathbreaking text, *The Black Jacobins* (1989 [1963]), was an analysis of the social origins and effects of democratic revolutions that sought to place the experiences of people of African descent at the center rather than the periphery of world history. The methodology James employed in the text was critically informed by his knowledge that comparisons among different revolutionary episodes generally served to highlight or even symbolize the supposed superiority of white, Western societies. Thus, the few studies that examined revolutions in the so-called Third World tended to reinforce the notion that revolutionary upheaval in the core countries was the result of internal dynamics while comparable events in the periphery could be explained as the result of either pressure from the West or the diffusion of Western ideals. *The*

Black Jacobins constituted a major challenge, therefore, in that it demonstrated how "the great Western revolutionaries of the modern world—the French in particular—needed the Africans as much as the Africans needed them" (Kelley 1996: 113). The text examines the history of the revolt of the slaves at St. Domingue in 1791 and the establishment of Haiti, the first independent Black nation in 1803. James describes how the slaves of St. Domingue were responsible for forcing the leaders of the French Revolution to debate the meaning of freedom and liberty as the natural rights of man. As James put it: "The slaves in St. Domingue by their insurrection had shown revolutionary France that they could fight and die for freedom" (1989 [1938]: 120). Thus, *The Black Jacobins* did not merely celebrate Black resistance, but "ultimately rewrote the history of the modern world" (Kelley 1996: 112).

The Black Jacobins can rightly be considered a founding text in what is currently called post-colonial studies. Post-colonial scholarship, in the words of Catherine Hall, seeks to demonstrate that "the political and institutional histories of 'the centre' and its outer circles [are] more mutually constituted than we used to think" (1996: 70). Recognizing that political ideas, ideals, and strategies cannot be confined to national or geographic boundaries, sociologists working within this tradition, in addition to comparing the experiences of different nations, also are interested in identifying, exploring, and explaining varying instances of dialogue across different nations. Thus, scholars such as Vron Ware (1992) and Anne McClintock (1995) have examined the connections among anti-racist, anti-imperialist, and feminist politics in Britain and its former empire. Scholars like Ann Stoler (1995), Jean and John Comaroff (1992), and Susan Thorne (1999) have looked at the ways in which empire shaped the British working and middle classes, while scholars like Howard Winant (2002), David Theo Goldberg (2002), and Stuart Hall (1996) have examined the transnational circulation of racist ideologies and practices.

The idea that "societies" are not always coterminous with nations and, thus, that the nation-state need not always be the privileged unit of analysis critically informed the work of New World African thinkers like William Wells Brown (1863), Robert Benjamin Lewis (1844), and Alexander Crummell (1891). Post-colonial scholarship has borrowed heavily from this tradition and, in the process, put forth a significant challenge to traditional thinking in macro-sociology. As was mentioned above, comparative-historical sociologists have been strongly committed to identifying independent units for use in comparative assessments. For the most part nation-states, which were seen as geographically bounded and independent wholes, have been the preferred cases. However, sociologists whose work is informed by post-colonialism, such as Paul Gilroy (1993) and Barnor Hesse (2001), have all focused on diaspora populations and transnational communities. In so doing, they draw upon a long tradition of scholars and activists who defined themselves as part of a larger international Black community and thus sought to "devise a theoretical framework or conception of history that treat[ed] the African diaspora as a whole" (Kelley 1996: 103).

Viewing societies as transnational rather than national phenomena has important methodological implications. Although it is possible to envision a study that compares the origins and historical trajectories of different diaspora populations by juxtaposing aspects of a small number of cases, most diaspora scholars eschew such an approach in favor of one that seeks to understand the culturally embedded intentions of individual and group actors, with the idea that parallel situations exist in different geographical areas. Thus, scholarship on the African diaspora, for example, seeks to explore the specific situations of Black people in different geographical areas while remaining cognizant of the "Black world" as a totality. Methodologically this has meant that the act of drawing historical comparisons has been supplanted by a search for historical parallels and a more thorough exploration of what Stuart Hall termed processes of "transculturation" or "cultural translation." According to Hall, post-colonialism is a method of analysis that "obliges us to re-read the very binary form in which the colonial encounter has for so long itself been represented. It obliges us to re-read the binaries as forms of transculturation, of cultural translation, destined to trouble the here/there cultural boundaries forever" (1996: 247). Some historical sociologists whose current work falls within this ambit (although they would not necessarily classify themselves as "post-colonialists") are Karen Barkey (1994), who has used the case of the Ottoman Empire to challenge Charles Tilly's work on state centralization; Miguel Centeno (2002), who has written on state formation in Latin America; and Timothy Wickham-Crowley (1992), who has done work on comparative revolutions in Latin America.

One of the strongest ways in which contemporary thinkers have carried forth the traditions of historical sociology launched by Weber and Durkheim has been in their continued use of concepts such as "Western civilization," "democracy," and "rationalization" to establish the particular features of historical cases. These analytic constructs function as epistemological instruments, which form the basis for comparisons among cases, and signposts, which orient the narration of historical events and patterns. Since these concepts are often the starting points for the construction of theory, they have traditionally been presented as politically neutral and objective. The final challenge to traditional historical sociology thus emerges in critiques of colonialism that simultaneously work to refute many of the core concepts that have traditionally guided the selection and presentation of historical patterns in macro-sociology.

Edward Said has argued that the "idea of Europe" is "a collective notion identifying 'us' Europeans against all 'those' non-Europeans . . . the idea of European identity as a superior one in comparison with all the non-European peoples and cultures . . . usually overriding the possibility that a more independent, or more skeptical, thinker might have had different views on the matter" (1979: 7). These "more skeptical" thinkers could be found among the ranks of the colonized. These were people who "bore the imprint of European civilization [but nevertheless] were not dazzled by European civilization" (Césaire 1972 [1955]: 76). Thus, in the recovery of their voices and stories it was possible to mount a historiographical revolution of sorts.

Critiques of European colonialism, such as those articulated by scholars working in the Negritude tradition, operated, in effect, as challenges to this idea of Europe as a kind of ideal and unchanging abstraction that possessed a set of indisputable and readily identifiable positive traits. Negritude, originally a literary and ideological movement of French-speaking Black intellectuals, reflects an important and comprehensive reaction to the colonial situation. This movement, which influenced Africans as well as Blacks around the world, specifically rejects the political, social, and moral domination of the West. The term, which has been used in a general sense to describe the Black world in opposition to the West, assumes the total consciousness of belonging to the Black race.

Aimé Césaire, the founder of the Negritude movement, questioned the objectivity of concepts such as "rationality" and "civilization," arguing that they were based upon an ontological and epistemological distinction between "the West" and "the Rest" that was by no means objective. Césaire maintained that the barbarism of the Third World and the civilization of Europe were discursive effects produced when Africa, Asia, and Latin America were looked at through the categories of modern European social science. Hence, he railed against the conceptual categories developed by bourgeois European intellectuals, which he saw as national myths that provided "the appearance of historical narrative to what was in actuality part fact and part class-serving rationales" (Robinson 1983: 267). As Césaire put it: "One of the values invented by the bourgeoisie in former times and launched throughout the world was *man*—and we have seen what has become of that. The other was the nation. It is a fact: the *nation* is a bourgeois phenomenon" (1972 [1955]: 57). Thus, in his *Discourse on Colonialism*, Césaire argued that there was no such thing as "Western civilization": "At the present time the barbarism of Western Europe has reached an incredibly high level, being only surpassed—far surpassed, it is true—by the barbarism of the United

States" (p. 26). According to Césaire, Europe, rather than being an exemplar of rationality, had actually "undermined civilization, destroyed countries, ruined nationalities, and extirpated the root of diversity" (p. 59).

The themes first explored by Césaire have been taken up and refined by scholars who identify themselves with the subaltern studies school, which "operates within the discipline as a kind of insurgency with respect to conventional academic forms of history" (R. J. C. Young 1990: 160). The Subaltern Studies Collective, founded in 1982, was begun with the goal of establishing a new critique of both colonialist and nationalist perspectives in the historiography of colonized countries. Its most famous members—Gayatri Spivak and Partha Chatterjee, among others—were instrumental in establishing the discipline best known as post-colonial studies.

The goal of the subaltern historian is to "bring hegemonic historiography to a crisis" by locating instances of insurgency among the colonized (Spivak 1987: 198). Thus, in his recent book, *Provincializing Europe*, Dipesh Chakrabarty (2000), one of the founders of the subaltern school, critiqued the mystical figure of Europe, which has been viewed as the original site of the modern in many histories of capitalist transition in non-Western countries. He argued that the practice of looking at India through the categories of modern European social science continually produces India as a residual category whose only function is to validate arguments about the unique dynamism of the West. Ranajit Guha (2002), on the other hand, has offered a critique of mainstream historiography by exploring the ways in which the Hegelian concept of world history reduces the world to Europe. Guha has argued that Hegel's concept of world history overlooked the narratives of the colonized and thus introduced a statist bias into historical research. Like the scholars who identified themselves with Negritude, historians working within the subaltern tradition have focused on creating a historical practice that uncovers "the contribution made by the people *on their own*, that is, *independently of the elite*" (Guha 1982: 3; emphasis in original).

When it comes to the issue of how theoretical ideas and historical evidence are brought to bear on one another, scholars working within the subaltern school share many affinities with post-colonialists. Like post-colonialists, their preferred units of analysis are neither nations nor societies but rather the discourses, ideologies, and representations through which European culture was able to produce, manage, and exploit the Third World. Subaltern scholars' preferred methods of analysis are also akin to those used by post-colonialists. They, too, are less interested in clarifying the particularities of historical cases through contrasts than they are in tracing the dialogic emergence of social phenomena. Homi Bhabha, for example, has argued that the effect of colonial power is to produce "hybridization." In

"Signs Taken for Wonders," he maintained that one of the paradoxes of colonialism is that it continually enables "denied knowledges" (e.g., the knowledge produced by the colonized) to "enter upon the dominant discourse and estrange the basis of its authority" (1985: 156). Thus, democratic insurgency in the colonial context should be read not as an instance of "diffusion" from the core to the periphery but rather as an instance of articulation wherein "the words of the master become the site of hybridity" (p. 162).

Although historical sociologists whose work falls within the ambit of post-colonial studies and subaltern studies share many of the intellectual concerns of traditional macro-sociology, they are more interested in finding the most compelling conceptual lens to mediate between meaningful happenings in the past and the concerns of present-day audiences than they are in showing the repeated applicability of a single theoretical model or searching for causal regularities by using a hypothesis-testing approach. Thus, in their orientations they are much closer to E. P. Thompson, who did not ask specific causal questions about historical data or attempt to validate theoretical hypotheses about causes, than to a scholar such as Barrington Moore, who strongly believed that historical comparisons could be used not only to test the validity of existing theoretical models, but also to develop new causal generalizations. Scholars whose work falls into this vein include George Steinmetz (2003a), who has written on the development of German colonialism in southwest Africa; Ming-cheng M. Lo (2002), who has written on the changing role of Taiwanese doctors as "agents of modernity" under Japanese colonial rule; Julian Go (2000) and Emily Ignacio (2004), who have both written about U.S. colonial rule in the Phillipines; and Nader Sohrabi (2002), who has done comparative work on revolutions in the Ottoman Empire, Iran, and Russia.

Future Directions in Historical Sociology

Much of the work currently being done in comparative-historical sociology relies on very different types of evidence and methods of analysis than those pursued by either classical theorists or twentieth-century scholars such as Skocpol, Moore, and Wallerstein. This shift reflects important changes in the research agendas and methods pursued by contemporary macro-sociologists. As was shown above, an important trend has emerged in historical sociology whereby scholars are less wedded to a vision of society as an essentially closed system and instead have become open to the idea that societies are constituted by relations of exchange and are marked by a significant degree of interpenetration. Since macro-sociologists can no longer treat societies as independent units, they have had to search for alternative methodologies. The comparative method, whereby contrasts are made among cases in order to either highlight features particular to discrete historical contexts or establish causal regularities, has been shown to be inadequate in those instances where cases cannot be viewed as essentially independent. As a result, scholars have opened themselves up to alternative methods, many of which owe a strong debt to post-modernism and post-structuralism. Thus, discursive analysis, Foucauldian 'archaeological' approaches, and deconstruction have all emerged as alternate research strategies in historical sociology.

One important corollary and consequence of the shift from comparative analytical devices is that macro-sociologists have been less inclined to search for general explanatory models that can be applied equally well to an infinite array of instances spanning different times and places. Much of the work emanating from the alternative traditions explored above is similar in orientation to interpretive historical sociology, which Skocpol described as being "skeptical of the usefulness of either applying theoretical models to history or using a hypothesis-testing approach to establish causal generalizations about large-scale structures and patterns of change" (Skocpol, ed. 1984: 368). Instead, these scholars seek meaningful interpretations of history, in two intertwined senses of the word "meaningful." First, careful attention is paid to the culturally embedded intentions of individual or group actors in the historical settings under investigation. Michael Goldman's forthcoming ethnographic study of the World Bank as a disciplinary apparatus is one notable example of this type of work. Second, both the topic chosen for historical study and the kinds of arguments developed about it are culturally or politically "significant" in the present. Jan Pieterse's (2001) work on the different meanings of "international development" over time, which places the discussion of contemporary trends in a historical context, is exemplary in this regard. The shift to interpretive methods thus leaves open the question as to whether maco-theorists who choose to explore alternative organizing frameworks for their work must also, necessarily, eschew the search for generalizable explanatory principles. Steve Brechin's (1999) work on global environmentalism, which explores how and why public concern for the environment has spread across the globe, clearly does not, as his stated goal is to develop a generalizable theoretical understanding of the rise and spread of environmentalism. However, studies like Zsuzsa Gille's (1999, 2000) on ecology in Eastern Europe are much less concerned with examining the variations of history in order to identify invariant causal regularities than with highlighting the features particular to the case under study (in Gill's case, Hungary).

Comparative-historical sociologists have begun to relinquish their attachments to the idea that societies have clearly defined "insides" and "outsides" that are coterminous with the geographical boundaries of the nation-state. One can, for example, point to Emily Ignacio's (2004) study of Filipino communities in cyberspace or Winifred Poster's (1998, 2001, 2002) work on gender and globalization. They have also begun to seriously rethink notions of social change as natural and internal to societies and to question the validity of the "rise of the West" as an organizing framework for macro-sociology (see Go 2000). All the while, however, they have retained a commitment to developing adequate explanations for outcomes and patterns in history and exploring the validity of alternative explanatory arguments.

A work of analytical sociology such as Theda Skocpol's *States and Social Revolutions*, for example, could have been greatly improved had she turned her analytical gaze outside of Europe's borders. Despite her claim that "transnational relations have contributed to the emergence of all social-revolutionary crises and have invariably helped to shape revolutionary outcomes" and that "all modern social revolutions, in fact, must be seen as closely related in their causes and accomplishments to the internationally uneven spread of capitalist economic development and nation-state formation on a world scale" (Skocpol 1979: 19), *States and Social Revolutions* had nothing to say about France's colonial empire and its probable impact on the course of the French Revolution. According to Skocpol, "those who opposed the traditional constitution and favored a unified National Assembly . . . included not only the representatives of the Third Estate but also a hefty minority of the nobility—with a disproportionate number of nobles who were acclimated by birth and/or regular residence to urban life and culture. In fact, some of the key leaders of the 'revolutionary bourgeoisie/Third Estate' were aristocrats" (p. 66). Skocpol did not give any serious consideration to the various means by which this class had acquired its wealth and the role that this played in the launching of the revolution. However, as was demonstrated in the work of C. L. R. James, "the slave trade and slavery were the economic basis of the French Revolution. . . . The fortunes created at Nantes, by the slave trade, gave to the bourgeoisie that pride which needed liberty and contributed to human emancipation" (1989 [1963]: 47). According to yet another scholar working within the post-colonial tradition, not only did colonial wealth play a major role in the growth of bourgeois power in port cities such as Bordeaux and Nantes, but also a significant number of National Assembly members relied on colonial trade (one in five members were owners of colonial property) and a much larger number were linked to the colonies through trade or administration (Malik 1996). A more careful consideration of the fact that France was a colonial power would have not only added more complexity to Skocpol's causal variables, but also could have enriched her discussion of the causes and outcomes of political crisis and conflict in modernizing agrarian states.

Likewise, abandoning what Stoler calls the "origin myths of European culture" (1995: 14), which assumed a "self referential western culture [that is] bounded by Europe's geographic parameters" does not mean that macro-sociology has to abandon its traditional preoccupation with uncovering the social origins and effects of Europe's industrial and democratic revolutions, the rise of the working class, the democratization of politics, or the bu-reacratization of states. Rather, it means that these phenomena should be understood as having arisen in the context of transnational, rather than strictly national, social and economic dynamics. As Stoler observed, recent work in colonial discourse analysis suggests that many of the "key symbols of modern western societies—liberalism, nationalism, state welfare, citizen-ship, culture, and 'Europeaness' itself—were clarified among Europe's colo-nial exiles and by those colonized classes caught in their pedagogic net in Asia, Africa, and Latin America and only then brought 'home' " (1995: 16). Thus, anyone wishing to understand the dynamics that informed the spread of democratic politics in Britain must consider the role of the Morant Bay Rebellion in Jamaica on the discussions of the 1867 Reform Act (C. Hall 1992) or the Anglo-Boer War on the suffrage movement (Burton 2000). To understand the evolution of bureaucratic structures in France it may be necessary to take a detour through Algeria, where a number of strategies were worked out prior to their introduction in the metropole (Prochaska 1990). And a thorough understanding of the disciplinary strategies of large-scale industrial production in Europe requires an analysis of the organiza-tion of plantation labor in the Caribbean (S. W. Mintz 1985).

The effort to rid sociology of its Eurocentrism has introduced signifi-cant tensions into scholarship—different questions must be asked, different sources of evidence must be drawn upon, and different analytical methods must be developed. These tensions have, on the whole, been productive rather than disabling. Current moves to understand what Said called our "overlapping territories and intertwined histories" (1994: 4) have had a pro-found impact on the practice of historical sociology—mostly for the better. Theda Skocpol concluded *Vision and Method in Historical Sociology* with the observation that "the stream of historical sociology has deepened into a river and spread out into eddies running through all parts of the sociological enterprise" (Skocpol, ed. 1984: 356). One might make the same observation about studies of Asia, Africa, and Latin America: they too have deepened into a river and spread out into eddies running through all parts of historical sociology.

GEORGE STEINMETZ

The Epistemological Unconscious of U.S. Sociology and the Transition to Post-Fordism: The Case of Historical Sociology

The Domestication of Historical Sociology?

In a much discussed essay, Craig Calhoun (1996) argued that American historical sociology was "domesticated" in its search for professional legitimacy. Sociologists' turn to history during the 1970s and 1980s initially challenged some of mainstream sociology's entrenched methodological and epistemological assumptions. Yet historical sociologists, according to Calhoun, elected to "play on the turf of their mainstream colleagues, not just in placing an emphasis on empirical research ahead of theory and epistemological critique" (p. 309), but also in promoting a research framework that was compatible with the dominant meta-position in postwar American sociology. In this chapter I analyze this position, which I call *methodological positivism*.

This chapter first examines the consolidation of methodological positivism as the *epistemological unconscious* of American sociology in the postwar period and then looks at the historic turn in American sociology since the 1960s, exploring its partial domestication and its contemporary condition, which I will describe as epistemically unsettled and far less monolithic than Calhoun predicted in 1996. In trying to understand how historical sociology had moved through stages of historical critique, partial recuperation, and present dispersion, I propose a *historical sociology of sociological knowledge,*

Thanks for comments to all of the participants in the Evanston workshop at which this chapter was first presented; to Julia Adams, Lis Clemens, and Ann Orloff for detailed comments; and to Julia Hell, Nader Sohrabi, and the Power, History, and Social Change workshop at the University of Michigan. Craig Calhoun, David Featherman, Mark Mizruchi, William Sewell Jr., and Mayer Zald also provided invaluable information used in this essay. I would also like to thank Raphael Allen for help in obtaining source material.

focusing on the period since World War II and placing historical sociological research within the broader framework of postwar American sociology. My account differs from others by emphasizing the changing *structures of plausibility* of different ways of thinking about the social. It is, to paraphrase Pierre Bourdieu, an analysis of the "spontaneous epistemology" of sociologists qua social actors. Drawing on regulation theory (Jessop 1999, 2001; Steinmetz 1993, 1994b, 1997b), I will argue that the patterning of social life by modes of regulation—specifically by Fordism and later by post-Fordism (both of which are defined and discussed below)—has important implications for sociologists' conceptions of social epistemology. Concepts like "capitalism" and "modernity" are too broad-gauged to explain medium-term shifts in sociologists' metaphysical and epistemological assumptions, despite the claims of Marxists like Lukács (1968: 110–148), who saw modern "bourgeois" philosophy as a product of reified consciousness per se. After all, Marxism, logical positivism, and post-structuralism are *all* historical products of one and the same "capitalist modernity." By attending to the shifting structures of social regulation, we can make sense of the specific *timing* of epistemological challenges within social thinking and sociology, including the upsurge of adherence to positivism after 1945 and the rise of the various non-positivist movements since the late 1960s. We can also understand something about the *depth of sympathy* for these movements and their particular *emphases*. My overarching theoretical model thus concerns the impact of modes of regulation and societalization on the relative plausibility of different social epistemologies.

    This is not to deny that the factors emphasized in earlier work by historians and sociologists on the rise of positivism explain a great deal about the dynamics of domesticating historical sociology. Such forces include the pressures of professional legitimation and the priorities of funding agencies on sociologists (Kleinman 1995; D. Ross 1991; Schwendinger and Schwendinger 1974; S. P. Turner and Turner 1990). Other factors include the "hysteresis" of epistemological habitus (Bourdieu 1984); the dynamics of patronage and gatekeeping (S. Cole 1983; H. A. Zuckerman and Merton 1973); and enlisting allies (Latour 1987). Although these factors have been especially important in accounting for the ongoing *recuperation* of critical intellectual movements in the discipline of sociology, they cannot explain the emergence of these movements or their specific substantive focus. Nor can these approaches make sense of the partial expansion of non-positivist forms of sociology during the past decade, both within historical sociology and in other subfields. Professional legitimacy and funding priorities have *not* shifted to non-positivist forms in this period. Although a "taste for necessity" (Bourdieu 1984: ch. 7)

of hysteresis distortion

might account for the adoption of non-positivist epistemologies among dominated fractions of sociology, this structural mechanism cannot explain the *increase* in non-positivist positions over time. *Maybe positivism got exhausted.*

As noted, this chapter begins by reconstructing the consolidation of American sociology's *epistemological unconscious* around the assumptions of methodological positivism (summarized in table 1) in the three decades between 1945 and 1975. I then examine the historical turn in sociology during the 1970s, emphasizing its connections to the shifting structures of social plausibility, which were themselves related to the ongoing collapse of Fordism. Like the other critical movements in American sociology that initially challenged methodological positivism, historical sociology was indeed, as Calhoun argued, partly recuperated. But the *shearing pressure* between the social structures of plausibility and the recuperative enticements in the scientific field has become more intense in recent years. One result is that even texts that intend to defend positivist orthodoxy are often torn between positivist and non-positivist positions, becoming incoherent and internally contradictory as a result. The conclusion analyzes one such exemplary text in detail. The entire field of sociology in the United States is not moving in a post-positivist direction; rather, the methodologically positivist position that used to be *doxic* has been forced to become more explicit and *orthodox* or else has diluted its claims, taking on board some elements of non-positivism (see Bourdieu 1977: 167–169 on the distinction among doxa, orthodoxy, and heterodoxy).

Methodological Positivism Defined

The intellectual formation I am calling *methodological positivism* contains, first of all, a set of *ontological* assumptions about the nature of social reality, objects, and causality. Closely articulated with these ontological foundations is a set of *epistemological* precepts concerning the way in which social facts can be known. A third element of this formation is a *scientistic-naturalist* belief in the unity of the social and the natural sciences. A final set of assumptions concerns social science methodology and the form in which social science should present itself. *Methodological positivism* can be juxtaposed to several other understandings of social science, including critical realism and conventionalist idealism.[1] These contending formations and their individual components are summarized in table 1.

1. Conventionalism is the doctrine that the success or failure of scientific theories in achieving acceptance is based on convention—that is, on considerations other than the correspondence between theory and the object of knowledge. Bourdieu (1988) is conventionalist insofar as his account of the

This is not an ideal-typical definition but a realist one that attempts to capture the central elements of the actual practices of sociologists.[2] Disaggregating the ontological, epistemological, and methodological dimensions of this formation makes it possible to distinguish the different kinds of *partial* breaks with methodological positivism that have characterized historical sociology in different periods since the 1970s. Carefully defining this conglomerate position also makes it possible to identify latent positivist positions *symptomatically* within texts that avoid the explicit language of positivism. Such avoidance of the language of positivism has been the usual situation in sociology since the 1950s.

Empiricism is an *ontological* position according to which "there is no real difference between 'essence' and 'phenomenon' " (Kolakowski 1968: 3). Empiricism therefore rejects the invocation of theoretical, abstract, and unobservable entities. Empiricism suggests that the explanatory elements of an explanation—the explanans—are located at the same phenomenal or actual level of reality as their explananda (Hempel and Oppenheimer 1948).[3] Empiricism holds that reality, or at least any reality that can be legitimately included in a scientific account, is observable using current observation technologies (R. W. Miller 1987: 359–363). As Andrew Collier pointed out, empiricism in the social sciences is most often expressed as the denial of the existence, plausibility, or usefulness of conceiving of "underlying structures which determine events, and instead locates the succession of cause and effect at the level of events" (1994: 7). Empiricism is not necessarily associated with any concepts of causality—hence the need to distinguish between empiricism as a position within ontology and positivism as a position within epistemology. Indeed, Foucault and his followers often converge with older versions of empiricism in their proscriptions on "depth hermeneutics" and causality itself.[4] Actualism/empiricism can thus be contrasted with a depth realism, which begins from a vertically stratified picture of reality. Differentiating the levels of the empirical and real allows for disjunctures (*counter-*

---

domination of specific scientific fields focuses exclusively on considerations of power (capital) and not on the correspondence between scientific beliefs and the objects of which they are theories. Bourdieu (1990) recognized correspondence only as a sort of utopian horizon.

2. The theoretical basis for my definition of methodological positivism is critical realism (Archer 1995; Bhaskar 1979, 1986, 1989, 1994, 1997; A. Collier 1994; A. Sayer 1992; Steinmetz 1998; Steinmetz and Chae 2002).

3. Bhaskar (1997: ch. 2) called this proscription on ontological depth *actualism*; Kolakowski (1968) called it *phenomenalism*.

4. See, for example, Foucault, whose "archaeological" approach "reveals relations" that are "*not* intended to . . . isolate mechanisms of causality" (1972: 162; my emphasis).

phenomenality) between underlying causal mechanisms or deep structures and observable phenomena.[5] Depth realism also allows for a *horizontal* stratification of causal mechanisms, suggesting that in *open systems* like the social, a multiplicity of mechanisms will typically combine in conjunctural ways to produce any empirical event (Bhaskar 1986: 110; A. Collier forthcoming).[6]

Positivism is a well-established philosophical position with particular importance for sociology due to the role of Auguste Comte in coining and popularizing the terms "sociology" and "positivism" (Comte 1975 [1830–1842]); Giere and Richardson, eds. 1996; Halfpenny 1982; Kolakowski 1968; Scharff 1995). Yet self-identification as positivist has come to seem unfashionable, even curmudgeonly, within sociology, something best avoided (Despy-Meyer and Devriese, eds. 1999: 95–143). More widespread than identification with positivism or any other explicit epistemological position is the simple avoidance of all such discussions. Indeed, the central sites for the communication of positivism to sociology students for many years have been introductory textbooks on sociology, statistics, and methods (e.g., Blalock 1964; Hanushek and Jackson 1977; Lundberg, Schrag, and Larsen 1954).[7] The communication of methodological orthodoxy is also embedded or embodied within research monographs and papers. Defining positivism in philosophical terms allows us to avoid using the term as an epithet and to distinguish between sociologists' explicit or manifest descriptions of their position and the latent assumptions expressed in their texts.

Positivism, by contrast, is a position within *epistemology*. It insists that scientific explanation take the general form "if A, then B" or some more elaborate version of the Humean "Constant Conjunction of Events." According to Hume, "we may define a cause to be *an object, followed by another, and where all the objects similar to the first are followed by objects similar to the second*" (1975 [1748]: 76; emphasis in original). Such statements presuppose the *invariance* of empirical relationships. Invariance is rendered possible in

---

5. Although the term "mechanism" runs the risk of sounding mechanistic, it is preferable to all of the alternatives, such as "deep structure," with its roots in French structuralism, and "causal entities," with its Platonic connotations. The conceptual goal in making such a distinction is to signal a difference between (a) relatively enduring social structures that are capable of being reproduced unintentionally and without the conscious awareness of social actors, and (b) the empirical effects these structures are capable of producing. The best illustration of the difference between "events" and "mechanisms" is the psychoanalytic imagery of the generation of symptoms by the unconscious (Rustin 1991, 1999).

6. J. R. Hall complained that "it remains for metaphysical realism [including critical realism] to offer the social ontology that it would claim to warrant" (1990: 344). Bhaskar's (1979) critical realism does, in fact, sketch out the basic lineaments of such a social ontology.

7. Key texts from the 1960s and early 1970s are cited in Gartrell and Gartrell (1996: 144); for a critical discussion of Blalock, see R. W. Miller (1987: 240–241 n. 11).

Table 1 Different Understandings of Social Science

Three approaches to social science

Premises about core aspects of Social Science	Methodological Positivism	Critical Realism	Conventionalist Idealism
Epistemology	Positivism Search for constant conjunctions of events (i.e., general laws)	Conjunctural and contingent causality is assumed to be the norm in open systems Distinguish between theory and explanation	Conventionalism Theories are accepted or rejected due to convention, not to correspondence with their objects No rules for explanation
Ontology	Empiricism Assume irrelevance or nonexistence of non-phenomenal level Assume concept-independence of practice Assume time-independence of social-theoretical concepts Assume space-independence of social concepts	Transcendental Realism Assume disjuncture between phenomenal and real levels Assume concept-dependence of practice Assume time and space dependence of social concepts	Idealism Theories of the world create states of affairs in the world
Stance on Scientific Naturalism	Scientism Natural and social sciences are identical Values and facts are radically distinct Sociology as a technical *Hilfswissenschaft*	Critical Naturalism Social sciences differ from natural ones: social mechanisms are only relatively enduring Social and natural sciences similar insofar as social and natural systems are both open ones	Critical Anti-Naturalism Social sciences are assumed to be radically different from natural sciences, although some versions are conventionalist in treating the natural sciences as equally socially determined
Methodology	Hempel's Deductive-nomological model Privilege given to quantitative methods and experimentation	Denies fact/value distinction Methods should be appropriate to the object of study	"Anything Goes"

two different ways. One is the ontological assumption of phenomenalism or actualism. But it is possible to retain the rule of invariance even if one embraces depth realism—that is, if one breaks with empiricism—as long as the relevant underlying explanans are uniform across all instances of a given explanandum. This sort of *depth-realist positivism* (not presented in table 1) can be found in some versions of traditional or Hegelian Marxism (see Althusser 1990 [1965]; Postone 1993), those versions that posit a unitary cause of all instances of a given type of empirical event. As Somers (1998) has argued, this hybrid position is also characteristic of many rational choice approaches that are realist about ontology but positivist about epistemology.[8] Although empiricism and positivism have been closely interwoven historically, they have also periodically diverged (Harding 1999). Some rational choice theorists have also moved away from assumptions of general or universal laws, however (see Elster 1998), while others embed models of rational decision making within broader contexts of contingent cultural rules (Laitin 1986, 1999).

As noted, the third constituent element of methodological positivism is its adherence to a strong version of scientific naturalism. "Naturalism" in this context refers not to aesthetics but to the philosophical assumption that the social world can be studied in the same manner as the natural one. *Scientism* is a more stringent variant of naturalism that "claims a complete unity" between the natural and social sciences (Bhaskar 1994: 89). Scientism is therefore closely linked to assumptions about ontology and epistemology, but it has additional implications for sociological methodology (row 4 in table 1) and ontology (row 2 in table 1). Due to the central place of quantification, experiment, and prediction in the natural sciences and because natural science is often incorrectly assumed by sociologists to be both empiricist and positivist, many social scientists have assumed that these are appropriate and feasible goals for their own work.

Sociological scientism had three consequential implications for social ontology. Scientism militates against the recognition of the *concept-*, *time-*, and *space-dependence* of social structures and practices. The notion of "concept-dependency" refers here to the claim that human practices and social structures do not exist independently of human theories about them. Social practices are not "brute facts" (C. Taylor 1975: ch. 3; 1979), in other words. Without taking the signifying dimensions of social practices into account, we literally cannot tell what sort of behaviors they are, as Geertz famously illustrated with his discussion of the indeterminate and context-bound meaning

---

8. Of course many rational choice theorists are not realist about the concept of human rationality but describe it as a heuristic device and a fiction (e.g., Friedman 1953).

of a rapid contraction of the eyelids (see below). The meaningful dimension and its material substrate are as inseparable in human practice as two sides of a sheet of paper, in Charles Taylor's effective image (1979). As Herbert Blumer pointed out, "when current variable analysis deals with matters or areas of human group life which involve the process of interpretation, it is markedly disposed to ignore the [interpretive] process" (1956: 686). The scientistic premise of *concept-independence* pushed sociology toward a construal of social processes as connections between empirical, thinglike "variables." Assuming that social action is always suspended within webs of signification suggests that a hermeneutic or interpretive dimension is intrinsic to social research, while concept-*in*dependence suggests, in Emile Durkheim's famously misleading phrase, that sociology's "first and most fundamental rule" is to "*consider social facts as things*" (1982 [1907]: 60; emphasis in original).

Postwar sociology's avoidance of problems of concept-dependency was abetted by the fact that most natural phenomena are not in fact concept-dependent in the same way as human practice. Natural objects are "intransitive," in Bhaskar's terms; or, as Hacking puts it, quarks "do not form an *interactive kind*; the idea of the quark does not interact with quarks"; they "are not aware that they are quarks and are not altered simply by being classified as quarks" (1999: 32; my emphasis). Positivist sociology hoped to inform policy, but this relied on a view of politics as simply taking advantage of intransitively existing, invariant social laws (Fitzgerald 2002). Awareness of the existence of "looping effects" (Hacking 1995, 1999) between scientific theories and the objects of which they are the theories crept into social psychology and survey research in the guise of technical questions (for example, in discussions of "interviewer effects" on respondents). But methodological positivism has not acknowledged that *all* social realities are ubiquitously shaped by social knowledge. The discussion of interviewer effects gestures toward only the tip of the iceberg, acknowledging looping effects in the laboratory or the survey while disavowing the pervasive effects of social science (including survey results themselves) on the supposedly intransitive social realities that social knowledge is supposed to grasp. Recognizing concept-dependency would undermine the scientistic identification of the social sciences and the natural sciences and remind sociologists of their "illegitimate birth" in a space "between literature and science" (Lepenies 1988). More constructively, it would suggest that sociology students should receive serious training in hermeneutics, semiotics, and textual interpretation.

Sociology's scientism also led to a radical underestimation of the time- and space-dependence of social structures. Again, the regulative model here was the natural sciences. Obviously, the causal mechanisms of nature change much more slowly than social ones, if at all, and do not change as we move from one city, country, or continent to the next. Sociological writing often reveals an underlying assumption that social structures and forms of practice exist trans-historically and trans-spatially—that concepts such as "class" or "social development" can be unproblematically applied to earlier periods and disparate places. As Sewell suggested, this is linked to a view of historical sociology as "merely the sociology of the past" and as "valuable above all because it increases the number of data points" (1996b: 246). The insights of ethnosociologists who suggest analyzing India through Hindu categories (see Marriott 1990), or of historians who challenge the direct application of Western concepts like "civil society" to Chinese society (see P. C. C. Huang 1993, 1998), have fallen largely on deaf ears in sociology.[9]

Another dimension of sociological scientism was its attempt to banish values from science. As Habermas notes, early positivism placed "scientific-technical progress" itself "in the place of the epistemological subject" (1971: 73). Thus was a meta-value enshrined for all science: the injunction that it be predictive and technically utilizable. Against this understanding of "value-freedom," Bourdieu countered that the "scientific field itself *produces and presupposes* a specific form of interest"—an interest that inevitably prevents science from being "disinterested" or value-free (1981: 258; emphasis in original). The alternative to assumptions of value-freedom would be to acknowledge the inevitable presence of values in all phases of social scientific work; to analyze systematically the knowledge-constitutive interests of social scientists, the ways in which descriptions of social states of affairs may legitimate or even help to constitute those affairs (Harding 1991); and to explore the possibilities of nonarbitrary ways of "deriving value and practical judgments from deep explanatory social theories" (Bhaskar 1991: 145). But the fact/value distinction was enshrined in some of the earliest statements of sociology's mission (Rammstedt 1988; M. Weber 1949) and was then reasserted in post–World War II American sociology and later periods of epistemological-political unrest as a supposedly necessary component of democratic liberal-

---

9. To the extent that sociologists have discussed *scope conditions*, they have acknowledged time-dependence. Unlike the term "path dependency," which I criticize below, the notion of "scope conditions" does not necessarily imply that certain social processes are *exempt* from this form of historicity. Of course, the notion of scope conditions has sometimes been used in an empiricist way to refer simply to the chronological limits of constant conjunctions, rather than compelling the analyst to make theoretical sense of the historical and spatial limits of underlying causal mechanisms. Some writers also combine the idea of scope conditions with a neo-positivist "falsificationism" (see Walker and Cohen 1985). Because of counter-phenomenality, falsification is an inadequate and misleading criterion for theory choice.

ism (Mihic, Engelmann, and Wingrove 2005).[10] Arguments about the possible connection between positivist notions of value-freedom and the totalitarian "banality of evil" (Adorno and Horkheimer 1986 [1944]; Arendt 1965) were already largely dismissed or ignored during the cold war as antipositivism was brought into unsavory correlation with fascism.

Research methods in the narrower sense are both selected and limited by these three basic scientist assumptions (see table 1, row 4). Qualitative data and methods are compatible with positivism and empiricism, just as quantitative data and methods are in some cases compatible with non-positivist (realist or idealist) epistemologies. Sociology's particular understanding of the natural sciences led it to privilege quantitative methods, however, as well as experimentation, even though true experiments are logically impossible within open systems like the social.[11] That quantitative methods do not flow necessarily from a commitment to positivism and empiricism underscores the fact that the actually existing set of rules is a contingently hammered-together *dispositif* or assemblage of rules.[12]

Finally, particular ways of representing the social textually and visually tended to be associated with methodological positivism. Statistical and tabular forms of presentation are understood as preferable to textuality; narrative or experimental forms of textuality were widely dismissed as unscientific. Just as vision itself was denigrated in twentieth-century thought and diminished specifically within social theory (Jay 1993; Woodiwiss 2001), visual forms and media (other than tables and statistics) were dismissed in sociology as amateurish. One seemingly trivial but still revealing example of the scientism of postwar sociological modes of representation is the way in which the *American Sociological Review* (*ASR*) has emulated "hard science" journals by presenting its text as two tightly wrapped columns on each page. A more general representational issue is the shift from books and book chapters to short journal articles as the field's defining format. Ceteris paribus, short articles do not allow authors to develop complex narratives or arguments that interweave multiple strands of causality. A final issue is the marginalization of authorial voice. The implicit message that individual

10. For a recent example, consider the criticism of linkages between social movements and academic research associated with the National Association of Scholars (see Coleman 1992).

11. See Camic and Xie (1994) on the emergence of statistics as a discipline-defining technique at the turn of the twentieth century. The timing of their argument is not antithetical to mine, since I differentiate between the creation of the raw materials for a later positivist orthodoxy during the pre–World War II decades and the actual consolidation of that orthodoxy. (They also focus specifically on Columbia and not on the entire field of American sociology.)

12. See Layder (1988) for an interesting discussion of the "interdependencies" among specific methods, epistemologies, and theoretical discourses.

voice or interpretation was less significant than standardized analytical techniques and modes of representation was reinforced by sociologists' increasing emulation of the "hard science" practice of publishing articles with a rotating list of authors drawn from a large group. The distrust of authorial voice as subjective was initially linked to the distinction between facts and values, but the voiceless style soon became established in sociology and was reproduced without reference to its original philosophical-political motives.

The combination of positivism, empiricism, and scientism is best described as methodological positivism's center of gravity rather than its common denominator. The cluster's constitutive parts have been differentially emphasized in various periods, sociological subfields, departments, and texts. In recent years, for instance, mainstream American sociology has clung more to positivism and scientism than to empiricism, which has been rejected even by many quantitative sociologists. These differing versions of methodological positivism can still be seen as having family resemblances with one another, as comprising a single category despite their differences of emphasis. If there is a common denominator, it is positivist epistemology, which has allowed even historical, Marxist, and cultural sociology to be presented in the form of closed-system generalizations.

American Sociology's Postwar *Rifondazione* (Refounding) and the Consolidation of Methodological Positivist Orthodoxy

One of the first issues that needs to be addressed in a reconstruction of the genealogy of positivist orthodoxy in U.S. sociology during the postwar period is the fact that many of its discursive and material-institutional building blocks were already in place before World War II.[13] Many of the nineteenth-century founders of sociology worshiped at the altar of the natural sciences. The specific cluster of naturalism, empiricism, and positivism had been promoted by Comte, whose "hierarchy of the positive sciences" placed mathematics, astronomy, physics, chemistry, and physiology before "social physics" (Comte 1975 [1830–1842]: 101).[14] Spencer (1972) assumed that natu-

---

13. This section is a much condensed version of an analytical historical sociology of the postwar period on which I elaborate in more detail in Steinmetz (forthcoming a). (I use the term *Rifondazione* in a loose analogy to preservation of traditionally communist positions by the Italian Communist Refoundation Party (Partito della Rifondazione Comunista), formed in 1991 after the dissolution of the old Italian Communist Party. Similarly, American sociology consolidated a positivist orthodoxy in the postwar period, just as philosophers of science were beginning to move away from positivism.

14. Although Comte introduced the term "positivism," the differences between his definition and the one that prevailed in the twentieth century are extensive (C. Bryant 1985).

ral species provided a grid for taxonomizing different types of societies, and Durkheim (1915: 486) elevated science itself to an object of quasi-religious worship. The philosophical writings of Ernst Mach (1886), the godfather of logical positivism, were extremely important for early American sociology. Founders of American sociology such as Franklin Giddings drew on Mach's empiricist theory, according to which science and knowledge in general were based entirely on sense impressions (see also Bannister 1987: 72–73; D. Ross 1991: 227; Toulmin 1969: 33–35). Karl Pearson, who promoted a positivist, empiricist, and naturalistic understanding of the social sciences, was also influential. Pearson's 1892 *The Grammar of Science* was adopted by many of the first generation of American sociologists in their self-transformation from reformers and social evolutionists into social technicians (Bannister 1987: 151; G. Levine 1996). In that book, Pearson reproduced a sketch by Mach of the view from inside the scientist's head, looking out at the world, to illustrate the argument that sense perception was the sole source of knowledge (see fig. 1). Pearson also argued that science found its "fullest expression" in statistics (Bannister 1987: 151). The scientific naturalism of early founders of American sociology, like Giddings at Columbia University or Albion Small at the University of Chicago, was explicit (Dibble 1975; W. T. O'Connor 1942; Vidich 1985: ch. 8).

Positivist approaches were also actively promoted by the Laura Spelman Rockefeller Foundation during the 1920s and 1930s, under the guise of making sociology less theoretical and political and more scientific, applied, and similar to the natural sciences. Major grants were made to a number of sociology departments, the list of which is startlingly similar to the roster of top-ranking departments today (Bulmer 1982; Fisher 1993; D. Ross 1991). Ahmad (1991) supports Fisher's (1993) conclusion that the Laura Spelman Rockefeller Foundation rewarded a positivist version of social science with an orientation toward predictions and practical applications for business and the state (but compare Bulmer 1982, 1984).

Nevertheless, American sociology was epistemically unsettled during the entire period from the Gilded Age to 1945, lacking any consensus about criteria for scientific authority and distinction. Many leading figures in early American sociology, including Sumner, Mead, Cooley, Veblen, Parsons, and Howard P. Becker, rejected some version of positivism. Non-positivists had a voice in the *American Journal of Sociology* (*AJS*) and the ASR, which began publication in 1936. In 1939, the ASR carried a critique of Comtean positivism by the founder of an earlier version of critical realism, the philosopher Roy Wood Sellars (1916). The first two volumes of ASR also carried essays on cultural theory, psychoanalysis, Lenin's theory of revolution, and the topic of "imagination in social science." Even the Sociological Research

Figure 1

Association, an elite, invitation-only professional group that was formed in 1936 in response to battles within the American Sociological Society between "value-free" positivists and "humanistic" social activists, was itself divided between theoretical and more positivist wings (Bannister 1987: 189, 218). At the end of the 1930s, American sociology was not yet a "scientific field" in the Bourdieuian sense of the term—that is, it was a fragmented field, not one in which all actors shared a set of criteria, conscious or unconscious, defining scientific capital (Bourdieu 1985, 2001; S. P. Turner and Turner 1990: 75).

Parsons began his discussion of the positivist tradition in 1937 with the question, "Why has it died?" Parsons (1993) also produced some of his most historical and non-positivist work in his wartime writing on Germany and Nazism. Ironically, this was the swan song of anti-positivism in American sociology. In defiance of Parsons's performative speech act, positivism came roaring back to life immediately after the war and soon came to dominate

American sociology.[15] Indeed, it persisted as *doxa* until sometime between the late 1960s and the mid-1970s and still functions as *orthodoxy* within the field today. How can we account for this rapid and overwhelming consolidation of positivist doxa?

Scientific Captial, Modes of Regulation, and Ideological Resonance

Bourdieu's notion of the field (*champ*) is a useful starting point for analyzing postwar changes in U.S. sociology. A field contains diverse positions and viewpoints but is nonetheless clearly structured, such that certain positions are recognized by the dominant and the dominated alike as the most *distinguished* (see Bourdieu 1981, 1984, 1985, 1986, 1988). Bourdieu notes that epistemological differences are a central axis of distinction within scientific fields, writing that "a survey on power in the scientific field could perfectly well consist of . . . epistemological questions alone" (1981).[16] Certain methodological positions have more *scientific capital* than others, all other things being equal. All participants in a well-structured field recognize a common definition of scientific authority and competence, a hierarchy of distinguished and less distinguished positions, even as the dominated develop a somewhat perverse taste for their own domination. My argument, for which I can provide only partial evidence here, is that sociological scientific authority increasingly accrued to methodologically positivist positions during the postwar decades.

Unlike earlier anthropological notions of culture, this imagery of structured fields does not require any assumption of cultural uniformity. Unlike Gramscian hegemony, it does not suggest that alternative positions are unthinkable. Instead, it suggests that alternative *valuations* of heterodox positions are unworkable. Epistemological alternatives were never absent in postwar American sociology. Marxism, cultural sociology, and the sociology of science all had prewar precursors, and all of them continued to lead at least a desultory existence throughout the cold war period.

It is also important to keep in mind that what counts as distinguished is field-specific. What counted as cultural capital within sociology certainly would not have been recognized as such in the broader arena of American cultural life during the cold war. Positivism has had no eminent

---

15. In the field of psychology, by contrast, positivism already flourished during the war as a result of wartime policies (Herman 1996); here, behaviorism was stronger than epistemically analagous positions within sociology (Buckley 1989).

16. Interestingly, Bourdieu is discussing American sociology here.

defenders in philosophy for many decades; already in the early 1950s philosophers observed that "the words 'positivist' and 'positivism' seem to be in general disfavour . . . as a result of incriminating overtones which accrued to them in the twenties and thirties" (J. W. Smith 1952: 190). The dominance of positivism within sociology might also seem to contradict Bourdieu's general thesis that distinguished positions tend to exhibit a greater degree of "distance from necessity." Yet we should not necessarily define such distance in aesthetic terms. *Empiricism* is indeed more concrete than realist ontologies, and thus in one respect it is closer to "necessity" in Bourdieu's sense. From another perspective, however, *positivism* understands itself as less concerned with details than the other epistemological positions. Positivism's *abstractness* applies to the explanans as well as the explanandum. By declaring itself uninterested in the idiographic—that is, in the details (or even the identity) of the specific case—positivism keeps the concrete at arm's length. In the social sciences this typically involves replacing place names or proper names with the names of variables. And by emphasizing constant conjunctions, positivism avoids the concrete "messiness" of explanatory strategies that are open to constantly changing concatenations of mechanisms.

This is not to suggest that non-positivist approaches could not have defined themselves as distinguished. Emphasis could have been placed on the fact that simple, parsimonious explanations are actually closer to commonsense understandings of the social, for example. So why was methodological positivism so successful in its bid for leadership? Although Bourdieu helps us to clarify the general sorts of arguments that must be used by *any* position trying to govern a given field, his approach cannot explain why specific definitions of distinction are more successful than others in any given time and place. Obviously economic (and social) capital can enhance the value of cultural capital, at least indirectly. The resources offered by private and government sources to sociologists who agreed to configure their work along the lines of the natural sciences played a key role. But these resources were also available during the prewar period, and they still exist today, yet their ability to shape the discipline has varied over this entire period.

Bourdieu's theory allows us to understand the operation of cultural capital in consolidated, settled fields, but it is poorly equipped to explain why particular ways of describing society come to be recognized as more distinguished than others. Bourdieu's relatively ahistorical and conventionalist account of science needs to be reformulated in order to understand the changing *conditions of plausibility* of different ontologies and epistemologies of the social.[17] To explain why certain visions of the social seem more intuitively reasonable than others, to understand why some intellectual challenges are able to emerge and seize the imaginations of social scientists despite entrenched interests, habituses, and the preferences of external agencies, we need to consider the overall context of social regularities. It is possible to argue that certain ways of seeing the social world are *empowered* in particular historical epochs by their resonance with that world without thereby reducing them to a simple reflection of some external reality (Peirce 1955: ch. 7).

This suggests that we need a theory of the aspects of the social worlds that are most relevant to social epistemology. We also require a theory that is able to make epochal distinctions within the broad period of capitalist modernity, if social structures are to account for social epistemologies, given that the latter have changed and evolved over the timeframes designated as "modernity" and "capitalism." Regulation theory is one of the few social perspectives able to fulfill both of these requirements. The distinction between Fordism and post-Fordism within this framework (see below) underscores the theory's goal of periodizing analytically *within* the broader epoch of capitalism. Regulation theory has also emphasized the influence of system-level regularities on subjectivity and culture (Hardt and Negri 2000; Harvey 1989; Hirsch and Roth 1986; Steinmetz 1994a, 1994b, 1997b). We can extend this to the investigation of system-level effects on spontaneous social epistemologies.

My argument does not reduce to a reflectionist theory of social perception in which ideologies are understood as mirrors or as partial, blurry, or inverted images of reality. A mirror (or *camera obscura*) approach would involve the absurd claim that post-Fordist restructuring is leading social actors to become spontaneous regulation theorists (if we assume, for the sake of argument, that regulation theory best captures these ongoing social changes). Instead, as theorists such as Jameson (1984) and Roudinesco (2001) have argued, contemporary social transformations are more likely to be expressed in subjective forms such as feelings of ephemerality and depthlessness. By arguing that positivism and post-structuralism are the spontaneous social epistemologies of the Fordist and post-Fordist eras respectively, for instance, one is not claiming that these are *adequate* forms of knowledge.

The connection between social epistemology and Fordism should not be understood as a difference between a dependent cultural realm and an independent acultural one but as a relationship of *resonance* between two dif-

---

17. While the present chapter *supplements* Bourdieu's approach via a theoretical account of macro-social patterns of societalization, elsewhere I have reformulated Bourdieu's underlying theory of subjectivity in psychoanalytic terms (Steinmetz 2002, 2003a, forthcoming b).

ferent formations of practice. Resonance suggests formal and structural homologies rather than any sort of direct mimesis. Regulation theory avoids a reifying language according to which Fordism or post-Fordism would be reducible to brute material or narrowly economic practices (Jessop 1999). The concept of modes of regulation is centered on rates of profit and exploitation, but it encompasses an entire array of patterned cultural, social, spatial, temporal, and political practices as well. It is these broader aspects of Fordism and post-Fordism that are most relevant to explaining the fluctuating degrees of plausibility of positivist and non-positivist epistemology in sociology. Social knowledge may register the shifts in these regulatory modes in oblique and indirect ways. To take a simple example: social crisis may be more resonant with epistemologies that emphasize *discontinuity* than with epistemologies insisting on repeated, general social laws (Bourdieu 1977: 170; 1984: 168). By attending to the changing modes of regulation and societalization, it is possible to periodize the waxing and waning influence of spontaneous social epistemologies.

The determinants of sociologists' social epistemologies can be heuristically described as being external or internal to the scientific field. In explanations of the development of science, the adjective "external" has typically been used to refer to all influences on science that do not relate to the intellectual question of the fit between theory and object (Breslau 2003; R. A. Hall 1963). I draw the boundary between internal and external influences at a different point, with the *inside* encompassing subfields, disciplines, universities, research institutions, and funding agencies. The *outside* then refers to other sociocultural factors that influence science, as well as branches of the government concerned with science.[18] This is not to deny that each of these separate levels may have its own distinctive fieldlike properties. But the sociology of sociology has not paid enough attention to the extra-scientific sources of social epistemologies, focusing instead on intra-scientific dynamics and on interventions by government and private funding agencies (Ahmad 1991; Fisher 1993; S. P. Turner and Turner 1990; D. Ross 1991). The impact of broader social structures on sociologists' epistemological leanings—a field of inquiry suggested by Marx and Engels in *The German Ideology* (1970)—has been left largely unexamined.

The Bourdieuian theory of fields and scientific capital, combined with a regulation-theoretic sociology of social knowledge, allows us to move beyond the usual focus on material blandishments and sanctions in explaining

---

18. Examples of such external sources would include Puritanism and pietism in Merton's (1936) classic study of seventeenth-century science and the social role of the "gentleman" in Shapin's (1994) study of the same period.

the dominance of methodological positivism and the timing of its consolidation. We can now understand how the intellectual raw materials of methodological positivism could have existed for many decades before becoming dominant. Fordism may have lent credence to methodological positivism, but it did not create it.[19] By the same token, the post-Fordist mode of regulation that is currently being consolidated resonates with non-positivist forms of social knowledge production without having given rise to those forms, and it may help explain the stepwise and piecemeal dissolution of positivist doxa in recent years.[20]

The Postwar Conjuncture and Positivist Social Science

The postwar period saw an enormous rise in resources for social science research from the state sector (Featherman and Vinovskis 2001; Gieryn 1999: 65–114; Klausner 1986; Kleinman 1995; Larsen 1992; J. T. Wilson 1983). Leading sociological figures, from Talcott Parsons to Philip Hauser, understood this conjuncture as an opportunity to establish sociology more firmly as a discipline. This would require epistemological convergence, however. The direction of this convergence was suggested initially by the National Science Foundation (NSF), which made funding available to sociologists provided they were willing to generate "social laws" and predictions (Hauser 1946: 382). Parsons wrote a paper in 1948 for the Social Science Research Council that argued that "the same philosophical principles that guided the natural sciences were at the heart of the social sciences" (Klausner and Lidz, eds. 1986: viii). In 1954, the NSF mandate was expanded to include the social sciences. Conditions were laid out defining which sociologists would be permitted to receive funding (Alpert 1954, 1955a, 1955b, 1957; see also Lundberg 1947). The first condition was "the *criterion of science*" specified to mean the "convergence of the natural sciences and the social sciences" (Alpert 1955a: 656). Sociologists were cautioned that access to future funding depended "largely on their capacity to prove themselves by their deeds" (p. 660). During the years 1945–1949, the proportion of articles in *AJS, ASR,* and *Social Forces* acknowledging outside sources of funding was 17.4 percent; by 1960–1964 this figure had risen to 52.5 percent (McCartney 1971: 388).

The positivist camp was strengthened by other institutional factors (Featherman and Vinovskis 2001). The wartime mobilization brought social scien-

19. For a similar argument about the ways Fordism "bundles" and reinforces specific forms of practice without actually giving rise to them, see Steinmetz (1994a).

20. See P. Anderson (1998), for example, who traces the origins of "post-modernism" as an aesthetic category to the 1930s and as an epochal category to 1954.

tists into the ambit of the state (Kleinman 1995: ch. 3). After the war many new recruits were brought into sociology from government agencies and hard science disciplines, tending to reinforce methodological positivism (S. P. Turner and Turner 1990: 86–88). Another critical factor was the rise of freestanding research institutions such as the National Opinion Research Center in Chicago and the Institute for Social Research at the University of Michigan (Frantilla 1998). These new research institutes were often physically separated from the extant sociology departments, but they were still able to intervene in the ongoing redefinition of the discipline's identity.

The scope of these postwar ambitions was expressed in a 1948 paper by Paul Lazarsfeld that C. Wright Mills (1959: 59–63) quoted extensively. Students were to stop studying "the history of institutions and ideas" and focus on "the concrete behavior of peoples" and contemporary events—an empiricist preference. Lazarsfeld called for "studying social situations and problems which repeat themselves rather than those which occur only once"—a direct restatement of the positivist definition of science as the search for constant conjunctions. Methodologically, sociology was to cease being an artisanal activity practiced by "the individual observer" and to become more like "organized, full-fledged empirical science" (p. 61). And "basic techniques for finding explanations," according to Lazarsfeld, were "statistical" (p. 63).

What explains this powerful surge of methodological positivism after World War II? While some of the influences were internal to social science— the influx of funding and recruits oriented toward a natural science model, the creation of freestanding centers of "abstracted empiricism" (Mills 1959: ch. 3)—other factors were external. The positivist position was encouraged, first, by an association of anti-science irrationalism with the rise of Nazism and Soviet totalitarianism. Adorno and Horkheimer's 1944 *Dialectic of Enlightenment* (1986) had moved dialectically from a Heideggerian critique of positivism to an explanation of anti-Semitism and Nazism. In the context of the wartime triumph of science and the postwar confrontation with the Soviet Union, however, it became more difficult for anti-fascists to criticize the spirit of modern science itself. Indeed, it was widely argued that it was precisely the *lack* of a modern scientific culture that had contributed to fascism. Suspicion was now cast backward retroactively on the entire non-positivist tradition, running from Hegel and the German Romantics through to Marx, Dilthey, Nietzsche, and the critical theorists of the interwar period. This was doubly damaging to anti-positivist arguments, since most of these thinkers had emerged from the German-speaking context and could therefore be linked, if only by a vague sort of "guilt by association," with German exceptionalism and hence with Nazism (Steinmetz 1997a).

The 1950s thus saw an accumulation of pressures conducive to positivism. Nonetheless, methodological positivism became dominant only at the end of the 1950s and during the 1960s, after a considerable period in which its basic picture of the social had been ratified by the consolidated Fordist mode of regulation. It is to those processes of ratification, or resonance, that I will now turn.

The Resonance of Fordism with the Positivist Social Imaginary

Fordism can be understood as a contingently arrived-at regulatory dispositif, a mixture of social, cultural, political, and economic arrangements that provided a temporary solution to the problems of capitalist instability and profits.[21] Fordism arose in the United States and elsewhere in the advanced capitalist world through processes of trial and error, and not due to some functional logic or central coordination. As Fordism proved attractive to a wide array of powerful actors and institutions, they began to orient themselves toward reproducing it, and it prevailed as a dominant form of social regulation for several decades. Although Fordism was never all-encompassing, its logics had a wide reach and were able to shape the subjectivities and practices of many people (Aglietta 1987; Boyer 1990; Gramsci 1971; Lipietz 1987).

Fordism's dominance in the 1950s and 1960s was not unconnected to the cold war boom in science funding. The Fordist state relied to a greater extent than earlier forms of regulation on positivist social science to track the economy, regulate business cycles and labor markets, survey the population, and bring social practices into conformity with the regularities of mass production and mass consumption. It is more than ironic in this respect that, just as Henry Ford's social system in southeastern Michigan was a microcosm of the all-encompassing postwar mode of regulation, so Ford had created his own Sociological Department in 1913 to promote Americanization, health, and a wholesome family life among his workers through inquisitorial visits to workers' homes and paternalistic interventions (Nevins 1957, vol. 2: 332–354).

American sociology and Fordism were thus connected from the start, and sociologists were among the creators of Fordism as a mode of regulation.

---

21. See Aglietta (1987) for the first, more economistic statement of regulation theory and a definition of Fordism. The important thing to remember in the current context is that Fordism is not the same as Ford, even if some of the elements of the Fordist social formation were strongly associated with Henry Ford in the U.S. context (high wages, the assembly line, vertically integrated production, attempts to police and control workers' private lives, etc.). Fordism as a social formation is associated most strongly with the postwar period, culminating in the 1960s in most of Western Europe and North America.

But I want to focus on the causal arrows running from Fordism to sociology. Specifically, the array of sociocultural changes that regulation theory gathers under the heading of Fordism contributed to the *plausibility* of positivist approaches to sociological research and writing. The state-organized wartime regime in which many sociologists were involved provided a glimpse of this more orderly life that emerged in the 1950s and 1960s. The world wrought by Fordism seemed increasingly to correspond to a positivist representation of social phenomena as repeated and invariant across time and space, as rational, acultural, predictable, and controllable.

The first aspect of American Fordism that resonated with positivism was the management of economic crisis and the corresponding sense of the end of (economic) history. Fordism seemed to bring capitalist instability under control through a combination of high wages, Keynesian demand stabilization, and social benefits. The muting of capitalist crisis made it increasingly plausible that social practices really were repeatable in ways that could be captured by statistical models and replicable experiments. One could imagine that a wide range of human practices could be construed as constant conjunctions of events while ignoring the historical conditions of possibility of this patterning. The specifically Keynesian-Fordist strategies for dampening the effects of the business cycle lent support to theoretical approaches premised on synchronic rather than diachronic analysis.[22] In contrast to the chaotic social conditions of the Great Depression, organized Fordist societalization seemed to be coherently serial and cyclically repetitive.

A second way in which Fordism shaped sociologists' spontaneous perceptions of social ontology involved the homogenization of consumer tastes, subjectivities, and everyday life. Behaviorist and economic models of psychology, surveys, and statistical approaches seemed appropriate to an increasingly flattened out and standardized culture. The infantilization of the consumer-citizen (Adorno and Horkheimer 1986 [1944]; Berlant 1997) helped to convince social scientists, who were consumers and citizens themselves, that individual consumers and producers were in fact interchangeable. It made increasing sense for undergraduate social psychology laboratory subjects to stand in for the generic American. American intercollegiate football could be compared to "tribal" African cultures and described as another example of a "culture complex" (Lundberg, Schrag, and Larsen

---

22. Even under Fordism, history could not be ignored completely, of course, given the nonsynchronized spaces of communism and the nonaligned post-colonial world. But modernization theories folded these recalcitrant worlds into the dominant narrative, defining them as earlier stages of the normative Western trajectory.

1954; 196–197). Surveys and statistical modeling approaches to human be-havior both assumed and rhetorically implied that the units of analysis—individuals—were fundamentally the same with respect to their decision-making processes. And as subjectivities and social practices became sta-bilized, *prediction* itself started to seem feasible.

The third implication of Fordism for sociologists' spontaneous social philosophy relates to its synchronization of the scale of activities within the contours of the nation-state. As Jessop (1999) and other regulation theorists have argued, Fordism organized economic development and economic flows mainly within and between national states. Neil Brenner (1998) demon-strates that Fordism effected a relative reduction in levels of uneven develop-ment within the contours of the national territory. The resulting taken-for-grantedness of the *nation-state space* as the fundamental frame, or container, for social practices made it easier to believe that social events actually did occur in constant conjunctions. By contrast, the idea of social regularities is much less plausible where each type or dimension of social practice has a different spatial reach and location, as is increasingly the case under "glocal-izing" post-Fordism, with its myriad spatial reshufflings (N. Brenner 1999; S. Graham and Marvin 2001).[23] Fordism's geosocial character was thus con-ducive in myriad ways to methodological positivism.

The importance of the spatial organization of capitalism and social life more generally for the social sciences can also be seen in the division be-tween the putatively nomothetic social science disciplines and the sup-posedly idiographic fields of area studies. Although spatial scale was rela-tively settled within the capitalist core countries (and the East European socialist ones) during the Fordist era, it remained less so in the so-called Third World. Seemingly continual changes in the location of international borders were one aspect of peripheral spatial uncertainty. The naturalness of the nation-state as the obvious scale for economic, political, and cultural practices was continually called into question in the Third World by interna-tional labor migrations and anti-systemic movements (pan-Arabism, pan-Africanism, communism) that partly transcended national boundaries. The nation-state was not only too small to capture the main dynamics of the periphery; it was also too big. Social activities in the periphery often seemed to be more local in their focus, and economic development continued to be more uneven within nation-states. These differences undergirded the divi-sion between area studies and the generalizing, supposedly context-free so-

23. "Glocal" refers to the mixing up of the global and local scalar levels in contemporary post-Fordism, as opposed to the "containerization" of most social practices within the scale of the nation-state under Fordism (P. J. Taylor 2003).

cial sciences. Prediction seemed less conceivable in a Third World because Fordism was absent or only partially instantiated there (Lipietz 1987). Other factors played a role in staving off positivist dominance within area studies, including the pervasive view of the non-West as less rational and more cultural; this was conducive to hermeneutic methodological approaches (see Bierstedt 1949: 590; Steinmetz 1999).[24] Positivist forms of social science knowledge that promised to fold the non-West into a generalizing explanatory framework were not entirely lacking, of course, especially where U.S. economic and security interests were at stake.

In sum, while the Fordist state directly subsidized positivist regimes of social knowledge, Fordism as a mode of social regulation and way of life provided sustenance to the positivist social imagination.

Sociology Becomes a Full-Fledged Field

The outcome of this postwar conjuncture was that U.S. sociology had become a well-structured field by the early 1960s. Despite differences of taste or viewpoint, all of the players in a field agree on common stakes and legitimate definitions of field-specific capital. Reputational, social, and economic capital in sociology tended now to accrue to more positivist positions. Fluency in positivist methodological positions began to function as a field-specific form of scientific capital. Even those who rejected positivism often colluded in its rise to preeminence. Talcott Parsons, who had forcefully opposed positivism in the 1930s (and who is currently associated with an antipositivist strand of social theory; see J. C. Alexander 1982), accommodated to the new doxa.[25] Those who did not conform often "emigrated" to less influential sociology departments (Abbott 1999).

A system of rules that guided the creation of knowledge, the channeling of resources, and the inscription of boundaries within sociology and against other disciplines was thus institutionalized and internalized. The initial period of consolidation in the 1940s and 1950s was still characterized by occasional skirmishing over foundational questions, but by the early 1960s these

---

24. The orientation of area studies fields toward a fetishization of language and "translation" problematics promoted an atheoretical approach that critics of these fields sometimes label "positivism" (Dutton 2002); this is not equivalent to positivism as defined here.

25. I am not following Gouldner (1970) here; see Steinmetz and Chae (2002) for a critique of his conception of American sociological positivism. Elsewhere (Steinmetz forthcoming a), I discuss Parsons's prewar and postwar theories in detail, finding an increasing compatibility with methodological positivism. Robert Merton played a key role in translating Parsonian grand theory into terms that were compatible with methodological positivism, especially with his highly influential empiricist-positivist notion of "middle-range" theory.

rules had become largely habitual and commonsensical. Positivist method-ological positions won the battle to define field-specific cultural capital, becoming doxic.

Historical Sociology and Other Challenges to Methodological Positivism since the 1960s

The dissident movements that emerged within sociology during the late 1960s marked the first challenge to the discipline's postwar common sense. The incipient collapse of Fordism after the economic and oil crisis of 1973 entailed the disappearance of the social regularities that had indirectly sup-ported a spontaneous positivism in the vision of sociologists. Yet method-ological positivism remained dominant in the field, if not doxic, well into the 1990s. American sociology remained well structured as a field, with scientific capital continuing to accrue to more positivist positions. The dom-inance of this framework was still recognized by most sociologists, whether or not they stood to profit from it (S. Cole 1983: 137). But the emergence of post-Fordism created a disjuncture between the overall structuring of social-epistemological plausibility and the continuing adherence of much of the discipline to the older model. In recent years, methodological positivism has been forced to become more explicit and orthodox or else has relinquished one or more of the tenets that had been central.

Historical sociology is one of a series of challenges to methodological positivism that began in the late 1960s. There have been at least four such movements: critical sociology (neo-Marxism and feminism and, somewhat later, critical race theory); historical sociology, starting in the second half of the 1970s; cultural sociology, reemerging in the 1980s; and the epistemologi-cal turn, which was located especially within science studies but not re-stricted to them, in the 1990s.[26] Each of these movements initially rejected one or more of the mainstays of methodological positivism. Although each of them was partially recuperated by positivism, they were not fully domes-ticated, *pace* Calhoun, and have been able to recover some of their non-positivist potential in recent years. There is enough space here to discuss only the second of these challenges, the historical turn in sociology. But the

26. In addition to these four challenges, Gouldner (1970) pointed to the work of Goffman and Garfinkel as having the potential, along with humanistic Marxism, to displace positivism and to introduce a more reflexive approach into American sociology. Both of these theorists provided impor-tant sources of continuity with the hermeneutic tradition, and Goffman (1974) was adopted in the 1980s by social movement theorists who were trying to think their way out of their subfield's en-trenched aculturalism (Snow et al. 1986).

contributions of the other movements to the critique of methodological orthodoxy can be briefly summarized.[27]

The first challenge came from *neo-Marxism, feminism/gender studies,* and *critical race studies.* Neo-Marxist sociology emerged just a few years after methodological positivism had become enshrined as doxa. Some of the earliest Marxist interventions attacked empiricist ontology by insisting on the legitimacy of unobservable causal mechanisms and theoretical concepts like reification, commodity fetishism, surplus value extraction and the value form, the political unconscious, modes of production, and ideological inter-pellation. Some neo-Marxists also rejected the scientistic assumption of the temporal invariance of theoretical concepts, arguing that their own central explanatory concepts (such as social class) were time-dependent and not necessarily applicable across all social formations. Feminists and critical race theorists also deployed theoretical, nonempiricist concepts such as patriarchy and mimicry. Theorists called attention to the social construction and geohistorical variability (time dependence) of gender, race, and sexuality.

The *historical turn* in sociology since the 1970s (discussed by the editors of this volume as the "second wave" of historical sociology), like neo-Marxism and feminism, promised to make sociologists aware of the historical mutability of their theoretical categories. Unlike Marxism and feminism, it also emphasized the ubiquity of conjunctural and contingent causality. In formal terms, historical sociology was open to *narrative emplotment.* There was also an emphasis on historicity itself, on time and process, that had been almost entirely lacking during the preceding period (Aminzade 1992; Sewell 1996b). These messages about contingency, conjuncture, figurational analysis, narrative, the historicity of concepts, temporal process, and the category-dependence of social practice ran up against the deeply entrenched dominant epistemic habitus in sociology.

The *cultural turn* in sociology since the 1980s signals a broad-gauged interest in the role of signification and subjectivity in all types of social practice, along with a reinvigoration of the older sociological tradition of studying more narrowly defined cultural "objects" (Griswold 1987; Wuthnow 1989). The main critique of methodological positivism emanating from the recent cultural turn, familiar from earlier interventions dating back to the nineteenth-century *Methodenstreit* (methods dispute), is the insistence that human practice is always an entanglement of meanings and material

27. See Steinmetz (forthcoming a) for further elaboration and references.

substrates.[28] In ontological terms, this militates against the scientistic assumption of concept-independence and against behaviorist or one-sidedly materialist theories. Insofar as it analyzed subjectivity and culture as mutable, diverse, and complex, the culturalist turn discouraged sociologists from looking for trans-historically valid conjunctions of events.

The ongoing *critical epistemological upheaval* within the contemporary human sciences, including sociology, is centered around a reinvigoration of interest in philosophy and social theory, a renewal of Critical Theory's emphasis on self-reflexivity, and the specific subfield of the new science studies.[29] Many of the participants in this literature reject the entire set of assumptions of methodological positivism, although they are divided with respect to alternatives. Some embrace the ideas presented in the second or third columns in table 1 (critical realism or conventionalist idealism). More explicit defenses of positivism, empiricism, and scientism are also emerging in response to this challenge (e.g., Stinchcombe 2002; J. H. Turner 1993). The central axis of debate generally pits defenders of various sorts of philosophical realism against an array of constructivist, conventionalist, and idealist positions that are radically skeptical about the possibility of choosing rationally among contending theories (i.e., that embrace the position known as judgmental relativism; see Bhaskar 1986, 1997 [1975]). This configuration of debate is quite different from that found in the first half of the twentieth century, which was dominated by disputes between positivism and various forms of realism.

Like the rise of methodological positivism during the postwar period, we can understand the emergence of positions critical of positivism only by considering the ways they have been encouraged by the overall mode of societalization. Both the timing of these critical movements and their particular substantive emphases partly reflect the environing structures of social regulation. Again, this is not to downplay the significance of material rewards, allies, patronage, gatekeeping, or sheer habit. These factors have been especially central to the domestication of critical turns (Calhoun 1996; Flacks 1989: 355; Gouldner 1970: 445; Wright 1994: 1–15). But it is difficult to see how they could explain the *emergence* of new paradigms. A competition-based theory of science can account for the continual generation of new challengers, but it cannot explain the specific *contents* of their challenges, except in a formalistic way, as the simple negation or inversion of earlier

---

28. The Methodenstreit, or "methods dispute," pitted natural science against humanities as models for the social sciences; see Dilthey (1910).

29. See Shapin (1995) for an overview of science studies and the sociology of science.

positions.[30] Nor can a purely internalist approach explain why the current epistemological challenge seems to be less easily assimilable than the critical, historical, and cultural turns. This resistence by the epistemological turn to cooptation cannot be traced to the nature of the object of study itself, since American sociology demonstrated in earlier periods that science could be studied in a positivist manner. Indeed, the second half of the 1960s was a crucial watershed for a shift toward a sociology of science focused on the quantifiable aspects of science, such as citations, discoveries, and rewards, and away from the more historical and interpretive emphasis that still characterized this field in the first half of the 1960s (see Barber 1962; Ben-David 1960a, 1960b, 1971; Ben-David and Collins 1966).

The differences in the trajectories of the four critical turns can be understood in terms of the shifting conjunctures of internal and external determinants. The early neo-Marxists and second-wave feminists in sociology confronted a positivist doxa that was still buttressed by the conforming social regularities of Fordism, whose collapse did not really begin until the 1970s. These critical movements encompassed a fundamental critique of sociology's dominant epistemology, but at the same time, they themselves had been shaped by the Fordist conditions that underwrote methodological positivism. These critical challenges were contemporaneous with, and in many ways parallel to, the first wave of new social movements. Social movements of the late 1960s and early 1970s such as anti-consumerism and environmentalism were directed *against* aspects of Fordism, but in many ways they were also shaped by the very forms of subjectivity that Fordism had generated. Fordism was most likely to become a central target of widespread, vehement protest among those who had experienced at first hand the degrading side of standardization and mass consumerism and whose subjectivity was correspondingly shaped by it (Hirsch and Roth 1986; Steinmetz 1994a, b).[31] Similarly, the critical sociologists of the period before the mid-1970s were motivated by their opposition to a disciplinary formation that had shaped their own intellectual formation. At the same time, this superego dimension of original symbolic identifications introduced re-

30. Neither Karl Popper nor Thomas Kuhn provides a social account of the contents of new theories or paradigms. For Kuhn, a paradigm shift is stimulated by the accumulation of anomalies. But since he is concerned with the natural and physical world, which he assumes is the *same* world before and after the scientific revolution (1970: 129), he cannot use that world to explain the contents of the new paradigm.

31. Conversely, certain strands in the current anti-globalization and far right movements look back nostalgically to a Fordism they never knew, enhancing its positive virtues (see Steinmetz forthcoming c).

cuperative pressures into the confrontation. And the ongoing regularities of domestic Fordism overshadowed the challenges to regulated order emanating from the Third World (Vietnam), reinforcing the positivist social worldview for many critical sociologists.

Taken together, these factors hampered the ability of the early critical antipositivism to capture the imagination of most sociologists. It was on this terrain, coupled with the internal dynamics of hiring, firing, funding, and direct political repression, that the initial critical turns were partly reintegrated. Marxism's epistemological critique of positivism and scientism was divorced from its substantive claims, some of which found their way into mainstream sociological research under the guise of "independent variables." This was perhaps a political victory, but it was an epistemological setback.

The style of Marxist and feminist research that became prevalent in American sociology was thus oriented toward the search for *constant conjunctions of events*—or constant conjunctions between underlying mechanisms and surface events (the position I call depth-realist positivism; see Steinmetz 2004). Marxists and feminists tended to assume away the horizontal openness of the social, rejecting the ontological assumption of a multiplicity of causal mechanisms in favor of arguments for the causal primacy of a single mechanism (capital, class, or patriarchy) or a constant subset of several mechanisms (as in so-called dual-systems theory; see Hartmann 1981).

The most recent critical movements, by contrast, have arisen in a thoroughly post-Fordist environment (A. Amin, ed. 1994; Harvey 1989; Lipietz 1992). Unlike the earlier movements, these critics do not share social conditions of birth with their main opponents. Nor do the new post-Fordist conditions seem to confirm or conform to the positivist perspective to the same extent as Fordism. In many ways, post-Fordism is actually more compatible with non-positivist than with positivist social epistemologies. Post-Fordism has entailed a new set of demands on the individual personality, which is compelled to become more adaptable, flexible, self-promoting, and reflexive and to be able to read social practices hermeneutically, as texts, in order simply to function properly in everyday life (U. Beck, Giddens, and Lash 1994; Lash and Urry 1994; Wernick 1991). In methodological terms, these developments tend to direct people's attention toward the concept-dependence of social practice.

The attempt to define "culture" restrictively as a delimited range of objects is undercut by the generalized "becoming cultural of the economic, and the becoming economic of the cultural" in this more recent period (Jameson 1998: 58, 63). In other words, conditions internal to the sociological discipline may still disproportionately reward positivism, but the world that sociology purports to study does not provide the same level of resonant affirmation. Critical sociology would thus not appear to be as susceptible to recuperation as the neo-Marxism and feminism of the 1960s and 1970s.

The idea of "domestication" is too simple and sweeping to describe what happened to the earlier critical movements in U.S. sociology. First of all, none of these developments was internally homogeneous. Not even during the heyday of multivariate Marxism and quasi-experimental historical sociology in the 1970s and 1980s did historical sociologists adopt the positivist approach en masse. Furthermore, many books and articles that seemed to adopt a discourse that was superficially positivist were punctuated by moments or latent levels that were less positivist.[32] Second, we have to distinguish these critical movements' conditions of emergence and early reincorporation from their subsequent trajectories. In more recent years, for instance, Marxist sociology has rearticulated itself through the lenses of post-structuralism, semiotics, narrative analysis, and Lacanian psychoanalysis and rediscovered the anti-positivist traditions of the Frankfurt school. Gender and queer studies, both influenced by Foucault, have emerged out of feminist sociology, and there has been some rapprochement among sociological feminism, post-structuralism, and psychoanalysis. Cultural sociology is moving beyond its earlier restrictive focus on so-called cultural objects, with some practioners returning to the hermeneutic tradition and others embracing the approaches of Bourdieu or Birmingham-style cultural studies, all of which were formerly found mainly in Europe and Britain. The new visual sociology (Woodiwiss 2001) breaks with the early frameworks emphasis on text, number, and diagram.

The Historical Turn in Sociology

The wave of historical sociological research that began in the 1970s had a handful of antecedents during the postwar period, including Bendix (1964), Lipset (1963), Moore (1966), Roth (1963), Smelser (1959b), Swanson (1960, 1967), Tilly (1964), and Wallerstein, ed. (1966). But historical sociology was not recognized as a distinct subfield in this period. The ASR carried almost no historical articles between 1945 and 1970 and historical sociologists such as Smelser never before the end of the war (in 1944 and February 1945). Only at the end of the 1970s did sociology start opening up to intellectual traditions and methodological strategies associated with the field of history. The importance of this opening should not be underestimated. Historians'

---

32. This includes, according to Burawoy (1989) and Sewell (1996b), Skocpol (1979), which manifestly adopted an "experimental" methodology. Burawoy argued that Skocpol's text in fact adopted a "conjunctural analysis in which political crises have different causes" despite her manifest adherence to the positivist "method of difference and agreement" (1989: 772).

approaches had been defined as antithetical to sociology since the late-nineteenth-century Methodenstreit. Even during the interwar period, few American sociologists were as historically oriented as European sociologists like Weber and Elias.[33]

Since there was only a handful of American sociologists who could be "recovered" for the historical opening in the 1970s and early 1980s, courses in historical sociology typically contained a large proportion of European "classics" and works by historians. One result of the lack of an indigenous tradition, paradoxically, was a greater willingness to read work written before or outside of American sociology's positivist culture. And these external sources provided crucial resources for unthinking positivism. Although Weber had insisted on what critical realists call the concept-dependency of social practice—the unavoidable hermeneutic dimension of social analysis—this had been lost or suppressed in the American translation of his work. Some of the discussions around culture, language, and practice that were beginning among historians in the 1970s and 1980s, for instance (e.g., Sewell 1980), seeped into sociology.

Historians offered sociologists important lessons about the historicity of conceptual categories. This was especially visible in work on class formation. Sociologists tried to make sense of E. P. Thompson's insistence that social class was not some simple material structure but rather something that "happens when some men, as a result of common experiences . . . feel or articulate the identity of their interests as between themselves, and as against other men" (1966: 9).

The opening to historiography also promised to make sociologists more aware of the horizontal openness of the social and hence of the ubiquity of conjunctural and contingent causality. Drawing a series of methodological lessons from this first period of historical sociology, the sociologist Philip Abrams (1982: ch. 9) recognized the special significance of the category of *contingency*. In a direct refutation of the distinction between a supposedly idiographic historiography and a more nomothetic sociology, Abrams (1982: 195–196; 1972, 1980) pointed out that the individual event was amenable to (sociological) explanation, even if this explanation involved a plurality of mechanisms operating in a contingent conjunction. As Abrams noted, "what is unique about an event is the conjunction of elements it embodies" (1982: 197). During the same period, Norbert Elias's (1978) proposal for a "figurational sociology" translated a central epistemological lesson from the

---

33. One of the major exceptions was Merton, who published historical essays on science and Puritanism during the second half of the 1930s (e.g., Merton 1936).

field of history into sociology by arguing for "figurations" rather than "invariant laws."[34]

Somewhat later, historical sociologists began to discuss narrative emplotment as a distinct and sometimes privileged means of presenting complex historical conjunctures and representing the braiding together of the meaningful and material aspects of social life.[35] From historians such as Louis Mink (1987), they learned about the unique cognitive and interpretive contributions of narrative form, understanding the importance of reading beneath the textual surface for the "content of the form" (Hayden White 1973, 1987) or the textual "unconscious" (Jameson 1981). This helped historical sociologists to *unlearn* the simplifying accounts of narrative that had been proffered in earlier decades by positivist philosophers—arguments that reduced complex narratives to a series of simple lawlike statements or probabilistic generalizations (e.g., Hempel 1966; Mandelbaum 1961; Nagel 1979 [1961]: ch. 15).

These lessons about the historicity of concepts, the concept-dependency of social practice, contingency, conjuncture, figurational analysis, and narrative ran up against American sociology's entrenched positivism. During the foundational postwar period, figures such as Lazarsfeld had insisted on the hoary distinction between history and social science and between idiographic and nomothetic knowledge. Even Parsons, despite his critique of positivism, empiricism, and scientism, insisted again and again on the distinction between "the historical and the analytical sciences" (1937, vol. 2: 759–760). Rather than learning from historiography, many postwar sociologists assumed that they had lessons to provide historians.[36] An entire lexicon of terms was elaborated to keep "idiographic" history at arm's length. Work that paid too much attention to the meaningful dimensions of social practice was referred to as "wishy-washy," "loosey-goosey," "fuzzy," "soft," "parasitical," "airy-fairy," and, mirabile dictu, "poetry." Writing that attended to sequence and conjuncture was often dismissed as "journalism" and "just-so stories."

How was the "second wave" of historical sociology related to broader de-

---

34. On conjuncture and contingency, see also Itzkowitz (1996), Sewell (1996b), and especially Althusser (1990, 1994) for the concepts of conjuncture and "aleatory materialism."

35. See the special issue of *Social Science History* (16:3, 1992) on narrative.

36. Compare the tutelary approach of Lipset (1968) or postwar sociologists' favorite philosopher, Hempel (1966), with the comments about the relationship between the disciplines by G. S. Jones (1976). Even Immanuel Wallerstein, who has contributed to current discussions of "unthinking" the limits of positivist social science, continues to use the concept of the "idiographic" when discussing historiography (1991: 252).

velopments in the discipline and society at large? Periodization is crucial here. Dissertations and books began to appear in numbers sufficient to speak of a "second wave" of historical sociology only at the end of the 1970s.[37] Some sociologists became *more* historical during the 1970s. *The Formation of National States in Western Europe* (C. Tilly, ed.), published in 1975, was not organized around the search for a uniform model of state formation but offered instead a series of sensitizing concepts. Wallerstein's *The Modern World-System* (1974) may have presented its arguments in a realist-positivist mode, but its complex historical narrative undermined any simple monocausal argumentative structure.[38] Indeed, the so-called waves of research in historical sociology have to be seen as referring as much to epistemic formations as to generations or individuals.[39] But a serious boom in historical sociology began only after a half-decade of socioeconomic crisis in the United States, a period that saw the unraveling of the Fordist mode of regulation and a postwar nadir of American imperialist projection overseas (Steinmetz 2003b). In this respect, and in contrast to the earlier neo-Marxist and feminist movements, historical sociology was faced with a mainstream episteme whose sociopolitical conditions of support were already beginning to crumble. The patterned Fordist regularities of time, subjectivity, and space, which had ratified sociologists' positivist worldview in earlier decades, were disappearing. Under these conditions, timeless sociological laws—statements of regular conjunctions of social events—seemed inherently less believable. With respect to more immediate supports for positivism, the state and private foundations also were scaling back their demands for social science research in the late 1970s and 1980s, in contrast to the full-bore welfare-warfare state clientelism that social scientists had experienced during the 1960s.[40]

As with the earlier wave of critical sociology in the 1960s, there was a

---

37. This involved people such as Aminzade (1981), Arjomand (1984), Block (1977), Bonnell (1983), Calhoun (1982), D. Clawson (1980), P. B. Evans (1979), Lachmann (1987), McAdam (1982), Sewell (1980), Skocpol (1979), Starr (1982), Traugott (1985), Trimberger (1978), and Zaret (1985). See Adams, Clemens, and Orloff (this volume) for the idea of a "second wave" of historical sociology.

38. Bendix (1978) is another example from this period of an opening to history, but Bendix had already been exceptional on this count, orienting himself more toward the Weberian tradition and historiography (compare Bendix 1960, 1964).

39. One of the most historical studies in this period, Schwendinger and Schwendinger (1974), was concerned with the discipline of sociology itself. Historical books in this period included Chirot (1976), Hechter (1975), Paige (1975), and Schwartz (1976). Paige's work is an interesting seismograph of change. His 1968 dissertation was concerned with the 1967 urban riots in Newark and Detroit. Paige's (1975) Sorokin Award–winning book, by contrast, was more historical and nonempiricist in its use of the concept of the mode of production; at the same time, however, it was mono-causalist and acultural. His most recent book (1997) is multi-causal and concerned with cultural meaning.

40. See the special issue of *American Sociologist* (17:4, November 1982) on financing sociological research.

structural parallel during the late 1970s and the 1980s between the historical turn in sociology and social movements in society at large. This was the era of a generation that had arrived "after the revolt" (R. Mohr 1992), too late for the optimistic upheaval of the 1960s. These social movements unfolded in a period of double-digit unemployment and academic retrenchment, behind the paradoxically historicist slogan, "no future." As Louis Menand remarked, "the economic value of a college degree began to fall" around 1975, and "the income differential between college graduates and high school graduates dropped from 61 percent to 48 percent" over the decade (2001a: 4; compare E. A. Duffy and Goldberg 1998; Lazerson 1998). This period also saw a shift from the more united politics of the old and new left, both of them committed to the idea of a "revolutionary subject," to the fragmented politics of the shifting coalitions, continually rearticulated identities, and nontotalizing "snake-like" forms of protest (Hardt and Negri 2000: 57–58; Laclau and Mouffe 1985).

These social and political developments were paralleled by a turn within sociology toward more conjunctural ways of thinking about social change. The decline of triumphalist social narratives of progress that resulted from the economic recession, the energy crisis, Watergate, the U.S. loss of the Vietnam War, and the splintering of the left was echoed intellectually not just by a post-modernist "suspicion of grand narratives" (Lyotard 1984 [1979]), but also by sociologists' turn toward history. The grand narrative of sociology's own unfolding as a cumulative science had become as unconvincing as the modernization-theoretic and Marxist meta-narratives of social development. The turn toward history thus represented an embrace of anti-teleological and ironic modes of thought—even if historical sociologists sometimes took detours through historical methods and meta-narratives that historians already considered outmoded. The turn to history also meant that sociologists were seeking rapprochement not with one of the "harder" sciences, as had been the case during each of the discipline's earlier phases, but with a more humanistic discipline. History had not enjoyed the largesse of the "post-historical" Fordist science-and-security state and had produced some of the harshest critics of sociological scientism during that period.

Despite social conditions conducive to the historical turn, however, a period of domestication set in quite quickly, as noted by Calhoun (1996). The epistemological disruptions coming from the new historical sociology were countered by efforts to make the subfield conform with existing conventions. This involved, first, forcing historical research back into the procrustean bed of the covering-law format. Methodological discussions within historical sociology were dominated for years by single-mechanism explanations or models in which a single interaction term was repeated across contexts. Theda Skocpol influentially recommended that qualitative historical sociologists adopt John Stuart Mill's "Method of Difference and Agreement" and seek "invariant causal configurations" (Skocpol 1984a: 378; 1979; also Orloff and Skocpol 1984; Skocpol and Somers 1980). This promised to provide qualitative historical sociologists with a simulacrum of quantitative statistical design, although quantitative sociologists gleefully called the historical sociologists' bluff, insisting on the inferiority and logical flaws of these small-n comparisons in comparison to standard statistical models (Goldthorpe 1991; Lieberson 1991; Steinmetz 2004). It also meant that historical sociologists were rejecting notions of the openness of the social system and eschewing methods attuned to shifting conjunctural overdetermination. Compared to the method of difference and agreement, multivariate statistical methods were much better equipped for dealing with complex interaction terms; indeed, this was one reason some historical sociologists turned to quantitative methods. In doing so, however, they reinforced a tendency to relate to history as a source of data. They were also unable to deal with shifting conjunctures (but see Ragin 1987).

There was also a tendency to redefine historical sociology in empiricist and anti-realist terms. This was partly due to the adoption of statistical methods, which tended to collapse indicators into the mechanisms that they were supposed to measure—no matter how often statistical methodologists warned against this. Similarly, Skocpol's method of induction tended to "[reduce] causal processes to causal associations," as Burawoy (1989: 783) noted, pushing it away from a realism of mechanisms. Finally, historical sociologists tended to accept the mainstream refusal of "interpretivism," which they often associated with earlier essentializing and politically conservative cultural approaches. The adoption of statistical methods played a role here as well, since culture is intrinsically resistant to measurement.

Although domestication was largely self-imposed, historical sociologists were also facing a still powerful positivist mainstream. Research funding, publication in the main journals, and hiring and promotion decisions continued to be dominated by this approach. Indeed, some major sociology departments moved even further in this direction during the 1980s, as Neil Smelser (1986) pointed out. The initial disruption to sociological positivism sparked by the trembling foundations of Fordist normalcy during the 1970s seemed to have been contained by the early 1980s. And without equating the three waves of historical sociology with generations, we must not overlook the continuing domination of most sociology departments during the 1980s by the generation that had come of age intellectually during the 1950s and 1960s.

Despite these recuperations, however, historical sociology was not completely reconciled with methodological positivism. Some sociologists from the so-called second wave continued to relate in an unencumbered way to historicity and historians and to take seriously ideas such as conjuncture, context, narrative, persistence, and culture. Studies of working-class politics by historical sociologists in this period, for example, were often culturally or semiotically oriented (see Aminzade 1981; Calhoun 1982; Sewell 1980). Ronald Aminzade's 1981 book was organized around a cultural-Marxist theoretical framework of hegemony and was methodologically similar to the work of social historians; Calhoun (1982) and Sewell (1980) were organized around theoretical discussions in cultural anthropology and social history. A background outside the mainstream of American sociology may have been the differentia specifica in some of these cases.[41] The subfield of class formation was also protected from positivism to some extent by the fact that many influential books on the subject, even during the 1950s and 1960s, rejected aculturalism (compare Gouldner 1954; Thompson 1966; Willis 1977), in contrast to research on topics like state formation or social policy.

The Unsettled State of Historical Sociology Today

The cluster of social changes signaled by the concept of post-Fordism has tended to push sociologists' spontaneous social epistemologies away from the assumptions of positivism. The sheer accumulation of critical movements within sociology, furthermore, has helped to preserve the vision of a less positivist discipline. Yet entrenched disciplinary interests and habits continue to pull in the opposite direction. This straining in opposing directions produces multi-accentual and internally contradictory texts and unexpected epistemological hybrids.

A recent attempt to take stock of comparative-historical analysis by Mahoney and Rueschemeyer (2003) underscores both the persistence of meth-

---

41. Sewell's Ph.D. was in history rather than sociology, despite his strong positivist background (see Sewell's own comments on this in Sewell forthcoming), and Calhoun had earned an Oxford D.Phil. in social sciences, with an anthropologist and a historian as advisers (personal communication). At the same time, Sewell was a member of the Sociology Department at the University of Michigan between 1985 and 1990 (with an appointment in history as well); Calhoun was appointed in sociology departments at the University of North Carolina and New York University. Aminzade earned his Ph.D. in sociology at Michigan, with Charles Tilly as adviser. As noted above, Tilly was one of just a handful of American sociologists whose work became increasingly oriented toward historiography and historians during the 1970s.

odological positivism, and the changes in sensibility since the 1980s.[42] To illustrate the polycentrism and multi-accentuality of present-day American historical sociology one might also have selected the introduction to the present collection, but it is located at a greater distance from sociology's positivist center of gravity.

At the manifest level, Mahoney and Rueschemeyer's text is an attempt to channel the subfield back toward the predilections of the "second wave." Yet a closer examination of the text reveals a certain level of epistemic multi-vocality in which the manifest positivist aspects are combined with latent non-positivist ones. This epistemological dualism reflects the increasing presence of non-positivist alternatives in other subfields of sociology, as well as the collapse of the environing social regularities associated with Fordism and the emergence of post-Fordism. Despite Calhoun's pessimistic diagnosis, then, it appears that the project of domestication has not been entirely successful, even among the would-be domesticators. Although the recuperative processes identified by Calhoun are obviously still operating, the dialogism of Mahoney and Rueschemeyer's text is indicative of an unsettled field—unsettled in the sense of not being united around shared recognition of a particular definition of scientific capital or "distinguished" types of research.

Skocpol's (1984a) concluding essay in *Vision and Method in Historical Sociology* serves as the template for Mahoney and Rueschemeyer's article, making it instructive to map the continuities and deviations from the earlier text to the present one. Mahoney and Rueschemeyer follow Skocpol explicitly in singling out three features of historical sociology for praise: *attention to temporal processes, causal explanation*, and *comparison*.

Temporality/Historicity

The first facet of Mahoney and Rueschemeyer's definition of "comparative-historical analysis" is an *emphasis on processes over time* (2003: 8). This seems, on the one hand, to reveal a difference from the static, pseudo-

42. I will treat Mahoney and Rueschemeyer's text with respect to historical sociology, ignoring the fact that part of their agenda is to conjure up an object intermediate between sociology and political science that they call comparative-historical analysis. This seems fair since both authors are sociologists. I should also note that an early reviewer of this article asked me to discuss Mahoney and Rueschemeyer's chapter, while a subsequent reviewer wondered why I would devote so much space to it. Hopefully this treatment falls somewhere in between their expectations. My sense is that Mahoney and Rueschemeyer's piece does exemplify the way in which the multi-accentuality of epistemological discussions in contemporary sociology can undercut arguments that attempt to hew a more unified positivist line.

no dominant paradigm ...

experimental model of historical sociology advocated earlier. Yet the authors draw back from acknowledging the full epistemological consequences of a genuinely historical approach to temporality. They seem to feel compelled, for example, to avoid established historiographic terms for temporal processes, preferring scientific alternatives such as "path dependence." Historians might well ask why they should replace their own rich lexicon, which includes notions such as persistence, continuity, memory, process, and the return of the repressed—not to mention historicity and "history" itself—with this rather rebarbative phrase. More to the point, "path dependence" makes sense as a distinct concept only if one retains some background belief in a "normal" path of development from which deviations may be plotted. But one of the fundamental arguments derived from critical realism—and a commonplace among most historians—is the untenability of any notion of "normal" and "deviant" development paths (see Blackbourn and Eley 1985; Steinmetz 1997a). Historical events are *always* produced by contingent conjunctures of causal mechanisms. Earlier conjunctures influence the intensity or particular value of any given mechanism in the present; they also co-determine whether a particular mechanism will be suppressed or expressed. What this means is that *all* events are partly shaped by earlier conjunctures, via historical "paths." Path dependency is thus a synonym for historical change *tout court*. It is only necessary as a separate term if one retains some belief in general social laws. As a figure of thought, path dependency has the structure of a fetish (Freud 1963 [1927]), with the subject's anxiety in this case being fixated on proximity to the humanistic, less scientific field of history. Like a fetish, the idea of path dependency disavows the sociologist's identity with the historian while at the same time covertly acknowledging it.

Winking and Blinking:
Erklärendes Veistehen (explanatory interpretation) and
Verstehendes Erklären (interpretive explanation)

Mahoney and Rueschemeyer's discussion of *theory and explanation* reveals a similarly uneasy mingling of positivism and non-positivism. On the non-positivist side of the ledger, they decry the "poverty of universalizing theoretical approaches," which are said to generate "ahistorical concepts and propositions that are often too general to be usefully applied in explanation" (2003: 7). Against general (that is, reductionist) theory, they advocate a pluralistic approach to explanation, as well as a "dialogue between theory and history" in many iterations of analysis and a combination of "induction and deduction" as concepts are formed and refined in light of evidence (ibid.: 20). Although they do not spell out what they mean by either "theory" or "explanation," Mahoney has elsewhere (2001a) embraced a form of realism, arguing that social theories are about underlying causal mechanisms and cannot be equated with empirical correlations between empirical events. This explicit endorsement of conjunctural causality and realism and of a distinction between theory and explanation suggests a distancing of historical sociology from older versions of positivism.

At the same time, however, much of Mahoney and Rueschemeyer's discussion of causal explanation is continuous with methodological positivism. They embrace the so-called *macro-causal* style of analysis presented in Skocpol and Somers (1980), which is based on Mill's "Method of Difference and Agreement." This approach is at odds not just with the idea of "contextual" comparison, which attends to the varying effects of a given mechanism within differing contexts, but also with the realist program of specifying and elaborating on underlying mechanisms.

Another site of continuity with the positivist framework is the authors' definition of theory as "mid-range generalizations that apply to particular times and places" (Mahoney and Rueschemeyer 2003: 19). As I have argued elsewhere (Steinmetz and Chae 2002; Steinmetz 2004), the Mertonian idea of *middle-range theory* is ultimately indefensible, a compromise formation that reduces to a semi-empiricist positivism. Social theories are about causal mechanisms, and these do not exist in some nebulous purgatory realm of intermediate causal forms. The fact that the causal purview of a social mechanism is limited temporally and spatially is intrinsic to its very nature as a *social* mechanism and does not automatically cast it into a putative middle ontological range. *its not that the reality of context*

The centerpiece of Mahoney and Rueschemeyer's discussion, however, involves an opposition between explanation and interpretation. Accentuating Skocpol's declared intention to "rise above" the viewpoints of social actors in accounting for their actions and her professed lack of interest in psychic or ideological factors (but see Skocpol 1985b, 1992, and Adams and Padamsee-Garrett 2001), the authors erect a Berlin Wall between causal explanation and cultural interpretation. Although they are most adamant about this particular point, it is also the least coherent part of their argument, in both linguistic and philosophical terms. First, as Calhoun (1998: 864) notes, a non-sociologist would have a difficult time understanding what exactly is being differentiated from what here, at the level of ordinary language. After all, the *Oxford English Dictionary* (OED) initially defines interpretation very precisely as *explanation*. Similarly, Gadamer noted that "in the early tradition," hermeneutics "was divided up in the following way: a distinction was made between *subtilitas intelligendi* (understanding), and *subtilitas explicandi* (interpretation)" (1975: 274). Note here that "subtilitas

compare this to my recommendation for greater context in intro notes...

explicandi" is translated as "interpretation" and not juxtaposed to it. Two of the OED's subdefinitions seem to bring us closer to the typical usage of "interpretation" in the human sciences: (1) a "construction put upon actions, purposes, etc."; and (2) "a translation or rendering." If interpretation in the human sciences involves a *translation* from one symbolic system into another, this suggests that one level of reality, the empirical or phenomenal level of appearances, is being rendered or recoded in a more theoretical language. Even the most basic redescription of empirical phenomena into a quantitative language is thus a form of interpretation.

Interpretation and causal explanation are interwoven at another level. Even the most straightforward realist account of (social) science requires a combination of what positivists refer to as interpretation and explanation. The core of a causal theory is a picture, image, or narrative about a theoretical entity that may produce effects (Bhaskar 1986; Peirce 1955). Postulating such an object is, for a realist, key to science. Is the creation of such a model to be understood as an act of interpretation or as explanation? To create such a model, one needs to move beyond the immediately visible or descriptive level; this movement from one sort of description to another is thus interpretive, insofar as it involves putting a construction on something, engaging in a sort of translation. One also needs to assign to this mechanism some sort of hypothetical power, some putative ability to produce empirical effects. This "retroductive" act is also an interpretation, but one with directly causal or explanatory implications.

Even if we were to accept the authors' definitions of these terms, however, there are other aporias in their argument. Due to the concept-ladenness of human practice, even the simplest empirical description in the social sciences is inherently interpretive. Bhaskar puts this succinctly: "social life is pre-interpreted" (1998: xv). Ironically, this is the central point made by Geertz in the essay that Mahoney and Rueschemeyer use to fabricate an artificial boundary between interpretation and explanation. The authors associate interpretation with a supposed *hostility* to science, quoting as evidence Geertz's statement that anthropology is "not an experimental science in search of law but an interpretive one in search of meaning" (1973: 5). Yet Mahoney and Rueschemeyer should have been more careful in their *explication de texte*. In this exact sentence, Geertz is describing anthropology as an interpretive *science* and not as something *other* than science: "interpretive" is an adjective modifying a noun—"science." Like critical realists, Geertz is attacking the idea of invariant social laws tested via experiment, not the idea of science itself. More to the point, Geertz is rejecting the mirage of a social science based on causal laws determined independently of any interpretation of meaning. In this argument for the centrality of interpretation, Geertz

is doubted, but rather that the truthfulness of theory is uncertain. without ideal-types/simplification observation ensues.

develops his famous example of the rapid contraction of an eyelid, a gesture that is completely illegible at the purely behavioral level—is it a wink, a twitch, a parody of someone else's wink or twitch, a rehearsal of such a parody, a fake winking or blinking, or what? If empirical description is impossible without interpretation, the same must be true, ipso facto, of explanation. Explanation and interpretation are complementary dimensions of all social analysis.

The impetus to polarize interpretation and explanation, like the contrary insistence that the two are inextricably linked, reaches back much farther into sociology's history than any recent confrontation between science and post-modernism, to the debates among Dilthey, Windelband, and other partici-pants in the nineteenth-century German methods dispute and also to the *Methodenstreit* "positivist dispute" of the 1960s (Adorno et al. 1976). Sociologists are rou-tinely taught about Weber's struggle to rearticulate the sundered strands of interpretive (*verstehende*) hermeneutics and the "causal-explanatory" ap-proach that he associated with "rationalistic interpretations" (1978, vol. 1: 7). Weber's alternative to this binarism was "explanatory understanding" (*erklärendes Verstehen*). This formula actually sounds quite similar to Geertz's "interpretive science." We should not retreat backward epistemolog-ically to positions that flourished before Weber but try to advance beyond his still unsatisfactory solutions.[43]

Once we turn our attention to the present-day context, we can start to reconstruct the animus motivating Mahoney and Rueschemeyer to divide the Red Sea of interpretation and explanation. The authors equate inter-pretation with the "cultural or linguistic turn," and in a jarring string of epithets, they call cultural analysis anti-scientific, post-modern, nonrigor-ous, unsystematic, speculative, "willfully selective" with regard to evidence, and even lazy.[44] The authors warn ominously of the "danger" to "young researchers" of "not taking sides" against the cultural-interpretivist tempta-tion (Mahoney and Rueschemeyer 2003: 22–23). Most of these charges, reminiscent of popular media reporting on the "science wars" in the 1990s and of many other moral campaigns, are themselves too "willful" to warrant

43. Weber's famous methodological solution of the *ideal type* differs from a critical realist position, for example, insofar as it does not seek first to resolve a complex event into its components through abstraction (A. Collier 1994: 163–164; A. Sayer 1992), proceeding from there, via the process of retroduction, to descriptions of regular relations between these events and some underlying, postu-lated mechanisms (Bhaskar 1986: 68). The telos of concept formation for critical realism might be the *real type* rather than the ideal type, even if it is acknowledged that knowledge is necessarily provisional and theory choice inevitably shaped by social factors.

44. Interestingly, rational choice theory is associated with "ambition" (Mahoney and Rueschemeyer 2003: 7) rather than "ease," even if it is rejected on substantive grounds.

much of a response. But some of them are helpfully diagnostic. Mahoney and Rueschemeyer trace the interpretivists' "willful selectivity" in the use of evidence to a "preoccupation" with the "critique of power" (p. 23). Here we can detect in a highly reduced form that old chestnut, "value-free" social science. In the general context of vehement attacks on "anti-science postmodernism," such a taunt automatically dredges up the entire polemic against fields "associated with a social movement," in which "a 'politically correct' agenda of research" arises because "the criterion of how best to advance knowledge has been replaced by the criterion of how best to advance the cause of the movement" (Coleman 1992: 8).

Mahoney and Rueschemeyer also misleadingly elide "post-modernism" with post-structuralism and equate the latter with judgmental relativism. While post-structuralism does reject the possibility of choosing rationally among contending interpretations, post-modernism is best construed not as an epistemological position but as the name of a historical epoch or cultural and subjective condition. Various analysts have traced post-modernity causally to "realist" mechanisms such as late capitalism, post-Fordism, or time-space compression; post-structuralism is itself sometimes included as part of this overarching post-modern condition that needs explaining (Harvey 1989; Jameson 1984, 1991; also Hardt and Negri 2000).

The most peculiar aspect of Mahoney and Rueschemeyer's critique, however, is the contrast between the strangled rhetoric of their discussion of the cultural turn and the measured tone they adopt when discussing the two other alternatives to comparative-historical analysis. In a striking concession to rational choice theory, for instance, they write that their differences do "not revolve around the assumption that actors are rational" (2003: 20–21). This throwaway comment completely overlooks the legions of sociologists and political scientists who have problematized this exact assumption. Subtle critiques of rational choice theory have been published by one of the founders of the *Journal of Historical Sociology* (D. Sayer 1987), by a recent chairperson of the comparative-historical section of the American Sociological Association (Somers 1998), and by one of the editors of this volume (Adams 1999). Historical sociologists since Elias (1994 [1939]) have analyzed the social operations of forms of subjectivity other than formal rationality, whether unconscious, affective, or habitual (Adams 1994, forthcoming; Berezin 1999; Bourdieu 1977; Steinmetz 2002, 2003a).

Apples and Oranges: Toward a Non-Cannibalistic Comparativism

The third criterion Mahoney and Rueschemeyer use to identify comparative-historical analysis is "contextualized comparison [,] typically limited to a small number of cases" (2003: 14)— a concept they draw from Richard Locke and Kathleen Thelen (1995). This format is juxtaposed with two other types: "statistical studies of large numbers of countries" and so-called *idiographic* studies (Mahoney and Rueschemeyer 2003: 13, 17). Their critique of the first approach is well taken; the problem lies at the other delimiting boundary. Why is "comparison" a necessary component of any and all "analytic" historical research? It is critical to their project to define an area called *comparative-historical analysis* and to mark a distance from merely *historical* sociology.

The key term here is *comparison*. Comparison would seem to be logically indispensable to assessing the plausibility of theory for critical realism (see Lawson 1997; Steinmetz 2004). Investigation of a single case provides less assurance that the causal mechanisms of interest actually exist. So what is wrong with Mahoney and Rueschemeyer's argument?

On the one hand, I am struck by the bad faith of sociologists who continue to construct a lineage of comparative macro-history purged of historians' contributions. Mahoney and Rueschemeyer do not include a single book or article by a historian in their category of comparative-historical analysis. It is as if our discipline believed that Max Weber invented history and that it did not reappear until sociologists became interested again in the 1960s. In fact, comparative-historical social science originated in history, and most of the classics are by historians. One has only to think of Ranke's universal history and his works on French, German, English, Spanish, Roman, and Ottoman history. One immediately thinks of classics by Perry Anderson, Marc Bloch, Fernand Braudel, Robert Brenner, Otto Hintze, Eric Hobsbawm, and Ernst Kantorowicz, and of more recent comparative work by Geoff Eley, Michael Geyer, Jürgen Kocka, Charles Maier, and Jürgen Osterhammel. The longest lived journal of comparative-historical social studies, *Comparative Studies in Society and History* (1958–present), has been edited by historians.

The bigger problem, however, lies with Mahoney and Rueschemeyer's attempt to restrict properly "scientific" macro-social inquiry to the comparative type. Against this, we should recognize that the ontological and epistemological characteristics of social life make the case study the precondition for any comparative assessment of theory. Within an open system like the social, and in contrast to artificially closed systems like the scientific experiment, empirical events are inevitably multiply overdetermined by a plurality of conjuncturally interacting causal mechanisms. Because genuine experiments cannot be conducted in the human sciences, one has no other choice than to investigate the expression of underlying causal mechanisms within complex constellations in concert with other mechanisms. Moreover, the mechanisms making up the formative constellation will vary from case to case. Causal mechanisms in social sciences usually exist in hybrid rather than a simple, uncombined form (Bhaskar 1986: 111–113). An empirical contrast may reflect two differing combinations of the same set of mechanisms, rather than the presence or absence of a single mechanism. Due to *counter-phenomenality*, an empirical contrast may also result, not from the variable presence of a single mechanism, but from its varying ability to be expressed at the level of the actual. Both of these considerations undermine the notion that a comparison of two or more cases is necessarily more conclusive than a case study.

Social events are unique or unrepeatable in the sense that they cannot be explained in terms of a universal law, even if there are partial regularities at the level of events (Lawson 1997). The usual deployment of the terms "idiographic" and "nomothetic" is thus an incoherent intellectual survival—or if we must retain these terms, then we have to admit that social explanation is necessarily idiographic. One can gain access to causal mechanisms only through the study of unique events, specific individuals, etc. Since the basic object of an explanation is the individual event or case, it makes no sense to set case studies against explanation. Indeed, excluding case studies from historical sociology would be equivalent to excluding explanation from historical sociology.

Social knowledge necessarily involves movement between case studies and theory; and comparisons among case studies. In Peirce's terms, discovering any regularity requires movement from induction to retroduction to "deductions from retroductive suggestions" (Peirce 1931–1932, vol. 2: 491). *Explanation* concerns the unique phenomenon, *theory* concerns underlying mechanisms, and the *evaluation of theory* requires an accumulation of cases—that is, comparison. Comparison may therefore be "indispensable" given an "analytic interest in causal explanation," as Mahoney and Rueschemeyer claim, but it cannot be *identified* with explanation. Indeed, there is no philosophical program, *not even positivism*, in which the two are equated. For Popper, to "give a *causal explanation* of an event means to deduce a statement which describes it, using as premises of the deduction one or more *universal laws*, held together with certain singular statements" (1992 [1934]: 59; emphasis in original). A single event, in other words, *can* be explained. Similarly, Nagel insisted that "explanations may be offered for individual occurrences" (1979 [1961]: 15) and developed an example involving an individual historical event (pp. 552 passim).

It is also unclear exactly what sort of comparative method Mahoney and Rueschemeyer endorse. They recommend "contextualized comparison," which is summarized as a method of exploring "how variables may have different causal effects across heterogeneous contexts" (2003: 13). This procedure would seem to be compatible with critical realism, as long as there is no assumption that causal mechanisms are empirical or that explanation is concerned with constant conjunctions of events involving clusters of causal factors. Yet the authors also endorse "macro-causal analysis," which suggests an understanding of explanation as involving constant relations of dependence between clusters of determining causal factors and specific outcomes. For critical realism, by contrast, comparison might involve a group of empirical phenomena having little in common at the empirical level other than the hypothetical impact of a given underlying causal mechanism. The goal of explanation would be to investigate the vicissitudes of the underlying causal mechanism in differing empirical contexts (Steinmetz 2004).

I am not making the statisticians' criticism of selection on the dependent variable. There is nothing wrong with organizing comparisons around phenomena that are similar at the empirical level; this is an alternative to comparing phenomena that have little in common at the empirical level other than the putative effect of some causal mechanism of interest. Indeed, many historians would prefer comparisons among entities that are historically connected to one another in this way (Bloch 1953; Grew 1980; Sewell 1967). There may also be ethical or political reasons for organizing a comparison among phenomenally similar events or objects.

Others have rejected the idea of comparison from the standpoint of incommensurability (see Keane forthcoming; Lambek 1991; Nancy 2000; Povinelli 2001; Yengoyan forthcoming). These arguments cannot be dismissed as the ravings of a "camp" of politically driven, unsystematic, anti-science postmodernists—especially since this argument can be traced back historically at least as far as Kant's theory of the "sublime" and German Romanticism. Due to the concept-dependence of human action, comparison necessarily involves problems of translation into a meta-language. Translation may repress the incommensurable aspects of the translated culture or force differing cases into categories determined by the more powerful. Conceptual categories used in comparisons with the non-West often treat parochial or geohistorically limited categories as if they were universal (Chakrabarty 2000).

It is obvious that "difficulties of translation" will arise between theorists of incommensurability and positivistically inclined social science. Like positivists, critical realists are willing to deploy theoretical categories and languages to designate mechanisms that may not be consciously perceived by the actors in question. But critical realism does not require that mechanisms be universal to all societies. Nor does it insist that the empirical level of events be redescribable in a theoretical meta-language. By contrast, positivism and so-called macro-causal analysis seem willing to redescribe disparate empirical events using universal conceptual categories. For critical realism, abstract conceptual language would be deployed when discussing putative causal mechanisms, but not necessarily with respect to the empirical level of events.[45] This breaks with the "cannibalistic" tradition of positivist comparison in which the concrete historical individual is disaggregated into a heap of variables and devoured.

L'Objet Petit n: Big N's and Bigger Cases

If sociology as a field suffers from a kind of "economics envy," historical sociology has often displayed signs of an inferiority complex vis-à-vis the more positivistic sectors of the discipline. The domination of the field by methodological positivism in earlier decades accounts in large part for the self-recuperative tendency of the so-called second wave. There is also more than a hint of this identification with the aggressor in Mahoney and Rueschemeyer's article. At one point they seem to concede that historical sociologists'—their own—work entails "some reduction of ambition" (2003: 7). Elsewhere, they describe comparative-historical sociology as a "bargain," making it sound like the Wal-Mart of social science (p. 11). But a historical explanation that weaves together a large number of causal factors, attempting to place the proper weight on each of them and to trace their intricate imbrications and overdeterminations—like Rueschemeyer's own study with Stephens and Stephens (1992) of the relations between capitalist development and democracy—is every bit as ambitious as the most universal theory. Mahoney and Rueschemeyer both are certainly aware that such research is no "bargain" for those who undertake it.

The most striking indication of a sense of historical sociology's dominated status is the authors' clamorous identification with "big" and "important" questions. Comparative-historical analysis is defined by its focus on "large-scale outcomes" (Mahoney and Rueschemeyer 2003: 5). Although there have certainly been good political reasons in the past for historical sociologists to emphasize topics such as revolution or the rise of capitalism, the continuing insistence on a narrowly delimited set of topics is a dead

---

45. This does not contradict the above discussion of Geertz and concept-dependency. The translation of an eyelid contraction into a wink, for instance, is a translation into a sign that is itself also culturally specific. On a different, more abstract level, winking may also be explained in terms of theories of communication, twitching in terms of psychological theories, etc.

weight on the shoulders of current researchers. Charles Tilly's *Big Structures, Large Processes, Huge Comparisons* opens with the sentence, "We bear the nineteenth century like an incubus" (1984: 1). The incubus pressing down upon us today has a more recent origin in the second wave of historical sociology, which was overwhelmingly informed by Marxism or by a Weberianism that was itself a reaction-formation to Marxism.

The insistent mobilization of adjectives such as "big" and "important" also suggests the competitive pressures of a discipline that is still perceived as dominated by quantitative sociologists with "big N's." This seems to be an almost masochistic sort of "symbolic identification" (Lacan 1991: 134; Laplanche and Ponatalis 1973 [1967]: 144), an identification with an *external location* from which historical sociologists think they are being observed. We should instead be seeking a more pleasurable "imaginary identification" with an image of " 'what we would like to be' " (Žižek 1989: 105). What many of us would like to be is students of a small number of cases. This could be called historical sociology *à la recherche de l'objet petit n*. The quantitative connotations of "big" in this discussion cannot be dissociated from the socio-historical context of Fordist big science, the era in which methodological positivism came to the fore. Both the wielders of the "big N" and their counterparts, with their equally "big" and "macroscopic" cases (Skocpol 2003), seem somehow fixated on the gigantism of this now bygone Fordist era. This gigantesque sociology seems more at home in the Russian Magnitogorsk or in Komsomolsk-on-Amur in the Russian Far East, or in Ford's River Rouge, than in the post-Fordist twenty-first century.

Delimiting "big" topics in a commonsensical way seems especially inappropriate within a branch of sociology that defines itself as historical. One need only compare the topics that were considered important in American sociology four decades ago to topics that are currently big, such as culture, nationalism, space, post-colonialism, sexuality, human rights, religion, and globalization; the current themes were nearly invisible in American sociology during the middle decades of the cold war. While adjectives like "big" and "important" serve to mark off a distance from the merely fashionable, the selection of themes in historical sociology has always been presentist—it is no surprise, for instance, that historical studies of revolution became popular during a period of worldwide revolution.

Something has changed between 1984, when Skocpol's *Vision and Method* appeared, and the present. The newly destabilized conditions seem to be compelling some social scientists to insist more dogmatically on the positivist position, given that it is no longer doxic. Indeed, their version is not even an *orthodox* one, but rather a new mixture of elements. The text's multi-vocality is suggestive of the epistemologically unsettled character of the field. The prominence of methodological positivism within this hybrid mix, however, underscores that position's continuing power in the discipline as a whole.[46]

Conclusion: Post-Positivism Eternally Deferred?

In this chapter I have emphasized the conformity of Fordism with the methodologically positivist social worldview and the conformity of post-Fordism with certain aspects of the historical, cultural, critical, and epistemological turns in sociology. The non-positivist elements in these intellectual movements resonate in particular ways with the flexibilized and information-centered society of the post-Fordist "new economy" and might therefore be expected to have some staying power. Positivism would also seem to be weakened by the decline in state funding for research, the waning of postwar fears of totalitarianism, and the collapse of Fordist regularities in sociocultural life. One possible prediction, then, would be a continuing weakening of positivism.

The analysis of modes of regulation is not just another name for social control or disciplining, however, but is embedded within an overarching analysis of capitalism. And while regulation theory has jettisoned the earlier Marxist functionalism and teleology that seemed to guarantee that capitalism would resolve its crises in a quasi-automatic fashion, in favor of a "Marxism without guarantees" (S. Hall 1983), it is actually more focused than earlier Marxisms on the notions of contradiction and crisis. The point is that while post-Fordism may be more improvisational, flexible, self-reflexive, deterritorializing, and culture-centered—tendencies that seem to resonate with postpositivist social epistemologies—it is no less oriented than earlier modes of regulation toward increasing the rate of extraction of surplus value. Although the post-Fordist strategies of deregulating and flexibilizing production and markets and recommodifying labor differ from earlier Fordist strategies of shoring up accumulation, these aspects of post-Fordism could be seen as resonating in different ways with positivist forms of social knowledge. Economic flexibilization has involved the imposition of uniform neo-liberal economic models to all places and situations. These projects depend upon a decontextualized economic model of human sub-

---

46. Mahoney and Rueschemeyer's (2003) text contrasts interestingly with similar programmatic statements in political science, such as G. King, Keohane, and Verba (1994), which makes fewer concessions to non-positivism (see Mihic, Engelmann, and Wingrove forthcoming; Wedeen forthcoming).

jectivity and behavior, even if it is a model of "rational man" rather than the "behaviorist man" of the Fordist era. Post-Fordist states continue to favor positivistically packaged social science, as do private foundations and social movements, even as the overarching social structures of this new mode of regulation render methodological positivism less and less plausible.[47]

And while this paper has emphasized the overall external social context, especially the mode of regulation, as a determinant of sociologists' spontaneous social epistemologies, one cannot overlook the abiding and profound implantation of methodological positivism within disciplinary institutions, patterns of socialization, and scientific habituses. Sociology is relatively autonomous from external pressures and events, like any other field. One can expect a lag, or *non-simultaneity*, between the unraveling of Fordism and the disruption of methodological positivism within sociology due to the *hysteresis of the scientific habitus* (to paraphrase Bourdieu)—that is, the fact that intellectual paradigms are not simply intangible discourses but are instead embodied practices.

Another scenario, then, would see positivism changing its form without disappearing. The increased interest in rational choice theory in political science and parts of sociology, for instance, places the active social agent at the center of social analysis, corresponding to the felt increase in demands on the individual to be self-promoting and self-reflexive. At the same time, rational choice analysis promotes a universal model of subjectivity and retains an orientation toward the prediction of social action. The shift from a behaviorist black-box image of subjectivity to a universalizing view of the subject as agent resonates with the changed structures of plausibility in post-Fordism.

Given my acknowledgment of the contradictory epistemic signals sent by post-Fordism and my more general critique of the notion of invariant patterns of social behavior, it would be foolish and paradoxical to predict which direction (historical) sociology will take. But one plausible scenario, at least, includes an increased space for non-positivist alternatives. Gouldner's (1970) prediction three decades ago that American sociology would move

47. Even in the current period, the state (considered at all of its scalar levels) is still the superordinate coordinator for regulatory initiatives, and it continues to organize most of the familiar legal, infrastructural, and welfare-statist interventions. During the 1990s, when the post-Fordist regime seemed to attain a certain level of consolidation, state funding for science began again to increase but with new emphases. Where the National Institutes of Health, National Institute of Mental Health, and the National Science Foundation were previously at the core of government funding for social science, the life sciences now became more central. The social sciences are again being encouraged to repackage themselves along the lines of the natural sciences; witness the recently renewed interest in "sociobiology" and genetic explanations of behavior.

through a period of crisis characterized by the collapse of theoretical hegemony to a less positivist and more reflexive polycentrism might turn out to have been correct, if premature (see also J. C. Alexander 1982). Historical sociology, along with critical sociology, cultural studies, and the sociology of science, would have contributed in no small part to such a future.

PHILIP S. GORSKI

The Return of the Repressed: Religion and the Political Unconscious of Historical Sociology

Comparative-historical sociology has enjoyed a remarkable efflorescence over the last quarter century, so much so, in fact, that one (participant-) observer has spoken of this period as a "golden age" of macro-social analysis (R. Collins 1999). It is generally agreed that this efflorescence has had two intellectual sources. The first was a reaction against modernization theory and structural functionalism, the perspectives that had dominated macro-style work in sociology (as well as political science and anthropology) during the 1950s and 1960s. The second was the "crisis of Marxism," precipitated by the events of the late 1960s in Eastern and Western Europe. These two currents flowed together in the work of scholars such as Perry Anderson and Immanuel Wallerstein, who sought to develop a materialist alternative to modernization theory *and* a historically informed reconstruction of Marxist theory.

Since then, of course, comparative-historical sociology has broadened out considerably. It has taken up new subjects, such as revolution, class formation, and the welfare state. And it has absorbed new perspectives, from Weber and Hintze to cultural and feminist theory. Still, one might well ask whether it has broadened out enough. For however much the field may have developed, the core questions that animate the comparative-historical project are still inspired by the strategic concerns of Marxist politics: state and revolution, class consciousness, and social provision. In this sense, one might speak of comparative-historical sociology as having a political superego that is Marxist, and insofar as Marxism is also modernist, perhaps also at a still deeper level, a theoretical superego that is distinctly modernist.

If this premise is correct, then one goal of the present volume—to continue the metaphor—must be to undo the state of political and theoretical repression, which is the work of this Marxist and modernist superego. In this essay, I will focus on an object that has undergone a particularly and perhaps even uniquely powerful process of repression—namely, religion. That such a process of repression has occurred can hardly be denied. In its early years, sociology displayed a keen interest in things religious. Indeed, for Durkheim and Weber, the founding figures of modern sociology, religion occupied an absolutely central place. In their view, it was at the origins of social life as such (Durkheim) and at the root of developmental and civilizational differences as well (Weber). Accordingly, religion was also the object to which they devoted their greatest energies and their magnos opera (*The Elementary Forms of the Religious Life* [1912] and *The Collected Essays on the Sociology of Religion* [1920], respectively). Thus, it would not be entirely inaccurate to say that the comparative study of religion and society is the mother of comparative-historical sociology and of macro-sociology more generally. But as close as they may have been at one time, historical sociology and the sociology of religion drifted apart over the years and now have little to do with one another. Religion rarely figures into the explanatory accounts of historical sociologists and almost never appears as an object of analysis in its own right. And historical materials and methods are rarely found in social-scientific works on religion. For their part, sociologists of religion typically prefer the present to the past and ethnography and surveys to libraries and archives.[1]

Why? What explains the estrangement of history and religion in sociology? And what might we learn by reuniting them? What would it mean to do a historical sociology of religion? And how might greater attention to religion enrich or reframe historical sociology? The purpose of this chapter is to answer these questions, if only in a tentative and provisional way. The chapter is in four parts. In the first two, I look briefly at the recent history of historical sociology and the sociology of religion in an attempt to understand when and why the two fields diverged from one another—and from their common roots. I will argue that the divergence was conditioned by independent developments within both fields. In the last two, I will discuss the effects that this divergence has had on each field. I will argue that work in each field would be deepened and enriched through greater interaction with the other.

---

1. To all these rules, there are, of course, exceptions. The role of confessional parties figures prominently in recent works such as Rueschemeyer, Stephens, and Stephens (1992). For an example of historical sociology that takes religion as the "dependent variable," see Gorski (2000a). An example of historical work in the sociology of religion is R. Stark (1996). The work of Robert Wuthnow constitutes an important exception to all these rules, tacking, as it has, between the sociology of religion and historical sociology.

How History Lost Its Religion

When and why did historical sociology part ways with the sociology of religion? The "when" question is relatively easy to answer: during the 1970s. In the 1950s and 1960s, there were a number of prominent historical sociologists working actively on religion. Shmuel Eisenstadt's (1963) initial work on ancient empires and world civilizations is an excellent example. Conversely, there were also prominent sociologists of religion who did historical work. Here, one thinks particularly of Robert Bellah's early writings on "religious evolution" and of his book on religion and capitalism in Japan (1957). Religion also figured into the analyses of people who did not work on religion per se, as in Seymour Lipset's original work on "American exceptionalism" (1963, 1996), Stein Rokkan's (1970) analyses of "political development" in Western Europe, or their joint researches on "cleavage structures" in electoral politics (Lipset and Rokkan, eds. 1967). Nor would it be difficult to expand this list. Daniel Bell's (1980) essays on the "cultural contradictions of capitalism" and "the return of the sacred" come to mind. One might even include Karl Polanyi's (1957c [1944]) monograph on "the great transformation," which was inspired by a Christian Democratic stance toward the ethos of modern capitalism. More striking, perhaps, is the fact that prominent Marxists from this period also felt obliged to incorporate religion into their work. E. P. Thompson's (1963) grudging acknowledgment of the influence of Methodism on the English working class provides a good example, while Christopher Hill's (e.g., 1958) lifelong concern with the relationship between Puritanism and revolution represents an even better one. During the 1970s, however, a new generation of scholars emerged onto the scene. Unlike their predecessors, these scholars were utterly uninterested in religion, not only as a subject in its own right, but also as a factor in historical development. A brief examination of the seminal works from this decade is sufficient to confirm this. Consider Wallerstein's *Modern World-System* (1974–1989), Perry Anderson's *Lineages of the Absolutist State* (1974a), Charles Tilly, ed., *Formation of National States* (1975), and Skocpol's *States and Social Revolutions* (1979). One must look hard to find a single reference to religion in any of these books, a fact that is all the more remarkable when one considers that the influence of religion on capitalism, states, revolutions, and social provision was—and remained—an article of faith for the preceding generation.[2]

This brings us to the "why" question, which we can now reformulate as follows: Why were the seminal figures of the new historical sociology of the

2. A partial exception to this rule may be found in works on nationalism from this period. Here I am thinking particularly of Breuilly (1982) and B. Anderson (1983).

1970s so uninterested in, even dismissive of, religion? The first answer that comes to mind is "Marxism," and this answer is by no means incorrect. Three of the five figures in question—Wallerstein, Perry Anderson, and Esping-Andersen—were avowed Marxists, while a fourth, Theda Skocpol, had been deeply influenced by Marxism during earlier years. Only one, Charles Tilly, lacked a Marxist pedigree (which is not to say that he did not take Marx seriously). And yet this answer is by no means complete either. After all, it is quite possible for a committed Marxist to appreciate the historical impact of religion, as the examples of Thompson and Hill make clear. The common denominator among these scholars is not Marxism as such, but a specific *tradition* of Marxism that owes more to *The Communist Manifesto* (K. Marx and Engels 1998 [1848]) than to *The Eighteenth Brumaire* (K. Marx 1963 [1852]), a kind of Marxism that sees "the material" (production, classes, interests, etc.) as the "really real" and "the ideal" (culture, religion, ideology, etc.) as a mere mask or veil that is used to conceal the real from the downtrodden and the ignorant. What one finds in all of these works is not so much a specific prejudice against religion as an unspoken conviction that "the ideal," however conceived, does not really matter in history.

But why was this new generation of scholars so attracted to this particular kind of Marxism? And why were they so inclined to downplay the significance of "ideal factors"? I would like to suggest two hypotheses. The first focuses on the intellectual field in the strict sense. From this perspective, one might see the rise of Marxism and anti-idealism more generally as a(n) (over)reaction to the dominance of structural functionalism, with its emphasis on norms and values. The second focuses on the political field more broadly construed. From this perspective, one might see the rise of Marxism and anti-idealism as the result of events and debates outside the academy, of revolts and revolutions inside and outside the West, in which Marxist intellectuals and activists played a leading role. Obviously, these hypotheses are not necessarily exclusive of one another. In fact, one could see them as complementary. One could argue that it was a confluence of intellectual and political developments that led to the triumph of strict materialism within American macro-sociology. To see why, consider the following counterfactuals. Imagine that postwar American sociology had come to be dominated by a different theoretical perspective, one that was better able to explain, and perhaps also more sympathetic to, the events of the late 1960s and early 1970s than structural functionalism but that also left more conceptual space for "the role of ideas in history"—a Gramscian version of Marxism, say, or perhaps a certain type of "left Weberianism." In that case, developments outside the academy might not have provoked a paradigm shift within sociology.[3] Or imagine, quite simply, that the 1960s had never happened: no student movement, no Vietnam, no Third World revolutions. In that case, the Oedipal conflict within American sociology might have taken a less dramatic form, and the move away from structural functionalism might have been more incremental and "reformist."

Of course, the influence of Marxism has waned considerably since the mid-1970s, not only within historical sociology, but within the world more generally, and other theoretical perspectives have gained ground over the years, most notably Weberianism, feminism, and cultural sociology, in roughly that order. Given the centrality of religion in Weber's work and, indeed, in the history of culture, one might well have expected religion to make a comeback within historical sociology—and cultural sociology—during the 1980s and 1990s. And, indeed, one does find some examples of such a shift, such as the attention to religious parties and ideas in Rueschemeyer, Stephens, and Stephens's (1992) work on democratization and Esping-Andersen's later work (1990) on the welfare state, or the focus on religion and discipline in my own work on early modern state formation (Gorski 2003a). Still, the engagement with religion was nowhere near as deep or as widespread as it had been during the 1950s and 1960s. The number of works that incorporated religion remained small, and the number that focused on religion per se was smaller still.[4]

Why did religion remain on the margins of our vision in the 1980s and 1990s? Once again, let me suggest two possible explanations. The first concerns the framing effects exerted by figures such as Skocpol and Tilly. In retrospect, it is quite clear that the subfield of comparative-historical sociology that emerged during the 1980s was (and to a large extent still is) defined not only by a particular set of methods, but also by a certain set of questions regarding class and state, revolution and reform (a.k.a. class formation, state formation, social revolution, and the welfare state).[5] Of course, the answers we now give to these questions are no longer (strictly) Marxist. But the questions themselves are. And questions about religion are not on the list. In this sense, the question of religion has become a part of our political unconscious. My second hypothesis concerns the impact of modernity and modernism, both as a period and a project. There has always been a strand of thought within sociology that sees modernity and religion as antagonistic

3. This hypothesis could be tested by comparing American sociology with various European sociologies.

4. More detailed data and discussion on this point will be presented in the following section and table 2.

5. There is nothing inherently wrong with this; as Weber recognized long ago, the framing of research questions is inevitably influenced by the values of the researchers.

and views modernity (in the guise of scientific rationality) as the inevitable victor. This is not the only strand of thought, to be sure, but it is an influential one that stretches from Comte and Saint-Simon through Durkheim and Weber to modernization theory and neo-Marxism.[6] Historical sociology is, in part, a reaction against this way of thinking, and historical sociologists have worked hard to disentangle themselves from it, replacing teleology with "contingency," determinism with "probabilism," convergence with "path dependence," and so on. But they have not been entirely successful. Indeed, one might even argue that the current generation of macro-sociologists has undergone a process of regression vis-à-vis their forebears, insofar as they have written religion out of the past as well as the present, unwittingly aligning themselves with the most trenchant voices of the Enlightenment and positivism. The roots of the repression would therefore seem to be cultural as well as Oedipal. But it would be wrong to lay all of the blame on historical sociology. Both partners are usually at fault when a relationship fails, and as we will see directly, this relationship is no exception to that rule.

How Religion Kept Its History

Let us now turn the tables and examine the place of historical research within the sociology of religion. At first glance, it might seem small or even marginal. During the years 1990–1999—a period of revitalization in the sociology of religion—the flagship journals (the *AJS* and the *ASR*) published a total of twelve articles in the field.[7] An examination of *Social Forces*, another well-known general interest journal, yields a similar result: eight articles on the sociology of religion, seven of which used quantitative methods.[8] Nor does the picture change when we turn to other journals that publish historical work, such as *Theory and Society* or the *Journal of Historical Sociology*.[9] Based on this evidence, we might conclude that sociologists of

6. This position has always had its critics, however, and one could (re)construct another strand of thought stretching from Spencer, Simmel, and Scheler, through Parsons, Bellah, and Berger, to Joas and Taylor.

7. This figure is based on searches for the keywords "sociology of religion" in ASR and AJS for the period 1990–1999 in the Proquest Research Library database.

8. This figure is based on a search for the keywords "sociology of religion" in *Social Forces* for the period 1990–1999 in the Proquest Research Library database and a cursory review of the articles retrieved.

9. This assessment is based on a search for the keywords "sociology of religion" in *Theory and Society* for the period 1990–1999 in the "J-stor" database and a manual search through all issues of the *Journal of Historical Sociology* through 2000. The first search retrieved no articles; the second search turned up one.

Table 1   Journal Articles in *Sociological Abstracts*: Selected Topics by Decade

Search Categories	Period			
	1960–69	1970–79	1980–89	1990–99
All "sociology"	27,649	52,761	108,467	173,655
All "historical sociology"	33	64	472	9,101
All "sociology of religion"	1,404	2,208	6,023	9,973
All "political sociology"	3,099	6,778	9,975	22,854
"historical sociology" and "sociology of religion"	0	0	18	279
"historical sociology" and "religion"	0	0	25	473
"historical sociology" and "politics"	0	0	106	1,925
"sociology of religion" and "religion"	119	309	644	1,456
"sociology of religion" and "politics"	42	117	491	1,365

religion are averse to historical methods and/or uninterested in historical questions.

Upon closer inspection, however, this picture proves to be deceptive.[10] A search of a more extensive database, *Sociological Abstracts*, suggests that historical research has always been an important part of the postwar sociology of religion—and one that grew substantially during the 1990s (see tables 1 and 2). Turning to undergraduate textbooks, we come to a similar conclusion: from the 1950s to the present, most have included a substantial number of historical materials—typically related to the themes of Durkheim's and Weber's work in the area (e.g., "primitive" religion, church and sect, the Protestant ethic, and the world religions).[11] Unfortunately, a comprehensive search of scholarly monographs is not feasible. However, the fact that many prominent sociologists of religion (e.g., Bellah 1957; D. Martin 1979; Wuthnow 1988, 1989; R. Stark 1996; Finke and Stark 1992) have produced historical works suggests that this is an important—and prestigious—style of research within the field. Sociologists of religion also appear to be avid consumers of

10. It probably reflects the selection bias of the mainstream journals toward quantitative methods and the bias of historical researchers away from the topic of religion, leading to publication rates that do not reflect the publication mix within the field as a whole.

11. This is based on cursory readings of the following sociology of religion textbooks, all published between 1950 and 2002: Yinger (1957); Hoult (1958); Vernon (1962); O'Dea (1966); Robertson, comp. (1969); Hargrove (1979); Bruce, ed. (1995); M. Hamilton (1995); Fenn, ed. (2001).

Table 2   Selected Topics as a Percentage of Field

Topic and Area	Period			
	1960–69	1970–79	1980–89	1990–99
"sociology of religion" as a percentage of all "sociology"	5.1	4.2	5.5	5.7
"historical sociology" as a percentage of all "sociology"	0.1	0.1	0.4	5.2
"political sociology" as a percentage of all "sociology"	11.2	12.8	9.2	13.1
"historical sociology" and "religion" as a percentage of all "historical sociology"	0	0	5.3	4.7
"sociology of religion" and "history" as a percentage of all "sociology of religion"	8.5	14.0	10.7	14.6
"historical sociology" and "politics" as a percentage of all "historical sociology"	0	0	22.4	21.2

historical research. Or such at least is the inference one might draw from the book review section of the *Journal for the Scientific Study of Religion*, probably the most important journal in the field: between 1960 and 2000, the proportion of books that could be coded as "historical" remained more or less constant from one decade to the next at around 15 percent, despite frequent changes in the journal's editorship. While the evidence I have presented here is hardly conclusive, it does suggest that historical research occupies an important—and growing—place within the sociology of religion. Thus, while historical sociologists can fairly be accused of neglecting religion, the reverse does not appear to hold.[12]

What explains the importance and persistence of historical inquiry among sociologists of religion? Its importance probably has a great deal to do with the continuing effects exerted by the works of Durkheim and, even more, of Weber, works that continue to figure centrally in the training of all sociolo-

12. Based on a rough coding of books that were reviewed from 1961 to 2001. For the first two decades, I relied on the "books reviewed" section of the cumulative index for the years 1961–1980. For the years 1981–2001, I inspected the book review sections of individual journals. The coding was done solely by title. If the title contained date ranges (e.g., "1800–1914") or certain keywords (e.g., "history," "development"), I coded it as historical. This coding method was imperfect; it led to the omission of some titles that I personally knew to be historical works. However, I applied it consistently across the entire period, so perhaps the errors canceled each other out.

gists and works that have exemplified a historical approach to the study of religion, posing a set of questions demanding historical answers. While the Marxist founders of historical sociology tended to marginalize religion, the Weberian current within the sociology of religion was apt to embrace history. And while the political turmoil of the late 1960s probably did have an effect on the sociology of religion, it seems to have been more quantitative than qualitative: the (relative) decline in research output during the 1970s strongly suggests a decline of interest in—and recruitment into—the field, but the fact that the *proportion* of historical work within the field remained constant suggests that its importance was (relatively) unchanged.

Or was it? A closer inspection of the search results discussed above suggests that a large and growing percentage of the historical work on the sociology of religion was published outside of sociology. This could reflect a tendency for people working within historical sociology to publish outside the discipline. Or it could reflect a tendency for people employing historical approaches to the sociology of religion to be employed outside of sociology. Further research would be necessary to clarify this point.[13] In either event, it suggests a perception among researchers that sociology is not the most hospitable locale for historical research—and that the sociology of religion is not quite as historical as it seems. And as we will see directly, this is not the only evidence—or the most important symptom—of incomplete historicization within the sociology of religion.

The Limits of Historicization

If one were looking for evidence that sociologists of religion had missed the historical turn—and had continued straight down the modernist superhighway—then the latest chapter in the secularization debate would be a good place to start. It pits defenders of classical secularization theory against

---

13. However, the limited evidence I have compiled suggests the latter. For example, of the 77 articles from the 1960s retrieved in a broad search for the terms "sociology of religion" and "history," 45 appeared in sociology journals. By contrast, of the 69 articles from the 1990s retrieved in a narrower search for "historical sociology" and "sociology of religion," only 16 appeared in sociology journals, as compared with 22 in history journals, 13 in area studies journals, and 13 in interdisciplinary journals. Of course, it could be that this reflects a general tendency of people working within historical sociology to publish outside the discipline. And, indeed, a closer examination of articles published during the 1990s containing the strings "political sociology" and "historical sociology" confirms this suspicion: of the 224 total articles, 94 appeared in sociology journals, 10 in other social science journals, 36 in history journals, 32 area studies journals, and 52 in interdisciplinary journals. That said, it is striking that almost 42 percent of these articles appeared in sociology journals, as compared to about 23 percent of the religion articles.

advocates of the religious economies approach. Despite the historical character of both schools' object of study, neither is particularly historical in its approach.

Classical secularization theorists have defined secularization in many different ways—as a decline in religious beliefs, a privatization of religious practices, or an increase in social differentiation.[14] But they have tended to see its causes in strikingly similar terms—namely, as an inevitable and irreversible result of "modernization" in all its guises (industrialization, urbanization, rationalization, etc.) Because it assumes a singular notion of, and trajectory toward, "modernity," which (necessarily!) coincides with the road to secularity, this perspective leaves little room for comparative or historical research, except perhaps as a source of corroboration for its initial presuppositions. And indeed one finds little evidence of a serious or sustained engagement with historical literatures or materials in the classic works of secularization theory written during the 1960s—or in their subsequent reformulations.[15] Most simply assume what they would need to demonstrate—namely, that religious institutions, practices, and beliefs have undergone a steady and pervasive decline since the onset of the modern age.

To their credit, advocates of the religious economies approach have taken secularization theory to task for this. They have pointed out, quite rightly, that there are significant variations in religiosity—across space and time—that are not easily accounted for in terms of classical secularization theory. The central exhibit in their case against secularization theory is the United States, by most measures one of the most "modern" countries in the Western world but also one of the most religious. The religious economists argue that the "religious vitality" of the United States is the result of a "free religious market" in which churches compete for members without any interference by the state. And they attribute the low levels of religious vitality (typically operationalized as church attendance or church membership) that can be observed in European countries to the existence of "religious monopolies" (i.e., state churches) and "religious regulation" (i.e., state repression or sponsorship of particular churches).

Although much of the research produced by proponents of this approach *has* been comparative and historical in the sense that it deals with other countries and with the past, it has not been especially comparative or histor-

14. The best treatment—both historical and conceptual—of classical secularization theory is Tschannen (1992). For a brief overview in English, see Gorski (2000a).

15. This is true not only of relatively ahistorical works such as B. Wilson (1967) and Bruce (1996). It is even true of works that attempt to describe secularization in somewhat more concrete and historical terms, such as Berger (1967) or D. Martin (1979). One of the few books that attempts to compile some hard evidence for the secularization thesis is Bruce (1999).

ical in terms of data or methods. Most of the evidence on religious vitality presented in these studies is cross-sectional data from individual countries—typically the United States—and most of the studies focus on a single, national case.[16] And on those rare occasions where religious vitality is studied across time, the analysis itself displays little sensitivity to historical context. For example, in their much touted book, Finke and Stark (1992) fail to consider the possibility that increasing levels of church membership in the United States might be the result of decreasing levels of stringency in admissions criteria (rather than of increasing competition and/or decreasing regulation) (see Holifield 1994). A similar propensity for anachronism is evident in a discussion of late medieval and early modern Christianity, which interprets the widely observed decrease of magical beliefs and practices during the Reformation era as evidence for an increase in religiosity per se (R. Stark and Iannaccone 1994). The problem with this analysis, of course, is that it measures medieval religiosity in terms of a modern metric—theological orthodoxy—and thereby ignores the possibility that medieval and modern religiosity are quite different, not in quantity, but in *quality*.[17]

The problem with the religious economies model goes deeper than a lack of historical evidence or interpretive acumen, however. It goes to the very pretensions of the model to erect a "general theory" of religious change that would be valid for all times and places. Models of this sort have not fared well in historical sociology and social history. They have foundered again and again on the complexities of social life and the contingencies of historical change. And they have been duly abandoned by most historical sociologists, who have left behind the grandiose quest for "closed theories" and "developmental laws" and embarked on a less ambitious mission: the search for "narrative accounts" and "causal mechanisms."[18] Not surprisingly, perhaps, the religious economies model has not fared particularly well either. The bulk of the evidence now suggests that its central hypothesis—that religious pluralism increases religious vitality—is simply not correct.[19]

Insensitivity to historical context, a hankering for social laws—these selfsame criticisms could also be leveled at classical secularization theory. For its

---

16. See, for example, Finke, Guest, and Stark (1996) and Finke and Stark (1988). For a comprehensive bibliography (and critical review), see Chaves and Gorski (2001).

17. This point is discussed in Gorski (2000a: 144–150).

18. On the antinomies of "general theory" and historical explanation, see Somers (1998). For an attempt—unsuccessful, in my view—to bridge the gap between a priori, deductive theorizing and historical and narrative explanation, see Bates et al. (1998). For an excellent discussion of social mechanisms, consonant with the way that term is used here, see Elster (1999: ch. 1).

19. For a comprehensive review of the evidence, see Chaves and Gorski (2001). For a devastating methodological critique and an empirical refutation, see D. V. Olson (1999).

engagement with history has also been quite superficial, although in a somewhat different way. While proponents of the religious economies model have paid insufficient attention to the historicity of religion, to changes in its very character, defenders of classical secularization theory have ignored the conjunctural character of religiosity, its historical ebbs and flows.[20]

Why this deep-seated resistance to a genuinely historical approach to the problem of religious change? To answer this question, we must look at the history of the sociology of religion itself and, more specifically, at the legacy of Comtean positivism.

The Persistence of Positivism, or the Secret Life of Auguste Comte

Comtean positivism had two basic tenets (Comte 1975). The first was that human history consisted of three stages of development: the religious, the metaphysical, and the scientific. The second was that science was the highest form of knowledge—and sociology the queen of the sciences. For Comte, then, the emergence of sociology was the culmination of human history (a seductive fantasy!), and religion was an inferior form of knowledge that belonged to a bygone era. From this perspective, there was little need for a "sociology of religion." Of course, sociology *could* explain religion in scientific terms. But its real task was to *replace* religion as a source of moral and political principles. Since religion belonged to the past, its study was the preserve of dilettantes and antiquarians, not sociologists and other serious scientists.

The emergence of "modern" sociology and psychology in the decades around the *fin de siècle* was accompanied in some quarters by a partial break with the tenets of Comtean positivism concerning religion. This break took two different forms. Some argued that religion was a false interpretation of real experiences. This is the position taken by Durkheim (1995 [1915]) where he argues that "primitive religions" arise out of supernatural (mis)interpretations of "collective effervescence," in which the very real powers of "society" are (wrongly) attributed to a sacred symbol, such as a "totem." From this perspective, religious belief was still a cognitive error but one that was entirely comprehensible and even half true, insofar as it involved the operation of a real force—society. Freud advanced a similar argument in *The Future of an Illusion* (1975) and various other writings. The social world, he contended, is a cruel and chaotic place in which instinct and desire are, and must be, repressed. Religion is a means of coping with, and giving meaning to, these realities. It is an illusion that fulfills infantile desires and dulls the

20. For an excellent discussion of this point, see R. Stark and Bainbridge (1985).

edge of reality. We might call this the social-psychological interpretation of religion, in contrast to a second position, which was epistemological in nature. It was inspired by the philosophy of Immanual Kant and rested on the view that the question of religious truth is beyond the purview of scientific reason.[21] This is the basic stance that underlies Weber's writings on the sociology of religion.[22] However skeptical he may have been, Weber adopted a studied neutrality toward the problem of "ultimate meaning" in his "scientific" writings on religion. This same stance can also be seen in the writings of William James and Charles Peirce, who combined a deep personal faith (of sorts) with a studied methodological agnosticism.[23] The epistemological argument involved an even sharper break with Comtean positivism than the social-psychological argument insofar as it bracketed the question of truth—the question, that is, of whether the religious worldview might be correct.

But sharp as it was, the fin-de-siècle break with the positivist legacy was still far from complete, especially in the case of Durkheim and Weber, who are rightly regarded as the founders not only of sociology, but also of the sociology of religion. For while Durkheim recognized that religion was grounded in real experiences and Weber emphasized that science could not answer questions of value and meaning, both still assumed, if only tacitly, that the future of religion was either extinction (Durkheim) or drastic decline (Weber). Of course, this was already a widely held view among European intellectuals, so perhaps we should not be surprised that they shared it.[24] Still, it is interesting to note that the inner logic of their views on religion could actually have led to very different conclusions and that it did in fact inject certain ambiguities and inconsistencies into their arguments. Consider Durkheim. He was convinced that religion in the narrower sense of the Judeo-Christian tradition was destined to decline. But he was equally convinced that religion in the broader sense of "the sacred" and "the collective conscience" was a functional necessity of social life. This led him to the view—not altogether unlike the later Comte—that the "old religions" would have to be replaced with "new religions," meaning civil religions, and with other sources of "mechanical solidarity," such as occupational associations. So it is unclear whether we should view Durkheim as a theorist of religious decline or a theorist of religious transformation. As for Weber, his belief that the human species has a deep and perhaps inborn desire for meaning and his recognition that science cannot provide this meaning, except perhaps to

21. Kant's position on this issue is laid out most clearly and succinctly in Kant (1960).
22. This position is most explicit in M. Weber (1946c: esp. 142–143).
23. Their views on religion are discussed at length in Menand (2001b).
24. For an entertaining if anecdotal account, see A. N. Wilson (1999).

its practitioners, seems very much at odds with the view that religious believers would soon become a tiny minority of the weak-willed, and it might have led him to a conclusion somewhat like Freud's—namely, that religion has a bright future even if it is an illusion. Thus, there is a tension between Weber's anthropology and his sociology, between his understanding of human nature and his prognoses about the future of religion.

Notes Toward a Post-positivist Sociology of Religion

Eschatological Agnosticism, or Bracketing the Future

Partial though it was, the break with Comte and the radical Enlightenment was enormously fruitful, because it allowed—indeed impelled—social scientists to ask new and important questions. The recognition that religion was grounded in real experiences and the willingness of some to bracket the question of religious truth opened up new avenues of theorizing and research regarding the psychological dynamics of religious life and the social and historical origins of particular systems of religious belief. The result was an enormous outpouring of scholarly work in the sociology of religion and in the social sciences more generally, work that continues to serve as a source of concepts and questions even today. But it is hard to escape the impression that the creative torrent has ebbed and perhaps even reached an impasse, at least in certain areas such as the debate about secularization, where professional debates about the religious past are too often a Trojan horse for metaphysical quarrels about the religious future.

Various remedies have been proposed, of course, a strong dose of economic theory being the most vigorously recommended one. But they have not proven as effective as their proponents had promised. My own view is that a more radical course of treatment is called for—namely, a second (and final?) break with Comtean positivism and the radical Enlightenment. At the most general level, such a break would involve the recognition that there are no universal laws or stages of historical development and that the social sciences are incapable of forecasting the future with any reasonable degree of accuracy. Put more positively, it would mean focusing on *patterns* of historical change and searching for the *causal mechanisms* that underlie them. This is clearly the direction in which sociology as a whole is moving, and it would be wise for sociologists of religion to follow. Within the sociology of religion per se, a complete break with Comteanism would involve stripping the theory of secularization of its teleological trappings and recognizing that secularization is neither the sole dimension of religious change nor the only direction such change can take. In positive terms, it would mean treating *secularization as a conceptual variable*, rather than a developmental trend, and explaining it in contingent and historical terms instead of teleological and nomothetical ones. And it would mean searching for patterns of religious transformation other than secularization—changes in the organizational structure of religious groups or the predominant types of religious actors, for example—and the reasons for such shifts. If this agenda had a slogan, it would be, "Bracket the future." Just as Weber and James adhered to a position of methodological agnosticism, which banned the question of religious truth from the sphere of scholarly debate, so should we adopt a stance of *eschatological agnosticism*, which brackets the question of the religious future in the sociology of religion—and for much the same reasons: just as Weber and James recognized that science could not adjudicate questions of "ultimate meaning," so we have come to understand that social science cannot reveal the telos of history (or the lack thereof). While we have been quick to recognize the consequences that this has in other areas of the discipline, we have been slower to admit the consequences that it has for the study of religion. The Comtean fantasy dies hard.

This, in broad outlines, is what a post-Comtean sociology of religion might look like. But what could historical sociology contribute to it? That is the question to which I now turn.

Add Politics and Stir: Thoughts on a New "New Paradigm" of Religious Change

The style of comparative-historical sociology that has taken shape within the United States and Great Britain over the last three decades has a number of distinctive features, some of which are identified in its name. It is "comparative" in the sense that it uses comparisons of large socio-political units (usually nation-states) to identify and account for historical events (e.g., revolutions) and structural variations (e.g., among states). And it is "historical" in the sense that it focuses on the past and makes (increasing) use of historical sources (e.g., archival records) and in the sense that it eschews the search for developmental laws or general theories in favor of the search for causal mechanisms and historical explanations of particular (sets of) events or variations. But comparative-historical sociology also has another feature that is not so clearly identified in its name and that I already highlighted above: a concern with the state and with the political more generally, both as the *explanans* and the *explanandum*.

As we have seen, the sociology of religion never really lost its comparative and historical dimensions. It continued the tradition of cross-civilizational comparison and added a cross-national approach. And it continued to wrestle with the historical questions first posed by Durkheim and Weber. But however strong it was, the comparative and historical approach never penetrated to the paradigmatic core of the field: the theory of secularization. Much the same might be said of political sociology. Here, too, there is a long and fruitful tradition of interaction and cross-fertilization. Studies of religious movements often employ the tools of political sociology. For their part, social movement scholars have been attentive to the impact of religion. And in recent years, researchers working at the intersection of the two fields have begun asking whether there are any fundamental differences between religious and nonreligious movements.[25] Some political sociologists have also begun studying the effects of religious belief on voting behavior again, a topic that had gradually become the preserve of political scientists, while some sociologists of religion have begun to examine the effects of political beliefs on religious behavior (see Manza and Brooks 1997; Hout and Fischer 2002).

Where secularization theory is concerned, however, comparison, history, and politics are notable mainly for their absence. Most versions of classical secularization theory remain wedded to a modernization-theoretical framework in which variations in secularity are treated as variations in modernity—as successive stages along a single path—and secularization itself is traced to deep-seated social processes that occur beneath the feet of historical actors and without their knowledge, like slow seismic shifts. It is an approach that leaves little room for historical particularity and no room for the possibility—the certainty, really—that secularization was (also) a political program that was consciously pursued by certain groups or organizations.[26] If some sociologists of religion have been slow to recognize this, perhaps it is because they are loath to abandon the positivist philosophy of history—and their privileged place within it.

The religious economists cannot be accused of ignoring variations in secularity or of treating secularization as an inevitable and irreversible process. But they cannot be accused of paying much attention to politics, either. Politics for them enters only from without, as an artificial disturbance (religious regulation) that disrupts the "natural" operations of religious markets. The idea that politics could itself be a source of ultimate values that compete with religious values, or that free markets are not natural occur-

25. The work of Christian Smith and his students provides a good example of the use of social movement theory to study religious movements. See, for example, C. Smith (1991). Attention to religion has been particularly pronounced in works on the civil rights movements. See A. Morris (1984) and McAdam (1988). On the differences between religious and nonreligious movements, see Warren (2001) and R. L. Wood (2002).
26. This is the central message of C. Smith, ed. (2003).

rences but political constructions, is as foreign to them as it is to their friends in economics.[27]

The study of secularization and of religious change more generally is thus one area in which closer collaboration between historical sociologists and sociologists of religion promises to be particularly fruitful. Recent work by historians of religion suggests the shape such research might take.

Since the publication of David Martin's (1979) landmark study, English-speaking sociologists have not produced very much historical work on secularization.[28] This cannot be said of historians, however, who have generated a steady stream of edited books and monographs on the subject. The central figure in this field is British historian Hugh McLeod. Historians have long known that the decades around the fin de siècle were a period of religious disaffection and disaffiliation in many parts of Western Europe, a period in which church attendance, Easter observances, and other indicators of religious vitality were on the decline. McLeod and his various collaborators have attempted to account for the variations and rhythms of this mass withdrawal from the churches.[29] And like David Martin, they have generally concluded that religious pluralism and state-church relations are the key factors that explain these variations. At first glance, this argument is strikingly similar to that of the religious economists, who often invoke Martin. But in fact the resemblance is only superficial. For Martin and McLeod focused on religious pluralism and state-church relations not because of the effects they might have on "religious markets," but because of the effects they had on the socio-political struggles of the period, especially the three-cornered struggle among liberal, socialist, and confessional parties.

I have suggested elsewhere (Gorski forthcoming b) that the approach pioneered by Marin and McLeod might be dubbed the "socio-political conflict model" (henceforth SPCM). Extrapolating from their empirical analyses, one could summarize its central theses as follows. Where a state-controlled church exercised a religious monopoly, as in Scandinavia, religious officials and institutions were unable or unwilling to support or ally with progressive or opposition political parties and movements, and laypeople were forced to choose between organized religion and social reform. Many opted for reform and against religion. By contrast, where church and state were fully

---

27. These are hardly new insights. The possibility that politics could be a source of ultimate values was already clearly recognized in M. Weber (1946b: 333–338). On the political construction of markets, the locus classicus remains Polanyi (1957c [1944]).

28. A partial exception to this rule, which focuses on one dimension of secularity (church/state relations), is Demerath (2001).

29. See especially McLeod (2000) and McLeod, ed. (1995). Similar arguments may be found in F. Höllinger (1996).

separate and no church exercised a religious monopoly, as in the United States, religious officials and institutions were not as strongly bound to a conservative establishment, and some clergy and churches sided with the forces of reform. This meant that laypeople were not necessarily forced to choose between religion and reform, and the result, it appears, was a lower rate of disaffiliation and disaffection from organized religion. Based on this model, we would expect that countries where state-supported churches did not possess religious monopolies, such as England and the Netherlands, would exhibit moderate levels of religious vitality that fell between those found in Scandinavia and the United States. And, in fact, this does appear to be the case. We would also expect that countries characterized by a high degree of religious monopoly and a moderate degree of church-state separation, such as the Catholic countries of Latin Europe, would also exhibit moderate levels of religious vitality. This, however, does not appear to be the case. With the exception of France, these countries exhibit fairly high levels of religious vitality. One possible explanation for this anomaly, which accords well with the SPCM, is the emergence of strong Christian Democratic movements in many European countries (e.g., Italy, Austria, southern Germany, Spain), but not in France, and the relative weakness of confessional movements in most areas of Protestant Europe. Another weakness of the SPCM, as I have presented it here, is that it does not address secularization as a structural process—the removal of various cultural and institutional domains from ecclesiastical influence and control—and its relationship with the micro level of religious vitality. The paradox here is that many state churches in Europe still retain considerable power in the social and cultural realms (e.g., in the provision of social services and education), even in countries where few people espouse orthodox Christian beliefs and fewer still participate in traditional Christian worship. Nor is it clear if, or how, the SPCM could be extended to explain other episodes of secularization, such as those that occurred in many parts of the West during the 1960s. So while it appears quite promising, the SPCM is still in need of further development and testing.

Beyond Secularization: Neo-Weberian Paths Toward
a Sociological History of Religious Change

While historicizing the secularization debate brings us some distance toward a post-positivist sociology of religion, it is only a first step. The next step is to transcend the question of secularization by integrating it into a more general and multifaceted understanding of religious change. This means reconceiving the problem of religious change as a question of "what kind" rather than just a question of "how much." Obviously, I cannot answer this question here. Instead, I will suggest various ways in which one might pose it, taking Weber as my point of departure.

a) Changing patterns of "religious leadership" and "lay community." In "The Sociology of Religion," Weber (1978 [1922]) distinguished various types of religious leaders and the sorts of lay communities that tend to form around them (see also M. Weber 1978, vol. 1: 422–480; Bourdieu 1987). The purpose of this exercise was to identify the kinds of religious leadership and lay community that characterized Western Christendom and certain recurring patterns of interaction between them, as a means of explaining the genesis of "innerworldly asceticism" and other peculiarities of Western religious development. In essence, Weber argued that the religious history of the West was characterized by a triadic interaction among priests, prophets, and congregations that resulted in twin tendencies toward theoretical and practical rationalization. Christian priests attempted to monopolize access to the means of salvation by defining these means in sacramental terms and organizing the universal church into an "institutionalized provider of grace" (*Gnadenanstalt*). They were repeatedly challenged by prophetic preachers, usually drawn from the laity, who sought to define the means to salvation in ethical terms. Often, although not always, prophetic movements were "routinized" into sectarian communities—gathered communities of like-minded believers. Prior to the Reformation, these communities usually consisted of clergymen and took a monastic form; following the Reformation, "congregations" of laypeople also emerged. They demanded greater influence in church governance—and greater attention to their "religious needs." Confronted with these challenges, the priestly caste responded in two ways: (1) by developing formal systems of religious doctrines and closed canons of religious scriptures that would insulate them from prophetic assault, and (2) by developing systems of practical ethics and pastoral care that would assuage the demands of the laity.

For Weber, then, the discussion of priests, prophets, and laity served an explanatory function. But it can also be used as a heuristic device—as a conceptual lens for tracking changes in the dominant forms of religious leadership and religious community. Viewed through this lens, from a bird's-eye perspective, the history of Western Christianity can be see in two different but complementary ways. The first picture looks roughly as follows: during the first millennium of Western Christendom (ca. 500–ca. 1500) priestly authority and churchly community were on the ascendant, and prophetic challengers were integrated into the church through the establishment of clerical orders under papal supervision. Following the Reformation, priestly authority and churchly community eroded considerably, partly as a result of prophetic and lay challenges from within the church and the consequent emergence of congregational and sectarian forms of religious community, and partly as a result of challenges from outside the church, both by secular "experts" claiming jurisdiction over social functions long monopolized by the church (e.g., the provision of charity and education, the production of natural and ethical truth, and even the cure of souls) and by non-Christian purveyors of ultimate meaning and individual salvation. This is the standard reading among secularization theorists. But it is by no means the only reading possible. If we widen our conceptual focus and lengthen our historical perspective, a rather different picture comes into view. Looking back to pre-Christian Rome, we discover a religious world populated not only by priests and prophets leading churches and sects, but by many other figures as well—"magicians," "teachers of social ethics," "exemplary prophets," "gurus," "mystagogues," and, indeed, the full panoply of religious and quasi-religious purveyors of meaning discussed by Weber. A world, in other words, that is strikingly similar to our own. In this picture, it is the millennium of priestly hegemony and churchly monopoly that appears strange.[30] And the weakening of traditional Christianity appears not as a decline of religion per se, but as a *return to polytheism* or, to put it more precisely, a return to polysemism, since the new worldviews are not uniformly theistic. This suggests a second optic of religious change.

b) The end of the Axial Age? Changing structures of religious belief. In his essay "Religious Rejections of the World and Their Directions" (1946b) Weber argued that modern Western society was divided into distinct and competing "value-spheres" or "life-orders"—religious, economic, political, aesthetic, erotic, and intellectual—constituted by clear and irreconcilable standards of "ultimate value" that were "carried" by antagonistic groups of virtuoso practitioners. Weber did not regard these processes of institutional differentiation and theoretical rationalization as unique to the West, but he did believe that they had gone farthest there. Not surprisingly, he attributed this fact to certain distinctive features of Western religion, whose origins could be traced back to the "Axial Age," the twelve-hundred-year period marked by the birth of the Buddha (563 B.C.E.) and the death of Mohammed (632 C.E.), when the various world religions took shape.[31] Weber began by drawing a distinction between "world-affirming" and "world-rejecting" religions—that is, between religions that see worldly life as the real and the

---

30. For a similar reading of the period, see Hopkins (1999).

31. Weber himself does not use the term "Axial Age." It was originally coined by Karl Jaspers (1949), a close friend and great admirer of Weber's. For an excellent discussion of this concept, with empirical applications and critical assessments, see Eisenstadt, ed. (1986).

good (e.g., the religions of ancient Greece and classical Japan) and those that see it as illusory or corrupt (e.g., Hinduism, Buddhism, Christianity, and Islam). In the former, Weber suggested, the primordial unity of the world was preserved.[32] In the latter, by contrast, the world was rent in two, into a lower, mundane realm and a higher, transcendent one. The two realms were inevitably in tension with one another. But the *degree* of tension, Weber suggested, was highly variable and depended, above all, on the way in which transcendence was conceived and, more specifically, on the mundane means through which it could be obtained.[33] In "cosmocentric" religions (e.g., Hinduism, Buddhism, and Confucianism), these means were typically (though not invariably) ritual or contemplative. The usual results were "flight from the world," in the case of religious virtuosos, or "indifference to the world," in the case of the religiously "mediocre." Conflicts between the mundane and the transcendent realms were minimized both by the withdrawal of the virtuosos from everyday life and by the compartmentalization of religious practice. By contrast, in "theocentric" religions, particularly those that espoused a personal, creator God (e.g., Judaism, Christianity, and Islam), the means to salvation were predominantly (although not exclusively) ascetic and ethical. Here, complete disengagement from worldly activity and total indifference to worldly goods were impossible, even for religious virtuosos, such as monks, who could obtain salvation only by struggling with the world and overcoming its temptations. But the highest level of tension, said Weber, arises when the path to the monastery is closed and the religious virtuoso is forced to live "in the world," as were the lay sects that emerged after the Reformation. As the demands of religion on the world become more intense, worldly elites respond by defending the autonomy of their own spheres of action, not only from religion, but also from other spheres. The result is increasing differentiation among the value-spheres and increasing rationalization within them. Thus it is, Weber concluded, that the religious rejection of the world culminates in the fragmentation of social life.

Like his discussion of "Priests, Prophets and Laity," Weber's "Religious Rejections" can be read in two rather different ways. In the first reading, which is the standard one, it is an essay about the paradoxical sense in which religion is itself the root cause of secularization (see, e.g., Berger 1990 [1967]: esp. ch. 5; Schluchter 1989: 249–264). By increasing the tension between religion and the world beyond the breaking point, the argument goes, West-

---

32. On the peculiarities of the one society in which this "primordial unity" remains more or less intact, see Eisenstadt (1995).

33. A limpid exegesis of Weber's analysis of the world religions may be found in Schluchter (1989: chs. 3–6). On the scholarly background of Weber's comparative sociology of religion, see especially Kippenberg (forthcoming).

ern Christianity contributed mightily—if unintentionally—to its own demise. In the second reading, which I am suggesting here, it is an essay about the collapse of the Axial Age synthesis, in which Western civilization was unified by a widely shared—and firmly institutionalized—vision of transcendence and the (re)emergence of religious pluralism, not simply in the banal sense of competing (Christian) denominations, but also in the radical sense of competing visions and levels of transcendence. In the post-Axial West, theistic visions of transcendence are forced to make room for explicitly cosmocentric ones. Some, such as Buddhism, are themselves the products of other Axial Age civilizations. But others, such as environmentalism, are both modern and indigenous.[34] For is not environmentalism, with its language of "natural balances," "sacred cycles," and "mother earth," a religion of sorts, that has its "virtuoso" practitioners (e.g., Earth Firsters and tree sitters), as well as its mass followers (check-writing members of the Sierra Club and the World Wildlife Fund)? It is, at the very least, the most vibrant political religion of the twenty-first century in most of the West. Nor is this the only competition faced by theistic religiosity. Even more pervasive, perhaps, is the smorgasbord of "little transcendences" commonly grouped together under the rubric of "spirituality" and the various "aesthetics of existence" propagated by health and beauty gurus of one sort or another.[35] Nor should one overlook the widespread popularity of magical practices, from astrology through psychic healing to voodoo. Of course, nontheistic worldviews and popular magical practices never disappeared from Western culture, despite the efforts of the post-Reformation churches to suppress them. But the collapse of the Christian monopoly seems to have given them more room to grow. Thus, disenchantment in some quarters has given way to re-enchantment in others. The size and composition of the West's new "magic garden" is, of course, an empirical question.

c) *Religion and subjectivity: From asceticism to aestheticism?* In his most famous—and most controversial—work, *The Protestant Ethic and the Spirit of Capitalism*, Weber argued that there was an "elective affinity" between "ascetic Protestanism" and "modern capitalism."[36] More specifically, he argued that the Protestant ethic forged a new type of person, a disciplined and methodical person who found spiritual solace in self-renunciation and unremitting labor—a person who was thus ideally suited by outlook and dis-

34. For an engaging study of a virtuoso sect of radical environmentalists, see Gelber and Cook (1990).
35. The terms "little transcendences" and "aesthetics of existence" are borrowed from Luckmann (1990) and Foucault (1990) respectively.
36. For the original (1905) version of this essay, see M. Weber (2002b). For a recent retranslation of the revised (1920) version see M. Weber (2002a).

position to the tasks of capital accumulation and economic rationalization. It did so, said Weber, by making diligence in a worldly calling (i.e., a trade or profession) a key "mark" or "sign" of one's spiritual fate (salvation or damnation). In a later essay, "The Protestant Sects and the Spirit of Capitalism," Weber suggested another source for this new personality type: the system of communal discipline pioneered by Reformed churches and Baptist sects during the Reformation era.[37] By linking personal morality to social honor and ideal interests to material ones, Weber emphasized, communal discipline created extraordinarily powerful incentives for righteous conduct.

What is of interest to us here is not the importance of this personality type for the genesis of capitalism, which is quite controversial, but rather the importance of religion for the genesis of this personality type, which is much less so.[38] For what Weber's analysis suggests is that the "modern subject" qua "rational actor"—an individual who possesses consistent and explicit goals and pursues them in a systematic and calculating fashion—is not an ontological universal but a "historical individual" who emerges out of a particular context, in this case, the combination of a particular soteriology—an ethical path to otherworldly salvation—with a particular ecclesiology—a system of communally embedded social surveillance. From this perspective, it is no coincidence that the philosophers most responsible for articulating the "philosophy of the subject" in both its Anglo-American and Continental varieties—namely, Locke, Descartes, and Kant—lived and worked in times and places strongly inflected by ascetic Protestantism: Oxford, Amsterdam, and Königsberg.

Today, of course, this context no longer exists on anything like a mass scale, at least not in the West.[39] Here, communal discipline is seen as a historical anachronism (such as in the case of the Amish) or as social deviance (such as in the case of "cults"). And except among certain traditionalists and fundamentalists, the old ethical soteriology of the "wages of sin" has been displaced by a feel-good philosophy of afterlife-for-everybody. This raises an important question: what implications do these shifts have for the

37. An English translation of this essay appears in Gerth and Mills, eds. (1946) and is reprinted in M. Weber (2002a).

38. Weber may well have been wrong about the economic significance of this personality type, but he seems to have been right about its inner dynamics and their religious roots. The English Puritans and their spiritual kin really were "innerworldly ascetics" who combined a fierce work ethic with a rejection of sensual pleasure. This, at least, is the conclusion in the most thorough and even-handed assessment of "the Weber thesis" in light of the existing evidence: G. Marshall (1982: esp. ch. 4). Marshall focuses mainly on the British Isles, but similar conclusions may be found in a recent study of the New England case: Innes (1995).

39. However, it can be found in other areas of the world, such as the Middle East.

structure of personality and subjectivity? Will the "modern subject" and the "rational actor" disappear with the context that brought them into being? Or are they simply being reproduced through other means?

Weber himself was ambivalent on this score. At the end of *The Protestant Ethic*, he famously suggested that the discipline of the calling, now loosened from its religious moorings, would find a new support in the capitalist division of labor, which forces us to renounce "the Faustian universality of life" in favor of a life of specialized work. Based on this argument, one might conclude that the signal task of the individual subject is to break free of the "iron cage" of modern rationality—through aesthetic or erotic experiences, for example.[40] In other writings, however, such as "Science as a Vocation" (1946c: esp. 148–149), Weber suggested that the weakening of Christianity had ushered in a new era or, rather, brought us back to an older era in which the numerous gods—of love and mammon, of truth and power, of war and family—all vied for our souls. From this perspective, the great challenge for the modern subject is not so much to break free of the iron cage as to choose the cage that suits her best—not just as a form of self-confinement, but also as a means of protection from internal and external chaos.

But different as they are, both scenarios suggest that modern "subjectivity," in the sense in which that term was originally understood, will become more difficult to achieve, at the individual level, and less predominant, at the social level. In this sense, Weber's diagnosis is quite consonant with the one delivered up by post-modernist theorists, who portray the Kantian subject as a historical figure whose time has now passed. Weber's explanation for this state of affairs is quite different. Unlike the deconstructionists, who trace the death of the subject to philosophical and cultural developments—the destabilization of the sign, the end of master narratives, and so on—Weber drew our attention to the role of social structure, and in particular social differentiation, in the fragmentation and decentering of subjectivity.[41] And unlike Marxist post-modernists, who do grasp the structural side of the equation, Weber suggested that capitalism is only part of the story.[42] Most important, perhaps, Weber's approach made the problem of subjectivity into a problem that can be researched. Following his lead, we might ask what patterns of life conduct and what sorts of subjective experi-

40. This was more or less the conclusion of those who followed this line of thought to its logical conclusion—namely, Theodor Adorno, Max Horkheimer, Herbert Marcuse, and other members of the Frankfurt School.
41. The seminal works in the deconstructionist vein are, of course, Lyotard (1984 [1979]) and Derrida (1982).
42. For Marxist post-modernists, see especially Harvey (1989) and Jameson (1991).

ence are likely to emerge in a society of multiple transcendences, theocentric and cosmocentric, great and small, where otherwordly salvation competes with worldly experience but where God no longer competes with the devil, and so on.

Thus far, I have considered what it would mean to study religion in a truly historical way. I now turn my attention to the related question of what it would mean to study history with greater attention to religion.

The Recovery of the Repressed: The Religious Factor in Historical Change and the Future of Historical Sociology

The repression of religion into the political unconscious of historical sociology spanned two full generations. It began with the generation that rejected structural functionalism and embraced Marxism during the 1970s. And it continued into the next generation, the generation of the 1980s and early 1990s, which distanced itself from Marxist theory but remained focused on Marxist questions about state, class, revolution, and reform. Since that time, however, religion has crept back into the consciousness of historical sociologists, both young and old. The purpose of this section is to review some of that work and explore some of its implications for the field as a whole. Having asked what the sociology of religion might learn from a more serious engagement with historical sociology, I will now reflect on what historical sociology might learn from more sustained attention to religion.

Let me begin with my own area of expertise, the study of early modern state formation. Like most areas of historical sociology, it was originally dominated by neo-Marxists and later conquered by neo-Weberians. The most important representatives of the neo-Marxist position were Perry Anderson (1974a), who argued that the early modern state was a "recharged apparatus of feudal domination" (1979a: 18) based on a quid pro quo between crown and nobility, and Immanuel Wallerstein (1974–1989), who argued that the structure and strength of early modern states was a function of their position within the global economy. They were succeeded by neo-Weberians such as Brian Downing (1992) and Thomas Ertman (1997), who focused on the impact of geopolitical competition on state administration and of the structure of representative institutions on conflict between crown and estates. Since the mid-1990s, however, a growing number of historical sociologists and early modern historians have attempted to put religion back into the story of early modern state formation. They have emphasized the impact of confessional divisions on the socio-political struggles that concerned the neo-Marxists and on the institutional transformations that occupied the neo-Weberians.[43] These scholars have emphasized the role that confessional conflict played on the type of regime and the form of administration that emerged in various parts of early modern Europe.

The evolution of comparative-historical work on the welfare state has been similar. It, too, was initially dominated by a group of neo-Marxists, known as the "power resources school," who argued that levels of welfare expenditure were directly tied to levels of class organization. They were subsequently challenged by neo-Weberians, who emphasized the importance of political conflict and state structure.[44] Religion did not figure prominently—or even marginally—in either of these perspectives. In recent years, leading scholars in this area have come to recognize that there is a Christian Democratic variant of the welfare state that is quite different from liberal and social democratic welfare regimes in terms of both its organization and its goals (Esping-Andersen 1990; Huber and Stephens 2001; Kersbergen 1995). At the same time, a group of revisionist historians has returned to the once unfashionable view that social welfare evolved quite differently in Protestant and Catholic states.[45] Juxtaposing these two findings raises a number of interesting questions. For example, one might ask whether there was not some deep continuity in the social policies of Catholic states from the early modern to the modern era. Similarly, one might ask whether the liberal welfare regimes of England and America might not have had Calvinist roots and why it was in the Lutheran countries of Scandinavia that the social democratic version of welfare took hold most deeply. In other words, one might ask to what degree contemporary variations in welfare regimes are the product of historical differences antedating the emergence of capitalism. Similarly, one might ask how religious cleavages and parties figured into the socio-political struggles of the nineteenth and twentieth centuries. These are important questions that have not, to my knowledge, been the subject of systematic and comparative research.

The study of nationalism has also taken a religious turn in recent years. This turn is particularly evident (at least to me) among specialists in early modern history and literature, who have come to see confession, and religion more generally, as one source, and perhaps *the* source, of national identity in the centuries before the French Revolution.[46] It is also evident in

---

43. See, for example, te Brake (1998); R. J. W. Evans and T. V. Thomas, eds. (1991); Gorski (2001, 2003a); and Braddick (2000).

44. The classic statement of the power resources perspective is Korpi (1983). For an example of the neo-Weberian perspective, also known as the "state-centered" approach, see Weir and Skocpol (1985).

45. See Grell and Cunningham with Arrizabalaga, eds. (1999) and Grell and Cunningham, eds. (1997). Similar views and additional literature may be found in Gorski (2003a: ch. 4).

46. A comprehensive review of these literatures, along with a comparative discussion of several cases,

more recent work on Poland (Zubrzycki 2001) and Ireland (C. C. O'Brien 1988), where nationalism and religion are still tightly intertwined. These two streams of research challenge the received wisdom, still dominant in historical sociology and political science, that nationalism is a product of the French Revolution and represents a secular alternative to revealed religion. What is more, they suggest that Western nationalism may well be rooted in narratives of the Old Testament and the notion of the "chosen people" and that this particular strand of discourse is still operative today, both explicitly and implicitly. If this is correct, it would represent a major challenge to the received orthodoxy regarding the relationship among religion, nationalism, and modernity.

What about work on revolution? Here, too, we discover a familiar pattern. During the 1960s, a number of prominent scholars focused attention on this topic, arguing, in effect, that radical religion was the midwife of revolutionary politics and that revolution was a product of the Reformation or even of the Axial Age (see, e.g., Hill 1958; Walzer 1965, 1985; Eisenstadt 1978a, 1978b). During the 1970s, religion disappeared from the view of historical sociologists as attention turned to modern revolutions (cf. Skocpol 1979; C. Tilly 1978). Over the last decade, however, it has returned, first in work on Latin America and the Middle East and, more recently, in work on early modern Europe.[47] One wonders whether the greater willingness of social scientists to consider religious factors in Third World cases might be the result of a strange marriage of positivism and post-modernism in which cultural relativism serves as cover for a deep-seated modernism that still sees religion as a symptom of backwardness. Further grounds for these suspicions can be found in work on social movements. Here, too, the emphasis on religion, and on culture more generally, seems to have been greater in work on racial Others, such as African Americans, than in work on native-born whites.

The ongoing work of Michael Young (e.g., 2002) represents one attempt to fill this lacuna. *Pace* the contentious politics approach, Young argued that the emergence of national-level social movements in the nineteenth-century United States was largely the result of the growth of national-level religious organizations and that these organizations played a crucial role in the mobilization of native-born whites into national-level politics.

Traditionally, students of working-class history have either ignored religion altogether or treated it as a barrier to class consciousness. This is still

---

may be found in Gorski (2000b). The early modern roots of modern nationalism are also emphasized in Greenfeld (1992), albeit with undue emphasis on the English case.

47. I am thinking here especially of work on "liberation theology" and the Iranian Revolution. See, for example, Neuhouser (1989) and Arjomand (1988). On religion and revolution in early modern Europe, see, for example, te Brake (1998) and Gorski (2001).

the dominant view, even today. But perhaps it is time to question it. Clearly, religious dissent could go together with political opposition—and often did—not only in Christian Democratic countries such as Belgium and Italy, but even in Protestant countries such as England and the United States, albeit not with the same results. Thus, the fact that Christianity was often at odds with socialism should not lead us to assume that it was at odds with class formation per se. On the contrary, if one contrasted the Christian Democratic countries of Western Europe not with the social democratic polities of Scandinavia but with the liberal polities of the Anglo-American world, one might reach the very opposite conclusion: that it was the lack of religiously based class mobilization that hindered class formation.

Conclusion

Writing on the place of religion in the social sciences, Craig Calhoun (1999) remarked that there is probably no topic that matters so much to the average American yet receives such short shrift from American sociologists. As we have seen, historical sociology is no exception to this rule. Despite the central place that religion occupied in the work of Durkheim and Weber and in macro-sociological work during the 1950s and 1960s, it disappeared from view during the 1970s and 1980s and continues to be severely understudied even today. I have argued that this decline of interest in religion resulted from four nested causes: (1) the impact of the 1960s on the internal politics of the academy, insofar as it helped bring about (2) the rejection of the Parsonsian synthesis in favor of theories that emphasized the material over the ideal, insofar as it contributed to (3) the emergence of a new generation of macro-sociologists whose research interests were directly or indirectly inspired by Marxist politics. Their conviction that religion was irrelevant was further reinforced by (4) the dip in traditional religious belief and practice that occurred during the early 1970s. Taken together, these four developments made work on religion look theoretically unimportant, politically irrelevant, and historically outmoded and helped erase religion from the agenda of historical sociology.

Religion may have been repressed into the political unconscious of historical sociology. But it did not cease to exert certain effects. Rather, it returned, in good Freudian fashion, in the form of symptoms. Sometimes these symptoms took the form of empirical anomalies generated by the willful neglect of the religious, as in theories of early modern state formation that ignored the Reformation. Other times, they took the form of historical nearsightedness, as when various scholars insisted that revolution, nationalism, and welfare states were inherently modern phenomena with entirely secular causes. A third, and less obvious, symptom was the growing estrangement between historical sociology and the sociology of religion, two fields, as we have seen, that had been closely allied. This estrangement was detrimental to both fields, since it allowed historical sociologists to be superficial in their analyses of culture by reducing it to the study of ideology and allowed sociologists of religion to be superficial in their analyses of history by reducing it to the study of "the past."

Fortunately, there are signs that the tide has now turned. The number of scholars working at the intersection of the two fields has increased significantly during the last decade. The causes of this (re)turn to religion in the social sciences are several: (1) the decline of Whiggish modernism and materialist Marxism and the concomitant rise of post-modern skepticism and radical multiculturalism, both inside and outside the academy; (2) the "cultural turn" in the social sciences and growth of cultural sociology; (3) the emergence of a third generation of macro-sociologists, whose intellectual and political agendas were formed during the 1990s, after the fall of communism; and (4) the resurgence of religious belief in general and of politicized religion in particular, both in the United States and abroad. Skepticism about Enlightenment views of science and rationality, greater concern with culture and values, a changing of the guard, the rise of fundamentalism—all of these have suddenly made religion seem more relevant again theoretically, historically, and politically.

This is not to say that sociologists have entirely freed themselves from their positivist reflexes. On the contrary, these reflexes were on full display in the academic discussions of terrorism prompted by the events of September 11, 2001—and not only among historical and political sociologists. The overwhelming majority of these analyses took a blatantly reductionistic or Whiggish form. "Islamic fundamentalism" was either traced back to something else (e.g., poverty or imperialism in the case of the lower classes, blocked ascendancy or political ambition among the elites), or it was treated as resistance—vain, of course—to the march of cultural, economic, and political modernization (a.k.a. globalization) and thus as a shadowy anachronism that will disappear as the light of reason spreads. This is not to say that imperialism and ambition are irrelevant or that religious "fundamentalism" is not, in part, a backlash against Western "modernity." It is merely to insist that religion first be analyzed on its own terms and that sociologists stop trying to wish it away simply because they do not like it. To do so would be a political error as well as an intellectual one.

ANN SHOLA ORLOFF

Social Provision and Regulation: Theories of
States, Social Policies, and Modernity

Social provision and regulation have taken on many public and mixed pub-
lic/private forms, from poor relief and publicly subsidized charity to "workingmen's insurance" and pensions, "social security," "the welfare state,"
"welfare capitalism," "the social state," and "*l'etat providence*." They have
been a central focus of politics across the West in the centuries since modernizing states first began to challenge the church for control of the functions of relieving those in distress, disciplining subjects, and maintaining
order and found relief and other forms of welfare useful in larger projects
of regulating and mobilizing populations. Indeed, some *public* (or quasi-
public) form of social provision has been a distinctive feature of modern,
Western capitalist societies for a very long time, although in the last half
century public social security systems have spread to all corners of the
globe.[1] These systems have come to be the principal domestic undertaking

Many thanks to colleagues who have read and commented on earlier versions of this essay, including
those at the initial "Remaking Modernity" conference held at Northwestern University in spring 2001
and those at the August 2003 meeting of the International Sociological Association's Research Committee 19 on Poverty, Social Welfare, and Social Policy. I am grateful to the alleged *apparatchiks* for
reminding me of the constructed nature of the line between "state discourse" and "social science." Lis
Clemens, Lynne Haney, Alain Noel, and Rianne Mahon offered especially useful critiques and suggestions. Julia Adams was more than a co-editor: she read countless versions of the draft (and particularly
difficult paragraphs, relayed back and forth over e-mail); made insightful comments; and offered
helpful rewordings, citations, and arguments, all the while convincing me that this essay could indeed
be written under unusual circumstances. (The curious may ask me in person about the roast pig, the
printer that is "just like a woman," and how I worked under the sign of *torno subito*.) I am grateful to
the Weinberg College of Arts and Sciences at Northwestern University for support of a sabbatical
leave, during which I wrote this essay.
1. Outside the developed world, however, the proportions of the population covered are quite small,

of states in the West—and after World War II have trumped even military operations (in terms of spending), except in the United States. Social provision has centrally defined the relations among states, capital, and labor (the "social partners" in Euro-lingo) and between states and citizens/subjects, and it has been critical to the viability of markets and the reproduction of populations. It is essential to the constitution of politically salient groups, identities, and goals and of moral and cultural orders. Systems of state social provision and regulation are quintessentially modern in their linkage with capitalist industrial orders and the emergence and regulation of the realm of "the social."

Social scientists, including sociologists at the end of the nineteenth and the beginning of the twentieth centuries, were deeply concerned with the "social question." The question grew out of elites' difficulties in maintaining social integration and order as growing urban working classes emerged as political actors in the context of increasing democracy and the development of new forms of risk and inequality. The character of social provision was significant, for these developments emerged in a context in which accepting relief implied a loss of citizenship rights—a situation understood to contribute to workers' unrest (Orloff 1993b: chs. 4–5). Indeed, sociology as an academic discipline developed alongside the social question and its successors (e.g., the "urban crisis" of the 1960s or the "welfare mess" of the 1980s in the United States; see, e.g., Steinmetz, this volume). The varied answers to the social question, which centrally involved social insurance, pensions, other forms of assistance, and novel forms of state regulation, depended on the new knowledges produced by the social sciences (see, e.g., Burchell, Gordon, and Miller, eds. 1991; Horn 1994; Rueschemeyer and Skocpol, eds. 1996). Systems of social provision and regulation have been an enduring focus of social scientific scholarship ever since.

Social science scholarship on these systems has been in two not altogether separate veins. First, there is scholarship directed at helping states "regulate the social" through analyses of social problems and policy. Some of this work bears the stamp of the research *apparatchik*; some of it has far greater intellectual legitimacy, even if it is often more directly political than work produced for academic audiences.[2] However, I will not here cover the vast

---

usually limited to civil servants and, sometimes, members of urbanized working and middle classes. As industrialization proceeds, economies grow, and the model of state modernity spreads, social security expands, as has been the case in East Asia and Latin America—evidence that earlier theories of the expansion of social provision on the "logic of industrialism" (Wilensky 2002) were not entirely incorrect, even as they must be modified to encompass the political and cultural concomitants of modernity.

2. See historian Alice O'Connor's brilliant dissection of the production of "poverty knowledge" (the title of her 2001 book) in twentieth-century America. She makes clear that the ways "poverty knowl-

bodies of information produced by social scientists in the direct employ of the state or working in the closely related government-funded university research projects; these might be best understood as varieties of state discourse. Second, there is scholarship—including that by historical sociologists—that aims to understand the relations among capitalism, modernity, and systems of social provision and regulation; the contributions of welfare to relations of power, difference, and inequality; and the character of modern institutions. It is this latter work that most interests me. My central focus is on U.S. historical sociologists and the ways in which second-wave debates have given way to potential third-wave challenges and new theoretical controversies, but no survey of this field can afford to ignore the contributions of historical-institutionalist political scientists or scholars from outside of the United States.

For many years—even before being formalized in modernization theories—changes in the character of social provision were seen as part and parcel of the development of "modern" capitalist societies. Responsibilities for social protection were seen to have shifted from families and communities to the national state. This occurred alongside a shift away from deterrent and punitive poor relief toward social protections as rights of citizenship that took the form of what was then thought to be an ever-widening and linked set of provisions that came to be called the "welfare state" in the post–World War II era.[3] This was captured in book titles such as *From Poor Law to Welfare State* (Trattner 1999 [1974]). The story differed somewhat in accounts influenced by Marxism, in that these shifts were seen as the products of class struggle. But the progressive cast of the story was similar, with a similar end point: social citizenship and greater material equality, even if these were understood as a "ransom from capital" to maintain social stability and economic productivity. It was expected that all countries would eventually wind up with a "complete" set of programs to deal with social risks, because welfare states were seen to be essential features of modern democratic capitalism. There were also distinctive national subplots: the United States as welfare laggard (e.g., Rimlinger 1971) or the egalitarian

---

edge" so often functions to reinforce the policy status quo have little to do with the intentions of the rank and file researchers in the projects of state bureaucracies and much more to do with the political constraints under which their scholarship must be produced. A key theme of her book is the way in which the demands for "scientific" standards from funding agencies reinforced tendencies for individualist explanations of poverty.

3. Deterrent and local forms of social assistance were dominant in the early years of capitalist industrialization. They have diminished in importance relative to contributory social insurance or universal benefits, yet they remain (variably) significant components of social provision everywhere (Eardley et al. 1996a, 1996b). Modernization analyses have tended to construe these as "remnants" of "traditional" provision that would eventually disappear. No sign of this as yet.

Swedish welfare state helping to lay the foundations for socialism, for example (e.g., Stephens 1979).

Things began to change after the 1970s, with various political attacks on core programs of social provision and more or less serious policy changes, variously described as dismantling or restructuring welfare states (e.g., Pierson 1994; Huber and Stephens 2001). The overarching progressive story has been unraveled and replaced by a more complex story of uneven changes. After decades of a belief in the irreversibility of welfare states, a host of political, economic, and social trends shook this assumption: the emergence of neo-liberalism and the elections of "anti-welfare warriors" Margaret Thatcher and Ronald Reagan; the fall of "actually existing socialism" and its extensive systems of paternalist-authoritarian social protection; and the rise of newly industrializing states whose competitive economic advantage stemmed in part from lower social spending. Moreover, the factors that had been traditionally associated with the emergence of modern welfare states also have been profoundly changed, as we see the expansion of service sectors and the decline of manufacturing; the decline of breadwinner/full-time caregiver marriage-based households and the increase of nonmarital births and single-person and dual-earner households; and expanded capital mobility and concomitant concerns about employers' increased capacities to demand lower taxes and social spending. This progressive story was not undermined only by events, of course. Theoretical developments have been important as well. Many accounts of welfare states and social provision feature "new" actors (new to social scientists, that is)—women and men (as gendered persons), Whites and Blacks, natives and immigrants, pronatalists and eugenicists, and so on—in addition to workers, capitalists, and political elites; for some of these actors the story of progressive expansion does not hold even for the period before the "crises." Attention to discourse and culture has increased. And less benign visions of social policy have emerged: Piven and Cloward (1971) famously proclaimed that welfare was directed at "regulating the poor," while a Foucauldian strain of work emphasized darker (if still "productive") aspects of social policy: bio-politics, surveillance, discipline, classification.

This essay provides an overview of the theoretical battles that have raged across the terrain of modern systems of social provision and regulation—the "modern welfare state." I will make the case that we could use some fraternization (that is, greater theoretical complexity) across the battle lines and that feminist work provides an admirable example of theoretical hybridity, drawing on the significant theoretical resources associated with Weberian, Foucauldian, culturalist, and Marxist analytic traditions. I also argue that we need to exorcise more fully the spirits I take the liberty of associating with

Marx—particularly those of social determination—which live on in this area of scholarship, but today, as a mostly unacknowledged presence.

Hovering over the theoretical debates around modern welfare systems—something like the Heavenly Father in Veronese's paintings of Venice's battles with its foes—is the spirit of Marx, whose vision of industrial capitalism and its social conflicts informs many accounts of modern social provision (including those reacting against Marxism). But rather than sticking to Marxist doctrine about class struggles and the state, it would be preferable to historicize the Marxist (and socialist) elements that have shaped the development of modern systems of social provision.[4] Marxist influences abound, for it was Marxism in its political guises—the "spectre haunting Europe"—that was one of the most important forces shaping developments of modern social provision and regulation. Indeed, one can read the development of the modern welfare state as "socialism by other means" or as reform functioning as the alternative to revolution. Early working-class movements inspired by Marxist and other forms of socialism worried elites, some of whom turned to social policy to deter revolution. More mature movements staked their political fortunes on expanding social provision for their constituents. For Western political elites, the Soviet bloc with its full employment and extensive welfare provision was to be combated by the welfare state along with the military means of the cold war. Weber's spirit appears as well, guiding our understandings of the development of state bureaucracies and, at times, the cultural dispositions that guide our experiences of capitalism and risk. More recently, the dark jester of modern social

---

4. In the course of circulating earlier drafts of this essay to colleagues who, like me, were "brought up" intellectually in a Marxist context—or at least in one heavily influenced by Marxism—I was told more than once that I was being "too hard" on Marx. After all, Marxism is multifaceted, encompassing, for example, on the subject of ideology, not only clunky Lukacsian social determinism, but also sophisticated Gramscian indeterminism. Now, I will admit that I like Gramsci as much as the next woman, but I am too unsettled by the demise of "actually existing" socialism and relevations about the grave defects to which it gave rise—yes, in the land where my grandmother and her sisters fought for the October Revolution and in the lands where others fought the good fight against fascism—to ever be comfortable again in invoking Marx without a slew of qualifications. In particular, the ongoing revelations (pioneered, of course, by dissidents before the "fall") of how state power was corrupted to serve foul ends mandate—at the least—caution before we accept Marxist accounts of politics, including social politics. "Exorcism" of intellectual spirits strikes me as a rather mild form of de-Marxification. No doubt others have come to question Marxism via other, perhaps more exclusively theoretical/analytical, routes; I have found these compelling as well. Like David Stark and Laszlo Bruszt (2001) in the recent debate over sociological theory and the end of communism, I believe that Marxism's monopoly on critical theory has been decisively broken; like Eyal, Szelényi, and Townsley (2001) in that same volume, I would argue for an "immanent critique" of capitalisms (and "their" welfare states). For a somewhat different take on these theoretical dilemmas, see Nancy Fraser's wittily titled *Justice Interruptus* (1997).

theory—Michel Foucault—has come to haunt the field. His followers scoff at the Enlightenment modernism of the Weberian variety while allowing the *Marxisant* vision of elites and populace, now discipliners and disciplined, to remain, still hoping for "resistance," if not revolution. Culturalist approaches to politics have emerged across a range of arenas, offering non-materialist understandings of the formation of identities and goals and the mobilization of actors. But the stolid mainstream studies of pensions, workers' health insurance funds, and welfare bureaucracies continue, almost unaffected by these developments in the "superstructure." The dominant perspectives in the field—most now identifiable as institutionalist—mix different portions of Marx and Weber, sticking fairly closely to a materialist understanding of politics; among more marginal approaches, we find those who take their Foucault more or less straight, as well as those with a range of culturalist understandings. This field would benefit from some theoretical hybridization, partly because it offers a way to break more fully with materialism, but also because there are insights to be gleaned from both mainstream and more marginal perspectives. Feminist work provides a model of productive hybridity.

Feminists are gathered under diverse theoretical banners to disrupt the masculinist stories of welfare states as involving only capitalists, bureaucrats, and workers (gender unmarked but clearly men, whether wearing suits or overalls) or the similarly masculinist if otherwise more perverse narratives of the Foucauldians. If one must pick one theorizing woman to guide us, let it be Simone de Beauvoir, who famously avowed that "one is not born, but rather becomes, a woman" and whose analyses ushered in the fertile outpouring of feminist scholarship on the social (and political) construction of gender that has nourished scholars of welfare, along with many others.[5] Gender scholars have raided many theoretical armories to fight their battles and to develop understandings of how gender, class, "race," and other forms of inequality, difference, and power are implicated in the developments that have given us modern welfare states and how in turn those relations are shaped by—indeed constituted with—welfare systems.[6] Their approaches have tended to take culture and signification more seriously than have mainstream perspectives, while they are simultaneously more attuned to the

5. Using de Beauvoir as a signifier for feminist work on welfare states is more than a little ironic, given that her theoretical contribution was in the construction of gender and not at all around the labor, emotions, or political claims associated with care, which has been a hallmark of many gendered analyses of systems of social provision and regulation.

6. I here employ the convention of putting scare quotes around race to indicate that racial groups are social constructions, not biological entities; this should be understood whenever race is invoked in the rest of the essay.

classic issues of political economy, family, and state than are many culturalists and Foucauldians (feminist or not). Yet while such theoretical cross-
breeding might be useful, it is hard to imagine that all of the institutionalist
mainstream, especially those drawing ever closer to rational choice perspectives, will take this up. But for those willing to listen, I offer this narrative,
animated by hopes for hybridity, or at least tolerance.

Defining the Modern Welfare State

Before we enter the story of the various theoretical debates that make up the
literatures on modern welfare systems, I want for a moment to consider the
object of our study, "the modern welfare state"—how it has been variously
defined and what problems attend to the possible alternative definitions.
Among many U.S. comparative and historical sociologists, the term "welfare
state" has functioned as an accepted, if often anachronistic, shorthand for
systems of social provision in the developed capitalist world (and sometimes
even beyond). A typical definition of the welfare state was "a state commitment of some degree which modifies the play of market forces in the attempt
to achieve a greater measure of social equality" (Ruggie 1984: 11). Modernization theorists took for granted the political claim embedded in the very term
"welfare state": that states were committed to citizens' welfare. More politically critical Marxists and others might not accept that claim but still tended
to view the welfare state as a more or less unified project of state and
bourgeois elites to secure their rule by extending material benefits to the less
advantaged, notwithstanding claims about the contradictory demands of
legitimacy and accumulation. Yet this would seem to accept what should be
proven—that social provision results in something that can legitimately be
called "welfare." Even if one does not wholeheartedly endorse the Foucauldian or social control visions of welfare, these analysts have unearthed material that undermines any easy or unmodified acceptance of the modernist,
progressive view of welfare—for example, the eugenicist policies that accompanied positive welfare in almost every Western country (yes, even Sweden).

Perhaps as troubling is the inattention to the historical and national
specificity of the term "welfare state." The shorthand may be convenient, but
it occludes the significant cross-national and historical variation in the
meaning attached to and the content of the various programs that scholars
today group together as welfare states. The British coined the phrase "welfare
state" in 1939 to counterpose the Nazi "warfare state," grouping under this
umbrella several heretofore separate social insurance, social assistance, and
universal citizenship programs (R. Williams 1976). Following the defeat of
fascism, Britain and most other European countries reformed and expanded

their systems of social provision in the direction of universal coverage for workers; at the same time, social provision was articulated with the political goal of "equality," understood in class terms, in the concept of a welfare state (see, e.g., Esping-Andersen 1990, 1999; Huber and Stephens 2001; Korpi 1978). The modernism, statism, and progressivism of the term are apparent. The gendered aspects of this articulation are also now clear; social insurance covered workers, who were mostly men, with spousal coverage for most women; protection focused on loss of income, not care (J. Lewis 1992; Sassoon, ed. 1987; for the Swedish [partial] exception, see J. Lewis and Åstrom 1992). Even after the long Thatcherite attack, the "welfare state" still has resonance in the United Kingdom, while Western Europeans define themselves partly through their attachment to the welfare state: "social Europe" or the "European social model" (Hemerijk 2002). The term certainly has never had similar resonance in the United States, where "welfare" is politically despised, although "social security"—initiated by Franklin Roosevelt—is still popular (Skocpol 1988a). And before the term "welfare state" gained currency, social analysts, reformers, and politicians referred to "relief," "workingmen's" or social insurance and pensions, or the "social state" (see, e.g., Rubinow 1913). These terms and the systems they referenced reflected different politics, targets of policy, and sets of state activities than do contemporary systems (see, e.g., Steinmetz 1993 on the German case). Even if some of these might eventually have metamorphosed into today's programs, it may be assuming too much to speak of the "origins of the welfare state," and it is certainly misleading to speak of the "early welfare state."

Most analysts of systems of social provision and regulation have studied the origins, historical development, or "crisis" of the welfare state by focusing on a standardized array of programs given quasi-official definition by states and international organizations themselves (e.g., in the United States, *Social Security Programs throughout the World* [U.S. Social Security Administration, Office of Policy 1999] or the publications of the International Labour Organization): old-age and survivors' insurance, disability and sickness insurance, workers' compensation, unemployment insurance, family benefits, social assistance, and, sometimes, maternity insurance and parental leave. Modernization analysts were interested in the relationship between levels of industrialization and "welfare state generosity," the proportions of GNP devoted to social spending—that is, to this standard group of programs (or, even more crudely, to all nonmilitary public spending). Even today some scholars use these measures, while others find the focus on spending inadequate and have instead developed concepts such as de-commodification, social citizenship rights, stratification, extent of public versus private provision, the male breadwinner model, de-familialization, or personal independence (Esping-Andersen 1990: ch. 1; Korpi 2000; J. Lewis 1992; Lister 1997; Julia O'Connor, Orloff, and Shaver 1999: ch. 1; Orloff 1993a). But when these concepts have found their way into empirical analyses, they have almost always been operationalized from data on that same standard array of social programs.

In taking such programs as definitive of "modern welfare," analysts also take on the embedded understandings of what is a "risk" and which risks are legitimately *social*, against which states ought to provide protection. Modernization theorists have assumed that systems of social provision are functional arrangements for dealing with conditions to which all humans are subject—old age, sickness, accident—and that leave them with needs for protection and care that must be solved collectively. Once people are reliant on wages, these problems become understood as risks of income insecurity, and there is a new risk, unemployment; then interest centers on the social programs dealing with those risks: old-age pensions, workers' compensation, unemployment and health insurance, and survivors' insurance. Of course, analysts do not accept even this minimal definition of risks as entirely unproblematic; indeed, the progressive narrative of the development of the welfare state assumes a transition from "traditional" familized or communal ways of dealing with needs to "modern" public and collective means (Baldwin 1990). The more politically oriented scholars of historical sociology's second wave and their successors have seen the extent to which needs and risks are dealt with publicly rather than privately as a reflection of the class (or gender, or other) balance of power (among other things). To some extent, this insight has become embodied in the notion of a "welfare regime," which gained currency in the 1990s; rather than focusing solely on *state* provision, regime analysts examine the interdependent provisioning from states, markets (e.g., employer benefits and private insurance), and families (and sometimes communities) and argue that the institutional location in which different needs are met reflects and in turn influences balances of power. One should also note the gendered dimensions of these definitions: the focus is on cash and risks of losing income because of an inability to find or undertake employment—but not on care or services and risks of losing income because of having to undertake care or due to the dissolution of family relationships that underwrite caregiving.[7]

While mainstream analyses admit an irreducibly *political* component to

7. Feminists have unmasked the ways in which discussion of needs for support on the part of "dependents" often conflates what they have called "inevitable" and "derived" dependency. The former refers to dependency that "flows from the status and situation of being a child, and often accompanies aging, illness or disability," while the latter "flows from the role of caretaker and the need for resources [the] caretaking generates" (Fineman 1995: 162).

defining need and risk, they have been less interested in their (simultaneously) *cultural* or *discursive* constitution. For some analysts, this is genealogical work on the modern system of social provision, its styles of thought, and its (cultural) contribution to capitalism. For example, François Ewald described the emergence of the epistemological transformation—the "philosophy of risk"—that displaces juridical notions of fault and accompanies the birth of social insurance: "Insurance . . . signifies at once an ensemble of institutions and the diagram with which industrial societies conceive their principle of organization, functioning and regulation" (1991: 210; see also Ewald 1986). Morever, there are classificatory processes that bring groups into political being and, further, the political and cultural discursive work through which their "needs," "risks," or possibly "rights" are defined within existing systems of social provision, as in Fraser's (1989) influential analysis. All take the very categories of analysis of the earlier referenced authors as the objects to be explained. For many of these analysts, it is not the welfare state that is the object of scrutiny, but the invention and regulation of "the social," a constitutively modern sphere or "arena located 'between' the economy and state" (Steinmetz 1993: 55) or "that modern domain of knowledge and intervention carved out by statistics, sociology, social hygiene and social work" (Horn 1994: 4). This invention is constitutive of modern capitalism rather than its functional byproduct or the effect of the class politics it spawns. And the welfare state became a primary mode of regulating this sphere in the twentieth century (although whether it will continue is at least open to question).

In this essay, when making general references, I will use the phrase "systems of social provision and regulation" rather than "welfare states." I include "regulation" as well as "provision" to underline that benefits are never delivered without some sort of discipline, regulation, or categorization. But where one could make a reasonable claim that welfare states—states responding to the claims by citizens and denizens for protection against some of the risks of modern industrial and family life—do exist, I will use the term. And where I am describing theoretical perspectives that do not focus on regulatory issues, I will refer simply to work on "systems of social provision or protection." Finally, for variety and simplicity, I will sometimes allow myself the shorthand terms "welfare," "welfare regime," or "welfare systems."

Explaining State Social Provision and Regulation

Scholarship on modern social provision surely ranks as one of the success stories of historical sociology of the second wave and beyond. This work exemplifies the advances of the second wave and its friendly institutionalist successors in establishing that "politics matters," historicizing accounts of social provision, giving greater attention to political processes and to states, and producing richer and less economistic understandings of interests, goals, and identities. Analyses of systems of social provision and regulation were not a theme of the classical theorists of the first wave (welfare states were not yet invented).[8] However, they have been a major battleground in several major scholarly controversies involving historical sociologists since the 1970s: between modernization theorists and scholars interested in conflictual politics; between researchers in the "society-centered" power resources tradition and "state-centered" scholars; between institutionalists and ahistorical rational choicers (more prominent among political scientists than sociologists); and within the research community of institutionalists and advocates of power resources theory, between those who do and do not incorporate gender into their analyses. Some nationally based narratives have been substantially altered in part due to the work of historical sociologists: a signal achievement here is the recasting of the U.S. narrative, recognizing its lead in early-twentieth-century "maternalist" social politics and provision even as its adoption of protections for workingmen took place later than in other industrializing countries. The gendered theme has also been pushed forward in studies of postwar welfare regimes and has contributed to the reorientation of mainstream scholarship to incorporate relations among states, markets, and families in examining work, fertility, and politics. In addition, one can point to a historicizing transformation of the whole field of scholarship on social provision and regulation. The dominant paradigms in the field make historical arguments about the influence of factors such as class coalitions, patterns of partisan dominance, state structures, and policy legacies on past and contemporary social politics and policies (for an excellent literature review, see Myles and Quadagno 2002). Some analysts explicitly invoke the language of path dependency, but the historical move is even more widespread.

In tracing the lineage of contemporary debates, we should note the different statuses of the contending intellectual currents. The second-wave historical sociologists were not displaced as the dominant forces within the

8. The classical sociologists did not develop theoretical interpretations of the legislation and programs now understood as precursors of modern welfare states. Indeed, Marx's famously ambiguous musings on the state or on the passage of factory legislation—which he saw as a kind of functional necessity for capitalist society—helped to give rise to wildly divergent orientations among neo-Marxists writing on the capitalist state in the 1970s and 1980s. Marx, suitably revised, was also a key resource for theorizing reformist social democratic projects. Weber advocated certain types of protective labor legislation while opposing Bismarck's paternalistic approach, but he did not theorize social protection (Steinmetz 1993: 23). Neo-Weberians have drawn on his more general insights about bureaucracy, war, and rationality for accounts of social policy developments.

field; rather, their new intellectual formation—institutionalism—became the new core of scholarship on welfare states and other systems of social provision. Feminists, those taking the cultural or discursive turn, and scholars arguing for the significance of race, ethnicity, or nation are challengers whose work has been taken more or less seriously by the institutionalist mainstream. And in this field of scholarship, one also sees the continuing deficiencies of institutionalism, even at its historicized, processual best: utilitarian assumptions about interests and identities; a focus on the political economy to the exclusion of other social arenas; a thin understanding of how culture shapes politics; and exclusions of the sexual, racial, ethnic, and national elements in welfare even as some limited headway has been made with respect to gender. Feminist scholars have introduced questions about informal labor, care, dependency, dominance, and bodies into work on welfare. But to the extent that work on gender has penetrated the mainstream, it has been on materialist grounds and on the terrain of work rather than dominance, bodies, or sexuality. And while continuing to resist analysis of race and nation, work on welfare systems is spreading beyond the (West) European–white settler society core to Latin America, post-socialist Eastern Europe and Asia, and East Asia, and the ways in which the multifaceted phenomenon of "globalization" shapes contemporary welfare have attracted a good deal of attention (see, e.g., Esping-Andersen, ed. 1996; Gough 1999; Pierson 2001; Pierson, ed. 2001; Scharpf and Schmidt, eds. 2000; J. B. Williamson and Pampel 1993).

Culturist or disciplinary examinations of social provision have been in a quite separate intellectual space, identifying a different object of study, utilizing different analytic strategies than the mainstream, and locating their work on the broader terrain of culture and politics or governmentality rather than on the ground of the welfare state *tout court*. (This may have contributed to lessening their impact on mainstream scholarship, although I believe it is more a case of mutual intellectual incompatibility.) Many scholars influenced by the cultural turns have shown how discourses about the poor, paupers, workers, the unemployed, teenage mothers, and other problematized categories shape social welfare practices and social policies (e.g., Fraser 1989; Haney 1996, 2002; J. Mohr 1994; J. Mohr and Duquenne 1997; Steinmetz 1993; historical anthropologist Ann Stoler 2002a takes up these issues in the colonial context).[9] The shift from sovereignty to governmen-

---

9. World systems analysts in the John Meyer school take the spread of social security programs to all corners of the globe, often in purely formal terms, as evidence of cultural diffusion of the emblems of modernity and modern states, but they show little interest in the power of categorization or the capillaries of power that have intrigued Foucauldians.

tality and associated changes in the character of power, with the emergence of surveillance, "biopolitics," and population as targets of state activities, have fascinated Foucauldians. Sometimes these are associated with the "welfare state" but more often with the regulatory or supervisory professional practices occurring on its outskirts (see Burchell, Gordon, and Miller, eds. 1991; Horn 1994). Historical sociologists have probed the interface of practices, discourses, and institutions of welfare provision and the regulation of various deviant categories of individuals, as in David Garland's (1985) work on nineteenth-century Britain or John Sutton's (1988) examination of the emergence of juvenile courts and "justice" in early-twentieth-century America. But Ewald, Foucault's intellectual and professional heir, did subject the emergence of *l'état providence* (in France, at least) to a fully Foucauldian analysis, arguing that the invention of the social, and of insurance as technique and discourse for regulating it, was constitutive of capitalist modernity; as Colin Gordon described it, "capitalism's Faustian daring depends on this capacity [of insurance] of taking the risk out of risk" (1991: 39). This may be. But these intriguing insights are lost for the mainstream when they cannot be (or are not) connected to the Marxist-Weberian apparatus of welfare states.

The culturalist challenge has mainly been ignored, even as institutionalism has accepted a greater role for "ideas" and the role of interpretation in the development of identities and interests.[10] Institutionalists continue to neglect the deeper cultural foundations of social provision—such as the perceived racial and religious homogeneity of the Scandinavian welfare meccas in their "golden age" or, indeed, rationality and risk themselves. Some mainstream analysts argue that these matters can be taken as settled for the purposes of their studies (e.g., Baldwin 1990: 12 n. 10) or simply carry on as if they did not matter. Yet one might well doubt the fixity of categories of risk, the status of citizenship, and citizen claims based on even a cursory familiarity with contemporary political debates about immigration, Islam, and the (Christian) religious and (homogeneously white European) ethnic basis of the welfare states of Europe or their counterparts in the United States and other settler societies (where ethnic, racial, and religious diversity has a different status) (F. Williams 1995; Yuval-Davis 1997). But while this potentially unsettling message falls on deaf ears in some corners of the field, culturalist and discursive perspectives are influencing feminist work in productive ways, a subject to which I return below.

---

10. This interest in the role of "ideas" or "policy paradigms" is stronger in political science institutionalism than in sociological versions, where broader conceptions of culture and discourse are more likely to be invoked.

Historical sociologists of the second wave first entered the fray about welfare states in the late 1970s and 1980s, when apolitical modernization approaches focusing on the "needs" of "society" held sway, countered by a naive pluralism or a radical structural Marxism that focused on the "needs" of "capital." With allies among other political sociologists and political scientists, they dismantled modernization accounts thoroughly, showing that social policy developments have not been "automatic" responses to social change, nor have they followed a progressive line of development. Politics matters for the character of social provision in modern societies but in ways not fully captured by pluralism. They also argued against the structuralist Marxist account, along lines similar to their anti-modernization critique—especially in stressing politics and variation among capitalist countries. But they took structuralist Marxism more seriously than modernization theory—they were, after all, more or less on the same side of the intellectual and political barricades of the time—and also took for granted the "structural" and "instrumental" power of capital and capitalists. And Marxism still defined the puzzles they were trying to solve.

Second-wave historical sociologists were joined by others who were as critical of the welfare state itself as of social science accounts of it. For example, Piven and Cloward's (1971, 1977) influential analyses held that social provision "regulates the poor" in the interests of capital and political elites, although there are transitory moments—ushered in by "poor people's movements"—when the poor could get something from the state.[11] More important to a later generation of historical sociologists taking the cultural turn were the works of Michel Foucault and his followers, first appearing in the 1970s. These offered a much darker vision of what welfare represented, linking welfare with the penal system (Garland 1985), other disciplinary technologies, and a eugenic concern with population. However, Foucauldians and their fellow travelers have remained at odds with the institutionalist successors to the second wave. For while second wavers, institutionalists, and power resources analysts recognized that systems of social provision were initially created by political elites with the interests of business and state in mind, they have stressed the post–World War II face of welfare as also a

---

11. Piven and Cloward focused on English poor relief and U.S. welfare (AFDC, or Aid to Families with Dependent Children) rather than the social insurance programs targeting employed workers that interested other analysts, especially in Europe. Their view can be understood as reflecting the peculiarities of U.S. politics and social policy, but it has been extended by some to refer to the social control aspect of all welfare systems. They were not historical sociologists in the vein of the second wave, for they used historical materials illustratively rather than to assess alternative explanatory claims; indeed, their argument that state social spending expands and contracts in response to the rise and fall of popular disruption was more directly derived from 1960s welfare rights politics.

significant social right of citizenship, an accomplishment of social democratic politics, and a link to greater class equality and social protection.[12] In short, they held to a modernist and progressive vision, however qualified. The second wavers battled modernization theory and quasi-functionalist Marxist accounts, but it was not because they saw welfare states in anti-Enlightenment terms.

One could tell the story of these developments in a number of ways. I will tell it as I now understand my experiences of living through it, beginning my narrative with the second wave (where I began my scholarly career), then moving to its institutionalist successors, and finally to some of its more successful critics—the feminists (among whom I am now spending time), who are creating a channel through which discursive and culturalist work may yet reshape the mainstream. I close with some brief thoughts about other challenging intellectual currents that have appeared in the field of welfare state studies.

The key debates of the second wave around welfare states took off from Marxist theories of *the* state, which posited that social policies would ultimately be functional for capitalism, if only by preventing revolution, and which assumed that capitalist states were fundamentally similar. This did not mean that the state was literally the "executive committee of the bourgeoisie," for Marxists also believed in the "relative autonomy of the state," which allowed "state managers" to act against the explicit preferences of capitalists in order to pursue the long-range interests of capitalism. The autonomy, however, was always "relative," for state managers would always ultimately be limited by structural constraints: the need to respond to the demands of legitimation and accumulation faced by all capitalist states. (The canonical texts cited for these positions are Gough 1979, James O'Connor 1973, and Offe 1984; the view, however, was widespread.) Structuralist Marxists posed welfare as a functional but contradictory and crisis-engendering solution to these demands; welfare bought off popular unrest, thereby securing legitimacy. It also promoted capitalist accumulation and the commodification of labor by ensuring labor force stability and productivity when welfare programs siphoned off unproductive workers and demanded discipline and steady work histories for entitlement. But it was expensive, triggering fiscal crises, or, if cheaper but inadequate, legitimacy crises (for a

12. A number of recent studies in political science have stressed the role of business elites and firms in creating economic coordination and social policies that under certain circumstances—such as those obtaining in Sweden or much of continental Europe—might result in more egalitarian outcomes than has been the case where the market is less constrained (e.g., the United States) (P. A. Hall and Soskice, eds. 2001; Swenson 2002). Welfare states are still seen as progressive accomplishments, even if the actors responsible are different from those identified in the social democratic model.

review of the literature on fiscal crisis, see Block 1981). In these accounts, "crises" were more or less constant, or at least imminent, but in the meantime, critique of welfare was a necessary exercise of demystification.

These highly general and abstract Marxist accounts could not easily deal with the multiplicity of social policy profiles to be seen across the advanced capitalist world (see, e.g., Block 1986; Skocpol 1980); why, for example, did Sweden's workers demand so much higher a proportion of state spending than America's to secure their (presumed) docility? Nor were these theories of much use in explaining instances of policymaking that seemed to go against the interests of capital, such as the Wagner Act, which empowered U.S. unionists to organize with some state protection. And what allowed state managers to be so much more farsighted than the capitalists in whose ultimate interests they toiled? What political mechanism (as opposed to logically induced necessity) actually guaranteed that state managers would not transgress the limits set by accumulation and legitimation? The problem of the state's "relative" or "potential" autonomy—a problem that made sense only within the Marxists' theoretical frame, which still animated the second wavers even as they attacked it—inspired a debate between so-called society-centered (social democratic or "power resources") theories and state-centered (neo-Weberian, later "institutionalist") analyses about the role of the state in social policy developments. The former drew upon a social democratic reading of Marx, augmented by Karl Polanyi and T. H. Marshall; the latter mixed their Marx with large doses of Weber, Tocqueville, and a dash of Hintze.

Walter Korpi, John Stephens, John Myles, and Gøsta Esping-Andersen, the intellectual progenitors of the power resources or social democratic approach, first mobilized to take on structuralist Marxism and political Leninism, which assumed that welfare states "serve capitalist interests" and that social democracy is just a "milder version of capitalist politics as usual" (Esping-Andersen 1985: xiii; see also Korpi 1978, 1989; Myles 1984; Stephens 1979; key texts of this analytic school and their critics are in Julia O'Connor and Olsen, eds. 1998). For these analysts, the potential for state autonomy *from capital* was critical, but full autonomy would be problematic; they asserted that parliaments could control states, for workers through social democratic parties could win control of parliaments, then progress down the parliamentary road to socialism. They drew on the social democratic traditions of Marxism—Bernstein, Kautsky, the Austro-Marxists, and contemporary Scandinavian social democrats—along with T. H. Marshall and Karl Polanyi, iconoclastic scholars writing in mid-century Britain about the development of citizenship, the embeddedness of markets, and the need for social protection. Polanyi (1957c [1944]) was critical in revealing the centrality of the commodification of labor to the functioning of capitalist markets while simultaneously insisting on the social embeddedness of the market, which is self-regulating only in the fantasies of economists and ideological liberals. Social provision—partly in the form of what Esping-Andersen would later call "de-commodifying" benefits—was necessary for "society" to protect itself from the market, even as the inherent tensions between the two would continue to influence politics (see also Block and Somers 1984). T. H. Marshall (1950) was called upon for his account of the historical development of citizenship rights, in which he argued that political rights (e.g., suffrage, rights to organize) could be used to claim social rights, which offer protections against the market. Thus, welfare states reveal the possibilities of "politics against markets": social rights, won by workers in the democratic arena, work to counter capitalist economic power and—most important— affect the very character of the class structure, augmenting the power resources available to workers, who then push for even greater concessions— perhaps on into socialism. As Esping-Andersen put it, the "ultimate instrument of social democratic class formation . . . is state policy" (1985: 33). Here is one key source for the institutionalist approach to social politics, showing the constitutive role of state policy.

Led by Theda Skocpol, the state-centered analysts—of whom I was one— broke with neo-Marxist views about the relative—that is, ultimately limited—autonomy of the state and about the sources of group formation, using welfare states as a proving ground. As we note in the introduction, Skocpol's 1980 article on the New Deal and neo-Marxist theories of the state was a key switching point in the second wave, ushering in work on critical political junctures and the patterns of social policy development without relying on teleological Marxism.[13] Following on the heels of *States and Social Revolutions* (Skocpol 1979), this work established Weberian- and Tocquevillian-inspired scholarship on states—with welfare states taking center stage—as a contender with academic Marxism or social democratic approaches. (Much of this literature, along with contending perspectives, is reviewed in Skocpol and Amenta 1986; Orloff 1993b: chs. 1–2; and Weir, Orloff, and Skocpol, eds. 1988: ch. 1.) It was not only the possibility for state policy to break with capitalist preferences or the "structural prerequisites" of capitalism that interested us, although we tried to examine this question empirically. We could agree with the social democratic analysts that under some circumstances, working-class political forces might well affect policy developments,

13. See Fred Block's (1987) classic essays on relative autonomy, state managers, and "the ruling class that does not rule" for a similar break with functionalist tendencies that remained within the Marxist framework.

but we viewed their understanding of political possibilities as too narrow and economistic. Rather, we looked at the ways in which state elites might pursue projects beyond any suggested by "social" actors (that is, actors "outside" the state). State and other political elites, we argued, were not only situated with respect to domestic class structures, but also participated in transnational networks, considered the geopolitical situation, and worried about electoral and organizational issues. They were influenced by the organizational or fiscal capacities and structures of the state: an institutional mediation of political strategizing. (This opening to geopolitical or "global" concerns has yet to be exploited fully.) We broke with economistic, socially determinist accounts of the formation of collective political actors by examining what we would now call the institutional constitution of actors—that is, the ways states influenced patterns of group formation, including interests and political identities. All of this provided an opening to considering different kinds of politics not based on class—those of fraternal orders, religious groups, feminists or "maternalists," and so on. Considerations of culture were not too far away.

The state-centered attack engendered its own critique from those who would bring "class" or "society" "back in" or from those who had remained steadfastly convinced of the explanatory power of U.S. business interests (e.g., Domhoff 1996). Many historical sociologists insisted on the efficacy of capitalists' or, less often, workers' political efforts vis-à-vis U.S. social (and labor) policy, usually turning to different elements of the New Deal policy arena to prove their points (Manza 2000 provides a review; see also Gilbert and Howe 1991; C. J. Jenkins and Brents 1989). Quadagno (1988) offered an intriguing explanation for U.S. policy developments that relied partly on the power of capital but even more significantly on the institutionally mediated and historically changing role of white Southern planter elites. Yet many single-case studies made no use of historical or comparative variation to check their explanations of policy developments (Amenta 1998; Orloff 1993b); other institutionalist accounts challenged their interpretations (see, e.g., Finegold and Skocpol 1995; Hooks 1990a). Ultimately, however, the charges and countercharges could not be resolved on the ground of the New Deal alone.

Scholars in the power resources group struck back, emphasizing the determinative significance of social democratic partisan strength in shaping welfare outcomes and the limits imposed on state officials by the "societal power structure" (Korpi 1989: 324). Many critics and reviewers used specifications of the key premises of the state-centered approach that were inadequate at best, misleading at worst. Often, it boiled down to a public-choice-style set of assumptions, including that "number of bureaucrats" that tapped our construct of "state autonomy," since increasing their own numbers allegedly represented state elites' core interests. In other instances, the state-centered approach was caricatured as arguing that the state *is* autonomous and powerful, rather than that this is one potential. Of course, I would argue that the key insights encompassed both potential autonomy and the structuring role of states (autonomous or not). Luckily, institutionalism soon brought a more sophisticated understanding of states and other political institutions shaping policy while moving beyond debates about state autonomy that were unlikely ever to yield to empirical resolution.

Institutionalism built on the intellectual innovations of second-wave analysis, particularly the break from economic determinism to a broader social and political terrain. At least implicitly responding to critiques of their work as lacking attention to process and agency, in the late 1980s and early 1990s leading second-wave scholars of social provision developed new lines of research that foregrounded the development of social policy over time and the activities of political actors, contributing to historically contingent outcomes. The shift from the state-centered and society-centered perspectives of the second wave to institutionalism occurred against the backdrop of the intellectual decline of paradigms inspired by Marxism and the political demise of socialism after 1989. As Marxism lost force, the animating spark for the debates around state autonomy was also extinguished. Moreover, both sides relaxed the weakest parts of their arguments. State-centered scholars first moved to the terminology of "political institutionalism" in order to make clear our analytical interest in the whole range of political institutions (not just the state) and to legislate against misreadings of the perspective as being opposed to the influence of "social" factors. The society-centered group admitted the structuring and mediating influence of the state and other political institutions on class actors (while remaining recalcitrant—or steadfast—on the subject of potential state autonomy). Both sides could meet on "institutionalist" ground, the Tocquevillian issues of the institutional constitution of political actors, identities, and interests and the variable conditions for successful institutional innovation or stability. Furthermore, different foes were emerging—neo-liberalism politically (from the Thatcher and Reagan elections of 1979 and 1980) and (certain varieties of) rational choice intellectually. Here, the debates pitted the former foes (state-centered and society-centered analysts), now friendly cooperators in the institutionalist project, against those assuming exogenous "preferences" and pre-political identities in political "games" seemingly undistorted by power asymmetries.

Institutionalist work on systems of social provision has been particularly strong in two areas: comparative and at least implicitly historical analyses of the modern, Western welfare states, or "regimes," and historical and at least implicitly comparative studies of the development of U.S. social policies, which have overlapped significantly with studies of American political development, largely located in political science. And there have been as well two key intellectual orientations in explaining social policy developments, claiming ancestry from the social democratic/power resources approach and the neo-Weberian or state-centered approach respectively, although—as outlined above—they are less sharply demarcated than in the past. Two spectacularly influential works of the early 1990s, Esping-Andersen (1990) and Skocpol (1992), capture the new institutionalist spirit in these two streams and in the two intellectual idioms. All of this work reflects the interests of politically engaged scholars concerned with social equality, which could no longer be imagined to be reliably guaranteed—much less attained—through revolution; welfare states could be understood as contributing to an evolutionary version of progress toward equality and were linked to the still attractive politics of challenging groups. Yet there was a far broader understanding of those challenger politics. The social democratic/power resources analysts, while retaining a focus on working classes and a basically materialist approach, broke with the notion that their interests could be identified only with socialism; under certain circumstances they might be identified with Christian Democratic or liberal-labor forces. The neo-Weberian institutionalists made a stronger break with class determinism, if not necessarily material determinations, allowing for a very wide range of ways in which identities and political claims may be realized. They all built on the second-wave insight that there were multiple forms of capitalism, exploring the conjunctural and multiple causation involved in distinctive policy and political outcomes. Finally, all have accepted the significance of history for explaining contemporary as well as past developments; this is often referenced in the phrase "policy creates politics" or in the notion of path dependency.

Esping-Andersen's (1990) innovative formulation of "three worlds of welfare capitalism" set the terms for comparative and historical work on the eighteen-plus advanced capitalist democracies, drawing on power resources or social democratic analysis but moving it in identifiably institutionalist directions (see also E. Carroll 1999; Esping-Andersen 1999; Esping-Andersen, ed. 1996; Esping-Andersen et al. 2002; Hicks 1999; Hicks and Misra 1993; Huber, Ragin, and Stephens 1993; Huber and Stephens 2001; Korpi and Palme 1998; Wennemo 1994). Welfare is viewed as varying qualitatively; differences among states are not unilinear—more or less generous, as in older formulations—but configurational.[14] Building on the work of Rich-

---

14. This genre of work on social provision retains a quantitative analytic orientation and has been the site for post-positivist methodological experimentation (e.g., for those using Charles Ragin's Qualita-

ard Titmuss and his own collaborative work with Korpi, Esping-Andersen famously argued that capitalist welfare comes in three distinctive forms or "regime types": liberal, conservative, and social democratic; these reflect the dominant political force in each and feature distinctive profiles of state-society, or public-private, divisions of responsibility for provisioning; stratification; and levels of the de-commodification of labor. The concept of welfare regimes has sometimes given rise to typological arguments, thus continuing the "comparative statics" that characterized much second-wave historical work. But more significant, there are also notions of policy feedback and path dependency, in which policy creates politics—the implicit history of this wing of scholarship on welfare provision—and here regime analysis encourages more processual thinking. Regime types can be seen as distinctive political-institutional opportunity structures, producing historically and nationally specific sets of interests or preferences, identities, and coalitions (and, neo-Weberians would add, administrative capacities) that influence social politics in path-dependent ways. Moreover, the different "worlds of welfare capitalism" are the products of different political-institutional histories, featuring distinctive class coalitions, profiles of partisan dominance, and state structures.

Skocpol's (1992) pathbreaking revisioning of U.S. social provision introduced social scientists to America's "maternalist" reformers and their efforts to develop a maternalist system of social provision for mothers and their children; it further expanded knowledge about America's "precocious" social spending program, Civil War pensions for a large percentage of the late-nineteenth-century nation's elderly men in the North (see also Orloff and Skocpol 1984). The book showed that U.S. patterns differed qualitatively from European ones, rather than being simply a tardy, incomplete version; even while focusing on a single national case, Skocpol located it fully in comparative context. The book reoriented the field in multiple ways, notably in the encouragement given to the institutionalist emphasis on politics as process (especially through "policy feedback").[15] But perhaps most notable

---

tive Comparative Analysis [QCA], see Amenta and Poulsen 1994, 1996; Amenta, Carruthers, and Zylan 1992; Huber, Ragin, and Stephens 1993; Huber and Stephens 2001).

15. Theda Skocpol had consolidated her position as a leading figure in historical sociology's second wave with her work on social provision (e.g., Orloff and Skocpol 1984; Skocpol and Amenta 1985; Skocpol and Ikenberry 1983). The turn to "institutionalism" dates from 1988, with the publication of an edited volume of essays, many by her students, on the politics of social policy in the United States (Weir, Orloff, and Skocpol, eds. 1988). In this volume, we further developed the concept of policy feedback, which has come to be significant in institutionalist accounts of systems of social provision; policy shaped subsequent politics in terms of state capacities, understandings of social problems, and

was the way that gender was brought onto the same analytic ground as class, community, and ethnicity—that is, as a potential basis for the development of identity and political goals, given specific social, cultural, and political-institutional conditions. Skocpol's work on maternalism proved to be inspiring for new generations of historical social scientists and historians (of women) to explore gender issues in welfare (about which, more below). My own work on the comparative politics of pensions (Orloff 1993b) examined the ways in which "needs" were constituted through the lens of ideology and mediated by existing social provision and then were rendered effective politically in historically specific ways, conditional on the particular political-institutional context. Amenta (1998) questioned the dominant understanding of the U.S. system of social provision as ever-lagging and stingy, showing that during the Roosevelt administration, the United States was (briefly) the world leader in social spending and developed a great deal of innovative social policy such as the Works Progress Administration. The institutionalist perspective also found adherents among political scientists examining, for example, the connections among policy ideas, policy feedback, and state capacities in the area of employment (Weir 1992); the dismantling or retrenchment of welfare in a new era of crisis (Pierson 1994); the political sources of ineffectiveness in unemployment policies in the United States and Britain (D. King 1995); the relationship between the "tax state" and the "expenditure state" (C. Howard 1997); the development of a gendered and "divided" citizenship (Mettler 1998); the symbiotic relationship between public and private provision (Hacker 2002); transformations in European welfare states (Ferrera and Rhodes, eds. 2000); the shaping of U.S. social provision by racial inequality (M. Brown 1999; Lieberman 1998); and the critical role of capitalists and firms in the development of alternative models of welfare provision (Swenson 2002; P. A. Hall and Soskice, eds. 2001)—to name only a few.

Investigations of how racial factors led to the underdevelopment of the U.S. system of social provision have assumed greater prominence within institutionalist and political-economic scholarship (Manza 2000; Misra 2002: esp. 28–31; Quadagno 2000). For example, Quadagno (1988, 1994) explored the racial power and racism underlying the Southern political economy and its institutional mediation in Congress and traced the ways in which U.S. welfare was racialized during the period from the New Deal

---

development of constituencies. Policy feedback was joined analytically with state structures and capacities and patterns of democratic political involvements, related to patterns of class formation and mobilization.

through the Great Society (see also M. Brown 1999; Lieberman 1998; Reese 2001). Dorothy Roberts (1993, 1995) showed how the devaluation of African Americans' reproduction was expressed in hostility to Black women's motherwork (a theme also taken up in G. Mink 1998). This work tends to take racial groups as already constituted, then examines how racial hierarchies have been consolidated and restructured through social provision. Some feminst work, discussed below, has been more likely to take a constructionist view of racial (or national) categories, which are understood as simultaneously gendered (e.g., Boris 1995; Glenn 2002; Koven and Michel 1993; G. Lewis 2000; F. Williams 1995).

The fruitful line of institutionalist work continues today, making contributions especially in showing the relevance of historicizing analysis with the concepts of path dependency and policy feedback. It seems clear that the economic difficulties of the 1970s and the political attacks on welfare that followed, most dramatically in the English-speaking world, helped to undermine the progressive story of expanding welfare states that had heretofore held sway. A number of studies have attempted to understand how programs unravel (Hooks 1990a; Reese 2001; Soule and Zylan 1997; Stryker 1989). With reference to the most recent rounds of unraveling, it was soon clear that not all programs were equally vulnerable to attack and that there was a great deal of resilience to modern welfarc states. Paul Pierson (1994) subjected the patterns in the United States and United Kingdom to systematic analysis and concluded that policy had created politics in the sense of creating constituencies that would defend "their" programs from attack. Thus, politicians would engage in "blame avoidance" and stealth politics in order to cut certain programs that, while popular, were tempting targets for budgetary savings or rolling back state activities that offended other important constituencies. Esping-Andersen used his regime analysis for similar purposes: regimes were understood as putting into place distinctive sets of constituencies and interests (anchored to what was referred to as "welfare state stratification"), which then produced distinctive patterns of social politics. Thus, for example, universalistic welfare states such as the social democratic regimes of Scandinavia are seen to give rise to a broader-based popular support than the residual states of the liberal (mainly English-speaking countries') regimes, in which the limited coverage of state protection leaves most citizens dependent on private provision and indifferent if not hostile to state welfare. There is now a thriving literature investigating the resilience—or lack thereof—of welfare states against the threats usually represented as globalization, neo-liberalism, and the associated liberal (or "Anglo-Saxon") model of welfare or some assortment of domestic pressures (e.g., Ferrara and Rhodes, eds. 2000; Huber and Stephens 2001; Kuhnle, ed. 2000; Mishra

1999; Pierson 2000; Scharpf and Schmidt, eds. 2000; Swank 2002; Sykes, Palier, and Prior, eds. 2001).[16]

The phenomenon of policy creating politics has come to be encompassed in the broader concept of path dependency, the idea that once countries begin certain trajectories, there is a kind of "lock in" created by constituencies with interests to defend in the status quo and even increasing returns to established lines of development (Pierson 2000). The concept, while promising in the encouragement it gives to examining the historical origins of modern programs and politics, is hardly above reproach. The Weir, Orloff, and Skocpol, eds. (1988) formulation of policy feedback—an ancestor or cousin of path dependency—insisted on the potential *multivalence* of reactions to past policies; to take only one example, U.S. Civil War pensions certainly created a constituency devoted to defending the program but also produced extreme reluctance on the part of elite reformers to enter into alliances with working-class organizations to enact new social spending programs (see also Skocpol 1992: part 1; Orloff 1993b: chs. 5, 7, 9). Path dependency has too often been interpreted as literally ensuring lock-in, making it difficult to understand disjunctures in policy and politics. Kathleen Thelen (1999) argues that there are limits to analogizing to politics from the technological literature, which is the source of ideas of lock-in and increasing returns; most things political are not contingent at the outset, nor are decisions, once made, protected in perpetuity against recontestation, as losers do not typically disappear. Fiona Ross (2000), among others, documents continuing partisan battles over the course of welfare restructuring; Julia O'Connor, Orloff, and Shaver (1999) highlight partisan differences (linked to different versions of liberal ideologies) within "liberal" regimes with respect to gender policies. And, as Steinmetz points out (this volume), the term "path dependence" obscures the fact that *all* politics (and policies) are dependent on the past, as the past gives us the only materials out of which we make the present.

Institutionalism could become more compelling if scholars address some

16. The embedded nationalistic and racialized thinking that goes into the term "Anglo-Saxon welfare model" has always struck me as ripe for deconstructive analysis. The country that allegedly represents this model best—the United States—is the most racially and ethnically diverse among the developed countries. "Anglo-Saxons," if we accept the term for a moment, do not even represent an ethnic majority among white Americans. Even the United Kingdom, putative ancestral home to "Anglo-Saxons," features much greater heterogeneity than the term allows. Furthermore, what is it about "Anglo-Saxonness" that is thought to be associated with the allegedly stingy welfare systems of the United States and United Kingdom? I expect it would be more productive to investigate the links among levels of ethnic/"racial" heterogeneity, social solidarity, and the character of social provision. Contemporary debates about immigration in Europe offer a new ground on which to examine these issues (see, e.g., G. Lewis 2000; Pred 2000; F. Williams 1995).

continuing problems, particularly the thinness of understandings of culture in the construction of identities and goals and in the very development of the categories of state welfare. The prevailing weakly utilitarian understanding of actors either should be toughened up with more explicit links to utilitarianism and rational actor perspectives or, as I would prefer, discarded for a more fully culturally situated conception of selves. Gendered scholarship on welfare has highlighted the significance of care in human development and productivity, but care cannot easily be fully commodified and rationalized, posing theoretical difficulties for analytic models that depend on narrowly utilitarian, rationalistic conceptions, a point to which I return below. Ethnicity and race have begun to receive attention, but this could be more systematic, and the uses of welfare in building and sustaining nations could be given greater play. And finally, the global, geopolitical concerns affecting political elites and others—first noticed in the state-centered period—should be more effectively integrated with studies of American or Western developments. In particular, scholars could explore the ways in which cold war commitments were significant for the postwar expansion of welfare and the ways in which the demise of socialism has affected the welfare states that were understood as providing important alternatives to it.

Feminist work on systems of social provision first emerged concurrently with the second-wave historical sociologists, offering a parallel critique and revision of Marxist accounts.[17] Feminists (usually also "socialist" in this area of scholarship) highlighted "social reproduction," gender, and family as sources of interests and solidarities, along with the class and production politics that concerned Marxist analysts of welfare (for a pioneering analysis, see Jenson 1986; much of this work is reviewed in B. Laslett and Brenner 1989). By the late 1980s and early 1990s, historical investigations of women's

17. Among feminist scholars engaging Marxism, welfare states were only one of a number of sites for critical analysis. "Feminist theories of the state" focused on men's control of women's sexuality and associated violence (e.g., MacKinnon 1989) or on men's control of the distribution of productive and reproductive labor, in both strands of scholarship raising explicit parallels to Marxism. The socialist feminists, following Hartmann (1981), memorably discussed the "unhappy marriage of Marxism and feminism" (see essays in Sargent, ed. 1981). All raised questions about the necessary connection between states and male dominance. This latter strand of scholarship soon linked up with studies of the welfare state (McIntosh 1978), which was at first understood as reproducing patriarchy (e.g., Pateman's [1988a] analysis of the "patriarchal welfare state," which joined the "sexual contract" with gendered citizenship forms based largely on wage labor and unpaid domestic labor). This mainly negative view of welfare states was countered by Scandinavian and other scholars, including Hernes (1987), with her influential formulation about the "woman-friendly" potential of some states (for a review, see Borchorst 1994). The work of Connell (1987, 1995) can be read as an attempt to incorporate some of these lines of thinking into an encompassing but still historically situated analysis of gender relations, including states. I review these debates at greater length elsewhere (Orloff 1997; also Julia O'Connor, Orloff, and Shaver 1999: ch. 1).

politics pushed scholars beyond the deductive, materialist, and naturalistic understandings of "women," "men," and their interests that characterized socialist feminism. Here, historical sociologists have made key contributions. Skocpol's work on maternalism reflected the conceptual broadening of gender scholarship on policy developments in the United States and elsewhere. Around the same time, a number of feminist sociologists critiqued mainstream comparative institutionalist scholars, notably Esping-Andersen, unveiling the gendered (masculinist) assumptions about actors and political goals parading as (universal) class actors and interests and specifying the ways in which gender shaped social provision (Hobson 1990; J. Lewis 1992; Julia O'Connor 1993; Orloff 1993a; Sainsbury, ed. 1994). (Thus, paralleling gender-free institutionalist work, there are two hubs of activity among feminists: historical investigations of U.S. social policy development, with a focus on maternalism and its successors, and comparative work on welfare regimes, sometimes but not always historical.) Research on welfare and men—as gendered persons rather than as "universal" citizens or workers—is still in its infancy (but see, e.g., Coltrane and Galt 2000; Connell 1987, 1995; L. Haas 1992; Hobson, ed. 2002; Leira 2002; Orloff 1991; Orloff 1993b; Orloff and Monson 2002). Yet as in the task of "provincializing Europe" or other analytic moves to investigate dominant and unmarked categories, this work will need to be pushed forward to develop a fully gendered understanding of state social provision and regulation.

Theda Skocpol (1992), Seth Koven and Sonya Michel (1993), Linda Gordon (1994) and Susan Pedersen (1993), among others, developed the concept of maternalism to describe women's political activities around the turn of the century in a number of industrializing democracies in which women entered politics on the basis of "difference," made claims to citizenship based on their capacities to mother, and idealized a maternalist state that could care for its citizens, especially mothers and their children (see also Bock and Thane, eds. 1991, a very useful collection of historians' essays on different countries' maternalisms). This scholarship sharply disagreed with presentist notions of "women's interests," common among mainstream researchers, as solely consisting in entry to the paid labor force and the development of public provision of care services; moreover, gendered "difference" was understood as socially and culturally constructed. These works provide a model for comparative analyses sensitive to national and regional (or, in the United States, state-level) differences in how women were understood as, and encouraged to be, "mothers" as opposed to "workers," a theme that has continued into investigations of contemporary social policies and politics (e.g., Duncan and Edwards, eds. 1997; Leira 1992; J. Lewis, ed. 1997). To explain divergent policies about maternal and infant health, public provision of child care, or maternity leaves, scholars call upon factors such as employers' demands for women's labor; trade union men's capacities to command a "family wage"; state officials' interests in promoting fertility; and women's organizations' demands for economic independence, protection of motherhood, and/or entry to particular occupations—all of which are simultaneously discursive or "cultural" as well as "material." In the contemporary period, I would argue that we are collectively saying "farewell to maternalism," with the shift to social policies encouraging employment for mothers as well as others and citizenship claims made on the basis of gender "sameness" or employment (Orloff forthcoming).

Many feminist analysts of U.S. policy history have built on Skocpol's work on maternalism and work on the gendered U.S. welfare state, with masculine and feminine "streams," "channels," or tiers, shaped by gendered assumptions about work, citizenship, and supervision and reflecting and recreating a pervasive gendered inequality (Fraser 1989; Nelson 1990). There has been a good deal of research on the development of the "feminine" policy stream that flowed from the state-level mothers' pension programs initiated in the 1910s and 1920s to the establishment, expansion, and recent demise of Aid to Families with Dependent Children (AFDC, or "welfare" in American terms) and the successor program, Temporary Aid to Needy Families (TANF, still "welfare"). This research has uncovered the gendered—and simultaneously raced and classed—assumptions guiding U.S. social policy, especially with reference to motherhood and (paid) work and policies' gendered, and stratifying, effects.[18] Scholars have been concerned especially with the racially and sexually exclusionary character of mothers' pensions (and other maternalist social provision) and AFDC, arguing that welfare has been constitutive of (historically variable) racial and ethnic inequalities and differences (Bellingham and Mathis 1994; Glenn 2002; Naples 1997; Quadagno 1994; Reese 2001).

Work on gendered welfare regimes and comparative gender policies emerged in the context of an interdisciplinary, international community of gender scholars, including many historical sociologists. Inspired by mainstream comparative analysis, institutionalist work, and gender studies and building on earlier work on social reproduction, analysts have carried out both feminist critique and empirical research on programs and policies seen

18. Yet in certain respects some of this scholarship—unlike the works that inspired it—seems quite decontextualized: it relies on the idea of a gendered, "two-tier" state but does not situate the U.S. feminine stream with respect to any sustained analysis of the "masculine" stream, which is treated more or less as an ideal-typical foil to demonstrate gender inequality. Nor does it pay attention to the comparative or historical context. In this way, it parallels some of the research on state autonomy and class politics in the U.S. New Deal. Both suffer from a ferocious U.S. centrism.

as especially relevant to the political construction of gender. I would call attention to several aspects of this work: its inductive and historicizing approach; its insistence on the continuing significance of central state institutions in constituting gender relations; its qualified modernist embrace of emancipatory feminist goals; its doggedly comparative approach; its provisional acceptance of the regime concept; its simultaneous engagement with gender studies and the institutionalist mainstream of comparative welfare state scholarship; and its opening to culture and discourse (see, e.g., Bergqvist et al., eds. 2000; Hobson and Lindholm 1997; Julia O'Connor, Orloff, and Shaver 1999).

Since many scholars use the regime concept, it may be worth assessing how this compares to mainstream work. Welfare regimes are understood as reflecting particular political configurations—class coalitions expressed in partisan alliances above all—of predominant liberalism, social democracy, or Christian democracy (conservativism/corporatism in the original formulation); they express more or less unified logics with respect to (de-)commodification, stratification, and the institutional locus of welfare provision (state, market, or family). Gendering the regime concept has not left us with a strictly parallel notion, however. Unless one accepts the deeply problematic notion of a "gender contract" between men and women, there are no gender analogues to class coalitions.[19] Instead, we have only the unmasking of the gendered aspects of the political forces explicitly involved in legislating welfare provision and, sometimes, the bringing to light of previously ignored actors.[20] And yet we have all looked for ways to compare, systematically, across difference. In my own work (e.g., Orloff 1993a), I have tried to develop some understanding of what would be a dimension of analysis and political intervention that would allow for such systematic comparison and would simultaneously index the emancipatory potential of welfare states vis-à-vis women—parallel to Esping-Andersen's de-commodification for workers. Eschewing the deductive, Marxist approaches of my youth, I instead attempted

19. Some scholars—Simon Duncan and Rosalind Edwards come to mind—do utilize the concept of a "gender contract" to (as they say, ironically) parallel "the idea of the social-democratic contract, or 'historical compromise,' between capital and labour" deployed by social democratic analysts in the tradition of Esping-Andersen (Duncan and Edwards 1999: 223). They trace the concept to Hirdman (1991). They go on to argue for a compound concept combining the gender and capital-labor contracts: "genderfare." This strikes me as merely compounding the dehistoricizing tendencies to be found in all these notions of contract! For a deconstructive and historicized analysis of a gendered "social contract" in recent U.S. social policy, see Naples (1997).

20. For example, Bismarck is Bismarck, Roosevelt is Roosevelt, the Social Democrats are the Social Democrats, whether understood in terms of class, gender, or some other characteristic. Of course, this is not to deny the importance of documenting the activities of "maternalists," "femocrats," and women's movements of the first and second waves.

to read the historical record of women's demands on state systems of provision across a number of Western countries. While feminist political claims differed cross-nationally and over time, especially with respect to questions of mothers' paid work and (unpaid) care, it struck me that there was a common core in demands for the means to ensure personal independence and the capacity to enter or leave familial or marital relations on the basis of choice rather than necessity (to be secured in different ways, to be sure—state benefits or access to paid work and services).[21] Similarly inspired notions—of personal independence or "defamilization"—have been put forward by other feminist sociologists (e.g., Lister 1997; Julia O'Connor 1993). Moreover, the notion of "gender logics" may be a useful analytic tool—revealed through explorations of the *articulation* of policies as, for example, Julia O'Connor, Sheila Shaver, and I (1999) carried out vis-à-vis biological and social reproduction and the labor market in four "liberal" regimes. But our approach is not at odds with Adams and Padamsee's (2001) warning that one cannot assume that each nation-state has a single, coherent regime—a simplifying shorthand rampant in all the literatures on modern systems of social provision and regulation that we would all do well to be on guard against.

The conversation between feminist and mainstream institutionalists has been relatively productive, and many of the leading figures of institutionalist welfare regime analysis have of late incorporated gender into their analytic models, with Esping-Andersen (1999; Esping-Andersen et al. 2002) taking up feminists' concepts of "defamilization," exploring the "household economy," and arguing for a "new gender contract";[22] Korpi (2000) investigating the politics of different gendered family models in social policy; and Huber and Stephens (2000) exploring the political sources of Scandinavia's "woman-friendly" provision of public services. Interestingly, this is one of the few substantive areas in which mainstream political analysts have acknowledged the significance (first brought to light by feminist scholars) of women's political participation, paid work/unpaid care work trade-offs, and family dynamics—however inadequate their appreciation of the full significance of gender. Perhaps this is because there are such notable and unsettling post-modern or post-industrial changes in labor and capital markets, with the decline of the standard (male) industrial worker and the increase in

---

21. This approach has been referred to by some, dismissively, as modernist. Perhaps so; it certainly does (deliberately) recognize the link between modernity and contemporary Western feminism.

22. And, I cannot resist pointing out, in the 2002 book performatively contradicting the more explicit commitment to gender equality (as compared with the 1999 book) by failing to cite any of the feminist texts (yes, mine included) that were the inspiration for the notion that we need more egalitarian gender arrangements (however it has been modified in rational choice directions). To give credit where it is due, Korpi, Huber, and Stephens have been more equitable in their citation practices.

capital mobility; families, with the decline of male breadwinner/female full-time caregiver households and the increase in different household forms; and states, with the decline in national state capacities vis-à-vis capital. And women service workers may be the next best hope for the social democratic project.

Yet the conversation has not been entirely satisfactory, not simply because certain voices are "heard" (that is, cited) more than others. Mainstream scholars' conceptions of gender are fairly thin—often confined to ideas about the "reconciliation of work and family"—especially when it comes to bodies, violence, sex, dependency, or the cultural concepts of masculinities and femininities, which are notable by their absence (Adams and Padamsee 2001; Brush 2002). Men appear not to even *have* a gender. Mainstream analysts rely upon a particular conception of political subjects as rational, autonomous, unburdened by care, impervious to invasions of bodily integrity and therefore (heterosexual and) masculine. Indeed, their work on women shoehorns them into this ill-fitting conception (which may improve upon structuralist accounts in recognizing women's agency but falls short in other ways). We see this, for example, in their writings on the new "gender contract" we are now supposed to need (Esping-Andersen et al. 2002). This concept calls upon the notions of freely-choosing individuals of liberal social contract theory—individuals whose existence is as illusory as that of self-regulating markets (which, as good institutionalists and social democrats, these analysts do recognize as fantasy!). The complexities, burdens, and joys of care, about which feminists have written so eloquently, are simply dissolved in the assumption that we can commodify care sufficiently to allow all adults to enter paid labor.[23] Such a "solution" to women's disproportionate share of the household division of labor and concomitant difficulties in

---

23. The feminist scholarship on care, particularly among political philosophers, is as voluminous as it has been innovative and inspiring for sociologists; for a small sampling of these rich analyses with particular relevance for welfare and citizenship, see Fineman (1995); Kittay (1999); Noddings (2002); Sevenhuijsen (1998); Tronto (1993). Feminist sociologists pioneered the study of care and welfare—in terms of both the relations of caring and the provision of care-related services (see, e.g., Balbo 1982; Finch and Groves, eds. 1983; Land 1978; Sassoon, ed. 1987; Waerness 1984). Among these pioneers, Hilary Graham memorably argued that "Caring is experienced as a labour of love . . . whose form and content is shaped (and continually reshaped) by our intimate social and sexual relationships" (1983: 30) and connected caring to women's development as *social* beings. But, of course, care is not only about love, but also work and the conditions of that work. An influential sociological analysis of "rights to time to care" is found in Knijn and Kremer (1997); Daly and Lewis (2000) examine how "social care" has been used in studies of welfare states; Antonen and Sipila (1996) consider care and regime typologies. M. H. Meyer, ed. (2000) collects essays, some historical, dealing with care and welfare. Empirical work on child-care arrangements and gender is another expansive literature (see, e.g., Michel and Mahon, eds. 2002). Finally, one can mention work on the (economic) "costs of caring" (e.g., England and Folbre 1999; Joshi 1990).

entering and staying in the labor market could not hold up under serious scrutiny; it would be far too expensive given current budgetary constraints, even if it were "optimal" for those doing the caring and those who receive care—which it does not seem to be (see, e.g., Ungerson 1997). And, of course, these conceptions should not pretend to be innocent of the deeply gendered historical developments through which modern political subjects were birthed (see, e.g., J. Landes 1988; Lister 1997; Pateman 1989; Zerilli 1994). Citizenship has always been, and remains, gendered, and neither past nor contemporary social politics can be understood without reference to the (diverse) masculine and feminine characters of different political identities. But unfortunately, the mainstream's thin concept of gender is likely to be stretched even thinner as these scholars draw closer to rational choice formulations of risks, preferences, and agents. Meanwhile, many feminist historical sociologists seem poised to move in quite opposite directions—precisely toward understanding the cultural and discursive processes that are integral to gendering welfare.

Feminist historical sociologists of welfare are increasingly open to analyses of culture, discourse, and signification through interchanges with historians of women and gender, political theorists, and others. Especially influential have been Nancy Fraser's (1989, 1997) works on the (discursive, cultural) "politics of needs interpretation" and, with Linda Gordon, analyses of the genealogy of key welfare concepts such as "dependency," "contract," and "citizenship" (Fraser and Gordon 1992, 1994a). Opening up to scrutiny the "risks" and "needs" to which welfare is addressed has been immensely productive, allowing scholars to examine the creation of categories of clients or beneficiaries, as well as the creation of demand for the services and expertise of various professionals connected to the welfare and disciplinary bureaucracies. (Scholars would do well, however, to pay more attention to the agency of the "discipliners," as Steinmetz 1993 argued.) Lynne Haney's (2002) work on "the invention of the needy" in post-socialist Hungary develops these ideas, showing the ways in which understandings of women's needs and associated policy strategies and administrative organizations changed over the course of several distinct phases of social politics from the 1940s through the present. Haney's combined ethnographic and comparative-historical project, like her work investigating the local implementation of AFDC-related programs (Haney 1996), also highlights the payoffs of analyzing the different levels of welfare politics and administration, with their potentially contradictory exigencies and effects. These are not exactly Foucauldian analyses of the "capillaries," but they do draw on the insights about the normalizing techniques of power; yet one must stress the need to remain cognizant of the structuring role of national state policies. Adams and

Padamsee have suggested a systematic reworking of the regimes concept to highlight signification and culture, encompassing "signs, subjects, strategies, and sanctions": "A state policy regime, then, can be defined as a set of policies with accompanying sanctions, which are in turn the precipitates of subjects' actions undertaken on the basis of ordered signs" (2001: 16). They offer illustrations from the literature on maternalism, arguing against various socially determinist accounts that offer variants of a "standpoint" approach that links political ideologies and goals to social location. They contend that "initially, making the claim that maternalist ideas matter in politics involves showing how the sign of 'motherhood' organizes and links together a number of otherwise separate and subordinate signs" (p. 11); then they go on to investigate the "hailing" or recruitment of subjects, their strategic policy-making, and the sanctions or capacities they may call on to enforce strategies.

The historical construction of gendered divides between public and private—which changes over time—is a critical moment in the gendering of welfare, fixing (temporarily) which needs may be addressed through public social policy and which are to be left to the family, charity, or the market (Gal and Kligman 2000; Julia O'Connor, Orloff, and Shaver 1999). A number of scholars have examined the provision of child care through this lens; when the care of children is understood to be women's "natural" vocation, or a "labor of love," state provision is ruled out and women must find private solutions if they must or want to enter the paid labor force (see, e.g., Michel 1999; Michel and Mahon, eds. 2002). Meanwhile, when masculinity is defined in opposition to caregiving activities, changes in familial divisions of labor are stymied and fathers may resist taking up parental leaves—even those designed to encourage their participation (Hobson, ed. 2002; Leira 2002). In taking up the cultural turn, these scholars have not, it would seem, abandoned progressive understandings of welfare as a potentially emancipatory weapon in the political struggle for gender equality. While the insights of Foucault and others have proved useful in calling attention to the significance of discourse and categorization and to the capillary and productive character of power, they reject the political implications of Foucault's analysis—which leaves us with "resistance" and little else.[24]

24. In hilarious form Marshall Sahlins (2002: 52) in *Waiting for Foucault, Still* skewers the bastardized "Foucauldian" impulses one sometimes finds behind the call for "resistance":

Ever since Gramsci, posing the notion of hegemony has entailed the equal and opposite discovery of the resistance of the oppressed. So the anthropologist [or sociologist!] who relates the so-called grand narrative of Western domination is also likely to subvert it by invoking "weapons of the weak," "hidden transcripts" or some such local discourse of cultural defiance. In any case, this is a no-lose strategy since the two characterizations, domination and resistance, are contradictory and in some combination will cover any and every historical eventuality.

Feminist scholarship on Western systems of social provision and regulation has been, arguably, at its most radical in deconstructing the subject of welfare states and welfare state scholarship and in highlighting the significance for "public" welfare of practices—particularly care work—that take place in the "private" sphere (for recent debate around these issues, see, e.g., Adams and Padamsee 2001; Brush 2002; Jenson 1997; J. Lewis 1997, 2001; Orloff 1997; Padamsee and Adams 2002; Shaver 2002). But until recently, this work has remained focused on the Western welfare states.[25] Yet there are interesting parallels—in opening up private spaces to analytic scrutiny—to feminist work on colonial and post-colonial, socialist and post-socialist states. For example, Foucauldian inspiration is evident in analyses stressing the significance of "the intimate" and "carnal knowledge" to colonial rule, to borrow the evocative terms of Ann Stoler (2002). Stoler examined Dutch colonial welfare administration in the Indies, tracing relationships of domination and (sometimes) intimacy among women and men across "race," nation, and class and excavating racial and gendered classificatory schemes from the documentary traces of institutions of social provision and regulation. Susan Gal and Gail Kligman (2000; Gal and Kligman, eds. 2000), among others, have developed gendered themes in novel analyses of the socialist and post-socialist states, in which questions of "public" and "private," the political significance of reproduction (biological and social), and gendered patterns of labor all take on forms that upset settled understandings based on Western experiences (see also Emigh and Szelényi, eds. 2001; Fodor 2003; Haney 2002; Kligman 1998). For example, why was abortion—either when it had been available on demand (e.g., Poland) or when it had been outlawed (Romania)—one of the first questions taken up for political debate after the fall of socialist regimes? Work on gender and social policy in post-colonial states is similarly challenging to accepted views about women and (welfare) states (see, e.g., Charrad 2001; Haney and Pollard, eds. 2003). In all of these contexts, modernity, with its associated institutional forms—such as welfare states—is articulated in complex ways with imperialism, and "women's status," as expressed in family law, civil rights, and social provision, is often the flashpoint for tensions around these connections, as when women's labor force participation can signify modern gender equality, capitulation to imperialism, or the capitalist degradation of the family! We would surely benefit from more explicit comparisons of gendered patterns of work and welfare across time and space.

---

25. Or at least it has been limited to welfare states in industrialized countries; gendered welfare arrangements in Japan have attracted considerable attention; see, for example, Peng (2002), linking gender, demography, and postwar developments in the Japanese welfare state.

Conclusion

In studies of modern systems of social provision and regulation, Marx has met Weber (metaphorically). I have suggested that we need to perform a kind of collective exorcism of Marxism, if I can call on "Marx" to signify the whole set of socially determinist analytic approaches that have held us back from making a cultural turn in this field, as well as a politics that takes for granted the identity, goals, and goodness of working-class mobilizations (to say nothing of an often sentimental and unjustified evaluation of the former Soviet bloc). Yet I also want to historicize the Marxist contribution to the development of modern welfare, to investigate how certain sets of ideas derived ultimately from (more or less adulterated versions of) Marx have guided both the politics and analysis of welfare states; how the threat of socialism, socialist movements, and parties pressured elites to enact social reforms; and how actually existing socialist states—and then their demise—shaped and continue to shape Western welfare provision. This would suggest that we need to probe more deeply into the geopolitical elements of the context in which contemporary systems of social provision and regulation developed. It also should encourage greater attention to the ways "welfare" was provided in the socialist bloc and how socialist modes of provision and regulation have influenced ongoing transitions to capitalism.

But why stop with Eastern Europe? We clearly need to understand social provision and regulation outside the heartland of social Europe, in the rapidly developing capitalisms of Latin America, East Asia, and South Asia, as well as in past colonial outposts of the European metropoles for what this can tell us about welfare's multiple forms and sources and its relationship to diverse forms of capitalism, including that in the "core." This means, among other things, situating modern social provision wherever it has developed more fully with respect to nation, race, and ethnicity (G. Lewis 2000; Quadagno 2000; Stoler 2000; F. Williams 1995). In contexts where industrialization is not fully established and modern systems of social provision and regulation are embryonic, we can hardly expect a level of interest in pensions—the perhaps-too-thin lifeblood of welfare state studies—comparable to that found across the developed world.[26] After all, "welfare states" are only one possible institutional form for more widespread activities of reproduction.

I would also like to encourage the ongoing encounter between Weber and Foucault, if I can call on "Foucault" to signify the whole set of regulatory,

---

26. As someone whose dissertation and first book concerned pensions, I hope no one will take offense at this suggestion that pensions may not be of equivalent interest in all times and places.

capillary, disciplinary, and discursive analytic themes that have enriched studies of politics in many areas and "Weber" to stand in for attention to both states and the "means of administration" and the deeply contradictory effects of modernity on modern subjectivities and relationships. State-centered work and then the broader institutionalist movement have drawn principally on Weber's administrative themes to enrich understandings of welfare states as products of class politics. But as I have argued above, this leaves out significant dimensions of social politics and provision, even within the Weberian tradition—such as the development of modern disposi-tions. Foucauldian scholarship has insisted on the fact that provision is never free of classification, regulation, and discipline. This is not to say these are always bad things to be resisted, although in many cases they are—fascist or eugenicist racial classification comes to mind (on Nazi politics and gen-der, see, e.g., Bock 1991; Koonz 1987). Rather, it is to say that their character is consequential for politics and culture. In many cases (in democratic or democratizing contexts particularly), categories of provision and regulation are bases for mobilization. And here one could foresee a fruitful linkage to Weberian-inspired studies of "policy creating politics" and the role of state and political structures.

I would especially like all of these "gentlemen" to meet de Beauvoir, signifying the gendered contribution, to enliven studies of welfare with considerations of bodies, gendered identities, reproduction, and care. But, of course, my true concern is with the real men and women working under the signs of "Marx, Weber, Foucault" or, alternatively, under the sign of "de Beauvoir." In a number of venues, conversations have begun, but they could go much further in a theoretical vein. How does incorporating gender change our understandings of the historical trajectories of systems of social provision and regulation and of capitalist modernities? Having learned a great deal about gender and modern welfare systems—for example, the relationships among families, markets, and states; the role of women service workers in post-industrial transformations; or the ways assumptions about masculinities and femininities have informed social policies—we can, and should, engage fundamental questions of agency, power, structure, and mo-dernity. In short, I repeat the calls made as a co-author of the introduction for more talk across theoretical and analytic divides and especially more openness to subjects formerly excluded or repressed.

EDGAR KISER AND JUSTIN BAER

The Bureaucratization of States:
Toward an Analytical Weberianism

Historical reality involves a continuous, though for the most part latent, conflict between chiefs and their administrative staffs for appropriation and expropriation in relation to one another.—Max Weber

Bureaucratic organization is one of the most ubiquitous features of the modern world; one could argue that it is the organizational embodiment of modernity. Bureaucracy is the institutional aspect of legal-rational authority, the culmination of the rationalization process described by Weber.[1] Analyzing its initial development thus provides important insights into the birth of modernity. This chapter has two main goals. Substantively, we develop a model of the causes of the bureaucratization of states and use it to explain aspects of the development of several pre-modern states. Theoretically, addressing a central Weberian question using contemporary theoretical tools allows us to both illustrate what we can learn from the classics and gauge how far our theories have progressed since then.

This chapter illustrates one neo-Weberian approach to historical sociology.[2] Like earlier readings of Weber (Bendix 1977; Collins 1986; Parsons

We would like to thank Jen Edwards, Gary Hamilton, Steve Hanson, members of the Macrosociology Workshop at the University of Washington, and the editors of and contributors to this volume for helpful comments.

1. Bureaucracy is only one aspect of rationalization; a full account of the many other facets of rationalization is beyond the scope of this chapter.

2. To paraphrase Randall Collins (1986: 3), we do not propose our interpretation as the one "true" Weber, and we are not concerned with demonstrating that other interpretations are wrong. Like all interpretations, ours stresses some features of Weber's complex ideas and downplays others. We simply offer a new interpretation of Weber that may serve as a useful model for contemporary scholars.

1937), our interpretation is shaped by our own theoretical perspective. We believe that the core of Weber's approach to historical analysis corresponds to emerging developments in sociological versions of rational choice theory (Adams 1996; M. Brinton 1988; Brustein 1996; Coleman 1990; Hechter 1987; Hechter and Kanazawa 1997; Kiser 1994, 1999; Levi 1988, 1997). Both perspectives rely on methodological individualism, assumptions about intentional action, and the use of abstract models of organizational and institutional structures. Our rational choice interpretation of Weber is roughly analogous in its intent to interpretations of Marx proposed by Elster (1985) and Roemer (1986). Just as they outlined an "Analytical Marxism," this chapter is a preliminary attempt to illustrate an "Analytical Weberianism."

Instead of attempting to specify the research strategy suggested by this Analytical Weberian approach in abstract terms (see Kiser and Hechter 1998; Norkus 2001), we provide an extended illustration. We explore the main causes of the bureaucratization of states in the two arenas that dominated early modern state structures: tax administration and armies. Our arguments begin with insights from Weber, which are further developed using the analytical tools of contemporary agency theory. However, our goal is not to turn Weber into a contemporary economist but just the opposite: to use Weber to broaden the scope and explanatory power of agency theory.

Prior Work on Bureaucratization

In spite of the impressive early work of Weber and Otto Hintze (1975 [1902]), analyses of state bureaucratization were not a central part of the revival of historical sociology in the 1960s and 1970s (see the introduction for a much more detailed discussion). There are two main reasons for this. First, the revival of historical sociology drew its main questions more from Marx than from Weber, so there was a greater focus on class-state relations (was the state relatively or potentially autonomous?) than on the internal dynamics of states. Second, Parsons's (1937) interpretation of Weber was still dominant; *The Protestant Ethic and the Spirit of Capitalism* (1930) was seen as Weber's most important work, and as a result he was understood mainly as an idealist counterpoint to Marx, who advocated an interpretive methodology (*verstehen*).

Although these factors pushed the focus of most historical work away from bureaucratization, there was still some important work on this topic, and interest in it has increased recently. The earliest work used Weber's typology of bureaucracy but situated it within a Parsonian functionalist framework (Eisenstadt 1963; Hoselitz 1963; La Palombara 1963). This work paid little attention to either the micro-level or to the details of history, tending instead to focus on the development of typologies and propositions at such a high level of abstraction that they were difficult to test. Reactions against this loosely Weberian functionalism came from "second-wave" structuralists (stressing material conditions and group conflict) and cultural Weberians (who wanted to bring the micro-level back in using a verstehen methodology). Although bureaucratization was generally not their primary concern, structuralists (see many of the essays in C. Tilly, ed. 1975; Skocpol 1979) showed how many of the group conflicts involved in state making and unmaking (revolution) shaped the development of civil and military administrations. Recently Ertman (1997) argued that both group power and democratization affected the timing of bureaucratization across Europe. The main limitation of this work is its neglect (in some cases explicit rejection [Skocpol 1979]) of human agency. Cultural Weberians (Bendix 1977; Gorski 1993; G. G. Hamilton 1984, 1989; see also Thompson 1963 on factories) who have studied bureaucracy have stressed its cultural and historical determinants. Although they have provided rich and detailed analyses of the cultural (especially religious, elaborating on Weber's argument about Protestantism) and historical factors affecting both the development and effectiveness of bureaucracy, they have generally been unable to construct general, testable models of the process.

The most general problem with prior work on bureaucratization, which we think Analytical Weberianism can at least mitigate if not solve, is the inability to include complex (multiple) micro-foundations in a clear, testable model. Culturally oriented Weberians have done the former but not the latter, whereas structuralists and standard rational choice theorists have retained the latter but at the cost of ignoring or oversimplifying the former.

Two factors have laid the foundation for the development of Analytical Weberianism: a renewed focus on the micro-level and a new interpretation of Weber. The first developed out of a series of criticisms of structuralist historical sociology. Both culturally oriented narrativists and rational choice theorists argued that structuralists paid too little attention to human agency (Griffin 1992; Kiser 1996; Somers 1996b; see also the introduction to this volume). This re-incorporation of the micro-level of analysis naturally increased interest in Weber (the classical advocate of methodological individualism), and especially in his typology of social action. However, cultural and rational choice critiques of structuralism suggested very different appropriations of Weber, with the former focused on value rationality and the latter focused on instrumental rationality.

The second foundation of Analytical Weberianism is a new interpretation of his work, based more on *Economy and Society* (1978 [1922]) than on his work on the religious foundations of capitalism (R. Collins 1986; Mann 1986; Norkus 2001; Swedberg 1998). This interpretation sees Weber as a primarily materialist conflict theorist who usually (but certainly not always) used instrumentalist micro-foundations, rather than as a verstehen-based cultural sociologist. Analytical Weberianism is an elaboration of this view of Weber. It differs from prior Weberian arguments due to its greater stress on testability and its emphasis on the analytical primacy of instrumental rationality, and it differs from most versions of rational choice theory by stressing the importance of retaining multiple micro-foundations.

An Application of Analytical Weberianism to the Bureaucratization of States

For Weber, the relationship between rulers and their administrative and military staffs is essential to understanding political history. His model of this relationship shares many features with contemporary agency theory. Rulers (as principals) must delegate authority to some staff of state officials (as agents) in order to implement any of their policies. Weber stresses the fact that rulers face a problem in controlling these agents, because the interests of the agents often differ from theirs. Weber (1978 [1922]: 225, 991–999) also realized that agents are often able to get away with actions contrary to the interests of principals because they have better information concerning the quality of their performance than principals do. This is a classic statement of an agency problem: delegation of authority leading to problems of control due to conflicting interests between principals and agents and informational asymmetries favoring agents.

Weber's ideal types of state organization (patrimonialism, bureaucracy) are abstract models of particular types of agency relations.[3] They describe common configurations of recruitment, monitoring, and sanctioning strategies.[4] Weber's arguments about the causes of variations in forms of administration foreshadowed those of contemporary agency theory in that they

---

3. Weber argued that "sociology seeks to formulate type concepts and generalized uniformities of empirical process. This distinguishes it from history, which is oriented to the causal analysis and explanation of individual actions, structures, and personalities possessing cultural significance" (1978 [1922]: 19). He also had a clear preference for abstract over historically specific models: "The more sharply and precisely the ideal type has been constructed, thus the more abstract and unrealistic in this sense it is, the better it is able to perform its functions in formulating terminology, classifications, and hypotheses" (p. 21).

4. These ideal types are also closely linked to more general forms of domination and legitimation in Weber's work, but those issues are not the focus of this chapter.

tended to stress efficacy or efficiency. He argued that "the decisive reason for the advance of bureaucratic organization has always been its purely technical superiority over any other form of organization" (1978 [1922]: 973).

Weber's model of the agency relation between rulers and their staffs was not just an early formulation of the economic theory of agency; it was fundamentally sociological in the sense that it included both a rich depiction of the structural context within which agency relations were embedded and a more complex view of the micro-foundations of action. For Weber, ruler-staff agency relations are always embedded in a structural and historical context (including general systems of legitimate domination). Analyzing these relations thus requires not only the use of abstract ideal types (patrimonialism, bureaucracy, etc.), but concrete knowledge of historical conditions as well. Analytical Weberianism thus responds to Granovetter's (1985) powerful criticism of economic rational choice theory by including these structural factors.

As a methodological individualist, Weber (1978 [1922]: 4, 13) believed that any complete explanation must include an account of the motives of actors. The second difference between Weber's approach to agency relations and that of most economists is that he had a broader conception of action, including noninstrumental motivations. Weber argued that it would be *analytically useful* to begin all work by assuming instrumental micro-foundations.[5] His model was not limited to instrumental action, however, but also included values, emotions, and habits.[6] Weber (p. 264) thought that the problem caused by the conflicting interest of rulers and their agents could be mitigated in two main ways: (1) by constructing organizational forms that make it in the instrumental interests of officials to comply with the orders of rulers (by using appropriate forms of monitoring and sanctions); and/or (2) by fostering a belief in officials that the authority of the ruler is legitimate and thus that it is their moral duty to obey. The micro-foundations Weber used to model civil and military administration were thus based on a combination of instrumental rationality and value rationality.

The key question raised but not answered in Weber's model is under

---

5. "For the purposes of a typological scientific analysis it is convenient to treat all irrational, affectually determined elements of behavior as factors of deviation from a conceptually pure type of rational action" (M. Weber 1978 [1922]: 6). The fact that Weber began his analysis with instrumental micro-foundations does not mean that he thought instrumental rationality was ontologically primary; the choice was based on analytical utility. The issue of the ontological primacy of instrumental rationality in different times and places is obviously an empirical question.

6. We focus only on values and emotions in this chapter, because we believe that habits can be explained instrumentally (see Becker 1976).

what conditions these different micro-foundations (instrumental rationality, values, emotions) will be important. Lacking a satisfactory answer to this question, contemporary Weberians have either focused on only one aspect or combined them in ad hoc ways. Some rely mainly or exclusively on organizational structure and incentives, the side of Weber most consistent with rational choice (Adams 1996; Ertman 1997; Hintze 1975 [1902]; Kiser 1994; Kiser and Schneider 1994), whereas others incorporate values and legitimacy into their analyses of agency relations, thus going beyond the bounds of mainstream rational choice theory (Bendix 1977; Gorski 1993; G. G. Hamilton and Biggart 1980, 1984). Our intention is to show that these two paths out of second-wave structuralism (see the introduction to this volume), usually seen as conflicting, can be made compatible. We take Weber's advice by beginning with instrumental micro-foundations, but we then specify the conditions under which values and emotions must also be incorporated.

Rational choice theory focuses on the intentions of actors, as does Weber's methodology of verstehen, but there are important differences between the two. Verstehen combines theoretical assumptions (there are four types of social action; we can begin by assuming instrumental motivations) with empirical analysis (using historical sources such as diaries, letters, and memoirs) to get a detailed picture of what and how historical actors thought. This is an extremely difficult methodology and as a result quite rare in contemporary historical sociology. Rational choice theory generally relies only on the former, in part because data on motivations are often unavailable for most historical actors, and in part because these data are frequently unreliable (since people often go to great lengths to conceal their true motivations and feelings) (Kiser and Hechter 1998).

Does verstehen have any place in Analytical Weberianism? Following Weber we do not think it is necessary for understanding "rationally purposive action," because it has the "highest degree of verifiable certainty"; all of us "can understand what a person is doing when he tries to achieve certain ends by choosing appropriate means" (1978 [1922]: 5). The same is not true of particular values, because they vary across time and space, and it is especially difficult to understand rare or idiosyncratic values. Therefore, verstehen is especially useful when analyzing particular actors in positions of power—such as the rulers of states—since their personal idiosyncrasies (values, emotions) could have an important impact on outcomes. Weber realized that the principals could engage in "appropriation and expropriation" of the resources of agents, a problem that Perrow (1990) correctly noted is ignored by contemporary agency theorists in economics. This is one of the many ways

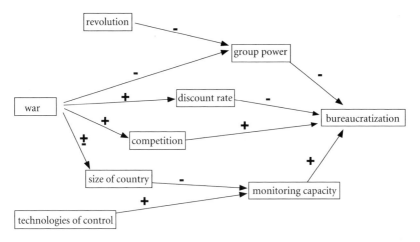

Figure 1

in which Weber's analysis is more substantively sophisticated, even if much less precise and formal, than contemporary economic agency theory. We argue that there are two reasons to think that the verstehen method may be more useful for understanding the motives of principals than those of agents in state administration: (1) rulers usually left many more empirical records of their motives than their subjects did; and (2) individual idiosyncrasies generally wash out in large groups (such as all agents in state administration), but most pre-modern principals were single individuals, and in some cases unique personalities may have had important effects on historical outcomes. Any historical Analytical Weberian study of bureaucratization should thus use verstehen to understand the choices of individual rulers. However, space limitations prevent us from doing so in this chapter, so we will simply assume that rulers were instrumental actors interested in wealth and power.

Figure 1 provides our general model of the bureaucratization process, building on Weber. Our chapter is organized around the main causal processes outlined in the figure. We begin by discussing the causes and consequences of variations in monitoring capacity, the agency theory core of our model. We next focus on the conditions under which values and/or emotions are important in accounting for bureaucratization, and we conclude that they are essential for bureaucratic armies. We then describe the effects of several structural factors highlighted by both Weber and contemporary historical sociologists—group power, war, and revolution.

Size of Country, Technologies of Control, and Monitoring Capacity

The size, geography, and climate of a country affect the efficiency of administration by affecting the cost and difficulty of monitoring agents. Monitoring requires the movement of people and information across space, and characteristics of the natural environment in part determine the speed and cost of these movements. Since monitoring problems increase with distance, the farther officials get from the ruler, the more they "[evade] the ruler's influence" (M. Weber 1978 [1922]: 1051).

The effects of these aspects of the natural environment on the efficiency of tax collection are contingent on the level of development of technologies of communication, transportation, and information processing. The costs and effectiveness of monitoring are primarily determined by these technical factors, since they determine the ease with which principals can acquire information about agents (M. Weber 1978 [1922]: 224). We will refer to these as *technologies of control*, since they are the main technologies affecting the ability of rulers to control tax agents and taxpayers. The higher the level of development of technologies of control, the greater the monitoring capacity of rulers.

Whether rulers choose different types or aspects of patrimonial or bureaucratic administration depends first and foremost on their monitoring capacity.[7] When monitoring is poor, stronger sanctions are necessary to compensate (Becker and Stigler 1974). Since bureaucracy relies on fairly weak positive and negative sanctions (fixed salaries and the threat of dismissal), it will be efficient only when monitoring capacity is well developed. When monitoring capacity is poor, two types of patrimonial systems will outperform centralized bureaucracy: (1) forms that include the stronger sanctions necessary to induce agents to comply, such as tax farming (privatized tax collection in which agents retain the profits or take the losses) or severe negative sanctions (see Kiser 1994; Kiser and Schneider 1994); and/or

---

7. Patrimonialism and bureaucracy are complex combinations of several features. Most of the choices pre-modern rulers made were among different types of patrimonialism. The shift to bureaucratic organization rarely occurs all at once—different aspects of bureaucracy develop at different rates (Kiser and Kane 2001).

Economic factors are also preconditions of bureaucracy. Prior to monetization of the economy, officials cannot be paid money salaries but must be compensated in nonpecuniary ways (usually status and/or land) that are less effective positive sanctions. Economic development is one of the main determinants of the level of literacy and education in societies and thus affects the availability of trained potential agents (M. Weber 1978 [1922]: 973). The availability of trained agents is also endogenously determined, however, since rulers can create and fund schools or other training centers (as the case of Han China illustrates).

(2) a decentralized administration that makes central monitoring less important, such as feudalism or prebendalism (payment in land or the profits from land) (see Barkey 1994 on the Ottoman Empire).[8] The development of adequate monitoring capacity is thus a necessary condition for bureaucracy.

Monitoring Capacity and the Bureaucratization of Tax Administration

The relationship among size, technology, and monitoring capacity allows us to explain a great deal of the variation in the bureaucratization of tax administration in empires and states. England developed aspects of bureaucratic administration (especially in excise taxation) prior to other European states (Brewer 1988) due mainly to its relatively small size and more rapid development of effective communications and transportation systems (Geiger 1994: 19; Szostak 1991: 55–57).[9] Technological shifts also explain the general temporal pattern of bureaucratization. Most civil administrations bureaucratized in the eighteenth and nineteenth centuries because transportation speeds began to significantly increase only in the late eighteenth century; prior to that time early modern states could move information and officials no faster than they could in the Roman Empire (Braudel 1949: 369; Wachter 1987: 96). One reason that bureaucratization was not a linear process in the West is that the development of transportation technologies was not linear.

Another general implication of our argument is that bureaucratization generally begins at the top, in central administration located in the capital.[10] Top officials are much easier to monitor—they are less numerous and less distant than lower-level officials. The main problem with controlling high-level officials was their power (as the section on group power illustrates); when this obstacle was removed, bureaucratization at the top generally followed.

8. Another way to strengthen sanctions is to hire agents for whom existing sanctions will be more costly. The clearest case of this is hiring dependent agents who have fewer opportunities or resources other than state employment (injured military veterans in Prussia, slaves in the Ottoman and Roman Empires). Weber (1978 [1922]: 993, 1015–1018, 1043) was especially interested in the role of dependence in agency relations, since the more dependent the agents, the more likely they are to comply with the principal's orders (see also Adams 1996; Kiser and Schneider 1994).

9. Overall, the English state in the eighteenth century was both more bureaucratic and more efficient than its continental counterparts. For example, corruption in eighteenth-century France was "at least four times higher" than in England (Brewer 1988: 73).

10. European military organization followed the same pattern, with bureaucratized war offices and officer training preceding any bureaucratization of lower levels (Lynn 1996: 527; G. Parker 1995 [1979]: 40).

Are Noninstrumental Motivations Important in the Bureaucratization of Tax Administration?

In what type of situation should an Analytical Weberian look to values and/ or emotions in explaining compliance in agency relations? In general, principals will always try to motivate their agents in the most efficient way possible, so factors affecting values and emotions will always be used when their net benefits for compliance are greater than their costs. We argue that values and emotions will be especially important when highly motivated agents are necessary (due to poor monitoring capacity) and when instrumental motivations are ineffective. When the costs of compliance are high and the benefits of compliance are low (because it is inefficient to shift residual claimancy to agents), principals will seek noninstrumental ways to motivate agents; thus values and/or emotions will be important.[11] The costs of compliance are much higher in armies, where compliance can result in death, than in tax administration, where it means forgoing corrupt earnings. We thus expect values and emotions to be less important in tax administration than in armies.

There are two general ways in which rulers can promote noninstrumental compliance: (1) by recruiting agents who already hold values or emotions consistent with the principal; or (2) by creating a situation in which agents acquire these values or emotions in training or job performance. Gorski (1993) gave an example of the former, from a cultural Weberian perspective, from civil administration. He argued that one of the main causes of the efficiency of administration in Prussia and Holland was that rulers selected agents on the basis of religious affiliation, and their religious values inhibited corruption. In the language of agency theory, Gorski concentrates on the consequences of hiring agents of different types, differentiated by religious affiliation (an indication of religious values). Gorski has added to these economic models by making agent type endogenous. Instead of simply stipulating that agent "type" is given by "nature," he argued that it is derived from religious affiliation.[12]

The ongoing debate about the causes of the efficiency of early modern Prussian tax administration illustrates the limitations of Gorski's cultural

---

11. Another interesting possibility is that values and emotions will be more important in conditions of high uncertainty, since instrumental calculation will be more difficult (Mann 1986).

12. Gorski (1993) also suggested an additional causal mechanism linking religious affiliation with low corruption: third-party monitoring and sanctioning by churches. If corruption is contrary to religious as well as state rules and churches enforce those rules, they are indirectly acting as a control mechanism for the state. This part of Gorski's argument not only does not contradict agency theory, it also provides additional evidence for the large literature in political science on third-party monitoring (Kiewiet and McCubbins 1991; Weingast 1983).

Weberianism (Gorski 1993, 1995; Kiser and Schnieder 1994, 1995). Theoretically, he failed to analytically separate the effects of instrumental rationality and values. Empirically, the tendency of cultural Weberians to overstate the effects of values also distorts his conclusions: hiring on the basis of religious affiliation was common only for high-level officials and only for a short period (roughly 1700–1750); thus its effects on the efficiency of Prussian tax administration could not have been as great as Gorski claimed (Kiser and Schneider 1995).

An example of the second strategy, using training periods to create pro-compliance values, comes from the Chinese state.[13] The long period of education required of potential Chinese officials was geared more toward instilling pro-state Confucian values than teaching accounting skills. Although this attempt at indoctrination may have been successful to some extent, it had an important unintended consequence. The Chinese bureaucracy was permeated by factional and patronage ties that inhibited monitoring and created widespread collusion (Fairbank 1986: 43; see also J. T. C. Liu 1967 on the Sung period). Collusion started during the long process of education necessary to pass exams (Fairbank 1986: 31). The ties made during agents' collective education were reinforced throughout the careers of officials (R. Huang 1974: 206) and served to insulate individuals within factions from monitoring by peers and superiors. The attempt to instill values of good official behavior actually increased corruption (Kiser and Tong 1992).

As both the Prussian and Chinese examples illustrate, there is no consensus regarding the importance of values or emotions in the bureaucratization of tax administration. Cultural Weberians tend to overestimate these factors, whereas rational choice theorists generally ignore them. Analytical Weberianism attempts to avoid both problems by more clearly specifying the conditions under which they will be important. In this case, instrumental motivations were probably sufficient.

The Anomaly of Bureaucratized Armies:
The Role of Values and Emotions

The effects of monitoring capacity on the bureaucratization of armies are less straightforward because agents in the military differ from agents in civil administration in at least three significant respects: (1) it is more difficult to

13. Another example is the use of indoctrinated slaves in the Ottoman Empire. These slaves were generally Christian children who were given an Islamic education and then given jobs (including the highest-ranking positions) in the military or civil administration. However, this example is complicated by their slave status: their high level of dependence (and not their education) could account for their compliance.

measure their "output"; (2) they are more mobile and more distant, often on foreign soil; and (3) they have very strong incentives for noncompliance (avoiding death). These factors make monitoring extremely difficult. The key monitoring problem is in the relationship between the high command and the troops in the field: local monitoring will be essential here since central monitoring will be ineffective. It is well known that soldiers fight for others in their units, not for their generals. Centralized monitoring is thus not as important a factor in the military as it is in tax administration.

Because of the difficulty and importance of monitoring, it is clear that highly motivated agents are even more essential in the military than in tax administration. There are essentially two ways to get highly motivated agents in this setting. The first is to make them residual claimants, similar to the tax farming (privatized collection) solution for taxation, by allowing them to "pay" themselves with war booty. This was a common solution for most of military history (in feudal and mercenary armies), but it implies a nonbureaucratic organization and comes at the price of low central control of military activities.

What happens when the need to have a more highly organized army (due to increases in the size of armies, more use of infantry, and new weapons) demands a shift to a bureaucratic organization based on hierarchical monitoring and relatively weak incentives (fixed salaries, dismissal for noncompliance)? In this situation, compliance by instrumentally motivated agents will be low—only agents with high dependence on their job in the military (people facing unemployment and likely starvation if they were dismissed) would be willing to risk death just to keep their fixed salaries. Since we observe much higher rates of compliance in armies than this argument suggests, something else must account for it.

Instrumentally based compliance will be ineffective in a bureaucratic military because agents cannot be made residual claimants, so rulers will be forced to find other ways to motivate them (or suffer consistent losses at war).[14] One way they do this is to use much more severe negative sanctions (such as shooting soldiers who desert or fail to attack), but there are limits to how often these sanctions can be used. Moreover, the threat of severe negative sanctions can produce compliance but not the heroic actions often found in battle. This suggests a general proposition: the shift away from

14. Because the effectiveness of armies had such an important impact on the wealth and power of rulers, rulers are expected to attempt to enhance effectiveness whenever possible. Moreover, wars will work as selection mechanisms that will eliminate rulers (and their states) if they do not maintain effective armies.

feudal and mercenary armies, in which agents are residual claimants, to bureaucratized armies should lead to attempts to develop mechanisms to provide agents with noninstrumental motivations. The institutional rationalization of modern armies is not linked to more instrumental action, but just the contrary: it decreases the level of instrumental rationality and increases the importance of values and emotions.

How were noninstrumental motivations created and maintained in armies? In the West, the key factor seems to be the use of repeated drills, made necessary by the shift to more systematic, bureaucratized army units beginning with Maurice of Orange in the sixteenth century and Gustav Adolphus in the early seventeenth century.[15] Drilling army recruits made them more efficient in battle, but "an additional advantage was that it became safe to arm even the poorest classes, pay them a pittance, and still expect and secure obedience [because] the emotional resonance of daily and prolonged close-order drill created such a lively *esprit de corps* among the poverty-stricken recruits and urban outcasts who came to constitute the rank and file of European armies, that other social ties faded to insignificance among them" (McNeill 1995: 3). This effect was strengthened by the fact that Maurice divided his troops into smaller units, in which "primary personal ties, extending from commanding officer to newest recruit, could also establish themselves among the members" (McNeill 1982: 130). The creation of shared values and emotional attachments in these small groups mitigated monitoring problems.[16] The causal mechanism here seems to be the same one Durkheim (1995 [1915]) identified in tribal religions: repeated participation in collective rituals creates a strong emotional sense of group solidarity. It is no wonder that all European armies soon imitated these innovations.[17]

Our argument suggests that the increasing importance of drill should be roughly correlated with the decreasing importance of plunder and booty in military operations, and this seems to have been the case. The "military revolution" brought together both the use of drill and an increased attention

15. Weber calls Maurice's military "one of the first modern, disciplined armies" (1978 [1922]: 1152). Drill was used by Athens, Sparta, Rome, and China long before it was adopted in early modern Western Europe (McNeill 1995; M. Weber 1978 [1922]: 1152), and Maurice's innovations were inspired by his reading of Greek and Roman history. However, drill had not been used extensively by either the feudal or the mercenary armies that were the dominant forms after the fall of the Roman Empire.

16. "Equally remarkable was the way in which army units obeyed the will of invisible superiors with about equal precision, whether they were located over the nearest hill crest or half the globe away" (McNeill 1982: 133).

17. It is not clear whether or not rulers were aware of this positive effect of drill; it could have been an unintended consequence that was selected for after the fact.

to the logistics of army supply, replacing plunder with centralized provisioning (Downing 1992: 70–72). The strong incentives provided by the prospect of war booty were replaced by the emotional and value-based solidarity created in small military units.

Some may argue that this account ignores the motivational changes brought about by the rise of nationalism. This transformation in the nature of armies, and thus in the micro-foundations of military action, cannot be explained by purely cultural arguments such as the rise of nationalism and the resulting shift in the identities of soldiers. Nationalism became a dominant force in Europe only in the nineteenth century (Hechter 2001, 218), centuries after the basic changes described here.

So why was the use of collective training successful in European armies but unsuccessful (mainly producing collusive corruption) in Chinese tax administration? Both cases produced group solidarity, but why did the army case not produce collusive corruption in which small military units all agreed not to fight? In some military cases it did (see Axelrod's 1984 discussion of trench warfare in World War I and Bearman's 1991 discussion of desertion in the Civil War). However, Axelrod's (1984) work showed why this is rare in the military: noncompliance generally involves collusion with the enemy as well as with fellow soldiers (although this is often not true of desertion), and this is very difficult to create and maintain; trench warfare in World War I was a special case (and even then collusion was limited to certain times of day).

Group Power

Weber was well aware that hiring agents of certain types would affect the extent of control problems in ruler-staff agency relations. He argued (1978 [1922]: 264, 994, 1043) that efficiency could be enhanced by hiring agents with high ability, using formal examination systems to identify merit. This form of recruitment is one cause of the efficiency of bureaucracy. Weber (pp. 232–333, 257, 1007) also discussed the ways in which the process of agent selection affected the relative power of principals and agents. If the support of powerful groups is necessary for security of rule, these groups can often obtain a monopoly (closure) of profitable positions in the tax administration (pp. 1058–1059). For example, nobles in many early modern states used their power to monopolize positions in the tax administration (by demanding ascriptive recruitment based on noble status) and used those positions to increase their wealth at the expense of both rulers and peasants.

Group power was one of the primary impediments to bureaucratic reforms.[18] Since reforms would break group monopoly on positions (by opening up to merit) and remove many lucrative opportunities for corrupt profits, groups with entrenched power often try to block bureaucratizing reforms.[19] Rulers in pre-modern states frequently become dependent on these powerful patrimonial agents. In some feudal and prebendal cases they were necessary for maintaining rulers' power, in others they had purchased offices that rulers lacked the resources to buy back (France and Spain are classic cases), and sometimes they operated large tax farms that rulers lacked the skill or capital to operate (in both late republican Rome [Levi 1988] and early modern England and France [Kiser 1994]); each of these types of agents usually had the power to block reforms contrary to their interests. Weber (1978 [1922]: 981) thus concluded that the bureaucratization of armies always occurs with a shift from propertied to propertyless agents. The next two sections, on war and revolution, document the main ways in which group power is broken, facilitating bureaucratization.

War and Bureaucratization

As figure 1 shows, war is a broad causal factor, with multiple diverse effects. Weber (1978 [1922]: 291, 966) argued that war often affects the form of agency relations between rulers and agents. His main proposition was that competition hastens the development of more efficient forms, in this case bureaucracy. Isolated states do not face such pressure to increase efficiency, so they are expected to maintain inefficient systems longer. For example, Weber (p. 291) suggested that England maintained administration by notables longer than continental states because geographical isolation resulted in less pressure to bureaucratize. Our model suggests an interaction effect between military competition and monitoring capacity: military competition will lead to bureaucratization only if monitoring capacity is developed enough to make bureaucracy more efficient than other forms of organization.

18. There are other important impediments to reform, most important the transaction costs of shifting from one system to another.

19. Entrenched group power is not the only structural factor blocking bureaucratizing reforms. One of the most significant structural constraints on rulers' strategies is a lack of resources (M. Weber 1978 [1922]: 973). It is costly to control agents, and rulers often do not have the resources to invest in control mechanisms. When rulers lack resources, they will often be unable to hire a sufficient number of agents. Sanctions will also be weak when resources are inadequate. Sufficient resources are a necessary condition for the development of bureaucracy, since agents must regularly be paid fixed monetary salaries (p. 1059).

Weber also realized that war could decrease administrative efficiency. For example, he saw the sale of offices as primarily caused by war: "the direct purchase of offices . . . occurs when the lord finds himself in a position in which he requires not only a current income but money capital—for instance, for warfare or debt payments" (1978 [1922]: 966). War tends to increase the discount rates of rulers because it threatens their security of rule, thus making them more likely to alter tax administration in ways that produce short-term increases in revenue at the expense of long-term efficiency (Levi 1988). Perhaps the best example of this is that war increased the sale of offices in early modern Europe (Swart 1949: 21), creating an entrenched group of officials that blocked reforms. In England, with far less military pressure due to insular geography, the sale of offices was much less common (Brewer 1988: 20–24).

War can affect bureaucratization in a third way: it can break the power of entrenched officials to block reforms (Kiser and Schneider 1994). Long and devastating wars, or those resulting in severe loss, can sweep away entrenched powerful agents.[20] Drastic reforms, in which much of the existing administrative structure is removed, can often result from external pressures that both reveal the necessity for reform and redistribute power to facilitate reform. How could the Chinese aristocrats be dislodged from their profitable positions in the patrimonial state several centuries before their European counterparts? As a result of the duration and severity of warfare in the Spring and Autumn Period (722–481 B.C.) and the Warring States era (480–221 B.C.), landed aristocrats in China were much weaker than their European counterparts. These wars devastated the aristocracy, literally killing the main barrier to administrative reform (Kiser and Cai 2003).

War also affects both of the structural causes of monitoring capacity. First, war often determines the size of states and changes in size over time. Success at war often increases monitoring problems by increasing the size of the country, whereas losing land as a result of war often decreases monitoring problems and thus facilitates bureaucratization. Second, war can have a direct impact on technologies of control. Certain types of war can facilitate the development of infrastructure that can also be useful for administration. Wars of conquest, for example, generate huge logistical problems in premodern societies. In order to be able to move troops and equipment more effectively, Roman armies of conquest often built roads and bridges (Mann 1986). Roads built for the military served to decrease transportation times,

---

20. Mancur Olson's (1982) argument about interest groups that produce inefficiencies in politics also made this connection: both revolutions and losses at war are seen as necessary conditions for eliminating entrenched interest groups.

thus unintentionally facilitating both centralization and bureaucratization of civil administration.

The effects of military competition and war on the bureaucratization of armies are even stronger than their effects on tax administration. Armies come into direct contact, which (1) facilitates information transfer (it is easier to see what other states are doing differently); (2) makes the selection mechanism punishing poor organization much stronger (as C. Tilly, ed. 1975 noted, Europe went from around five hundred political units to around fifty in the early modern era); and (3) creates clear "demonstration effects" as to which forms are more effective. Defeat in battle, when it did not eliminate a state, often resulted in reform of the army (McNeill 1982: 161). For these reasons, "armies that fight each other tend to resemble one another . . . more than any other institution" (Lynn 1996: 509).[21] Although it is generally agreed that the Dutch and Swedish armies were leaders in bureaucratization (McNeill 1982: 117–124; M. Roberts 1995 [1967])—supporting our argument that small states should bureaucratize prior to large ones—the "military revolution" quickly diffused to several places (G. Parker 1995 [1979]).

The stronger selection pressure of war on military organization is the main reason that armies generally bureaucratized prior to the civil administration (Downing 1992: 70). It is difficult to date the bureaucratization of armies exactly, because in the military some aspects of bureaucratic organization date as far back as the Assyrians in 1000 B.C., whereas others do not develop until the late nineteenth century (the same is true of civil administration). Roughly, however, many aspects of bureaucracy in armies developed during the military revolution in Europe in the late sixteenth and seventeenth centuries (McNeill 1982; G. Parker 1995 [1979]), whereas tax administration did not bureaucratize in most of Europe until the late eighteenth and nineteenth centuries (English excise administration in the late seventeenth century is an outlier). In fact, bureaucratic military organization served as a model for bureaucratizing civil administration, in Prussia and elsewhere (Gorski 1993: 298).

Differences in the pressure of war also help explain why England was so late to bureaucratize its military. England's insular geography muted the effects of war on its military organization. To take just one example, people could purchase officer positions in the British military up until 1871, while other European states had abandoned that practice just after the Napoleonic Wars at the beginning of the nineteenth century (D. W. Allen 1998). England

---

21. There is never a complete convergence of forms, since some countries are relatively isolated and others lack the resources to imitate successful innovations or face social or structural constraints that prevent their adoption (Lynn 1996: 511–512).

was somewhat isolated from the Napoleonic devastation, so these wars had less effect on it.[22]

Revolution and Bureaucratization

The relationship between revolution and bureaucratization is complicated, as the English and French cases illustrate. Revolutions did have important impacts on bureaucratization in both England and France, but some reforms in that direction occurred prior to both revolutions, and some aspects of tax administration were not bureaucratized for more than a century afterward (Kiser and Kane 2001). For example, direct taxation did not significantly bureaucratize in either country until over a century after their revolutions.[23] The same was true of the English military, which remained primarily patrimonial until late in the nineteenth century (D. W. Allen 1998; Lynn 1996: 511). In France, bureaucratization of the army began in the late seventeenth century (C. Jones 1995 [1980]: 160), and after the Seven Years' War (1756–1763) the French army had developed most "principals of bureaucratic rationality" (McNeill 1982: 164–165).

Revolution was clearly neither a necessary nor a sufficient condition for bureaucratization, but it did have some important effects. The main effects of revolution are on recruitment, through breaking the power of entrenched groups. Perhaps the most important impact of both the English and the French Revolutions was to end both tax farming and the sale of offices, two of the most significant patrimonial elements in the pre-revolutionary states.

Is the effect of revolution due to the removal of obstacles to reform or to proto-democratization? The relationship between proto-democratization and bureaucratization is not strong in France or England. In France, bureaucratization began prior to the revolution under the control of private tax farmers, was carried much further by the revolutionaries (especially

22. Particular wars had important effects on bureaucratization. The Thirty Years' War (1618–1648), because it brought all of the European great powers together, spurred important organizational innovations (McNeill 1982: 161). Sweden's startling success (given its weak resource base) in the Thirty Years' War made it a model that several defeated countries would emulate (and the same was true of Prussia after the Seven Years' War) (Lynn 1996: 514). The Napoleonic Wars also had important effects. For example, the proximate cause of bureaucratization in Prussian tax administration was Napoleon's invasion (Kiser and Schneider 1994). The Crimean War resulted in broad administrative reforms in both Russia and the Ottoman Empire.

23. This demonstrates the fact that assessment and monitoring problems were the main barriers to bureaucratization. It would take the significant improvements in communications and transportation in England in the late eighteenth century and in France in the late nineteenth to set the stage for bureaucratic administration of direct taxes and the introduction of the income tax.

under the Directorate), and developed more in Napoleon's autocratic empire. In England, some of the most important moves toward bureaucratization, such as the abolition of tax farming and the centralization of monitoring in the hands of the treasury, occurred under monarchal government during the Restoration era (1660–1688) (Brewer 1988: 92–93; Prest 1998: 310). Monarchs and emperors seem just as responsible for bureaucratization as parliaments. The most important effect seems to be the one stressed by Skocpol (1979) and Goldstone (1991: 437): revolutions can sweep away entrenched officials opposed to reform.[24]

The Bureaucratization of Contemporary States

All states look to the administrative systems used by apparently successful states as models and often attempt to imitate them. In many cases this borrowing is very useful, but there is one recurring problem: the organizational forms that are most efficient in the most developed (successful) states often do not work well in the very different structural conditions present in less-developed states. As Weber (1978 [1922]) recognized and sociological versions of agency theory stress, the effectiveness of any type of agency relation depends on the structural context in which it is embedded.

One of the best examples of this problem comes from tax administration in contemporary less-developed countries. Most less-developed countries have attempted to model their administrative systems on the bureaucracies of the developed West, and almost all of them have found that this type of reform significantly increases the costs of administration without decreasing either tax evasion or official corruption (Gillis 1989; G. Shaw 1981: 149). It is easy to see why this would be the case: the technologies of control (transportation, communications, record keeping) in most contemporary less-developed countries are more like those in early modern states than those in contemporary developed states. These countries might be right to imitate Europe, but they would do better imitating the administrative systems of early modern rather than modern Europe (Kiser and Baker 1994). As it is, much of their inefficiency is due to over-bureaucratization. One of the most

24. Proto-democratization probably did have some effect (Ertman 1997). Voting institutions allowed some taxpayers to voice complaints about administrative corruption and gave them the power to do something about it. Brewer (1988: 70, 78–79) also suggested that the strength of the English Parliament after 1688 produced both better monitoring (Parliamentary "inquiries") and greater accountability of officials to the public, both of which lowered corruption. Perhaps most dramatically, the French Revolution opened the way for the use of a mass conscript army, which certainly would not have been possible under the absolute monarchy.

interesting questions this raises is why they over-bureaucratize. Arguments from John W. Meyer et al. (1997) and DiMaggio and Powell (1983) about imitation and institutional isomorphism may provide the best answer.

The problems with imitating more-developed states are by no means limited to contemporary less-developed countries. For example, Findley (1980: 156–161) argued that problems with the bureaucratizing Tanzimat reform in the early-nineteenth-century Ottoman Empire stemmed from an over-reliance on Western models in the much different Ottoman context (coupled with a lack of resources to consistently pay adequate salaries and too few trained personnel). The Ottoman Empire in the nineteenth century found that what had worked in France did not work as well for it. The reforms of Peter the Great (1696–1725) in Russia met a fairly similar fate. His attempts to Westernize his administration by adopting some aspects of bureaucracy largely failed, due mainly to differences in Russian context (Peterson 1979). Neither Ottoman nor Russian structural conditions could support a centralized bureaucracy.

Conclusion

This chapter has illustrated an Analytical Weberian approach to the study of bureaucratization. Analytical Weberianism begins with the central questions Weber posed, so, first of all, its substantive concerns are Weberian. At the micro-level, it assumes that individual action is a necessary component of any complete explanation (methodological individualism). It begins with instrumental rationality, but unlike most rational choice approaches it also assumes that other types of motivations (values, emotions) are sometimes important. It then attempts to specify the conditions under which non-instrumental motivations are likely to be important. The last feature is by far the most difficult, and our short discussion of the role of values and emotions in the military has provided only a small part of the answer.

Analytical Weberianism also has an important macro-level component. It attempts to specify the context of action using abstract models (ideal types) of forms of social relations and institutions. Agency theory and Weber's ideal types of patrimonialism and bureaucracy are only a few of the many models available to Analytical Weberians. Combining these micro-foundations and macro-level models, the goal of Analytical Weberianism is to produce both general propositions with abstract scope conditions and concrete analyses of particular historical events and outcomes.

We have shown that both macro-level structural factors and multiple micro-foundations combined to explain bureaucratization in tax administration and armies. Our argument thus combined insights from three camps often thought of as incompatible: second-wave structuralists, rational choice theorists, and cultural sociologists. One of our most counterintuitive and ironic conclusions was that the rise of bureaucratic armies entailed an increase in noninstrumental micro-foundations. In other words, rationalization in this realm at the macro-level produced a move away from rationality at the micro-level. This sort of ironic conclusion is also essentially Weberian: just as an increase in deep religious conviction was associated with the rise of rational capitalism, so too an increase in emotional motivations accompanied the rise of rationalized armies.

The further development of Analytical Weberianism will require a great deal of additional empirical and theoretical work. Our discussion of Analytical Weberianism has been based on only one illustration, the process of bureaucratization in states. Moreover, one could argue that this empirical illustration is one of the easiest for Analytical Weberianism, both because Weber's models of bureaucracy and patrimonialism are very close to contemporary agency theory and because instrumental rationality is dominant (although far from universally used) in his account of bureaucratization. It will no doubt be more difficult to apply Analytical Weberianism to some of Weber's more cultural concerns, such as the role of religion in political and economic development or problems of legitimacy. Just as agency theory has allowed us to increase the precision of Weber's ideal types of patrimonialism and bureaucracy, we will need to draw on other contemporary models to improve upon Weber's analyses of other substantive issues. How far we can get with this is still unclear; additional empirical work will be necessary to clarify the scope of Analytical Weberianism.

The theoretical tasks necessary for the further development of Analytical Weberianism are also daunting. This chapter has begun the process of defining the scope of instrumental rationality, but the larger task of specifying abstract scope conditions for the other significant micro-foundations of social action (values, emotions, and habits) is still ahead. In order to be able to develop and test precise propositions, we must eventually be able to specify the scope of all four sources of social action, and that will require a synthesis of work across the social sciences. In addition and perhaps even more difficult, we must be able to model the interactions among different micro-level causal mechanisms, as they are unlikely to occur in isolation in most cases. Even standing on the shoulders of a giant like Weber, we still have a long way to go before reaching our goal of developing a theoretical model that is both broad enough to capture the complexities of human action and social development and precise enough to generate the testable propositions that facilitate the cumulation of knowledge.

PART III   History and Political Contention

MEYER KESTNBAUM

Mars Revealed: The Entry of Ordinary People into War among States

Sorting through the historical and comparative sociology of state building, revolution, nationalism, social movements, and even social provision, the reader cannot help but notice the important part given to warfare among states. Yet within this same broad tradition of scholarly inquiry, from its roots in classical sociological theory more or less through the 1990s, only rarely and never systematically has armed conflict been subject to scrutiny on its own terms. Warfare plays a role marking time, defining conjunctures, and perhaps catalyzing change. Left largely unaddressed, however, is whether war has an internal logic and structure that may vary in sociologically significant ways. Never asked is how warfare actually works.

Over the last fifteen or so years, however, another scholarly voice has emerged with increasing power. Some fairly small number of sociologists but also historians, political scientists, anthropologists, and even scholars of literature and the arts have produced provocative and compelling research that takes warfare as its central object of inquiry and explicitly examines what difference it makes for states and societies precisely how war is waged. Although frequently produced (and consumed!) with little awareness of other work written in different disciplines, this range of scholarship forms the foundation on which we may begin to construct an emergent sociology of war—one that is simultaneously socially, institutionally, and historically sensitive. Why has the study of war been largely marginalized in historical

My thanks to Julia Adams, Lis Clemens, and Ann Orloff, organizers of the conference at Northwestern University, March 30–April 1, 2001, and to Bruce Carruthers, Rebecca Emigh, Philip Gorski, Roger Gould, Edgar Kiser, Peggy Somers, George Steinmetz, and the other participants for their helpful suggestions. My appreciation also goes to Cynthia R. Cook and James Murphy for their continued and fruitful engagement with this project over many, many months.

sociology, and to what effect? How does scholarship from other fields enable us to ground a new historical sociology of war? What are the main contours and contributions of this emerging field of inquiry? These are some of the questions the following chapter will take up. But first we must ask: What distinguishes the new treatment of war in historical research?

Specifying a Historical Sociology of War

The emerging historical sociology of war takes as its point of departure Max Weber's seminal formulation of the distinctiveness of the state, on which so much of contemporary political sociology depends. The state—understood as a set of administrative, tax-collecting, judicial, and military organizations claiming rule over territory and the people within it—acquires its distinctive quality only when it additionally claims a monopoly over the legitimate use of force.[1] Weber's construction draws attention not to a single moment, but rather to a complex historical process achieved to greater or lesser extent in different historical cases, in which the means of violence are concentrated in a set of coherent organizations—the armed forces—over which the state gains control.[2] Taken to its absolute extreme, the result of this process is a disarming of society and what Robert Bates (2001) and Norbert Elias (1982) before him have characterized as a taming of violence, transforming it from private injury into public force.

If we turn our attention from the state to armed conflict, however, we discover a critical counter-current somewhat obscured by Weber's formulation. Between the beginning of the sixteenth and the end of the eighteenth centuries, while European states attempted to eliminate private as well as contract armed forces and to replace both with standing armies staffed and administered by state officials and maintained by state revenues, warfare certainly fell hard upon ordinary people. Nontrivial numbers were recruited

1. M. Weber (1978, vol. 1: 50–56; vol. 2: 901–904). Cf. Skocpol (1985a: 6); C. Tilly (1990); and Mann (1993)—all of whom explicitly relax the monopoly claim while retaining a focus on territoriality and the organizational structure of the state apparatus.

2. This process is dual in character. First, standing armies became the foundation of war among states, state builders, and rivals for state control. Not only were military organizations increasingly maintained on a permanent basis, but also this shift effected the separation of the warrior from the means of war, concentrating control over war making in the hands of the military commander. Second, European state makers eliminated private as well as contract armed forces. By demilitarizing internal elites and forming a standing army maintained and staffed from the center, European state makers worked to consolidate something approaching an effective monopoly over force, although this was rarely if ever achieved in fact. On the interaction of these two processes, see Kiser and Baer (this volume). On the former process, see especially Redlich (1964–1965). On the latter, see also C. Tilly (1990); Mann (1986, 1993).

for long service into the armed forces, and the lives and livelihoods of many more were ruined or lost when they came into direct contact with military forces, whether at peace or at war. In the main, however, inter-state warfare in this period neither solicited nor depended upon the involvement of "the people" at large, nor were they its primary targets (see Corvisier 1979; C. Duffy 1987; M. Howard 1976; M. Howard, Andreopoulos, and Shulman, eds. 1994: esp. chs. 4, 6; Redlich 1979). Around the end of the eighteenth century, however, this was all to change. In the midst of what historians of the Atlantic world R. R. Palmer (1959–1964) and Jacques Godechot (1983 [1956]) have called "the age of democratic revolutions," ordinary people were brought to the very center of war among states. Whether mobilized by the state into armed conflict or transformed into an enemy to be targeted and attacked, "the people" were inextricably bound up with the conduct of hostilities, and conflicts themselves took on popular meaning and significance that could barely have been imagined only a few decades before (see Best 1980, 1882; Black 1991, 1994, 2001; Paret 1992). These newly institutionalized relationships and practices, as well as models of conceptualizing and making war, marked a true sea change. From their birthplace in a European and North American environment embroiled by revolution and war, they spread ultimately across the entire globe, carried by warring states and imperial powers and adapted by local resisters of foreign incursions. Since the end of the eighteenth century, the particular place of ordinary people in war among states has certainly been subject to change. But the centrality of "the people" has been repeatedly affirmed wherever the terrible toll of armed conflict has fallen upon civilians and other noncombatants and wherever authorities have elicited popular involvement in armed conflict—from wars of independence, ethnic rivalry, national self-definition, and revolution to the commitment of conventional forces dependent on widespread political support.

How are we to capture this world-historical transformation? In the classical idiom, warfare after the eighteenth century may be distinguished by the loss of any pretense that the state maintains a monopoly over the practice of war making. Instead, monopoly claims are replaced by the state's thoroughgoing and often publicly enunciated reliance upon the wide swath of "the people" in armed conflict. This is not to imply a diminution of the state's role as prosecutor of hostilities, for once standing military forces have been formed, the state is always implicated in the organized use of force—whether it is a question of war waged by the state or state challengers. Rather, it is to suggest that what is constitutive of modern warfare is the variety of ways in which the state turns to the ordinary people over whom it rules to act on its own behalf: to take up arms; to produce the matériel and provide the resources necessary for armed conflict; to support a war effort; and ultimately to endure dislocation and devastation; to become casualties and victims; and to comprise the ranks of the lost and the fallen. In Clausewitz's memorable phrase, "war again became the business of the people" (1976 [1832]: 592)—their contribution essential, its impact upon them inescapable.

The historical entry of ordinary people into war has tremendous theoretical significance for the study of armed conflict. It provides the defining core of the emerging historical sociology of war, from which we can draw five central propositions specifying not only the broad domain, but also the mode of inquiry. Let us look at them in turn.

First, the central object of the emerging field is to grasp how the state wages war in fact, appreciating precisely how the waging of war may vary both within and among states. That is to say, not only is warfare a complex social process with its own logic or set of logics, its own peculiar social organization, and its own dynamics and central relationships, but also that logic, that social organization, those dynamics, and the relations on which they are built are historically variable. Such research is defined by the two principal questions it addresses: Why does warfare operate the way it does at different historical junctures? And what difference does it make for states and societies that war is or has been waged in that particular manner? This view of war, in turn, must be distinguished from an analytic focus on war initiation, diffusion, and cessation characteristic of research on international relations or diplomatic-strategic analysis, whether in political science or history.[3] The emerging sociology of war is not primarily concerned with why wars start or why some states wage war against others, but rather with how wars work once opponents are engaged. This is a matter of looking at war *from the inside*, as states, militaries, and societies make sense of it, as each attempts to shape the course of state-organized coercion, and as each is forced to grapple with the experience of armed conflict.

Second, the key to making sense of how warfare works at any historical juncture is the precise manner in which ordinary people are drawn into

3. There are, of course, two important points of intersection between these broad lines of research: when questions of the distinctive logics of states at war produce grounds on which conflicts may expand or contract in scope or may conclude, and when the conclusion of war yields an international settlement upon which ways of war making or the aftereffects of war making may be predicated. These complementarities and points of intersection make scholarship on issues of war initiation and cessation a valuable *adjunct* to the emerging sociology of war but not constitutive of its analytic core. Among historical approaches to international relations, see especially Kagan (1995) and Schroeder (1994). Among political science approaches, see especially Ikenberry (2001); Reiter and Stam (2002); Walt (1996); and Zakaria (1998). For a compelling discussion of how these political science and historical approaches interconnect, see Elman and Elman, eds. (2001).

armed conflicts. Explaining shifts in the place of the people in war and addressing the myriad consequences of such shifts comprise the central directive of this research and provide its substantive unity. Focusing attention upon the place of the people in conflict sensitizes the analyst to questions of the social-structural locations of those drawn into armed conflict, as well as the particular respects in which war envelops them. In the latter regard, two sets of distinctions take on special salience. At issue is not only how ordinary people are drawn into war as armed combatants, but also the host of other ways in which they may enter conflicts, either voluntarily or against their will, as laborers, supporters, association members, bystanders, protesters, and so forth. Further, it is not merely a matter of those mobilized by the state or by state challengers; it is also a question of those designated as the enemy against whom mobilizations are directed and who are, more to the point, the targets of the use of organized and often deadly force.

Third, examining the manner in which ordinary people enter war reveals its promise as an analytic device when scholarly inquiry adopts a self-consciously relational approach, capturing its dynamic and interactive quality.[4] The point of departure for this relationality lies in the observation that preparing for conflict, waging war, and the aftermath of recovery serve to forge, reaffirm, or transform relations among the state, the armed forces, and society. That these relations are frequently expressed not in the idiom of one or another realm of social life but rather in terms of the formation of new and multiple articulations or fusions among the political, the military, and the cultural, for example, makes the relational quality constitutive of the emerging sociology of war deeper still. But armed conflict on this account involves more than the dynamic and fluctuating renegotiation of relations and linkages among institutionally circumscribed actors and social realms. The very means of explanation for these renegotiations, linkages, and fusions is caught up in shifting and contingent alignments between the political and the military occasioned by war, for example, and the formation of new institutional arrangements.

Such a relational approach may be distinguished from a more clearly differentialist strategy for examining war. Differentialist analysis does not ignore relational considerations—far from it. Instead, it focuses primarily on questions of organizational structure, implicitly underscoring the social differentiation such organization necessarily involves. The distinction between approaches is largely a matter of emphasis. The emerging sociology of

4. Cf. Margaret Somers's call for a "relational realism" in Somers (1998: esp. 766ff.) and Emirbayer (1997).

war focuses not on organizational structure per se but rather on linkages, alignments, fusions, and the complex intertwining of relations bound up with organizational structure in institutionally variegated contexts.

Fourth, the analytic power of the relational approach is dependent upon understanding war as both a complex social process and an extraordinary series of events in the lives and histories of peoples and states. The processual quality of war is central to grasping how war is structured by patterns of social relations, and how it expresses certain linkages and alignments and forges new ones. The eventful quality of war is the key to capturing contingency and the distinctiveness of particular conflicts, permitting the analyst to grasp how war unfolds in a given case, as well as the way it is experienced by those caught up in it and the legacies of that unique experience. The processual and eventful qualities of war form its two faces, each of which informs the other in analysis.

The relational focus on ordinary people in armed conflict points to a fifth proposition. National citizenship, understood as categorical membership in a political community of fellow nationals, helps us to understand not only how "the people" came to be involved in war, but also the many and sometimes contradictory meanings given to that involvement by multiple parties to a conflict.[5] National citizenship provides a kind of organizing principle—in Brubaker's words, by way of Bourdieu, "a principle of vision and division" (1996: 3ff.)—in terms of which the involvement of ordinary people in armed conflict is articulated and given meaning; relations among the state, the military, and society are constructed and their valence derived; realms of social life are linked together; and wars themselves are framed. By either its invocation or rejection, national citizenship helps us to disentangle and make sense of the particular relationality of war making since the end of the eighteenth century.

Historical Sociology and the Question of Warfare

Scholarship on war reflecting these five principles—a focus on how wars are waged, ordinary people, relationality, process and event, and national citizenship—builds on a substantial legacy in historical sociology that can be traced back to its birth in classical theory. Nowhere is this clearer than in the works of Karl Marx, Alexis de Tocqueville, and Max Weber. Even among these three grandfathers of the discipline, however, armed conflict and the use of organized coercion by the state or state agents are treated in unsystematic and largely secondary terms. One need only examine the nu-

5. On citizenship as membership, see Brubaker (1992); Walzer (1983: 29–34, 40–51; 1970).

merous passages within their wider work in which particular wars comprise organizing or galvanizing moments. There, the ability of specific armed struggles to produce the pertinent effect is all that matters. How the effect may be explained and whether one might expect other wars to work in a similar fashion go entirely unexamined.

The marginal and unsystematic treatment of war is further reinforced in sustained arguments concerning the direction and movement of history. For Marx, Tocqueville, and Weber, warfare merely punctuates history's march, serving at different junctures to advance what each conceives of as the master processes of history. Unique among the troika in question, Tocqueville is almost entirely silent with respect to how the equality of social conditions or the fall of the old regime was influenced or shaped by warfare.[6] For Marx—from discussions of class conflict as the motor of history to his examination of the origins of capitalism "red in tooth and claw"—organized coercion plays a role as harbinger or even handmaiden of economic change (K. Marx 1977 [1894]; K. Marx and Engels 1978). Coercive force is clearly polyvalent, however, for in the hands of reactionary elements it offers the tool by which the forces of revolution may be suppressed (K. Marx 1963 [1852]). Whether employed for revolution or reaction, violence remains the largely undifferentiated and entirely episodic means employed at different junctures by some social actors to effect or retard transitions in economic formations or patterns of class rule. No different fundamentally is the treatment offered by Weber. Weber provided three arguments concerning the ways in which war drove rationalization broadly: by producing limitations on subsistence and therefore compelling rationalization of economic activity; through victory in war that led to secularization and thus rationalization of lawmaking and law finding (formulated in distinctly pre-modern terms); or through military rivalry that produced the competitive selection of bureaucratic forms of organization (1978, vol. 1: 70; vol. 2: 771, 971–982). More than the others, he specified a range of mechanisms by which the use of organized coercion might shape the movement of history, but as in the case of Tocqueville and Marx, the distinctive logic or logics of war making per se did not enter into these discussions.

Why do Marx, Tocqueville, and Weber place the analysis of war at the margins of their theoretical projects? The varied consequences of particular wars are undeniable, but that their myriad causes and effects are interlinked in an enormous range of ways across individual cases offers a nearly insuperable challenge to general theorizing. As a consequence, all three treat specific conflicts in largely ad hoc terms and make sense of the effects of wars upon

6. See Tocqueville (1955, 1969); and especially Herr (1962: 78–80, 122–124).

other central regularities, such as the pattern of social relations or institutional structure, as so much exogenous shock. If specific wars are intractable, war in general may still be understood—but only as the servant of some other overarching historical process with its own distinctive logic. For Weber and Tocqueville, as one of potentially innumerable elements contributing to a larger pattern of change, by virtue of its subordinate status war does not merit systematic examination in its own right. For Marx, insofar as armed conflict may be understood to have a logic, that logic is not its own but instead a reflection of some underlying economic process. For all three, what is important about warfare is not foremost its inner workings or how these hang together, but rather the effects of the eruption of violence. In the end, it is the classical theorists' ascription of a problematic autonomy to armed conflict—great in the case of individual wars, practically none in the case of warfare overall—that helps explain their partial and unsystematic treatment.[7]

Marx, Tocqueville, and Weber gained somewhat more purchase on war, however, when they turned their attention directly upon the organization of the armed forces. The key lies in their efforts to forge a link between a historically specific understanding of how societies organize for war and particular ways of war making. Marx began in promising fashion in his analysis of the Bonapartist coup d'état in France after 1848. The identification of components of the armed forces with particular class segments and political parties determined what role those components played in political struggles, the bargaining leverage of class actors, and the character of the ruling regime overall.[8] That the organizational components of the military may constitute both sites and instruments of class struggle is quite suggestive but ultimately unsatisfying, however, since Marx stopped short of linking one or another pattern of military organization to particular ways of waging war. Tocqueville, in contrast, made precisely this connection. Under democratic social conditions the nation at large and the rank and file of the armed forces remain close, sharing the same mores and beliefs, as well as the same stake in social and political arrangements. This set of circumstances, Tocqueville contended (1969: 645–652, 657–658, 662–663; see also 230, 235–236, 244), has a powerful impact on the concertedness and scale of warfare waged by democratic societies. Since armed conflict endangers that com-

---

7. There is another aspect of wars' autonomy inimical to analysis. The actual use of coercive force, even when organized, is by its very nature destructive of order. Unlike sometimes violent and equally destructive transformations such as revolutions, violence as a tool can do no more than break, and so it is not without other consideration that structure emerges.

8. Perhaps the clearest example is offered by the distinction between regular military troops representing the party of order and the National Guard. See K. Marx (1963 [1852]: 56–59, 120–124).

mon stake in society, one can expect that democratic nations will be slow to enter war. Once embroiled, however, they will be unusually focused upon it, especially when a say in politics has given the people a common interest in their country's fate and war threatens to strip them of their political power. For Weber (1978, vol. 1: 50–56; vol. 2: 901–904), the military is mainly an issue of the organizational structure of coercive force in a given political association. Whether his arguments were formulated in terms of the bureaucratization of the armed forces (vol. 2: 980–982), the acquisition of a monopoly over the means of violence (vol. 2: 904–910; 1988 passim), or the development of discipline (1978, vol. 2: 1150–1155), Weber returned repeatedly to the historical "separation of the warrior from the means of war" and the "concentration of control over the means of war in the hands of the warlord."[9] The link between organization and war making, however, is most clear in Weber's discussion of discipline: in conjunction with gunpowder weapons, discipline in the professional standing military precipitated a transformation in war such that armies eclipsed horsemen and acquired the capacity to wage offensive wars overwhelming an opponent, a transformation that continued through the French revolutionary period and up to the outbreak of World War I.

If Tocqueville and Weber linked the organization of the armed forces to particular ways of waging war in suggestive ways, it is critical to note that in doing so, they offered perhaps the first specification of the relational and differentialist approaches to analysis that have come to dominate much sociological examination of warfare. Weber attended closely to organizational differentiation and the forms of social distinctiveness to which it gives rise. His differentialism is clear in his focus on the formation of the state as a set of organizations distinct from society and the development of particular institutions. Tocqueville, on the other hand, primarily examined the linkages among institutionally situated persons in democratic social conditions, in particular the bonds of sentiment and interest forged between the armed forces and society. His approach placed primary emphasis on the ways in which the state and society come into finite, patterned relations.

The resurgence of historical sociology in the 1970s and 1980s brought warfare from its position at the margins of inquiry much closer to the center. Seminal work on state building by Charles Tilly (1985, 1990; C. Tilly, ed. 1975)

9. For further elaboration, see also M. Weber (1978, vol. 2: 1223–1226, 1260–1262, 1311–1314, 1359–1362, and 1988: esp. 60–61, 288–289, 319, 405, as well as 154–155, 164–167, 341, 346–347). The discussion in the latter work is divided into three sets of issues: self-equipment vs. provision of equipment; political participation and military role corresponding to self-equipment (e.g., *polis*); and military pressure leading to bureaucratization. The first two sets of issues are discussed at some length as well in M. Weber (1981: 320–321, 324–325, 331–332).

and Michael Mann (1986, 1993, 1998) and on social revolution by Theda Skocpol (1979) contended that warfare is critical to the processes in question. Tilly formulated this claim in six short words that stand as a rallying point around which an entire scholarly orthodoxy emerged: "war makes states, and vice versa" (1990: 67).[10] Although his arguments are nuanced and complex, at their core lies the proposition that the organizational structures comprising the state developed out of the demands placed upon rulers to extract the resources and to develop the organizational capacities necessary to wage war. Conversely, Skocpol argued that the exigencies of foreign war may precipitate fractures in or disintegration of those very same state structures, providing the revolutionary openings through which popular uprisings erupt. And in a fashion echoing Mann and Tilly, Skocpol went on to argue that the subsequent pressure placed on revolutionaries who have seized power to defend their regime by force spurs further state building.

The construction of these arguments suggests a complex appropriation of the classical legacy. Where Tilly, Mann, and Skocpol each accorded warfare a central place in analysis, it becomes solely a means of explaining their primary object of inquiry. While the placement of war in the account is reminiscent of the classical treatment of the master processes of history, war making for Tilly, Mann, and Skocpol is understood as a process characterized by some intrinsic regularities whose nature is central either to state building (through resource extraction) or social revolution (as it precipitates political and organizational cleavages). By taking this step, all three avoided the problem assailing the classical theorists of focusing on the effects of war in entirely particularistic terms.

At the same time, however, this analytic move has several other significant implications. First, Tilly, Mann, and Skocpol offered a rather thin processual conception of war. Warfare is transformed from a complex and socially comprehensive set of practices undertaken by the state into a constant environmental condition—geopolitical competition—with which all states must contend. Second, war making is understood to vary chiefly in terms of the organizational structure of the armed forces. In this respect, each embraces Weber's differentialist orientation toward war, expressed in what Mann (1986) called the very organizational materialism that comprises one of the greatest virtues of this kind of research. Yet when read in the strongest terms, such differentialism with regard to armed conflict suggests that warfare in effect may be reduced to the military; insofar as other elements are introduced into the analysis of change, they are treated in an entirely ad hoc manner. Third, as they looked at the broad historical sweep of warfare, all

10. For other variants, see C. Tilly (1990: 14–15), and C. Tilly, ed. (1975: 42).

three suggested that the great historical turning point came with the formation of standing armies under state control. After this moment, armies and war changed in ways they work into their particular analyses, but these changes did not fundamentally alter the pattern of state building or social revolution.[11] And fourth, the curious product of this analytic position is that it offers little or no room to examine systematically the ways in which particular wars may play a special or distinctive role in wider patterns of change. It is not the case that these sociologists fail to recognize historical variation or particularity in war. Rather, they do not theorize what it means to take individual wars seriously as unique and influential events caught in the wider processes of geopolitical competition, nor do they attempt to link variation in war making itself to the outcomes on which they focus. The net result is that while the seminal work of the 1970s and 1980s elevated war to the center of analysis as a driving force in history, it tended to treat armed conflict more or less as a black box whose internal logic and structure are reduced to military organization and whose varying effects have little to do with changing ways of war making themselves.

The scholarly response to this generative moment in historical sociology prepared the way for the emerging sociology of war, in some respects forming its initial steps. We can best make sense of this response along two lines, the first of which takes the form of internal critique. The point of departure among such critiques can be found in Brian Downing (1992). Building his causal account around the same transformation in military organization to which Tilly and Mann drew attention, Downing subjected this shift to sustained analysis. The "military revolution," as he and the historians on whom he draws contended, is foremost a "qualitative and quantitative change in military organization" (1992: 73) unfolding according to its own logic across Europe roughly between 1500 and 1650. Its result was the dominance of comparatively large, standing infantry forces whose cost placed tremendous financial and organizational burdens upon the states that maintained them. Warfare waged by means of this new military organization undermined vestigial forms of constitutionalism and tended to build military-bureaucratic forms of government in those cases where the costs of war required the extraction of very significant proportions of domestic resources. When war did not require such deep and repeated domestic resource extraction, constitutionalism flourished. What is especially important about the causal logic of this account is not merely that it suggests warfare may shape regime as well as state structure, but that waging war in different ways and to

---

11. The important exception to this last assertion lies in Mann's (1993) often neglected account of military power and its bureaucratic "shell."

different degrees—even if these ways are defined primarily in terms of military organization—may have differential effects on political institutions precisely because they involve distinct social relations of extraction.

Miguel Centeno (1997) took issue with the implication in Tilly's early work, carried through *Coercion, Capital, and European States*, that war making in the early modern and modern periods invariably led to state making.[12] The key to his case lies in turning analytic attention from Europe to Latin America, where it becomes clear that war leads to something like a coherent national state only when substantial organizational infrastructure already in place is joined by the availability of appropriate social alliances and a reliance on domestic resource extraction to wage war. When these conditions are not met, the "extraction-coercion cycle" will be broken, leaving states generally incapable of extracting domestically the resources necessary to maintain their independence and ultimately leaving them cut off from their societies. Like Downing, therefore, Centeno underscored what is at best only implicit in the work of Tilly, Mann, and Skocpol: not only is war making linked to a range of political outcomes, including the pattern of relations between state and society, but precisely how the state mobilizes resources in different institutional contexts is what chiefly determines the political effects of war.

The second significant response to historical sociology's consideration of war in the 1970s and 1980s comes from some of its core contributors, whose subsequent work turns explicitly to the question of military mass mobilization. Mann (1987a) contended that governmental and popular orientations toward warfare have been strongly shaped by different experiences of armed conflict. The state's understanding of war as a rational policy instrument comes from the limited conflicts that were common up to the end of the nineteenth century and that returned after World War II. The popular sense of war, however, is rooted in the historical experience of mass-mobilizing conflicts, derived most especially from the two world wars but including the French Revolution and the American Civil War. In those moments, war offered an appeal to the people because it could be justified readily as the act of a self-consciously political nation and as a key to achieving and consolidating both democratic citizenship and nationhood.

Theda Skocpol (1994) focused as well on relations between the state and society in the midst of extensive and socially comprehensive warfare but suggested that the peculiar qualities of this relationship have everything to

---

12. See also Centeno (2002), where the argument is broadened substantially and in ways that make this strand of research clearly central to the new sociology of war.

do with its revolutionary origins. Rather than producing something that approximates democracy, Skocpol argued, social revolutions have proven most adept at generating mass-mobilizing authoritarianisms, in which those previously excluded from politics are drawn into public life by competing elites but are denied anything amounting to meaningful rights of political participation. The key to the construction of mass-mobilizing authoritarianism, in turn, proves to be the striking consistency with which revolutionary regimes direct the popular classes into protracted and humanly costly war.

As with their internal critiques of war and state making, Mann and Skocpol sensitize us to questions of precisely how the state mobilizes for war and what difference the character of mobilization makes for political outcomes. Unlike the preceding line of critique, however, when attention turns away from professional standing armies, the question is no longer primarily one of material resources but rather of the masses of the people mobilized into armed conflict. And when we are talking about the masses of the people, suddenly not only are questions of popular and revolutionary politics brought to center stage, but also mass-mobilizing warfare itself brings into sharp focus the articulation of popular voice, democratic political institutions, and military participation, suggesting a way of explaining their historical variation. The importance of this move cannot be overstated. By focusing on the way in which mass war forges or alternately expresses particular relations among the state, the military, and society and in turn represents a realignment of the political and military in some respect for the masses, Mann and Skocpol departed from the differentialist focus typical of historical sociology and instead suggested the power of a more relational approach to the analysis of warfare.

If the generative moment of the 1970s and 1980s treated armed conflict more or less as a black box, subsequent research questioning the straightforward link between war and state building and focusing on mass military mobilization goes some length toward prying open that box. Peering inside, we see that warfare may be sufficiently salient and variable a process that its inner workings deserve to be made the central object of analysis on their own terms. The point of departure for such an examination lies in attending to warfare's specifically relational dimensions. The comparative frame allowing us to make sense of war in this manner, however, cannot be limited to the two and a half centuries marking "the military revolution" as well as its immediate aftermath, nor can the extra-European world be ignored, precisely because the social relationships constitutive of war making vary dramatically and in telling ways across these boundaries.

War in Theory

How are we to give substance to the promise revealed by these critiques and extensions? The key lies in refining our understanding of the logic or logics by which war operates and more clearly specifying the array of relationships comprising the social organization of warfare. Such an interior view is the province of broadly theoretical scholarship bearing on historical patterns of war making, much of which is largely disjoint from historical sociology. Work of this sort ranges across a vast terrain, but we may gain some purchase by examining its successive emphases on interaction, organization, and participation. Each offers a lens focusing analytic attention on armed conflict in a distinctive way, underscoring the dynamics of a different dimension of war making, as well as the central relationships in terms of which these dynamics unfold.

The interactionist orientation is perhaps most powerfully advanced in Carl von Clausewitz's *On War*. For Clausewitz, war may be distinguished from all other human activities precisely because it is "an act of force to compel our enemy to do our will" (1976 [1832]: 75). What is critical on this account, however, is not merely a focus on force and compulsion, but rather the particular qualities of the relationship between two parties in which each uses coercion to render the other powerless. Warfare always presumes "the collision of two living forces" (p. 77), each at risk of being overthrown by its opponent, each dictated to by the other until one side emerges victorious. Central to this collision, in turn, are questions of state mobilization, or "the effort to be made."[13] Clausewitz contended that while war in the abstract may appear to drive belligerents inexorably toward their maximum exertion of strength, in real war a range of factors inhibits such precocious escalation. Real war is never an isolated or autonomous act, but rather is waged by states within constraints imposed by their own social and institutional structures and distinctive histories and subordinate to the political object war is intended to serve. To understand the workings of real war and to make sense of mobilization in particular, Clausewitz argued further that for each belligerent we must appreciate war's fundamentally trinitarian character. Real war involves the interaction of violence and passion; uncertainty,

---

13. If the tendency toward extremes manifest in terms of the escalating exertion of military strength is insufficient to underscore a focus on mobilization, one need only consult Clausewitz's most self-consciously historical writing in *On War*, especially the part that forms the bookend and complement to the largely abstract opening chapters. There, in a section entitled "Scale of the Military Objective and of the Effort to Be Made" (1976 [1832]: 585–594), Clausewitz made clear how the expansion of real war and the senses in which it approached the absolute were mainly made sense of in terms of the resources available to the state that were in turn mobilized into armed conflict.

chance, and probability; and political purpose and effect. Clausewitz identified these three elements respectively with the people, the military, and the
government, whose interrelationships form the key to waging any particular
war (see Paret 1992: 110–111; cf. Roxborough 1994).

Where Clausewitz emphasized the logic of military mobilization and the
structure of relations within combatant nations, Carl Schmitt (1976 [1927])
drove the interactionist perspective self-consciously across state borders.
Just as for Clausewitz, for Schmitt the relationship between belligerents
defines the special province of war. And like for Clausewitz, war's fundamentally political character is paramount. Schmitt, however, introduced a
distinctive analytic emphasis. War derives its political character not from
its subordination to policies of state, but rather from the fundamentally
political character of the opposition between friend and foe. In one stroke,
Schmitt made "the enemy" the key to war. The enemy conceived in this
manner is not fixed, but instead may be defined more or less inclusively. The
tendency to define the enemy in expansive terms—in particular equating it
with a nation or even a civilization—is itself a reflection of the political unity
of a people behind a warring state and the extensiveness of the state's own
military mobilization (Schmitt 1976 [1927]: 44–46). Furthermore, such a
focus on the enemy raises a question, also touched upon by Clausewitz,
concerning dramatic variation in the coercive measures or means of attack
that warring states direct at their opponents. Where Clausewitz suggested
these were governed primarily by the political intent of the conflict, Schmitt
argued that the character of the enemy—in particular the threat it posed—
determined the military measures that may be both required and justified.

Embracing the interactionist claim that war is necessarily caught up with
political association and subordinate in powerful terms to politics, the second cluster of scholarship turned its attention from relations among combatant countries to the centrality of military organization in war. Few more
powerful examples of this orientation can be found than Raymond Aron
(1966). Aron contended that war may be distinguished from other forms of
violence because it necessarily involved the organization of violent action by
political collectivities in conflict. Warfare as a result is foremost a question of
maintaining the capacity to use organized force and of disrupting or disor-
ganizing an opponent's capacity to do the same. As such, the armed forces
stand at the center of war as practiced on the ground. To put it another
way: one cannot speak about war without speaking about patterns of military organization, from their structure to their potentially fluctuating coherence. The significance of these claims can be seen in their wide application—
for example, forming the basis of eminent military historian John Keegan's
(1976) analysis of how things military become regimented and how military

units collapse in combat, as well as comprising the kernel around which Randall Collins (1989) has sought to theorize the relationship between war and other destructive phenomena.

The focus on military organization leads in two different directions. The first may be identified with Morris Janowitz (1971 [1960]) and Samuel Huntington (1957). For both, the question is not one of waging war in broad historical sweep but of how to ensure the civilian control of the military. Janowitz contended it is through tying the military closely to society; Huntington identifies the key in the structure of political institutions. Either way, the analysis centers upon the peculiar qualities of the military as an institution, fundamentally distinguished from other social institutions by virtue of its focus on war making and its concentrated coercive capacities, in terms of which its links to either state or society become absolutely central. Attention to the distinctiveness of the military characterizes the vast bulk of the research following in this tradition. However, among its most notable contributors—from Charles Moskos, to David and Mady Segal, to James Burk—the preponderance of this work attends to the lower rather than upper reaches of the armed forces, focusing on rank-and-file soldiers and the ways in which they are tied to the wider society.[14]

The second thread following from the organizational turn adopts a broad sweep and focuses on a series of arguments of fit among the structure of the military, the organization of society, and war. Taking Weber to the logical extreme, Stanislav Andreski (1971) argued that the structure of the armed forces takes primacy, determining the manner in which society is stratified, on the one side, and the way it wages war, on the other. Andreski was primarily interested in how military organization—especially the proportion of the society that could expect to be mobilized during armed conflicts—determined the steepness or gradient of social stratification. On the warfare side, however, he made an important leap. He suggested that what distinguished among ways in which societies wage war could be found in the interaction of formal military organization and rates of military participation. By this means Andreski, like the Segals, Burk, and Moskos, ultimately drew attention to the organizational channels linking society to the armed forces through military service.

Precisely this attention to the patterned ties between the military and society links the organizational to the participatory move in the study of war. Scholarship on participation places analytic emphasis squarely on the regular people whose commitments and fears, whose resolve, and ultimately

14. See, for example, Burk (1992); Burk, ed. (1994); Moskos (1970); Moskos and Wood (1989); D. R. Segal (1989); D. R. Segal and Segal (1993).

whose lives are caught up and made the stuff of armed conflict. This perspective is brought to a high state of theoretical elaboration by Elaine Scarry (1985). Scarry took issue with Clausewitz's simplifying assumption that war was fundamentally a duel, pitting two opponents against one another. It is not Clausewitz's interactionism she found problematic, but rather the presumption that single combat works anything like war, in which opponents are comprised, in her terms, of multitudes. For Scarry, the distinctiveness of war lies in the fact that it is a peculiar kind of contest, and the participation of large numbers of people—and not merely their participation, but the surrendering of their bodies to pain, injury, and death—is required to substantiate the designation of winner and loser. That is, bodily injury suffered by multitudes gives the conflict substance and confers upon the resolution of that conflict a reality that all sides accept as incontrovertible.[15] Such an analysis, in turn, has important political implications, raising the question of how and even whether ordinary people authorize what they give their lives to substantiate.

Turning Scarry's materialist examination on its head, Victor Davis Hanson's (1999) account of the centrality of popular participation to warfare gave primacy to politics.[16] For Hanson, the issue is not how war marks bodies, but rather how democracy transforms war. The crux of the argument can be found in the extraordinary political power Hanson ascribed to armies of free men on a march of liberation, mustered quickly and in significant numbers only to disperse after they are no longer needed. For Hanson, the mission of liberation is absolutely central: expressive of the democratic values suffusing the soldier and the political order, it justifies the extraordinary sacrifices demanded by the state, as well as the extent of mobilization for war; confers on soldiers an abiding sense of the moral high ground in their pursuit; and makes clear when their task is accomplished and they may return home. It is this mission that fosters the terrible intensity with which democratic armies wage war, giving them the capacity to overthrow tyranny and the slave regimes against which they fight. Taken together, for Scarry and Hanson the key to understanding the logic of war lies in both the material and the moral potentialities embodied in the people and the various senses in which their commitments and their lives define the conflict.

15. Scarry captures the unique power of bodily injury to substantiate victory and defeat thus: "the visible and experienceable alteration of injury has a *compelling and vivid reality* because it resides in the human body, the original site of reality, and more specifically because of the 'extremity' and 'endurance' of the alteration" (1985: 121; emphasis in original).

16. See also Hanson (1989), in which the author first put forward arguments concerning free men waging war for their political community.

Understood as complementary lenses of analysis, interactionist, organizational, and participatory scholarship suggests we must simultaneously attend to the way in which relations among belligerents define the terrain of inquiry and give it its distinctive quality; how military organization and its articulations with both state and society are central to these relationships; and the fact that in all of those relationships the participation of the people in war has special and potentially multiple salience. Taken together, these treatments suggest a strong relational understanding of warfare—focusing not only on linkages among state, military, and society and among warring states, but also between "the political" and "the military" most especially—grounded in a refined sense of institutional arrangements and organizational structure. Such a relational emphasis, in turn, highlights and is in important ways contingent upon the particular role of ordinary people in war among states.

Capturing War as Process and Event

To fully realize the potential of a relational approach to war making informed by interactionist, organizational, and participatory scholarship, it is necessary to give serious theoretical attention to war as simultaneously a process and an event. Only by keeping in tension the senses in which war is a process structured by patterns of relations as well as a string of contingent events can we hope to grasp the complexity and richness of armed struggle in dynamic and interactive terms. This involves bringing together two often disjoint strands of analysis, uniting more conventional institutionalist and more clearly culturalist components. If we do so, it is possible to reappropriate in systematic fashion the sense offered by Tocqueville and Weber that warfare varies in sociologically significant ways subject to explanation *and* that some wars or some points in wars possess truly transformative power.

We may start from the contention that warfare is a social process embedded in a set of institutions that give the practice of war structure and a measure of intelligibility. To paraphrase Karl Polanyi's (1957b: 248–250) substantive institutionalist characterization of the economy, war itself is an *instituted process*. The rich, complex "process" sense of warfare is quite clear. If we take Polanyi's lead, process suggests analysis in terms of motion. Much may be set in motion during war: not only soldiers, statesmen, and officials, but also persons in an enormous array of other structural positions or roles, as well as resources and matériel, and even such nonmaterial but no less substantial things as political support, consent, or authority. Put another way, not only state structures but also the economy, the polity, and civil society at large may all be set in motion in the midst of armed conflict. Movement of this sort necessarily involves recurrent interaction, not only among states and between states and persons, but also between persons and the organizational, institutional, material, and cultural features of their environment.

Such movements are given unity and stability by their particular "institutedness." It is the instituting of motion that "produces a structure with a definite function in society; it [establishes] the place of the process in society, thus adding significance to its history" (Polanyi 1957b: 249–250). Our ability to make sense of the interdependence of the multiplicity of movements and to analyze their potential independence, relies upon grasping the particular manner in which those movements are instituted.[17]

While war may be understood as an instituted process, it must also be appreciated as an event. We can see the affinity between these two formulations at first blush, simply by noting that the movements constituting war as a process can be rendered as chains of discrete occurrences. In this limited sense, seeing war as an event is an exhortation to decompose the multiple movements of which it is comprised and to appreciate the historical particularity of its constituent elements, as well as their sequence and timing. This is important, but it is not all that is meant by understanding war as a series of events—unique, sequenced, arrayed in particular historical configurations, and forming particular temporal orderings. As William Sewell Jr. (1996b: esp. 262–263) and Andrew Abbott (1992) have argued in more general terms, taking something like war seriously as a series of events suggests it is important to recognize the contingent quality of its constituent elements. Among forms of contingency, path dependence looms especially large, in which what happens at one moment in time affects at least the possible outcomes of events at subsequent moments in time. Wars are made up of myriad path dependencies, the understanding of which deepens and enriches our grasp of the processual dynamics of war. Notable among the sources of paths are the outcomes of wars themselves—victory or defeat, glory or humiliation. Each of these outcomes may be invested with spectacular and even terrible significance, potentially on a global scale, as we have witnessed in the twentieth century.

---

17. That war is an instituted process has two broader implications of note. The study of the shifting place occupied by warfare in society is therefore nothing other than the study of the manner in which the process of war waging is instituted at different times and places. What is more, in a fashion analogous to what economic sociologists such as Mark Granovetter have powerfully argued is Polanyi's legacy for economic analysis, warfare is embedded in institutions both military and nonmilitary. The full array of institutions—economic, political, religious, etc.—must be taken into account, precisely because they may be and have been as important as expressly military institutions for the structure or operation of warfare. It is in this regard that state service, obligation, and citizenship, just to touch on a few, can be comprehended and brought into the center of a historical sociology of war.

That the outcomes of particular wars influence subsequent events in a path-dependent fashion also suggests an even deeper implication of seeing armed conflict as eventful. Not only are wars arrayed in temporal orderings, but they also have the power at certain junctures to shape or define the very orderings—temporal or otherwise—in which they are embedded. One need think only of the way in which the Great War offers a point of orientation for individuals as well as entire nations in Europe or the manner in which "postwar" in the United States requires no elaboration whatsoever to indicate the period since World War II. In both cases, given wars in their particularity affected people in powerful ways, making of those events themselves an acknowledged and collectively understood point of reference. This is a powerful illustration of one of the senses in which Sewell suggested that "events" matter: they have the capacity to transform structures, not simply "the balance of causal forces operating [in any one moment] but the very logic by which consequences follow from occurrences or circumstances" (1996b: 263; see also Sewell 1996a). Events attain this power to alter the causalities in play because they may transform cultural categories by (re)defining either their content, their salience, or their valorization. Such reshaped cultural categories then may be instituted in the central processes of warfare, forming a distinctive mechanism by which particular conflicts may be invested with extraordinary transformative power that lives well beyond the conflict in question.

The processual and eventful quality of armed conflict helps to set the parameters of historical inquiry into the place of ordinary people in war, focusing attention on the instituted and contingent dimensions of armed conflict as an unfolding process with the capacity to produce varied legacies. These boundaries in place, treatments of war in historical sociology, in theory, and in war studies more broadly drive two clusters of questions to the fore. The first explores why states wage war the way they do, seeking to explain shifts in state-led mobilization, as well as the definition and treatment of the enemy. The second investigates the political and cultural consequences of different kinds of war making, exploring how mobilization and treatment of the enemy shape inclusion in civil society and the polity, as well as the way individuals and nations remember and give meaning to the experience of war. These four problematiques or thematic areas—mobilization, the enemy, inclusion, and memory—constitute the substantive core of the new historical sociology of war. Each inscribes a domain with its own peculiar puzzles and accounts.

In the remainder of this chapter, I will examine noteworthy research within each of these four domains in order to illustrate the distinctive character and contribution of scholarship characteristic of this emergent field of inquiry.[18] I will focus my discussion on the long arc of change linking the democratic revolutions at the end of the eighteenth century to the era of the world wars, dwelling primarily on developments in the Atlantic world. I do this not only because the pattern and logic of change revealed in this manner is of significance in itself, but also because this examination allows me to underscore the issues that emerge as central to the transformation of war making across the globe from the sixteenth century all the way up to the present. Such a temporal and geographic focus should not be taken to suggest that scholarship on other times and places is not powerful—and even less that puzzles or cases outside these bounds are unimportant or somehow not amenable to this kind of analysis. Indeed, the opposite is the case. This selection permits the identification of precisely those analytic issues in the sociology of war that transcend historical moment or geographic location and that for this very reason find broad and telling parallels in other locales and at other junctures. Wherever states and state challengers raise the people in arms or use deadly force against entire populations defined in partisan, national, ethnic, or racialist terms, the value of these central arguments is affirmed, and each such instance provides a remarkable opportunity to refine the kind of analysis that follows, sensitive to variation in historical, social, and institutional setting.

Mobilizing the People into War

The point of departure for a consideration of military mobilization in early modern Europe lies in Geoffrey Parker's (1976, 1988) and William McNeill's (1982, 1989) equally influential formulations of "the military revolution" (as occurring between 1530 and 1710) and "the age of gunpowder empires" (running roughly from 1450 to 1800) respectively.[19] Both accounts centered upon the development of professional standing armies equipped with gunpowder weapons, employing drill and discipline, and maintained by the state. For both, the roots of the transformation are technological: McNeill traced everything to gunpowder weapons in the hands of infantrymen, while Parker suggested the roots of change lay in a new mode of fortification particularly resistant to artillery bombardment. Either way, the effect was to render professional standing armies militarily dominant over other kinds of

---

18. Cf. Caplow and Hicks (2002), a wide-ranging and powerful synthesis of scholarship that, while attending to questions in some of these same domains, does not generally attempt to identify large-scale patterns of historical change or to develop a relational analysis sensitive to variation in historical, social, and institutional setting.

19. For a brilliant rendering of the historical and historiographical debate to which Parker's work has given rise, see Rogers, ed. (1995), which includes Parker's response to his critics.

forces and to spur a significant increase in their size. Both Parker and McNeill also focused on the political consequences of this transformation, echoing the war-and-state-making line of scholarship and in some cases— notably with respect to Downing—providing specific substantiation for its arguments. Parker examined not only how the logistical and financial challenges posed by the military revolution spurred the expansion of state administration, but also how naval gunnery and the fortification of European enclaves abroad gave European states a decisive advantage in their attempts to expand. McNeill was interested primarily in how failure to monopolize gunpowder weapons in Europe precipitated high levels of military competition, accelerating the pace of military innovation and prompting the formation of multiple states, each with a core administration of some substance. The result, McNeill argued, was that when European states came in contact abroad with extensive empires unified under gunpowder weapons monopolized at the center, those non-European empires fell more or less easily before the military might of European powers.[20]

In stark contrast to the claims of Parker and McNeill, Peter Paret drew attention to a subsequent moment of historical transformation that he argued was no less important: "the revolution in war at the end of the eighteenth century" (1992: 3–4; see also pp. 16–17, 26–27, 32–38, 77–80, 136, 151, and Paret 1986). Paret acknowledged the significance of the professional standing army to the history of European warfare. He suggested, however, that to understand military mobilization in the broad sweep—and in particular to understand how warfare broke from the shackles that the maintenance of large professional armies had placed upon it—we must look beyond the organizational structure of the armed forces per se and attend to "new methods of raising forces and organizing armed forces . . . that could add tremendous power to the policies of state" (1992: 3). What were these methods, so different from those employed in the *ancien régime*? They amounted to nothing less than the state's mobilization of the wide swath of "the people" into inter-state war, reorganizing war making around the masses. By making this analytic move and identifying this as the turning point in the history of warfare, Paret assumes a central place in the emerging historical sociology of war. But he is not alone. To varying degrees, historians Omer Bartov (1996a), Jeremy Black (1991, 1994) and Michael Howard (1976: ch. 5), and political scientists Deborah Avant (2000) and Barry Posen (1993), as well as contemporary observers such as Clausewitz (1976 [1832]: esp. 587–594; 1992), echo the sentiment: what we see at the turn of the

20. On the complementary process by which this form of military organization diffused beyond Europe, and to what effect, see Ralston (1990).

eighteenth century is a dramatic break from the past, one that ultimately unleashed tremendous and even terrible military power, born of the new role assumed by the people in armed conflict.

The revolution in warfare at the end of the eighteenth century can be understood most clearly if we see it in four closely related senses. In the first, the recruitment of the people made possible the formation of a new type of military organization: the mass army. Second, the mass army became the centerpiece and focal point of state-led military mass mobilization, extending well beyond merely the raising of troops to the mobilization of the economy and political support for war, employing both compulsion and appeals for voluntary assistance. Third, military mass mobilization had the effect of producing a nationalization of war among states. Not only did the state increasingly direct its appeals explicitly at members of the national community, but as it did so, it began to exclude non-nationals from service and other forms of military participation (see Avant 2000; S. F. Scott 1984, 1986; Thomson 1994). Fourth, the effect of the foregoing was to expand the scale and intensity of war making. War of this type was quite literally more encompassing in social and political terms, mobilizing people from a broader array of social locations to participate actively in a war effort extending over longer periods of time than had previously been the case on either side of the Atlantic. Mass-mobilizing war was distinguished by political goals—liberty, democracy, revolution—of unprecedented breadth and magnitude. The multivalence and popular appeal of these political goals enabled the formation of broad, cross-class coalitions in support of their achievement. But just as important, the difficulty of attaining such abstract aims and their identification with highly charged political stances demanded as well as justified extensive mobilization and sacrifice.

In contrast to the technological roots of the military revolution and the age of gunpowder empires, explanations for the revolution in war at the end of the eighteenth century hinge on politics. But the real issue is, precisely how? Here, my own work becomes salient. I argue that the key to the revolution in warfare lies in the institution of citizen conscription that emerged in the United States, France, and Prussia between 1778 and 1814.[21] Conscription provided the state with the means to construct the mass army, even against resistance; it helped refashion war into a collective endeavor whose success or failure depended upon the contributions of the people; and as it did so, it redefined war among states in terms of the masses mobilized to wage it and the sweeping and popular goals mass-mobilizing war was to achieve.

21. For this and the next four paragraphs on citizen conscription, see Kestnbaum (2000, 2002, n.d. a).

Citizen conscription's transformative power rests in the way it linked the organization of politics to the organization of war, binding the newly emerging institution of national citizenship to state mobilization through a principle of obligatory service.[22] By raising the people to serve in the armed forces explicitly in their capacity *as citizens*, mobilizing them into armed conflict as members of a single political community in whose defense they were obligated to fight, pitting them against foes from whom they were distinguished based on their membership in a national community, and having them fight over issues identified with that political community, military conscription, especially on an extensive scale, helped remake warfare along distinctly national lines (see also Bartov 1994; Brubaker 1992; Scarry 1996; E. Weber 1979). At the same time, conscription helped to make national citizenship an organizing principle of politics. Embodied in authoritative policy and implemented by the state, conscription gave national citizenship a particular political valence and rendered it socially consequential in the most visceral and immediate of terms, helping to forge "national citizen" into a meaningful practical category.[23] But just as conscription injected citizenship into war, it also inserted war into citizenship. Where national citizenship was defined inclusively in class terms, corresponding to the participation of the urban and rural masses in this new kind of war, its gender-exclusive character was affirmed at the same time, excluding from the citizenry or from full political participation women and girls who were formally restricted from bearing arms for the state.

Comparative scholarship on the origins of citizen conscription is quite limited, but my own research contends that the key to its birth resides in a particular and unprecedented historical conjuncture that emerged around the end of the eighteenth century in North America and Europe—a conjuncture defined by the mobilization of the previously excluded popular classes into national politics during a war in which the future of the state and the independence of its people were both at stake. At that moment, popular political mobilization within national states became an integral part of

22. National citizenship was understood not in terms of one's place in a society of estates and orders based upon privilege. Rather, it was understood in terms of the individual's unmediated and explicitly political relationship to the state as the sole legitimate possessor of territorial rule, the authority of which derived in turn from the people themselves as a sovereign nation. Citizenship, then, meant membership in the political community of fellow nationals. In contrast to corporative understandings of membership, it was formally egalitarian, although national citizenship's social inclusiveness might vary, for example, in terms of whether the mercantile or laboring classes formed part of the sovereign collective (Brubaker 1992: 14–15, 27–29, 35–49; on the revolutionary understanding of the nation in expressly political terms, see also Hobsbawm 1990 and especially B. Anderson 1983).

23. I am indebted for this construction to Brubaker (1996: esp. 13–22).

armed struggle to seize, maintain, or re-acquire state power in war against other states. Facing extensive political mobilization and inter-state war together, political and military elites were confronted with a new set of urgent imperatives: to build a viable regime around the popular classes while also organizing and deploying the force of arms. Under these conditions, coalitions of reformers, regardless of their constitutional orientation, determined that the conscription of national citizens was a *politically desirable* response to the host of challenges they faced. By incorporating the wide swath of "the people" as citizens, conscription offered a way to build popular support for the regime in power while also gaining a measure of central direction over those newly mobilized into politics. Bringing the people into the regime as citizens, binding them into a political community and to the state through obligation—*that* was the key to consolidating a regime suddenly dependent on popular mobilization, strengthening the hold of elites over state power, and building the military means necessary to contend with the crises they faced.[24]

We can see how both reformers and the representatives of those newly mobilized into politics understood citizen conscription to help consolidate a politically mass-mobilizing regime in three distinct ways, each corresponding to a different sense in which the policy incorporated the people as citizens. By leveling social differences in the military and political spheres, conscription rendered all (male) citizens formally equal. By breaking down the insulation of the line army from society and instead bringing the army closer to the people, conscription integrated the people and their state into a single polity. And by making military service an obligation of national citizenship, conscription politicized relations of citizens to one another, the state, and armed conflict, transforming military service into *the* constitutive political act and military mobilization itself into a form of political mobilization on behalf of the regime in power.

What national conscription offered reformers was a way to foster and channel the mobilization of the popular classes, broadening the social foundation of the regime in power while undercutting threats to its stability. What it offered the masses was political recognition if not democracy, a way to participate in at least one of the state's chief endeavors, and a way—perhaps only symbolically—to appropriate the state as their own. In any particular historical crystallization, elements of popular participation or state control received priority in the aspirations of reformers and popular

---

24. For this paragraph and the two following, in addition to previously cited work by Kestnbaum, see also Kestnbaum (n.d. b).

groups, as well as in the implementation of the policy on the ground. In all cases, however, it was the way in which conscription incorporated the people as citizens that held out its promise as a tool of war.

Such an account of the politics of conscription receives additional support from other recent research on the development of citizen service across the nineteenth century in which political logics are emphasized generally at the expense of more military-centered accounts. Deborah Avant (2000) contended that the spread of the citizen army in the early part of the nineteenth century was due just as much to efforts by regimes in power to legitimate their rule as to the strategic advantage that might follow from implementing the policy. Conscription as a policy also underwent substantial reform across the nineteenth century, approaching something like universal male service. Margaret Levi (1997) argued that polities eliminated mechanisms of buying out of service obligations, however, not under military pressure or in accord with the expansion of the franchise, but only when standards of fairness understood in terms of equal service and sacrifice were embraced by lawmakers, either because those standards had become widely diffused or because they were imposed from above by reformist ministers. It is important that both of these accounts reinforce a distinction in practice between citizenship and political democracy. For Avant, legitimating rule in terms of citizen service had less to do with democratic institutions than with the way it signaled acceptance of the principle of popular sovereignty among citizens and other states. For Levi, the franchise per se was not the issue, but rather how the ideology of universalism came to shape the actions of lawmakers.

The Opponent: States and Peoples as the Enemy

Implicit in the examination of the revolution in war at the end of the eighteenth century is a second set of questions focusing on the cultural construction of the opponent in war and its relationship to the *jus in bello*, or the actual practices of armed forces in conflict. The point of departure for this line of inquiry can be found in the analysis of the laws of war governing treatment of the enemy, framed normatively by Michael Walzer (1977) and examined in terms of concrete practices and institutions by Geoffrey Best (1980; see also Best 1994). Both focused upon the historically variable link between the protections afforded persons comprising the opponent in war and the particular roles those persons played in the opponent's war effort.

Such a formulation draws attention to two kinds of deviation from late-seventeenth-century theory and practice, which dictated states wage war against opposing states and their militaries within specific confines and not against civilians. The first is the extent to which basic protections such as humane treatment after capture were systematically denied combatants. The second is the extent to which noncombatants were exposed to direct and especially deadly attack from military forces. Both are questions of the failure to accord minimum protections to particular categories of participants in war mobilizations. Each is associated with brutality, war crimes, and ultimately the commission of atrocities. The second sort of deviation received particular attention from Walzer and Best because of its terrible consequences for civilian populations. And for the emergent historical sociology of war, this second sort of deviation also comes to center stage because of what it says about how broadly "the enemy" is defined. At issue is the practical elimination of noncombatant immunity, either because civilians are intentionally targeted for the application of coercion or because military forces fail to discriminate between combatants and noncombatants in their use of force.

It is perhaps surprising that none of the shifts in state mobilization that occurred at the end of the eighteenth century—the development of the mass army, mass military mobilization, the nationalization of war, or the enlarged scope of conflict—precipitated an immediate relaxation or redefinition of the protections afforded soldiers or civilians that had prevailed since the end of the prior century (see Best 1980; M. Howard, Andreopoulos, and Shulman, eds. 1994). They did, however, yield the guerrilla fighter, waging war by popular uprising, whose anomalous position as neither soldier nor civilian created new challenges for mass-mobilizing forces that faced one another in war.[25]

An important collection entitled *On the Road to Total War* (Förster and Nagler, eds. 1997) identified a turning point in the treatment of the enemy during the American Civil War, which revealed a notable lack of restraint with respect to guerrillas in conjunction with a willingness to destroy private property, including property in slaves. As James McPherson argued in this collection, both the harsh treatment of guerrillas and the intentional destruction of property by armed forces owed their origins to the especially bloody war fought in Missouri. There, guerrillas refused to conduct themselves as soldiers, simply disappearing only to reappear as an even greater threat; and there, it became clear that destroying property was a potent way to deny resources vital to the opposing military while simultaneously undermining popular support for the opponent's war effort. With that pattern of mobilization and that degree of bloodshed, both the scope of the enemy and acceptable recourse shifted. The experience of Missouri "predisposed them

25. See Clausewitz (1976 [1832]: 479–483). On the triangular nature of conflict that gave rise to the guerrilla, see Shy (1973: 126ff.).

[Grant, Sherman, and Sheridan] toward the conviction that, in Sherman's words, 'we are not only fighting hostile armies, but a hostile people,' and must make them 'feel the hard hand of war'" (McPherson 1997: 302).[26] By this means, the Civil War and the German Wars of Unification shortly after initiated a long historical process in which states waging mass-mobilizing war against equally mass-mobilizing opponents began to target as a matter of course not just their opponent's instrument of war making—the armed forces—but their opponent's *capacity to make war*—the resources, economy, and political support on which mass war depended.

The link between conceptions of the enemy and protections afforded that enemy is perhaps most clearly forged in the work of Omer Bartov (1996b, 2000) and John Dower (1986) on World War II, a moment that raised these issues in high relief and exposed their potentially horrific consequences. For both, the erosion of noncombatant protections and the lumping together of the opponent's population into a homogeneous and dehumanized enemy precipitated a barbarization of war that expressed itself in unprecedented slaughter, massive dislocation of entire populations during and after conflict, and genocide. Dower argued, simply put, that the racialization of ethnic differences permitted a precocious escalation of brutal acts by American and Japanese troops against one another in the Pacific theater, as well as the willingness, for example, of the United States to intern Japanese Americans on U.S. soil. The key, for Dower, lay in the way such racialized enemies could be readily demonized, rendering them objects of extraordinary fear or dread and making wartime acts of brutality appear both reasonable and necessary.

Bartov (esp. 1992) echoed these same arguments in his examination of the European theater of World War II, but in *Murder in Our Midst* (1996b) and the later *Mirrors of Destruction* (2000) he built upon them in significant ways, drawing in arguments similar to those developed by McPherson. For Bartov, the origins of the Holocaust, as well as the murder of hundreds of thousands of non-Jewish civilians by the Nazi regime, lay in the experience of World War I. In Bartov's terms, World War I saw the emergence of "industrial killing," the "mechanized, rational, impersonal, and sustained mass destruction of human beings, organized and administered by states, legitimized and set in motion by scientists and jurists, sanctioned and popularized by academics and intellectuals" (1996b: 3–4). The experience of industrial killing in World War I forced Europeans to reformulate their understanding of war and its relationship to society. This new conception amounted to a radicalized version of industrial killing in which the question—at least for

26. For an extended account along these lines, see especially Royster (1991).

Germans—was not how to prevent it, but rather how to master it. In extreme form, this view held that "the only way to prevent the annihilation of the individual and the collective to which he belonged was to further perfect the techniques of killing and to more strenuously mold the mind of the individual so as to accomplish the total extermination of the enemy" (Bartov n.d.: 2; see also Bartov 1996b: 26). What is critical here is that because World War I had mobilized the vast majority of populations in national terms, the only way to prevent similar destruction in the future was to bring about the total annihilation of entire peoples perceived as the nation's enemies. When the enemy was identified not only with states waging war against Germany, but also with a systematically racialized and dehumanized Other defined in contradistinction to the German nation—lurking even within the territorial confines of the Nazi state—industrial killing expanded to encompass what Bartov characterizes as "militarized genocide."

Backlash against the horrors of World War II, the Holocaust, and the use of weapons of mass destruction, as well as the military defeat and dismantling of totalizing regimes, goes some way toward explaining retreat from the homogeneous enemy and a reassertion of the strong distinction between combatants and noncombatants in the aftermath of World War II (see Best 1994). Much the same can be said about the period three centuries before, following the Thirty Years' War, when first the theory and then the practice of noncombatant immunity were firmly established (G. Parker 1994). What McPherson, Dower, and Bartov suggested, however, was that the potential for precocious expansion of the enemy resided in conflicts characterized by guerrilla war and the multiplication of nonconventional combatant roles, the radical confessionalization or racialization of parties to the conflict, and a conviction for historical or ideological reasons that only by indulging in brutality oneself could an opponent's penchant for committing atrocities be overcome.

Inclusion and Exclusion in War

The processes of group definition arising from war—whether in terms of the designation of the enemy or the "we" who fight together against a common foe—help explain both the dominance of a national idiom since the revolution in war at the end of the eighteenth century and conjunctures at which nationality acquires an ethno-religious or racialist cast and becomes decoupled from (or not entirely dependent upon) the territorial state at war.[27]

---

27. On variations within the national idiom, see the provocative treatment offered in Brubaker (1996), and especially the distinction Brubaker credits to Michael Mann of state-framed versus counter-state understandings of nationhood.

If we turn this national mapping inward, looking not at relations among belligerents but instead at relations within the country at war, our attention is drawn to questions of differential inclusion in the polity and to democratic political participation. Arthur Marwick (1974) framed the issue in its seminal form. Echoing Andreski, he focused analytic attention on the participation of the people in the war effort and suggested that the form of their military participation had everything to do with how they were included in the civic or political life of the wider society.

Marwick's concerns have found expression in two different lines of scholarship. The first examines how the pattern of state mobilization of persons drawn from particular categorically defined social groups shapes the way in which those groups are included in civil society or the polity. The second looks at how the incidence of war or state mobilization interacts with the formation of voluntary associations and social movements as expressions of democratic participation.

Skocpol's (1994) argument that social revolutions tend not to produce democracies but rather mass-mobilizing authoritarianisms provides a powerful grounding for research along the first line. Nested in her account is the claim that formal inclusion in the polity as a citizen is not itself a guarantee of meaningful political participation. Two important issues arise from this formulation. Skocpol underscored a recurrent theme in research: inclusion due to military mobilization is often partial and contingent on the maintenance of elite and formal institutional supports. At the same time, she highlighted the political dynamic driving whatever inclusion does follow from mobilization. While not producing democracy, revolution gives the masses previously excluded from politics influence over political outcomes because their support is pivotal to revolutionary elites. James Burk (2001), Margaret Levi (1997), and Elaine Scarry (1985: 104–105, 153–157, 345–346; 1990; 1991) explicitly translate this argument into the domain of armed conflict. Once the wide swath of "the people" is drawn into war, it is the people themselves who must authorize the state's war making precisely because it is they who carry arms on the state's behalf. In short, war depends on the consent of the warriors. Because the state relies upon the support of those it brings into armed conflict, military mobilization confers a type of political power on those mobilized with which they may advance or defend a claim to be included in civil society or the polity and to which other political actors must respond.

The foundation for claims of inclusion, however, comes from another source altogether. One product of the close association of national citizenship's birth with forms of mass military mobilization has been that in a wide variety of settings, performing military service for the state has offered a compelling and politically resonant basis on which to stake claims for full citizenship rights. In democratic contexts, this has had powerful but differential effects on political inclusion and produced markedly different citizenship dynamics for different groups mobilized into war.[28] For African Americans during the U.S. Civil War, the link between military service and citizenship claims meant initial resistance to permitting free or freed Blacks to serve in the Union Army for fear of the political implications; a requirement of separate and subordinate service once they were inducted; and after formal emancipation a strong reluctance, rooted in long-standing racial discrimination and the political compromises that produced a reunification of the United States after Reconstruction, to accord even those Blacks who had served in the armed forces anything approaching political equality with whites in the South (Berlin et al. 1979; see also Valelly 1993). But it also meant that as African Americans served in the armed forces in significant numbers, military service itself constituted a powerful argument for the receipt of voting rights, pensions, and other benefits from the state based on veteran status (see Skocpol 1992, 1997).

Traditional exclusions of women from the soldiery based on gender meant that when national citizenship was first articulated in socially expansive terms during mass-mobilizing war at the end of the eighteenth century, women were not only excluded from the citizenry in any meaningful political sense, but also were prevented from laying claim to the status of citizen through military service.[29] The simultaneous institutionalization of what Jean Bethke Elshtain (1987: 121) has characterized as the notion of "civic virtue as armed and bellicose" and women's formal exclusion from bearing arms for the state has been expressed in the dominance of discourses characterizing women not as warriors fighting and dying, but rather as the "noncombatant many" who play an auxiliary or pacific role with regard to war and may comprise its victims. That women were excluded from the franchise as well as military service, however, did not prevent many in fact from seeking a more active role in war, nor did it impede the state from calling upon them during war in other capacities.[30] Severing the link between citizenship and military service for women, however, forged an entirely new relationship between war and political participation. It spurred the formula-

28. See Burk (1995). On the historical origins of the principle of civic militarism, see Hanson (1989; 2001: esp. 99–134).

29. Refer to my earlier formulation with respect to the manner in which citizen conscription injected war into citizenship.

30. In addition to Elshtain (1987, especially see pp. 47–159, 163–171, 180–193, and passim) for women's roles in war and the military, see especially M. W. Segal (1995); De Pauw (1998); and Goldstein (2001: esp. ch. 2).

tion of alternative foundations for citizenship and grounds for the extension of suffrage and social provision to women, rooted not in war fighting but instead in women's roles as laborers or mothers (Elshtain 1987; see also Skocpol 1992). And it exposed a powerful duality in the conjuncture defined by war: an opportunity to participate in a national endeavor and to illustrate publicly women's ability to contribute in a variety of realms, from the family to voluntary associations to paid labor and even uniformed service (see, e.g., D. Campbell 1984); war was also something against which women and men could mobilize since pacifism no longer necessarily implied surrendering the claim to participation in the polity.

The second line of scholarship on inclusion in many ways picks up where the first leaves off, focusing on how patterns of state mobilization for war are linked to the formation of voluntary associations and associational networks. Some of the most powerful underscore the manner in which war as a particular kind of historical event intervenes in processes of movement formation. Take, for example, Elisabeth Clemens's (1999b) provocative examination of the women's movement up to World War I. On Clemens's account, state entry into armed conflict not only spurred pacifist opposition, but also fundamentally altered the *intersection* between suffrage and pacifist networks comprising the women's movement. Whereas joint membership in associations was unproblematic before the war, with the advent of hostilities each network was rent in two: the latter between peace and "women's peace," the former between suffrage and suffragists for peace. John Horne (1994, 2000), by contrast, examined the other side of the process during World War I, focusing on how the specific demands of state mobilization dramatically altered the organization of labor and its articulation with the state. For Horne, industrial mass-mobilizing warfare prompted the French and English states to accelerate the organization of labor, albeit in a subordinate position, to ensure continuous production and labor peace. This had the effect of turning labor's attention away from management and toward the state as the locus of redress of grievances, and in conjunction with the bargaining power that came from organized labor's central role in the war effort, it led labor to reformulate its demands in terms of policy reform.

As part of their broader research on large membership associations in the United States, Theda Skocpol and her collaborators (Skocpol et al. 2000) took the logic of Clemens and Horne and extended it across many American armed conflicts, looking at how wars have shaped associational formation broadly (see also Skocpol et al. 2002). Much of their effort was devoted to explaining the extraordinary expansion of associationalism in the aftermath of the U.S. Civil War. Reliance on local elites to form military units rooted in the community to wage the war retarded association formation throughout the conflict, but the national war effort created strong ties among elites at the center and provided them with a model of how to organize associations based on the federal state, which together prompted associational formation at the end of hostilities. Associational expansion or contraction surrounding the world wars had everything to do with which national, federated associations the state enlisted to support or assist in the war effort, providing resources and visibility, and which associations instead were explicitly or implicitly identified with the enemy in the conflict.

The strong relationship between military mobilization and inclusion becomes even clearer in scholarship examining how the very stimulus provided by war to associational growth feeds back into the way states mobilize for mass war. My own work illuminates this issue. At the end of the eighteenth century, the confluence of popular politics and war that gave rise to citizen conscription also produced an efflorescence of politically engaged and locally rooted organizations, from citizen militias and revolutionary committees to political clubs, popular societies, and fraternal and other voluntary associations. As networks developed among these local partisan bodies, they formed much of the organizational backbone for the mobilization of the previously excluded popular classes into national politics. When the onset of war forged strong links between the emerging associational structure and public authorities, the locally rooted partisan organizations were loosely tied together into an extensive network of networks, bound at the center and reaching down to the locality. It was this network of networks, comprised of and held together by public authorities, quasi-public bodies, and voluntary associations, that provided much of the organizational capacity necessary to mobilize the breadth of the people into war. Thus, in one important sense, associationalism made the revolution in war—and citizen conscription in particular—organizationally possible (Kestnbaum 2000, n.d. b).

Similarly, John Horne's (1997) seminal edited collection underscored the many ways in which European states relied upon voluntary associations and quasi-public commissions to organize and administer much of the local and municipal apparatus of the centrally directed war effort (see also Horne 1989). Just as important was the extraordinary degree to which the state left the maintenance of order and morale to those at home, as well as the provision of some social services and the raising of public funds through bond sales, for example, to volunteer efforts. Scholarship on the role of women contributing to the maintenance of the family as well as volunteer efforts complements this strand of research, forming somewhat of a recurring theme: mobilization for mass war has been in many ways constituted by its dependence on voluntary associations and other nonstate agencies.[31]

The Memory and Meaning of War

If participation in war may yield political inclusion, armed conflict's darker face is no less significant. The experience of mass-mobilizing warfare can be shattering, not only in a material and institutional sense, but also insofar as it destroys deeply rooted understandings of social or political order and the nature of armed conflict itself. Faced with such an extraordinary and cataclysmic event, soldiers and citizens no less than states attempt to come to grips with what they have been through, assigning meaning or significance to sacrifice, horror, and loss, as well as victory, cause, and heroism. Such efforts to make sense and find meaning are representational, played out during particular conflicts but, just as important, continuing long after, as nations reappropriate a war, fixing that conflict and its significance in memory that must be reaffirmed and is subject to reevaluation.

Recent scholarship on representation and memory in war is distinguished by a focus on the dynamic relationship between the community of those who fight and the defining qualities of mass war. Emphasis on one or the other side of this relationship defines two basic approaches. Jay Winter (1995) occupies a central place among studies underscoring how the experience of mass war shaped the "we" who have fought (see also Winter and Siran, eds. 1999). Winter proposed to examine the extraordinarily complex impact of World War I on European cultural history broadly by focusing on a single central theme: the form and content of mourning for the dead. For Winter, the catastrophe of war was most clearly expressed and acutely felt in the extraordinary loss of life, the scale and scope of which drove almost all towns and villages in the major European combatant countries to become communities of bereavement: shocked by death, painfully trying to understand what had happened, ultimately accepting loss. In the study, grounded in an analysis of associational life focused on commemoration of the dead and assistance for those the dead had left behind, Winter argued that forms of "fictive kinship" emerged from this common mourning, matching the brutality that war brought into social life to a range of social solidarities within which compassion and ultimately consolation were available to those who mourned.

George Mosse (1990) is an exemplar of the alternative approach, placing

---

31. In addition to those works previously cited with respect to associational contributions to war, see Eisner (2000) and Keller (1977).

emphasis rather on how the experience of armed conflict produced new understandings of war itself. Mosse examined the emergence, transformation, and ultimate collapse of a single, powerful "myth of the war experience" from the period of the French Revolution to World War II. The reality of war confronted by ordinary people was of something uncontrolled and uncontrollable, unintelligible, horrible, and terrifying. By contrast, the myth amounted to a simple claim: war was purposeful and glorious, fought on behalf of the nation by its patriotic and willing citizens. As a consequence, war for the nation gave meaning to the lives of those who waged it, and most especially the myth conferred meaning and significance upon the tremendous loss of life such war produced. The myth's appeal lay in the consolation it offered in the face of mass death, providing a means of transcending the experience. By emphasizing war as a test of manliness, the special camaraderie that came from engaging in that test together, and the exceptionality that flowed from participating in what was constructed as a sacred endeavor, the myth not only linked national to personal regeneration, but also bound state-organized violence on a massive scale to the achievement of political goals and to national self-definition.[32]

The myth emerged during the revolution in war at the end of the eighteenth century, and its power was still clearly in evidence in the extraordinary enthusiasm for war on the eve of 1914. Confrontation with the reality of what Bartov has called industrial killing and the disillusionment that followed, however, drove warring states to explore ways to mitigate the horror of mass war. Most distinctive were states' attempts to derive meaning from the very scale of the killing itself. The result was the cult of the fallen soldier, which in Germany took the form of sanctifying the youth who sacrificed themselves joyously for the fatherland. In this, youth was symbolic of manhood, virility, and strength, and death was not to be understood as death at all but as sacrifice and resurrection. The recognition that both personal and collective redemption lay in the death of their fellows offered a way to help overcome the fear of those who witnessed it first hand and a way for all to grapple with the horror and loss of war.

The awful irony in this process, according to Mosse, is that while the development of the myth of the war experience allowed the myth to weather the Great War, retaining its power to unify and motivate, it also had the effect of making mass death itself acceptable. Most notably in Germany, this process precipitated a brutalization of politics in which the means and methods typical of war were imported into domestic politics and on which

32. Cf. Elshtain (1987), for whom the myth of armed civic virtue is somewhat more broadly construed and in that form has substantially older roots, although it is expressed in an equally masculine idiom.

the political ascendance of the Nazi party and its promulgation of the "final solution" rested. Here we can see both the affinity between Mosse and Bartov and an important source of disagreement. Bartov contended that rather than militarizing politics, industrial killing politicized war in new and terrible ways, especially for Germany. It shattered any illusions of individual worth or chivalry and heroism in war, depriving armed conflict of those sources of meaning. Instead, it led to the forging of a new ideology and the production of a new imagery of heroism and liberation organized around the extermination of whole populations by military means (Bartov 1996b). This debate aside, for Mosse the defeat of the Nazi dictatorship in World War II broke the power of the myth in Germany. The postwar German state represented war as tragic rather than glorious; commemoration focused upon its many victims rather than its perpetrators. Ultimately, at least in Germany, war was severed from its purported power to regenerate either the individual or the nation, although the same could not be said necessarily for the states that emerged victorious from World War II.

Both approaches to representation underscore the centrality of mass death, consolation, and brutality to the memory of war in the twentieth century, but they highlight very different intersections. For Winter, a focus on community is tightly bound up with receiving consolation for the mass death experienced by ordinary people. Community in this account is nationally circumscribed but locally defined. In turn, where public authorities are involved, this is largely an issue of how local groups experience and negotiate the process. For Mosse and Bartov, a focus on understanding war suggests that the experience of mass death demands a response but that the product of that response ultimately is to orient those who have experienced the horrors of mass death toward inflicting something even more horrible and brutal on their enemies. For both, the experience of mass death forges an especially powerful form of militant nationalism, and in turn, the dynamics of mass war focus primarily upon the central state.

Winter, Mosse, and Bartov come together, however, in their understanding of the development of the means to represent the experience of mass death. For all three, it is an issue of elaborating cultural codes and finding a language of mourning and commemoration within established genres. This has involved developing particular ways of "seeing" the dead, based on older motifs and images of sacrifice, death, and resurrection, as well as masculinity, strength, and youth. Such efforts were complicated, however, by historical, national, and genre-specific challenges facing those attempting to endow representational narratives of heroism, victimhood, and slaughter with wider meaning.

Conclusion

Perhaps the greatest contribution of the emerging historical sociology of war comes in offering a vantage point from which to assess the nature of modernity. More than fifty years ago, John Nef (1950) fixed the terrain for such considerations by asking about the relationship between war and human progress. Fully relational examinations of state mobilization, the enemy, inclusion, and memory suggest one response. Since the introduction of ordinary people into war among states, armed conflict has been constituted by a central antimony between the progressive potential of concerted action by united peoples and the terrifying and horrific destructive power that very concert unleashes. War fuses together democracy, citizenship, nationhood, and collective political will. It brings terror, subjugation, horror, and death. It joins meaning and meaninglessness.

The capacity of warfare to be both world making and world breaking makes it leap off the historical landscape for analytic attention, forcing us to attempt to make sense of it. Today, from the killing fields of Rwanda, to the breakup of the former Yugoslavia and the emergence of ethnic cleansing, to war in Iraq, not only ravaged generations and genocide, but also revolution, the struggle for political independence, and the destruction of tyrannies great and small by force of arms keep warfare on the agenda. These are the potentialities residing within war as both process and unique event. Making sense of these potentialities—explaining how and why states mobilize the people as they do, how the enemy is constructed and treated in conflict, how societies at war redefine the boundaries of political inclusion and cope with the terror and destruction they must endure—is precisely what the emerging historical sociology of war sets as its task. Insofar as this new domain of inquiry pushes further and deeper, we may better appreciate the tension between war's destructive and constructive faces, which have together bequeathed to modernity one of its most distinctive qualities.

ROGER V. GOULD

Historical Sociology and Collective Action

It is slightly inappropriate, in a revealing way, to provisionally identify the subject of this chapter as "the historical sociology of social movements."[1] The phrase contains a glaring anachronism. The concept "social movement" is usually taken to apply to an ongoing, organized effort at social transformation identifiable not by the content of the intended transformation, but by its form—notably, its reliance on collective action of a noninstitutional or even disruptive sort. This sort of collective action is so thoroughly a feature of twentieth-century industrial society that coupling it with the phrase "historical sociology" is a little like putting a book about the Crusades in the international relations section of the bookstore. Still, the anachronism offers a hint at one of the contributions historical sociology has made to the study of contentious politics. To adumbrate that contribution, I will switch to the term "contentious collective action," under whose semantic umbrella I suggest we include contemporary social movements along with peasant *jacqueries*, bread riots and grain seizures, slave revolts, "rough music," eighteenth- and nineteenth-century democratic societies, urban uprisings, artisanal blacklists and workshop turnouts, and revolutionary sects. By thus expanding the field on which the sociological study of protest may be thought to operate, I aim to highlight the way historical knowledge obliges us to pull back from familiar, present-day phenomena and construct more abstract, hence theoretical, categories. Historians often experience acute discomfort upon encountering such abstractions or, more accurately, upon hearing sociologists employ them explicitly; historical sociologists are more likely to experience them as

1. The final editing on this chapter was done by Peter Bearman.

an essential tension, a gap between concept and referent that stimulates and sometimes clarifies our thinking.[2]

For the moment, the relevance of the anachronism lies in the fact that it is one of several reasons why the affinity between the study of political contention (or "protest" or "contentious collective action"), on the one hand, and historical sociology, on the other, is less obvious than is the case for many of the subjects historical sociologists have conventionally addressed. Consider the major phenomena around which much of comparative and historical sociology has crystallized: the formation of national states, transitions to capitalism, the enactment of social provision as a political right, and even the cognate subject of revolutions. All of these topics involve either long-term, macroscopic shifts from one institutional form to another (monarchy to parliamentary government; feudalism to capitalism; capitalism to—in theory—socialism; laissez-faire states to market-regulating welfare states, etc.) or the appearance, whether over short or long periods, of novel but highly durable institutional forms (constitutions, nation-states, corporatist bargaining, labor laws, and so forth). In contrast, contentious collective action occurs episodically and on a wide range of scales (most of the time local, very rarely societywide), is by definition *not* institutionalized, and, perhaps most significant, is typically seen by both participants and commentators not as a social outcome with value in its own right but instead as a means to some such outcome.[3]

Contentious collective action, then, is unlike capitalism, welfare institutions, parliamentary democracy, urbanization, or bureaucratization in the following respect: there is no massively taken-for-granted present state of political contention whose explanation social scientists are naturally interested in proposing. There emphatically *is* an institutionalized current state of affairs in the case of capitalism, democracy, and state-run social provision, even when these seem to be under challenge. Given these states of affairs, social scientists usually hope not just to describe them, but moreover to account for them. And there is, accordingly, an impulse to historicize in

2. I do not wish to be too harsh in my portrayal of historians, even though they are sometimes merciless when writing about the work of historical sociologists. Nonetheless, it is worth remembering that abstractions like "modernity," "capitalism," "feudalism," "urbanization," "class," "gender," and "the state" abound in the writings of historians. The difference, I believe, is that sociologists tend to spend more time thinking in terms of these abstractions, returning occasionally to concrete cases for illustrative purposes; historians are much more likely to stay close to the empirical ground, paying only brief visits to the rarefied stratosphere of concepts.

3. This last statement is not true of all social movements scholars, notably those who speak of the current emergence of a "social movement society." I will return to this issue below.

such cases—that is, to point out that matters have not always been thus, that there is a story to tell concerning how we arrived at the present from the past, and (more controversially) that that story is a necessary part of any adequate *explanation* of the present. The prima facie case for a historically grounded account of "the formative years" of social movements is harder to make. Indeed, contemporary social movements are among the most modern of sociological explananda in that their self-representations usually include vehement renunciations of the past along with enthusiastic evocations of futures not yet realized.

A second basis for the distinctiveness of contentious collective action in this context is the relative marginality of the topic to the modernization framework. As Adams, Clemens, and Orloff note in their introductory chapter, the account of modernity inherited from T. H. Marshall, Parsons, Lipset, Smelser, the Rostows, and others made strong claims about cross-national convergence toward a universalistic, liberal-democratic, capitalist social order—claims that furnished a ready-made falsificationist foil for "second-wave" historical sociologists writing about paths to capitalism, democracy, and the welfare state. Scholars writing within the modernization framework had less to say about patterns in political contention and mass mobilization, usually seeing such phenomena as growing pains—difficult adolescent moments en route to the maturity and stability modernization ultimately entailed (Huntington 1968) but not central, or even necessary, to the process.

Even orthodox Marxism, which on the matter of teleology differed from structural functionalism primarily in positing one additional stage in the Enlightenment saga, relegated contentious collective action to a secondary and transitional role. To be sure, Marxist social science was, and remains, committed to the idea that some sort of mobilized working class is an indispensable ingredient in toppling industrial capitalism—and in that respect, Marxian thinking offered a clear prediction about the conditions and consequences of mass (class-based) mobilization under capitalist society. Again, though, in this version of the story of Progress, contentious collective action is an instrument, not an aim, of social transformation. It is certainly, to extend Trotsky's metaphor, the dynamite bringing down the old building; it might be a source of energy in erecting the new one; but in no way is it an element in the new building's design. The end of the story is also the end of struggle.

In short, the relevance of historical sociology for the study of political contention is less clear-cut than in the case of a range of other topics covered in this volume. Political contention is not a "big," world historical phenomenon, even if it sometimes coincides with other "big" phenomena, such as social revolutions. Social movements, a contemporary form of political contention, are not self-evidently the descendants of some earlier form, at least not in a way that makes it easy to say that history matters. And the social theories against which much of historical sociology has positioned itself did not offer a lot of guidance (positive or negative) concerning how to talk about contentious collective action. In a sense, historical sociology has backed into the area—and for their part, many students of contemporary social movements have not paid that much attention to the intrusion.[4]

I hope to treat this challenge as an opportunity. The less straightforward the connection between historical research and sociological theorizing, the more self-conscious one has to be in making the case for it. So here goes— beginning with the reason "social movements" became "contentious collective action."

Historicizing Protest

Imagine you have two rival theories about modern society—here I use the term "theory" loosely, to refer to any relatively coherent system of propositions about the world—from which to derive predictions about developments in mass mobilization. One of the theories can be shown to imply that in the long term, protest should wane as the mass of the population is absorbed, culturally and practically speaking, into the institutions of liberal-democratic market society. Older dimensions of conflict, like ethnic and sectarian differences, will vanish first as people sensibly abandon ascription and embrace achievement as the determinant of social position. Newer ones—notably over labor's share of income, working conditions, and other issues of material well-being—should eventually decline as well, as institutions for managing such conflicts take shape and prosperity replaces tense, zero-sum struggles with more pleasant plus-sum negotiations.

The second theory expresses a different sort of optimism—a breaking-eggs-to-make-an-omelette sort. This theory also predicts a decline in ascription-based conflicts (except where clever bourgeois ideologues, as in the post-bellum American South, offer them as distractions from the true conflict), offset by ever-sharper struggles over labor's share of income, leading ultimately to the creation of mass working-class parties. The coming

---

4. I do not mean that social movements scholars never cite or read historical sociologists who study political contention. At a minimum, the towering presence of Charles Tilly's (1978) work in the social movements literature is undeniable. At the same time, there is nothing particularly historicist about the way Tilly's work has been folded into the sociology of social movements. Indeed, there is a notable tendency for the reception of Tilly's writing to concentrate on theoretical claims and to disregard historical ones.

crisis of capitalism will lead either to successful working-class revolutions, perhaps with the aid of educated vanguards (Lenin 1926), or in the short term to fascist dictatorships relying on coercion, ideological seduction, and imperialist adventures to control and distract the proletariat in the service of capitalism (Marx 1976 [1852]; Neumann 1944; Marcuse 1964).

Because neither "theory" says exactly when the predicted state of affairs will come about, neither prediction is strictly speaking falsifiable. Sects proclaiming that the end is near can hold out for longer than those announcing that the end is tomorrow. Nonetheless, while awaiting either outcome— social peace or total social upheaval—you might find yourself seeking a third approach. Your sense that a third way might be preferable will be amplified by the constant accumulation, made possible by a glut of doctoral dissertations, of empirical evidence concerning existing and past political struggles. In the first place, the essentially linear progression your two theories prepared you to observe—toward either increasing social accommodation or intensifying conflict—is not to be found. Instead, the evidence reveals no obvious trend. Labor struggles coexist with all sorts of conflicts you had been led to believe were obsolete. In some cases, material conflicts wane while sectarian, nationalist, ethnic, and racial ones, thought to have subsided, reemerge.

Even in the struggles you expected to find, moreover, the cast of characters and the lines they utter are not what you anticipated. Social histories of industrialization in Europe and North America caused trouble for the class-polarization story by documenting the centrality of skilled artisans, rather than unskilled proletarians, in the urban upheavals, revolts, and organized labor actions of the nineteenth century (Gossez 1956; Hobsbawm 1975; Moss 1978; Rudé 1964; Soboul and Markov 1957; Thompson 1963). Studies of both rural and urban strife undermined the modernization story by showing that participants in unrest were hard to portray either as uprooted, disoriented victims of economic dislocation or as defenders of an obsolete social order who opposed progress because they did not understand it or because it threatened their entrenched position. Rural protest was not confined to "underdeveloped" regions, and peasant revolts were not necessarily retrograde in their apparent goals (Rudé 1964; C. Tilly 1963). And although political unrest was frequently backward looking in both content and form— employing traditional tactics, for instance, in resisting the incursion of market relations into local moral economies—it was often simultaneously progressive, selectively embracing aspects of the new industrial order and articulating a variety of utopian alternatives (for a thorough historiographical review, see Prothero 1997).

In addition, of course, all of this historical complexity was coming to light at the same time that an entirely new population of social movements was coming into being, simultaneously identifying and mounting challenges to dimensions of oppression orthogonal to the material dimension that had occupied almost everyone's attention.[5] And, as if the rise of new dimensions of conflict and mobilization were not enough to confuse matters, these self-appointed "new" social movements also at times allied themselves with the "old" labor movement—which reasserted itself with considerable force, to the surprise of many, in the late 1960s. In the face of this diversity and nonlinearity, you would be forgiven for losing interest in the search for a "maturing" working class or for the alternative grail, a steady decline in social unrest.

The question to answer, then, is what theoretical framework to adopt in place of the apocalyptic and the Whig narratives that had proved unsatisfactory. Instead of rival determinisms, historians elected to follow Thompson's (1963) lead in tracing the path of "class formation," offering ordinary folk the opportunity to define their experience of industrialization, marketization, and urbanization rather than defining it on their behalf. Class—and later gender, race, ethnicity, coloniality, and other "dimensions of difference"—became receptacles into which diverse experiences could be poured, rather than sieves designed to filter out that very diversity in pursuit of a parsimonious theory of history.[6]

Many sociologists, on the other hand, were more prone to follow Charles Tilly's example and continued to look for a framework within which to search for general patterns in protest, old and new. And it is here that the idea of generalizing from "social movements" to "contentious collective action" gained its justification. The idea was straightforward, even if its execution has not been. Recognizing that protest has undergone significant

5. One of the most interesting aspects of the trajectory of 1960s activism in the West is the "discovery" of these alternative dimensions by activists steeped in Marxist categories. The challenges to the dominant order that emerged in the postwar period, from feminism to indigenous rights movements to the unionization of Chicano agricultural laborers in California's Central Valley, almost always began with a class-based analysis. Needless to say, scholars and activists alike quickly became frustrated in their efforts to talk about patriarchy, apartheid, ethnic marginalization, homophobia, and short-sighted uses of natural resources as forms of class exploitation. I would venture that the astonishing impact of Michel Foucault's writing, beginning in the 1970s, was in large part due to Foucault's having arrived on the continental intellectual scene just as politically engaged writers were experiencing these frustrations.

6. On the professional plane, this is an excellent idea. When the pursuit of parsimony is supplanted by the goal of celebrating the diversity of experience, it is better to have more local studies, more particularity, less generalization, and therefore more dissertations.

changes from, say, 1600 to the present does not preclude the search for patterns that hold across diverse contexts and forms of protest. In fact, it adds a dimension to the search: having adopted the more abstract category of contentious collective action, we can now talk about patterns in the way protest shifts from one form to another. The true historicist would balk at such a maneuver, arguing that each protest form belonged to its own time and place. For the historicist, it might make sense to document changes in contention over time and even to construct a narrative (as Thompson, Hobsbawm, and other historians surely did) tracing these changes in a particular county, town, or nation. But it is primarily the sociologists who think it worthwhile to seek *general explanations* of such changes or of the emergence of mass mobilization in some conditions and not others, and it is only the sociologists (not even all of them) who see such explanations as in principle applicable in historical contexts other than those for which they were first proposed.[7]

I do not think it is possible in a single chapter to defend the principle behind this generalizing impulse; programmatic arguments of that sort tend to persuade only those who already wish to be persuaded. Instead, I shall lay out some examples of general theoretical claims for which historical sociologists examining contentious collective action in diverse times and places think they have found evidence. It would be preferable to see these claims as stylized facts—that is, propositions that do not hold anywhere precisely but that appear to hold broadly in a rough way. (As a caveat, however, I confess on behalf of my colleagues that replication is scant in this research area; we are wont to start talking generally about, say, the "role of elite fragmentation in mobilization" when only one or two studies have documented it.)

The best starting point, because it sets the stage for further findings, is the matter of grievances. Stated crudely, the implicit basis for both Marxist and modernization stories about mass mobilization is that protest occurs when people are angry. This might happen when life is hard—in Marx's evocative phrase, when "the forest of uplifted arms demanding work becomes ever thicker, while the arms themselves become ever thinner" (K. Marx and

---

7. It is occasionally argued, and I think correctly, that anyone claiming to offer a "causal" explanation of something—even an obviously singular occurrence—is implicitly committing to some general principle. If I say that sharecroppers in the post-bellum American South joined the Southern Farmers' Alliance *because* their experience of the crop lien system resonated with the alliance's account of that system as exploitative (see Schwartz 1976), I am making a claim at least about the conditions under which sharecroppers are likely to join cooperative farming arrangements. I am also quite possibly making a claim about the conditions under which agricultural workers are likely to join movements that challenge agrarian economic systems. I may even be making a claim about the conditions under which people join protest movements.

Engels 1978: 216). Alternatively, it might happen when people expect life to improve but it does not, or when people see conditions improving for others but not themselves (J. C. Davies 1962; Gurr 1969).

Historical research has cast doubt on these claims, although they continue to dominate commonsense and journalistic accounts of strife. Rather than selecting instances of contention, listening to the grievances expressed therein, and concluding that grievances were the reason (i.e., "cause") for contention, historical sociologists elected to examine variation over time in levels of contention—and to correlate them with indices of poverty, inequality, unemployment, growth/decline in real wages, and so forth. They found that the correlations were weak. Protest sometimes rose when material conditions improved; sometimes it declined when they improved; sometimes it remained the same (Bohstedt 1983; McAdam 1982; Shorter and C. Tilly, eds. 1974; C. Tilly, eds. 1974; C. Tilly, Tilly and Tilly 1975). Crude interpretations have often concluded from this series of findings that grievances are therefore not a factor in protest. Such a conclusion is as unreasonable as finding a weak correlation between the presence of gravity and the rate at which people fall down stairs and concluding that gravity is not a factor in falling down stairs. Grievances are weakly correlated with rates of protest because they do not vary as much as protest does.

That is a negative finding, of course, and negative findings are a dime a dozen (even if they are more important than is ordinarily acknowledged). But the negative result came with some important positive ones. In the first place, one very good predictor of rates of contentious collective action, across a range of studies and time periods, is political instability. Although the romantic revolutionary image teaches us to expect that insurgency brings down regimes, it is more accurate to say that vulnerable regimes invite insurgency: numerous historical cases and analyses of time series data indicate that states that are off balance (due to external pressures, political transition, or internal fragmentation) are more likely not only to be overthrown by insurgencies, but also to become the targets of insurgency. Peasant revolts, workers' strikes, urban riots, and guerrilla wars are both more likely to occur and, more self-evidently, more likely to bring about political collapse during moments of political instability.

What makes this observation more than a tautology is that "instability" can be defined and measured independently of insurgency: it may take the form of a close election, a foreign invasion, or even the accidental death of a dictator. (Not that it always *is* measured independently of insurgency. A recent article in the *American Sociological Review* stated that the prerevolutionary Ottoman state "seems to have been particularly susceptible to a series of crises" [Barkey 1991: 710].) More broadly, there is evidence that mobilization increases in response to signals of sympathy on the part of a segment of the ruling elite—as occurred, for instance, when the U.S. Supreme Court made a number of rulings favoring civil rights for Blacks in the 1940s and 1950s (McAdam 1982). Because of this heterogeneity in what might be called "invitations" to mobilize, social movements scholars outside the historical sociology camp have in recent years begun talking regularly of "political opportunity." Although there is, as I noted, a danger of circularity, wherein "political opportunity" turns out to be anything associated with increased rates of mobilization, it is fair to regard as a major discovery the observation that levels of protest are more sensitive to climates hospitable to protest than to the underlying discontent protest is thought to express.

A second robust finding bears a similar relationship to the matter of grievances in that it once again suggests the secondary importance of discontent as a predictor of mobilization. The predictor in question might be termed "social organization," again reflecting an effort to speak generally (with the attendant risk of vacuity). Social organization can be realized in a wide variety of ways, including collective ownership of land in peasant societies (Skocpol 1979), guildlike corporate bodies in the case of urban craft workers (Aminzade 1981; Sewell 1980); and clanlike kinship groups among immigrants (Katznelson 1981; Morawska 1998). The core idea is that mobilization of contentious collective action takes place primarily through patterned social relationships that predate whatever the overt political issue is and only secondarily through organizations deliberately founded by activists. (Again, this proposition counters the "revolutionary vanguard" model popular with professional activists [Alinsky 1963; Lenin 1926], according to which organized, militant leaderships turn inchoate discontent into focused, purposeful collective action.)

This is not to say that formal organizations do not matter in sustaining political contention; on the contrary, there is good reason to believe that they do. But formal organizations specifically designed for activism, like unions, protest organizations, and political parties, both grow out of preexisting social structures and depend heavily on those structures, at least early on, for their efficacy. Formalized protest organizations do not substitute for, but instead interact with, those structures, in bringing about and patterning mobilization. In particular, there is evidence that formal organizations are significant in establishing social contacts across conventional social boundaries, inducing large-scale interdependencies in mobilizations that might otherwise remain isolated. Hence the concentration of social network analysis in the exploration of these issues (Bearman 1991; Fernandez and McAdam 1988; Gould 1991).

Historical sociologists again preceded students of contemporary social movements in documenting the importance of social organization, beginning with the fact of militancy during the industrialization of just those occupational groups that were hardest to characterize as proletarians. Given the Marx-inspired prediction that worker militancy would be most advanced where proletarianization had proceeded the furthest, the discovery that skilled craft workers were consistently more radical than semiskilled factory workers constituted an anomaly.[8] The overrepresentation in militancy of skilled craft workers was explained by pointing out that militancy is collective action and that collective action is hard to achieve in the absence of social relationships discouraging free riders. In the reformulated account of political and economic mobilization during industrialization, what mattered most was not the amount of misery industrial development inflicted on various categories of people (including women engaged in household production, who were probably the most miserable—and least militant—of all), but the social resources available to these categories. Craft organizations, through which skilled journeymen already acted collectively to control training and the supply of labor, were readily adapted for more confrontational actions against employers who were introducing new technology, hiring female laborers, cutting workers' share of income by speeding up work, and otherwise extending control over the labor process.

Like the political opportunity argument, the idea that social organization is a precondition for mobilization has migrated to other contexts, many of them connected to such contemporary social movements as feminism, environmentalism, and peace activism. Taylor's (1989) examination of the American women's movement in the twentieth century, for instance, contends that "abeyance structures" maintained commitment to feminism among a core group of activists through dry spells in mobilization. Here again, there is a danger that extensions of the finding shade into tautology: inasmuch as the concept of "social movement" by definition *presupposes* the existence of durable groups of committed, mobilized challengers to the social order, it would be hard to falsify the proposition that durable groups of committed activists are necessary to social movement mobilization. Nevertheless, so long as one is careful not to adopt a conception of social organization that is equivalent to the outcome it is hypothesized to influence, there is a significant lesson to be gained here. And, illustrating again the distinctive contri-

---

8. Literature reviews often cast such disjunctures between theoretical prediction and evidence as indications of the "failure" of the theory in question. I sharply disagree with this characterization of theoretical development. In the absence of the proletarianization thesis, which was derived from the Marxian framework, there would have been no reason to be surprised or intrigued by the significance of artisanal laborers in nineteenth-century European militancy. Progress in theorizing worker activism therefore proceeded because of, not despite, the "incorrect" predictions of the Marxian approach.

bution historical sociology makes, the insight emerged through investigations of contentious collective action in an era predating the emergence of professionalized social movement organizations.

There is a third area, pertaining to the formation of collective perceptions and group identities, in which historical sociologists have assembled theoretical knowledge of a similar kind. I hesitate, however, to discuss it in this section, because it is also the area in which most of the "cultural turn" scholarship of the last two decades has been concentrated. Summarizing this large body of research in the form of stylized facts, as if the goal were the scientific one of accumulating propositions and identifying mechanisms that hold over a range of contexts, would come across as naive. At best, it would convey the mistaken impression that historical sociologists who work in an interpretivist mode are engaged in clumsy or ineffective social science, when in fact many of them are willful about *not* participating in the scientific enterprise. There are some sociologists studying collective identities (including myself) who are interested in producing specifically scientific knowledge on this subject, but to concentrate on the work these scholars consider important would be to substitute the perspective of the minority for that of the majority. Consequently, I will present the minoritarian version in the next section, against the background of the more common culturalist version.

Contentious Collective Action and the Discursive Turn

Historians, as I noted above, began to write about collective action as "culture" as soon as they discovered that the consciousness expressed during unrest did not neatly conform to pre-established theoretical models. Presumably, if peasants, slaves, abolitionists, religious sect members, artisans, factory workers, women's suffrage activists, and mobilized ethnic groups offered their own accounts of who they were, what they wanted, and why they were entitled to what they wanted, then it was the job of social scientists to document these representations and make sense of them on their own terms, not to measure how far they deviated from some idealized conception (G. S. Jones 1983; Sewell 1980; Thompson 1963). "Making sense" then came to mean something like *Verstehen*, in which the analyst's role was to employ the symbolic and discursive behavior of historical actors to render a satisfactory account, in light of everything else known about the context, of their subjective experiences. In the specific case of contentious politics, the experiences in question most often involved (1) grievances concerning disjunctures between actual social conditions and social conditions recognized as just, as in protests over corruption among political and religious elites (G. S.

Jones 1983; Zaret 1980b); (2) grievances concerning actual and supposedly just conditions newly viewed as unjust, as in the demand for political representation of women or propertyless persons, the emancipation of slaves or serfs, or the rights of workers to organize; and, more radically, (3) the people whose grievances presupposed their conceptual organization into collectivities.

Even with the legacy of Tilly and other science-oriented writers, the study of contentious politics has been a particularly hospitable environment for constructivist inquiry. The reason is that political contention necessarily entails the representation of some set of interests or entitlements as common to some aggregation of people. Because every person's position and experience are unique, such aggregations cannot be said to exist in reality but only insofar as they are posited to exist—and thereby brought into being—through political rhetoric and coordinated action, contentious or otherwise. It was therefore natural that historical sociologists interested in contentious collective action would seize the opportunity offered by the scholarly turn toward culture and discourse to engage in a different sort of sociological study in which the goal was not to generalize across contexts about how and when contentious collective action occurs, and with what effects, but instead to investigate precisely the variability that the constructedness of social categories (races, sexes, classes, ethnicities, hierarchies, inequalities, interests, rights, capacities, desires, and so forth) allows. Recognition that schemata for representing the social world and its elements are human creations, rather than natural givens, led to a way of talking about historical developments in contentious collective action that celebrated agency over determination, variability over generality, and finally, because agency frustrates determination, interpretation over causal explanation. Crudely speaking, interpretive studies of contention operate on the premise that women and men do not merely make their own history; they also, by the power of interpretation, through which all objective conditions are filtered, make the circumstances in which their history is made (Ellingson 1995; Frank and Steinberg eds. 2001; Sewell 1992).

One benefit of this reframing of the enterprise is that there is now a clear case for historicism, in a way that (I have suggested) was not so readily available to sociologists interested in testable theories of contentious collective action. Even with the newly discovered importance of context, historical sociologists have recognized that there are profound questions worth asking about how people who have made one version of the world for themselves and engaged in a series of contentious political events both expressing and reaffirming that version of the world nonetheless can find themselves entering or making a new one. Such questions, it turns out, are hard to answer in anything but a descriptive way. The most common result is to document transformation—from *charivari* to strikes or protest marches (Frank and Steinberg, eds. 1994; C. Tilly, ed. 1995), from guerrilla war to accommodation or the reverse (Paige 1997), or from communal radicalism to trade union reformism (Calhoun 1982)—and then to weave a tale concerning "why" the first gave way or led to the second. In the absence of disciplined counterfactuals, it is difficult to make such tales meet any test more stringent than that of plausibility. Nevertheless, sociologists interested in analytical narratives are making the attempt. For present purposes, it is important that the attention to *temporal process* that many historical sociologists see as a hallmark of what they do was not a central part of the historical sociology of contentious collective action until after social science turned to culture.

Some Concluding Remarks

With the rejection of determinism, and along with it the project of causal explanation of outcomes, it is unsurprising that recent participants in the historical sociology of contention are not trying to build general, positive theories of protest. This is not to say that the current generation has abandoned abstraction, even if the abstractions are different ("spaces of contention," "injustice frames," and "zones of exclusion" are more likely to crop up, for instance, than "selective incentives," "opportunity structures," and "probabilities of success"). Rather, it is that the purpose of abstraction is more to array disparate cases alongside each other and to draw metaphorical parallels or intriguing contrasts across contexts than to build a formal language with reference to which general theories can be formulated, hypotheses derived, and empirical tests performed.

Post–discursive turn scholars typically argue that things have to be this way: once one acknowledges the constructedness of interests, social categories, and dimensions of social conflict, one is bound to abandon the scientific enterprise and embrace the interpretivist one. (Coexisting with this conviction is another, according to which the effort to capture the subjective experience of militants, oppressed groups, and disenfranchised women [among others] is an emancipatory—and hence not a scientific—project. Whether science or interpretation is more likely to bring about emancipation is, it seems to me, an entirely open question; in any event, it is orthogonal to the present subject.) This argument seems to me to be wrongheaded, because it mistakenly supposes that if interpretation—i.e., the way historical actors make and act on meaning—is the object of analysis, then interpretation must be the method employed. Just as ethnographers have generated interesting knowledge by directing their interpretive gaze at the practice of science, sociologists can fruitfully direct their scientific gaze at meaning-laden social practice.

In my own research, this choice has taken the form of trying to derive systematic propositions about the conditions under which people will arrive at one commonly held definition of their situation rather than another—a class identity rather than a communal one, for example, or a definition of conflict as collective rather than individual (Gould 1995, 1999). Recognizing that more than one outcome is in principle possible, in other words, does not require one to accept either that all outcomes are *equally* possible or that the outcome that ensues is purely a matter of chance or free will. To the extent that social conditions push people (in the cases in Gould 1995 and 1999, nineteenth-century Parisians and nineteenth-century Corsican villagers respectively) more toward one outcome than toward another, leading to unequal likelihoods across possible outcomes, it is reasonable to make scientific claims about the determinants of collective interpretations. To say that the scientific enterprise is inapplicable to the processes by which human beings construct meaningful accounts of their actions is as unreasonable as it is to say that poets should not write about trees because trees do not appreciate poetry.

In any event, the supposition appears to have led to two historical sociologies of political contention: one in which abstract categories are the building blocks for general theory, and one in which they are (as I said they were for cultural historians) conceptual receptacles or dimensions along which to arrange the varied versions of the human experience. This bifurcation is in my view a shame, all the more because it is a contingent rather than necessary outcome of the process by which academic collective identifications are formed. Students of protest have learned from history to theorize more broadly, because historical research showed that concepts like "social movement" are context-bound. But their initial focus on "resources" and "opportunities" underlay a surprisingly unhistorical (which is to say non-temporal) theory-building project. On the other hand, historical sociologists interested in the cultural or discursive side of protest have been eminently conscious of temporality and context. But this sensitivity has come with a reluctance to generalize that, while understandable, is not in fact a necessary concomitant of respect for history, context, and the "meaningful" character of human action. An enormously productive synthesis might well follow from recognizing the contingency of this division.

NADER SOHRABI

Revolutions as Pathways to Modernity

Since the French Revolution of 1789, a bewildering mixture of social classes, groups, and actors has taken part in revolutions in the widest array of settings around the globe, yet these variegated groups have rallied around only a small number of revolutionary doctrines. The small number of choices in such a wide range of contexts is undoubtedly a sociological puzzle in need of explanation—a puzzle because it goes against our Marxian, Durkheimian, or rational choice intuitions that ideologies are byproducts of bounded social contexts. Bounded contexts, depending on one's theoretical orientation, may mean social structure, division of labor, or local interactions, yet if these have indeed varied so greatly across time and space, how can we explain the uniformity of revolutionary doctrines across the spectrum? If revolutionaries have put to use only a limited number of doctrines in broad historical and geographical contexts, perhaps we need to reexamine whether ideologies are a pure reflection of bounded contexts.

That ideologies matter in revolutions is a topic that still remains controversial in revolution studies. In fact, there is little consensus that ideologies affect the timing, form, process, goals, and outcomes of revolutions. Nor has it appeared surprising to many that there have been so few revolutionary ideologies, perhaps because they have not been viewed as consequential. In balance, however, the sociology of revolution, in keeping with the social sciences in general, has in recent years seen greater openness toward analysis of meaning, subjectivities, ideologies, and culture (Foran 1993b; Goldstone 2001b). The overdue convergence of theories of revolution and social movements (Aminzade et al. 2001; McAdam, Tarrow, and Tilly 2001), for example, has been in part due to the realization that slow-changing structures of the long run, in the final analysis, elucidate only the "conditions of possibility" of revolutions but not the dynamics of mobilization, confrontation strategies, processes, or their final shapes. For these, we need to know a good deal more about the subjectivity of actors in context and their imagined visions of the past, present, and future.

The emphasis on subjectivities has also afforded a more dynamic view of resources. Revolutionaries need weak states, networks, and organizations to succeed, necessities that cannot be created purely out of ideology or willpower. Yet there is a large gap between potential resources and those that are mobilized for action, a gap filled by human agency. More and more is the revolutionary arena thought of as a field crowded with skilled and unskilled revolutionaries and counter-revolutionaries engaged in mobilizing and de-mobilizing by struggles over labeling as moral or immoral, legitimate or illegitimate; appealing by speaking the right language or offending with inappropriate choice of words or opportunistic or sluggish maneuvering; and selecting and attracting the right choice of partners to a coalition or missing opportunities. It is in this context that resources become available or unavailable, correct methods of warfare are learned or missed out upon, and weak states are made stronger or more vulnerable depending on how the insurgents or their adversaries succeed or fail in each of these tasks.

Without a doubt, revolutions require many structural conditions. Chief among these are the financial crisis and political weakness of states, both domestic and international. The best state-centered studies of revolutions (Goldstone 1991; Goodwin 2001; Skocpol 1979; C. Tilly 1978, 1993b) have expanded a good deal on Crane Brinton's (1952) original insights about state weakness as the core issue of revolution. From these, two authors have been centrally concerned with the impact of forms of states on the shape of revolutions. On the one hand, Charles Tilly (1993b), in his wide-ranging analysis of European revolutions, argues that as states progressively monopolized the means of coercion or laid claim to such a monopoly, concentrated power in one location, penetrated to deeper layers of the social, and claimed greater control, they progressively made themselves the natural targets of grievances and protests, with revolutions being the most forceful expression of protest against the power wielded by states in modern times. As a corollary, with increasing globalization and the gradual diffusion of powers of states in the future, what we know as modern revolutions will disappear with them.

Building on these insights in a detailed and equally admirable study, Goodwin (2001) attributes the historical character of "Third World" revolutionary movements in the cold war era to highly specific forms of states that leave "no other way out" for their citizens but to smash and overtake the state to inaugurate an era of radical social transformation. Thus, in what

Goodwin labels as the "state-constructivist" approach, he argues that particular kinds of states—those that fulfill five criteria—create revolutionary subjectivities bent on destroying them with actors that resort to an essentially Leninist takeover of the state: they are left with "no other way out."[1] Like other context-based explanations that reduce subjectivities to exigencies of social structure, Goodwin's contends that the five criteria create the necessary subjectivity for seizing the state in a sudden overthrow.

Goodwin's formulation, however, ignores the subjective dimensions of Leninism; overemphasizes it as a response to purely objective conditions; and although it considers it to be limited to a particular historical period, it attributes the peculiarity of the era to the structural rather than ideological characteristics of the period. Yet actors caught in the same set of structural conditions have not always opted for a Leninist-style overtaking of states. The subjective state of "no other way out" never results entirely from conditions created by states. Even when actors found themselves in circumstances such as those outlined by Goodwin, they did not follow the Leninist route prior to 1917, nor would they do so after 1991.[2] This is not because the "objective" conditions for Leninist revolutions did not exist across the globe prior to 1917 or suddenly ceased to exist after 1991, but because Leninism is only partially a creature of states. More than that, it is a historical/subjective template for action and reaction for both revolutionaries and governments, a template that held sway for a limited historical era whose time now seems to be over. The states that fulfill the five criteria have not disappeared. What accounts for lack of Leninist revolutions is that Leninism has lost its appeal as a confrontational and liberation doctrine.

Charles Tilly (1993b) has *historicized* revolution by exposing the recent origin of modern states to which revolutions have been a relatively new and violent reaction. I argue here that the concept may be historicized further by emphasizing that the reaction to the power of modern states is conditioned

---

1. According to Goodwin (2001: 44–50), the population becomes attracted to radical ideologies under the following conditions: (1) when states sponsor or protect unpopular economic or social arrangements: thus, the states that reform and regulate and abolish perceived economic and social injustices are less likely to become the targets of political demands, revolutionary or otherwise; (2) when states repress and/or exclude mobilized groups from state power and resources—that is, lack of opportunities tends to push certain groups and individuals toward radical politics; (3) when states indiscriminately but not overwhelmingly use violence against mobilized groups; (4) when states have weak policing capacities and infrastructural power—in other words, repression works and revolutionaries do not stand a chance against overwhelming power, but arbitrarily repressive states with weak capacity are vulnerable to revolution; (5) when states are corrupt and personalistic and thus alienate, weaken, or divide their potential supporters among the elite.

2. Exceptions are those revolutionaries who were already locked into the Leninist trajectory before 1991.

more by the available global templates for action than the conditions created by states. Different templates create essential differences among revolutions. Revolutions are pathways to modernity, and the ideological framework under which they unfold exposes revolutionary societies to widely different modernities. Contrary to our sociological intuition, I suggest that revolutionaries choose their paths *irrespective* of local conflicts. That is, a socialist-Leninist or a constitutionalist path, two of the most popular routes to modernity, is chosen almost entirely *independently* of local problems or grievances against the old regimes. This choice is even independent of social classes/actors involved in the conflict.[3] Rather, the greatest influence comes from the global templates in vogue at the time of conflict and the local perception of their success.

The historicized approach suggests that world time (history) dictates the broad/general goals and categories under which revolutions unfold. These broad outlines are far from trivial and impact the dynamics of confrontation and transformation. The revolutionaries who tend to emulate the French model—they could be called constitutionalists—aim at forcing their governments to grant constitutional assemblies but stop far short of state or monarchical overthrows at the beginning. If they succeed, a crucial period of legal activity and temporary ceasefire begins during which various parties, including monarchies, mobilize new resources and build new coalitions. The principle of popular sovereignty is established through constitutions, parliaments, elections, and explicit contractual statements about the relations among the ruler, state, and citizens. The government is divided into various branches, most commonly three; checks and balances are introduced; legal frameworks and court systems are transformed; and private property and individual rights are reorganized. Even when these ideals remain far from realized, as long as the actors call themselves constitutionalists, they operate within the broad set of rules specified by such a polity. It is significant that a large part of the post-revolutionary conflicts are transformed into constitutional ones and channeled through parliaments and the new legal framework. These include the conflicts over radical social and institutional reforms and the redefinition of rights.

This is a distinctively different strategy than that of the Leninist (or its close variant, the Maoist) model, which was constructed in explicit rivalry

---

3. There is in fact an emerging consensus in studies of revolution from a variety of orientations that revolutionary proclivities are not the exclusive domains of particular groups or social classes (Goodwin 2001; McAdam and Sewell 2001; C. Tilly 1993b). This does not imply of course that all groups or classes have equal revolutionary potential or are as willing to participate in constitutional revolutions as they are in Leninist types of uprisings. Yet it is important to note that this is far from the earlier Marxian search for the truly revolutionary class.

with the constitutional template (Lenin 1992). Revolutions *after* the Bolshevik example of 1917 mobilized for a sudden overthrow from the very beginning without any prospect of a temporary ceasefire and diversion of struggles through a new legal framework. Here, the basis of sovereignty is not the popular will but the will of the proletariat (even though only "temporarily"), expressed not through a constitutive assembly in the name of the "nation" but through a political party in the name of a class. Thus, if one revolution establishes parliament and divides the state into various branches, the differing conception of politics and rights disbands parliaments and unites branches into one (Lenin 1992: 43), and if one revolution strengthens property rights, the differing conception of the social abolishes them. In short, the dynamics of struggle and the conception of the political and the social are different in these two types of revolutions, affecting both processes and outcomes (McAdam and Sewell 2001; Sewell 1985; Sohrabi 1995).[4]

Despite the critical importance of macro-structural conditions, an exclusive reliance on them prohibits exploration of many essential features of revolutions. But even if reference to ideological templates allows for a more precise explanation, one still needs to account for why revolutionaries adopt them, what is understood by them, and how mobilization takes place through them. Help may be at hand in concepts that emphasize the subjective and interpretive dimension of social movements such as framing (Goffman 1974); frame extension by "movement entrepreneurs" and master templates (McAdam and Sewell 2001; Snow and Benford 1992; Snow et al. 1986; Tarrow 1992, 1994); the invention of tradition (Hobsbawm and Ranger, eds. 1983); waves (Huntington 1991; Markoff 1994, 1996b, 1999; Tarrow 1994); repertoires (C. Tilly 1993a, 1999; Traugott 1993); agency (Sewell 1985, 1996a, 1996b); and interaction of the global with the local (Chabot and Duyvendak 2002; Sohrabi 1999, 2002). Without abandoning the previous emphasis on states and resources, these concepts have allowed more precise explanation of form, process, and outcome and have better dealt with the complexity of revolutions as pathways to modernity.

In the empirical section that follows I concentrate on the global-local dimension of social movements, a more encompassing rubric under which other theoretical frameworks may be considered. The recent focus on globalization has sensitized us to the cross-border flow of ideologies from one

---

4. It may be tempting to trivialize the differences and explain these differing strategies as two distinct but analogous instances of multiple sovereignty or essentially a struggle over the domination of states through different methods, yet this collapses the essentially differing conception of goals and the divergent trajectory of each type of revolution in to an oversimplified brute struggle over state domination.

national context to another, a flow that challenges our context-based explanations. Yet the flow here should be distinguished from the organizational diffusion theory and modernization theory or their more sophisticated variant, world society theory (Boli 1987; Boli-Bennett 1979; J. W. Meyer 1999; J. W. Meyer et al. 1997). The difference is that none of these has adequately considered the complex dynamics at the point of reception, and they have ignored the mechanisms of absorption and transformation of ideologies or institutions in their local contexts.

From the time of the invention of the modern concept of revolution in France, with help from England and America (K. M. Baker 1990; Sewell 1990, 1994), revolutions have been discovered to be of very limited types. The few modular global master templates (B. Anderson 1991; McAdam and Sewell 2001) have imposed profound uniformities upon the dynamics of revolutionary mobilization and confrontation (Sohrabi 1995), as well as the shapes of regimes that have come into being afterward. Thus, world society theory's emphasis on the uniformities caused by diffusion is well placed, but when the empirical contexts are explored more closely, we recognize deep differences that need to be explored individually.

These differences are due to global-local interaction and the complexities generated at the local level, complexities that diffusion advocates tend to ignore. I am concerned in particular with three interrelated issues. First, the actors, due to their vantage point within social contexts, interpret global doctrines in a manner most advantageous to their own situation. This has an indigenizing effect upon global ideologies. Second, global ideologies are hardly ever impressed upon a tabula rasa where no previous ideologies existed before; they collide and interact with indigenous notions and change as a result. Actors make sense of global doctrines by localizing, or indigenizing, them based on their own received categories. This interaction and the consequent transformation may be strategic and agent-driven; the revolutionary elite may make the global notions more palpable to a local audience by couching them in the language of custom and tradition, an intentional act that may have important unintended consequences in the future. Or the transformation can be unintentional, especially in the case of popular revolutions, when the public spontaneously interprets global doctrines in familiar local terms, leading to a clash of rather coherent sign systems that may generate a new and unexpected system of signs and meanings. Last, problems, grievances, and injustices at the point of reception have their own way of indigenizing the global. In order to mobilize the public, the revolutionary elite is forced to address parochial concerns and, by doing so, assimilate local issues into its offered global solutions.

To sum up, the historicized approach is critical of diffusion theories and the supposed one-way flow of ideas, models, and institutions. While taking account of the unifying effect of diffusion, one should take note of new, hybrid forms generated in interaction with varied social contexts. All three factors enumerated above—the reception of global notions by interested and competing actors, interaction with pre-existing local ideological and cultural notions, and assimilation of local problems to global solutions— transform and localize global ideologies. As actors, pre-existing cultural notions, and problems differ in each context, the same global ideologies take on different forms.

This historicized approach has an ironic implication: revolutions are imagined here as primarily local phenomena that take on a uniform global form. Even more ironic, revolutions are a conjunction of various smaller local revolts over particular issues that come together and are expressed collectively as a single event in the name of an all-encompassing abstract set of demands that is recognizable globally. There is an affinity here with Lefebvre (1947) and others (McAdam and Sewell 2001; C. Tilly 1993b) who consider the French Revolution or revolutions in general not as a single, uniform, grand uprising but a conjunction of autonomous rebellions that come together to constitute a seemingly single event. There is also an affinity with the earliest generation of theorists, who repeatedly distinguished be-tween revolts and revolutions by pointing to the ideological leap from the particular to the general, from the specific, target-oriented revolts to the far broader goals of revolutions. New here is the claim that the transition from particular to general is one from local to global; the choices are informed by modular world historical master templates, which are far fewer in number than the indigenous progression to generality depicted by the earlier genera-tion. The local, global progression contributes to the multi-vocality (Vol-osinov 1973) of slogans and demands, and ultimately to their somewhat ambiguous nature. This is not a negative trait but a flexibility that provides a broad range of interpretive possibilities, allowing a wide array of actors to identify with them. In accord with the earliest generation of theorists, it should be noted that it is the intelligentsia that is primarily responsible for wedding concrete demands to various strands of culture and discourse and for making the local language a global one. Thus, the emphasis on the centrality of the intelligentsia—much to the dislike of the "structuralists," who dismissed it on the grounds of idealism—was well placed (C. Brinton 1952; Edwards 1970; Pettee 1938, among many others). This does not mean that the study of revolutions should be reduced to intellectual history, as Furet (1981) subtly implied in his influential study of the French Revolution. But neither can it afford to be captivated exclusively by concern for the economy, resources, networks, organizations, states, or methods of warfare at the expense of the subjective/interpretive dimension that impacts mobilization at the level not only of ideology, but also of organization, confrontation strategies, and outcomes.

To illustrate the importance of the subjective dimension, I turn to two revolutions outside the European core whose broad contours were defined by the grand narrative of Western constitutionalism. These revolutions, in Iran in 1906 and in the Ottoman Empire in 1908, were part of a long wave of constitutional revolutions that began with the English, American, and French Revolutions and included such exemplary cases as the 1848 revolutions in Europe and the Meiji Restoration in Japan in 1868. They were also part of a short wave of constitutional movements that included Russia (1905), Mexico (1910), and China (1911), and that was brought to an end with the Russian Revolution of 1917, an event that gave socialism a revolutionary strategy. Iran and the Ottoman Empire, non-Western but also noncolonial societies, are particularly good sites for investigating the global-local link and the diffusion and local assimilation of global ideologies. The written constitutions of these two societies were deeply influenced by the Belgian constitution, and their revolutionary processes were also marked by striking similarities informed by the constitutional master frame (Sohrabi 1995). Yet in the process of negotiation with local concerns and familiar forms of action, the constitutional master frame underwent creative transformations that resulted in new, hybrid forms. As to why the constitutional model was undermined, one should note that a major source of its appeal in the non-European world was its promise of rapid material progress, the same kind of association made by the later Leninist model after the Russian Revolution had seemingly proven that it had drastically changed Russia's destiny from being Europe's backwater. The Communist revolution in China that emulated the Leninist model only magnified this promise and the Russian and Chinese examples helped to overshadow constitutionalism as the most effective way to magically propel nations at the margins into the center.

An investigation of global-local connections would not be possible without a systematic reference to agents, the links between global models and the locality. Yet rather than proceed with a conventional comparative analysis, in this short treatment I have chosen two nonparallel instances of revolutionary drama. These examples highlight two contrasting ways in which agency operated to localize the global. Starting with the Young Turk revolution in the Ottoman Empire, I will emphasize why the revolutionaries became committed to constitutionalism and what they understood by it. Furthermore, I will show how the revolutionary wave influenced the dynamics of mobilization in the locality and the way in which the global master frame was transformed to help mobilization. The Young Turk instance exemplifies a voluntaristic conception of agency in which actors negotiated global paradigms with local traditions and blended past repertoires with present global examples to mobilize and force the old regime to grant a constitutional assembly. Agency here purposefully made itself part of a global wave and did not stumble upon revolution. I will follow this with an analysis of the post-constitutional period in Iran and the struggles over the definition of the National Assembly between the representatives and the monarchy, on the one hand, and among actors with differing conceptions of the assembly, on the other. The emphasis here is on the unintended transformation of the global template, when the clashing understandings of constitutionalism in the course of a popular revolution came to create a new synthesis in practice.

The flow of political notions from the nineteenth century and the loosening of terms and images across the world from their previously held coherence in the Euro-American narrative have been captured by Appadurai (1996: 36) in terms of ideoscapes. Ideoscapes have provided nation-states with a set of keywords around which they organize political cultures but that evoke different meanings in their diasporic context. An advantage of a comparative exercise of this kind is that it highlights the distinctiveness of each diasporic context within which the language of constitutionalism is employed. We regularly qualify the global master frames with distinctive local referents and speak of Cuban socialism, Russian Marxism, Chinese communism, and the like. Approaching the topic from an interpretive-comparative angle is an opportunity to observe the similarities that result from operating within the confines of a single global master frame but also to tease out the effects of local histories, cultures, concerns, and interests that leave their imprint upon the global doctrines in each context.

The approach of Max Weber (1958, 1946d) holds the most promise for coming to terms with the complexity of global-local interaction as it does not reduce the core elements of ideologies to material structures, as would, for instance, even a flexible Marxian notion of relative autonomy. Equally appealing are its emphasis on the distinction between natural and human sciences, its assumption that social life is characterized by meaning that calls for interpretation, and its attention to the interaction of ideational and material structures. This does not entail dismissing the fundamental Marxist insight about broad unity in the consciousness of social classes or their pursuit of material interests in conflict with others. This insight in fact lends greater power to the concept of revolution as a conjuncture of autonomous sets of smaller-scale revolts by various groups in pursuit of their particular interests, but it emphasizes that the overarching ideational frames around which various classes rally are not to be reduced to class consciousness. Likewise, modernization or world society theory's emphasis on diffusion may not be ignored, but equal attention should be paid to the dynamics of indigenization at the point of reception. Even rational choice theory's consistent emphasis on interests and optimizing logic are useful, but its individualistic slant, its assumption about the emergence of ideologies (and norms) out of insulated local interactions, and its reduction of ideologies to interests without need for their hermeneutic recovery make it a less attractive choice here.

Comparative analysis has taken a turn away from rigidly isolating a limited set of variables to explain revolutions. In the face of accumulating empirical evidence that challenges the scientistically precise and parsimonious results of previous studies, the search for causes has become more oriented toward processes and mechanisms (Aminzade et al. 2001; Goldstone 2001b; McAdam, Tarrow, and Tilly 2001). Given this new orientation, now may be the time to pay closer attention to what actors define as problems, the manner in which the intelligentsia seeks to solve local problems by recourse to global ideals, and the local vernaculars and cultures in which the global master frames are couched. This approach would not privilege the actors' point of view, and it insists on breaking with the "native" from the privileged vantage point of the sociologist/historian. Yet it encourages such a break only after descent into the local experience and not a priori and out of false fears of becoming duped (and confused?) by the object of analysis. Methodologically this standpoint shares Bourdieu's (1977) quest to integrate hermeneutic and structuralist viewpoints by taking simultaneous account of both positions, as well as the critical realist perspective that views interpretation as integral to the comparative approach without a need to suppress the unique (Steinmetz 2004, this volume).

Making Revolution in the Ottoman Empire

Gaining access to the world historical context of revolutions is not simply a matter of identifying a state's geopolitical position within the system of states, but also of recovering how that standing is subjectively experienced by those making a revolution, an essential step for understanding why and how agents commit to action and to specific programs. The analysis of revolutionary literature allows one to decipher, in terms understood by actors themselves, the place they assign their societies in historical and contemporary world contexts, their diagnosis of major problems, their reasoning as to why other states were not burdened by them, which political system is desirable from the available range of possibilities, which revolutionary strategy is the most viable and suited to their conditions, and why a revolution would rectify matters. Looking at the Young Turk commentary about world events when grappling with the above issues, we can recover how they made themselves part of a global wave of revolution.

Before attending to these issues, however, we should take note of the "material-structural" conditions predating the revolution. Here we should note that the conditions necessary for revolution listed by state-centered theorists (e.g., Skocpol 1979)—even the more restrictive ones outlined by Goodwin (2001: 44–50)—existed in the pre-revolutionary Ottoman Empire. The severe financial, international, and domestic political problems of the late Ottoman state, the so-called "sick man of Europe," are well known, and there is no need to dwell on them here. One structural condition that needs to be highlighted, however, is the severe conflict between the mid-level modernist-Westernist sectors of the Ottoman army and bureaucracy and the patrimonial and neo-patrimonial sectors of the same institutions. The Young Turks, as the new emerging middle class in the military and bureaucracy, were in conflict, first, with equals and superiors who possessed inferior "modernist" credentials, and, second, with the less educated ranks below them because of the drain their inflated numbers placed on state resources. All were considered vestiges of a traditional, nonrational bureaucracy that was to be reformed. The Young Turks' grievances, aside from unhappiness with the myriad budgetary and compensation problems that plague all states in crisis, centered around their slow or blocked mobility and the unfair structure of rewards and compensations. They thus vehemently attacked the sultan and his administration for arbitrary rule, personalistic appointments and conduct, exclusionary style, and corruption. Given the sultan's transfer of all power to the palace secretariat, his strong inclination toward neo-patrimonial appointments, his emphasis on personal loyalty (in deviation from the previous era of modernizing reforms), and the persistence of traditional patrimonialism in some sectors, the sultan had become the main target of criticisms. The vehemence of criticism was partly the product of an extreme rationalist perspective intolerant of the slightest deviation from the European military and administrative manuals. The criticism extended to blaming the sultan and the administrative system he upheld for all the empire's problems, including poor economic performance, diplomatic failures, and internal ethno-religious conflicts.

Despite financial shortages, the sultan's notorious spy system was so successful that initially the Young Turks could not organize an effective opposition from within the empire and were forced abroad, mainly to France. Opportunity for internal organization arose in 1903, however, when in the aftermath of Bulgarian revolts in Ottoman Macedonia, the European powers placed the area under intense supervision and created a semi-autonomous region that could not be as easily controlled from Istanbul. In the less supervised Macedonia, the disaffected military and bureaucratic ranks and their peers from abroad came together to successfully organize an extensive opposition, complete with wide-ranging village networks and the unwavering loyalty of the deeply entrenched middle ranks of the bureaucracy and military. Their popular uprising in June–July 1908 was so extensive and effective that it forced the sultan to grant a constitution in less than a month after the uprising had started. Internal military and administrative conflict proved essential in mobilizing civil and military cadres who, in pursuit of their own interests, took it upon themselves to stage a revolution to prevent the empire's disintegration through radical reforms. The aggressive post-revolutionary purges, a hallmark of the Young Turk regime, transformed the state into a streamlined, rationalized machine but also attended to the demands of this emerging class.[5] Both aims happily coincided.

In fact, if one were to make a list of conditions necessary for a revolution according to major strands of state-centered theory, the 1908 Ottoman Empire would seem to have fulfilled them all: financial and political weakness brought about by geopolitical competition, a motivated group of actors pursuing material/class interests, a new opportunity for action and lowered costs of mobilization that explained the timing of the revolution, and discontented villagers who could be readily organized into networks—in addition to the more specific conditions outlined by Goodwin, such as the exclusionary policies associated with neo-patrimonialism. If this is the case, why go beyond this parsimonious structuralist/materialist explanation? Why make this simple story confusing and muddled by entering the minds of the actors? Why invoke fuzzy concepts like "wave," "repertoire," and "frame" when we can get a perfectly good explanation with the straightforward states and resources model? There are many good reasons. Contrary to the expectation raised by Goodwin, the Young Turk opposition did not opt for a Leninist overthrow of the state but chose the constitutional route, despite its clear martial ability and awareness that the state could be overtaken. The Young Turks were aware of their ability and the state's weakness and proved it when they defeated the counter-revolution in 1909 in less than ten days. If we are convinced that the constitutional route was a significant choice both for the later trajectory of revolution and for the kind of changes effected afterward, then we should be centrally concerned with the choice.

Furthermore, there are a host of other important issues that may not be

---

5. For this conflict from the contemporaries' point of view, see Murad (1891); Niyazi (1908: 18–19, 25–26, 34–35); Nuri (1911); Refik (1908); Tahsin Paşa (1931); and the newspapers *Şura-yi Ümmet* (Cairo, Paris), *Volkan* (Istanbul), and *Tanin* (Istanbul). For an analysis of its development, see Findley (1980, 1989); Hanioğlu (1986, 2001).

understood without grasping the frame of mind of the Young Turks. The most obvious is, why constitutionalism? What did they understand by it? How was it expected to solve the problems of the ailing empire and cater to the needs of the burgeoning middle class? To make matters more complicated, how did they convince themselves and the public—villagers no less—to rally behind this notion, given its obvious origins as a European import that could violate the cultural and religious traditions of the empire and indeed could easily be labeled as a violation by its opponents? Furthermore, what was their working definition of "constitutionalism," a definition that was critical for post-revolutionary construction? Finally, why and how did they become populists? Their traditional repertoire of Ottoman history called for military action alone, and they themselves had for years been committed advocates of Comtean evolutionary positivism and shared Le Bon's distaste for mass movements; most critical of all, they were fully aware that waging a popular movement was the most dangerous strategy to pursue in the multi-ethnic context of Macedonia, one that could cause ethno-religious clashes to flare and invite foreign intervention and the collapse of the empire.

The Young Turks' comments on world revolutionary events that appeared in their journals, declarations, and memoirs (among other sources) demonstrate how they localized the global master frame and broadened its appeal through frame extension and a rediscovery of forgotten Islamic roots of constitutionalism. Such a transformation allowed for wider mobilization by legitimizing the movement based on an invented tradition, and also an inventive incorporation of additional elements, as would a *bricoleur* (Lévi-Straus 1966: 16–33), to create a local mythology (by reworking the global myth) that facilitated constitutionalism's metamorphosis into a panacea for all the problems of the empire. In addition, their comments show the process by which they negotiated the global populist agenda with the traditional repertoire of Ottoman history, strategically extending a repertoire that called for military action alone to make themselves part of a global wave of constitutional revolutions.

The historic decline of the empire, its shrinking borders, and the impending possibility of its breakup were at the forefront of Young Turk thought. The most pressing issue for them was how to get on the "high road of civilization," catch up with Europe to stave off its expansion in the age of imperialism, and recapture the empire's lost glory. A second goal was to bring an end to the nationalist separatist movements and the endemic ethnic conflict that provided the impetus for breakup from within. Greece, Serbia, and Bulgaria had already broken away from the empire, and the ties between the newly established adjoining nation-states and their brethren in Ottoman

Macedonia were a constant source of conflict. The intervention of the Great Powers in these disputes only worsened the situation.

In the Young Turk imagination, the progress of West European nations had resulted from their political-administrative systems, all of which were constitutional. The same reasoning explained why great empires such as the Russian, the Chinese, and the Ottoman had fallen behind. Within this context it was not too difficult to conclude that modernity and strength, political and military, derived from a constitutional administrative system. Furthermore, constitutionalism was seen as a solution for the ethno-religious conflicts. If representation were given to all ethnic and religious groups within the Chamber of Deputies, it was thought, the ideal of Ottomanism in the form espoused at least since 1839 would be fully realized for the first time.

Imagining Revolution

It was no wonder that the Young Turks expressed ambivalence toward the French Revolution, even when they held it up as the most important event in modern history. In their minds France owed its prosperity and order—as indeed did most of Europe that followed in its footsteps—to this first constitutional revolution. Yet as late as 1904 the Young Turks feared its violence and condemned it accordingly. The gains of the French Revolution, they argued, would have been possible without the Terror and without Robespierre, who exemplified the bloodthirsty masses in revolution (*Şura-yi Ümmet* 55, July 14, 1904, p. 3).

If France had gained its constitution through violence, they wondered, was violence the unavoidable fate of all similar movements? The Meiji Restoration of 1868, another purportedly constitutional revolution, had sidestepped mass participation and bloodshed yet had attained its political goal and immense progress. This was not the only reason why Japan had captured the Young Turks' imagination more than France. After 1868, Japan had begun a period of tremendous progress and had "evolved" from a "backward" nation in Asia to a major world power in the early twentieth century, even defeating a powerful European enemy—Russia—on land and sea in 1905. The Young Turks were hopeful that the Ottomans too could usher in progress in the blink of an eye, stave off the Great Powers' aggression, and stop the encroachments of Russia, their archenemy. They consistently upheld constitutions and parliaments as responsible for such amazing progress and professed their plans to emulate Japan. Not only had the Meiji Restoration been bloodless, but also an alliance between modernist sectors of the military and the bureaucracy had made it possible (*Şura-yi Ümmet* 52, May 1, 1904, pp. 3–4). The Young Turks, drawn from the same sectors, took

Japan as a guide for both their goals and their strategy.[6] In early 1906 they wrote: "Knowledge and progress is transferred from one country to another, and from one nation to the other, gradually. Yet at some times and under some circumstances the law of evolution can be speeded up. The Grand Mikado and the advanced Japanese are the reason for our opinion. We are ceaseless supporters of revolutions in minds, schools, industry, and knowledge, but not in the streets" (*Şura-yi Ümmet* 88, February 25, 1906, p. 1).

The Young Turks found support for a constitution and the Japanese strategy in the Young Ottoman movement of 1867–1876, the first constitutional movement in the Middle East. In 1876 a coalition of high-ranking military men and bureaucrats, in couplike fashion, had placed a new sultan on the throne and inaugurated the empire's first constitutional period. A parliament sat for two legislative periods (less than six months in sum) before the new sultan, using the excuse of Russian advancements to the outskirts of the capital, suspended it in 1878. Despite the movement's eventual defeat, the strategy of revolution from above had proven to be sound and possible. Equally important was the ideological contribution of the movement. Reacting to challenges of imperial decline, ethnic conflict, Western interference, and reform and Westernization, the Young Ottomans had sought to solve the empire's problems by resorting to constitutionalism. Their most original ideological contribution was to indigenize the constitutional doctrine by systematically relating it to Islam and tracing its roots to the *Qur'an,* prophetic traditions, and traditions such as the Circle of Justice (discussed below). The rhetoric and language of political opposition was thus heavily Islamicized. By recourse to it the opposition could argue that far from deviating from tradition and grasping at a Western solution, it was instead reviving the old notions of consultation and justice that were reasons for the very success of the empire in its earlier phase. The Young Ottomans' attempt at localization of the global through an invention of tradition was not a consciously designed manipulative act, but it certainly paralleled the best attempts of political practitioners to gain hegemony or extend frames. In contrast to the sincere intent of their predecessors, the Young Turks clearly used their rhetoric in a manipulative fashion, as their belief in the Islamic lineage of constitutionalism had lessened a good deal. Equally important, they could claim that constitutionalism resolved the problem of ethno-religious inequality within the empire, an issue for which they were severely pressed by the Great Powers, so there remained no reason for for-

6. *Şura-yi Ümmet* 29, May 28, 1903, pp. 3–4; 46, February 2, 1904, pp. 1–2; 64, November 23, 1904, p. 4; 85, October 30, 1905, pp. 2–3; 88, February 25, 1906, pp. 1–2; 123, October 15, 1907, pp. 1–2; 104, November 30, 1906, p. 3.

eign demands for reform. Thus, three principal ideological notions survived into the Young Turk period: a constitution was the source of progress, it was an Islamic notion (and thus not alien to the fundamental traditions of the empire), and it facilitated the transformation of subjects into citizens, with equal rights and obligations guaranteed and expressed through parliamentary representation (Devereux 1963: 28, 74–77, 80–97; Mardin 1962).

In 1905 and 1906, constitutional revolutions in two neighboring countries, first in Russia and then in Iran, confirmed that the Young Turks were on the right track. These revolutions placed the Ottomans in close proximity to the revolutionary wave. Without a doubt the Russian revolution was the more important influence, though one characteristic it shared with Iran was a source of discomfort: both events had involved the public, in sharp contrast to the strategy of limited revolution from above. Two contemporary popular constitutional revolutions in adjacent territories could not be easily ignored or argued away by recourse to theory or history.

If Japan served as a model, Russia served as an example of everything that could be wrong in a nonconstitutional empire (Şura-yi Ümmet 75, May 20, 1905, p. 1). This view was reinforced when tiny, constitutional, Asian Japan defeated the nonconstitutional European empire of Russia in 1905 (Şura-yi Ümmet 99, August 31, 1906, p. 4). Although it was quite an exaggeration to argue that the Russian state was not rationalized, that its army was entirely disorganized, or that its leaders were unaccountable because they were not elected by the public, these accusations were hurled by many, including Russia's own internal opposition, and the Young Turks repeated them with vehemence. Russia, they argued, had declined under the weight of an autocratic ruler and a nonrational administration, and it was no wonder that it now faced widespread constitutional opposition.[7]

Yet the success of a popular revolution created explanatory problems for the Young Turks. Initially they resisted acknowledging the significance of public participation and tried hard to cast the Russian events in the mold of an elite-directed and controlled uprising, arguing that its few assassins were more effective than the large crowds it turned out (Şura-yi Ümmet 73, April 21, 1905, p. 4). By mid-1905, however, contradictory statements about the Russian events betrayed a split within the Young Turks' ranks (Şura-yi Ümmet 75, May 20, 1905, pp. 1–2; 86, November 13, 1905, pp. 1–2). Some still held to the notion that a revolution from above could set all matters right, while others began to argue more forcefully for a more wide-ranging movement that involved the public. Certainly the receding danger of Russia and

---

7. Şura-yi Ümmet 52, May 1, 1904, pp. 3–4; 54, May 30, 1904, pp. 2–4; 57, August 13, 1904, pp. 3–4; 64, November 23, 1904, p. 4; 71, March 22, 1905, pp. 1–3; 73, April 21, 1905, p. 4; Ascher (1988: 43).

the diminishing possibility that it might repeat an invasion similar to one that had brought the Young Ottoman movement to an end was encouraging for the faction that leaned toward mass participation. But even more convincing was witnessing the power of revolutionary organizations that in the Young Turks' own estimation had brought an army as massive as Russia's to its knees.[8] The centrality of revolutionary organizations and popular participation became key lessons of the Russian revolution for many of the Young Turks, and progressively this became the majority opinion.

Further support for the faction favoring mass participation came from Iran, where the 1906 revolution was popular, constitutional, and had followed in the Young Ottomans' footsteps by using an Islamic rhetoric similar to theirs to localize the global. Moreover, the revolution's populism had not degenerated into violence, and the ease with which the shah had granted constitutionalism astonished everyone. The Young Turks thus congratulated the Iranians for having joined the company of civilized nations and adopting the Islamic principle of consultation, and they openly argued that if Iran, a "backward" Muslim nation, could adopt such an "advanced" political system, surely the Ottomans, who lived under a more "developed" administration, were ready for it as well.[9]

Did this mean the Young Turks were now ready for mass action because of Russia and Iran? The majority within the Committee of Union and Progress (CUP), the Young Turk party located in Paris, began to make the case for greater public participation. But how convincing could the Russian and Iranian examples be in light of the serious danger of foreign intervention, the weight of the historical Ottoman repertoire, and the Young Turks' previous intellectual justifications against mass action? Moreover, no previous mass action or organization had indicated that a popular uprising was feasible in the empire.

A series of internal uprisings, although materially unrelated to final revolutionary action, further emboldened the Young Turks about the possibility of mass mobilization. In 1906 and 1907 sporadic tax rebellions took place in Anatolia (the Asian Turkey of today). These revolts were staged by the Turkish population and were surprising because of the population's meager

8. For contradictory expressions but ones that eventually gave way to strong support for mass uprising, violence, and revolutionary organization, see *Şura-yi Ümmet* 87, February 10, 1906 [February 9, 1906], pp. 1–2; 75, May 20, 1905, pp. 1–2; 73, April 21, 1905, pp. 1–2; 76, June 5, 1905, pp. 2–3; 88, February 25, 1906, p. 3; 94, May 25, 1906, pp. 1–2; 95, June 23, 1906, pp. 2–3; 96–97, August 1, 1906, pp. 1–2, 7–8, 96–97; 99, August 31, 1906, pp. 1–3.

9. *Şura-yi Ümmet* 100, September 15, 1906, p. 4; 101, October 1, 1906, pp. 1–2 and 4; 102, October 15, 1906, pp. 2–3; 104, November 30, 1906, p. 3; 106, December 15, 1906, p. 3; 108, January 30, 1907, pp. 2–3; 115, June 1, 1907, p. 2; 118, July 15, 1907, pp. 1–2; 124, October 31, 1907, pp. 3–4.

history of anti-state activity; somewhat violent, they did not devolve into ethnic warfare. The events carried enormous symbolic significance, even though their organizational contribution was nil.[10] By August 1906, the combined effect of Russian, Iranian, and Anatolian uprisings prompted the CUP to issue substantive and direct calls to the public for a mass uprising (Şura-yi Ümmet 99, August 31, 1906, pp. 1–3).

The major organizational breakthrough came in September 1907, when the CUP united with an organization of the so-called action-oriented revolutionary officers in Macedonia. With this alliance, the organizational structure of the CUP as a whole was dramatically transformed (Hanioğlu 2001: 217–230; Niyazi 1908: 36–37). The CUP immediately began issuing orders to officers to organize Macedonian villagers (Greeks and Bulgarians in particular), on the model of rebellious Christian bands active in Macedonia (Enver 1991: 57, 61–69, 72; Hanioğlu 2001: 217, 221–227; Niyazi 1908: 34, 40–41, 43–44, 51–61), into units of ten to fifteen members to begin liberating territories (Şura-yi Ümmet 123, October 15, 1907, pp. 3–4). The mobilization of Muslim villagers in Macedonia, and hence a more broadly based movement, was now openly advocated. With the emphasis on officer leadership, the CUP worked out a compromise between mass mobilization and military action.[11] In this manner, under officer command, it brought together all the disparate Muslim bands that had been formed to defend villages against Christian bands in Macedonia, including those created by action-oriented officers. After the alliance organizational activities among villagers and other spheres expanded greatly. The CUP officers promised the villagers greater immediate protection from ethnic warfare and a permanent end to ethnic conflict, as well as a restructuring of their unjust taxes under the future constitutional administration. Although somewhat reluctant at the beginning, they gradually made the same appeals to the Bulgarian, Greek, and Serbian bands with some success. When appeals did not work, they did not hesitate to use threats. The cooperation of the Christian villages, although late and limited, was interpreted nonetheless as a positive sign of a future without ethnic clashes under the constitutional administration (Enver 1991: 118–122; Hanioğlu 2001: 242–254; Niyazi 1908: 49–50). The cooperation between external and internal organizations had transformed the CUP as a whole into a

---

10. Şura-yi Ümmet 89, March 11, 1906, p. 4; 89, March 11, 1906, pp. 3–4; 94, May 25, 1906, pp. 1–2; 104, November 30, 1906, p. 4; 106, December 15, 1906, p. 1; 108, January 30, 1907, pp. 3–4; 118, July 15, 1907, p. 1; 123, October 15, 1907, p. 4. For a different view of their organizational importance, see Kansu (1997: 29–72).

11. Even here, organizational learning may have played a role. Greek bands did include the clandestine presence of Greek army officers who crossed in from the border. Yet obviously their scope of action, organization, and mobilization capacity were lower than officers who engaged in subversive activities from within the territories of their own state.

true revolutionary party (Hanioğlu 2001: 210–232). It was no surprise then that the Young Turk Congress, which convened in the closing days of 1907, openly declared itself revolutionary and advocated a series of revolutionary and passive methods of resistance. It declared in unambiguous terms that nonviolent methods had proven insufficient and that now armed resistance and public uprising were enthusiastically endorsed.[12]

The documentary evidence from the last, most intensive days of the revolution provides a picture of widespread uprising in Macedonia, with quite extensive involvement on the part of villagers and the general public and under the tight control of military officers.[13] The mobilization capacity of the CUP proved to be outstanding. The entire military force in Macedonia, with minor exceptions, had been won over. The government reacted quickly when it found itself incapacitated by mass outpourings, threats against its officials, and a CUP promise of a march to the capital within forty-eight hours. The generals and top civil officials pleaded with the sultan to grant a constitution, and he begrudgingly did so on July 23, 1908, after openly admitting the extent of the popular and military uprising in Macedonia.[14]

There are a number of reasons to believe that the CUP turn to radicalism and populism was not simply the result of a pragmatic alliance with the action-oriented officers inside the empire. First, as the careful timing established here demonstrates, the shift in strategy predated the alliance. Second, at the time of the alliance the two groups (inside and outside the empire) held views far more similar than hitherto acknowledged, and the faction abroad even had a stronger desire for radical, popular action. If the timing for organizational transformation and revolutionary activism coincided with the wave of revolutions and predated the alliance, and if the individuals responsible for the alliance justified their departure from conservatism by propagandizing based on the revolutionary events around them, we do not need better proof that it was the wave that swayed them in the direction of armed popular rebellion. It is indeed curious that an organization with such passive credentials that had disparaged violence and populism until 1905

12. Under the congress's Ottomanist mantra, only one major non-Turkish revolutionary group, the Armenians, participated, even though the congress's propagandist proclamations made far wider claims. *Şura-yi Ümmet* 128–129, February 1, 1908, pp. 1–5.

13. For a firsthand account of the activities of the action-oriented officers and their methods of mobilization of villagers, one may refer to the memoirs of officers who emerged as heroes of the revolution (Enver 1991: 102–121; Karabekir 1995; Niyazi 1908: 30–31, 35, 95–120, 141–149, 173–181).

14. This observation is based on the large number of files in the Rumeli Müfettişliği Tasnifi and Yıldız collection in the prime ministry archives of Istanbul that are too numerous to cite here. See also Hanioğlu (2001) and Sohrabi (2002). For the content of the sultan's decree, see *Düstur* (Istanbul), second series, vol. 1, July 23, 1908, pp. 1–2.

would suddenly turn into a full-fledged revolutionary force in a short period between 1905 and 1908.

Coming to Terms with the Puzzle in the Ottoman Empire

What did the Young Turks expect to gain from a constitution? A constitution for them was both a symbol and the cause of Western progress, materially and civilizationally. By adopting it, the state was expected to undergo fundamental organizational restructuring and turn into a streamlined, efficient machine of intervention against social ills. Part of this project would be blissfully self-serving: by purging patrimonial and neo-patrimonial sectors it opened channels of mobility and catered to the interests of the emerging middle class in the name of greater efficiency and rationality. The anticipated strength would improve the state's standing in the international power rivalry. Furthermore, the constitution would help cure ethnic and religious separatist movements and conflict and allow the full realization of Ottoman citizenship for the first time. These were all to work together to make foreign intervention more difficult and to stave off the empire's breakdown as the result of forces acting from within or without. Finally, the constitution was linked to an invented Islamic tradition of representative government. Thus, the Young Turks made the global master frame relevant and legitimate to a broad spectrum by linking it to the empire-wide problems and cultural traditions. By doing so they gained public confidence and mobilized their support for revolution, but at the cost of de-emphasizing constitutionalism's major components such as limiting the powers of the state, emphasis on natural rights, and sanctity of popular sovereignty. Instead they turned it into a statist doctrine.

Agency was the link between the global ideology of constitutionalism and its local metamorphosis, and in the Ottoman Empire it also connected a clandestine movement with a global wave of constitutional revolutions. With the coming of the wave, the movement's rhetoric and organization underwent transformations that made it populist and revolutionary. Agency did not create revolutionary organizations without pre-existing potentialities, but it recognized the domestic possibilities after receiving clues from the international context. Departing from its previous conservatism, the movement brought together disparate, disorganized elements under one cohesive whole to stage a revolution that could be characterized as organized, planned, and executed from above and assisted by energetic mass action from below.

We are now in a position to explain why there has been so little variation in revolutionary doctrines. On the one hand, if skillful local actors can mold and shape global notions according to local exigencies, as did the Young Turks, then the global doctrines are indeed different concepts locally. On the other hand, one may not overlook that a commitment to the same discourse, although seemingly superficial, will have dramatic consequences, and the global master frames do exert tremendous weight in bringing uniformity to the framing, processes, and outcomes of revolutions.

The CUP was in a position to overtake the state in July 1908, but its constitutional language forced it instead to settle for exerting its influence through a clandestine, extra-legal party that operated in support of the Chamber of Deputies but in violation of constitutional principles. Nine months later, when forced out of power in a counter-revolution, the CUP made a quick recovery by making good on its promise of capturing the capital with the help of the military in Macedonia. This time it openly professed its intent not to leave affairs in the hands of the tyrannical administrators of the old regime. Condemning its own indecisiveness after the revolution, it spoke of its failure to fire the administrators of the old regime and its refusal to shape public opinion out of a naive belief that doing so violated constitutional articles and the letter of the law.[15] The subsequent purges, the CUP's bolder interference, and its domination over the Chamber of Deputies attested to the new style of politics after the defeat of the counter-revolution. Yet the initial commitment to the discourse of constitutionalism continued to exert an influence through elections, constitutional struggles with the monarchy and government, operating space for political opposition (however limited), and the pursuit of social programs, such as the creation of a new bourgeoisie (to name a few). It is significant that because of the constitutional trajectory within which it had locked itself, the CUP could not abolish the Chamber of Deputies and begin to rule in the name of the nation. Regardless of the abuses that constitutionalism suffered under the Young Turks or the subsequent republican government, from 1908 the Chamber of Deputies became a staple of Turkish life, firmly engrained in the fabric of politics and a rallying point for an opposition intent on bringing constitutionalism closer to the global master frame.

The Revolution in 1906 Iran

Rarely are revolutions as well planned and executed as the Young Turk revolution. And rarely are we able to trace the shifts in strategy and planning and the influence of the revolutionary wave in so precise a manner. In Iran, by contrast, there were no organized parties, no central organ of revolution,

15. For a bold statement to this effect see, for example, *Tanin* 252, April 26, 1909, p. 1.

and no planning. Yet constitutionalism as an idea was by no means new in 1906. There was even widespread eyewitness reporting of the impact of the 1905 Russian revolution. But to trace the wave's precise influence is a futile endeavor because, as noted, an organized revolutionary party, a central organ that reflected its every mood, and long-term planning simply were not there. What began as a spontaneous popular revolt turned into a constitutional revolution at the very last minute, thanks to the constitutionalist intelligentsia who rose to leadership and the recent Russian events that encouraged it. Thus, although the global wave did not affect the strategy of revolution in Iran, the global master frame left its imprint by way of the constitutional goal the revolution set itself, the framing of conflict in pursuit of that goal, and the revolutionary process thereafter.

Constitutionalism was localized in Iran in a fashion strikingly similar to the Ottoman context. Its rhetoric was Islamicized, and the constitution not only symbolized modernity and progress, but was considered to be their cause as well. It was no accident, then, that the 1905 Japanese victory over Russia was perceived through very much the same lenses (Haag-Higuchi 1996; Pistor-Hatam 1996). Similarly, the constitution was expected to take administrative rationality to new heights and make the state the major instrument of change through purposive intervention. One major difference from the Ottomans, however, was that a constitution was not imagined as a remedy for disunity among various ethnic and religious communities. In Iran, the ethno-religious communities were not politicized nearly to the same extent as in the Ottoman Empire. In the age of nationalism, Iran was not imagined as an empire with a *remembered* history of conquest and subjugation, and hence the idea of constitution was not reconstructed as a cure for ethno-religious disunity. Another difference was that the revolution in Iran involved the public in larger numbers and over a longer duration. A far weaker and less institutionalized Iranian state made public participation more consequential, especially in the urban centers. Furthermore, the public was not under the control of an organized party, and popular mobilization actually gathered momentum after the granting of the constitution rather than dying out as in the Ottoman case. This made for a multi-class, multi-actor, de-centered revolution rife with conflicts and contradictions.

Again we are ready to consider the two major themes of this essay: global-local interaction and agency. In keeping with my critique of modernization and world society theories, here I concentrate on the dynamic interaction of constitutionalism with the local discourse of justice. This interaction, or even clash, gave rise to confusions and confrontations that finally resulted in a new synthesis that cannot be explained through linear diffusion. The synthesis required intervention by active agents, but the most consequential agents here were not the intelligentsia of the Young Turk revolution with its voluntarist intervention. Although the presence of the intelligentsia was crucial in Iran as well—the concepts of constitution and assembly would not have been known without them—the most consequential actor was the rebellious public, which was not in pursuit of a grand constitutional plan. A consideration here of the public allows us to address how global doctrines effect change in local doctrines and are themselves transformed in an unintended fashion.[16]

The Local Idiom of Politics: The Circle of Justice

After protests by clerics, a Westernist intelligentsia, merchants, statesmen, and a significant number of urban guilds in 1906, the shah of Iran agreed to grant a constitutional assembly. Yet it was surprising that such a broad movement for representative government had taken place at all; aside from the intelligentsia, few had knowledge of constitutional politics. Thanks to the Young Ottomans, constitutionalism in Iran was also heavily Islamicized, and the localization of the global master frame partially accounted for its broad appeal.[17] But the public dedication to the cause went beyond intellectual appeals. Even though public energy was tapped for the constitutional cause, the public's language and forms of action signaled that it was not following a constitutional script but a more familiar script of politics in search of justice. Here I argue that the local discourse of justice provided the public with an opportunity to legitimize an anti-state revolt in the guise of loyalty to the shah. The internal peculiarities of the familiar discourse of justice allowed the public to manipulate it in this new circumstance, but in the presence of a competing discourse, manipulation provided a dynamic that led to the synthesis of global and local discourses of politics, a transformation that went beyond the intentions of all the actors.

The history of uprisings is rife with examples of the crowd's pursuit of justice. The more interesting question, however, is what "justice" means in each context and what actors do to attain it. In Iran, the discourse of justice was contained within the Irano-Islamic theory of kingship, known as the Circle of Justice, a combination of pre-Islamic and Islamic notions accord-

16. The issues raised here are relevant to all considerations of culture: are actors/agents ever able to transcend their local categories? If not, are they prisoners of culture, or can they manipulate certain aspects of it, and if so, what is the extent and limit of their manipulative capacity? Furthermore, at what point do cultures, with their language-like resiliency, undergo radical transformations?
17. On the Islamicization of constitutionalism, see, for example, Mustashar al-Dawlah (1985) or the newspapers *Akhtar* and *Qanun*.

ing to which the king was sacred, in touch with divinity, and the source of justice.[18] The pre-Islamic treatises on rule, or "mirrors for princes," devised a hierarchical ordering among the various estates and advised the ruler not to allow those at the highest social rungs to coerce those at the lower. Justice held the estates in their God-given positions and in stable relations with one another and guaranteed the shah's position at the top of the circle. The handbooks recounted to the shah the benefits of justice and the hazards of injustice and established a direct link among justice, order, and prosperity, as well as their reverse—injustice, disorder, and destitution. They also emphasized that balance in the circle was preserved and dissemination of justice assured only when ordinary subjects could come into unmediated contact with the shah; if unmediated contact was jeopardized, the social order would break down and crisis befall the realm. Although the shah was ultimately responsible for breakdown and injustice, the mirrors consistently elaborated a scheme that allowed the ruler to shift responsibility to mischievous courtiers, viziers, and grand viziers who surrounded and isolated him and left him unaware of his subjects' grievances and the injustices inflicted by the powerful estates. This official ideology of the center was practiced—the grand viziers, viziers, and courtiers were dismissed or killed at times of crisis—to preserve the charismatic legitimacy of the shahs (Abbas, ed. 1969; Boyce, ed. 1968; Ghazzali Tusi 1938; Tusi 1964).

This thinking survived in the "mirrors" of the late nineteenth century (Adamiyat and Natiq 1977). It was also strongly reflected in the works of contemporary statesmen, who drew extensively from their vocabulary and logic to explain the rapid decline that had gripped the Qajar monarchy: they laid responsibility for the crisis on those surrounding the shahs but insisted on the innocence of the reigning monarchs (I'timad al-Saltanah 1969; Majd al-Mulk 1979). Also, the institutions introduced at this period—such as the practice of reading petitions to the shah on a weekly basis, the implementation of the Box of Justice in the capital and provinces,[19] and the creation of the Council for the Investigation of Grievances—indicated the mirrors' presence, as they were all intended to bring about unmediated contact between subjects and shah (Adamiyat 1972; Adamiyat and Natiq 1977; Damghani, ed. 1978; Ettehadieh 1989; Mustawfi 1945).

In conformity with the mirrors' teachings, the revolution began by targeting the grand vizier, who, the clerical leaders declared, "stands as an obstacle between the shah and his subjects and does not allow our petitions

---

18. For a discussion of the synthesis of Muslim, Iranian, and Greek traditions, see Marlow (1997).

19. The Box of Justice was a place where complaints could be dropped for the shah to later read.

to reach the shah" (M. N. Kirmani 1983, vol. 1: 293). It is also significant that the public, instead of demanding a parliament, asked for a House of Justice in each province "to attend to subjects' petitions and grievances and to treat them with justice and equity" (p. 358). In fact, after the National Assembly began its work, the public mistook it for a House of Justice, flooded it with petitions, and took sanctuary in its compound or in telegraph offices around the country in order to come into direct contact with the "source of justice" (*Habl al-Matin* 16, May 16, 1907, pp. 3–4; *Anjuman* 90, June 1, 1907, pp. 1–4; 91, June 2, 1907, pp. 1–4; 92, June 3, 1907, pp. 1–4). Even some deputies in the National Assembly thought the solution to crisis lay in bypassing the "traitor" grand vizier and other intermediaries who, by feigning loyalty to the innocent shah, had led him astray; to establish direct contact, they suggested an exclusive telephone line between the assembly and the shah or a permanent assembly delegate for regular visits with him (*Ruznamah-'i Majlis*, January 3, 1907, pp. 41–42; January 22, 1907, pp. 59–60; February 28, 1907, p. 97; April 13, 1907, p. 132; August 26, 1907, p. 262).

The local transformation of constitutionalism, however, was not confined to the public perception and treatment of the National Assembly in familiar terms (e.g., petitioning, establishing direct contact with the shah). The transformation was more fundamental and involved a more intricate process. To understand this process fully, it is critical to note that although the public followed the cultural script, it took advantage of its interpretive possibilities or loopholes to manipulate it to its own advantage. Initially the public withheld direct attack on the shah and praised him with intensely "naive" expressions of loyalty (Field 1989) as the symbol of justice and an innocent victim of his ministers and associates. Yet even from the beginning, when we move from front to back stage (J. C. Scott 1985, 1990) and into anonymous domains—the ubiquitous unsigned leaflets, the popular forums, the lesser known newspapers—it is clear that the treatment of the shah is harsher. In such leaflets, the shah's purity of character was called into doubt and his fitness for kingship questioned, and sometimes, though indirectly, he was threatened with death (A. M. Kirmani 1968: 96, 367; M. N. Kirmani 1983, vol. 1: 360–361; Sharif Kashani 1983: 21–22, 77–81). As we move forward in time, the divide between public and private domains becomes less pronounced and attacks begin to surface in public forums. Frequently the newspapers upheld the myth of the shah's innocence and reported mass gatherings at which the public expressed loyalty to the shah, praised his adamant support of the constitution, and condemned the shortsighted swindlers around him. But often the very same issues contained references to the shah as a conceited tyrant adamantly opposed to the constitution and deserving of death.[20]

The divide between assertions favorable to the shah and hostile proclamations and actions was far too sharp to be attributed to expected oscillations between belief and disbelief in unstable times. This wavering is better explained through James Scott's (1985, 1990) notion of public and hidden transcripts and the sharp divide of opinion between public and nonpublic spheres, although Scott ultimately adheres to a notion of radical agency that fails to grant sufficient weight to political culture as a *doxic* realm (Bourdieu 1977: 165–168). Even when the public became convinced of the shah's absolute opposition to its movement, it connivingly continued to profess loyalty to the shah to divide and confuse authorities about its intentions, to delay and to soften their reactions and to allow the shah room to change his ways and side with the movement without fear of losing face. Yet even in the most radical moments, the public did not intend to radically reorganize the entire institution of kingship, with its traditional functions and responsibilities, but at most to replace an unjust shah with a just one. In other words, the public did not discard the familiar idiom of kingship but rejected only the shah.

To use a structuralist distinction drawn by Gluckman (1963) and Kantorowicz (1957), when the public denounced the shah, it denounced the "person" and not the "position," the individual and not the office.[21] Yet although the public had not intended to reject or change the larger discursive framework of local politics, and even though its agency operated within the familiar confines of the discourse of kingship and justice, paradoxically its practice transformed the culture of politics.

20. *Anjuman* 42, February 11, 1907, p. 1; 43, February 13, 1907, pp. 2–4; 44, February 14, 1907, pp. 1–4; 75, May 6, 1907, pp. 1–2; 80, May 14, 1907, p. 3; *Azarbaijan* 2, February 28, 1907, pp. 1–4; 4, March 16, 1907, pp. 1–2; 10, April 28, 1907, pp. 4–5; 13, May 28, 1907, pp. 1–2; 15, June 26, 1907, pp. 1–4; 16, September 30, 1907, pp. 2–4; 17, October 11, 1907, p. 3; *Hasharat al-'Arz* 6, April 23, 1908, p. 4; 9, May 16, 1908, pp. 1–4; 11, May 30, 1908, p. 2.

21. Revolting against the state while professing absolute loyalty to the head of the state was quite advantageous. The Russian peasants had done the same by invoking the locally invented myth of the Tsar the Deliverer, a phenomenon that appeared to be "naive monarchism" to outside observers when they took the peasants at their word. For peasants it was a strategy that divided authorities, bought themselves time, and reduced punishments for their evasive activities (Field 1989). The Circle of Justice doctrine was even more amenable to manipulation than the Tsar the Deliverer: its truth was never disputed because it had not been invented by the public, but was the ideology by which the center had presented itself to the public for centuries. When it was invoked, the tacit knowledge of the rules of the political game were immediately apparent to the dominated and dominant. The contenders, in their "symbolic jujitsu" (J. C. Scott 1985: 333) with the state, drew strength from the doctrine of kingship to fight the shah himself.

In contrast to the popular classes, the constitutionalists challenged the position of the shah rather than his person—a far more thorough affront that questioned the entirety of the traditional idiom of politics and the shah's position within it. Despite their efforts, the constitutionalists ultimately failed to dissociate the National Assembly from a House of Justice. What they did manage was to make it known that the assembly was not a mere transition point between the public and the shah and subordinated to him, but that it stood on its own. This was a crucial ingredient for the transformation of political culture.

The simultaneous petitioning of the National Assembly and the shah created confusion about the location of the "source of justice." When the public petitioned the defiant assembly, it placed the traditional practice of petitioning the source of justice at risk (Sahlins 1981). This challenge was so apparent that during the ultimately abortive counter-revolution of mid-December 1907, the shah ordered the setup of a telegraph machine in the midst of disgruntled counter-revolutionary crowds so that he could be petitioned directly in competition with the assembly (Dawlatabadi 1983: 114). If the public, acting within the confines of the traditional theory of rule, had challenged the person but not the position of the shah, in this new circumstance the public practice of petitioning the assembly *unwittingly* challenged the position of the shah as well.

What ultimately ended the confusion and pitted the crowds against the shah in the midst of this ambiguous situation was the assassination of the grand vizier in August 1907, an act rife with symbolic implications in the context of the Circle of Justice paradigm. This was not a gradual evolutionary radicalization but an event that forced various groups into diametrically opposed camps that ultimately transformed the structure of culture (Sewell 1996a). Even this act was initially portrayed as an expression of loyalty: explicitly it had rid the shah of the principal traitor, and implicitly it had given him a chance to back away from confrontation and side with the public. Instead the shah introduced a handpicked, hostile cabinet. This was ousted by the assembly shortly after and replaced with one sympathetic to the constitution. In reaction, the shah abruptly dismissed the new cabinet, sent the new grand vizier into exile, and unleashed his first attempt at a counter-revolution (the attempt failed).

With the assassination, matters had taken a clear turn. Future grand viziers could no longer be the subjects of dissimulation in the public's fight against the state; the shah had rejected the public's choice after it had saved him from the principal "traitor." From then on, voices that argued for the shah's innocence became fainter, and telegrams from around the country began to openly threaten the shah and his dynasty, culminating in a popularly supported assassination attempt against the shah himself in February 1908. These developments led the shah to make a second attempt at counter-revolution in June 1908. He succeeded in ousting the assembly, but for only a year. When the Assembly was restored in July 1909 after a year of fighting, the shah was deposed and replaced with his powerless eleven-year-old son. Now the new assembly was in a position to reign without the monarch's interference.

The Assembly as a Synthesis

What emerged from the clash of constitutionalism with the local language of politics was both familiar and unexpected. It was familiar because the public demanded justice and not representation, and it petitioned for it directly. It was unfamiliar because now the public did not petition the shah for justice but rather demanded it from an institution independent of him. The outcome was just as novel for the constitutionalists, who had partially succeeded in replacing the shah with the National Assembly in the public mind but were still far from establishing a representative assembly with constitutional functions.

What began as reproduction ended in cultural transformation. The resulting synthesis, being continuous with and divergent from both cultures of politics, was "at once conservative and innovative" (Sahlins 1981: 67–68). Practice led to cultural transformation. Agency, in the guise of the "naive royalism" of the public, was not the cause of this cultural shift, though it initiated it and transformation would not have been possible without it. The new discourse of politics, by inserting an assembly with independent powers into the structure of traditional political culture, transformed the "tradition," yet the synthesis was in many ways still within the bounds of tradition.

The far-reaching consequences of such transformation cannot be underestimated. What was new at the end was not only a different monarch or a formally constitutional government. The position of the shah had been replaced by an institution composed of individuals, and the political culture had been transformed at the popular level from one with a strong faith in monarchy to one that believed in the assembly as the new source of justice. Although the assembly was not engaged in representation, the exercise of authority by such an institution and its popular acceptance were without precedent and served as potential building blocks for a future full-fledged representative parliament. More immediately, the altered conception of state spelled the end of monarchy. This may explain not only the ease with which the Qajar monarchy was abolished, but also the crisis of legitimacy that the Pahlavis, who supplanted the Qajars, suffered until the end of their rule in 1979.

Revolution in the Ottoman Empire and Iran

Although I have concentrated on different episodes in the Ottoman and Iranian revolutions, the general lessons remain the same: the doctrine of constitutionalism, despite its uniform appearance at the global level, was transformed in the locality. Because of cultural affinity, geographic proximity, a shared experience of decline, and European encroachment, the Ottomans and Iranians localized constitutionalism in quite similar ways. The strong association of constitutionalism with strength, regeneration, rationalization, and state centralization was the dominant theme for the modernist elite in both locations, and it came at the expense of the liberal dimensions of constitutionalism. Yet as each context is unique, the global master frames were localized with new elements, or different weight was assigned to the elements the two locations shared. For example, in Iran, where ethno-religious relations were far less politicized, constitutionalism was not imagined as a cure for ethnic disunity. Similarly, the consistently populist dimension of revolution in Iran, the lack of an organized political party, and in general the far less institutionalized aspects of governance and social life allowed a populist, less intellectualized, local interpretation of the global master frame. Strong associations were thus made between constitutionalism and the Circle of Justice in Iran; in the Ottoman context, such an ideology, while it did also exist, never was a forceful presence and remained more or less without consequence.

Concern with localization should not detract from attention to the universalizing aspects of revolutionary doctrines, although the latter dimension was not examined here. Commitment to the global discourse on constitutionalism focused revolutionary conflicts around the creation and defense of an assembly, popular sovereignty, constitutional rights, and assembly-initiated reforms. The global frame fundamentally altered the form of conflict between revolutionaries and the old regimes in both the Ottoman Empire and Iran and endowed their constitutional struggles with strikingly similar processes (Sohrabi 1995).

Finally, in both cases the intelligentsia played a significant role in translating global doctrines into the local language and in transforming them into an elixir for local problems. In the Ottoman context, it played the additional role of altering the strategy of revolution and reshaping a semi-revolutionary party into a revolutionary one with the determination and means to mobilize the public. The Iranian intelligentsia performed many of the same functions but was only a shadow of its counterpart. Unlike the Young Turk intelligentsia, it could not determine the strategy of revolution but only influence its course; with some good fortune it turned an ordinary revolt into a nationwide constitutional revolution. Yet beyond the role of the intellectual elite, agency figured in a more subtle way in the Iranian context. The space created by revolution provided an opportunity for the public to exercise its agency and manipulate the local paradigm as a protective shield when opposing authority. However, because of the simultaneous presence of a new global paradigm, its actions unwittingly ended in the transformation of both the global and the local paradigms. This dealt a severe blow to the legitimacy of monarchy.

State-centered and resource mobilization theories have advanced our understanding of all aspects of revolution, and no analysis can afford to ignore their systematic insights. These theories, however, have erred on the side of a radical dissociation of the "ideal" and "material," the subjective and objective, and it consistently came at the expense of the first component of the dichotomy. Given that they were reacting to an often simpleminded idealism, perhaps their emphasis was largely justified and a necessary moment to advance a productive strand of theory. More recent revolution studies, however, in line with the broader social science turn toward "practice" (Ortner 1984), are moving beyond the rigid structural materialism of the previous generation and devising approaches that incorporate subjectivities. This is not an attempt to bring ideology, culture, symbols, etc. "back in" to locations from which they were banished, but to cultivate an approach that considers them as closely intertwined. The fluidity of revolutionary periods, moments when actors are engaged in casting their worlds anew, provides particularly good opportunities to trace the agents' pursuit of meaningful action and to watch at close hand how they transcend these apparent dichotomies. The insights generated here may even take us beyond these extraordinary episodes of history and into the nature of the social in general. Beyond that, as our two short treatments have demonstrated, it is hard to make general statements about how freely and consciously agents move within the bounds of their constraints and whether they can accomplish all that they had intended; such considerations should be evaluated empirically after intensive engagement with context. Revolutions also provide rare opportunities for examining the interaction of global master frames with local notions—a neglected aspect of these events. Beyond the homogenizing impact of global models, it is equally important to take note of the way in which local actors grapple with them and put into practice, rework, and reshape models in new contexts, with results that are intended or not.

PART IV   Capitalism, Modernity, and the Economic Realm

BRUCE G. CARRUTHERS

Historical Sociology and the Economy: Actors, Networks, and Context

Since sociology's origins in late-nineteenth-century Europe, sociologists have been deeply interested in the economy. In many respects, classical social theory was invented to understand modern industrial society and capitalist economic development (Giddens 1971). Furthermore, classical social theory was imbued with a strong appreciation of history, which in the cases of Marx and Weber literally meant an encyclopedic knowledge of economic history and how capitalism emerged. These two founders also studied formal economics and engaged the key debates of their time (the theory of value for Marx and marginalism and the *Methodenstreit* for Weber).

Sociology, economics, and economic history have since gone their separate ways. Partly this was due to the sharply divergent careers of economics and sociology as social sciences. It also occurred because of sociology's long retreat from the macro-historical concerns of the founders. Yet the recent "historical turn" in sociology has combined with the resurgence of economic sociology to reinvigorate sociological interest in economic history. Sociology's relation to economics became more salient as sociology split between enthusiasts who embraced rational choice theory and those who criticized economics. The current conjuncture of sociology and economic history offers the chance to revisit the old economic sociology, with its interest in history, and transform the new economic sociology's relationship

As always, Roger Gould's presence at the Northwestern University conference where this chapter was first presented greatly improved the discussion, and I shall miss his wit and wisdom. Thanks to Frank Dobbin, Ivan Evans, Tim Guinnane, David Weiman, and the conference organizers and participants for helpful suggestions and to Mariam Manichaikul for research assistance. I am especially grateful to Elisabeth Clemens for her editorial guidance. This chapter was written with the support of the Russell Sage Foundation and the Lochinvar Society.

with economics from schizophrenia (flattering imitation vs. unequivocal rejection) to a more productive one of appropriation, engagement, and revision.

Economic Sociology, Old and New

If economic sociology means the application of a sociological perspective to economic phenomena, then Marx, Durkheim, Simmel, and Weber all did it. In Marx's class analysis of capitalist society and the origins of value, Durkheim's discussion of social solidarity in industrial society, Simmel's analysis of money, and Weber's explanation of Western capitalism's emergence, sociological ideas were used to explain the economy. But this older economic sociology did not last because the emerging division of labor between economics and sociology meant that, particularly for American scholarship, economists studied the economy while sociologists studied other matters. In the 1950s and 1960s, Talcott Parsons and Neil Smelser were virtually alone in trying to maintain an economic sociology (Parsons and Smelser 1956; Smelser 1963), but their efforts had little influence in sociology and none in economics (Swedberg 1991: 266).[1] In the same period, Polanyi's writings (1944, 1957a) enjoyed much greater influence in anthropology than in sociology. Sociologists considered the economy only in connection with social stratification research.

The 1960s and 1970s witnessed a resurgence of neo-Marxist scholarship in sociology. Marx's analysis of capitalism renewed interest in the economy, construed in class terms and in its historical and political context. The divergence between sociology and neo-classical economics grew wider as the latter continued to develop mathematical models with little room for "exploitation," "legitimacy," or "social context." Furthermore, general equilibrium models assumed an institutional framework that economists themselves overlooked (Stiglitz 1994: 29–30). Rarely did they consider how private property rights, modern commercial laws, liquid capital markets, or wage labor came to be. Nor did economists reflect on the atomized, autonomous rational actors who in neo-classical models maximized utility. The ability to deploy such unrealistic simplifications in the explanation of market phenomena was considered not a blemish but rather a sign of the technical virtuosity of economists, rather like pulling rabbits out of hats (Friedman 1953).

Scholars such as Wallerstein (1979) and Cardoso and Faletto (1979) crit-

---

1. The problem seems to be guilt by association: Parsons and Smelser indirectly implicated economic sociology as their structural functionalist approach came under attack during the late 1960s.

icized Rostow's (1960) development economics for ignoring relations of interdependence. For Rostow, modernity consisted of a bundle of political and economic attributes that all countries could achieve independently as they moved from traditional society through "takeoff" and then to "maturity." Once started, economic growth became self-sustaining (Rostow 1960: 73–74). Wallerstein and others rejected modernization theory for its uncritical meliorism and, more important, for its inability to recognize that "success" in one part of the globe depended on "failure" elsewhere. Modernity was not a feature of nations but rather characterized relations among them.

Mark Granovetter's (1985) influential article marked the resurgence of economic sociology, not only because it challenged transaction cost economics (then a hot topic), but also because it combined Polanyi's (1957a) idea of embeddedness with network analysis to criticize economics more generally: economic actors are *embedded* in networks of social relations. They do not operate autonomously but only in relation to others. Thanks to network analysis techniques (e.g., Wasserman and Faust 1994; Harrison White, Boorman, and Breiger 1976), sociologists could offer empirically grounded, quantitatively rigorous explanations. Furthermore, Granovetter cautioned against simplistic contrasts between "modern" and "pre-modern" economies: embeddedness was to be found in both. Since 1985, the new economic sociology has extended Granovetter's argument but also revived the old economic sociology's concern for the preconditions of capitalist markets; the importance of institutions such as money, law, and property; and the centrality of power and conflict. The interest in institutions has been strongly reinforced by dramatic changes in the transitional economies of Central and Eastern Europe and by Third World attempts to "develop."

Today, economic sociology informs its study of the economy with a skepticism toward vacuous formal models and a growing appreciation of historical context. It problematizes rationality and insists on the importance of relationships among economic actors. Furthermore, it is concerned to understand *markets* and the *framework for markets* as institutions. These concerns derive not only from a critique of neo-classical economics, but also reflect the continuing influence of Marx, Weber, and Polanyi. Neo-liberal triumphalism in the post-1989 era has encouraged economic sociologists to examine the institutional foundations of market society with a skeptical eye. The engagement with economics remains strong, however, partly because economic sociology encompasses both sociology departments, with their typically critical outlook, and business schools, whose mission is to train managers and capitalists. The first group criticizes economics, while the second wishes to emulate its success, and the tension between them keeps their discrepant relations to economics in the spotlight.

Economic History at Present

During the "cliometric revolution" of the 1960s and 1970s, economic history fell into line with neo-classical economics and became dominated by scholars who analyzed large data sets using econometric methods to test formal models (see, e.g., Garber 2000; Hoffman, Postel-Vinay, and Rosenthal 2000; Neal 1990).[2] But recently the agenda for economists has changed, and economic history has moved toward sociology. There is now a renewed focus on institutions (North 1981, 1990; North and Weingast 1989), and ideas about path dependence and "lock-in" (Arthur 1989; David 1985) complicate simple predictions about the efficiency of economic outcomes. Furthermore, economic historians working on a large scale (D. S. Landes 1998; North 1981) invoke "culture" and "values" to account for long-run differences in economic development.

As theorized, the simple neo-classical market is like a frictionless, featureless plane on which supply and demand curves intersect. Real markets, by contrast, operate on much lumpier terrain, and economists have come to appreciate the importance of the lumps. Some lumps are informational or transactional (e.g., Stiglitz 2000; O. E. Williamson 1985), while others are cultural or institutional. It is the latter, in particular, that have caught the eye of economic historians, partly because of their effects on growth. North (1990: 3) defined institutions as the "rules of the game," including the state, property rights, kinship, and culture. He emphasized the effect of formal institutions, such as the state and property rights, on economic growth (e.g., North 1981). North and Weingast (1989), for instance, argued that the Glorious Revolution of 1689 made sovereign commitments more credible, foreclosed predatory behavior by the sovereign, and so encouraged the development of British capital markets. North inspired numerous analyses specifying how well-defined property rights encourage economic development (Eggertsson 1990).

The institutionalist turn encouraged economists to look outside the market for explanations. For example, Guinnane's (1994) study of the failed transplantation of rural credit cooperatives from Germany to Ireland underscored the need to place the economy in its social context. Agricultural credit cooperatives enjoyed great success in Germany, but despite the demand for rural credit and notwithstanding the efforts of the Irish Agricultural Organization Society, credit cooperatives did not take root in Ireland. Guinnane explained this failure in terms of the institutional structure of Irish cooperatives, the timing of their establishment, and social norms of rural Ireland.

---

2. For an insightful sociology of economics, see Fourcade-Gourinchas (2001).

Furthermore, thanks to ideas of path dependence and lock-in, economists now recognize that history matters, and efficient equilibria are not the inevitable outcome of economic change (David 1985: 332).[3] Rather, small differences in initial conditions can generate big differences in market outcomes. This broadening of economics has helped set the stage for renewed conversations with other social sciences (Mokyr 1990). As David Landes put it: "If we learn anything from the history of economic development, it is that culture makes all the difference. (Here Max Weber was right on.)" (1998: 516).

Historical Sociology of Markets

Classical economics and classical sociology both recognized the importance of the economy. But as they went their separate ways, economics kept custody of the economy. Now a re-engagement is afoot. The interface among economic sociology, historical sociology, and economic history offers great potential, although several key tensions remain. First, the interest in institutions and culture is substantially greater among sociologists than economists. Second, sociologists problematize rationality and overall market efficiency. Third, sociology de-emphasizes formal modeling and sociologists use textual or qualitative evidence more often than do economists. These differences mean that traffic among economics, historical sociology, and economic history will not simply blend these separate traditions into a composite. The interchange will most likely be partial and uneven.

Here I argue that historical sociology brings much to this juncture: its ability to problematize market actors, embed them in networks of relationships, and place markets in an institutional context of culture and politics.[4] In general, historical sociology examines what others take for granted. The first part of this section deals with the corporation, the most important market actor in modern capitalism, and extends Weber's emphasis on capitalist institutions (M. Weber 1978: 161–162; 1981). The second concerns relations among market actors. Corporations and firms are bound together in transactional, legal, and informal social networks, and among the social sciences sociology has progressed furthest in studying such networks. Next

---

3. See Cowan's (1990) study of light water technology in the civilian nuclear industry.

4. I am ignoring important topics that others address (e.g., transitions from feudalism to capitalism) and setting aside research on markets that uses historical data but does not engage historical sociology. The population ecology school, for example, studies organizations over long periods of time but uses a specific theoretical framework and focuses narrowly on "ecological" events and relationships (e.g., organizational births and deaths, density dependence). See Carroll and Hannan (1989); Hannan and Freeman (1988).

come markets, the loci in which economic networks are embedded, and the last part examines markets in their larger institutional contexts, including culture, law, and the state. At this level, research delves directly into the politics of markets, their institutional foundations, and their institutional boundaries.

The Rise of the Corporation

Starting with Weber, bureaucratic organizations have been an ongoing sociological topic (W. R. Scott 1998: 8–10), but in the 1970s historical sociology focused mostly on states, social revolutions, and class formation, overlooking the rise of the large corporation. The recent interest in corporations came partly in reaction to economics, but also from sociology's own recognition of the empirical importance of collective social actors (Coleman 1974) and from its general willingness to problematize institutions that are taken for granted in other fields.

As a historical puzzle, the rise of the modern corporation in the nineteenth century was famously researched by Chandler (1962, 1977). As a theoretical puzzle for economists, the existence of firms was conceptualized early on by Coase (1937). Theoretical and historical strands came together in Oliver Williamson's (1985) transaction cost framework, as well as in the nexus-of-contracts approach (Alchian and Demsetz 1972) and agency theory (Jensen and Meckling 1976). The basic idea was that firms exist because they are more efficient than alternative modes of governance. Some transactions are better governed within a large hierarchical organization than through arm's-length relationships in a market. When the U.S. economy expanded during the nineteenth century, various problems of coordination and control arose that could best be solved in firms.

The presumption of efficiency has not gone unchallenged. William Roy (1997: 27–38) disputed the "efficiency" explanation, testing arguments about the supposed functional and technological advantages of the corporate form. If efficiency were the main driving force, Roy argued, corporations should have emerged first in industries with high capital intensity, high productivity, and rapid growth. But this was not the case. Instead, Roy accounts for the emergence of corporations in terms of politics, power, law, and public policy.

Over the nineteenth century, American corporations straddled the boundary between public and private. The first corporations were created by special legislative acts, and in exchange for the privileges granted them (perpetual succession, limited liability, and the right to own property) corporations received a public charge: to settle new lands, run toll roads, build canals, etc.

Their quasi-public status made them politically accountable to the state that made them (Maier 1993: 55). Often, the law of incorporation explicitly laid out their public purpose. These special rights were granted not because corporations were inherently efficient but because they supported activities that markets on their own would not otherwise undertake (Roy 1997: 76). Furthermore, states derived revenue from incorporations, and a competitive "race to the bottom" unfolded in which states vied with each other to offer general corporation laws most favorable to investors (Grandy 1989: 677; Roy 1997: 164).

Roy's account of the rise of the large corporation recognizes the importance of politics and law in creating a new form of property. Power mattered more than efficiency, and Roy's narrative is filled with contingencies. Law and culture continued to shape U.S. corporations in later periods. In particular, Fligstein traced out the history of "conceptions of control," the cognitive models that pose what is deemed rational by corporate managers. The "direct control" conception preceded "manufacturing control," which gave way to "sales and marketing control" and most recently to "finance control" (1990: 12). Each conception entailed a distinct set of "rational" strategies. For example, the first begat predatory competition, cartelization, and the establishment of monopolies. The latest conception, ascendent since the 1960s, encourages diversification and a focus on financial measures of short-term performance (p. 251). Externally, these conceptions responded to public policy, such as anti-trust legislation. Internally, the career paths of chief executive officers (CEOS) influenced their predominance. For instance, growing numbers of CEOS with finance or accounting backgrounds help explain the rise of the financial conception of control.

Along with the rise of the multi-divisional firm came internal labor markets. The career mobility of individuals has become shaped by the organizational dynamics of large firms. Stovel, Savage, and Bearman (1996) describe the long-term impact of the shift from status-based to achievement-based employment within an organization. In the early decades of the twentieth century, American industrial firms shifted to internal labor markets built around features such as job ladders, standardized pay, formal job definitions, seniority rules, and centralized hiring (J. N. Baron, Jennings, and Dobbin 1988; Jacoby 1985). Firms stopped using the "inside contracting" system, in which workers were employed by a contractor rather than the firm (Buttrick 1952) and switched to more "bureaucratic" modes of labor management. This process was not driven simply by considerations of size or efficiency, but also by institutional and political forces (J. N. Baron, Dobbin, and Jennings 1986).

Other arguments against efficiency explanations have been offered by

Jonathan Zeitlin and Charles Sabel (1985). Their examination of nineteenth-century British industry suggested that the development of Fordist mass production was not a historical inevitability dictated by economic rationality. Networks of smaller firms were a real alternative to large, integrated corporations. Within corporations, Freeland (1996) used the case of General Motors (GM) to criticize efficiency explanations of the multi-divisional form. GM persistently diverged from the predictions of transaction cost theory (O. E. Williamson 1985) and yet remained a highly successful firm. Freeland argued that internal corporate structure helped to manage the political problem of managerial consent and helped bind managers to organizational goals (Cyert and March 1963).

Sociological analysis of the corporation has not focused much on events prior to the nineteenth century. Some historical sociologists have studied corporations like the Dutch East India Company (Adams 1996), the Bank of England, and the East India Company (Carruthers 1996), and Coleman (1974) tried to generate interest in the history of corporate actors, but there has been no general treatment of early modern firms. Weber stressed the importance of the *commenda* (a hybrid loan/partnership arrangement) as a vehicle for the mobilization of capital, but historical sociologists have not studied business organizations per se in the Middle Ages.[5] The central role played by joint stock companies in the colonization of British North America and the simultaneous "enfranchisement" of shareholders for corporate governance and "non-enfranchisement" of citizens for political governance suggest that further work could raise important questions for both economic and political sociology.

Relations among Economic Actors

Market actors are usually embedded in social networks and so do not behave like the atomized individuals of economic theory. It is not surprising that researchers exploit sociology's strength in the study of networks to examine relations among economic actors. Much work concerns intercorporate networks at the level of personnel, resource exchanges, and property relations. Consider, for example, the development of director interlocks (interlocks exist when two corporations share a common director). Roy (1983) studied U.S. corporate interlocks in the late nineteenth century and found a center-periphery structure with the railroads at the core of the network. Initially, central industries (railroads, coal, and telegraphs) were linked to each other, with peripheral industries joined to the center like spokes to a hub. Over

5. Among legal historians, see H. J. Berman (1983); Cooke (1951); Pryor (1977); Udovitch (1962).

time, interlocks increased in density, but the basic hub-and-spoke pattern persisted. Financial institutions proved crucial in the constitution of this network, and banks were among the most central. Subsequent research (Roy and Bonacich 1988) uncovered a more complex structure of corporate clusters, without a single center. Rather than a core-periphery contrast, the railroad industry possessed a Balkanized structure with no overall pattern of dominance and subordination. Other work on interlocks (B. Mintz and Schwartz 1985) suggested that financial institutions during the 1960s occupied central positions in American capitalism.

Historical sociologists have begun to examine transactional networks and develop causal accounts as well as descriptions. McLean and Padgett (1997) analyzed data from Renaissance Florence to test a model of "perfect competition" and found that despite the sophistication of the market, trading in Florence was neither anonymous nor impersonal. Carruthers (1996) studied trading in company shares on the London stock market in 1712, finding that trading networks were deeply influenced by political conflicts and ethno-religious differences. Such transactional evidence shows how social context influences rational markets, and it develops embeddedness arguments.

Analyzing the structure and dynamics of economic networks represents a special opportunity for sociology because of the sheer importance of market networks in the past and because sociology possesses the methods necessary to analyze them (Wasserman and Faust 1994). From the middle ages onward, it is clear that buying and selling were heavily structured by social relationships (Greif 1989, 1991), and network organizations were common (Powell 1990). Trading rarely occurred anonymously because merchants strongly preferred to deal with parties they knew and trusted. Frequently, ethnicity or religion determined the level of trust (see, e.g., Bosher 1995 on seventeenth-century Huguenot merchants). This network quality held for domestic and foreign trade (Breen 1985: 84; Earle 1989: 108–110), through the early modern era and into the industrial revolution (Grassby 1995: 89–90; Lamoreaux 1994: 4, 26; Tittler 1994), and for capital and goods markets (Beveridge 1985; Hancock, 1995: 83, 109; M. R. Hunt 1996: 22–23).

Industries, Markets, and Regions

Consistent with the ideas Granovetter drew from Polanyi, the analysis of embeddedness has been extended from relations among people to the macro-institutional level, opening up research that places the economy in the larger context of culture, law, and government (e.g., Schneiberg 1999). Industries, markets, and economic regions are conceived in sociology as sets (or fields) of interacting institutions and market actors, cumulated across multiple networks. This conceptualization highlights the contextual, configurational, and contingent aspects of economic phenomena. Dobbin (1994) and Dobbin and Dowd (1997, 2000) have examined the railroad industry in the United States and elsewhere. Dobbin's comparative study of U.S., British, and French railways underscores the crucial importance of public policy for industrial development. Even as government in the United States retreated from the promotion and funding of railroads to "mere" regulation, the industry was anything but laissez-faire. Dobbin and Dowd's studies of railways in Massachusetts showed that changes in public policy and the varying models of competition enshrined in policy affected foundings and acquisitions.

Looking across multiple markets and industries, Billings and Blee (2000) examined the long-term impoverishment of the Appalachian region, focusing on Kentucky in the nineteenth and twentieth centuries. Their analysis implicated three major causes: market activity, local culture, and the state. Under absentee ownership, firms in Kentucky supplied raw materials and low-value-added products to national markets. Local government involved such a high level of clientelism and corruption that the state could not pursue effective developmental strategies (p. 131). Local rural culture adhered to a "patriarchal moral economy" that, when combined with a system of partible inheritance, produced subsistence-level small-scale agriculture in only two or three generations (pp. 165, 194–196).

Granovetter and his collaborators have examined the origins of the U.S. electrical industry (Granovetter and McGuire 1998; Yakubovich, Granovetter, and McGuire 2000). They found that the system that had emerged by 1930 (centralized production and distribution of power by large-scale private corporations) was neither the only possibility, nor necessarily the most efficient (Hausman and Neufeld 1991). Other technical standards (e.g., direct rather than alternating current) and other organizational forms (public ownership rather than private ownership or distributed rather than centralized generation) were real possibilities foreclosed through political pressure, market clout, organizational muscle, and social networks. Extending embeddedness arguments from the dyadic level up to institutions and industries brings embeddedness to the same macro-level of analysis at which many comparative-historical arguments are pitched.

Culture and Markets

While some economists have tentatively begun to acknowledge the role of culture in the economy (and not just as a determinant of preferences; see Greif 1994; North 1990), sociologists have long recognized its importance

(M. Weber 1976). Culture influences the economy in many ways—by inducing status orderings, marking the distinction between legitimate and illegitimate action, and constituting the cognitive and normative categories economic actors use to interpret and evaluate their experiences. The inclusion of culture complicates models of economic action, much as the focus on embeddedness puts economic actors into networks.

At the industry level, Podolny and Scott Morton (1999) showed how social status operated within nineteenth-century British shipping cartels. When a rival firm tried to "break in," cartel members sometimes responded by cutting prices and driving the entrant out of business. Podolny and Scott Morton found that British shippers were more likely to respond aggressively to low-status entrants than those with high status, although both were equally threatening from a strictly economic standpoint. Biernacki's (1995) study of the German and British textile industries revealed strong cultural influences on labor compensation systems. Both industries used the same technology to manufacture the same product, using the same raw materials and on the basis of similar organizations, but wage determination worked very differently in the two countries. Workers in Germany and Britain were both paid on a piecework basis, but the measurement of output worked very differently. Biernacki (p. 73) concludes that this difference was rooted in distinctive cultural conceptions of labor.

Culture is the main explanatory factor in Alford's (1995) study of Chinese intellectual property law. Although China has taken recent steps to bring its patent, copyright, and trademark laws into conformity with Western standards, Alford wondered why intellectual property rights never took hold in China. He argued that Chinese political culture prevented the formation of indigenous intellectual property law, frustrated attempts by nineteenth-century European colonial powers to impose intellectual property law on China, and currently complicates the importation of such law from the West. The illegitimacy of the ownership of ideas played an important role in undermining the efficacy of formal property laws.

Culture determines market boundaries. In virtually all societies, particular objects and relationships are deemed uncommodifiable and so cannot legitimately be bought or sold (E. Anderson 1993). Such goods are considered "priceless," and their relationship to money becomes highly problematic and culturally charged (Zelizer 1985). Cultural categories therefore circumscribe the use of money (Zelizer 1994) and define separate spheres of exchange (Bohannan 1955; Parry 1989). Non-commodified goods still circulate, but their flow is not mediated by markets. Geary (1986), for example, shows how the distribution of sacred relics during the Middle Ages helped to fashion relations of obligation, subordination, and status within the church.

Conversely, the monetarization of goods can change their social meaning and allow people to use them in new ways.[6] According to Spufford (1988: 245), the monetarization of land in the Middle Ages encouraged people to view it as an economic resource to be exploited. Money and prices can themselves become political issues. Carruthers and Babb (1996) argued that post-bellum U.S. monetary controversies about greenbacks and the gold standard were, in part, political conflicts about the meaning of money. E. P. Thompson's (1967) classic article on the English "moral economy" showed how violation of "fair prices" in early modern England led to political strife. Cultural categories constitute the difference between gift exchange and market exchange. This difference is reflected in the problematic nature of money as a gift. In the contemporary United States, the use of money or cash as a gift is usually inappropriate, despite its obvious and considerable value (Webley and Wilson 1989).

Notions of legitimacy vary as cultural categories evolve over time. Cultural imperatives in contemporary Anglo-American society dictate strict separation of instrumental from intimate relationships (e.g., children are "priceless," payment for sex is wrong), but in the past instrumental considerations were paramount in making decisions about whom to marry. Like all such imperatives, however, their violation is inevitable and begets in response a combination of repression (in both the Freudian and political senses), impression management, and selective interpretation.[7]

States and Markets

The state has been a central topic for historical sociology and consequently its relation to markets represents a point of convergence between economic sociology and historical sociology. As Charles Tilly (1990) and others have noted, the emergence of capitalism involved a co-evolution of markets and nation-states, driven by war. A substantial body of research now exists on the rise of the state (e.g., Barkey 1994; Bensel 1990; Carruthers 1996; S. Clark 1995; Ertman 1997; Gorski 1993; Mann 1986; Skowronek 1982; 't Hart 1993; C. Tilly 1990), and it has unearthed several distinct linkages between states and markets: legal/regulatory, fiscal, monetary, and constitutive. Recognition of the ongoing importance of these links can help moderate contemporary neo-liberal claims about the self-sufficiency of markets in relation to laissez-faire states.

---

6. See Simmel's (1978) classic discussion of money.
7. See Ledeneva (1998) and Offer (1997) on the co-mingling of gift and market relationships in the West and Russia.

John Campbell and Leon Lindberg (1990) focused on property rights: the definition and protection of formal legal rights by the state. They pointed out that while "minimalist" states possess little capacity to regulate economic activity directly, using property rights they can nevertheless intervene dramatically in markets. As noted above, public policy has played a large role in the rise and development of large corporations (Dobbin 1994; Fligstein 1990; Roy 1997). Tigar and Levy's (1977) survey of the development of Western law noted the legal accommodation of commercial interests, and Horwitz (1977) argued that law played a leading part in fostering economic development in the United States. Commercial law often responds to the demands of powerful interest groups, who use the coercive power of the state to further their interests.[8] In encouraging capitalist development, the state frequently is not autonomous.

Fiscal relations between state and economy include taxation, expenditure, and debt (J. L. Campbell 1993). Levi's (1988) model of the state made "revenue-maximization" the central dynamic in the state-economy relationship (see also Kiser and Schneider 1994). Christopher Howard (1997) pointed out the importance of tax expenditures ("tax breaks") for a kind of invisible U.S. social policy. Various studies underscore the political origins of public spending (e.g., Amenta 1998; Devine 1983). Carruthers (1996) and Bensel (1990) argued for the political significance of the relationship between the state as a debtor and its creditors.

Money functions as the common denominator for market exchange. Historically, states and sovereigns have been the primary suppliers of money.[9] The monetarization of exchange is one way to subvert a subsistence economy and encourage capitalism (consider how colonial African governments created a cash economy; see Arhin 1976; Shipton 1989: 22). The creation of a uniform currency encourages commerce (see Hurst 1973: 18). However, extensive monetarization may violate cultural norms restricting or prohibiting the use of money in particular social spheres. Furthermore, different monetary standards benefit different interest groups, with important implications for political control over the economy (Carruthers and Babb 1996).

Finally, states act in a constitutive way, laying the political and institutional foundations for markets. Above and beyond law, the fisc, and money, states also "underwrite" the calculative rationality that animates markets. Such rationality requires that decision makers be able to assess and compare

8. See McCurdy (1978) on big business's use of the U.S. Supreme Court in 1875–1890 to establish a single, unitary national market. Law and regulation can also be used to squelch technological innovation (Mokyr 1992).

9. For more on money, see Ingham (1999).

alternatives. They have to evaluate commodities, prices, investments, etc. using some common denominator (e.g., utility, money, present value). States help create markets by setting and enforcing standards for this kind of evaluation. The historical role played by sovereigns in the promulgation of standardized weights and measures was one way to constitute such rationality (Kula 1986; Matson 1994: 399; McCusker 1973; Spruyt 1994: 121, 135, 159–160). Standardization goes beyond the physical, however. Liquidity in U.S. secondary mortgage markets was created, in part, by government agencies such as the Federal National Mortgage Association (Fannie Mae), which standardized mortgage underwriting and documentation (Carruthers and Stinchcombe 1999). U.S. government regulation over disclosure and filing requirements for publicly traded corporations has played an important role in the creation of credible and "transparent" information for U.S. capital markets. Various spatial and temporal coordination problems posed by the expansion of commerce were resolved by the standardization of time zones (Zerubavel 1982).[10]

States also lay the political foundations for markets. As Polanyi (1944) recognized, self-regulating markets cannot sustain themselves in the long run. Government intervention is needed to produce the preconditions for markets, and this may include "de-commodification" (Esping-Anderson 1990). Recognizing the full range of economy-state linkages is necessary to avoid underestimating the role of the state. Several studies redress mistaken impressions about which states do or do not have a large impact on the economy (Hooks 1990b; Novak 1996; Skocpol 1992). Developmental states clearly exploit these multiple linkages to encourage economic growth (P. B. Evans 1995; J.-E. Woo 1991). Such interventions, whether through law, regulation, spending, taxing, or borrowing, target growth, but they are often influenced by interest group politics.

Three New Problems

The issues discussed above remain far from exhausted. But rather than consider how these will develop in the future, I propose three other topics that intersect economic and historical sociology: property, information, and social relations. Private property is recognized as one of the core institutions of capitalism, and although property systems vary dramatically over time, historical sociologists have largely ceded the topic to lawyers and econo-

---

10. Standardization does not always increase efficiency. Consider the case of the telephone industry, in which local government regulations were exploited by the Bell system in the early twentieth century to squeeze out small competitors and establish a monopoly (Lipartito 1989; Weiman and Levin 1994).

mists. Information as a subject offers the chance for an especially productive interchange between economic and historical sociology. The economics of information is currently one of the most dynamic areas of economic research, but work consists mostly of formal modeling. Sociology can supplement this with empirical research, as well as with the recognition that information is a cultural object shaped by organizational practices. Finally, sociologists have been forceful in arguing that social relations matter in markets but less successful in explaining exactly how, why, and when they matter. Only by doing this can economic sociology sustain its claims about the importance of embeddedness.

Property

Property rights constitute the primary stuff of markets (for Marx, part of the "relations of production"). People trade property rights over things, not just the things themselves. These rights include usufruct (who may use the property and how), exclusivity (who may exclude others), and alienability/ heritability (who can transfer rights). Thus, as property rights have evolved, so have markets. Changes in property rights sometimes involve big transitions from one system to another (e.g., shifts from communal to private property).[11] Change also includes the extension of property rights to encompass things not formerly subject to such rights (i.e., commodification). Sometimes change entails the constitution of things qua things by virtue of their being subject to property law (intangible property). Finally, change may also involve the constitution of new classes of owners, whereby people (both real and fictive) become endowed with property rights. Each shift affects the development of markets and depends on various institutional and cultural processes. Changes in property rights involve the redistribution of wealth as new forms create possibilities for accumulation while the extinction of older forms inflicts losses on former owners.[12] The connection with economic inequality is, therefore, direct.[13]

One famous example of the transition from communal to private property is the British enclosure movement. Customary rights over the commons were nonexclusive and typically consisted of rights to graze animals (stint), gather wood (estover), cut turf (turbary), and so on (Simpson 1986: 107–

11. For a thoughtful discussion of the complexities of private property, see Robert Gordon (1995).

12. Consider the effects of the abolition of slavery on former slaveowners in the American South or the prohibition of venal offices in revolutionary France (Giesey 1983).

13. This connection holds even when property rights do not change: inheritance rules stipulate how property devolves from one generation to the next and so govern the reproduction of inequality (C. Tilly 1998a: 155–156). Inheritance also reflects noneconomic motives (McGranahan 2000).

108). Through the eighteenth and nineteenth centuries, these rights were curtailed and land ownership given into private hands. Between 1750 and 1820, almost one-third of all agricultural land in England was enclosed through act of Parliament (Neeson 1993: 329). Because enclosure extinguished valuable rights, it generated opposition from commoners (Humphries 1990). With the support of politically powerful groups, enclosure nevertheless proceeded. Despite arguments about the optimality of private property rights (they "internalize externalities" and solve the "tragedy of the commons"), evidence suggests that enclosure did not so much increase efficiency as redistribute wealth (R. C. Allen 1982). Traditional social regulation of the commons had mitigated the problem of over-exploitation (Neeson 1993: chs. 4–5). Enclosure also helped to proletarianize the rural population by increasing its dependence on wage labor (Humphries 1990; Neeson 1993).[14]

Private property rights have been extended over other things as well. The commodification of the electromagnetic spectrum in the twentieth century affected the development of the radio and television industries. Until advances in physics at the end of the nineteenth century, no one could understand electromagnetic radiation, let alone conceive of it as a form of property. But now it is, in discrete bandwidths and divided by geographical region. These extensions of property rights subject more and more of the natural environment to the logic of the marketplace and expose its use to highly uneven distributions of economic power.[15]

Although electromagnetic radiation independently preceded the property rights that now enmesh it, other forms of property do not. Unlike physical property, intangible property exists as a "fictional thing" whose "thing-ness" is constituted by property rights. For instance, copyright laws established property rights over ideas and texts and in effect turned these into "things" that could be bought and sold, like so many lumps of coal (T. Ross 1992). Patent laws transformed innovations into commodities (Ely 1992: 80; North 1981: 164–165). Corporation charters and law created company stock, which turned ownership over fictive individuals into alienable, divisible claims. Currently, intellectual property is subject to considerable international contention, especially between developed and developing nations (Sell 1995).

Property rights also change through the creation of new classes of owners. The emergence of modern corporations meant that these fictive individuals could, like real people, buy, sell, and own property. But corporations posed new problems for property law. As fictive persons, corporations can live

14. On property rights in the American West, see Libecap (1981, 1978).

15. See Firmin-Sellers (1995) on the extension of private property in colonial-era Africa.

forever, steadily accumulating property over the long run.[16] But when they do die (e.g., become bankrupt), inheritance law, which disposes of the property of dead real persons, does not apply. Real persons also acquire the right to own property. Traditionally, common law distinguished between married and unmarried women (*feme covert* vs. *feme sole*). A single woman possessed the same property rights as a man, but upon marriage her legal status changed and her economic independence ended (G. S. Alexander 1997: ch. 6; M. Salmon 1986). Technically, a married woman needed the permission of her husband to dispose of property.[17] This inequality was redressed in the United States through passage of state laws that modified married women's property rights and allowed them to become full-fledged owners (Lebsock 1977; M. Salmon 1986).

Property rights systems have changed dramatically over time and consequently have changed the markets in which such rights get exchanged. Each new development raised different issues about the legitimacy of property, the role of law in markets, the limits of commodification, the reproduction of social inequality, and the emergence of new market actors.[18] Since property rights are typically enforced through law, insights from the historical sociology of the state can be deployed to the study of property. John Campbell and Leon Lindberg (1990) opened up a line of research that has yet to be fully exploited.

Information

Within economics, models of perfect competition have been thoroughly upended by the economics of information. Many standard results (e.g., the fundamental theorems of welfare economics) fail in the presence of incomplete, imperfect, or asymmetric information (Stiglitz 2000). This development represents an opportunity for the cultural and organizational strands within historical sociology, for despite dramatic change in information technology, remarkably little has been learned about how economic actors acquire, store, and process information. Whether rational or not, decision making depends on information, and such research could explain much about economic behavior.

---

16. Consider the English law of *mortmain*, which dealt with the problem of a medieval church that steadily accumulated land but never died and so never released land from its grasp. See Goody (1983: 95); Simpson (1986: 53–54).

17. In practice, English and American married women possessed more autonomy than the strict *feme covert–feme sole* distinction implies (Gundersen and Gampel 1982; M. Salmon 1982; Staves 1990).

18. Many of these issues arise in transitional economies. See, for example, D. Stark (1996); Wank (1999).

Weber himself recognized the central importance of accounting information ("rational capital accounting"; see M. Weber 1978: 91; Swedberg 1998: 15, 19) in the rational calculus that animates capitalism (see also Sombart 1967). Ideally, double-entry bookkeeping (in which all transactions were entered as both debits and credits) allowed a businessperson to evaluate past decisions and assess his or her current situation. It is curious, however, that few merchants closely adhered to double-entry in practice, although it was the standard for centuries (Carruthers and Espeland 1991). This suggests other purposes for accounting information than just the ostensible technical ones.

The development of business information is not a history of steadily increasing efficiency. Competition did not force businesses to gather relevant information or use it rationally. Faulhaber and Baumol (1988) pointed out that firms took centuries to get their discount calculations correct. According to Daston (1987), insurance companies failed to use mathematical statistics, despite its relevance for the estimation of risks, because of cultural and political dictates that strictly separated gambling, insurance, and usury (see G. Clark 1999; 125). Cost accounting developed in Britain and the United States in response to political and regulatory requirements, not because of its technical superiority (Porter 1995: 97). Industry associations in the United States promulgated uniform cost-accounting standards as a way to collude on prices (Jucius 1943).

Quantitative information simultaneously discloses and conceals. Carliss Baldwin and Kim Clark (1994) argued that when U.S. firms incorporated the discounted cash flow formula into their capital budgeting systems, they underinvested in valuable but hard-to-quantify organizational capabilities. More generally, Porter (1995: 44, 47–48) pointed out that quantitative measures involve information loss since they require transforming what is being measured into countable objects through some process of standardization (see also Carruthers and Stinchcombe 1999). In the past, states have played a large role in the creation of a countable world. Information depends as much upon form as on content, but the formal qualities of the category systems used in markets have seldom been studied.[19]

The history of quantitative information in markets raises questions that seem ripe for sociological analysis (Guseva and Róna-Tás 2001). The framework offered by March (1994) is useful for understanding the nonrational uses of such information. Ezra Zuckerman (1999) has demonstrated the importance of the cognitive frameworks used by market analysts to apprehend the economic environment. Few historians or historical sociolo-

---

19. Douglas (1986) on wine is an exception, as are Cowan and Foray (1997) on codification. See also Bowker and Star (1999); Hacking (1990).

gists have examined the interplay between information technology and business organization (for a rare exception, see Yates 1989). Furthermore, it is clear that information flows have a large effect on capital flows (Baskin and Miranti 1997: 136, 226–227; Boderhorn 2000; Carlos and Lewis 1995). Understanding the pragmatics of business information and the conditions of its production and consumption, as well as the connection between genre and use, would shed enormous light on this critical aspect of economies. The cultural turn within historical sociology could be very useful in studying information.

Social Relations

Various reasons have been offered to explain why economic action is embedded in social relations: social relations resolve problems of trust, reduce transaction costs, provide credible information, support informal sanctioning mechanisms, and introduce noneconomic motives. But frequently such reasons are only imputed—there is no direct measurement of trust, transaction costs, information, and so on. However, historical evidence can offer unique insights into the modalities of embeddedness and show exactly how economy and society interpenetrate.

One starting point is to recognize that alternative social framings for exchange invoke different logics of appropriateness and consequence. Grierson's (1959) discussion of exchange in medieval Europe noted that goods circulated three ways: through market exchange, as gifts, and as plunder. The latter two were significant not only because of their greater frequency, but also because they functioned more effectively in the establishment of social relations of dominance, subordination, and reciprocity. William Miller (1986) and Marilyn Gerriets (1981) bore this out in their discussions of exchange in medieval Iceland and Ireland.[20] Miller pointed out that gift, commodity, and plunder were three alternative framings that could apply to the same physical goods and so did not demarcate distinct spheres of exchange. With great sophistication, social actors negotiated the meaning of the exchanges they undertook.[21] Each framing brought with it distinct implications for the significance of exchange, as well as varied social and economic consequences.

The rise of the state may have reduced the significance of plunder as a form of economic exchange, but gifts and commodities continue to coexist. In-

20. On gifts and commodities in ancient Greece, see I. Morris (1986).
21. See William Miller's (1986: 18–19) wonderful analysis of the discussion between Óspak and Þórir over the goods Óspak obtained from Álf.

deed, as Offer (1997) pointed out, their co-existence verges on the symbiotic: consider how many market exchanges are initiated by gift exchanges (client dinners, favors to customers, etc). Muldrew (1998) showed how debtor-creditor relationships in early modern England depended on "credit" in the sense of personal moral character. Loans were not simply business decisions, but also expressed the trust and trustworthiness that sustained a culture of credit. Loans functioned like gifts: they helped to maintain social relationships. Similarly, Christopher Clark (1990) distinguished between local exchange in nineteenth-century rural Massachusetts and long-distance trade: the former was embedded in the local social fabric, whereas the latter consisted of arms-length cash transactions.

In the twentieth century, businesses have maintained and even expanded the gift economy. Obscure martyrs were rehabilitated, traditions were invented, and dates such as St. Valentine's Day, Mother's Day, and Father's Day were transformed into occasions for potlatch-like presentations of greeting cards, flowers, and candy (Schmidt 1995). The economic consequences of gift giving are considerable (Caplow 1984).

Researchers have explained the overlap between market exchange and social relations in a number of ways (see, e.g., Lamoreaux 1994; Landa 1981; Montgomery 1992; M. A. Petersen and Rajan 1994; Uzzi 1996). They point out that social relations serve as channels for information and provide informal sanctions. Despite the plausibility of these explanations (or perhaps because of it), little historical research has been done on what kinds of information and informal sanctions different social relations offer and how these are mobilized in particular contexts. Ironically, relationships that involve the richest information and the strongest sanctions may be harder to exploit in the market precisely because their instrumental use seems inappropriate.

Conclusion

The new economic sociology has revealed much about business organizations, relations among market actors, the connection between economies and states, and the relationship between culture and markets. In doing so, it has drawn inspiration from Marx and Weber, who, not coincidentally, also founded historical sociology. But it has failed to say enough (in my opinion) about the role of property rights, information, and social relations in the historical evolution of markets. To its credit, the new economic sociology has not overdramatized the difference between "modern" and "premodern" economies, recognizing that significant differences exist but also substantial continuities. Embeddedness, networks, formal and informal institutions, governance structures, and multiple forms of exchange are found on both sides of the pre-modern/modern divide.

Historical sociology reminds us not to privilege present arrangements. Advanced markets possess an appearance of modernity that makes it easy to confuse contingency for necessity and to assume that what is now the case must necessarily have been so. Although pre-modern, modern, and post-modern economies are replete with formal and informal institutions, many features of modern economies did not exist in the past in their current form, including private property, legal systems, and money. Economic actors were different, as were the relationships that bound them together. And the events that transformed the past into the present were not driven by efficiency or rationality. To problematize the present is one valuable lesson that historical sociology offers to a sociology of the economy.

The insights of historical sociology are critical for understanding the past, but in some respects this past has caught up to the present. Current events bear out sociological interest in the connection among institutions, culture, the state, and markets. The transitional economies of Central and Eastern Europe pose as practical problems the necessary preconditions for modern capitalism. Equally striking, the reaction to the East Asian financial crisis of 1997–1998 had a distinctly Weberian quality as financial institutions such as the Asian Development Bank, International Monetary Fund, and World Bank embraced legal predictability and transparency and imposed these on debtor nations (Asian Development Bank 1998: 17; International Monetary Fund 1999; World Bank 2000: 38). So long as economic crises force experts to reappraise their assumptions, the perspective of historical sociology will possess continuing relevance.

Economic sociology sharply distinguishes itself from economics in its assumptions about methodological individualism and rationality and is reluctant to exalt formal mathematical modeling. Furthermore, economic sociology examines the connections between economic and noneconomic behavior without assuming that the latter functions to enhance economic efficiency. However, in defining itself so strongly against economics, economic sociology risks mirroring its opponent and letting it dictate the terms of debate. Particularly when based in a business school, economic sociologists are eager to prove that their ideas can profit corporate bottom lines. Similarly, mainstream economic sociology follows economics in adhering to a "normal science" research program: economic facts exist independent of the researcher who is able to measure and analyze them. Only when economic sociology draws on the sociology of culture does it consider meanings and hermeneutic circles. And only when it turns to historical sociology can it draw on the evidence that underscores the importance of institutional and social variation. The tension with economics has been a healthy and productive one but should not become a defining characteristic. A continued alliance with historical sociology and renewed interchange with the old economic sociology will help keep the new economic sociology from its reactive fixation on economics.

REBECCA JEAN EMIGH

The Great Debates: Transitions to Capitalisms

A volume about historical sociology and modernity is a most appropriate *not complete without a discussion of the transition to capitalism.* forum for discussing the use of historical referents in contemporary debates. Implicitly, such referents underlie fundamental social science concepts. The modern/post-modern divide is, after all, underpinned by "pre-modern." Arguing that historical referents are important, however, is different from explaining their use. Is history a "distant mirror" (Tuchman 1978) in which contemporary problems are dimly viewed? Are the "lessons" of history forgotten? Does history "repeat itself"?

I explore three possible answers. First, patterns of historical events may be repeated in toto. If so, historical referents apply directly to contemporary conditions. This use draws on a philosophical conception of reality in which there are relatively few differences between physical and social reality because initial conditions do not strongly affect outcomes.[1] The second position is the opposite: historical sequences are entirely unique. It draws on an opposite conception of reality in which the physical sciences and social sciences are fundamentally different because the unfolding of social reality depends completely on unrepeatable initial conditions. Thus, historical referents are useless because they describe events from starkly different social conditions. A third approach, between these two extremes, suggests that even if entire historical sequences are not repeated in toto, certain elements may be, and therefore the theorizable elements can be extracted from the

I would like to thank the editors of and contributors to this volume for their comments on my chapter, especially Julia Adams and Elisabeth Clemens, who gave me several sets of written comments; also thanks to Patricia Ahmed, who helped with the research. The market transition research was supported by grants by NSF (SES 9906120) and the Ford Foundation (990-0133-1).

1. For a discussion of these philosophical positions, see Steinmetz (this volume).

unique ones (at least in the abstract). A comparative method that looks for similarities and differences in historical sequences may be useful. Philosophically, this view corresponds to a realist position that attempts to theorize history but notes that theories will be underdetermined because social science data are context-specific, because much of the world's causal structure is unobservable, and because knowledge is concept-dependent, so knowledge of reality is different from reality itself (Lloyd 1986: 98, 119). This realist position provides the most powerful role for historical referents because they can be used comparatively to capture and theorize the repeatable dimensions of historical trajectories.

To discuss these possibilities, I review debates on transitions to capitalisms, past and present. Current debates, such as the so-called "market transition" in post-socialist Europe, can illustrate the contemporary relevance of historical referents. There is a common triumphalist reading of modern capitalism in both scholarly and everyday parlance: capitalism is the most efficient economic system and will spread inexorably from individual-level incentives or precipitous institutional arrangements. The collapse of socialism seems to confirm this interpretation (E. M. Wood 1999: 1), and it was explicitly advocated by the economic advisers in Central and Eastern Europe (e.g., Åslund 1995; Lipton and Sachs 1992; Sachs 1992). The first use of historical referents sometimes underlies this argument, emphasizing the inevitable and natural rise of English capitalism. For example, Åslund (1995: 8) suggested the contemporary relevance of historical Britain. This triumphalist reading of the transition to capitalism often emphasizes (1) its economic nature; (2) its inevitability; (3) successful, not failed, cases of it; (4) a normative assumption of its superiority; and (5) the possibility of repeating development models. This neo-liberal rhetoric recalls Rostow's (1960) "stages of history," through which all countries march, following England. The second use of historical referents also can be found. David Stark (1994: 67), for example, argued that general models of capitalism are not useful starting points for understanding the current market transition. Eyal, Szelényi, and Townsley (1998: 1–16, 47–52) argued for a variant of this second position; while they emphasized that the current market transition is fundamentally different from the general models of capitalism derived from Marx, Weber, and Smith, they hinted at better historical referents.

Åslund, an economist, suggested the usefulness of historical referents based on a view of the essentially repeatable, and thus completely theorizable, nature of social reality. In contrast, Stark, a sociologist, suggested that historical referents are inapplicable because social change is path-dependent and therefore essentially unrepeatable. The third, comparative use of historical referents goes beyond Eyal, Szelényi, and Townsley. In fact, with better historical knowledge of the historic rise of capitalism, it may indeed be the economists who reject historical referents and the sociologists who claim them!

The Playing Field: Classic Analyses of the Transition from Feudalism to Capitalism

Debates over the historic rise of capitalist economies in Europe form a well-developed literature that spans sociology, history, economics, and anthropology because the social sciences were largely founded on this topic. Because excellent reviews cover this literature up to the late 1980s (Holton 1985; Lachmann 1989), I review this material quickly. I focus primarily on qualitative shifts in economic forms, not on quantitative changes in growth.

The classic social scientists, such as Smith, Marx, Durkheim, and Weber, struggled to explain what they viewed as a profound shift from pre-industrial to industrial society. In some sense, Marx was reacting to, and building upon, Smith; similarly, Weber followed Marx (Kaye 1986: 172–173). They tended to "read backwards"—that is, to assume that pre-capitalist society was what capitalist society was not. Thus, they often provided better explanations of capitalist, not pre-capitalist, society. They worked in a tradition that assumed progress toward rationality and efficiency; consequently, they assumed that capitalism arose because of inherently advantageous conditions in England (D. Sayer 1992: 1382) and unfolded naturally thereafter. But they also viewed capitalism as inherently contradictory. From the Marxist position, capitalism holds its own demise (E. M. Wood 1991: 164–166). From the Weberian position, religious beliefs that might be necessary for the rise of capitalism might be unnecessary and even meaningless once it is established (Holton 1985: 113; Schluchter 1996: 239–243). Thus, the classics asked the question, "How and why did capitalism first develop in Western Europe (or England)?" (Lachmann 1989: 47). The so-called "second wave" (see the introduction to this volume) developed the classics' implications—the inevitabilities and contradictions of capitalism—producing the great "named debates" (Dobb, Sweezy, Brenner, etc.).

If a "loose third-wave coalition" (again, to borrow from this volume's editors) follows, its strength lies in asking different questions, providing new empirical evidence, using pluralistic theories, and employing new comparisons, thereby undermining the first and second waves' assumption of capitalism's inevitability and their sometimes scant knowledge of pre-industrial society. Relevant questions will generally, even if implicitly (often for the sake of euphony), assume a plural form: "What are capitalisms, were there transitions to capitalisms, and where were they?" (cf. Lachmann 1989: 47). Such work provides the best historical referents.

The View from Economic History

The precursor to much, if not all, of this literature is Adam Smith. His writing is more subtle than is often acknowledged, yet his central theme is still well captured by his phrase about individuals' natural propensity to "truck, barter, and exchange" (1961 [1776]: 13). Capitalism is an economic system that reflects, on an aggregate level, individual-level human nature. It unfolds naturally, following expansions in the division of labor that increase production, and, in turn, trade. Pirenne's (1914, 1952 [1925]) classic work in this tradition links trade and markets to the rise of cities and, eventually, industrial development. Macfarlane (1978) develops the idea of individualism, arguing that thirteenth-century England was largely capitalist, populated by self-interested economic actors.

In the 1950s and 1960s, the transition to be explained was from a preindustrial to an industrial economy. Economic growth theory (classic and neo-classical) emerging from Smith (e.g., Domar 1947; Harrod 1948; Kaldor 1960; W. A. Lewis 1955; Rostow 1960; Solow 1956) merged with Parsonian cultural analysis to produce modernization theory (e.g., Eisenstadt 1964; Hoselitz 1960; Inkeles and Smith 1974; Lerner 1958; see critiques in Apter 1987 and Binder 1986; for a positive reevaluation, see Inglehart and Baker 2000). The cultural dimension resonated with Durkheim's distinction between *Gemeinschaft* and *Gesellschaft*; the emphasis on the division of labor, with Smith and Marx.

Neo-institutionalist theories also emerged from this tradition. North and Thomas (1973) argued that states' enforcement of property rights facilitated the transition to capitalism by assuring that individuals who undertook risky or expensive innovations that eventually increased productivity benefited from them. In contrast to this thin view of the state, Polanyi (1957c) argued that the state's redistributive capabilities compensated for the self-destructive, commodifying effects of capitalism, thereby essentially allowing markets to operate.

Duby (1968), Habakkuk (1958), Le Roy Ladurie (1974), and Postan (1937, 1966) combined an emphasis on markets with demographic theory. Their explicitly neo-Malthusian and neo-Ricardian argument posited a homeostatic mechanism that regulated demographic and economic growth (Le Roy Ladurie 1985: 102). As population expanded, so did economic production, creating economic growth. But population growth generally outpaced

[handwritten note: what were the redistributive benefit the state offered to the residents of the Lander?]

economic resources, leading to eventual population collapse and a corresponding economic decline. Each cycle dissolved feudal relations, created a more efficient use of land and labor, and thus in the long run led to capitalism.

Another impulse from economic history—proto-industrialization theory—combined Marxism and demography (Mendels 1972). Rural proto-industry, often in the form of putting-out, was an important precursor to industrial and capitalist development (see also Kriedte, Medick, and Schlumbohm, eds. 1981 and review in Mastboom 1996). Proto-industry provided wages to supplement farm income, thereby altering demographic patterns by allowing offspring to marry earlier and without waiting for access to their parents' land. Another variant of demographic theory, following Hajnal (1965: 450; 1982), suggests that small, nuclear European families characterized by a relatively late age at marriage facilitated the rise of capitalism by limiting fertility or encouraging individualism (Hanley and Wolf, eds. 1985; P. Laslett 1988; D. Levine 2001: 14; for critical reviews see Goldstone 2000a: 177 and Goody 1996a, 1996b: 167–170). In contrast, Grassby (2001: 412) argued that family businesses and extended kinship networks facilitated market culture.

Marx and the Marxists

Though Marx did not fully develop his transition theory, it is clear that the central mechanism, class conflict, was generated through the increasing complexity of property relations (K. Marx and Engels 1970) or primitive accumulation (K. Marx 1964, 1977 [1894]: 873–930). This conflict allowed one class to secure a set of property rights that allowed it to extract surplus from some other class. If successful, it gained control over additional resources, allowing it to extract additional surplus, creating, eventually, a capitalist class. If not, it became part of the class from which surplus was extracted. Fully capitalist production required, first, that all individuals be separated from the means of their own reproduction (or subsistence) by becoming either capitalists or workers, and, second, that capitalists realize profit through surplus extraction via the sale of commodities produced by workers. These two requirements set the terms of Marxist debates. Starting from the requirement of separation from the means of reproduction, the "relations of production" school focused on social processes that transformed customary peasants and lords into wage laborers and capitalist tenants (R. Brenner 1985a; Dobb 1947). The "relations of exchange" school, starting from profit realization, focused on market expansion (Sweezy 1976; Wallerstein 1974). The latter thus had many affinities to Smith and Weber and therefore sparked debates across these paradigms (R. Brenner 1977, 1985b). Wallerstein (1974) shifted the unit of analysis to the "world system" by considering national and global profit realization.

These debates also had contemporary implications (Kaye 1986). Wallerstein (1974) and Frank (1966a) explicitly linked the historical rise of a capitalist world system to economic stagnation in the so-called Third World. Laclau (1971) retorted that, paradoxically, capitalism could create noncapitalist forms, giving rise to the "modes of production" literature (drawing heavily from Althusser and Balibar 1970) and unequal exchange (Amin 1976; Emmanuel 1972). Dobb (1947: last chapter; 1963: 387–393) referred to the economic conditions of the 1920s and 1930s and the rise of communism.

Weber and the Weberians

In *The Protestant Ethic,* Weber (1958) argued that the preconditions for capitalism were omnipresent, but the Calvinist doctrine of predestination sparked the transition only in Western Europe. Through hard work and frugality, Calvinists demonstrated their salvation, rationally reinvesting their profits and inadvertently creating perfect conditions for capitalism. Weber's idea is endlessly reevaluated (e.g., Barker and Carman 2000; Jere Cohen 2002; Delacroix and Nielson 2001; Innes 1995; Lachmann 2000: 204–227; Lessnoff 1994; J. F. Martin 1991; Newell 1998; Schluchter 1996). Much of this work shows that economic and religious actions are linked, but not in any singular direction.

Like Marx's, Weber's (1981) mature theory was incomplete and subject to multiple interpretations. While Marx emphasized class conflict, Randall Collins (1980, 1997a) argued that Weber focused on institutions that created the possibility of calculable actions. Universalistic religions, including Judaism, Christianity, and Buddhism, broke down barriers for economic participation and introduced disciplined religious practices. Weber also stressed the institutional preconditions—the military, coins, literate administrators, transportation, communication, writing, and record keeping—of what would become nation-states. These preconditions (Collins called them "ultimate conditions") set the stage for further institutional developments that facilitated rational economic action: a methodical, nondualistic economic ethic, calculable law, citizenship rights, and a bureaucratic state. In turn, these institutions enabled the rise of the elements of rational capitalism: the entrepreneurial organization of capital, rationalized technology, free labor, and unrestricted markets (R. Collins 1980: 931). Thus, for Weber, capitalism is an orientation toward profit-seeking behavior in markets. While it may have religious origins, once established, capitalism can operate independently.

Schluchter (1996: 179–243) used a different form of explanation to interpret Weber, based more on historical narrative than on separable factors (J. R. Hall 1999a: 217–218). He analyzed three historical transformations that produced capitalism (defined as formally free labor, the modern market economy, and a bourgeois mode of conduct). The first transformation consisted of three subsets of interrelated changes: a papal transformation that rationalized the church hierarchy; a feudal revolution that created systematically decentralized domination and a constant struggle between the central and local authorities; and an urban revolution that created new industry, commerce, and legal institutions (bonds, stocks, deeds, etc.). The second transformation created the bourgeois mode of conduct through the Protestant Ethic, which joined asceticism to rational, inner-worldly action. The third transformation was the objectification of economic life and social relationships. Schluchter's first transformation largely corresponds to Collins's institutional analysis, though Schluchter (1996: 325) maintained a unique role for the Protestant Ethic that Collins (1980) downplayed.

Chirot (1985: 181–190) developed a similar Weberian synthesis. He argued that the West had multiple advantages, including a geography that included a favorable climate and a land/labor ratio and relative freedom from war and other disasters. Political decentralization was related to geography. Unlike in China, where control of a few central river valleys virtually guaranteed political control, European political power was always fragmented, generating competition. Cities were also independent political and economic entities, fostering trade and economic activity. Finally, legal and religious rationality were important. Clearly defined laws, procedures, and stable property rights existed, and governments were bound by them.

Michael Mann (1986: 500–517), working in this broad Weberian perspective, considered how overlapping networks entailing the sources of social power—ideological, economic, political, and military—reinforced each other in the West, creating capitalism. Mann argued that comparative methods (e.g., R. Brenner 1985a) started too late in history and missed the links among power networks. Like Mann, John A. Hall (1986) and Jean Baechler (1988) made the essentially Weberian point that European advantage lay in relatively small political units, without the assurance of absolute internal power and arranged in conflictual and competitive (although diplomatically linked) international relations. Consequently, they analyzed the "European miracle" and downplayed English uniqueness. Because of the competition among states, economic changes spread quickly in Europe (Snooks 1994b: 18). Thus, if the Industrial Revolution had not occurred in Britain, it would have happened elsewhere in Europe (Snooks 1994b: 15). It also may have been focused within a few relatively advanced regions in England, France, and Belgium (Mokyr 1999: 30).

Perry Anderson (1974b) combined the Marxist ideas of a mode of production and social formation with a Weberian emphasis on the state's role in establishing preconditions for capitalist development, including civil law and property rights (see reviews in Holton 1985: 91–99; Lachmann 1989: 62–63; Mooers 1991: 37–40). The absolutist state protected aristocratic property and privileges but also simultaneously ensured the interests of the nascent mercantile and manufacturing classes (P. Anderson 1974b: 40). Marxist and Weberian combinations inspired a range of development literature connecting state strength and economic development, in particular suggesting that strong, developmentalist states produced capitalist development while predatory states produced economic stagnation. (For examples from varying viewpoints, see Amsden 1989; P. B. Evans 1995; O'Donnell 1978. For more general combinations of Marx, Weber, and Smith in the development literature, see Barrett and Whyte 1982; Cardoso and Faletto 1979 [1971]; Deyo, ed. 1987; Hirschman 1968; Shin 1998.)

Of course, my review cannot completely reconstruct the entire body of work in this field, which is undoubtedly much less schematic and more comprehensive. Nevertheless, these exemplars of second-wave work on historic transition debates shared a focus—though of course not exclusively—on working out the often underdeveloped classic theories. To a large extent, they stayed within these theoretical paradigms (sometimes by combining them) and were guided by the question of the classic authors that often assumed the inevitability and superiority of capitalism: "Why did capitalism arise in Europe?"

Recent Work

Since recent work on historic transition debates answers different questions than the classics posed, it falls less easily into standard theoretical camps, so I organize the review topically.

Capitalisms, Not Capitalism

There is an increased tendency—reflecting the influence of post-modernism—to use the plural forms "transitions" and "capitalisms" to emphasize their variability and complexity. For example, Radice (2000: 721–722) distinguished between contemporary national capitalisms, such as the liberal capitalisms of the United States and Britain, and the institutionalized capitalisms of Japan and Germany. Similarly, Blim's (2000: 28, 30) review of contemporary capitalism considered global capitalism, diaspora capitalism, *comprador* capitalism, bureaucratic capitalism, political capitalism, and booty capitalism. With respect to historic works, the terminology "the transition from feudalism to capitalism," which signals a single, replicable event, is usually changed to some indeterminate, plural form (Duplessis 1997; J. R. Hall 1999b; see my title of this essay). John R. Hall (1999b) suggested abandoning the transition terminology, arguing that it described a change in a "thing" and that neither feudalism nor capitalism was a single "thing." He argued for the term "recomposition"—that is, the adjustment and interpenetration of disparate and causally independent phenomena. Recomposition falls under the practice of "configurational history," which takes as its central task the description and decomposition of the object of inquiry into a series of historically emergent components that are contributory or necessary, but not sufficient, for that object (J. R. Hall 1999a: 217).

The recognition of multiple capitalisms calls for revisiting the multiple definitions of "capitalism" that were so central to the theoretical debates discussed above. Grassby (1999: 1–2) argued that so many definitions heralded a meaningless term. Furthermore, capitalism tends to be defined only by what it is not: a traditional, collective economy or a command-oriented socialist one. Because it arose in a particular historical context, it is not a universal, neutral descriptor. While Grassby called into question the coherence of the social science literature that cannot agree on the definition of its central term, it is also possible that the multiple definitions illustrate that capitalism has multiple forms or is a highly local, uneven process. Biernacki (1995: 2) made a similar point by arguing that taking the terms "the rise of market culture" and "the commodification of labor" out of context falsely objectifies their meaning. Wage labor, for example, meant embodied labor in Britain but labor power in Germany.

Duplessis (1997) emphasized multiple European transitions to capitalism, carefully pointing out the slow forward and backward trends toward full-scale industrial capitalism and arguing that the outcome was nowhere (including England) inevitable. Large, enclosed capitalist tenancies were characteristic of England, while small family farms predominated in the Low Countries, though both were highly productive and set the stage for further growth (p. 185). France was characterized by small-scale, labor-intensive industry and a strong high-quality sector (p. 243). English manufacturing was more industrialized, and because of higher agricultural productivity, more individuals were employed in industry, though it was not always more productive than elsewhere (p. 248). Bernstein (1994), following Byres (1991), outlined multiple paths of agrarian development alternatively based on capitalist farming, family farming, a continuation of peasant farming, petty commodity production, variants of large estates (feudal landholding, colonial or industrial plantations), or a strong state. Of course, it is not an entirely new idea that capitalism takes different forms in different places and times. Gerschenkron's (1962) argument that late developers followed different paths from early developers is just one classic example. Taken together, however, this recent work goes a step beyond Weber's recognition that capitalism is an ideal type (i.e., that it is a single phenomenon that looks different in different places) and calls into question the idea of a single ideal type. It moves away from second-wave debates, which suggested there should be a single definition, even if no one could agree what it was, toward the recognition of multiple forms.

Capitalism as a Political Agenda

If capitalism is assumed to be an efficient economic form that will unfold naturally, its failure to develop can be blamed on deficient cultural or political environments (E. M. Wood 1991: 163). Recent work suggests otherwise: capitalism is centrally a political and cultural creation. For example, Lachmann (2000) argued that conflicts among elites (not Marxist classes) within political units determine where and when capitalism arises. To transform economic relations, elites must have the capacity vis-à-vis other elites to exploit direct producers, and then they must create—unintentionally—capitalist relations. The English gentry created capitalist agricultural relations, thus laying the groundwork for the Industrial Revolution, by attacking peasants' rights to communal land and customary holdings to gain tactical advantages against other elites, the crown and the clergy. In France, endemic elite conflict and constantly shifting alliances never gave a single elite the capacity to transform agricultural relations extensively. The Habsburg political elite ruled the Spanish empire by allying with local aristocrats, thereby maintaining the existing pre-capitalist system. In the Netherlands, the lack of a clerical or noble elite created a strong and united urban elite that produced the Dutch Golden Age. Nevertheless, once these urban merchants gained power, they crystallized into a rigid, oligarchic class, thereby delaying a full-scale transition to capitalism. In Florence, though a single urban elite eventually triumphed, it refeudalized economic relations instead of creating capitalism.

While Lachmann argued that capitalism was a political agenda of the English gentry, Perelman (2000) claimed it was an agenda of the classic political economists. While economists such as Smith and Ricardo were on a theoretical level advocating laissez-faire policies, on a political level, they championed actions that actively deprived peasants of their livelihood. The creation of wage labor, far from being natural, was an outcome of their political agenda that favored the interests of capitalists above smallholders. Perelman (2000: 2–3) called this process the "secret history of primitive accumulation" to emphasize the similarity between these economists and Marx. Furthermore, capitalism was not necessarily efficient or rational, especially at its beginning. Subsistence or self-provisioning was often cheaper and more reliable for most peasants, who therefore had little incentive to shift to wage labor unless forced to do so. Thus, like Lachmann, Perelman argued that capitalism was more rational and efficient for particular individuals given concrete historical circumstances, not universally so. Similarly, Espeland (1998: 252) suggested emphasizing the process of rationalization—that is, the reinterpretation and reconstitution of interests and identities, not absolute levels of rationality. Carruthers (1996: 206) made the related point that markets do not simply coordinate the actions of self-interested actors but are created by political agents seeking multiple ends (political, ethnic, economic, etc.).

Robert Brenner (1985a, 1985b, 1993) developed his earlier argument about agrarian capitalism to highlight politics. He argued that an alliance between rural capitalist landlords and colonial merchants facilitated the rise of a strong, unified national state, based on parliamentary rule and control of taxation, that protected private property and monopolized force, therefore creating the basis of the commercial revolution (1993: 709, 713–715). Brenner then reversed the historical order of North and Thomas's (1973) argument by claiming that capitalists created a state capable of enforcing their property rights. In general, this work on capitalism as a political agenda, regardless of its historical ordering of the creation of classes and states, sees politics as actively creating capitalism, not simply establishing a few capitalist preconditions, as in the neo-institutionalist model.

Capitalism as Cultural Agenda

Weber's Protestant Ethic is commonly taken as the quintessential cultural theory of capitalism. Randall Collins (1997a) expanded on Weber by identifying a "Protestant Ethic" in Buddhism that contained the framework for shifts in agricultural production that led to Japanese industrialization. Collins extracted the generalizable elements of the Protestant Ethic, including ethical universalism; ascetic restraint on consumption; and an ethic of self-discipline that promoted economic activity, investment, and saving. By locating an Asian "rise of capitalism," Collins broke with the first and second waves' European (or English) focus. He also broke with Weber's assumption that many elements of Confucian culture were not conducive to capitalism (cf. Weller 1994: 313–314). Weller also argued that Confucian culture can contribute to capitalist practices. Family ties encouraged strategies of economic diversification and pooled resources, while filial piety encouraged hard work and cooperation. This echoes other research showing that the family is an asset to capitalist development, not its antithesis (see review in Creed 2000; Bruun 1993 and Farquhar 1994 highlight the importance of family entrepreneurship in China; see Whyte 1996 for a less enthusiastic assessment). Goldstone (1996: 7) noted one specific element of classical Chinese culture that may have discouraged industrialization: the division of labor that kept females inside the household.

While evaluating Weber's Protestant Ethic is important, it too often overshadows cultural studies of capitalism. The influence of culture cannot be understood through the examination of a single ethic or even through religion. For example, Biernacki (1995: 59, 479) demonstrated that a different cultural understanding of labor as a commodity in Britain and Germany had concrete social consequences. In Britain, employers treated labor in terms of what it produced—that is, as "embodied labor." In Germany, employers gauged labor by the amount of effort expended—that is, as "labor power." The daily German experience of buying and selling labor power led to an increased receptivity to Marxist economic theory's orientation toward the necessity of relieving the subordination of living labor. In contrast, in England, the focus on embodied labor meant that socialist unions emphasized the need to redistribute capital and access to labor. In Germany, women with family care responsibilities were allowed to leave earlier in the day, as German employers were accustomed to dividing labor power into units. In England, however, women were allowed to send substitutes to complete their shifts, since workdays were blocks that produced a set amount of goods.

Another important but underexplored avenue is the role of consumerism in the rise of capitalist economies. McKendrick, Brewer, and Plumb (1982) and Sidney Mintz (1985) showed that consumption is not inherent; English consumers, like workers (Thompson 1963), had to be made before consumerism could contribute to economic processes. Pendergast (1998: 26–29) reviewed work on consumerism, especially its relation to class and colonial identity, in seventeenth- and eighteenth-century England and the United States during the Industrial Revolution. Ruane (1995) showed how the adoption of Western dress in imperial Russia and the consumer culture that accompanied it were gendered, as women were the targets of fashion dictates that required several changes of clothing each day. But much research could be done, especially historically. For example, studies developing empirically grounded historical referents for Baudrillard's (1981) post-modern political economy of consumption or Hebdige's (1979) idea that the alteration of the use and exchange value of commodities constituted social protest would make valuable contributions. Research could also contribute historical referents to the Marxist genre of cultural studies examining reification and capitalism.

The relationship between knowledge and capitalism is also an underexplored Weberian topic. Clearly, there is some interplay among capitalism, numeracy, and literacy (Burke 1987; Carruthers and Espeland 1991; P. C. Cohen 1982: 41, 210; Crosby 1997; Starr 1987: 20–23), but the direction and the nature of the relationship can be further explored. For example, numeracy may have been widespread before capitalist markets in Tuscany (Emigh 2002). The cultural creation of states and markets is another useful research site, cutting across Weberian and Marxist research paradigms, following Philip Corrigan and Derek Sayer's (1985) and Sayer's (1992) argument that the English state and capitalism were cultural accomplishments. Similarly, the replacement of the local peasant markets by the Florentine market was not the result of the spread of rationality or efficiency but largely a result of political, personal, and cultural, as well as economic, domination (Emigh 2003: 1100–1102; cf. Raymond Williams 1975). The expansion of these research topics on historic capitalisms and culture would be useful redresses to a field dominated by Weber's Protestant Ethic.

Gradual Growth, Not Sudden Change

A central tenet of social science theory—stemming from Marx, Weber, and Durkheim—is that the transition to capitalism was sudden and dramatic. Recent work on the Industrial Revolution and economic growth, however, suggests the opposite—that it was slow and gradual. Furthermore, it challenges the assumption that capitalism and economic growth are synonymous. Like Smith's work, this work views economic growth as natural and, at least in the long run, inevitable (although it may be unpredictable in the short run). While a full review of economic growth and industrialization is beyond the scope of this essay, I will review a few recent developments directly related to capitalisms.

Economic growth is an increase in real per capita income (sometimes measured in Gross Domestic Product, or GDP). Moykr (1990: 4–6) distinguished among four sources of growth: (1) Solovian growth from increased capital stock; (2) Smithian growth from the expansion of trade, markets, and the division of labor; (3) scale effects from population growth (drawing on Malthus); and (4) Schumpeterian growth from technological innovation and increases in knowledge. The last, when financed through credit, is often associated with capitalist expansion (W. N. Parker 1984: 191, 211–213). Economic growth is thus conceptualized as broader than capitalism or industrialization because all four forms are genuine growth, but the first three do not necessarily lead to the fourth (W. Parker 1984: 212).

E. L. Jones (1994, 2000 [1988]) distinguished between extensive growth (rise in incomes) and intensive growth (any of the above four types that increases per capita income). There were multiple historical waves of intensive growth: in China from the tenth through the thirteenth centuries, in Japan in the seventeenth and eighteenth centuries, and in Western Europe in the medieval and early modern periods (Jones 2000 [1988]: xxxv). Jones (2000 [1988]: 189–191) located a political cause of these periods of Smithian growth: the dispersal of power among multiple rulers created competition. He therefore criticized advocates of dramatic, discontinuous growth and obsessions with the "great discontinuity paradigm" of "the unique European breakthrough" (1994: 25; 2000 [1988]: 188). Similarly, Snooks (1994a: 47–48; 1994b: 6) argued that the uniqueness of the Industrial Revolution was not in exceptionally high rates of economic growth; there were periods of rapid growth in pre-modern England. Hoffman (1996: 201) also emphasized the slow and gradual nature of the transition to capitalism by noting that traditional French agriculture had considerable dynamism and that peasants were actively engaged in markets. Some farming regions were highly productive, especially around Paris, the Beaujolais, and in Normandy, rivaling English farms. Such growth was largely Smithian—it occurred through trade and specialization (Hoffman 1996: 202–204).

De Vries and van der Woude (1997: 693) boldly argued that the Netherlands from the sixteenth to the eighteenth centuries had a fully modern economy characterized by (1) markets for commodities and factors of production, (2) a level of agricultural productivity high enough to support an extensive division of labor, (3) an effective state to enforce property rights and contracts, and (4) a level of technology capable of sustained development supporting market-oriented consumerism. Thus, they also dislodged the English Industrial Revolution from its pivotal place. Although the Industrial Revolution was important, it was only part of a larger process of modern economic growth in which the Netherlands was central (pp. 716–717).

Goldstone (2002: 333) claimed that Schumpeterian and Smithian economic growth occurred, usually together, throughout history. These outbursts of growth—"efflorescences"—were not usually self-sustaining but often lasted for generations. He distinguished this growth from modern, Kuznetzian economic growth, the continual and conscious application of scientific and technological progress to economic activity (p. 334). Such growth, located in England, driven by technology and science, produced the Industrial Revolution (p. 375). This emphasis on technology is distinct from the typical sociological emphasis on social relations (cf. Mokyr 1999: 39–45). Mokyr (1990: 6) detached technological growth associated with Schumpeterian growth from capitalism and industrialization in a different way by noting that technological growth predated capitalism. He characterized the Industrial Revolution not as a world-changing "macro-economic event" but as a series of small inventions with many historical continuities and precursors (1990: 82; 1994; cf. E. L. Jones 1994: 21). A related perspective, "endogenous growth theory," examines forces within an economy—often technology, research and development, and innovation—that produce sustained economic growth (see reviews in Pack 1994; Romer 1994; Solow 1994). The extent to which the British Industrial Revolution can be characterized by such endogenous growth is debated (Crafts and Mills 1997; Greasley and Oxley 1997a, 1997b).

The reevaluation of the Industrial Revolution also challenges the assumption that capitalism represented a dramatic rupture. Some historians argue that there was no industrial revolution; others downplay the scale of change (see reviews in Harley 1999; D. S. Landes 1999; Mokyr 1999: 1–6). One debate centers on whether the Industrial Revolution affected most of British society (Ashton 1997 [1948]; D. S. Landes 1969; Temin 1997, 2000) or just a few industries, such as cotton, wool, iron, and machinery (Cameron 1993; Crafts and Harley 1992; Harley and Crafts 2000). These debates seem far from settled; more important, however, is that they shift the question from "Why did dramatic change occur in England?" to "Did dramatic change occur in England?"

Contingency or Causality?

Like Duplessis (1997) and Lachmann (2000), who argued that the rise of capitalism was not a foregone conclusion, and John R. Hall (1999b), who argued for recomposition instead of transition, others highlight the contingent or conjunctural (perhaps even accidental) rise of capitalism, thereby diverging from an earlier emphasis on finding the finite "causes" of the transition (singular emphasized here) to capitalism. Such work invokes dramatically expanded comparisons, new empirical evidence, or synthetic theories. The comparisons, expanding earlier suggestions to look for "failures" (Krantz and Hohenberg 1975), often include cases in which the transition to capitalism did not occur, even in the presence of many capitalist preconditions (Aymard 1982; Emigh 1997a; Hopcroft 1999; E. L. Jones 2000 [1988]; Lachmann 2000; Pomeranz 2000; Wong 1997). As in much of historical sociology (Sewell 1996b: 272), there has been an increasing emphasis on primary sources and archival research (e.g., Biernacki 1995; Carruthers 1996;

Emigh 1997b) because such material can be directed toward the theoretical debate at hand more easily than secondary material, which might have been produced to answer second-wave questions or different historiographical debates. Primary material makes it much easier to investigate the pre-modern part of the modern/post-modern conceptual apparatus for under-pinning more accurate historical referents, which were more often assumed than empirically researched in first- and second-wave research.

Tuscany, for example, is an important negative case in which many of the preconditions for capitalism were present in the Middle Ages, but capitalism came relatively late to the region (Aymard 1982; Jere Cohen 1980, 1983; Holton 1983; Lachmann 2000). I have shown, using extensive archival evi-dence (Emigh 1998, 1999, 2000, 2003), that standard interpretations of the "failed Tuscan transition to capitalism"—stemming from a lack of capitalist tenants (Marx) or from the lack of a state-like political unit (Weber)—are largely inaccurate. If in the end sharecropping did not support the transition to capitalism within the Tuscan territorial state, it was not because it was inefficient, but because of sectoral relations that shaped its use in that politi-cal context: landlords were urbanites, while tenants were rural inhabitants (Emigh 2003). Thus, sharecropping tended to reproduce urban capitalism, not rural capitalism, because the economic interests of the more powerful, urban landlords were paramount.

Robert Allen (1992) and Rosemary Hopcroft (1994, 1999) questioned the standard Marxist interpretation that large tenant farmers formed the basis of English agrarian capitalism by showing that smallholders were more productive than large landholders. P. K. O'Brien and D. Heath (1994) con-curred by comparing France and England. Howkins (1994) argued that the large numbers of small farmers and farm servants fundamentally blurred the standard Marxist distinction among landlords, tenants, and laborers. Hopcroft (1999) used an impressive range of comparisons: England, the Netherlands, France, Germany, and Sweden. Her primary argument was that field institutions (how individuals held land rights and the physical organization of the fields) shaped the transition to capitalism. When land was held communally, difficulties and uncertainties in the enforcement of property rights decreased agricultural productivity. In contrast, in less com-munal regions, fewer difficulties in enforcing property rights allowed indi-viduals to focus on the efficient cultivation of their property. Although Hopcroft argued primarily from the neo-institutionist tradition, she drew in theoretically diverse factors to explain that rural development occurred where there were fewer communal field systems, little feudal control, favor-able ecologies, dense population, access to markets, impartial legal institu-tions, little rent seeking, and little warfare.

Other work, especially following Wallerstein (1974), shifts the temporal comparison. Arrighi (1994: 5–6, 86), instead of considering a shift from feudal to capitalist production, considered long-term cycles of capitalist expansion. Expanding Marx's analysis of the capitalist production process, in which capitalists use money to buy capital, which allows them to produce goods to make more money (i.e., Marx's general formula of capital: MCM', in which M stands for money capital and C stands for commodity capital), Arrighi analyzed alternating capitalist cycles of either material expansion (MC) or financial expansion (CM') historically and globally. Drawing on Abu-Lughod's (1989) idea of a pre-modern world system, Arrighi (1944: 87, 109) located the beginning of these cycles in thirteenth- and fourteenth-century Genoa. Frank (1998: xxii, 5) considered an even longer—five-thousand-year—world system in which Asia, not Europe, was usually at the center. European hegemony is, therefore, largely a myth, certainly before 1800, and is unlikely to continue. The temporary rise of the West was largely conditioned by the fall of the East through the coincidence of long-run economic and demographic cycles and the discovery of American gold and silver (pp. 276–277). The use of 1800 to periodize world history (Goldstone 2001a) breaks with Robert Brenner's (1985a, 1985b) use of the European Black Death in the 1350s as the point of divergent capitalist development within Europe or Wallerstein's (1974) dating of the world system to the end of the sixteenth century. David Levine (2001: 1) argued that Europe diverged from the rest of the world around the date 1000.

This comparison between European and East Asian history leads to another third-wave question: "Did capitalism arise in Western Europe?" The comparison itself is not new. Japan, probably because of its feudal past, was incorporated explicitly in second-wave debates (Takahashi 1976). Now, however, the East/West comparison is used not in the Weberian sense to explain causally the rise of the West (as among the second wavers), but to downplay Western predominance and highlight its contingent nature. Drawing on classics such as McNeill (1971) and Wolf (1982), world history is being rewritten from a non-Eurocentric view to stress global interconnections, the contributions of other regions to European culture, and comparisons not implicitly based on Europe (Pomeranz 2000; Alan Smith 1991; Wong 1997). This new version of world history argues against common historical themes, the "diffusion of European culture," or the "expansion of Europe" (Blaut 1993). For example, Goody (1996b) argued that Europeans had few cultural, familial, or economic advantages compared to Asians; furthermore, Eurasian societies diverged from a common base. Blaut (1993: 1–2) agreed that European civilization had no unique or internal historical advantage (except perhaps geographical), especially before 1492.

Wong (1997: 278), through careful comparisons that do not take European developments as the standard, showed that China and Europe, up to the seventeenth and eighteenth centuries, shared similar patterns of pre-industrial Smithian growth, including increased rural industries, increased agricultural productivity, and expanded commercial networks. There were, however, different political economies. China was an empire, constituted by a vertically integrated and unitary state aimed at spreading rule across a vast area. Thus, there was a continuum between state and society and an alliance between state officials and other elites. In contrast, Europe was characterized by the separation of state and society and the elaboration of functionally distinct and institutionally independent levels of government in which state officials and elites were forced to negotiate both with each other and with other states (pp. 280–283; cf. Zanden 2000). Wong argued that the clustering of inventions between 1780 and 1880 set the stage for the Industrial Revolution and interacted with this political and social context, but he argued that these were largely contingent events that cannot be explained causally. In the nineteenth century, economic development fit well with the European social context; in the twentieth century, industrialization fit the Chinese context (Wong 1997: 280). This provides a strong motivation for the argument that Asian and European capitalisms are different and that Asia is more "resurgent" than "newly industrializing" (Maddison 2001: 128). Thus, while Wong shares with second-wave Weberians an emphasis on the importance of state structure, he diverges from them by pointing to multiple transitions to capitalism.

Sanderson (1994) focused on a comparison between Japan and Europe and emphasized many of these same factors, but he argued that by the end of the Tokugawa period (1600–1868), Japan was capitalist. He stressed the similarities between medieval Japan and medieval Europe that allowed capitalism to develop in both places, including relatively small size, geography, climate, and political decentralization, as well as the context of the larger historical trend, expanding world commercialization that made it possible to capitalize on these advantages.

Pomeranz (2000) drew together these world history themes by arguing that there were few differences between Asia (primarily China and Japan) and Europe with respect to agriculture, industry, technology, population dynamics, and commerce before 1800 and that their subsequent divergence was explained by their interaction, not factors intrinsic to Europe (or England). European dominance stemmed from subtle interactions among small differences, including outlets for European population growth in the New World, the solution to energy shortages (coal supplies), and other geopolitical factors. By the eighteenth century, Europe had outpaced China and Japan with respect to labor-saving technologies, although not land-saving techniques. Without Europe's possibilities of overseas expansion and access to overseas resources (often through coercion), Europe and Asia might not have diverged. Thus, Pomeranz also emphasized the highly contingent rise of the West.

Goldstone (2000) has perhaps taken this argument the farthest, suggesting that England had no inherent advantages over Asia and was the first to industrialize mostly because of a series of accidents, including political compromises in 1689 between the Anglican Church and dissenters and between the Crown and Parliament; the adoption of Newtonian science; and technical developments in water pumping near coal mines. This new world history literature also echoes the work on the Industrial Revolution by stressing the technological roots of the divergence of East and West (Goldstone 2000; Pomeranz 2000; Vries 2002; Wong 1997). Vries (2002: 125–126) discounted even the differences in Eastern and Western state systems and emphasized that industrialization was driven by a set of technological and scientific breakthroughs. Thus, through new evidence and comparisons, as well as theoretical pluralism, this new work in world history calls into question the assumption that the rise of capitalism is an event that can be explained by a small set of causal factors.

The Market Transition

While the fall of socialism seems to reinforce the view that capitalism is natural, the recent work on the historic transition debates suggests that the "capitalism as triumph" lesson cannot be distilled from history. The economic literature suggests that privatization—the establishment of North and Thomas's (1973) neo-institutional preconditions, secure private property rights—is the path to post-socialist economic growth (Åslund 1995; Blanchard, Froot, and Sachs 1994; Kuboniwa and Gavrilenkov 1997; Lipton and Sachs 1992; S. Parker, Tritt, and Woo 1997: 4; Sachs 1992; Sachs and Pistor, eds. 1997). Privatization, however, is not a single phenomenon, nor is it easily established (Brada 1996; Clarke 1993b; D. Stark 1996; Verdery 1996: 135). Indeed, Kovács (1994: xi–xvii) argued that most reformers and politicians overestimated how easily capitalist economies could be erected. As David Stark (1994: 64) noted, the historic rise of capitalism was not designed; thus, it is unlikely it can be introduced exclusively by plan in post-socialist Europe. The historical literature illustrates these same points—the rise of capitalism was a slow, local, and highly contingent development even in the presence of multiple capitalist preconditions, and it had many cultural and political dimensions. As Cynthia Morris (1995: 223) noted, optimism about widespread and speedy returns from capitalist transformations cannot be based on Western history, where such changes were slow. One central task then, as Pickles and Smith (1998: xvii) have argued, is to understand this emerging triumphalism and universalism of transition theory. Historical sociology's complementary task is to examine both historic and contemporary transition debates.

Like John R. Hall (1999b), Kovács (1994: xiii–xv) and Gal and Kligman (2000: 10–12) pointed out that the word "transition" implies a common destination of Western capitalism and noted the use of the plural "transitions" to imply multiple paths. "Transformations" is often preferred to describe changes without direction and to suggest a variety of changes (cf. Böröcz 2001: 1157; Burawoy and Verdery 1999: 16; Róna-Tas 1997: 9; Adrian Smith and Pickles 1998: 15–16; Verdery 1996: 15–16). This idea of multiple paths to capitalism or multiple capitalisms is popular in Central Europe, with its "third way" tradition, once designating a route to modernization between socialism and capitalism (Burawoy and Lukács 1992: 168–173; Róna-Tas 1997: 184–185).

Similarly, the term "path dependent" describes how initial conditions shape outcomes (Mahoney 2000). Socialist society and class structure, for example, shape contemporary economic outcomes (Adrian Smith and Pickles 1998: 15). Adrian Smith and Adam Swain (1998) argued for the adoption of regulationist theory to understand these multiple paths out of socialism. The regulation of capitalist accumulation occurs not just through state and market, but through a variety of social mechanisms that arose historically and intersect in multiple ways. Thus, their change will be path dependent. David Stark (1994) showed how different models of privatization corresponded to different political paths during the market transition in the former East Germany, Hungary, Poland, and the Czech Republic. Nee and Cao (1999) highlighted a path-dependent effect of property rights on stratification in China.

Because of path dependency, David Stark (1996: 993) argued that different forms of capitalism would emerge in Eastern Europe, Western Europe, and East Asia. He thus echoed the historical arguments, such as Duplessis's, about multiple forms of capitalism. He reinforced the points of Wong, Frank, and Pomeranz, suggesting that China's path to a market economy may be quite different from that of Russia or Eastern Europe. Economic growth in China, far from being a paradoxical accompaniment to its socialist government, may be a relatively continuous historical development, especially in contrast to East European post-socialist countries, where underdevelopment or peripheral status seems to be relatively constant (cf. for Russia, see Derluguian 2001 and Adrian Smith and Pickles 1998: 9; for China and Russia, Lupher 1996; Burawoy and Lukács 1992: xi suggest comparisons to Latin America and Africa). The contemporary Asian/East European comparison is important (e.g., Burawoy 1997: 1434; Oberschall 1996; Szelényi and Kostello 1996; W. T. Woo, Parker, and Sachs, eds. 1997) and could be valuably informed by further, and more explicit, historical comparisons.

The debate over the role of politics and culture often follows the same lines of the historic transition debates; while economists tend to view politics and culture as exogenous forces that disrupt marketization, sociologists view them as intrinsic to capitalism. This debate has been particularly vivid with respect to Russia. Sociologists are deeply cynical of shock therapy (the extremely rapid, planned implementation of market institutions, such as privatization and the removal of price restraints) and dismiss economists' suggestions that failures of this policy occur only when it is implemented incorrectly or because culture and politics interfere (Burawoy 1997; Gerber and Hout 1998). Sociologists do often highlight the role of politics in Russia, especially in contrast to Central Europe (Eyal, Szelényi, and Townsley 1998: 4). Staniszkis (1991) used the term "political capitalism" to denote the use of political connections and offices to gain control of wealth and resources and to generate profit, especially in Russia. Drawing on Burawoy and Krotov (1992), Gerber and Hout (1998: 36–37) and Gerber (2002) argued that Russia is characterized by "merchant capitalism," the pursuit of short-term, windfall profits, instead of investment in productive enterprises.

The political nature of Russian capitalism, however, can be seen as the result of shock therapy, not the cause of its failure. Burawoy and Krotov (1992: 21) defined economic systems by examining, first, the relations of production (the mechanisms through which goods and services are appropriated and distributed); second, the relations in production (mechanisms that describe the production of these goods); and third, whether these are characterized by planning or lack thereof (that is, anarchy, the lack of any agent of superordinate control). State socialism is characterized by planning with respect to the relations of production and capitalism is characterized by planning in the relations in production. Russian merchant capitalism is characterized by neither, because the removal of the state simply eliminates planning at the level of relations of production but does not produce a market that would rely on coordinating the relations in production (i.e., there is no Polanyian state). Thus, Burawoy and Krotov (1992: 35–36) argued that the global market cannot compel a transition to capitalism in the absence of national agents who have both the interest and the capacity to create capitalism (cf. Burawoy 1997: 1442). Similarly, Nee (2000) outlined the Chinese state's role in creating positive economic reform, in sharp contrast to Russia, where the state has little ability to do so. As Woodruff (1999) pointed out, shock therapy created its own demise in Russia, because price liberalization essentially eliminated the opportunities to use financial instruments, forcing managers to use barter. Kogut and Zander (2000: 169) argued that technologically viable firms failed during the transition to capitalism because of the brutal shocks to the macroeconomic system; far from being a cure for the inefficiencies of socialism, rapid change was simply disruptive. Thus, like the historic transition literature (R. Brenner 1993; Lachmann 2000; Perelman 2000), this work on the contemporary market transition illustrates that markets are necessarily intertwined with, not divorced from, politics.

This invocation of merchant capitalism is a clear reference to historical transition debates, drawing on Marx's idea that increased trade was insufficient to bring about a transition to capitalism and that changes in the sphere of production were also necessary. Another use of historical referents might draw on insights of work stemming from Smith and Marx, which point out, respectively, that slow gradual growth and sudden dramatic change may both contribute to the rise of capitalism, although in different ways and in different places. Other interesting comparisons could be made by using Lachmann's elite theory as an alternative to class theory, perhaps in combination with the varieties of elite theory used in market transition debates (e.g., Szelényi and Szelényi 1995).

Like much of the third wave literature on historic capitalisms—and in contrast to the neo-liberal economists Åslund, Sachs, and Lipton—Róna-Tas (1997: 9) argued that capitalist economic transformations were gradual, contingent, and deeply influenced by political, social, and cultural factors. In particular, they stemmed from political contests among social groups (cf. Gerber 2002). Róna-Tas called the market transition the "Small Transformation" with respect to the "Great Transformation," thus using Polanyi to invoke the historical referent. He envisioned the collapse of socialism as the end of a modernist project of industrialization in which communist planners attempted to establish large-scale factory production, thereby modeling the capitalist industrial revolution. Thus, he views historic transitions as sudden and dramatic, in comparison to the slow and gradual post-socialist ones. The literature on the Industrial Revolution reviewed above, however, illustrates the smallness of this "Great Transformation," again suggesting the need for better historic referents.

Like Perelman (2000) and Lachmann (2000), Róna-Tas (1997: 180–181) denied that capitalism was inherently efficient. Socialism brought about, at least for a time, rapid growth. Thus, like the economic history literature, his work pointed to multiple processes of economic growth. Similarly, Burawoy (2001) pointed out that a transition from socialism to capitalism does not necessarily occur because the latter is more efficient but when the interests of political actors who can implement it are realized. Burawoy concurred that capitalism was initially less efficient than subsistence production. Thus, while it is common to assume that socialism collapsed because it was economically inefficient in comparison to capitalism or because of the economic pressures of globalization, this contemporary and historic evidence suggests otherwise. Clarke (1993a: 42), drawing on the Marxist idea of the contradictions inherent in capitalist production, argued that the collapse of the Soviet Union stemmed from the world capitalist system, of which it had been a part. Verdery (1996: 34–37) also argued that politics and culture were crucial to socialism's collapse; some international groups wanted to reduce the political power of socialist states through privatization. Capitalism and socialism collided because of two essentially different temporal orders, with corresponding notions of person and activity.

More generally, Burawoy and Verdery (1999: 2, 14) argued against the idea that culture and politics merely interfere with marketization by noting that on the micro-level, individuals' responses to new market initiatives often employ a language and symbols adopted from socialism, albeit to new senses and new ends. Thus, they explicated another mechanism by which the market transition is path-dependent. Verdery (1999: 50) argued that the reburial of bodies during the market transition illustrated how individuals reconfigure meaning during times of dramatic upheaval and disorienting change. Dead bodies are pressed into political service as cultural symbols for property restitution, political pluralization, religious renewal, and nation-state building. Individuals make claims to power and resources through these symbols (p. 52). Property restitution, for example, is a struggle of certain groups and persons to tie property down, against others who would keep it amorphous (Verdery 1996: 135).

Kennedy (2002: 272) also took a cultural approach, arguing that transition (from plan to market, from dictatorship to democracy) is about transition culture, which is undergirded by values and competencies centered in transnational organizations and national bodies. Thus, markets are discursive sites for identity construction: the rhetoric of markets signals a shift in identity for markets that need entrepreneurs and consumers (Kennedy 1994: 6). Kennedy echoed the historical point about the historical construction of workers and consumers (Biernacki 1995; McKendrick, Brewer, and Plumb 1982; S. W. Mintz 1985). Gal and Kligman (2000: 59–62) noted that economic changes also entail gender changes: men more than women are associated with the capitalist economic sector, thereby necessitating a reconstitution of socialist meanings of public and private space and gender.

Like Randall Collins, Eyal (2000) explicitly generalized Weber's argument about an ethical or ascetic spirit of capitalism. Eyal argued that there was an unlikely elective affinity coalition between dissident intellectuals and technocrats, who together bore the spirit of capitalism in the Czech Republic and therefore led the transition to capitalism. Eyal, Szelényi, and Townsley argued that contemporary Eastern Europe has "capitalism without capitalists" (1998: 1–2). While there is no capitalist class or economic bourgeoisie (nor a political elite), a cultural bourgeoisie, an intelligentsia that formed under socialism, is now developing capitalism. Thus, they argued that the current market transition was unlike the one analyzed by the classic authors, Marx, Weber, and Smith, who suggested that capitalists had to exist before capitalism.

Conclusions

Eyal, Szelényi, and Townsley's (1998: 16) call for a "neo-classical sociology" suggested that the classic sociologists, Weber, Marx, and Smith, analyzed a single, inevitable rise of capitalism (see comments by Böröcz 2001; Burawoy 2001; Eyal, Szelényi, and Townsley 2001; Kennedy 2001; D. Stark and Bruszt 2001). In contrast, neo-classical sociology would look at multiple transitions to capitalisms. Thus, Eyal, Szelényi, and Townsley (1998: 3) noted the need to shift away from the questions of the classics, which is also characteristic of third-wave research on historic transition debates like those reviewed above. They also suggested the need to develop further historical referents (pp. 47–54) that analyze the historic rise of capitalism without assuming the bourgeoisie's role. Yet to a large extent, they focused on the differences between the current market transition and historic transitions to capitalisms, thereby reinforcing the idea that historic debates provide relatively little information about contemporary ones. As Böröcz (2001: 1165) noted, their neo-classical sociology explores relatively little historical terrain. Therefore, Eyal, Szelényi, and Townsley follow, at least in large part, the second of the three uses of historical referents I outlined at the beginning of this essay, which emphasizes differences between past and present. While their call to revive topical interest in transitions to capitalism is important and timely, it could be more effective if the emphasis on first-wave work were supplemented with more recent, third-wave work on historic transition debates that is already oriented toward multiple historic transitions to capitalisms.

   This third-wave literature is reorienting the classic authors' questions with new comparisons, new evidence, and new theories. In the recent wave of theorizing, the "transition to capitalism" is rarely discussed as a singular, inevitable event to be explained by a single theory. While historic transition debates draw on standard social science perspectives derived from Smith, Marx, and Weber, most recent work combines these perspectives in innovative ways or goes beyond them and uses a variety of comparisons (or draws out the implications of cases discussed less frequently in the past), often based on new archival evidence. Much effort is spent asking what capitalism is, analyzing if and where it arose, and explaining the contingent nature of transitions to capitalisms. It emphasizes the political and cultural constitution of capitalisms. Furthermore, it employs, at least in large part, what I call the third use of historical referents, which draws on comparisons using both similarities and differences across time and space and between past and present. Such a method rejects the first use of historical referents—that history can be repeated in its entirety—but also rejects the second use—that historical sequences are entirely unique. Third-wave uses of East/West comparisons (e.g., Pomeranz 2000; Wong 1997) and comparisons within Europe of negative and positive cases (Emigh 2003; Hopcroft 1999; Lachmann 2000) carefully look for regional and temporal similarities and differences without assuming capitalism's inevitability.

A better understanding of the contemporary market transition can be developed through this third-wave research on historic transitions to capitalisms with this third use of historical referents. Much is certainly different about the historic rise of capitalist economies and the current market transition, including the degree of intentionality and planning, the level of technology, and global economic conditions. Nevertheless, as the preceding review shows, much is also similar. In fact, the similarities between past and present provide the sharpest critique of the neo-classical economic advice often implemented in Eastern and Central Europe and the common American cultural parlance that capitalism is the most efficient and rational economic system.

Indeed, the literature on historic capitalist economic change suggests that the contemporary market transition is unlikely to be a sudden, purely economic affair with a certain and inevitable outcome, swept into place because of a few capitalist preconditions. Instead, it suggests that transitions to capitalisms are highly local and gradual affairs, with different outcomes in different places, influenced by politics and culture. Perelman and Lachmann's work suggests—and Burawoy; Eyal, Szelényi, and Townsley; Gal and Kligman; Kennedy; and Verdery all confirm—that analyses should consider in whose interest it is to make capitalism. Far from being a neutral or efficient allocation mechanism, the market is generally advanced by those who find it to be in their short-term interest. Other work, such as that of E. L. Jones and Kenneth Pomeranz, suggests that sudden dramatic changes are rare indeed. While there is no denying the changes that occurred in Eastern Europe in 1989, in hindsight, the continuities may be more dramatic than the changes, as Róna-Tas suggests. To know for sure, however, how much change is a lot, historical sociologists must redouble their efforts to study historic transitions empirically, for it is the historical rise of capitalisms that provides the referents for the understanding of current market transitions. It is to be hoped that such work will continue to be diverse theoretically and empirically and to use multiple comparisons, moving away from the specific questions and assumptions of the classic authors while retaining their topical focus and ideas. By providing a better empirical understanding of what pre-modern is, historical sociology can provide a better understanding of what modern and post-modern are.

MING-CHENG M. LO

The Professions: Prodigal Daughters of Modernity

The history of the sociology of professions can be told as a tale about the contestation of modernity. Many scholars have long regarded professions as a form of institutionalized rationality and thus one of the designated carriers of modernity. Other studies of professions, however, challenge the assumed equation between rationality and modernity and question the role of professions in the social formation of modernity. The unsettled relationship between professions and modernity is not only central to the question of what professions are and how to theorize them in sociological writings, but is also symptomatic of certain contradictions in our discipline's formulation of the notion of modernity. This chapter is an attempt to draw a conceptual map for navigating through this unsettled relationship.

A map is by necessity incomplete—details are omitted, interesting background may be obscured, and important landmarks are not always incorporated, not because these things are deemed unimportant by the map maker, but rather because a map can serve only particular and limited purposes. My purpose here is to provide a framework for understanding the development of the sociology of professions in the past two decades by delineating the underlying debate regarding the nature of modernity. In this vein, I will start with a brief review of the frustrated conversations between the sociology of professions and historical sociology. I will then review the contributions of these writings to our understanding of the structural intersections of modern institutions. I suggest that as the field developed, a shift occurred from a focus on the professions' links to other modern institutions to their embeddedness in a broader array of (sometimes not so "modern") categories of identity. The recognition of the professions' social embeddedness presented a challenge, at least implicitly, to an enduring legacy of dualism in our discipline—namely, an oversimplified opposition between modernity (read "the rational") and tradition (read "the irrational"). It is a challenge that has been variously, and not always adequately, addressed. Building upon this discussion and drawing attention to some pioneering works, I will develop a broader notion of professionalism that facilitates a more coherent articulation of the rational and the relational aspects of professions.

The Professions and Their Discontents

The evolving course of the conceptualization of the professions in sociology is by now a familiar story (Abbott 1988; Macdonald 1995; Witz 1992). Until the 1960s, the overarching question in the scholarship on the professions was, by and large, how to define and describe their function in holding society together. Parsons conceptualized professions primarily in terms of their "functional specialties," motivating later scholars to specify—and debate about—the content of such specialties and study the steps involved in an occupation's becoming a profession (Wilensky 1964). The trait and process approaches, however, ultimately foundered "on the sheer diversity of elements that various authors identified as providing the essence of professions" (Witz 1992: 40), rendering the field fragmented and strained in its own self-definition.

But the unsuccessful endeavors of this functionalist approach also inspired and indeed called for greater historical sensitivity in the (re-) conceptualization of the professions. Aborting the search for a core set of traits or the defining steps of professionalization, scholars re-inserted professions in the historical transition to European modernity, viewing professionalization not as an independent process but a part of that macro-history. This "paradigm shift" in the sociology of professions in the 1970s and early 1980s also did not occur as an independent process; the comparative-historical renaissance—the emergence of the "second wavers" during the same years (see Adams, Clemens, and Orloff, this volume)—centralized a theoretical concern about the formal structures of the political economy with which students of the professions defined their new overarching question. Their writings thus conceptualized professions as institutionalized forms of power that, though based on knowledge and skills, were enabled and sustained *only* through particular institutional relationships with the modern state and the capitalist market.

To be sure, the sociological significance of the intricate interactions among the professions, the state, and the market was appraised quite differently by these scholars. Some conceptualized it as a process of professions achieving relative autonomy from the market and the state (Freidson 1970a, 1986), while others depicted it as a story of the professions becoming a tool of domination for capital and the ruling elites (Johnson 1972, 1993; Larson 1977). Nevertheless, the question about the place of the professions in the engendering of the moment of the modern—defined here in terms of the formal structures of the market and the state bureaucracy—formed their common point of departure. Later, Freidson characterized the second group of scholars as the collective agent responsible for developing the "power approach":

> By the early 1970s, two writers shifted the emphasis of subsequent theorizing about the professions away from their role in holding society together and toward issues of conflict and power. My books . . . emphasized the ideological character of professional claims, unjustified aspects of monopolistic privilege, and the way organized professional institutions create and sustain authority over clients, associated occupations, and the very way we think about deviant or undesirable behavior. Shortly afterwards Terence Johnson (1972) defined profession as a method of controlling work—one in which an occupation . . . exercises control over its work. And he emphasized the role of power in establishing and maintaining such control. Subsequent literature from both the United Kingdom and the United States was described by commentators as taking a "power approach" rather than the "trait approach" of earlier structural-functional writers. Later in the decade, Larson's *The Rise of Professionalism* (1977) brought both Marxist and Weberian theory to the fore in her analysis of professions, studying them as interest groups linked to the class system of capitalist societies and analyzing professionalization as a "collective mobility project" in which occupations seek to improve not only their economic position but also their social standing, or prestige (Freidson 1994: 3).

However, as the debate about the insitutional power of the professions continued, this central *problématique* soon proved to be rather troubling because the best answer always seemed to be, "It depends on the context." Rather than piecing together a general pattern that characterized the professions-state-market relationships, these studies yielded an unexpected—and perhaps somewhat frustrating for their time—realization that the professions as a conceptual category could be defined only contextually. For example, Freidson advised that "the future of professions lies in embracing the concept as an intrinsically ambiguous, multifaceted folk concept, of which no single definition and no attempt at isolating its essence will ever be generally persuasive" (1983: 32–33).[1] Similarly, Larson saw the professions as always a historically specific phenomenon. Profession is "a name we give to historically specific forms that establish *structural links between relatively high levels of formal education and relatively desirable positions and/or rewards in the social division of labor*" (Larson 1990: 30; emphasis in original). The contours and dynamics of such structural links, Larson maintained, could be specified only when properly contextualized.

The emphasis on contingency and context not only raised a question about the appropriate meeting ground for theory and history, but also, ironically, challenged the very assumptions about the primacy of social structures that had inspired many of these writings in the first place. In the end, efforts to delineate the professions as part of the structures of domination arrived at the realization that these structures were not discrete, universal, or enduring. Moreover, some of these studies directly challenged the central place of the state and the market in the making of modernity; even though students of the social formation of professions were fundamentally interested in the relations of the professions to the state and the market, they often presented findings that cautioned against any attempt to reduce the professions as a social institution to certain functions of the latter two. (Friedson's articulation of professionalism as "the third logic," distinct from the logic of the bureaucracy or the market, is a good example.)[2] Other writings, such as Abbott's monumental *The System of Professions* (1988), debunked the very assumption of structural determinism. Abbott suggested instead that professions should be studied "only within an interacting system, that a theory of professions had to embrace not only cultural and social

1. Apparently, after nearly two decades, Freidson did attempt to offer an elaborated definition of this "intrinsically ambiguous" concept in his thesis of "third logic"; see Freidson (2001).
2. The thesis of the third logic appears to be a revision of Freidson's earlier view of the professions as a folk concept. While the actual manifestations of this model are contingent upon social, political, and economic factors, in the third logic argument Freidson maintained that it is not only possible but also desirable to separate the abstract logic of professionalism from its concrete manifestations. This ideal-typical approach "can be intellectually useful even if present-day professions, crushed between private capital and the state, may be losing their special economic and social position as Krause claims, or if the 'organizational . . . dominance of expertise' will emerge, as Abbott . . . believes" (Freidson 2001: 9). Freidson specified five interdependent elements as the key components of such an ideal-typical model of professionalism: "(1) specialized work in the officially recognized economy . . . grounded in a body of theoretically based, discretionary knowledge and skill and . . . given special status in the labor force; (2) exclusive jurisdiction . . . created and controlled by occupational negotiation; (3) a sheltered position . . . based on qualifying credentials created by the occupation; (4) a formal training program . . . which is controlled by the occupation and associated with higher education; (5) an ideology that asserts greater commitment to doing good work than to economic gain" (p. 127).

structure but also intra-, inter-, and transprofessional forces, and that the development of professions would necessarily be a matter of complex conjunctures" (Abbott 1993: 204). These quarrels with class- and state-centered perspectives, as well as assumptions of structural determinism, which to some extent characterized the mainstream of the second wavers, eventually marginalized the studies of professions in historical sociology (see Adams, Clemens, and Orloff, this volume). Despite some occasional—and rather inspiring—attempts, the second wavers and the sociologists of professions who favored a more contingent, contextual mode of explanation never engaged in a full-fledged dialogue that might have explicitly addressed their epistemological differences and challenged the second wavers to reconsider their structuralist position.

If the second wavers in historical sociology have ignored the challenges raised by sociologists of professions, the latter group has not completely escaped the second wavers' definition of modernity. The sociologists of professions operate on a common belief in the modern-ness of the professions, as well as a specific understanding of modernity informed by a bifurcated notion of rationality and irrationality. While they differ on how to best explain the social formation and consequences of professions, "professions" are invariably the name given to the institutions that develop and provide rational and scientific solutions to social problems and are therefore unmistakably agents (or culprits) of modernity.[3] These scholars remain uncritical of the assumption of the great divide that characterizes the dualistic thinking of the second wavers—namely, the oversimplified opposition between the rationality of the "modern" and the irrationality of the "traditional" (see Adams, Clemens, and Orloff, this volume). Aligning professions with the category of the modern, they commonly assume that the work of professionals, however differently understood, transcends traditional or primordial categories such as race, ethnicity, or gender.[4] Larson (1977) explained that evolving notions of professionalism have established a dichotomy between professional and particular identities; these emphatically underscore the idea that "properly trained and socialized workers could (and should) transcend their particular differences when working together" (Woods 1993: 242). Sociological exchanges about the professions in the past two decades, therefore, both challenged and were constrained by the modernist framework that this volume seeks to problematize.

---

3. See Abbott (1988); Freidson (1986, 2001); Larson (1977). In addition, see Kimball (1992) and Krause (1996) for arguments about the pre-modern legacies in modern professions.
4. For a critical discussion of how race, nationality, ethnicity, and gender are conceptualized as primordial categories, see Brubaker (this volume).

Professions and the Messiness of Modernity

One can argue that comparative and historical studies of the professions in the past two decades have yielded an important yet incomplete understanding of the patterns and ambiguities of modernity. These insights, I will contend, have illuminated the complexity and contingency of the relationships among "modern" institutions and implicitly have problematized the modernist notion of agency and, by so doing, have provided grounds for addressing the oversimplified modern/traditional opposition. As the discussion in this section will show in some detail, the best examples in the sociology of professions recognize the trends of bureaucratization and capitalization of the professions, on the one hand, and on the other hand are sensitive to the irreducibility of professions to some combination of functions of these two master forces. Their understanding of the complex connections and conflicts within the institutions that we regard as "modern" brings to the fore the messiness of modernity. Such careful appreciation of the intersections of modern social structures, in turn, begins to raise issues about the multiple allegiances of social agents. Recognizing that professionals are often situated between intersecting, interpenetrating structures rather than dominated by the logic of any singular social institution, these scholars have to come to terms with the ambiguity of professionals' social identity. These writings contain the seeds for an argument—one that is yet to be explicitly articulated—against the very assumption upon which they stand—that is, the clear separation between the rational and the irrational.

Since the publication of two monumental works in the 1970s, Freidson (1970b) and Larson (1977), American sociologists' understandings of professions have largely progressed under an overarching question about the relationships of the professions to the state and the market. Freidson located the origin of professional power in the attainment of professional autonomy, or control over work, through state licensure and credentialism. Professional power manifests itself in the expanding professional "market shelters," where a profession monopolizes supply and the substance of demand within its jurisdiction. In response to his critics, Friedson (2001) acknowledged the "unpleasant truth" that such a credential-based, state-sanctioned market monopoly lies at the crux of the institutions of professionalism. Yet he viewed professionalism as a valuable solution to certain organizational problems in complex societies and found the reasonable position to lie not in damning the principle but in protecting its appropriate practice from abuse.

Larson (1977), on the other hand, distrusted the abstract neutrality of professionalism. Situating the phenomenon of expert authority in the historical stream of capitalist development, Larson emphasized the market incentives in the conversion of knowledge into property and the role of professionalism in the justification of the bourgeois ideology of meritocracy. Meanwhile, professions constitute themselves as agents of the state, define our needs, and, in a Foucauldian sense, develop a penetrating technology of power as a new form of discipline to which the citizenry is subject but of which it is barely aware (Larson 1984).

The dialogue between Freidson and Larson has shaped the framework of debate in the past two decades and motivated numerous sociological articulations of the subtlety of the professions' relationships to the state and the market. For example, Haskell positioned the professions in a unique relationship with the market. For him, "professional communities held strong appeal for anti-capitalist reformers. . . . [But] professions are 'countervailing markets,' capable of placing a modest premium on certain non-pecuniary dimensions of human performance—but finally cut from the same cloth of universal competition and rationalization as the market itself" (1984). These "countervailing markets" are thus to be regarded with suspicion, but not at the expense of understanding their epistemological efficacy. Haskell believes that although "truth" is produced by social conventions, not all social conventions are relative. "Social conventions arising from open and vigorous competition within a community that genuinely prizes criticism—which not all do, of course—are weighty and tenacious things. Certainly they possess more holding power than conventions that simply descend from past usage and tradition, or from arbitrary deference to a Hobbesian ruler" (p. xxxvii).

In turn, Halliday (1987) addressed the professions' ambivalent relations to the state. Maintaining that "the corrective pendulum of reaction against an overtly benign functionalism has swung too far," he wanted to hold in juxtaposition the two faces of professionalism—"the one monopolistic, even narcissistic, and the other benign, even altruistic" (p. 3). In this vein, Halliday departed from Larson's monopoly thesis to investigate the professions' contribution to state structure. He believed that "the centrality of monopoly to the professional enterprise has a developmental dimension" (p. 350). As a profession becomes established, its collective actions are seen as less geared toward maintaining monopoly and more centered upon shaping political policies, contributing its expertise to solving the crisis of "ungovernability" that is commonly faced by liberal democratic states. From this perspective, "bringing understanding to this tension of expert and representative authority is the mandate for the macrosociology of professions" (p. 376).

Taking a more radical departure from Larson, Abbott (1988) debunked the very concept of professionalization, shifting the focus from individual professions to professions as an interdependent system that, in Abbott's conceptualization, accommodates inter-professional competition, is affected by intra-professional differentiation, and is shaped by external social forces. In effect, Abbott's "jurisdictional competition" still shared with Larson's "monopoly" the same focus on the question of how and why professions came to dominate our world, and thus some readers would see it as not a rejection but an expansion of Larson's analysis (Macdonald 1995). But if Abbott shared some of the same questions that Larson had posed, his answers were radically different in that his system model aimed to achieve a theory of contingency rather than positing any specific trends and patterns of development.[5]

While Halliday discussed how professions helped alleviate the crisis of "ungovernability," Johnson questioned the very nature of "governmentality." Adopting a Foucauldian concept of governmentality, Johnson saw the professionalization of expertise as part and parcel of the process of governing.[6] The crystallization of expertise and the growth of professional associations in nineteenth-century Europe, argued Johnson, were directly linked to the rise of the modern state and its new techniques of ruling, which included "the classification and surveillance of populations, the normalization of the subject-citizen and the discipline of the aberrant subject. The establishment of the jurisdictions of professions like medicine, psychiatry, law and accountancy, were all . . . the product of government programmes and policies" (Johnson 1995: 11). From this perspective, the autonomy of expertise is granted to the professions only insofar as it works as a convenient and useful technique of state rule. The interests of the state, ironically and perhaps

---

5. For Abbott, his model "frees us entirely from the ideal type approach" and underscores the understanding of history as "a complex mass of contingent forces" (1988: 316).

6. Johnson offered a concise recapitulation of Foucault's concept of governmentality:

"Governmentality is a novel capacity for governing that gradually emerged in Europe from the sixteenth century onwards in association with the invention, operationalization and institutionalization of specific knowledge, disciplines, tactics and technologies. The period from the sixteenth until the eighteenth century was . . . notable for the appearance throughout Europe of a series of treaties on government: on the government of the soul and the self; on the government of children within the family; on the government of the state. . . . This rethinking of the various forms of governance was associated both with the early formation of the great territorial, administrative states and colonial empires, and with the disruptions of spiritual rule associated with the reformation and the counter-reformation." [This process signaled a radical break with the Machiavellian assumption that the power of the prince was best deployed in securing sovereignty. Rather, the new argument holds that] "governing was no more than the 'right disposition of things' leading to the 'common welfare and salvation for all.' This novel discourse which began to conceive of popular obedience to the law as the sole source of legitimate rule . . . also made it possible to identify . . . the means of governing, those tactics and knowledges developed in order to regulate territories and population" (1995: 8).

counter-intuitively, are best served by granting technical autonomy to professions rather than withholding it from them. Johnson thus cautioned against any assumptions about the neutrality or universality of professional autonomy. "We cannot understand what is happening to the professions today if we frame our questions around the issues of autonomy and intervention. . . . Freidson's view that the distinctive feature of a profession, autonomy in controlling its own technical work, is always contingent" (p. 21).

Johnson's view is similar to Larson's discussion of professions and power. Johnson and Larson also shared a Marxist perspective in their earlier works and later incorporated a Foucauldian notion of power. In contrast, critiques of the Foucauldian perspective maintain that it is theoretically undesirable and empirically invalid to collapse the distinctions between the institution of professions and the state. For example, Macdonald believed that "whilst one can certainly argue that the professions were part and parcel of a 'process of state formation' it is also the case that those of their actions which involved or impinged on the state were carried out for motives and with objectives which had nothing to do, consciously, with state formation" (1995: 119). Macdonald cited incidents of state-professions conflicts to make his point. Ultimately, he did not see profession formation as part of the state formation process; rather, he preferred to think that "the contemporary interventionist/corporate state invades nearly all institutions, and there is nothing unique in the way in which it regulates, incorporates and makes use of professional organizations. That is the spirit of our time" (p. 121). In this regard, Macdonald is similar to Freidson (2001), who set apart three distinct logics of organizations—managerialism, consumerism, and professionalism—and proposed to view the reality as a mixture of these three logics, interpenetrating but not mutually reducible.

Through a comparative study of the United States, Britain, France, Italy, and Germany, Krause observed a converging trend in the death of the professions' "guild power," both "because of external pressures . . . and because of the surrender of positive guild values—of collegiality, of concern for the group, of a higher professional ethic beyond mere profit—that has eroded the distinction between professions and any other occupation and thus left them together as the middle-level employees of capitalism" (1996: 281). Krause's sweeping conclusion about the professions' final surrender to capitalism presented a stronger version of several earlier critiques of Freidson's professional dominance thesis.[7] Both the professional dominance thesis and its critical evaluations, often referred to as the "professional decline perspective," present sophisticated accounts of the relations among the

7. For a thorough review of the exchange between Freidson and his critics, see Brint (1993).

professions, the state, and capitalism. While the professional decline perspective focuses on how professional autonomy has been eroded by the trends of bureaucratization and capitalization, the professional dominance thesis insists on professional autonomy, however constrained, as the basis for understanding the logic of professionalism.

The debate ultimately proves the either-or position to be rather futile; instead of a focus on whether professions are dominant or in decline, the key question becomes one about the interpenetration of the professions, bureaucracy, and the market. Freidson's analysis suggested that structural changes resulted in the formalization of unequal status and a declining collegiality within the professional world, but he argued that these changes did not alter the nature of professional power very much, even if that power was now shared unevenly by members of a profession. His critics, in turn, admitted to the autonomy of professionals in their technical decisions, but they insisted that because of the intervention of political and economic powers, such technical decisions were being formulated within a shrinking range of available options. Focusing on the case of medicine, Hafferty and McKinlay contended that "we need not claim that medicine faces restriction of choice within some range of currently acceptable alternatives. We do claim, however, that medicine faces a loss of discretion over what exists as a given range, something once solely established by claimed technical expertise and now facing the more explicit presence of economic or political considerations" (1993: 213). The authors argued that medical diagnostic and treatment options were established by medicine as science but that these options became available only if they were supported by critical resources, such as money, political mandates, and cultural authority. "If medicine is defined by what it does rather than what it can do, then the medicine we have today is meaningfully different from the medicine we had yesterday" (p. 214).

The sociological discussions of professions in the past two decades have, therefore, carefully depicted a picture of the intersections of the professions, the market, and the state. These diligent efforts to detect order therein, as we have seen, eventually led these authors—and us—to consider the messiness of modernity. Having situated professions in this extended web of institutional relationships, sociologists recognized the field of professions as complexly and quite diversely "structurated" not only through its own increasing organizational elaboration, but also through its deep embeddedness in the fields of the state and the market. Though an unpopular insight in its time, this appreciation of the messiness of modernity is potentially very useful for our understanding of the agency of professionals. More specifically, while professionals had thus far largely been assumed to be the unproblematic agents of professions, toward the end of the second wave they were beginning to be positioned in a more ambiguous, and therefore less predictable, structural location and recognized as potential agents of multiple institutions. Freidson (1984) considered the professionals' dual allegiance as a potential threat to professional hegemony. Hafferty and McKinlay prompted further discussions of this phenomenon via their work on the medical profession. They believed that "what is relevant here is the possibility that physicians have come to operate as agents of the state or other organizational interests, not as representatives of a professional community" (1993: 215). Though the agency issue remained a side note in the studies of professions during this time, the observation of the decoupling of the agency of professionals from their structural roles was a significant empirical finding that foregrounded later, more explicit theorization of the construction of modern social agency.[8]

Balzer, arguably a third waver, took a step further and considered the agency issue in terms of identity, questioning how to best understand the content of professionals' identities beyond specifying their (increasingly) ambiguous structural positions:

> Are we not dealing with a situation of multiple identities in increasingly complex societies? Even professionals employed in large universities or corporations may derive a significant part of their identity from their professional role, and their professional community may provide an important forum for political expression. . . . Professional identity . . . may be a status payoff that substitutes for material benefits; but it may also be a source of strength in confronting the organizational structures. Not enough attention has been paid to the enduring power of the professional specialist, even in seemingly rigid organizational settings (1996: 5).

Indeed, the structural in-betweenness of professionals—a variable quality, to be sure—begs the question of the nature of their agency and the social formation of their identity. Balzer was quite accurate in pointing out the scarcity of research in this area. The bulk of scholarship on the sociology of professions is devoted to the structural and organizational dimensions of this institution; until very recently, the identity of its agents had been treated by and large as an institutional derivative. But the meticulous works on the structural intersections of professions with the state and the market have

---

8. For example, John Meyer and Ronald Jepperson's (2000) theorization of agency provided a more elaborated and systematic articulation of the complex structuration of modern actors and their loose coupling to the structures of acting.

exposed this functionalistic assumption as well as its inadequacy. The agents of modernity, it would appear, follow no singular logic. This observation perhaps forms a basis where sociologists of professions can resume their suspended conversations with the third wave of historical sociologists.[9]

The Social Embeddedness of the Professions

The issue of the identity of professionals challenges us to move our focus from social structure to social embeddedness. Building upon our understanding of the ambiguous structural locations of professionals, we need to understand how professionals make sense of their positions and "embed" their professional practices in specific social contexts. This question pushes us to situate professions not only in an intricate web of relationships with the state and the market, but also at the intersection with social categories located on the other side of the modernity/tradition divide, such as race, ethnicity, and gender, that were previously deemed irrelevant to the social formation of professions. In turn, a fuller understanding of professionals' social embeddedness highlights the fluidity and mutual constitution of categories of identity, which can help us move toward a more rigorous perspective on the process of professional identity formation, as well as to treat it as a central question in the studies of professions. Instead of asking how professionals "choose" from their multiple allegiances, each assumed to imply a ready-made identity, we are compelled to study professions as sites of identity formation, where professionals come to terms with the meaning of their racial, ethnic, or gender identities in the context of their professional institution.

Ultimately, to focus on the mutual constitution of the professions and race, ethnicity, or gender cultivates a greater sense of historicity about the institution and practice of professions and, what is perhaps more significant, calls for an equally sensitive understanding about the historicity of our own theories of professions. To conceptualize professions as embedded in race, ethnicity, gender, and other social categories will lead to queries about why these categories were previously excluded from this scholarship and in turn will expose the assumptions upon which an asexual, nonethnic, nonracial (read white male) image of professionals in this scholarship was con-

---

9. As Adams, Clemens, and Orloff point out in the introduction to this volume, the third wave of historical sociology is also centrally concerned with the issue of identity formation, recognizing that the meaning of agency cannot simply be "read off of" social structures or derived from a notion of a "rational actor" that is largely assumed to be transcendent of historical contexts.

structed. To recognize and confront the particularistic roots of our own theories—to provincialize white European male professionals—demands that we take seriously the experiences of the formerly excluded, both at home and in the "non-West." This move toward the social embeddedness of professions does not, however, imply a theoretical gesture toward privileging the categories of gender, ethnicity, and race. Instead, the focus on these categories is itself historically specific, enabled and informed primarily by recent works in colonial studies and gender studies that have finally earned legitimacy as theoretical voices (as opposed to "just so stories") in critical dialogue with the mainstream of sociology. The notion of social embeddedness, then, will have to be continually revised and refined through the further understanding of other experiences on the periphery as those become thematized and potentially yield new conceptual categories.

In effect, one can argue that the shift of focus from social structure to social embeddedness is inevitable. If we scrutinize the professions' varying patterns of intersection with capitalism and state formation, then why ignore their intersections with other social processes? With this realization, what were previously viewed as informal mechanisms of exclusion, such as race, ethnicity, and gender (Freidson 1986), become recognized as threads of social fabric shaping patterns of professionalization. Balzer stated it succinctly: "Professionalization is not the single thread running through the fabric of modern society. . . . It must be viewed in the broader context of social history or it distorts more than it reveals" (1996: 5; see also Burrage 1990; Larson 1990; McClelland 1991).

Brint's survey of U.S. professionals gestured in the direction of greater contextualization, as he observed that professionals' attitudes come from their demographic backgrounds as much as from the inherent values of their profession. Professionals possess certain values because they "are more likely to be relatively young, highly educated, urban, and nonreligious" (1994: 102). Similarly, McClelland described the importance of race and ethnicity in shaping the contour of professional formation in Eastern Europe: "the smooth integration of the few modern professionals into the indigenous society was often encumbered by local conditions, so that Jews were disproportionately represented in the medical profession, and, as in Hungary, the impoverished lower nobility flocked into the law" (1991: 26). Through her analysis of occupational closure strategies, Witz studied how professionalization intersected with patriarchy, and she cautioned against the assumption "that exclusion on the grounds of gender and race is an 'informal' element of credentialing. . . . Rather . . . gendered exclusionary mechanisms were embedded in the formal credentialing process" (1992: 195). Celia Davies

(1996) further pointed out that beyond the discussion of exclusion, sociologists needed to better understand the particular forms of inclusion for women in the professional world.

These delineations of the social embeddedness of professions lend themselves to the question of the intersection of the allegedly modern institution of the profession and the presumably primordial categories of race, ethnicity, and gender. As professionalization is recognized to be a process that unfolds in close interaction with race, ethnicity, and gender, it becomes necessary to examine how certain gender, racial, and ethnic cultures and ideologies may become internalized in a profession's collective identity. In this vein, sociologists are challenged to separate the understanding of professional identity from the dominant narrative in the professions themselves, which conveys the image of a nonsexual, nonracial, and nonethnic professional (Woods 1993). In short, we are confronted with the question of how the collective identity of a profession is often gendered, ethnicized, and racialized yet rarely recognized as such.

We certainly would be mistaken to think that the role of gender, race, and ethnicity has never been studied in the sociology of professions; however, these studies primarily inform us of the ways in which minority professionals are *excluded* in the professional world rather than the patterns of how they might have been *included*.[10] The studies of minority professionals have therefore been ghettoized, given a space in the field but kept segregated from the more general and theoretical discussions. As such, we are still blind to the ways in which race matters to nonminority members of a profession; we are inadequately informed about how professionalization and professionalism are racialized; we have, in this sense, only partially understood how these social categories are mutually constitutive.[11]

---

10. For example, see Parlin (1976), who discussed how immigration laws attract immigrant professionals yet additional legislation does not protect them from discrimination and exclusion in the workplace. Stephanie Shaw (1996) also showed that Black professional women achieved high standing in their community and attained strong knowledge and skills in the profession, yet they remained excluded. These women "brought to their positions an agenda beyond establishing their own individual prestige. They also worked to raise the status of the race," but they remained "excluded by their professional peers, their alleged 'natural' allies" (p. 213).

11. Although they have also largely focused on the exclusion and discrimination of women in the professional world, feminist scholars have developed some important insights about how gender affects the overall structure and identity of the professions. In her now classic book, Kanter (1977) paid special attention to how and why women tended to be marginalized in the corporation. Using a powerful concept, "homosocial reproduction," Kanter explained how managers attempted to increase mutual trust in the workplace by homogenizing its personnel, resulting often in decisions to hire and promote their social peers, who shared their cultural backgrounds, assumptions, and communication styles. Similarly, focusing on the experiences of gay professionals in America, Woods (1993) explored

To fully de-ghettoize studies of race, ethnicity, and gender in the sociology of professions and to better understand their place in the social formation of professions, I argue that the professions should be conceptualized not only as a status category, but also as a site of identity formation. The roles of ethnicity, race, and/or gender may partially—but only partially—manifest themselves as the exclusionary mechanisms that Witz (1992) discussed. At a deeper level, professions adopt and normalize certain racial, ethnic, and gender norms in their institutional culture. Often, the marginalized racial, ethnic, or gender norms become the "Other" against which the professional "self" defines its culture and its social position. In this sense, the familiar stories about how women, gay people, and racial and ethnic minorities fight against native stereotypes in the professional world should also be read as a process of how professions construct and maintain the boundaries of their self-identities. Meanwhile, minority professionals, whose ethnicity, race, and/or gender differs from those dominant in their profession, are compelled to reconcile, integrate, and make choices about these competing sources of identity. For these "in-between" professionals, the profession becomes an institutional site of identity contestation that shapes their ethnic (and/or racial and gender) consciousness. Race/ethnicity/gender and professions, then, are mutually constitutive, each shaped by the other in an interactive process.

Informed by studies that have recognized and confronted the "default" of ethnicity, race, or gender in the professions as a structural problem (Kanter 1977; Woods 1993), I especially wish to advance the following argument: although the structural problems that ensue from such a "default" are most often experienced as profoundly and painfully personal issues and should be understood as such, it is crucial that these problems also be studied in the context of *collective* identity struggles. A structural problem calls for a collective solution. Thus, the organizations and submerged networks formed by groups of minority professionals can become important sites for collective and creative articulations of meaningful new identities. These identity narratives integrate, often with difficulties and ambiguities, the "deep structure" of their professions with the experiences and voices that are marginalized by it. We need to study the process through which the deep structure of a profession not only produces unequal opportunities, but, equally important, imposes a particular identity on those who do manage to obtain the

---

what the image of the "asexual professional" involved and how it in effect naturalized heterosexuality in the workplace. Illustrating a similar pattern, Gutek (1989) and Sheppard (1989) also discussed how professional women were encouraged to "desexualize" their dress, speech, and demeanor. Other examples include Bonner (1992), McIlwee and Robinson (1992), Riska and Weger, eds. (1993), and Stage and Vincent, eds. (1997).

opportunities normally unavailable to their group. We need more systematic research on the diverse manners in which these minority professionals come to terms with multiple and often conflicting identity narratives at an organizational level—for example, how and why particular groups of minority professionals are mobilized for collective action, how their collective identity claims may shape their articulations of professionalism, or, alternatively, how their blueprints for change and identity claims may be constrained or even deterred by their strategies of intra- and inter-professional jurisdictional competitions.

Through a study of the medical profession in Taiwan under Japanese colonialism, my own work (Lo 2002) offers a concept of "hybridization" for understanding the process through which these in-between minority professionals negotiate their collective identities. Informed by colonial and post-colonial studies, I conceptualized hybridization as the encounter, conflict, and/or blending of two ethnic or cultural categories that, while by no means pure and distinct in nature, tend to be understood and experienced as meaningful identity labels by members of these categories.[12] Since not every loop in the chain of hybridization is alike, a central question concerns how to differentiate among different kinds of hybrids, as we guard against excessive relativization of all experiences of the in-between. Drawing upon current discussions of hybridity, in *Doctors within Borders* I formulated the major parameters that would approximate the differences among the hybrids: their specific "relational configurations," formed by unequal social, political, and economic relationships; and their self-positioning and ontological narratives, articulated as they struggle to become "modern" (rather than being made modern). I analyzed the in-betweenness of Taiwanese doctors by tracing their changing structural locations, shaped by the intersection of the ethnic and professional communities, and by reconstructing the narrative articulations of these doctors' collective identity. Neither eth-

---

12. The term "hybridity," as it has been used throughout history, has multiple connotations. As Robert Young (1995) pointed out in his study of the genealogy of this term, the concept of hybridity is an integral part of the very colonial system that today's scholars seek to dismantle. According to Young, the usage of the term "hybridity" in the vocabulary of the Victorian extreme right presupposed the existence of "pure" and distinct racial categories and centered on the issue of the fertility of interracial "hybrids." Recent scholarship in post-colonial studies, however, has radically transformed the meaning of hybridity. The central concern here is about the creativity and cultural imagination of the hybrid that is located in between categories. This scholarship finds no reasons to assume hybridity as a blending of two *distinct* cultures, races, or ethnicities. For example, Paul Gilroy's (1993) discussion of the modernity of the Black Atlantic explicitly rejected any essentialist notion of ethnicity. For him, the two cultures that inform the "double consciousness" of intellectuals in the Black Atlantic are diverse, messy, and incoherent in and of themselves. It is in this latter tradition that I position my engagement with the concept of ethnic hybridity.

nic nor professional culture, interests, or organizations played a dominant part in the formation of this social group; ultimately, a meaningful collective identity came about as these doctors' collective imagination and struggles enabled them to discern coherence in their experiences of the in-between and to incorporate elements of their choosing into such changing identity narratives as "national physicians" and "medical modernists." At a more general level, the study developed through a historical case the theoretical argument for a move from social structures to social embeddedness in the study of professions; we learn more about the social formation of a profession from understanding its interaction with various social institutions than by limiting our analyses to its formal links to the state or the market.

Beyond contributing to an increasingly nuanced understanding of professionalization, greater attention to the social embeddedness and identity formation of professions cultivates a critical reflection upon the historicity of our theories of the professions. The salience of race, ethnicity, and gender from these perspectives forces upon us the obvious question of why these categories have been overlooked in theories of the professions. We thus are led to join and further earlier critiques of the theoretical malaise of Anglo-American ethnocentrism (Jarausch 1990; McClelland 1991). Burrage pointed out that until very recently, "most of them [British and American sociologists of professions] . . . were at their most insular or ethnocentric in these discussions, with never a glance to determine in what ways their own professions might be peculiar, never a hint that in order to explain the development or to construct generalizations about their own professions they might require comparative evidence from outside the English-speaking world" (1990: 4). In the last decade, a burgeoning number of historically sensitive and comparatively oriented studies have played an important role in bringing "the private Anglo-American discussion of the professions to an end" (p. 13). Thanks to these efforts, sociologists of professions are finally abandoning the assumption that "one can write about the institutions of one modern, capitalist society, about Britain, or France, or the United States, as though it was typical, more or less, of all the rest" (p. 20).

Critical reconsiderations of the marginalization of race, ethnicity, and gender push us to broaden this effort and take us beyond the West, where we must begin to interrogate how the genesis of modern professions is often embedded in the forces of colonialism. In these contexts, the professions are often explicit advocates and tools of certain racial and colonial ideologies. They are routinely instrumentalized by the colonial forces to help consolidate the racial hierarchies between whites and natives (Arnold 1993; Manderson 1996) and to control and contain the body and mind of the racial "Other" (Lo 2002; Stoler 1989). Because the professions are employed to service particular racist ideologies, the natives who are incorporated into the professions experience race and ethnicity as central dilemmas in their social existence (Fanon 1967).

Rather than dismissing the intersections of professionalization and colonialism as "mere histories" and therefore not very important, Western sociologists of professions can benefit from facing our ignorance about the rest of the world and considering how that ignorance qualifies the generalizability of our theories. By so doing, we may finally, to paraphrase Burrage, bring the private American-European discussions of the professions to an end. As one cannot escape the centrality of race and ethnicity in the social formation of professions under colonialism, such considerations can formulate a comparative question about the relationships of racism and professionalization elsewhere. Studies of the colonial experiences sensitize us to, and help us formulate questions about, the roles of professions in defining and oppressing the racial "Other" at home.[13] Much like the ways in which feminist scholarship has helped sociologists to see the need to "gender the agents" of professionalization (Witz 1992: 39), so can the previously understudied formations of colonial professions help "racialize the agents." To be sure, the focus on race, ethnicity, and gender in our current intellectual moment is brought about by the ways in which we position ourselves in certain histories of exclusion and moments of articulation. The awareness of the historicity of our own scholarship encourages us to continually investigate the complexity of the social embeddedness of professions, as other suppressed categories become thematized.

"The Rationality of Caring"

The social embeddedness of professions brings into sharp relief the connections between the scientific and the social. While professional solutions to human problems are claimed to be grounded in science, we must seek to better understand how they are shaped by and delivered through webs of social relationships. Students of professions, then, again need to separate their sociological insights from another dominant misconception held by the professions themselves—namely, an overemphasis on the technicality of

---

13. Colonial and post-colonial experiences may sometimes directly shape professional development in the metropole. For example, in my own fieldwork, I encountered some refugee children from Vietnam and Laos who came to the United States as "boat people." They have grown up to become social workers, nurses, and mental health professionals who are particularly dedicated to serving their ethnic communities and advocating for a culturally sensitive professionalism. In this case, the racial "Others" speak to the inadequacy of a race-blind professionalism not as passive victims but as active agents of the professions.

professional judgment and the impersonality of professional performance. Ultimately, this distinction exposes a hidden irony in the social formation of the professions: the institutionalized separation between relationality and rationality.

The social embeddedness of professions challenges us to properly situate institutionalized expert knowledge in broader contexts. More specifically, sociologists of professions are charged with the task to better understand the social context that sustains the authority of knowledge. Larson's pioneering work on this front provided an informative illustration of how the authority of knowledge depends on the existence of a lay public:

> The link between higher education and the social division of labor that we call "profession" has become, at least in capitalist societies, an almost ubiquitous way of *constituting expertise*—that is, creating, organizing, representing to both actors and spectators (or practitioners and clients) that here, vested in a person identified by particular badges, there is available specialized knowledge superior to that of other persons, who may well be even more knowledgeable and well-trained *but in other domains.* In fact, this way of constituting expertise presupposes the parallel constitution of *a lay public,* which cannot be composed of just anybody: lay men and women must have in common with the experts the knowledge that allows them to understand the marks of expertise, that is, the social/cognitive map on which the experts' "superiority" has been placed, or the code within which expertise must be attributed. . . . Lay men and women partake in their society's understanding of transgression, of reason and insanity (1990: 36; emphasis in original).

The emphasis on a lay public prompts us to engage in serious investigations of the social construction of expertise. Larson's perspective bridges studies of professions with the sociology of knowledge and, in so doing, brings into focus the role of professional encounters in maintaining the boundaries of expertise.

Although Larson's theoretical point is well taken, few empirical works have been produced in this area.[14] Perhaps such research is scarce because this new perspective radically debunks the professions' dominant belief about their own authority. Rather than regarding their authority as dependent upon the acquiescence of a lay public, professions vest their legitimacy primarily in an allegedly scientific, objective, and consequently unquestionable knowledge base. They are therefore inclined to position the institution

14. Abbott (1988) is a delightful exception to this observation.

of knowledge production at the core of the profession, from which the realm of practice is conceptualized as a derivative.[15] As social institutions, the professions subordinate the experiential to the theoretical and view their relationships with nonexperts as mostly inconsequential to the authority of knowledge. They share a tendency to "de-authorize non-expert speakers even when the issue at hand regards them . . . [which leads to] technocratic solutions of potentially political conflicts" (Larson 1990: 40). Any challenge to this construction of the professions-laity relationship threatens to "[transform] the boundaries of the discursive field" and thus tends "to be fueled and expanded from the outside or from the margins, by both unauthorized speakers and experts who abandon the professional mode" (p. 40). In short, professional authority as conceived by the professions is sustained by a particular construction of the professions-laity relationship, which, naturalized by the professions themselves, is to be problematized by sociologists.

Steven Epstein's voluminous study of AIDS activism offered a rare and valuable empirical examination of the politics of the professions-laity relationship as he investigated what happened when "the normal flow of trust and credibility between experts and laypeople [had] been disrupted" (1996: 17). Epstein studied the process of "knowledge-making from below" in a situation where AIDS activists, typically well educated, affluent, and young, took it upon themselves to become literate in the discussion of biomedical knowledge and thereby build for themselves a basis for questioning the experts' classifications, judgments, and truth claims. They brought the patients' experiences to bear upon the caretakers' theories, showing that professional judgment was but one possible informed decision, neither scientifically inevitable nor always socially responsible. As an unusual case in which the lay public challenged the neutrality of professional knowledge, Epstein's study illustrated both the difficulty and the importance for clients to enter into a meaningful discussion with professionals. Without denying the tenacious grip of institutionalized expertise, sociologists nevertheless have to acknowledge the leap required to reach certain judgments presented as scientific truth, as well as to confront the politics involved in the construction of its authority.

The critical consideration of the professions' truth claims is not meant to

15. Larson elaborated upon the ways in which the order of the "discursive field" of a profession is maintained: "The first and basic principle is the protection of something equivalent to what Bourdieu calls the doxa of scientific fields: the epistemological system by which claims to truth are recognized and validated. . . . A second principle is attached to the basic interdiction: the norm of containing controversy within the field. . . . The third principle is . . . the defense of professional authority" (1990: 39).

relativize all "truths"; most of us probably would not want to diagnose our own symptoms even if we understood how our doctors' authority was socially constructed. Rather, the de-naturalization of professional truth claims reminds us that based upon their institutionalized knowledge, professionals make judgments and that these judgments will be sounder with a greater level of inclusion of the perspectives of the concerned laity. Indeed, professionals distinguish themselves from technicians by, among other things, their command over a complex body of knowledge that cannot be standardized and therefore necessitates the exercise of discretion (Freidson 2001). This discretion, I argue, should be based upon not only the professionals' mastery of theory and accumulation of experience, but also a greater understanding and appreciation of the perspectives of the people to whom professional service is delivered.

The de-naturalization of professional authority further transforms our conceptualization of professional encounters. Taking a largely profession-centered perspective to understand professional encounters, current professional ideals and sociological theories undermine the importance of the active participation of patients, clients, or other service recipients. The relationships between professionals and their service recipients (individual-level encounters) and by extension communities (group-level encounters) are thus often ignored and understudied. But just as the authority of professional judgment depends on the existence of a lay public, the professionals' "autonomous" performance by necessity requires their service recipients to conform to a particular mode of encounter that is characterized by the features of impartiality and impersonality:

> The professional encounter . . . turns out to encompass . . . the features of impartiality and impersonality. . . . What is apparently attention to the fullest circumstances of the client/case, is in practice a sifting of information in terms of a diagnostic model using categories of action that fit established competencies. In terms of impersonality, there are often rules of eligibility to receive services that operate at a distance from the professional encounter itself and ensure that skills can be employed in an impersonal way. The portrayal of a professional concern, the proper "bedside manner" of the doctor, for example, keeps emotion at a distance. . . . *Professionals offer a detached "understanding" when clients, in what can be a highly charged context, frequently apologize for their fears and their tears* (C. Davies 1996: 67; my emphasis).

For professionals to sustain their understanding of a *relational* encounter as an *autonomous* performance, their clients, patients, or other service recipients have to cooperate in the marginalization of their own agency. After all, professionals can offer their detached understanding only "when clients . . . apologize for their fears and their tears." To de-naturalize this particular mode of professional encounter is not to devalue professional distance; it does not mean that we prefer our doctors to break down in tears when providing treatment. Rather, it encourages the perspective that proper professional distance is to be negotiated in concrete, specific professions-laity interaction and may be defined differently across different social and cultural contexts and shaped by the class, education, and cultural differences between the two sides. Furthermore, a relational understanding of professional encounters serves to sensitize us to the political implications therein. For example, scholarly attention to the relationships between the medical community and particular groups educated us about the medical treatment and mistreatment of African American communities or the difficult struggles of AIDS activists to inform the medical community of their firsthand experiences. Armed with a relational perspective, we thus open up questions about the possibilities of varying patterns of professions-laity interaction and the sociological meanings of such possibilities, underscoring the understanding that historical legacies and cultural differences are far from irrelevant to rational and scientific professional practices.

At a more macro level, as we restore the relational aspects in professional performance, we bring to the fore a hidden irony in the social formation of the professions. The professions, allegedly the institutional agents that serve and care for our needs, have institutionalized an impoverished notion of caring that is based on the separation of emotions and rationality. As feminist scholars have extensively documented, the historical juncture of masculinization and professionalization is largely responsible for this institutional development. For example, medical practices were "relocated" from a predominantly domestic and community arena to a predominantly market arena in the nineteenth and twentieth centuries. Meanwhile, men dominated in the institutions of the state and civil society that would regulate medical practices in the market arena. Caring was therefore de-feminized during this move, transformed from an act based on emotions and experiences to a trade enabled by knowledge and science (Witz 1992; see also Starr 1982). The gendered nature of the separation of the public and the private leaves an enduring legacy in the institutionalized dichotomy of emotions and rationality. Occupations that cannot completely institutionalize this dichotomy—that is, the caring professions—are in turn considered less than fully professionalized and awarded fewer material gains and less public respect.[16]

---

16. Although not explicitly discussing the issue of the caring professions, Sydney Halpern offered a similar observation. She situated pediatrics in the tradition of "social-problem based medical spe-

A serious consideration of the caring professions turns the question of professionalization on its head, however. Whereas the caring professions appear to be stumbling on their path to full professionalization, their difficulties raise questions about how well the model of professionalism can accommodate the act of caring in its entirety. With her detailed case study of nursing in Great Britain, Celia Davies confronted this very tension between professionalism and caring: "The vocabulary of professionalism . . . leave[s] no space to discuss the contradiction of care, and the paradox of daily experience" (1995: 145). More specifically, "emotional commitment to patients, caring about the outcomes, building a relationship so as to learn more about the person and hence adjust the environment" are repeated themes in nurses' daily experiences (p. 146), yet these elements are conceptualized as precisely those "irrational" elements that an occupation is to leave behind on its path toward professionalization.[17] Nursing, therefore, embodies the very irony of a professionalism that severs emotion from rationality. Yet instead of an analysis of how nursing can strive to conform to the model of professionalism, perhaps a more appropriate question is how sociologists can work the fertile ground of the experience of nurses and other caring professionals and in so doing reconsider the ideals of professionalism.

Celia Davies's empirical study offers a promising point of departure. Building upon existing feminist scholarship, Davies developed a new notion of professionalism:

> Waerness identifies the limited nature of scientific rationality and its embeddedness in a masculinist thinking that stresses a cognitive solution to problems via mastery of knowledge and control of its application. From this perspective, it is possible to begin to lay bare what she calls a "rationality of caring," an approach that is not driven by blind emotion and sentiment, but which has a describable logic of its own. . . . [*It means*] *accepting that emotions and commitments are part and parcel of the process of effective caregiving and recognizing that flexibility, adaptability and hence uncertainty are entailed by this work* (1995: 144; my emphasis).

---

cialties including psychiatry, public health, and obstetrics" and considered the differences between the segments of the profession that are more concerned with social problems and those devoted to the advancement of science (1988: 10–11). Halpern described these "social-problem based" segments of the profession as having common features, such as an association with reform movements, state sponsorship, lower income and status, and a larger proportion of female members.

17. Susan Reverby makes a similar observation in her now classic study of American nursing: "because of some deep understandings of the limited promise of equality and autonomy in a health-care system they see as flawed and harmful . . . nurses recognize that those who claim the autonomy of rights often run the risk of rejecting altruism and caring itself" (1987: 207).

Bringing this notion of the "rationality of caring" to bear upon Freidson's and others' theory of professionalism, we may redefine the meaning of professional discretion. As it is currently conceptualized, professional discretion gains its legitimacy from the professional's ability to command and apply knowledge as he or she sees fit in particular contexts. We may develop a richer conceptualization, informed by the "rationality of caring," by incorporating the elements of caring, commitment, and relationships with the clients into the basis of professional discretion.

One cautionary note needs to be added to the feminist intervention. Feminist scholarship critically examined the process in which, as professions became institutionalized, certain qualities were "weeded out" and simultaneously coded as "feminine." When seeking to restore some of these qualities to the ideal of professionalism, feminist scholars sometimes risk singularizing and essentializing their notions of femininity/masculinity, inadvertently taking what has been constructed as "feminine" and "masculine" as a given.[18] But we can hope for a new professionalism that is freer of gender biases if we are reminded that there are multiple types of femininity and masculinity. Our attempt is not to feminize the notion of professionalism, nor is it to simply address the issue of the exclusion of women.[19] Rather, we hope to move beyond the gendered division between the professional and the relational and thereby develop a vision of caring that grounds rationality in relationality. The professions, as well as the communities they serve, may all benefit from such a vision.

Conclusion

In this chapter, I have reviewed two decades of major writings in the sociology of professions through a discussion of how they are primarily informed by a modernist framework yet ultimately begin to push beyond the modernity/tradition divide. The best examples in the sociology of professions, influenced by the second wavers' concern with the formal structures of political economy, address with great sensitivity the complex structural intersections of professions with other modern social institutions. These

18. For example, Davies (1996) conceptualized professionalism as a masculine project.
19. Reverby very appropriately cautions us against any simplistic reading of women's oppression in the struggles of professionalization: "Nurses are neither the poor victims of hospital and physicians' oppression and the impotent descendants of a long line of women healers, nor the victors in a difficult and long struggle to gain professional recognition and status. Their history is more complicated than such simplistic analyses, built on either anger or romanticism. . . . Nursing's history provides us with a specific example of a group of women so divided by class that their common oppression based on gender could not unite them" (1987: 6).

works, although motivated by a modernist framework, become very informative about the messiness of modernity and inadvertently challenge us to
move our focus from social structure to social embeddedness.

The challenge pushes us to situate professions not only in an intricate web
of relationships with the state and the market, but also at the intersection
with social categories located on the other side of the modernity/tradition
divide, such as race, ethnicity, and gender, which were previously deemed
irrelevant to the social formation of professions. This move contributes to
the revision of the modernist frame in two senses. First, a fuller understanding of professionals' social embeddedness highlights the mutual composition of professional identity and "primordial" categories. Rather than assuming that particularistic identities will dissolve in the modern institution
of professionalism, I suggest that we recognize professions as sites of identity
formation, where professionals come to terms with the meaning of their
racial, ethnic, and/or gender identities in the context of their professional
institution.

Second, to focus on the mutual composition of the profession and race,
ethnicity, and/or gender demands a more nuanced understanding of the
historicity of our own theories of professions. For example, treating race
seriously in the story of professionalization demands we consider the intertwined histories of colonialism and professionalism in those parts of the
world labeled as non-Western. There the promise of modernity vested in the
professions appears more violent, more visibly tainted with certain racial
and colonial ideologies, and therefore more in need of qualification. Further
research in this direction will help us attain a greater sense of historicity
about our theories of professions, which are primarily grounded in Western
cases, and better recognition of their particularistic roots.

Ultimately, the social embeddedness of professions centralizes the connections between the scientific and the social. This understanding points to
the need—and offers a starting point—for further research in how professional authority is dependent on a specific professionals-laity relationship,
and how the marginalization of the relational aspects in professional performance perpetuates an impoverished notion of caring. Critiques of the
modernity of professions bear the promise for generating a vocabulary for
post-modern professionalism that allows for greater integration of scientific
knowledge and client perspectives, of professional practices and cultural
sensitivity, and, ultimately, of the rationality of caring and the concrete
relationship in which the caring takes place.

We may be witnessing the beginning of another paradigm shift in the study
of professions, and if this is so, the transition has a larger significance in that

it may form the basis for a renewed dialogue with historical sociology. The new paradigm shares with the third wavers in historical sociology many similar theoretical innovations—in the emphasis on social embeddedness over social structures, in the move to agency and identity, and in the inclusion of the voices of the non-West. But if our field has been striving not only to attend to the experiences of the periphery, but in effect also to, with our broadened perspective, revise the theories that have been produced at the center, then the marginalized place of the professions in historical sociology also can make a special contribution. Studies of the old topic of professions place qualifications on the newness of the third wave in suggesting perhaps greater continuities among the different waves. As the theoretical cultural turns in historical sociology seem to parallel, to some extent, an empirical subaltern turn that brings increasing attention to gender, emotion, religion, nation, and other previously ignored topics, we will benefit from a reminder that these new theoretical insights are equally relevant for older topics that are defined in terms of formal organizations. In this sense, the thesis of the social embeddedness of professions cautions us against the danger of decoupling second-wave topics from third-wave theories and instead suggests a more ambitious vision for the explanatory power of our new insights.

LYN SPILLMAN AND RUSSELL FAEGES

Nations

.

Nations are one of the most pervasive forms of modern social organization. "Nation-states" are normative in global politics, while "national" frames of reference shape routine domestic politics, as well as some of the most successful social movements of the last century. To the large extent that class and market relations are conditioned by political institutions, nations also structure economic action. Culturally, nationality remains an important dimension of identity formation and a common—although often unmarked—backdrop to most forms of discourse and practice, including a wide range of specialized cultural production processes from scholarship to mass media. In all these spheres, both conflict and consensus are organized primarily in national terms.

Sociology, too, is modern, formed to address issues generated by the emergence and spread of large-scale social differentiation, capitalist economic relations, and rationalization. Yet, paradoxically, scholarship on nations and nationalism has not been central to sociology, in comparison to work on topics such as inequality or deviance or religion. Even in comparative-historical sociology, scholarship on nations and nationalism is thin compared to work on topics such as class, the state, or revolution. Given the centrality of nations to modernity, and especially given comparative-historical sociology's focus on issues of long-term social change and large-

Special thanks to the editors of this volume and to the contributors for stimulating discussions in the course of its development. We also acknowledge the contributions of Reinhard Bendix, Victoria Bonnell, David Collier, Ernst Haas, Bill Kornhauser, Neil Smelser, and Kim Voss to the development of our thinking on this topic. Some of the work on this chapter was supported by a Guggenheim Fellowship and the Sociology Department, University of Arizona.

scale social organization, this absence is startling.[1] Meanwhile, students of nationalism confront an increasingly rich but chronically chaotic literature in which historians, political scientists, anthropologists, and humanists, but rarely comparative-historical sociologists, have made major contributions. The pertinent question here is what, if anything, the field's particular theoretical concerns and methodological sensibilities can contribute to understanding nations and nationalism.

We argue, first, that the general literature on nationalism is amorphous because of theoretical under-determination and definitional proliferation: even the delineation of the topic is constantly at issue. As a result, scholars talk past each other. Comparative-historical sociologists could address this problem but have not done so. Second, we discuss an unrecognized "canon" of works on nations and nationalism within the subdiscipline that offers important resources for a more sustained research program, although these contributions are disconnected, and without an explicit, common ground of discussion. Finally, we build on these arguments to formulate an agenda that brings the problem of the nation to the center of a revitalized comparative-historical sociology.

We suggest a new way of theorizing nations as political collective identities that can synthesize many of the insights generated in what the editors of this volume have identified as the first and second waves of comparative-historical sociology, and we also clarify contributions in what might be emerging as a third wave. This view draws on recent cultural sociology for conceptual resources to theorize collective identity by characterizing the nation as a discursive field. In addition to synthesizing previous contributions, it suggests two important avenues for future work. First, it suggests that competing theories of collective identity—grounded in "reflection" theories of culture, or rational choice—should generate different empirical predictions about nations and nationalism, providing a basis for fruitful dialogue. Second, it suggests a theoretical basis for linking work on nations to work on other forms of mobilizable collective identity, such as gender, class, and religion, generating an important new set of comparative questions.

Orienting Questions

Definitional proliferation plagues attempts to delimit the topic of nationalism. However, as a general guideline we specify here the sort of orienting

1. Anthony Smith noted that "sociologists from Comte to Marx to Parsons to Dahrendorf have neglected nationalism" (1983 [1971]: 3), and their relative contribution since has remained modest. Smith's own work is the important exception (e.g., 1986, 1998); see also *http://www.lse.ac.uk/collections/ASEN/* and, more generally, the journal *Nations and Nationalism*.

questions that concern those who study it. Many scholars, especially among social scientists, are most concerned with nationalism as political mobilization. They examine the nature, types, and causes of political projects that promote or entail the direct linkage of political authorities with groups of people sharing some distinguishing label. Both social movements and states are important actors in such political mobilizations. Scholars taking this line may emphasize state formation, societal modernization (division of labor, capitalism, rationalization), or inter-state relations as driving forces behind nationalism.

Other scholars, concerned with nations—nationalities, nation formation—as collective identities (analogous to religion, region, clan, or race), ask questions about collective identity formation, why and how collectivities come to think of themselves as "a people," how such identities differ from analogous collective identities, and how and why they differ from each other. Some accounts treat the formation of national identities as a direct reflection of changes in authority structures, mobilization, or industrialization. Other accounts emphasize the significance of pre-modern collective identities for nation formation. Still others suggest that the existence and nature of collective identities depend on processes of cultural production with their own dynamics, which may be either pre-modern or modern.

Theoretical Under-Determination and Definitional Proliferation

Any review of scholarship on nations and nationalism reveals not only ambiguity, but also ambivalence about its subject and disagreement about who does nations and when and how they happen. Often, however, competing positions on these questions are not really in competition, and there are no consensual criteria for judging them. This confusion is not due to any intrinsic feature of the topic itself but to two related problems of conceptualization. First, the classical social theorists provide too little guidance for theorizing nations and nationalism. We discuss this problem because a number of divergent leads drawn from these theorists have influenced the nationalism literature and because of their particularly strong influence in shaping comparative-historical sociology. Second, the general literature on nations and nationalism is afflicted by anarchic definitional proliferation of a sort that has been characterized as "vexing" (Weber), "stultifying" (Geertz), "tendentious" (Tilly), and "notorious" (Anthony Smith). We discuss this issue because of the rich, although confused, resources that this literature offers to comparative-historical sociologists. The common element linking these two problems is theoretical underdetermination.

Theoretical Underdetermination

Nations were not what philosophers of history call "central subjects" for the classical social theorists, nor did "the nation" play any significant role in their theoretical architectonics (P. James 1996). For Marxists, nations quickly became problematic. Durkheimian and Weberian ideas, by contrast, tended to leave nations theoretically unmarked, infusing them with a taken-for-granted quality, despite the grand historical and comparative sensibilities behind their social theories.

Marx's and Engels's scattered remarks took for granted the existence of "communities of 'language and natural sympathies,'" and they saw "the term 'nation' as equally applicable to polities from the Phoenicians to the Germans" (Anthony Smith 1998: 47; P. James 1996: 59). Some nationalisms could be progressive, but others were retrograde or irrelevant—indeed, some "historyless" peoples were destined to become, in Engels's sharp phrase, "ethnographic monuments" (cited in Anthony Smith 1983 [1971]: 73). Political actions, certainly those of the proletariat, would be less and less oriented by national identity; in the broad brush strokes of the "Manifesto," "modern industrial labour, modern subjection to capital, the same in England as in France, in America as in Germany, has stripped [the worker] of every trace of national character" (K. Marx and Engels 1978: 482).[2]

Marx's heirs found the national question more compelling; indeed, Anthony Smith suggested that the debates of Kautsky, Luxemburg, Bauer, and Lenin were the "most consistently sociological of the attempts to explain nationalism until the present decade" (1983 [1971]: 257). In the face of rising nationalism Luxemburg rejected concessions to nationality, versus class, as retrograde; Bauer saw nations as objectively given "communities of fate" and favored "national-cultural autonomy"; and Lenin saw federation as necessary to accommodate the reality of nations in the capitalist epoch but resolutely rejected "the principle of federation" in future communism. Lenin also attacked Kautsky's theory of "ultra-imperialism" (which hypothesized the imperialists of all nations uniting), because it broke a purported link between capitalism and nationalism and would delay the time when global revolution might be expected. Although the immediate political issues at stake in these debates are dated, the theoretical positions they generate still resonate in many ways with contemporary globalization debates (Breuilly 1993 [1982]: 40–41; Lenin 1980: 205–259; Nimni 1991: 119–84). Most influen-

2. On connections between class and nationalism, see Breuilly (1993 [1982]: 407–411). Scholars have explored Marx and Engels' treatment of nationalism for a century; for some recent accounts see E. Brenner (1995); Cummins (1980); P. James (1996: ch 3); Nimni (1991); Anthony Smith (1998: 11).

tial in the twentieth century, however, was a theory of anti-colonial nationalism deriving from the neo-Marxist theory of imperialism. Anti-colonial
nationalism was analogous to class conflict because of uneven capitalist
development, with the periphery playing proletariat to the center's bourgeoisie, and thus Marxism was associated with national liberation. The theoretical connection between uneven capitalist development and nationalism
remained an important influence in twentieth-century scholarship on the
topic (Lenin 1975: 204–274; see also Breuilly 1993 [1982]: ch. 7; Hechter 1999;
Nairn 1977; Anthony Smith 1983 [1971]: 65–85; 1998: 49–60).

Durkheim, too, neglected nationalism, but his sociology provides a coherent approach to its study. Empirical nations can be understood as occupy-
ing the middle reaches of a continuum defined by Durkheim's ideal-typical
models of segmented and organized society. Development of a segmented
society erodes differences and boundaries among its component segments,
while, reciprocally, increasing individuation within an increasing division of
labor will spread across the increasingly ghostly boundaries of increasingly
vestigial segments (Durkheim 1984: 127–139; Faeges 2001b). The result, empirically, is a sequence of increasingly larger societies—clan/tribal, local-
territorial, regional, national, supra-national, and, perhaps, global. For example, this process first produced, then eroded, distinctly Norman, Proven-
cal, and other such societies: "the Norman is less different [than earlier] from
the Gascon, and the Gascon from the Lorainer. . . . All share hardly more than
the characteristics common to all Frenchmen. But the diversity that Frenchmen exhibit as a whole had continually increased." But the national scale of
social organization is no more privileged than the regional, and "there is
tending to form . . . a European society that has even now some feeling of its
own identity and the beginnings of an organization." The ultimate implication is a single, global society, but Durkheim balked at this conclusion, saying
only that "there is nothing that demonstrates that the intellectual and moral
diversity of societies is destined to continue" (Durkheim 1984: 91, 337, 341 n.
6). Parallel to his understanding of nation-level social structures in terms of
his theory of social differentiation, Durkheim provided tools for understanding national identities in terms of his general theory of collective identity, symbolic representation, and ritual, worked out in *Elementary Forms*
through the study of religion in a segmented society: "What basic difference is
there between Christians' celebrating the principal dates of Christ's life . . .
and a citizens' meeting commemorating the advent of a new moral charter or
some other great event of national life?" (Durkheim 1995 [1915]: 429).[3]

3. Durkheim underemphasizes the relevance of "the Other"—in boundary formation and conflict—
for constructions of nationality, although he did note this mechanism elsewhere (P. James 1996: 86; cf.

Regardless of the degree to which analysts accept the grand narrative of modernity's organic differentiation, Durkheimian themes have persistently re-emerged in work on nationalism, from studies of modernization in the 1950s to recent theories such as Gellner's. Durkheim's theorization of the cultural mechanisms of collective identity formation has until recently been less influential but had an impact on studies of "political religion" (Apter 1968: 193–232; Deutsch 1966 [1953]; Gellner 1983).

Weber engaged nationalism more directly than either Marx or Durkheim, although he died before he could complete his intended work on the subject. The work that he completed turns on one of the enduring problems in the literature: the relationship among nationalism, ethnicity, and the state. On the one hand, Weber saw a family resemblance between nationality and ethnicity, for both share "the vague connotation that whatever is felt to be distinctively common must derive from common descent." The difference between them is a matter of action orientation. Whereas ethnicity leads to the most diverse types of action, or none at all, Weber saw nationality as distinguished by action oriented to political autonomy, the implication being that nations are politicized ethnic groups (M. Weber 1978, vol. 1: 395; cf. vol. 2: 926). On the other hand, he recognized that there are non-ethnic political communities, such as the Swiss, that are otherwise indistinguishable from ethnic nations, and he was tempted to define nations as political communities, regardless of the subjective basis of their action—indeed, regardless of the objective characteristics that they believe distinguish them from others: "the concept 'nation' seems to refer—if it refers at all to a uniform phenomenon—to a specific kind of pathos which is linked to the idea of a powerful political community of people who share a common language, or religion, or common customs, or political memories; such a state may already exist or it may be desired" (1978, vol. 1: 398). Then, to further complicate his picture of nations and nationalism, Weber also emphasized that patriotic fervor involved "sentiments of prestige" and that status interests motivated nationalism, especially among intellectuals. Moreover, political institutions are "held to have a responsibility of their own for the way in which power and prestige are distributed between their own and foreign polities" (1978, vol. 2: 921–922).[4]

Durkheim 1951: 205–206). He was drawn into propaganda efforts in World War I, although he more typically focused on progressive measures to improve domestic integration (M. M. Mitchell 1931). See also G. H. Mead (1964: 356) on conflict and collective effervescence. This and subsequent passages are partially based on Faeges (2001b, 2001c).

4. Like Durkheim, Weber was drawn into patriotic work in World War I (Beetham 1974: ch. 5; P. James 1996: ch. 4).

Like Durkheim's picture of modernization and collective identity formation, Weberian themes have profoundly shaped subsequent work. Some
theories and debates pursue the issue Weber identified of the complicated
and contingent association of ethnicity and claims for political autonomy.
The significance of international status and the importance of intellectuals
have also been persistent themes. More broadly, the theoretical connection
Weber drew between national identity and political action has become fundamental to the field, whether the political action is that of states, social
movements, or both.

Thus all these classical theorists, so influential in comparative-historical
sociology, spun different threads that have been woven into subsequent
approaches to nationalism, introducing themes of economic development,
social differentiation, collective identity formation, ethnicity, political action, the role of intellectuals, and international status. But Marx, Durkheim,
and Weber did not do the weaving themselves, and their contributions
radically under-determined later work. For instance, as Paul James suggested, "there was no analysis of the national form even distantly comparable to Max Weber's or Emile Durkheim's analyses of religion" (1996: 84–85).
Later work was empirically driven, mostly shaped by shifting contemporary
problems, and widely diverse in topical focus.

Apart from Marx's Second International heirs, the major analysts of nations and nationalism in the first half of the twentieth century were historians. At the beginning of the 1980s, a literature review still included the
work of historians such as Hayes, Snyder, Schafer, Ranum, and especially
Hans Kohn. Their focus was mostly European, and they tended to create
broad typologies with ethical overtones, such as Kohn's influential distinction between "Eastern" and "Western" nationalism. They also developed a
detailed chronology of nationalist ideologies and social movements in Europe, emphasizing the emergence of the first European nation-states, the
French Revolution, and the spread of claims about national identity as the
bases of political legitimacy in Europe in the nineteenth century (Kohn 1955,
1961 [1944]; Royal Institute of International Affairs 1939; cf. Deutsch 1966
[1953]: 7–14; A. W. Marx 2003; Anthony Smith 1998: 16–17).

World War II and the period of decolonization and anti-colonial struggle
that followed generated a new body of work on nations that expanded the
focus of analysis beyond Europe. Understanding nations and nationalism
was a necessary part of understanding and encouraging political development—or, indeed, "nation building." Comparative-historical sociologists
contributed to this literature, but it was, on the whole, an interdisciplinary
project involving primarily political scientists, psychologists, and anthropol-

ogists, as well as sociologists with a more contemporary focus. As would also be true later, specialists in "area studies" of different regions made significant general contributions.[5]

Another interdisciplinary attack on problems of nations and nationalism took shape in the 1980s. Important studies by Benedict Anderson (1991), Armstrong (1982), Billig (1995), Breuilly (1993 [1982]), Chatterjee (1999) Gellner (1983), Hobsbawm (1990), and Anthony Smith (1986), along with earlier work by Connor (1994), Hechter (1999 [1975]), and Nairn (1977), soon became standards in the field. The main "who, what, when, why, how" questions about nation issues are now (variously) framed in terms set by these scholars, in ways that are, on the whole, no longer driven by concerns about "political development." The ways nations and nationalism are related to uneven development and imperialism have been explored in new ways by Anderson, Chatterjee, Hobsbawm, and Nairn; the ways they are related to ethnicity, by Armstrong, Connor, and Smith; connections between political domination and nationalism are Breuilly's focus; and Gellner develops a new theory of nationalism and modernization.[6]

These and other recent writers provide a rich range of new empirical observations and arguments about nations and nationalism. But they differ widely in their disciplinary sensibilities and theoretical starting points, and they often speak past each other. In the most comprehensive recent overview, Anthony Smith concluded that "the field is so riven by basic disagreements and so divided by rival approaches, each of which addresses only one or other aspect of this vast field, that a unified approach must seem quite unrealistic and any general theory merely utopian" (1998: 223). Smith is unusual in even considering the possibility of a general theory, but it does not seem grandiose to hope for mutually intelligible dialogues and debates based on a set of theoretical perspectives whose relationships to each other, whether competing or complementary, would be clearly articulated. To achieve even this modest goal requires that we understand the nature of definitional proliferation.

Definitional Proliferation

Most scholars who have attempted to define nations and nationalism have commented on the difficulty of doing so, from Weber—"the nation, [which

5. See, for example, Almond and Verba (1963); Apter (1968); Eisenstadt (1966); Geertz, ed. (1963); Huntington (1973 [1968]); and the reflections in Pye (1991).
6. Useful collections include Balakrishnan, ed. (1996) and Hutchinson and Smith, eds. (1994). See also bibliographies assembled at *http://www.nationalismproject.org/*.

dissolves] as soon as we attempt a sociological definition" (1978, vol. 1: 395)—to Anthony Smith—"the notorious terminological difficulties in the field, and the failure to reach even a preliminary agreement on the definitions of key concepts" (1998: 221). Indeed, only one of the scholars surveyed for this chapter, Hobsbawm (1990: 9), chose to adopt the definition of another (Gellner), rather than cast his or her own.[7]

The reasons for this situation have been obscured by a tendency to reify nations and nationalism and by a general failure to recognize that definitions are crafted for a variety of purposes, using a variety of strategies. Addressing these causes and moving toward theoretically oriented definitions would greatly reduce the number of definitions aimed at nations and nationalism and would put those remaining into intelligible relationships with each other. The key questions are the following: What information do scholars seek to embody in their definitions, by what methods, and for what purposes? What is at stake when scholars craft, use, and debate definitions?[8]

Many scholars of nationalism have cited dictionary definitions as evidence of national phenomena (e.g., Greenfeld 1992: 31; Hobsbawm 1990: 14). Many have crafted such definitions themselves to explain nationalist discourse (e.g., Breuilly 1993 [1982]: 3; H. Kohn 1961 [1944]: 16). But the use of the term "nation" has varied so greatly that it is impossible to capture its meaning with a simple definition. For instance, Calhoun's investigation of "the rhetoric of nation" led him to assemble a list of ten definitions that together identify "the features of [this] rhetoric [that] seem most important, though none of them is precisely definitive" (1997: 4–5); no one or, indeed, any fixed combination of "features" is necessary and sufficient to explain all uses of the word "nation." The main reason for this variation is the variation in the claims that actors have made using "nation" and related terms, many of which are tactical "attempts to appropriate for one side, and to deny to the other, a potent word" (C. S. Lewis 1987: 19).

Definitions multiply further when they are aimed at the empirical situations that "the rhetoric of nation" purports to describe. For this purpose the proper criterion for judging definitions is, do they fit all and only those collectivities that are designated by ordinary use of "nation"? Regardless of how successful any given dictionary definition is for its intended purpose, it is unlikely to pass this test, for several reasons. According to Gellner (1983: 57), Renan (1994 [1882]), and many others, self-deception is essential to

7. Among the many similar observations are those of B. Anderson (1991: 3); Geertz (in Hutchinson and Smith, eds. 1994: 29); Greenfeld (1992: 7); and Seton-Watson (quoted in B. Anderson 1991: 3).

8. The following discussion draws on Faeges (1999, 2001a), which include more illustration and attention to other diagnoses of the problem and also on a more extended methodological analysis (Faeges n.d.).

nationalist discourse, so an accurate definition of this discourse must be inaccurate empirically; more generally, the use of contested terms to describe empirical situations varies not just with disagreements over their meaning, but also with actors' perceptions and values (Skinner 1989). An even more fundamental problem is that the empirical referents of "nation" are indeterminate and contested. Dictionary definitions of the term "nation" must account for any and all uses of that term, but must a definition aimed at the empirical situations denoted by that term accommodate such critical cases as Switzerland? Some observers have said no (e.g., Lenin 1964: 274), some have said yes (e.g., *Oxford English Dictionary* 1971: 1897), and some are uncertain (e.g., M. Weber 1978, vol. 2: 922).

In response to such situations many scholars resort to stipulative definitions in order to "demonstrate the limits of the field . . . to designate 'nationalist' phenomena, and give the term jurisdictional limits" (Anthony Smith 1983 [1971]: 165). This use of definitions is the opposite of the preceding two strategies. Rather than trying to account for the discourse and empirical referents of ordinary language use of a key term such as "nation," this strategy uses definitions to assemble groups of "comparable facts," because "only comparison affords explanation" (Durkheim 1951: 41). It eliminates the problems of indefinability and definitional proliferation that afflict the previous two strategies. It is also a source of definitional proliferation, but the reasons are different, and it is more manageable.

The stipulative use of definitions accepts that they sort the world differently than does ordinary language. What matters for this strategy is whether "the fact thus defined is of interest to the sociologist" (Durkheim 1951: 46). However, much confusion has occurred because scholars have used "nation" and related terms for a great many different, but closely related, classes of facts. This is not illegitimate, but it results in frequent quibbling, in which "the meaning of a term is changed as it changes hands, with a resultant argumentative distortion" (Fischer 1970: 275).

Is X a nation? Is Y a case of nationalism? Is Z a nation-state? When did nationalism begin? Did nationalism exist before the rise of the modern state? These might seem to be fundamental questions, but too many disputes about the answers have been nothing more than quibbling, because the participants have used different definitions of key terms. This is relatively clear in Anthony Smith's counter to Breuilly's claim that "to focus upon culture, ideology, identity, class or modernization is to neglect the fundamental point that nationalism is, above and beyond all else, about politics" (Breuilly 1993 [1982]: 1–2). According to Smith, "there have been 'pure' cultural nationalists who have either rejected or remained silent about the state and the need to capture state power. Breuilly consistently denies to such ideologies and movements the label 'nationalist'" (1998: 90). Note the phrase "the label 'nationalist.'" This dispute is terminological; it concerns the tactical use of a definition (C. S. Lewis 1987) rather than the theoretic or empirical relationships between movements that have labeled themselves with the "nationalist" label—or rejected it—and the definitions of the various scholars who say something about these movements. Some scholars do note the terminological nature of many of the debates in literature on nations (e.g., Greenfeld 1992: 8–9; E. Haas 1997: 23 n. 1), and some change terms to promote clarity (e.g., Anthony Smith 1983 [1971]: 167–168; B. Anderson 1991: 4), but this sort of clarity is rare.

This leaves theoretical under-determination as a cause of definitional proliferation. Theory-driven definition will not eliminate multiple definitions, but it will do two things. First, it will reduce the number of definitions relative to the eclectic and ad hoc strategies of definition that currently dominate the study of nations. Second, theory-driven definitions can be the subject of dialogue and debate in a way that eclectic and ad hoc definitions cannot. For example, Engels and Weber offered different definitions of "the state." Neither accounts for ordinary language, but both are correct, each within its own theoretic context, and they can be compared on that basis, which is a difference in theorization of the legitimacy of political violence. Similarly, Darwin's theory of natural selection indicated the relationship among the many different things that naturalists had defined under the label "species" (resemblance, sterility, descent, creation), such that most of those definitions were complementary, not competitors.

In the light of this analysis we suggest a turn away from attempts to define ordinary language use of "nation" and related terms and away from quibbles about their use as labels. Instead, for the purposes of this volume we suggest a turn in favor of theory-driven questions about the bases of political community. Such a turn directs renewed attention to theories of collective identity in relation to theories of political mobilization. It casts new light on the classical sociologists' under-determination of the study of nations—Marx and Weber, whose focus on subordinate economic groups and ethnic groups, respectively, were too narrow in their understanding of collective identity formation, while Durkheim's general theory of collective identity formation lacked a complementary theory of politics. And it suggests a way of making sense of the large body of knowledge that has accumulated on nation formation.

Comparative-historical sociology, as constituted in the United States since the 1950s, has emphasized the investigation of theory-driven questions about macro-social phenomena in historically sensitive and methodologically self-conscious ways. This work could contribute substantially to the construction of theory-driven understandings of nations and nationalism. In the next section we discuss some particular contributions of scholars working in American comparative-historical sociology who, while primarily concerned with broader issues of large-scale and long-term social change, have focused their attention on nations as significant forms of social organization. We examine these contributions for what they say about processes of collective identity formation that are analytically distinguishable from yet enmeshed with political processes. We then return to the issue of deriving theory-driven definitions of nations.

Comparative-Historical Sociology and the Nation

Communication and Authority

Nations interested American social scientists most deeply in the 1950s and early 1960s, when decolonization rapidly formed new states, to which the cold war gave domestic importance. In this context, cross-national studies of political change, economic development, and cultural modernization were valued. A rich array of empirical studies, including many of the main contributions to understanding nations from comparative-historical sociology, were developed to understand the conditions under which stable nation-states were formed.[9]

The works of Deutsch, Bendix, Lipset, and Znaniecki illustrate some of the key concerns of this "first wave." These works differ significantly in empirical focus, theoretical emphasis, and methodological approach, but they share two notable features. First, these works, and many others they represent, explicitly addressed contemporary nation formation and political development (e.g., Bendix 1977 [1964]: 1; Deutsch 1966 [1953]: 4; Lipset 1963: 2). Second, and less well recognized, these studies opposed modernization theory's supposed over-generalizations about historical development, value consensus, and so on. This is most evident in Bendix's work, especially "Tradition and Modernity Reconsidered" (1967), which made many of the points made anew by critics of modernist paradigms in the 1990s. But others are similarly circumspect. Deutsch presented a general approach for analyzing tendencies toward national integration or disintegration, but for him this theory helped identify factors to examine only "for each particular

---

9. On the related tradition of historically situated cross-national comparisons of aggregate individual values and attitudes, see, for example, Inkeles (1997); Inkeles and Smith (1974); Sasaki, ed. (1998); Schooler (1996); and more generally M. Kohn (1987).

situation" (1966 [1953]: 117; see also R. Collins 1973 [1968]: 42–67; Lipset 1963: 10; cf. C. Taylor 1999).

Deutsch's theory of the nation is essentially a theory of collective identity formation built on Durkheimian insights. For him, existing scholarship did not explain "why nationalist ideas met with wide and strong response at certain times and places, and with almost no response at others" and did not account for "just what makes a 'common' condition or experience"—such as history, language, or territory—"effectively common," since all could be interpreted differently (1966 [1953]: v, 19; cf. 27). Mining the social science literature and introducing concepts from communications engineering, Deutsch developed a "functional definition of nationality"; "membership in a people essentially consists in wide complementarity of social communication. It consists in the ability to communicate more effectively, and over a wider range of subjects, with members of one large group than with outsiders. This overall result can be achieved by a variety of functionally equivalent arrangements" (p. 97). Collective identity, then, is generated to the degree that lines of communication are dense, open, and complementary. What this means in modern stratified societies is that nationality is "an alignment of large numbers of individuals from the middle and lower classes linked to regional centers and leading social groups by channels of social communication and economic intercourse, both indirectly from link to link and directly with the center" (p. 101). A politicized nationality is a nation, and a successful nation becomes a nation-state (p. 105). No step in this development is historically necessary, but theorizing nationalism as fundamentally a matter of communications channels provides empirical leverage for understanding a wide variety of cases and offers numerous opportunities for measurement, an important goal of the study.

The theory extends Durkheim's approach to social integration in several ways. For instance, while an increasing division of labor will increase the population potentially "mobilizable" for nationality, this population can differ from the "assimilable" population if channels of communication are historically differentiated or weak (Deutsch 1966 [1953]: 128–130). Stratification and inequality are incorporated into the theory because they block communication and so limit national integration. And, Deutsch concluded emphatically, uneven development will determine the future of nationalism: "*not before the vast poverty of Asia and Africa will have been reduced . . . will the age of nationalism and national diversity see the beginning of its end*" (p. 191; emphasis in original).

Deutsch's theory also displays Durkheimian limitations. Political institutions and processes are epiphenomenal to nation formation, because political domination and legitimacy are conditioned by patterns of communication (1966 [1953]: 77–79). Meanings associated with nations are also epiphenomenal: "national consciousness . . . is the attachment of secondary symbols of nationality to primary items of information moving through channels of social communication . . . not just people, but 'our people' and 'the American people' " (p. 172). And, yet, the study suggested that a theory omitting politics and meaning would be inadequate for understanding national forms of collective identity. For instance, cases of "extreme nationalism"—of which, for Deutsch, Nazi Germany was only the most obvious case—occur when channels of communication are closed or perverted "in an extreme attempt to preserve unchanged a people with its institutions and policies" (p. 184). But who closes or perverts channels of communication, and why, cannot be addressed within this theory. Certainly, in providing a broad general theory, Deutsch need not address those who would wish to understand in more detail, for instance, how assimilated Jews came to be excluded from the German nation. But this inattention to processes of active exclusion ultimately suggested that inattention to politics and meaning-making also limited the adequacy of his theory of nations in less "extreme" cases.[10]

In contrast to Deutsch's implicitly Durkheimian perspective on nations, Bendix's is explicitly Weberian. For Bendix, nations were significant insofar as they expressed and legitimated authority relations that contrasted with aristocratic and monarchical rule—"the central fact of nation-building is the orderly exercise of a nationwide, public authority"—and he was mostly concerned with the contingent outcomes of tensions between authorities and publics inherent in "the formation and transformation of political communities which today we call nation-states" (1977 [1964]: 22). For instance, he claimed that "during the nineteenth century nationalism was so powerful in part because it could appeal directly to this longing of the common people for civic respectability, a longing . . . intensified by acute awareness of development in other countries" (p. 426).[11]

Unlike Deutsch, Bendix stressed the independent importance of the state

10. Deutsch commented extensively on numerous instances of exclusion, such as the treatment of Japanese Americans in World War II, typically attributing the exclusion to dominant groups; but such cases are theoretically peripheral—"pathological"—because he does not understand meaning itself as political (as a comparison of the treatment of Japanese Americans and German Americans might demonstrate racism in the constitution of collective identity). See also A. W. Marx (2003) on nationalism and exclusion.

11. Bendix's analysis traces in depth the institutional consequences of tensions among different principles of popular representation and between bureaucratic universalism and particularism, tensions central to the civic incorporation of lower classes in different historical contexts.

for nation formation. He criticized attempts to see politics and political institutions as "mere by-products" of economic structure or "interactions among individuals" (1977 [1964]: 88 n. 26). Later, he stressed "the importance of ideas and of government 'intervention' for an understanding of change" (1978: 269). Bendix also concluded that inter-state processes were key to the emergence and consolidation of nations, especially as external influences were mediated by war or by intellectuals. This theme emerged in his examination of political modernization in Japan and Germany, and was developed further in *Kings or People* (1978), where he argued that intellectuals, influenced by foreign developments, had an important impact on domestic political transformations. What this means is that "nationalism has become a universal condition . . . because the sense of backwardness in one's own country has led to ever new encounters with the 'advanced model' or development of another country" (1978: 5; cf. 1977 [1964]: 254–255). To the extent that Bendix believed transferable insights were generated by his cases, he wanted to stress that tensions underlying the constitution of authority relations, and international models, were key to the specific development of any particular case.

So Bendix attended to political process, unlike Deutsch, but he shed little light on the meaning-making processes that constitute nations: who are "the people," and how is this collective identity constituted? The ways in which "peoples" are constituted is central to authority relations in most nation-states and to the political claims of most nationalist movements. Only at the conclusion of *Kings or People* did Bendix mention the issue of "how 'the people' are to be defined": even "old states like those discussed here have grappled for centuries with internal divisions and the problems of political integration," and the issues are magnified in many ways in new states (1978: 599, 600).[12]

The contributions of Deutsch and Bendix can serve here to indicate, although not to fully represent, the richness of reflections on nations emerging from intellectual fields of the 1950s and early 1960s. Deutsch focused on the objective communicative conditions for the formation of nations as collective identities; Bendix emphasized the constitutive importance of tensions over political authority in nation formation and the role of the state and international position. To look into the literature on nations beyond Bendix and Deutsch would be, on the whole, to look more deeply into the

---

12. It is interesting that issues of collective identity formation for authority relations also emerge in Bendix's unusually Deutschian analysis of village integration in the Indian nation-state (e.g., 1977 [1964]: 256) and in a comparison of Russia with Western Europe (pp. 189–191).

infrastructural and political conditions of nations. Neither approach attends much to what nations actually mean to the peoples encompassed within such collective identities, and the active meaning-making involved in that encompassing; for Bendix, the question of "who are the people" appeared only at the boundaries of his project, and for Deutsch, national "conscious-ness" was a secondary formation likely to emerge naturally in the course of intensifying communication. However, a number of comparatively and his-torically grounded works of the period do address what national meaning-making might entail.

For instance, Lipset (1963) treated collective identity formation directly in his study of the United States, *The First Nation*. By problematizing American collective identity—often taken for granted in the political "development" literature—and by introducing a wide range of comparative evidence, he built a strong case that specific meanings (not simply communicative ties) do matter for how nations form as collective identities; he also made the stronger argument that foundational political values continue to influence the shape of political institutions. He understood culture as shared values and mostly limited his attention to values shaping authority relations. But key values are in fundamental tension, and they generate and regenerate opposing positions and opposing institutional solutions.[13]

Also worth mentioning here is Znaniecki's *Modern Nationalities* (1952), an investigation now almost lost from view. Znaniecki saw nations as forms of collective identity irreducible to states; "a solidary human collectivity of hundreds of thousands, even millions of people who share the same culture can exist for a long time without a common political government" (1952: ix). On the other hand, national solidarity is "not merely a matter of subjective mass psychology" because it involves "effective collective activities" (pp. 15–16). Drawing on a wide variety of cases, Znaniecki detailed how intellectuals of various types—"not constituted by any authoritative organized group"—generated organizations that spread national ideas (p. 24). Many students of nationalism have emphasized the role of intellectuals; Znaniecki differed in the way he located collective identity formation as a process independent of political institutions, a process of active organization of cultural production. Thus, whereas Lipset's work is valuable for emphasizing the variant mean-ings that might constitute national identities even given broadly similar political institutions, Znaniecki's contribution is to specify a nonpolitical level of social organization where those meanings are produced.

---

13. Other important claims include the central importance of founding moments, the forgotten shakiness of early American political development, and the consequences of value tensions in specific institutional locations. See also Lipset (1990).

These approaches, emphasizing patterns of communication, shifting forms of political authority, distinctive patterns of meaning, and their cultural production, do not constitute a coherent paradigm. However, they remain useful conceptual resources for comparative-historical work on nations. The concerns of these scholars differ significantly from those of scholars of the self-identified second wave of historical-comparative sociology that mostly emerged after the late 1960s.[14]

Domination and Mobilization

As Skocpol (1988b) illustrates, this generation of scholars, "self-consciously and loudly critical" of earlier work, drew strong symbolic boundaries between themselves and scholars active earlier. With a new set of predispositions and concerns emerging from their experience of American society in the late 1960s and early 1970s, they were attracted to conflict and interested in understanding "sources of domination" (1988b: 630–631; cf. Swartz 1988). In this intellectual field, a concern with understanding "the nation" as a collective identity was suspect, associated, rightly or wrongly, with assumptions of value consensus that at best were untenable and at worst were coercive, and probably were both. As cultural phenomena, "nations" were peripheral to the main historical forces shaping modernity, since structures of domination such as the state could account for such collective identity formation and change. It is also possible that collective identity formation—when it was not simply an ideological epiphenomenon—seemed theoretically unproblematic precisely because of the experience of generational "collective effervescence."[15]

Charles Tilly's introduction to the important collection he edited in 1975, *The Formation of National States in Western Europe*, illustrated the way questions about national collective identity formation were marginalized during the second wave:

14. Although these and other first-wave scholars shared some concerns that distinguish them from subsequent comparative-historical scholars, it is important to note that many continued to publish important works on similar themes for decades. Of these four, the work of Bendix and Lipset was probably best known to later historical sociologists.

15. This body of work did attend to "craft" and "gender" identities, especially in their relation to class consciousness. And the same period saw the renewal of critical theories of culture—the influence of Gramsci; the rediscovery of the young Marx, Marcuse, and the Frankfurt School; the work of Raymond Williams, the Birmingham School, Althusser, and others, including, a little later, Bourdieu—developments that affected the reconstruction of cultural sociology from the 1980s. However, this cultural theory was not, overall, a strong influence on the second-wave historical sociologists at the time.

We began our work intending to analyze state-making and the formation of nations interdependently. As our inquiry proceeded, we concentrated our attention increasingly on the development of states
rather than the building of nations. There were several reasons for this
drift. One was the greater ease with which we could arrive at some
working agreement on the meaning of the word "state." "Nation" remains one of the most puzzling and tendentious items in the political
lexicon. Another was our early fixation on the periods in which the
primacy of states was still open to serious challenge; they were not
generally periods of nationalism, of mass political identity or even of
great cultural homogeneity within the boundaries of a state. The third
was the bias in our original set of topics toward the extractive and
repressive activities of states (1975: 6).

Even so, Tilly assessed the importance of cultural homogeneity compared
to the factors stressed in the volume, concluding that "homogeneity itself
probably did not predispose Europe towards national states" (p. 28). Further, he suggested that an argument differentiating states according to their
mechanisms of collective identity formation "has rather a lot of consensus
and rather little coercion in the process by which states formed," but if
cultural homogeneity was understood in terms of "costs of securing compliance," it could fit the argument of the collection (p. 43; cf. 78–79). He also
noted that proto-states' failures to impose cultural homogeneity could increase their chances of failing, and he contrasted Southeastern with Northwestern Europe in this regard (p. 44). But why Southeast European proto-
states should be "tolerant of diversity" was of little interest within this
research program, since collective identity was relevant only to the extent
that it influenced the more or less rational actions generated by state-
forming projects.[16]

Tilly has recently engaged these sorts of issues more directly, moving away
from the central concerns evident in the second wave. On the classic question of why "only in the eighteenth century did nationalism become a salient
force in European politics" he has developed useful new evidence for "state-
centered" theories of nationalism, but he does not address how collective
identities are formed; his measures rely on "self-identified religious or ethnic
communities" (1994: 133, 134; 1998b). His later work also emphasizes that
states' projects of increasing central control involved important processes of

16. Around the same time, Tilly reflected, "When I began my long inquiry into conflict, protest and
collective action, I hoped to accumulate the evidence for a decisive refutation of the Durkheimian
line" (cited in Bonnell 1980: 161 n. 18).

cultural production (1994: 140). In other work he has increasingly addressed the constitutive cultural construction of nations and social movements, the fluid processes of claims-making they involve, and the relational rather than individualist epistemology necessary to understand them (e.g., 1998b, 2002).[17]

The major contribution to our understanding of nations from a comparative-historical sociologist during the second wave was Hechter's *Internal Colonialism* (1999 [1975]), which challenged the argument that cultural homogeneity and national integration ultimately follow from industrialization and modernization. Even in the United Kingdom, the Celtic periphery remained culturally distinct and continued to mobilize against the British state. Why? Far from generating similarity, political and economic modernization created regional exploitation and inequalities, which might, under some circumstances, be understood in terms of status rather than class, understandings that then could become powerful bases of political mobilization. Modernization theories fail to recognize "the utility of the maintenance of peripheral cultural identity as a form of political mobilization among groups perceiving themselves to be disadvantaged" (Hechter 1999 [1975]: 233). Hechter traced pre-industrial political incorporation and later economic incorporation of the Celtic fringe and their impact on economic inequality, cultural differentiation, and political mobilization.[18]

Hechter's work theorizes collective identity formation in a way that explicitly integrates political and cultural dimensions to provide an account of nations—at least of subordinate nationalist groups. Mobilizable "ethnic" identities are formed when "individuals are assigned to specific types of occupations and other social roles on the basis of observable cultural traits, or markers," so ethnic solidarity is "a response to the perception of patterns of structural discrimination in the society at large" and, in essence, a functional equivalent of class solidarity (Hechter 1999 [1975]: 314–315; 340). As Hechter expanded the theory later, "the configuration of the cultural division of labor will affect the relative salience of ethnic as against class cleav-

17. While these concerns fit with those of later scholars, described below, there is some difference in analytic emphasis. Tilly prioritizes social sites and transactions (2002: ix), whereas third-wave comparative-historical studies focus more on analyzing constitutive cultural frameworks and fluid cultural repertoires, which (as Tilly would recognize) may transcend particular sites and transactions. Cultural resources for political action may be very long-lasting; see, for instance, J. C. Alexander and Smith (1993); Brubaker (1992); Spillman (1998); and Swidler (1992).

18. Hechter's work further illustrates the generational dynamic Skocpol described (e.g., Hechter 1999 [1975]: xiii); however, his argument is more consistent with Deutsch's than is generally recognized (but see Hechter 1999 [1975]: 25 n. 1).

ages in the society as a whole" (1978: 312). In this perspective, meaning-making processes are often inherently political.[19]

Nevertheless, although Hechter did take issues of national collective identity formation seriously, unlike most second-wave comparative-historical sociologists, he spelled out the political dynamics much more clearly than the cultural dynamics. He recognized that his ecological data rested on what he called "assumptions about psychological processes," but he preferred to "treat the problem as if it were a black box" (1999 [1975]: 13; cf. 345). In short, processes of meaning-making are implied but not examined in his early work.[20] In his later work he further developed the thesis that "a cultural division of labor is decisive for the salience of national identity" (while providing a basically "state-centered" account of different types of nationalism). Groups form around "markers [that] systematically affect their incumbents' welfare" or among people sharing a common location. Group salience depends on "the differential stratification of groups, and their relative permeability" because the salience of groups to individuals depends on the degree to which they maximize self-esteem and the costs of exit (Hechter 2000: 96, 98, 99). Hechter thereby fills in the "black box" of collective identity formation by theorizing social-psychological mechanisms that heighten group salience, and by linking them to conditions that generate cultural stratification. These two levels of argument are unified by shared theoretical postulates about the relative costs and benefits of the different forms of action they entail. For Hechter, the only way of really understanding meaningfulness is to access individual subjectivity, and while social psychology provides some leads, the task is unmanageable without the postulates of rational choice theory.

Overall, then, the self-identified second wave of comparative-historical sociologists may have brought the state back in, but they pushed nations out of focus. Insofar as they addressed them, these scholars saw nations largely as outcomes or conditions of political mobilization and domination. More culturally grounded questions about nations as forms of collective identity

19. How dominant nationalities are constituted, and how the cultural division of labor emerges, remain more obscure in *Internal Colonialism*. Apparently, instrumental reasons account for the beginnings of the cycle of ethnocentrism, which ultimately leads to peripheral nationalisms (see Hechter 1999 [1975]: 164, 342).

20. Hechter's measures of cultural differentiation are religion and language, but he noted "many more subtle differences (customs, folklore, sports activities, dialects, and so forth) which cannot, unfortunately, be analyzed in a systematic fashion" (1999 [1975]: 207). This seems overly pessimistic about empirical investigation of the so-called "black box" of collective identity formation. Theories of culture that take seriously its public and intersubjective nature open this black box to empirical examination. See, for instance, Kane (2000), who problematizes the apparently inevitable emergence of Irish nationalism and investigates the discursive action by which it was formed.

were not addressed. The theory of meaning-making implied by a focus on questions of political domination was a simple theory of ideology (Spillman 1995; Wuthnow 1989). Where subordinate political mobilization was at issue, meaning-making was mostly taken as extrinsic to the central research problem, except by Hechter, whose later efforts to elaborate a theory of collective identity formation were grounded in individual interest rather than cultural processes (Hechter 1987, 2000).

Ideas and Idioms

Greater interest in nations stimulated new research beginning in the 1980s, leading to a wave of articles and monographs in the 1990s, by which time interest was also fueled by the collapse of the Soviet Union and the resurgence of nationalist conflict in several regions of the world (e.g., John Comaroff and Stern 1994; Tiryakian 1997). Central to the return of nations to the comparative-historical agenda were changing presuppositions about cultural analysis in late-twentieth-century scholarship, dissatisfaction with blind spots of structural-political explanation, and, for some, appeals to new conceptual tools drawn from cultural theory.[21]

Greenfeld (1992), who is unconcerned with the usual set of questions surrounding nationalist political mobilization, makes the sharpest break with second-wave approaches to nations. She focuses on the origins, nature, diffusion, and variants of the idea of "the nation" as a form of collective identity, equating nationalism with national identity. Her theory relies at each point on a macro-social account of status politics, highlighting emotional dynamics in national identities, especially *ressentiment* (cf. W. Bloom 1990).

For Greenfeld, one core idea distinguishes national identity from other collective identities: it "locates the source of individual identity within a 'people,' which is seen as the central object of loyalty and the basis of collective solidarity. The 'people' is the mass of a population whose boundaries and nature are defined in various ways, but which is usually perceived as larger than any concrete community and always as fundamentally homogeneous, and only superficially divided along the lines of status, class, or locality" (1990: 549). Moreover, "nationality . . . guarantees status. *National identity is, fundamentally, a matter of dignity*" (1992: 487; emphasis in original). This core idea was primarily an innovation of the sixteenth-century

21. See Steinmetz, ed. (1999). The reintroduction of cultural issues to the comparative-historical agenda is probably traceable as much to a lagged impact of the 1960s as to the events of 1989, especially the importance of identity politics in the late 1970s and 1980s. See also Tiryakian and Rogowski, eds. (1985).

Tudor aristocracy, who adopted it because of status ambiguities emerging from a sustained and intense period of elite social mobility.

The subsequent diffusion of the core idea was shaped by two distinguishable levels of status politics: "supra-societal" status in relation to the dominance of England or the West (thus echoing Bendix's argument), and internal status concerns of the specific indigenous elite groups promoting the idea. These forces created variant forms of national identity. Both English and American identity are instances of individualistic civic nationalisms; French national identity is civic but collective; German and Russian national identities are collective and ethnic (Greenfeld 1992; see also Greenfeld 2001 on the Netherlands and Japan). As for Lipset (1963), a single core and founding national identity characterizes each case, but these also involve emerging variants, contradictions, and challenges. Overall, although Greenfeld believes in principle that the emergence of nations and the forms they take are historically contingent, she tends to the conclusion that contention and variation are insignificant and little fundamental change is possible (e.g., Greenfeld 1992: 449–460, 472–484). However, such contradictions as American racial inequalities persist due to powerful interests: "of the available ideals and their possible interpretations, only those are selected and upheld at any given period which correspond to significant interests operating at the time . . . while others are at least temporarily discarded or put aside" (1992: 458–459). So founding ideals determine nations, but interests are introduced to explain the persistence of contradictions.

John Meyer and his colleagues also emphasize "supra-societal" forces and cultural determinism, but their understanding of culture is more cognitively grounded. Influential cultural models are ontological, "defining the nature and purposes of social actors and action"; embedded in social organization, they constitute actors, including nations, which achieve a "taken for granted status" (Boli and Thomas 1997: 172; Ramirez 1987: 323). McNeely demonstrates how such global cultural accounts affect the existence and recognition of nation-states, as well as providing models, norms, and prescriptions for "common organizational structures and practices" (1995: 151). It is important that global cultural accounts also influence domestic social movements, international organizations, and "epistemic communities" of experts; both states and nations operate in a broader organizational field. However, this research program subordinates domestic variation and conflict, because conflict implies shared cognitive models. There is also some evidence that endogenous influences (such as local social movement strength) weaken over time relative to global influences. From this point of view, many analysts have overemphasized sub-global structures and conflicts, at the expense of a longer-term and more consequential process of cultural change (J. W. Meyer et al. 1997).

More concerned with national distinctiveness, Brubaker (1996) brings the question of "who are the people" (which Bendix encountered at the margins of his investigation) into sharp focus. Emphasizing citizenship as an instrument of social closure, as well as a means of inclusion, Brubaker shows that consequential and persistent differences in understandings of nationality shape different citizenship policies in France and Germany. He traces over several centuries how "existing definitions of the citizenry—expansively combining *jus soli* and *jus sanguinis* in France, restrictively reflecting pure *jus sanguinis* in Germany—embody and express deeply rooted national self-understandings, more state-centered and assimilationist in France, more ethnocultural in Germany." Here, and as for Greenfeld, nations are persistently influential collective identities with important consequences for routine politics: "The nation-state is not only, or primarily, an ethno-demographic phenomenon, or a set of institutional arrangements: it is also, crucially, a way of thinking about and appraising political and social membership" (Brubaker 1992: 184, 188).

What distinguishes Brubaker's approach is the conceptualization of culture it brings to an issue that has most often been understood in terms of either ideas, values, or interests. Although Brubaker's argument is analogous to Greenfeld's and to Lipset's in the way he uncovers precise national differences and traces them to the influence of foundational versions of national qualities on political institutions, he characterizes these influences not as shared values or ideas but as "cultural idioms." This move allows a finer theoretical grasp of contention and variability in political claims-making. Indeed, Brubaker is careful to note that the dominant cultural idiom in each country represents "only one strand of a more complex national self-understanding," that both inclusionary and exclusionary claims are mobilized within each discourse, and that the " 'prevailing' idiom of nationhood has been contestatory and contested." These political vicissitudes of dominant cultural idioms can be of more interest than their always challengeable hegemony. Yet, at the same time, they are persistent over centuries and consequential because, on the whole, they limit the discursive field within which debates are conducted. Cultural understandings of the nation are, here, fundamentally political and, in some important ways, fluid and contested (1992: 14, 163; cf. 76, 98–102, 183–184). How exactly cultural persistence and cultural fluidity are to be reconciled, though, is not examined in depth.

Brubaker's approach also challenges the second-wave emphasis on state formation, not by counterposing a "naive culturalist approach," but by demonstrating in specific empirical contexts the ways meaning-making processes are central to state formation. Whereas second-wave comparative-historical sociologists implicitly relied on a theory of culture as ideology and interests, Brubaker makes a sustained challenge to such views:

> Understandings of nationhood and interests of state are not antithetical categories. State interests in an expansive or restrictive citizenry are not immediately given by economic, demographic, or military considerations. Rather, judgments of what is in the interest of the state are mediated by self-understandings, by cultural idioms, by ways of thinking and talking about nationhood.
>
> The more general analytic point is that cultural idioms are not neutral vehicles for the expression of preexisting interests; cultural idioms *constitute* interests as much as they express them. These culturally mediated and thereby culturally constituted interests are not prior to, or independent of, the cultural idioms in which they are expressed (1992: 16; emphasis in original).

Brubaker's later work, a more direct examination of political mobilization in state formation focusing on post-communist Europe, examines "nationhood as a political and cultural form institutionalized within and among states" and asks "how does nation work as a practical category, as classificatory scheme, as cognitive frame?" (1996: 8).

Spillman (1997) makes similar theoretical moves to address how nationality came to be taken for granted in two "new nations," the United States and Australia, in which neither nationalist movements nor state-led nationalizing projects were particularly influential. Conceptualizing nation formation as a process of cultural innovation, Spillman uses the comparison of similar cases to understand changes, similarities, and differences in national identity. National identities are understood as repertoires of symbols contingently mobilized in claims-making. These repertoires are distinguishable from and shaped by an underlying and persistent discursive field constituting nationality, a field that makes particular symbolic claims "national" (rather than, for instance, regional or ethnic) by situating them in relation to issues of internal integration, international standing, or both. This conceptualization addresses the potential contradiction between persistence and fluidity in Brubaker's notion of "cultural idioms" by distinguishing two different dimensions of culture, one more constitutive, another more contingent and, potentially, instrumental.

Cultural repertoires are profoundly shaped by discursive fields, but they are also formed and reformed in processes of cultural production. Cultural production of national identities is often at least in part the work of states or political movements, but the broader conceptualization is essential because, as Znaniecki pointed out, neither states nor social movements are always the central actors in this process. Nor are other cultural producers typically engaged in making strictly political challenges. Whatever its institutional location, though, cultural production of national identities is influenced by the competing claims of contesting—or resistant—cultural peripheries. Left unexamined in Spillman (1997) is precisely how the cultural dynamics it articulates operate in the context of more explicitly political nationalizing projects.

Recent comparative-historical work on nations, then, has returned to the issue of how nations are formed as collective identities. For Greenfeld, status politics at various levels and historical conjunctures is key to understanding such identities; John Meyer and his colleagues remind us of the impact of shared global models; Brubaker sees persistent and distinctive cultural idioms shaping claims-making and institutions; and Spillman sees national collective identities as repertoires of symbols invoked in claims-making and shaped by discursive fields and cultural production. These approaches do not theorize political mobilization as extensively as earlier work but suggest the inherently political dimensions of collective identity formation, on the one hand, and the meaning-making processes essential to mobilization, on the other. They also share the assumptions that culture is public and intersubjective, rather than confined to individual consciousness; that some strictly cultural dynamics, as well as political dynamics, influence claims-making about collective identities; and that both persistence and fluidity characterize cultural repertoires expressing collective identities (cf. Spillman 1995, 2002b). If a third wave of comparative-historical sociology were to be constituted, these positions would underlie its understanding of the nation.

At issue within such a paradigm would be the significance of the second-wave concerns about domination, resistance, structures, material interests, and the state. Both Greenfeld (1992: 17–21) and John Meyer and his colleagues (Thomas and Meyer 1984) distance themselves from these concerns. They adopt instead a direct cultural determinism (more emotional and more cognitive respectively) and examine very long-term, constitutive cultural forces. By contrast, Brubaker and Spillman emphasize more the inherently fluid, political nature of meaning-making processes, eschewing strong cultural determinism and combining the second wave's concern with power and conflict with a focus on the cultural constitution of interests and the cultural dynamics of claims-making.

More generally, comparative-historical work on nations and nationalism offers a number of theoretical formulations of issues of collective identity and political mobilization that provide a basis for future work in the area, even though this topic has not been central in the field. However, as in the nationalism literature more generally, there is little substantive dialogue among scholars. Only rarely do these works directly address other approaches, even though we have noted some shared themes and might have noted many other connections.

Conclusion and Agenda

Although nations and nationalism are central features of modernity, and although comparative-historical sociologists are fundamentally concerned with large-scale and long-term changes in political and social organization, we have contributed relatively little to the rich literature on the subject, and the studies that exist have not, on the whole, directly built on or challenged each other. The aim of this chapter has been to lay the foundations for doing both.

The literature on nations and nationalism is rich in deductions, inductive generalizations, hypotheses, guesses, and observations, but it is plagued by the related conceptual issues of theoretical under-determination and definitional proliferation. The classical social theorists neglected nations and nationalism, although they suggested a number of themes that have been taken up in later analysis. Perhaps as a result, most scholars have delineated their topics according to ordinary language or by ad hoc stipulation and frequently quibble with or talk past each other. But as Brubaker (1996: 8) has also suggested, "nation" is inadequate as an analytic category. What are needed are theoretical positions, competing or complementary, that do not reify the category of "the nation" but situate it in relation to other forms of collective identity and political mobilization. Perhaps comparative-historical sociologists could address this task.

As we have suggested throughout this chapter, understanding nations and nationalism requires the integration of theories of collective identity formation and theories of political mobilization. Some leads exist, but these are rare, and most theorists emphasize one dimension at the expense of the other. This reflects a larger and long-standing problem within sociology as a whole which has conceptualized culture in terms of either consensus or ideology.

However, recent understandings of culture challenge this oversimplification by providing conceptual resources to transcend the dichotomy (Spillman 1995). Cultural sociology translates the broader and more diffuse set of intellectual innovations in the cultural turn in ways that connect it with more traditional sociological concerns. Drawing on this body of theory and connecting it with contributions to our understanding of nations focusing on political mobilization, we propose the following definition:

"The nation" is a discursive field generated in the orientation of political action to claims-making about legitimate political authority,
claims-making about shared features of the putatively relevant population, and distinguishing that population from others.[22]

This definition unites the political mobilization and cultural dimensions of
nations. It leaves open to further investigation, both theoretical and empirical, a series of critical issues that are commonly treated by arbitrary definitional moves that close off the field a priori. Several implications of this
definition should be noted.

First, of course, it leaves open who are the actors creating and reproducing
the discursive field. Second, it also leaves open the specific symbolic elements—or "cultural idioms"—that may be mobilized in claims-making.
These are empirical issues. Third, it leaves open the question of timing; it is
consistent with arguments that national mobilization is very much more
frequent after state formation but does not require it by definition. Fourth,
this definition does distinguish between claims based on features of the
relevant authority (such as monarchical or imperial claims) and claims
based on putatively shared, distinguishing features of a population, except
insofar as the former are linked to the latter. Fifth, it does not presume
consensus but leaves this open to empirical investigation. Sixth, it is consistent with existing theories of political mobilization, except in the claim that
such mobilization is culturally constituted in important ways. Seventh, it
suggests that processes of cultural production are crucial to the emergence
and reproduction of the discursive field of "the nation." Eighth, it suggests
that national claims-making may be strongly associated with states, state
building, war, and contentious social movements but that, given routine
conditions of cultural production, "the nation" exists as a collective identity
beyond and between explicit mobilization. Finally, it does not foreclose by
definition the relationship of nations to other discursive fields generating
other collective identities (racial, gender, regional, class, etc.).

We suggested above that progress in understanding nations and nationalism requires a set of theory-driven definitions that do not reify "nations" but
allow scholars to debate the empirical power of respective theories rather
than the proper use of terms. In this spirit, we can note that the definition
above, driven by a theory of collective identity formation building on con-

22. Calhoun (1993b, 1993c, 1997) and Gorski (2000b) are others who have taken this basically discursive
view of the nation. Gorski, however, labels his approach post-modernist, while we emphasize that our
approach does not entail fragmentation and incommensurability in knowledge of the nation. A
theory of collective identity based on conceptual resources in cultural sociology enables an improved
modernism.

ceptual resources from cultural sociology, could be contrasted with definitions derived from a number of other theories of collective identity formation. We have already mentioned some points of difference within existing
culturalist positions. Further afield, two leading competitors, generated by
structuralist and individualist positions on collective identity, also exist. One
alternative would be grounded in a theory of collective identity formation as
ideology: social structural forces generate meanings that directly reflect
those forces through meso-level network processes (both dominant and
contesting); in this view, nations are the ideological counterparts to states,
and meaning-making processes can be factored out of explanations of nations and nationalism. Another alternative would be grounded in a theory of
collective identity formation in general, and nations in particular, as emerging from action based on individual interests. Future comparative-historical
work on the nation could be directed to assessing the empirical power of
these respective theories.

We also suggested above that theory-driven definition can and should sort
the "commonsense" world in new patterns and should not be rejected for
failure to reproduce commonsense categories. So far, most empirical work
on nations and nationalism, especially within sociology, has been designed
around categories of analysis taking nations as given, even if the thrust of the
analysis is explanatory. That is, most studies are designed, empirically, to
compare and contrast different nations, nation formations, nation-states,
and nationalist mobilizations. The definition of nations as discursive fields
emerging in the orientation of political action to claims-making about legitimate political authority suggests a different line of research: the explicit and
extended comparison of this form of collective identity and mobilization
with others, such as those based on cosmopolitanism, region, religion, gender, ethnicity, and class. It suggests that nations should be seen as one among
many forms of collective identity that can be created or absorbed in political processes and that they will be better understood in explicit comparison with other such forms of collective identity. Insofar as they all involve claims-making about legitimate political authority based on putatively
shared and distinguishing features, they are analogous, even if commonsense and many ideological claims say that they are mutually exclusive (and
regardless of what they are called). For instance, this suggestion provides
theoretical grounds to compare and contrast the nature, origins, mechanisms, mutual influences, and outcomes of late-nineteenth-century American feminist and nationalist mobilizations (see Ramirez, Soysal, and Shanahan 1997); Anthony Marx (1998) investigates an analogous question, as does
Roudometof (2002).

The more general point here is that a rich array of interesting questions for comparative-historical investigation emerge when the nation is conceptualized as—and not simply assumed to be—one among a number of common forms of mobilizable collective identities with fluid and contested relationships. Investigation of nations and nationalism does not require that our units of analysis all be nations or nationalist movements.

Meanwhile, many of the most theoretically sophisticated and empirically interesting studies of nations and nationalism are now being conducted on very different intellectual terrain, with presuppositions that take for granted the power of discursive regimes and examine their production, reproduction, and interaction, as well as the ways they are enmeshed in political action. We mention here only three intriguing examples of such investigations to demonstrate the relevance of this body of work. First, Waetjen (2001) has drawn on the extensive feminist literature detailing the fundamental connections between constructions of gender and constructions of the nation to argue that in the particular case of Zulu nationalism in late-twentieth-century South Africa, contested visions of Zulu masculinity were crucial in accounting for its failure. Second, Ong (1999) provides an account of how nation-states intersect with class and kinship regimes to explain the large proportion of elite Hong Kong Chinese who held multiple passports. Her analysis emphasizes both the continuing political significance of nationality and the important ways it intersects with other collective identities. Third, Rajogopal (2001) analyzes the significance of television's reconstitution of the public sphere for recent Hindu nationalism. These studies produce significant new knowledge about nations and nationalism and invite further comparative and historical investigation. Yet they could not have been produced within the confines of existing comparative-historical sociology.[23]

To fully explore this alternative intellectual terrain and what it offers for comparative-historical sociology would be the task of another essay. In highlighting here comparative-historical sociology's curious under-emphasis of the nation, examining the resources that do exist within the field, and suggesting a new theorization of nations, we hope to have opened lines of communication for the integration of this new work within the central concerns of the subdiscipline.

---

23. For an introduction to the extensive literature on gender and nationalism, see Enloe (1990); Jayawardena (1986); Kandiyoti, ed. (2000); West, ed. (1997).

MARGARET R. SOMERS

Citizenship Troubles: Genealogies of Struggle
for the Soul of the Social

When philosophy paints its gray on gray, then has a form of life grown old, and with gray on gray it cannot be rejuvenated, but only known; the Owl of Minerva first takes flight with twilight closing in.—G. W. F. Hegel

Perhaps only the Owl of Minerva would have predicted it: just when so many of the egalitarian ideals T. H. Marshall so brilliantly theorized in *Citizenship and Social Class* (1950) had been all but completely betrayed, his historical sociology of citizenship suddenly achieved canonical status. Forty-five years after its initial appearance and out of print for decades, the now legendary essay has reappeared—and with it a virtual explosion of interest in citizenship studies (T. H. Marshall and Bottomore 1992; Shafir, ed. 1998). Across all the disciplines, from law to comparative literature, from sociology to public health, the concept of citizenship seems to have overnight become one of the central organizing categories of our time. As the increasing momentum of interest rapidly produced a truly enormous body of literature, citizenship also quickly became one of those rare academic topics properly claimed by scholarship and the political public sphere alike (Archibugi et al. 1998; Blair 1996, 1998; Commission of the European Communities 1997; Eder and Giesen 2001; Fierlbeck 1991; Freedland 2001; HM Government

I am grateful to Weining Gao for research assistance, as well as to the editors of this volume for their comments on successive versions of this chapter. Many thanks also to the following friends and colleagues for their great generosity in sharing with me their thoughts and memories (and time) regarding the curious career of T. H. Marshall in the postwar social sciences: Fred Block, Craig Calhoun, Geoff Eley, Tony Giddens, Alex Hicks, Albert Hirschman, Engin Isin, Tom Janoski, Ira Katznelson, Mick Mann, Frank Michelman, Dietrich Rueschemeyer, Hiro Saito, Theda Skocpol, John Stevens, Richard Swedberg, Chuck Tilly, and Jeff Weintraub.

1991a, 1991b, 1991c; N. Lewis 1993; Marcella and Baxter 1999; Straw 1998; Tritter 1994; United Kingdom 1990).

Citations to Marshall himself can be used to track this expanding literature. The number of citations reported by the Social Science Citation Index (ssci) to Marshall from 1950 through 2002 underlines the point: after four decades of what are roughly steady rates of citation, in the early 1990s there is an upward spike that ends in a citation rate about thirty-seven times greater than that of the previous decades. To understand this shift, we need to begin with the conflicted and troubled genealogies of the problems of citizenship. Such a sudden eruption of interest in citizenship over the course of a little more than a decade makes the "discovery" of citizenship in the 1990s a true phenomenon of our time. This has been much commented upon. Indeed sometimes it seems to be unwritten law that no article or book on the subject is allowed to begin without this observation. Surprisingly, however, what have been virtually absent from the literature are engaged efforts to account for the many years of silence. The premise of this chapter is that developing such an account is a matter of compelling importance for both historical sociology and social analysis more generally. For despite the topic's current prominence, history shows us that citizenship has been only an occasional concern to social analysis, one with the strange habit of being discovered, forgotten, and rediscovered yet again. One does not have to be a sociologist of knowledge to puzzle over such oddity. Here is one of modernity's great signifiers—touching as it does on virtually every dimension of life from identity and the self to social provisioning and gender discrimination— making a significant appearance only once every fifty years. How do we explain this strange career of the concept of citizenship in historical sociology and the social sciences more broadly?

One way of thinking about it is through the eyes of Minerva's bearer of wisdom. Hegel used the legend to forewarn that the owl would bestow true knowledge of the world we live in only just as that world had become "a form of life grown old"—a view that gives meaning to what nonetheless seems tragic: much of the—relative—justice the democratization of citizenship rights made possible had to be left in shambles "with twilight closing in" before "philosophy" could "paint its gray on gray" and put citizenship rights back at the center of social thought. To be sure, depending on one's angle of political geographic vision, there will be different perceptions of just how much of the social provision state of Western Europe and the United States has been successfully dismantled—the usual continuum of demise being from Anglo-American societies at one end to the Scandinavian at the other, with continental Europe falling somewhere in between. Yet despite even once convincing arguments for the welfare state's institutional durability (Leibfried and Pierson 1995; Pierson 1994), a decade later there can be no gainsaying the effects of neoliberalism's global assault on what Marshall called social citizenship (Crouch 2001; Eder, Crouch and Tambini, eds. 2001; Esping-Andersen et al. 2002; Freedland 2001; Huber and Stephens 2001; Pierson, ed. 2001; Procacci 2001). It would be a mistake, moreover, to think that the "form of life grown old" is limited to social provisioning. Just as significant, especially in the United States, is the radical transformation of the federal judiciary over the last quarter century. With the exception of the rights of property and freedom of speech, a successful assault has been launched against virtually each and every civil right that Marshall made foundational to the very possibility of the democratization of citizenship rights. "To a degree that has been insufficiently appreciated, and is in some ways barely believable," according to one of today's most acclaimed legal scholars, "the contemporary federal courts are fundamentally different from the federal courts of just two decades ago" (Sunstein 2003: A2). Because they have a causally reciprocal relationship to each other, these legal challenges to civil and legal rights can in no way be separated from those of political and social rights. Any of today's neoliberal attacks on welfare and other forms of entitlement (L. M. Mead 1997; Murray 1984; Olasky 1992) place the blame on an "excess" of democracy for the reckless spread of a system of "hand outs."

Hegel would not have been all that off base in other ways as well. After all, it was history itself and *not* an autonomous, self-propelling burst of enlightenment that spurred the academic community to wake up to the significance of citizenship as an object of study. The spectacular appearance in Eastern Europe and Russia of new possibilities and processes of democratization made it impossible to any longer ignore an ideal and an institution that had become a central driving force of history, along with its associated vocabulary of civil society, the public sphere, and a democratic political culture. That the decline of the welfare state and the rise of democratic movements in Eastern Europe coincided with the rediscovery of citizenship is, in many respects, a familiar story. By contrast, my goal is to go beyond Hegel's theory of the twilight of history to a deeper understanding of the *absence* of citizenship from the sociological agenda, including the period of historical sociology's greatest strength in the 1970s and 1980s. This is in many ways unexplored territory.

Two themes will take center stage in my investigation: first, the peculiarities of twentieth-century social science, and, second, what I am calling the "troubles of citizenship." With respect to the former, the history of nineteenth- and twentieth-century social science reveals deep and recurring blind spots regarding the subject of citizenship. Much of the explanation for this lies with the genealogy of the social sciences in the context of political liberalism and the academic division of labor among the disciplines that ensued. In brief, in a struggle entailing the politics of epistemology, sociology's turf of the social required a triadic conceptual landscape. The public hegemony of political liberalism with its inseparable twin of economic liberalism, however, consistently superimposed its controlling and exclusive binary of public versus private, thus effacing the site of the social. In this context citizenship was eclipsed, at least as a sociological phenomenon rather than a purely legal category defined by nationality.

Not all of the blame can be placed on disciplinary troubles, however. Equally responsible are the deep and seemingly intractable "troubles of citizenship" inherent in the concept itself, a concept and a practice that is at once normative and deontological while also aspiring to full empirical status as an institutional mechanism of governance and nationality in the world order of sovereign states. This epistemological conflict, however, is a product of the concept's deeper ontological troubles. As a phenomenon of national inclusion, the concept of citizenship is inexorably tied to that of rights and duties—even if participatory and other rights to social justice are not among them.

Yet *citizenship* and *rights* have different and deeply conflicting ontological meanings rooted in their different genealogical and conceptual *sites*: citizenship is part of the public sphere, while rights are immutably of the private sphere and its autonomous self-propelling agents. Citizenship is a political and institutional artifice designed to overcome the dangers inherent in depoliticized free agency; rights are constitutive of individuals in the state of nature and thus are fiercely committed to a kind of governance produced not by men and women but by virtue of the balance of freedoms in their natural state, unhampered by political artifice. Citizenship is deeply bound to the particularism of place and membership and thus entails the privileges (not rights) of site-specific belonging; as such the privileges are immediately cancelled beyond the bounds of the polity. Natural rights, by contrast, are bound to no place at all but are deontologically *universal* and thus are utterly portable and indefeasible regardless of anything as arbitrary as political boundaries.

For much of its life course citizenship as a potential object of study has been trapped in these conflicting genealogies, which goes a long way toward explaining the puzzle of its previous absence. But there is also a moral to this story that has meaning for the history of the present. That it was history itself rather than autonomous intellectual developments that catalyzed the citizenship epiphany suggests to me that our enlightenment was gifted to us undeservedly, without our having to even recognize or engage directly these disciplinary blind spots and conceptual troubles. This in turn suggests that as long as these inherent conceptual irritants are still with us, the field of citizenship studies is at risk; if they once fueled its disappearance, there is no reason to believe that they could not do it again. We cannot rely on the Owl of Minerva to always do our work for us.

These, then, are the issues that frame this chapter. But several stipulations are in order before we proceed. The first concerns the relationship between T. H. Marshall's *Citizenship and Social Class* and the topic of citizenship more generally in the second half of the twentieth century. This is not an essay on T. H. Marshall, and it should not be read as such. But a central point of my argument is that from the moment that Marshall first delivered his famous lectures in 1949, *Citizenship and Social Class* and citizenship as a social science concept became one and the same. It is hard in today's context to understand that Marshall essentially invented the social approach to citizenship; once he did, in the absence of any preceding sociological heritage, he became its sole "owner."[1] To be sure, there was Reinhard Bendix's masterful *Nation-Building and Citizenship* (1964), and one would not want to compare Marshall's influence as a scholar more generally to Bendix's place in the pantheon of sociology's greatest. Nonetheless, Bendix's volume never came close to Marshall's in gaining the almost hard-wired association between the man and the subject.[2] Thus from the time of the original publication of *Citizenship and Social Class* at mid-century until a new generation of scholars finally came onto the scene at the century's end, T. H. Marshall essentially "owned" the historical study of citizenship.[3]

The second stipulation concerns the Anglo-American—even almost U.S.-centric—focus in my discussion of twentieth-century historical sociology, although Scandinavian and German scholarship play a central role in the overall story of Marshall's relationship to welfare state studies. The scholarship on welfare state policies of the 1970s and 1980s (see Orloff, this volume), quite simply, was not the same as today's citizenship studies (nor, not incidentally, did it define itself as such). In some respects it was precisely the great reach and influence of this partial aspect of citizenship that precluded attention to the concept as a whole. Welfare state studies and their immedi-

---

1. This is ironic since Marshall himself did not immediately continue the work on citizenship but shifted almost exclusively to public service and scholarship on social policy. He came back to it only later in life. See T. H. Marshall (1981).

2. A quarter century after Marshall, Ralf Dahrendorf—a sociology student of Marshall's at the London School of Economics (LSE) and a towering intellectual figure in his own right—briefly engaged Marshall's theory of citizenship (Bulmer and Rees 1996; Dahrendorf 1996).

3. Examples of other such "ownership" are few—for example, Marx and capitalism, Smith and the market, Weber and the Protestant Ethic.

ate association with Marshall's famous social citizenship should not be mistaken for citizenship *tout court* as theorized by Marshall himself and as it has developed today.

The Troubles of Citizenship: Genealogies and Contradictions

When Marshall paired citizenship with rights, he was quietly challenging three centuries of conflict between modern political liberalism's foundational concept of rights with its exclusive valorization of the private sphere of the individual and classical republicanism's foundational concept of citizenship with its exclusive valorization of the political. In republican citizenship theory as such, there exists no concept of rights. Conversely, and beyond rhetorical flourish (such as in that of the French Revolution), there is no substantial presence of citizenship in political liberalism's rights theory. None of this should surprise. The genealogy of citizenship and the genealogy of rights entail two distinct streams of thought, each with very different origins and processes, each with a different relationship to historical events, and indeed each with different degrees of influence in shaping history. Yet despite all these differences, as is so often the case, it is precisely because of how they developed in direct opposition to each other that makes their histories so deeply intertwined. Indeed once the discourse of rights entered the public sphere and the knowledge culture in the seventeenth century, the two streams of thought soon developed in explicit oppositional response, each refining and sharpening its own ontologies and epistemologies in an ongoing relationship of *agonistes*. If we are to understand the problematic relationship between citizenship studies and social science scholarship, we have to begin by recognizing this deep and fundamental fissure at the heart of the very idea of citizenship rights.

Republicanism and Citizenship

The idea of citizenship was born with classical Greece's mode of governance and social organization: through the institution of the *polis* human freedom was attached to the privilege of citizenship—collective (male and elite) participation in public life. Its civic ideal—"to rule and be ruled"—made all *meaningful* action synonymous with the political order. The "nonpolitical" universe was the *oikos*—the private domain that signified the site of economic life and "intimacy" under the control of the familial household. Considered little more than a (gendered) place of material and biological reproduction, the oikos could never be viewed as anything other than merely a zone of "necessity." So demeaned was this element of human life that it was excluded from the very definition of humanity itself. Meaningful agency and identity existed only in the context of citizenship and the active exercise of participatory political action in the public forum. Entirely missing from this world divided between public honor and private necessity was anything in between—a *public* sphere of the *social*. To be a republican citizen was to be exclusively a political being.

Like the rights tradition to follow, republican theory confounds the normative and the empirical. On the one hand, citizenship as an institution is a normative ideal; to gain membership in the public forum is not a right but a privilege and an honor that both reflects and endows virtue to those who earn it. Moreover, that its promise "to rule and be ruled" stands on a foundation of slavery and gender oppression has only strengthened the importance of its normative status—its very empirical failures only motivate more toward the ideal state of political equality. At the same time, theorists of republicanism refer to citizenship as a straightforwardly institutional mode of governance. Privileged, exclusive to be sure, but nonetheless amenable to empirical social science analysis. The problem, however, is this: because no such mode of governance has existed since the celebrated Italian city-states of the Renaissance, in modern political thought it is the normative dimension that has survived—but survived in the hands of its fiercest critics as much as in those of its advocates.

As republicanism ebbed and flowed over time—Rousseau was of course one of its greatest theorists—we see the first instance of a binary vision of the social world and its unhappy consequences for the possibility of a sociology of citizenship. Republicanism's single-minded normative valorization of the political and its demeaning of the private made it vulnerable to unwarranted accusations of responsibility for the Terror of the French Revolution by both conservative and utilitarian liberal critics. Almost two centuries later it would be blamed for "totalitarian statism" during the immediate postwar and cold war years. An indelible association thus formed between statist threats to individual freedom and citizenship—not as a formal legal status attached to a passport, but as a political *theory*. All of this added up to an inauspicious situation for a sociological appropriation of a theory of citizenship.

Citizen to Subject to Man:
Political Liberalism and Rights Theory

The rights half of the couplet of citizenship rights is in many ways the mirror image of that of citizenship—and with the same dichotomous result, one that excludes the social from its theory of both human freedom and political governance. Surely it is one of the weirdest facts of our modern knowledge culture that one searches in vain to find the words *citizen* or *citizenship* in political liberalism's founding texts.[4] In fact, in what I have elsewhere called "Anglo-American citizenship theory" there are no citizens; instead, there are only *rights-bearing individuals* who are ontologically fierce opponents of the very idea of human identity being embedded in *any* political processes, regardless of any putatively associated honor.[5] For sociologists, the great disappointment in Locke is how he first invents the very idea of civil society as a site of action and identity autonomous from the state but then immediately hijacks it back into not only the pre-political, but also the pre-social state of nature (Somers 1995a, 1999, 2001).

At first glance Locke's false promise appears to simply echo that of Hobbes, who had already changed the terms of discourse by locating the ontological origins of human identity not in political authority but in the state of nature. But Locke's treatise on political rights was actually a deep criticism of Hobbes for his sleight of hand. First, Hobbes takes a revolutionary stance against traditional absolutism by rejecting the notion that rights can only be *granted* by the positive law of the state, a position that relegates people to *subjects* rather than citizens. Instead he insists that people are born free and equal and endowed with *natural* rather than *conferred* rights. But what he gives with one hand, he steals back with the other. Ontologically predisposed to anarchy and violence, he has those very same rights-bearing individuals agree by social contract—in the interest of security and survival—to *forego* those very natural rights and relinquish them into the *artificial* hands of a political ruler. Once again, they have become subjects—only this time out of voluntary and rational self-interest.

Hobbes clearly had a leg in both worlds. On the one hand, he wants to start from a position of natural rights over and against the citizenship tradition of politically endowed identity. On the other hand, or leg, he thoroughly mistrusts people in their natural condition (the realm of necessity); only the artifice of political power could ensure order and security. But rather than endow them with the capacity to act together *socially* by creating the institutions of citizenship, he summarily demotes them to subjecthood with no right to resistance.

Locke's challenge to Hobbes is to reverse the legitimate source of enduring

---

4. See "An Essay Concerning the True Original, Extent, and End of Civil Government," in the section titled "Of the State of Nature" (Locke 1947), and, to a lesser extent, Hobbes's *Leviathan* (1968).

5. Not until L. T. Hobhouse (an important influence on Marshall) does liberalism directly address issues of citizenship; see Hobhouse (1964 [1911]).

authority from the positive power of the state to the natural rights of individual humans in the state of nature and their post–social contract naturalized version of civil society. But Locke has not freed Hobbes's subjects to become citizens. On the contrary, the true state of humankind is neither political nor social, and thus humans in their free and natural rights-bearing condition cannot be citizens—that is, social members—of any kind of "artificial" collective entity (Somers 1999, 2001): "To understand political power aright, and derive it from its original, we must consider what state all men are naturally in, and that it is a state of perfect freedom to order their actions and dispose of their possessions and persons as they see fit, within the bounds of the law of nature, without asking leave, or depending upon the will of any other man" (J. Locke 1947 [1690], book 2: 118).

So while Locke refuses Hobbes, he equally refuses citizenship; no ontological conception of political membership is possible in an individualistic conception of society and the state—both of which are no more than artificial entities created by social contract. For Locke, these are not men and women but Man—and thus rights-bearing by virtue of a universalistic, naturalized ontological individualism. Each individual is constitutively autonomous vis-à-vis any and all others and any and all relational entities, be they any society, political order, or particular nation or country in which they might happen to have been born and dwell. This leads us to a difficult question: When people are endowed with rights purely by virtue of being universal, abstract Man, rather than an English or French or Athenian "man," by what means can these natural rights-bearers defend themselves against violations by the state? The answer given by Locke is famously simply another right with no institutional foundation—namely, the *natural* right of the individual to resist the tyrannical artifice of the political.

Citizenship and the French Revolution. So much for citizenship in the origins of liberalism. But surely the two traditions came together in the French Revolution, one of history's most famous assertions of the natural rights of citizens? After all, it was that great event that for "about two centuries constituted the ideal model for those who fought for their own emancipation and the liberation of their people" (Bobbio 1996: 81). It *was* the principles of the *Declaration of the Rights of Man and the Citizen* (L. Hunt 1996) that constituted, "whether we like it or not, an obligatory reference point for the friends and foes of liberty" (Bobbio 1992: 81).

But when we turn to these founding documents of modern citizenship, things turn out to be not what they seem. Although every schoolchild associates the terms *citoyen* and *citoyenne* with the French Revolution (forever burned in memory by Dickens's sinister Madame Defarge and her infamous knitting needles), in fact the terms *citizen* and *citizenship* appear only a handful of times in the revolution's founding documents. Where they do appear, they are subordinate to abstract universal Man, who is free by natural right and not by membership in any sovereign popular body. It was the freedom of the state of nature of Locke's *Second Treatise*, Thomas Paine's *Rights of Man*, and Rousseau's "noble savage" that inspired this revolutionary statement. Not until one has read over one-third of the *Declaration* does the word "citizen" even make an appearance in Article 6, and there as merely a marker for the abstract Man. (L. Hunt 1996: 78).[6] Thus it was in the language and mandate of naturalistic, individual, pre-social, pre-political, and pre-membership rights and Man—not republicanism's citizen or citizenship—that the famous *Declaration* defined the new forms of political identity, individual liberties, and popular governance.[7]

Paradoxically, it was the reactionary rhetoric (Hirschman 1990) of conservatism that launched what was arguably the most republican-sounding criticism of the rights-based citizenship tradition. "I've never met Man," thundered Burke and others, "only English, French, Italian men." But Burke's commitment to free markets eventually overruled his traditionalism, and from J. S. Mill through the great liberal thinkers of the twentieth century, there has been no serious competition from republicanism.

In sum, the rights tradition is exhibit number two in the long-prevailing dominance of the binary depictions of the social universe. Just as in republicanism, the public versus private dichotomy exhausts the spectrum of any possible modes of governance and human agency. The difference between liberalism and republicanism is thus almost entirely normative rather than analytic. By mapping the privileged epistemology of social naturalism onto a fictive and privileged ontology of an originating aggregate of rights-bearing individuals, liberalism spins a metanarrative that invokes a "fear and loathing of the political" while it valorizes the private and "romances the market" (Somers 1999, 2001). Whereas in republicanism identity is collapsed into political citizenship, and the practices of reproductive necessities are de-

6. The "doctrinal nucleus" (Bobbio 1996: 82) of the *Declaration* can be found in the first three articles. The first asserts that individuals are born free and equal in rights as their natural condition, which thus precedes any formation of civil or political society; the second states that the sole purpose of political society, which is an outcome of individuals' consensual social contract, is the "preservation of the natural and imprescriptible rights of man"—namely, liberty, property, security, and resistance to oppression; and the third asserts that all "sovereignty rests essentially in the nation," which is explained to be the embodiment of the aggregate of the rights-bearing individuals.

7. As I suggested above, the connection between citizenship theory and the revolution *does* come to the fore, at least for its critics, once the Terror takes over the revolutionary process. No one has written more brilliantly than Balibar on the French Revolution's use of the conflicting concepts of "rights/liberty" and "citizenship/equality" (see, especially, Balibar 1994, pp. 39–69, 205–225). I read this work only after my essay had gone to press, and I am now completely convinced of his argument.

meaned, for liberalism human identity in natural rights is not only entirely pre-political. It is also entirely *pre-social,* an ontological condition invented for the very purpose of protection *against* the very political bodies so celebrated as the realm of freedom by the republican tradition. To be a rights-bearing "citizen," then, is not to be a member of any political or social entity, but an isolated individual whose self-interest alone contracts with others—reluctantly and contingently. Political liberalism's conception of citizenship remains entirely legalistic and formal and secondary to the constitutional liberties of individual rights and purely formal proceduralism.

The sociological implications of the rights tradition hardly make it a fertile ground for a sociology of citizenship. Once again, a binary universe over-determines the possibility of a domain of the social. Indeed one of the greatest ironies of political liberalism is that it actually *erases* the political as a site of human agency, identity, or even ethical institutional meaning. Instead it fashions a causal argument for the primacy of both the pre-political and the pre-social. Even the famous "social" in the social contract, then, is not truly social; rather, it is contingent, artificial, temporary, and voluntarily aggregated individual action. How curiously different this is from intuitively sociological notions of citizenship in which rights are held by virtue of membership in an entity that exists prior to the individual.

Like republicanism, rights theory is at once normative and institutional, with the normative usually trumping the institutional (thus explaining why its scholarship is limited to political and legal-constitutional theory rather than the empirical social sciences). To be sure, Charles Tilly (1998c) developed an empirically significant sociology of rights as "enforceable claims on the state"—an approach that contributes enormously to overcoming the long vacancy in sociological analyses of the institutional foundations for social and political movements (Giddens 1982; Somers 1993, 1994, 1995a; Steinberg 1999a; B. S. Turner 1986). The problem, however, is that much of the history of popular struggles for citizenship, social justice, and individual freedoms (which can be seen as civil, political, and social rights) is the *prehistory* of already established rights. It is largely one of efforts to achieve the recognition of such rights before they actually exist as enforceable claims on the state. This is the case regardless of whether the struggle is being waged for entirely new rights, for the extension and enlargement to a broader population of existing rights currently limited to some small element of the elite, or for a meaningful enforcement of such rights.

At issue, then, is the normativity inherent in the attempt to find foundations, even simply political justifications, for the rights-claims being exercised in any of the above types of struggles. Just as in republicanism's ontological resort to the political foundations of human agency, liberalism's resort to the state of nature is an appeal not to anything empirical but to a normative commitment. Again, like republicanism, it is one that cannot be used in the interest of analyzing the actual conditions that either support or disable human freedoms, political capacities, and social justice. Rather, the normative ideal is used as a discursive weapon of exhortation and attack against its enemies. This, too, makes liberalism no more likely a theoretical foundation for a sociology of citizenship.

Marxism and the Critique of Bourgeois Citizenship and Rights

As it happens it was not "statist" republicanism but Karl Marx who left us with the most enduring and influential critiques of political and economic liberalism. Arguably, at least in his early vision of the fundamentally *relational* nature of human "species-being" and with his various articulations of a post-capitalist world, Marx follows Hegel in setting up a *triadic* social universe. He thus holds out the promise of laying the groundwork for a sociological perspective. Unfortunately, he also follows Hegel in making that "third sphere" of civil society the site of market exchange and economic production; as a result, the idea of civil society is simply conflated into the private side of the public-private binary, making the third sphere not the social but, again like Hegel, the intimate sphere of the family.

So Marx disappoints the hope for a fundamental destabilization of the public-private dichotomy; but he has other fish to fry. He brilliantly pierces the illusions of bourgeois citizenship and all but leaves the entire idea of rights in shambles. Rather than Burke's concern for the *abstraction* of natural rights, for Marx the rights-bearing "Man" of Reason and individuality born in political liberalism's state of nature is too *particular*. Exhibiting a specious universalism, the only "natural" rights-bearers in modern capitalism were none other than the very *specific bourgeois men* who made up society's ruling class. Reflecting in the 1840s on the new constitutions produced by the American and French Revolutions, in "On the Jewish Question," Marx makes clear how he perceives the true meaning of modern political equality in a constitutional state:

> Nevertheless, the political annulment of private property not only fails to abolish private property but also even presupposes it. The state abolishes, in its own way, distinctions of birth, social rank, education, occupation, when it declares that birth, social rank, education, occupation, are non-political distinctions, when it proclaims, without regard to these distinctions, that every member of the nation is an *equal* participant in national sovereignty, when it treats all elements of the

real life of the nation from the standpoint of the state. Nevertheless, the state allows private property, education, occupation, to *act* in *their* way—*i.e.*, as private property, as education, as occupation, and to exert the influence of their *special* nature. Far from abolishing these real distinctions, the state only exists on the presupposition of their existence; it feels itself to be a political state and asserts its universality only in opposition to these elements of its being.[8]

In *Capital*, Marx extends the critique to the labor process by once again fiercely and polemically piercing the illusory "equality" endowed by constitutional political rights and the "voluntary" contract between autonomous and equal citizens in the labor market. Urging us to leave this world of "egalitarian illusion and rights" and to follow him "below," where the real causal mechanisms of bourgeois society are at work, he points us to the underlying truth of the equal rights of bourgeois law: there, behind the door that reads "only those here on business should enter," and in contrast to the "fair" labor market exchange that makes its appearance "above," we see the tyrannical and all-powerful capitalist employer striding forcefully, while behind him slinks in subordinated powerlessness the putatively equally rights-endowed working person looking pathetically meek and oppressed:

> In order that our owner of money may be able to find labour-power offered for sale as a commodity, various conditions must first be fulfilled. . . . [The worker] and the owner of money meet in the market, and deal with each other as on the basis of equal rights, with this difference alone, that one is buyer, the other seller; both, therefore, *equal in the eyes of the law.* . . . Accompanied by Mr. Moneybags and by the possessor of labour-power, we therefore take leave for a time of this noisy sphere, *where everything takes place on the surface and in view of all men,* and follow them both into the hidden abode of production, on whose threshold there stares us in the face "No admittance except on business." This sphere that we are deserting, within whose boundaries the sale and purchase of labour-power goes on, is in fact a *very Eden of the innate rights of man. There alone rule Freedom, Equality, Property and Bentham.* Freedom, because both buyer and seller of a commodity, say of labour-power, are constrained only by their own free will. They contract as free agents, and the agreement they come to, is but the form in which they give legal expression to their common will. Equality, because each enters into relation with the other, as with a simple owner of commodities, and they exchange equivalent for equivalent. Property,

---

8. *http://www.marxists.org/archive/marx/works/1844/jewish-question/index.htm.*

because each disposes only of what is his own. And Bentham, because each looks only to himself . . . and no one troubles himself about the rest, and just because they do so, do they all, in accordance with the *pre-established harmony of things,* or under the auspices of an *all-shrewd providence, work together to their mutual advantage, for the common weal and in the interest of all.*

On leaving this sphere of simple circulation or of exchange of commodities, which furnishes the "Free-trader Vulgaris" with his view and ideas, and with the standard by which he judges a society based on capital and wages, we think *we can perceive a change in the physiognomy of our dramatis personae.* He, who before was the money owner, now strides in front as capitalist; the possessor of labour-power follows as his labourer. *The one with an air of importance, smirking, intent on business; the other, timid and holding back, like one who is bringing his own hide to market and has nothing to expect but—a hiding* (K. Marx 1978, vol. 1: 337–342; italics in original).

In light of this it may surprise that Marx rejects the idea that modern bourgeois rights have achieved nothing. He sees them as "a big step forward," albeit a judgment he bases on the "limits of current conditions." "Within the prevailing scheme of things," bourgeois rights are the best that can be hoped for. This small concession is consistent with Marx's extraordinary admiration for capitalism as a necessary step toward communism.[9] Expressed lyrically in *The Manifesto's* famous encomium to the heroic progress of capitalism out of the slavery of feudalism, this nod to bourgeois rights is very much in line with Marx the ultra modernist, indeed, a pioneer of classical modernization theory. His depiction of teleological movement from "tradition" to "modernity," from feudalism to capitalism, converges with the developmental teleology that invented the dichotomous relationship between public and private. Until the mid-twentieth century, it is Marx's enduring image of the illusory quality of political rights that leaves the most lasting impression on the social sciences.[10]

Where Does This Leave Us?

It is time to take stock. Modern ideas of rights derive from natural law and are attached to people not as citizens of any particular political entity but as au-

---

9. For example, "Private Property and Communism"; "The Meaning of Human Requirements."

10. For the full list of social science citations on citizenship theory before Marshall, see Bain (1933); Branford (1906); Eldridge (1928); Hertz (1941); Hover (1932); Lancaster (1930); Mekeel (1944); Scruggs (1886); Sherwood (1923).

tonomous human beings with natural rights. As Locke first conceived them in the state of nature, these individuals exist independently and prior to any political or social body. By virtue of their pre-political foundations in human beings and in nature, these rights are thus indefeasible. Today's human rights movement finds its roots in this understanding of natural, not citizenship, rights.

But history has shown us that the idea of the normative rights-bearing subject is hopelessly abstract; after all, this is a subject whose very identity is rooted in the exclusively normative "state of nature," where no political power can actually *enforce* these rights and protect the bearer (Arendt 1951). In modernity, citizenship is wielded only by sovereign nation-states. On the basis of the sovereignty of nation-states to determine their internal affairs, rulers have slaughtered and tortured their "rights-holding" citizens with virtually complete immunity from without. At the same time, on the basis of the sovereign power of nation-states to control their own borders and population movements across them, untold numbers of stateless people—historically Jews, gypsies, and other ethnic minorities expelled and denaturalized by their own governments—have been served up to genocidal regimes as sovereign nations refuse asylum. These stateless peoples, as Arendt (1951) so brilliantly reminds us, were in full possession of their "natural rights" as they entered the gas chambers.

Citizenship, by contrast, is traced back to the Greek polis and the republican tradition of civic virtue, where it is available only to those with the privilege, not the right, of membership in a specific political body—itself an entity existing prior to and independent of any particular human beings. Looking from the outside in, citizenship is discriminatory and exclusive; once inside, it is a force for equality and inclusion.

When "natural rights" and "citizenship" are considered on their own terms alone, we are struck by the deficit of any sociological approach—both genealogies are forged through an erasure of the social. When they are coupled together, the political hegemony of liberalism has always required that individual rights trump the political equalities claimed by citizenship (e.g., Rawls 1971). That sociology's foundations lie deeply embedded in the juridical tradition of liberalism, a tradition characterized by a normative, naturalistic, individualistic, pre-social and pre-political rights-based approach to civic life, goes a long way to explaining the silencing of a serious sociological engagement with citizenship in the years before and leading up to Marshall.

Inventing a Sociological Citizenship

By the time T. H. Marshall's *Citizenship and Social Class* (1950) first appeared, the intellectual landscape had been transformed. The singular conflict between liberalism and republicanism was a distant memory. The intellectual and political fray was now characterized by three competing approaches to public life and social policy. Laissez-faire economic and political liberalism was of course still very much alive, but republicanism had been replaced by two versions of Marxism: Britain's postwar orthodox Communist Party, on the one hand, and, on the other, Fabian social democrats and others in the Labour Party who adhered to the ameliorative model of Marxism, or "reformism," as it had been called ever since it was used to characterize the German Social Democrats in the first decades of the twentieth century.

In this postwar Britain, it was the social democrats who had won the debate. The governing Labour Party had remarkable success instituting a social welfare state unprecedented in the breadth of its interference with the market in public goods and services (e.g., health and education), without in any way threatening to challenge capitalism as a system of governance (Eley 2002). Marshall, who in 1950 was one of Britain's leading social scientists, was an important friend of these social democratic policies (Halsey 1982). Thus when he transformed the idea of citizenship from a purely juridical status to a full-fledged *causally* dynamic institution extending from property to law to political participation to social policy, it is not surprising that his innovative concept of *social citizenship*, with its valorization of social and economic rights, gained the most attention. In the heated debate over the value of reformism in modern capitalist society *Citizenship and Social Class* was read as the theoretical imprimatur to the ruling social democratic regime.

The association was well deserved. Marshall *was* a man who dedicated more than half his adult life to public service in the interest of egalitarian social policy. He explicitly intended his interventions to endow political and moral legitimacy to public policy in the interest of *social* needs equal to that held by property rights, individual civil rights, and the democratic polity (Barbalet 1994; T. H. Marshall 1981).[11] *Citizenship and Social Class,* moreover, was organized around the central political debate of the day—namely, whether there were any measures short of Marx's revolution that could fundamentally improve the condition of the working classes in a modern capitalist society rent by class inequalities. Marshall's answer provided much to support the book's reading as both a political intervention and a historical and theoretical treatise on the developmental "fit" between the modern capitalist world and a "reformist" social democratic governance. Like the original Fabian sociologists who had been the intellectual "shop" of the

11. Although Marshall was a sociologist by degree, he spent the bulk of his time in the academy in the LSE's Department of Social Policy (T. H. Marshall 1981).

Labour Party, Marshall divided history into tradition versus modernity, localism versus the nation-state, particularism versus universalism. Like them (and equally wrongheadedly), he allowed only that which could be found on the "modern" side of history to count as real causal factors in the progression toward greater egalitarianism of modern society. And like theirs, his position was ambiguous with respect to the causal status his theory attributed to "pre-modern" working-class social movements and organizations such as guilds and proto-trade unions.

Yet it is the *differences* from these more familiar approaches that most help us understand why Marshall's theory of citizenship was not sufficiently recognized as either an original social theory or one that laid the ground for an entirely new field of social science and why the prevailing intellectual and political culture of mid-century Britain had negative implications more generally for the reception of *Citizenship and Social Class*. One of these was the now familiar problem of the "missing site of the social" across the entire spectrum of public discourse—an absence driven not by the obvious differences among liberalism, social democracy, and Marxism, but by what they had in common. Despite their opposing politics, all three approaches agreed that the "default" institutional and normative political landscape had been invented, shaped, delimited, dichotomized, and institutionalized by the rights tradition discussed above, and above all by political and economic liberalism's Manichean "great dichotomy" (Bobbio 1992), the now familiar fault line between the spheres of private and public that defined the very struggle between the competing norms of market freedoms and political regulations.

Even without republicanism, the basic picture remained the same: in the liberal vision of the world, the private sphere of natural individual rights, voluntary contract, rationality, choice, and independence endowed its individuals with moral autonomy and freedom from state tyranny by virtue of the natural rights of property and ontological autonomy. On the other side, the public sphere was equated with the menacing power of the "interventionist" state, which chronically threatened both the individual rights of property owners and the contractual norms of a free society. While for Marxists and social democrats the normative terms of debate were inverted from those of liberalism—the private, not the public, was the sphere of coercion and unfreedom—the ontology of the political universe was no less a Manichean dichotomy between the mode of production and the state, with the determining causal power attributed to the private and with no allowance for the social as an intervening substantive site on its own terms.

In this dichotomized world, the idea of citizenship as a social institution simply had not been invented. Instead it was a basic legal/political status defining nationality (and a xenophobic rallying cry in times of war), de-termined by one's relationship to the territorial nation-state. Citizenship rights were the rights to protection against other nation-states. If any given national citizenship included rights internal to the nation—and this is by no means something to be assumed—for liberalism their source was not membership per se but the long heritage of individual English liberties enshrined in common law—a legal and symbolic apparatus of *individual* protections against the state. For Marxists and social democrats, by contrast, the source of "rights" was capitalism's cunning trickery. The direction of power and authority in the distribution and nature of rights flowed from the private to the public. Blind to the yawning gulf of the social between the two, the spectrum of political discourse defined the foundations of state-protected citizenship in the pre-social and pre-political sphere of the private.

We should now be beginning to make sense of how *Citizenship and Social Class* was appropriated in the context of mid-century postwar British poli-tics and political culture. As a novel theory of citizenship, it was ignored not because it was evaluated as bad history, bad theory or even because it was ruled out of epistemological court for being nothing more than a speculative hypothesis unsupported by evidence. Rather, it did not fit into the prevailing categories of epistemological possibility at the time of its debut. In this knowledge culture of the absent social, there was no conceptual vocabulary available for Marshall's particular project of redefining citizenship through the social. Instead he was read through the prism of a political discourse that pitted reformist social democracy against more radical Marxism on its left, and laissez-faire free market theory on its right. It is thus not surprising, then, to find that his provocative work did not provoke a "following," nor did any major texts on the subject of citizenship and capitalism appear that implied a "Marshallian" influence. In the 1950s British sociology was busy emulating American postwar quantitative social science, and Marshall's text appeared old-fashioned in its qualitative and deceptively easy historical style. An American edition of *Citizenship and Social Class* was hardly considered at the time.

By the 1960s the world had become a very different place, both politically and in scholarship. Over the course of the 1950s Marshall's prodigious tal-ents as a teacher had produced a group of young sociologists that included some of the leading British and American social scientists of the postwar generation.[12] This, as well as his coterminous role as a leading public intel-lectual, led to a new appearance of the essay "Citizenship and Social Class"

---

12. Goldthorpe, Dahrendorf, Lipset, etc. (Bulmer and Rees 1996).

thirteen years after the first and fourteen years after the famous Marshall lectures. But it would be wrong to take this as a long overdue recognition of either Marshall as a path-breaking theorist of citizenship or the sociology of citizenship as an important new field of scholarship. In fact the new volume bundled the essay with a large collection of other essays and lectures and was tellingly renamed *Sociology at the Crossroads* (1963). Less than a new effort to foreground a new approach to citizenship, the repackaging was clearly marketing Marshall as a leading academic salesman for the infant discipline of British sociology. Perhaps for just this reason of a new legitimacy, in 1964 Seymour Martin Lipset (himself one of Marshall's crop of remarkable student protégés at the London School of Economics in the 1950s) convinced an American publisher to produce an American edition of the new volume. The story of this transmigration turns out to be a critical episode in the story of the long absence of a sociology of citizenship.

As has been well noted, twentieth-century American social science as a whole has been marked by its denial of political power. While very true of the post–World War II generation, a longer view of American social science suggests that this anti-statism was limited to only this generation of the mid-century on. By contrast, American social scientists from the end of the nineteenth century well into the interwar era focused extensively on the state (Cieplcy 2000). Many sought to engage policy and government; others had studied in Germany, where they had come under the influence of the now defunct German Historical School, a group of economic historians and sociologists who theorized the rise of capitalist modernity through the organizing theme of state and market.[13] The pragmatist movement in philosophy and its commitment to a "workable" society was also an influential part of the knowledge culture.

This explicit attention to the state came to a roaring halt with the emergence of European fascism and the outbreak of war in the 1940s. Under the broad rubric of "totalitarianism," a single signifier of Nazi and Stalinist state centralization almost single-handedly purged any neutral consideration of the state in postwar scholarship. Liberalism's foundational view of the state as an inexorable site of coercion and chronic threat to individual freedoms quickly came to dominate the postwar political and knowledge culture.[14]

---

13. The Historical School dominated the German academy at the time (until it was overcome by classical liberal social science in the early decades of the twentieth century) and at the turn of the century exercised enormous influence on the most important generation of English economic historians and the founders of the originally methodologically institutionalist *Economic History Review* (until these historians too were ousted by neo-classical economists and social scientists).

14. Emblematic of the age was a review of Polanyi's *Great Transformation* (2000 [1944]) by Hans Morgenthau, one of the foremost political scientists of his time. In direct reference to the Prussian

This was the context of the anti-statism characteristic of the generation of American postwar social scientists. Small wonder that they rebelled against the statism of the prewar social scientists. But why, then, would Lipset have adopted T. H. Marshall into their fold? After all, Marshall's citizenship theory considers the market-intervening state as a necessary and positive good. In a period in which the concept of totalitarianism had redesigned the conceptual map of American social science, it is not surprising that Lipset read Marshall as a variant of modernization theory—an essentially stateless, self-propelling explanation for "industrialization" and democracy. In this climate *Citizenship and Social Class* was read as an argument for inherent stability in an unequal society as long as it was mitigated by the illusion of political and social membership.

In his introduction, Lipset explained the first American edition of a fifteen-year-old book by arguing that Marshall deserved a wider social science audience than he had as yet received. This was not primarily because of his path-breaking sociological contribution to a historical theory of political rights and social justice or because of his exploration of the balance of power between the inequality of capitalism and the equalizing status of citizenship—as Marshall himself characterized his work. Instead, Lipset defined Marshall as first and foremost a true pioneer in the current (1960s) "renewed interest in historical and comparative sociology." Indeed it is in just these terms that he explained the long delay in the appearance of an American edition: when *Citizenship and Social Class* was first published in 1950, the social science community was fixated almost exclusively on "quantitative techniques and methodological rigor" (see Steinmetz, this volume); in that atmosphere, according to Lipset, Marshall was dismissed as an "example of the old-fashioned type of sociology that had characterized European scholarship before World War II . . . which regarded such men as Max Weber, Emile Durkheim, and Robert Michels as outmoded, representatives of the prescientific era of sociology." A decade or so later, "far from being a representative of the past, Marshall had proved to be a precursor of the future" (Lipset 1964: vi–vii).

As a theorist of citizenship rights whose discovery of Marshall and his citizenship theory in the late 1980s went on to shape my entire intellectual outlook, I find this to be heady stuff. And as a historical sociologist who came of age as such in the 1970s, I find it to be puzzling stuff. Not only do we *not* associate the revival of comparative-historical sociology with the 1960s (with the exception of Moore 1965), but here is Lipset—among the most

---

state, Morgenthau dubbed Polanyi's argument that political power was a necessary component of freedom as manifesting "the heavy hand of Hegel."

prominent targets of attack by the 1970s generation for precisely his "anti-historical" wrongheaded advocacy of modernization theory—sounding a siren for T. H. Marshall in exactly those terms. With this kind of advertising, one would have thought the book would have become one of the founding texts of the new historical sociology, which it very definitely did not.

The puzzle is perhaps solved by a closer look at the new moniker under which Lipset introduced T. H. Marshall to an American audience. In contrast to the British *Sociology at the Crossroads* (1963), the title *Class, Citizenship, and Social Development* (1964) reinstantiated *citizenship* as well as *class*. But it was Lipset's third term—"social development"—that proved to eclipse the others in its significance for how the work was received on this side of the pond. For it was *this* concept that Lipset put at the substantive core of that sociological approach he was so anxious to revive. "Comparative historical sociology," according to Lipset, "is a body of inquiry which, lacking a better label, has been called the sociology of development . . . sociologists interested in problems of societal modernization and nation building in Africa and Asia have come to recognize that the 'old states' of the world have much to tell us about these processes" (Lipset 1964: vii).

So "social development" was really a general form of "modernization theory"—in the 1960s a prestigious and enormously influential field of social science, and Lipset was among its most eminent and powerful practitioners. But for the generation to follow, whether under the guise of "development" or "modernization," it was a kind of intellectual imperialism. Modernization theorists imposed the yardstick of advanced Western industrial (capitalist) society as the measure against which to evaluate (and influence policy in) Third World countries around the globe—and inevitably to find them wanting.[15] Modernization theory, like the so-called "empirical theory of democracy" with which it was associated, thus conflated what was actually a normative "ought" with a putatively empirical "is." It deceptively concealed the truth of Western capitalist inequalities and racisms (among other failures) and instead invented and held up for the rest of the world to emulate a fictitious model of freedom and equality for all, unified not by hegemonic political ideologies but by a democratic "political culture"—itself defined as a set of psychological values committed not to any one set of political visions of the good but to political moderation and the procedural rule of law (see Somers 1995b, 1996c).

---

15. The critique of modernization theory is too enormous to even consider representing here. But among the most significant and influential discussions are Bendix (1964) and Grew (1985). See also Somers (1995b, 1996c) for discussion of the significance of modernization theory for the 1970s generation.

Surely there is a cruel paradox in Lipset's endorsement of T. H. Marshall as a pioneer in comparative-historical sociology.[16] By reducing the field to "social development" theory, which for the 1960s was interchangeable with modernization theory, Lipset ensured Marshall's recognition among the American social scientists of the 1960s but made Marshall a "marked man" for the next generation and his sociology of citizenship lost to another two generations. Modernization theory was about to meet its demise in the late 1960s, first under the unparalleled assault of Barrington Moore's comparative and class-based attack on its universalizing premises, and then under a stampede of the new 1968 generation of political and historical sociologists. Mistakenly aligned with this Lipset generation of "consensus"-driven modernization theorists, Marshall's star was extinguished virtually overnight.

The 1960s Generation of Historical Sociology:
A Knowledge Culture Is Born

Like all generations, the new generation of late 1960s historical sociologists was shaped by a combination of its historical context and a ritualistic patricide of the dominant mainstream scholarship. The opposition of these sociologists to the Vietnam War and other perceived forms of imperialism shaped their revulsion for the liberal government waging the war against peoples of the Third World. While "democracy" was part of their political culture, it was only in association with the demand for "participatory democracy" that emerged from the famous Port Huron Statement and the principles of Students for a Democratic Society (SDS). Beyond that, it was the inexorable coupling of capitalism with democracy that informed their outlook toward politics. For a generation living in a time of prosperity at home with no premonition of the neoliberalism to come, citizenship had little more meaning than that of the privileges of an American passport— hardly comparable with Marshall's driving force for social equality and justice.

The rejection of Lipset's definition of comparative-historical sociology may be best represented by a conference hosted at Harvard in 1980. The gathering had been organized by Theda Skocpol, one of the pioneers in the "state-centered" version of historical sociology, and included many of her generation's leading lights. Most interesting about both the conference and *Vision and Method in Historical Sociology* (Skocpol, ed. 1984), the book that followed, was that they were not organized around major sociological themes but around a number of twentieth-century social science's greatest

16. Which in retrospect he certainly was.

figures (e.g., Barrington Moore, Marc Bloch, Karl Polanyi, E. P. Thompson, Reinhard Bendix), each of whom in some way had inspired this new generation to once again bring history and comparison back into the heart of the social sciences.

Notably absent from these figures/mentors was the entire preceding generation of self-proclaimed comparative-historical sociologists, including Lipset and others of his generation.[17] Another surprising feature of the volume, in light of post hoc general impressions that it established a pantheon, was the minority status of Marxist theorists. Out of nine chapters, each dedicated to a different scholar, only two subjects (Anderson, Thompson), at most three (Wallerstein), could by any stretch of the imagination have been called Marxists. Even they, moreover, were involved in one form or another of a deep revisionism away from standard Marxism toward the state (Anderson), the market (Wallerstein), and working-class culture (Thompson).

One factor that triggered the link between the revival of comparative-historical sociology and the rediscovery of the state more generally was the confrontation with governmental power in the context of the Vietnam War. Not surprisingly, then, the view of the state that these pioneers of historical sociology brought into comparative-historical focus was staunchly Weberian and Hintzean, defined almost exclusively as the site of the monopoly of force, violence, coercion, and extraction—a considerable stretch from the historical analysis of the state as the site of the equalizing institutions of citizenship in their contest with the unimpeded powers of the market. Even Bendix's *Nation-Building and Citizenship* (1964) was read by the 1960s generation primarily as a rare holdout against structural functionalism and modernization theory, and Bendix himself was considered one of the lone sociologists who admired Weber for his tough-minded focus on domination and the state. Not a great deal of attention was directed to Bendix's work on citizenship.

Most important in the context of the broader problematic of this chapter, the connection between 1970s comparative-historical sociology and a state-centric theoretical approach contributed directly (albeit inadvertently) to the invisibility of citizenship. At issue is that nasty problem of the impossible "fit"—or lack thereof—between a sociology of citizenship's "third sphere" of the *social* and the now familiar great dichotomy foundational to almost all

17. This perceived slight did not go unnoticed. With the publication of *Vision and Method* in 1984, I received a note from David Landes, the great Harvard economic historian, congratulating me for my chapter on Karl Polanyi (Block and Somers 1984) but pointedly observing the absence of a long list of scholars from that generation associated primarily with modernization theory and the "end of ideology" but also an eclectic group of other "elders." Landes's list of the missing included Lipset, of course, but also Homans, Schumpeter, and Gerschenkron.

varieties of Western social thought—from republicanism to liberalism to all shades of Marxism. Bringing the state back in was very much a reaction against both the "society-centered" reductionism of the dominant pluralist approach to the political and the "socioeconomic" reductionism of Marxist approaches to the political as mere handmaiden to the mode of production. The rebellion was thus not merely against "anti-statism"; it was equally against the prevailing "society-centeredness" (read class and economy). In this context, a return to "society" was the furthest thing from their aims. At the same time, when the state took center stage in many of these earlier works, it did not have the effect of fundamentally destabilizing the dichotomy but just changed analytic allegiances (from economy to state) and the causal arrows (from reductionism to relative autonomy). Instead of only one master process of history (the mode of production, class interests, interest groups), there were now two relatively autonomous ones (economy plus state formation).[18] It would take history, not scholarship, for the real shake-up to occur with the rediscovery of civil society.

The Rediscovery of Citizenship

The rediscovery of citizenship in the last decade of the twentieth century was a product of history and scholarship. Although history played the greater part, the contribution of scholarship cannot be gainsaid. While no single intellectual product or world political-structural transformation or any particular event can be singled out as *the* flagship idea, event, or "citizenship moment," more than a decade after its initial burst on the scene, all of it has added up to the birth of a new field of *citizenship studies*.[19]

The 1960s historical sociologists themselves were spurred by the lack of fit between their theories and seemingly unprecedented world events to lead the way toward comparative-historical sociology's discovery of citizenship.[20] This is not all that surprising; after all, it was in the nature of their state

18. Before we leave this period in the story of the sociology of citizenship, it would be amiss not to call attention to the one great exception to its more general neglect in the 1970s and 1980s—the enormous body of work on the welfare state that flourished in Europe and the United States. In its initial phase this research was framed very much in Marxist terms as an analysis of the contradiction between "legitimacy and accumulation," in the influential language of the day. The "legitimacy" at issue was modern capitalist society's ideology of equality and justice for all; the "accumulation" was the reality of capitalism's unending need to accumulate, which inevitably produced such great class inequality. For an extended discussion, see Orloff (this volume).

19. Most notably in 1997 the new flagship journal *Citizenship Studies* began publication. See also Isin and Turner (2002).

20. Skocpol's and Skocpol and Orloff's work on the New Deal can be seen as an early example of this shift from a Weberian to a more Polanyite or even Marshallian approach (if not answer) to the state.

centrism to be propelled toward a broader set of questions about political institutions in relationship to the economy and social groups. It was a short step from there to move beyond the "two autonomous master processes" approach to one that hypothesized the state as causally implicated in market relations, or as Polanyi indicated, one that recognized the centrality of political institutional embeddedness—thus endowing the political with its full theoretical due in the shaping of history.[21] In light of the deep affinities between Marshall's work and Polanyi's explanation for mid-century social democracy (including the American New Deal), it was an easy slide from there to the very center of Marshall's analysis of citizenship—namely, the power of politics to reconfigure in fundamental ways, through equalizing institutions, the market-driven inequalities of social class. This new approach nudged welfare state studies toward a much broader *causal* conception of political/legal dynamics as political mechanisms of equality attached to a sociologically inflected conception of citizenship.

Comparative-historical sociology's rediscovery of citizenship was also signaled by the work of the leading state-formation theorists of the 1970s and 1980s—Mann (1986, 1987b) and Tilly (1995) in particular. Mann focused especially on the mechanisms and comparative processes of the extension of citizenship in the nineteenth century by state and dominant class elites, while Tilly developed a newly empirical and sociological definition of citizenship as the "rights and mutual obligations binding state agents and a category of persons defined exclusively by their legal attachment to the same state" (C. Tilly, ed. 1995: 369). Tilly also posed a number of still critical questions on the topic. In his discussion of what he considered to be Robert Dahl's definition of democratic citizenship, for example, he asked whether such a merely normative definition should be rejected because it was "empirically empty" in that no state or political community had ever met fully its requirements. Or do we justify it as a definition because it sets a standard against which we can array real political arrangements or even ask, "What political arrangements are worth sacrificing for?" (C. Tilly, ed. 1995: 370). That these are compelling questions that are still with us today demonstrates the complexity of a subject that so straddles the normative and the institutional.

Substantial contributions to the turn toward citizenship were also made by comparative-historical sociologists who in the 1970s and 1980s had combined their focus on state formation with research on class formation. Instant classics, such as Gareth Stedman Jones's (1983) influential essay on nineteenth-century English Chartism, demonstrated that even the most iconic of working-class movements at the height of the Industrial Revolu-

21. Some of us like to think that this transformation was an outcome of a greater reading of Polanyi.

tion were motivated by demands for participatory *political* inclusion and legal *rights* that were not reducible to class interests but driven by collective expectations of political and legal entitlements borne of the workers' rightful citizenship identities as "Freeborn Englishmen" (see also Thompson 1963 for the path-breaking Marxist analysis of the phenomenon).[22]

Inherited Marxist formulations were inadequate to capture this kind of political agency, and the new state-centric comparative-historical sociology had not turned its sights to this kind of fundamental political reformulation of class formation (e.g., Katznelson and Zolberg 1986; Somers 1989, 1996a). Finding a vocabulary for these politically driven movements inexorably led to an engagement with not only the language of rights, it also triggered a recognition that even in these classic moments of "class-for-itself," it was only through the prism of their constitutional rights as *citizens* that workers came to discover and articulate their "interests" in the first place (Somers 1993, 1994). For comparative-historical sociologists (along with other historically minded social scientists and theoretically oriented historians) in the late 1980s and early 1990s, recognizing popular social practices as expressions of citizenship identities brought together in an exciting new way the now well-accepted focus on state formation and political institutions with the study of class formation, a research area that had been relatively abandoned (and left to the social historians) with the more general critique of class and economic reductionism (Giddens 1982; B. S. Turner 1986).[23]

As important as these developments in comparative-historical sociology were, the rediscovery of citizenship was given an enormous boost by the remarkable changes that had been taking place in political theory for over three decades, changes above all oriented toward a rediscovery of *politics* as such and of *republicanism* in particular.[24] While this is obviously not the place to give adequate attention to the causes of its revival or the complexities and variations in approach, suffice it to say that it was founded on a critique of the hegemony of liberal theory—above all for its erasure of politics and social relationality through the postulate of the deontological

22. Polanyi also focuses on Chartism as a classic example of a non-interest-based social movement that sought to reclaim the institutional relationships that the Industrial Revolution was wrenching away.

23. That it was as early as 1982 that Giddens published his important article on the centrality of popular movements in the development of citizenship rights points to just how ahead of the curve he was with respect to an intellectual movement that only became fashionable a decade later. In retrospect and with just a hint of what was to follow, Giddens, along with Mann (1986, 1987b) and B. S. Turner (1986), were clearly harbingers of a scholarly reconsideration of citizenship in general and Marshall in particular.

24. This began as early as 1960 with Sheldon Wolin's (1960) lone voice in the wilderness, through Rawls's genuinely earthshaking *Theory of Justice* (1971), to Alasdair MacIntyre (1984), Michael Walzer (1983), and Charles Taylor (1985b, 1989).

pre-political and pre-social self-regarding utilitarian individual. Resurrecting the long-buried tenets of republicanism shifted the focus to political identities and practices based not on the isolated self but in the context of relationships, civil society, and, inevitably, citizenship and membership: All political philosophy presupposes a sociology (MacIntyre 1984). Long before sociology itself, historical or otherwise, political theory was guiding us toward a sociology of citizenship (Jean Cohen 1982; Jean Cohen and Arato 1992; MacIntyre 1984; Oldfield 1990; Sandel 1984, 1998; C. Taylor 1989; Walzer 1983, 1988; Wolin 1960).

Historical Eruptions

Developments in political theory and the logical maturation of comparative-historical sociology were only part of the story of the rediscovery of citizenship. The other necessary component was—with poetic justice—history itself. With numerous interpretations available, it is not necessary to rehearse all the possible configurations of social, political, and economic conditions that combined to trigger a new attention to the issue of citizenship.[25] I will simply touch on the issues upon which the field has settled as some of the most important catalysts of the new citizenship studies.

   Among the most important phenomena were the striking new patterns of immigration and movements of guest workers throughout the increasingly global labor market. Large numbers of immigrants and their descendants were becoming permanent denizens in advanced industrial societies, yet the status of citizenship remained either beyond reach or available in a less than complete form (Bauböck 1991, 1994; Bauböck et al. 1998; Joppke 1998; Soysal 1994). The permutations of this peculiar diaspora continue to be wide reaching and include the effects of ethnic differences on full political inclusion (Benhabib 2001; Oommen 1997a, 1997b). Often characterized as a conflict of particularistic identity movements asking for inclusion in (or in some cases withdrawal from) a polity defined by universalistic politico-juridical criteria, this has been theorized as a conflict between states that practice *ethnic* citizenship versus those that are built upon *civic* citizenship (Brubaker 1992; Rex 1996; Rex and Drury 1994).

   Regardless of a nation-state's juridical practices with respect to citizenship, however, there is no gainsaying that global labor movements of immi-

---

25. As I stated at the beginning of the essay, surveys of today's spectrum of approaches to citizenship can be found in the dozens. There is no reason for me to repeat them here, as they are not the point of this chapter.

grants from the poor to the rich countries, from post-colonial societies to the metropolis, means that all advanced Western societies have become irreversibly multicultural (D. A. Hollinger 1995). Attention to multiculturalism has been triggered not only by new immigrant arrivals, but also by indigenous peoples and national minority groups who, despite having the formal status of citizenship, have nonetheless long been excluded from most of its rights and privileges (Joppke 1998; Kymlicka 1995, 1997). The claims for full inclusion that many of these groups have expressed through social movements and other political mechanisms have been made almost exclusively in the language of *rights* and unfulfilled *obligations* on the part of the governing polity—a language immediately recognizable as that of the claims of citizenship. When specifically focused on rights to an increasing share of the economic and social pie, these are readily recognizable as claims to *redistribution* and so have triggered attention to Marshall's famous *social* citizenship. Marshall's contribution to parsing the heated debate between redistributive claims and property rights as a conflict between "warring principles" was also quickly recognized as still unsurpassed to date.

Completely beyond the universe of *Citizenship and Social Class*, however, was the explosive recognition that we were living in a new world of multiculturalism.[26] This has posed a strong challenge to traditional understandings of the rights and obligations of citizenship. Demands for inclusion have traditionally been made in the name of the *universal* principle of equal rights for all. New social movements, however, have mobilized under the relatively unfamiliar banner of a right to recognition based on *particular* identities and group *differences*. Supporters of these *identity movements* argue that they are piercing the illusory veil of universality and equal rights to reveal not Marx's conflictual economic foundation but the deep fissures of race, gender, sexuality, and ethnicity that comprise the fault lines of domination and privilege characteristic of virtually all contemporary advanced political cultures. Identity politics, from this perspective, are rightly pushing the limits of political/juridical citizenship and forcing it to accommodate such novelties as *group* rights based on group difference, the rights of institutions to practice diversity, and the right to recognition and protection for different expressions of sexuality (Benhabib 1996, 2002; Fraser 1997; Nussbaum 2000; Okin et al. 1999; I. M. Young 1990, 2000). The new attention to issues of inclusion, participation, and identity has thus vastly expanded the legitimate

26. Marshall himself was apparently *not* innocent of these issues, and his essays in Marshall (1981) reveal that he had for years been cognizant of how attention to race and ethnicity would impose significant adjustments on his earlier work.

scope of citizenship rights to include gender, sexuality, race, and even environmentalism—to name just a few (e.g., *Citizenship Studies* 2001; Isin and Wood 1999; Lister 1997; Voet 1998).

The uproar in the United States over recent Supreme Court decisions concerning sexuality and racial diversity prove just how deep a challenge these claims for recognition pose for existing definitions of citizenship. Critics of identity politics (from both the left and the right) are alarmed by the specter of group rights; the focus on difference and identity, they worry, threatens to tear asunder the principle of universality and egalitarianism that forms the very foundation of modern democratic citizenship. The idea that "primordial" attachments and loyalties to particular groups could trump the attachments of national *membership* in a polity held *in common* is felt by many liberals to threaten a "neo-nationalism" in which "questions of identity eclipse those of citizenship and democracy" (Morley and Robins 1995: 186). Others have famously worried that support for multiculturalism entails the "twilight of common dreams" (Gitlin 1995) and the "disuniting of America" (Schlesinger 1992, 1998). Even feminists who hold deeply shared commitments have debated this issue of "recognition versus redistribution" (Benhabib 1995; Fraser 1997; I. M. Young 2000). However one views the phenomenon, a central issue has emerged in the field of citizenship studies: a complex relationship, if not an irresolvable conflict, exists between citizenship and identity that demands deep intellectual engagement (Isin 1992, 2002; Isin and Wood 1999; Mouffe 1995; Preuss 1995; Procacci and Salamone 2000; Rajchman 1995; Trend 1996).

One of the most interesting challenges for citizenship is that of "post-nationalism." The term and the idea were generated by several transformations of the last decades. The first is the question of whether there is a new kind of citizenship that attaches to the formation of the European Union. Is there now such a thing as a "European citizenship" (Bellamy and Warleigh 2001)? If so, does it endow dual citizenship to the holder who maintains her original national status? Since there is now a "supra-national" legal entity, should it be able to trump the citizenship law, rights, and obligations of individual nation-states?[27] If so, what is left of the European system (the 1648 Treaty of Westphalia) that defined nation-states by their distinct territorial boundaries and thus made citizenship based on national membership based on those boundaries? A second reason for the idea of post-nationalist citizenship is the far-reaching implications of globalization, most important of which is the apparent shift of power away from nation-states, with their at least nominal systems of popular democratic decision making, toward the

27. This is the worry many have about the European Court of Justice in particular.

abstract, decentered global marketplace, where business and finance capital operate in a zone entirely outside the reach of any single polity or international political/legal entity (Sassen 2001). From the perspective of globalization, many scholars argue that not the state but the self-regulating market is functionally efficient not only for economic transactions, but also for the well-being of citizens more generally: "the problem with Marshall's theory is that it is no longer relevant to a period of disorganized capitalism. Marshall's theory assumed some form of nation-state autonomy in which governments were relatively immune from pressures within the world-system of capitalist nations" (B. S. Turner 1990: 195).

One last catalyst for post-nationalist citizenship theory is the extraordinary eruption of concern for human rights—rights that attach to the individual person qua person rather than being based on the rules and practices of nationality that are internal to any particular political entity. Since those concerned with human rights must of course confront the same problems that have long beleaguered liberal rights theorists—above all the absence of any legal or political institutions that can provide any clout to this new "human rights regime"—there has developed an exciting movement in citizenship theory that focuses on the possibilities for a "cosmopolitan citizenship" (e.g., Archibugi and Held 1995; Habermas 2001; Heater 1996; Held 1995, 1999; Held and McGrew 2002; Hutchings and Dannreuther 1999; Kymlicka 1997; Linklater 1990, 2000; Nussbaum and Cohen 1996; Sassen 1996, 1998; Walzer 1997).

As important as all of these events and processes were for the development of citizenship studies, for the purposes of this chapter the most significant was the rediscovery in the 1980s and early 1990s of the idea of a "third sphere" of civil society—one of three terms I have elsewhere dubbed *the citizenship concepts* (Somers 1999, 2001). The vehicles for this new attention to civil society were both practice-based and intellectual, and both have been discussed at great lengths by many (e.g., J. C. Alexander 1993; Calhoun 1993a; Jean Cohen and Arato 1992; Janoski 1998; Kennedy 1990b, 1991, 2002; Kymlicka and Norman 1995; Seligman 1992; Somers 1995b, 1999, 2001; C. Taylor 1990; Wolfe 1989). Suffice it to simply recall the political achievements of the civil society movements in Latin America, the trade unionist Solidarity movement in Poland, the widespread anti-authoritarian democratic revolutions of Eastern Europe, the 1989 fall of the Berlin Wall, and the collapse of the Russian state. Intellectually there was the emergence of a new "communitarianism," based on a critique of liberalism's excessive fixation on individualism (Etzioni 1997; Sandel 1998); the remarkable "discovery" of the importance of *social* (as opposed to just political and economic) relations in the form of something now fashionably called "social capital" (Becker 1996;

Bourdieu 1986; Coleman 2000 [1988]; Putnam 2000; Putnam et al. 1993); and even the emergence of revisionist approaches to West European democratiz-ation and citizenship formation that focused new attention on the impor-tance of civil society, the public sphere, and civic political participation (Beiner 1995; Habermas 1989; Putnam et al. 1993; Somers 1993, 1994; Walzer 1995).

All of these phenomena and many more contributed in some part to bringing citizenship back into political and academic focus by resurrecting the long-forgotten civil society concept. Recall how exciting it was to dis-cover a fresh political vocabulary free of the Manichean dichotomies with which the cold war intellectual landscape had for so long stifled us, a dyadic one (which we well know began centuries ago) with firm boundaries and epistemological closures between the mutually exclusive zones of public versus private, state versus market, that constituted Bobbio's now familiar great dichotomy of modern political thought. It was in the effort to break apart this dichotomous closure—one in between and independent of both markets and state authority, hence free of both coercion and competition—that East European intellectuals and political activists alike so resonated to the civil society concept. And it was for these reasons that civil society came to be seen as a "third sphere" situated in between, and not reducible to, either the ruthless individualism of unregulated capitalism or the bureau-cratic apparatus of the communist state.

In the context of the tyranny of the great dichotomy, it is easy to under-stand how the newly liberated "third sphere" provided such fertile ground for a rebirth and flourishing of the social in general, and a social approach to citizenship in particular. As such, it also made possible the expression of a renewed normative ideal—one that captured the desiderata of a durable social foundation for the democratic practices and collective solidarities of a "thick" participatory citizenship.

The revival of the civil society concept, however, was a product of a great deal more than a revolution in political language and normativity; it was also an attempt to define and make available for future social movements an empirial explanation of the causal mechanisms that made the revolution possible. Over and over again, empirical analysis pointed to the significance of *social organization* and *associational life*—both formal (e.g., trade unions) and informal ("underground" communities of shared resistance to the dominant regime). Only these social networks, civic associations, and com-munity solidarities could provide both the actual and the metaphorical foundations for the "third sphere." In turn, it was this seemingly novel political and social terrain that provided the springboard, and thus the necessary conditions, for those popular social movements and multiple forms of collective mobilization that successfully overturned oppressive re-gimes in the name of a participatory citizenship and democratic public life. In short, in empirical terms it was the terrain of civil society that made possible the "dynamics of contention" (McAdam et al. 2001), that made possible the remarkable revolutions of the 1980s and early 1990s, and that contributed mightily to a new empirical appreciation of citizenship as a *social* phenomenon.

Above all, then, it was the rediscovery of civil society both intellectually and as a practical site for democratic social action that broke apart seem-ingly immutable, age-old obstacles and transformed the parameters of pos-sibility in political discourse and policy. Suddenly the hegemony of the "great dichotomy" seemed to have given way to a long suppressed third sphere, and there emerged a new *social* site for citizenship practices. It is even more significant that these practices were expressed in the voice of *both* individual rights and civil liberties, taken from the liberal tradition *and* from the republican tradition, in the voice of a people not as isolated individuals with interests to be protected from the tyranny of the political but as citizens whose identities were shaped by their relationships to others in a larger, participatory political body. Only from the site of the social, moreover, could these views be expressed without being absorbed back into either the competitive chaos of market governance or the tyrannical domination of an administrative state. For the first time it looked like a *social* theory of *citizen-ship rights* would be able to transcend the centuries' old conflict between *citizenship* and *rights*.

Once again, perhaps only the Owl of Minerva would not be surprised by this turn of events. In response to the enlightenment signified by the owl's flight, we are currently blessed with an enormity of interest in citizenship—but with a host of unresolved conflicts, antinomies, threats, and challenges.

ROGERS BRUBAKER

Ethnicity without Groups

Commonsense Groupism

Few social science concepts would seem as basic, even indispensable, as that of group. In disciplinary terms, "group" would appear to be a core concept for sociology, political science, anthropology, demography, and social psychology. In substantive terms, it would seem to be fundamental to the study of political mobilization, cultural identity, economic interests, social class, status groups, collective action, kinship, gender, religion, ethnicity, race, multiculturalism, and minorities of every kind. Yet despite this seeming centrality, the concept "group" has remained curiously unscrutinized in recent years. There is, to be sure, a substantial social-psychological literature addressing the concept (D. L. Hamilton, Sherman, and Lickel 1998; McGrath 1984), but this has had little resonance outside that subdiscipline. Elsewhere in the social sciences, the recent literature addressing the concept is sparse, especially in comparison with the immense literature on such concepts as class, identity, gender, ethnicity, or multiculturalism—topics in which the concept "group" is implicated yet seldom analyzed in its own terms.[1]

This paper was originally published in *Archives européennes de sociologie* 53, 2 (2002). Earlier versions were presented at the conference "Facing Ethnic Conflicts," Center for Development Research, University of Bonn, December 14, 2000; the Working Group on Ethnicity and Nationalism, UCLA, January 13, 2001; the Anthropology Colloquium, University of Chicago, February 26, 2001; and the Central European University, Budapest, March 20, 2001. Thanks to participants in these events for their comments and criticisms and to Margit Feischmidt, Jon Fox, Liana Grancea, David Laitin, Mara Loveman, Emanuel Schegloff, Peter Stamatov, Peter Waldmann, and Andreas Wimmer for helpful written comments.

1. Foundational discussions include Cooley (1962 [1909]: ch. 3) and Homans (1950) in sociology; Nadel (1957: ch. 7) in anthropology; and Bentley (1908: ch. 7) and Truman (1951) in political science. More recent discussions include Hechter (1987), M. Olson (1965), and C. Tilly (1978).

"Group" functions as a seemingly unproblematic, taken-for-granted concept, apparently in no need of particular scrutiny or explication. As a result, we tend to take for granted not only the concept "group," but also "groups"—the putative things-in-the-world to which the concept refers.

My aim in this chapter is not to enter into conceptual or definitional casuistry about the concept of group. It is rather to address one problematic consequence of this tendency to take groups for granted in the study of ethnicity, race, and nationhood and in the study of ethnic, racial, and national conflict in particular. This is what I will call groupism: the tendency to take discrete, sharply differentiated, internally homogeneous, and externally bounded groups as basic constituents of social life, chief protagonists of social conflicts, and fundamental units of social analysis.[2] In the domain of ethnicity, nationalism, and race, I mean by "groupism" the tendency to treat ethnic groups, nations, and races as substantial entities to which interests and agency can be attributed. I mean the tendency to reify such groups, Serbs, Croats, Muslims, and Albanians in the former Yugoslavia, of Catholics and Protestants in Northern Ireland, of Jews and Palestinians in Israel and the occupied territories, of Turks and Kurds in Turkey, or of Blacks, Whites, Asians, Hispanics, and Native Americans in the United States as if they were internally homogeneous, externally bounded groups, even unitary collective actors with common purposes. I mean the tendency to represent the social and cultural world as a multichrome mosaic of monochrome ethnic, racial, or cultural blocs.

From the perspective of broader developments in social theory, the persisting strength of groupism in this sense is surprising. After all, several distinct traditions of social analysis have challenged the treatment of groups as real, substantial things-in-the-world. These include such sharply differing enterprises as ethnomethodology and conversation analysis, social network theory, cognitive theory, feminist theory, and individualist approaches such as rational choice and game theory. More generally, broadly structuralist approaches have yielded to a variety of more "constructivist" theoretical stances that tend—at the level of rhetoric, at least—to see groups as constructed, contingent, and fluctuating. And a diffuse post-modernist sensibility emphasizes the fragmentary, the ephemeral, and the erosion of fixed forms and clear boundaries. These developments are disparate, even contradictory in analytical style, methodological orientation, and epistemological

---

2. In this very general sense, groupism extends well beyond the domains of ethnicity, race, and nationalism to include accounts of putative groups based on gender, sexuality, age, class, abledness, religion, minority status, and any kind of "culture," as well as combinations of these categorical attributes. Yet while recognizing that it is a wider tendency in social analysis, I limit my discussion here to groupism in the study of ethnicity, race, and nationalism.

commitments. Network theory, with its methodological (and sometimes ontological) relationalism (Emirbayer and Goodwin 1994; Wellman 1988) is opposed to rational choice theory, with its methodological (and sometimes ontological) individualism; both are sharply and similarly opposed, in analytical style and epistemological commitments, to post-modernist approaches. Yet these and other developments have converged in problematizing groupness and undermining axioms of stable group being.

Challenges to "groupism," however, have been uneven. They have been striking—to take just one example—in the study of class, especially in the study of the working class, a term that is hard to use today without quotation marks or some other distancing device. Yet ethnic groups continue to be understood as entities and cast as actors. To be sure, constructivist approaches of one kind or another are now dominant in academic discussions of ethnicity. Yet everyday talk, policy analysis, media reports, and even much ostensibly constructivist academic writing routinely frame accounts of ethnic, racial, and national conflict in groupist terms as the struggles "of" ethnic groups, races, and nations.[3] Somehow, when we talk about ethnicity, and even more when we talk about ethnic conflict, we almost automatically find ourselves talking about ethnic groups.

Now it might be asked, "What's wrong with this?" After all, it seems to be mere common sense to treat ethnic struggles as the struggles of ethnic groups and ethnic conflict as conflict among such groups. I agree that this is the—or at least a—commonsense view of the matter. But we cannot rely on common sense here. Ethnic common sense—the tendency to partition the social world into putatively deeply constituted, quasi-natural intrinsic kinds (Hirschfeld 1996)—is a key part of what we want to explain, not what we want to explain *with*; it belongs to our empirical data, not to our analytical toolkit.[4] Cognitive anthropologists and social psychologists have accumulated a good deal of evidence about commonsense ways of carving up the social world—about what Hirschfeld (1996) has called "folk sociologies." The evidence suggests that some commonsense social categories—and nota-

3. For useful critical analyses of media representations of ethnic violence, see the collection of essays in T. Allen and Seaton, eds. (1999), as well as Seaton (1999).

4. This is perhaps too sharply put. To the extent that such intrinsic categories are indeed constitutive of commonsense understandings of the social world, are used as a resource for participants, and are demonstrably deployed or oriented to by participants in interaction, they can also serve as a resource for analysts. But as Emanuel Schegloff noted in another context, with respect to the category "interruption," the fact that this is a vernacular, commonsense category for participants "does not make it a first-order category usable for professional analysis. Rather than being employed *in* professional analysis, it is better treated as a target category *for* professional analysis" (2001: 307; emphasis added). The same might well be said of commonsense ethnic categories.

bly commonsense ethnic and racial categories—tend to be essentializing and naturalizing (Gil-White 1999; Hirschfeld 1996; Rothbart and Taylor 1992). They are the vehicles of what has been called a "participants' primordialism" (Anthony Smith 1998: 158) or a "psychological essentialism" (Medin 1989). We obviously cannot ignore such commonsense primordialism. But that does not mean we should simply replicate it in our scholarly analyses or policy assessments. As "analysts *of* naturalizers," we need not be "analytic naturalizers" (Gil-White 1999: 803). Instead, we need to break with vernacular categories and commonsense understandings. We need to break, for example, with the seemingly obvious and uncontroversial point that ethnic conflict involves conflict between ethnic groups. I want to suggest that ethnic conflict—or what might better be called ethnicized or ethnically framed conflict—need not, and should not, be understood as conflict *between ethnic groups*, just as racial or racially framed conflict need not be understood as conflict between *races* or nationally framed conflict as conflict among *nations.*

Participants indeed regularly do represent ethnic, racial, and national conflict in such groupist, even primordialist, terms. They often cast ethnic groups, races, or nations as the protagonists—the heroes and martyrs—of such struggles. But this is no warrant for analysts to do so. We must, of course, take vernacular categories and participants' understandings seriously, for they are partly constitutive of our objects of study. But we should not uncritically adopt *categories of ethnopolitical practice* as our *categories of social analysis.* Apart from the general unreliability of ethnic common sense as a guide for social analysis, we should remember that participants' accounts—especially those of specialists in ethnicity such as ethno-political entrepreneurs, who, unlike nonspecialists, may live "off" as well as "for" ethnicity—often have what Pierre Bourdieu has called a *performative* character. By *invoking* groups, they seek to *evoke* them, summon them, call them into being. Their categories are *for doing*—designed to stir, summon, justify, mobilize, kindle, and energize. By reifying groups, by treating them as substantial things-in-the-world, ethno-political entrepreneurs may, as Bourdieu noted, "contribute to producing what they apparently describe or designate" (1991a: 220).[5]

Reification is a social process, not simply an intellectual bad habit. As a social process, it is central to the *practice* of politicized ethnicity. And appropriately so. To criticize ethno-political entrepreneurs for reifying ethnic

---

5. Such performative, group-making practices, of course, are not specific to ethnic entrepreneurs but generic to political mobilization and representation (Bourdieu 1991c: 248–251).

groups would be a kind of category mistake. Reifying groups is precisely what ethno-political entrepreneurs are in the business of doing. When they are successful, the political fiction of the unified group can be momentarily yet powerfully realized in practice. As analysts, we should certainly try to *account* for the ways in which—and conditions under which—this practice of reification, this powerful crystallization of group feeling, can work. This may be one of the most important tasks of the theory of ethnic conflict. But we should avoid unintentionally *doubling* or *reinforcing* the reification of ethnic groups in ethno-political practice with a reification of such groups in social analysis.

Beyond Groupism

How, then, are we to understand ethnic conflict, if not in commonsense terms as conflict between ethnic groups? And how can we go beyond groupism? Here I sketch eight basic points and then, in the next section, draw out some implications of them. In the final section, I illustrate the argument by considering one empirical case.

Rethinking Ethnicity

We need to rethink not only ethnic conflict, but also what we mean by ethnicity itself. This is not a matter of seeking agreement on a definition. The intricate and ever-recommencing definitional casuistry in studies of ethnicity, race, and nationalism has done little to advance the discussion and indeed can be viewed as a symptom of the noncumulative nature of research in the field. It is rather a matter of critically scrutinizing our conceptual tools. Ethnicity, race, and nation should be conceptualized not as substances or things or entities or organisms or collective individuals—as the imagery of discrete, concrete, tangible, bounded, and enduring "groups" encourages us to do—but rather in relational, processual, dynamic, eventful, and disaggregated terms. This means thinking of ethnicity, race, and nation not in terms of substantial groups or entities but in terms of *practical categories, cultural idioms, cognitive schemas, discursive frames, organizational routines, institutional forms, political projects,* and *contingent events.* It means thinking of *ethnicization, racialization,* and *nationalization* as political, social, cultural, and psychological *processes.* And it means taking as a basic analytical category not the "group" as an entity but *groupness* as a contextually fluctuating conceptual variable. Stated baldly in this fashion, these are of course mere slogans; I will try to fill them out a bit in what follows.

The Reality of Ethnicity

To rethink ethnicity, race, and nationhood along these lines is in no way to dispute their reality, minimize their power, or discount their significance; it is to construe their reality, power, and significance in a different way. Understanding the reality of race, for example, does not require us to posit the existence of races. Racial idioms, ideologies, narratives, categories, and systems of classification and racialized ways of seeing, thinking, talking, and framing claims are real and consequential, especially when they are embedded in powerful organizations. But the reality of race—and even its overwhelming coercive power in some settings—does not depend on the existence of "races." Similarly, the reality of ethnicity and nationhood—and the overriding power of ethnic and national identifications in some settings—does not depend on the existence of ethnic groups or nations as substantial groups or entities.

Groupness as Event

Shifting attention from groups to groupness and treating groupness as variable and contingent rather than fixed and given allows us to take account of—and potentially to account for—phases of extraordinary cohesion and moments of intensely felt collective solidarity without implicitly treating high levels of groupness as constant, enduring, or definitionally present.[6] It allows us to treat groupness as an *event*, as something that "happens," as E. P. Thompson famously said about class. At the same time, it keeps us analytically attuned to the possibility that groupness may *not* happen, that high levels of groupness may *fail* to crystallize, despite the group-making efforts of ethno-political entrepreneurs and even in situations of intense elite-level ethno-political conflict. Being analytically attuned to "negative" instances in this way, enlarges the domain of relevant cases and helps correct for the bias in the literature toward the study of striking instances of high groupness, successful mobilization, or conspicuous violence—a bias that can engender an "over-ethnicized" view of the social world, a distorted representation of whole world regions as "seething cauldrons" of ethnic tension (Brubaker 1998), and an over-estimation of the incidence of ethnic violence (Fearon

---

6. For accounts (not focused specifically on ethnicity) that treat groupness as variable, see D. L. Hamilton, Sherman, and Lickel (1998); Hechter (1987: 8); C. Tilly (1978: 62ff.). These accounts, very different from one another, focus on variability in groupness across cases; my concern is primarily with variability in groupness over time.

and Laitin 1996). Sensitivity to such negative instances can also direct potentially fruitful analytical attention toward the problem of explaining failed efforts at ethno-political mobilization.

Groups and Categories

Much talk about ethnic, racial, or national groups is obscured by the failure to distinguish between groups and categories. If by "group" we mean a mutually interacting, mutually recognizing, mutually oriented, effectively communicating, bounded collectivity with a sense of solidarity, corporate identity, and capacity for concerted action, or even if we adopt a less exigent understanding of "group," it should be clear that a category is not a group (Handelman 1977; R. Jenkins 1997: 53ff.; McKay and Lewins 1978; Sacks 1995, vol. 1: 41, 401).[7] It is at best a potential basis for group formation or "groupness."[8]

By distinguishing consistently between categories and groups, we can problematize—rather than presume—the relation between them. We can ask about the degree of groupness associated with a particular category in a particular setting and about the political, social, cultural, and psychological processes through which categories get invested with groupness (W. Petersen 1987). We can ask how people—and organizations—*do things* with categories. This includes limiting access to scarce resources or particular domains of activity by excluding categorically distinguished outsiders (W. Petersen 1987: 341ff.; Barth 1969; Brubaker 1992; C. Tilly 1998a; M. Weber 1978 [1922]: 43ff.), but it also includes more mundane actions such as identifying or classifying oneself or others (H. B. Levine 1999) or simply "doing being ethnic" in an ethnomethodological sense (Moerman 1968). We can analyze the organizational and discursive careers of categories—the processes through which they become institutionalized and entrenched in administrative routines (C. Tilly 1998a) and embedded in culturally powerful and symbolically resonant myths, memories, and narratives (Armstrong

---

7. Fredrik Barth's (1969) introductory essay to the collection *Ethnic Groups and Boundaries* was extraordinarily influential in directing attention to the workings of categories of self- and other-ascription. But Barth did not distinguish sharply or consistently between categories and groups, and his central metaphor of "boundary" carried with it connotations of boundedness, entitativity, and groupness.

8. This point was already made by Max Weber, albeit in somewhat different terms. As Weber argued— in a passage obscured in the English translation—ethnic commonality, based on a belief in common descent, is "in itself mere (putative) commonality [(*geglaubte*) *Gemeinsamkeit*], not community [*Gemeinschaft*] . . . but only a factor facilitating communal action [*Vergemeinschaftung*]" (1964: 307; cf. 1978 [1922]: 389). Ethnic commonality means more than mere category membership for Weber. It is—or rather involves—a category that is employed by members themselves. But this shows that even self-categorization does not create a "group."

1982; Anthony Smith 1986). We can study the politics of categories from both above and below. From above, we can focus on the ways in which categories are proposed, propagated, imposed, institutionalized, discursively articulated, organizationally entrenched, and generally embedded in multifarious forms of "governmentality" (Brubaker 1994; Noiriel 1991; Slezkine 1994; Torpey 2000; T. Martin 2001). From below, we can study the "micropolitics" of categories, the ways in which the categorized appropriate, internalize, subvert, evade, or transform the categories that are imposed on them (Domínguez 1986). And drawing on advances in cognitive research, ethnomethodology, and conversation analysis, we can study the socio-cognitive and interactional processes through which categories are used by individuals to make sense of the social world,[9] linked to stereotypical beliefs and expectations about category members,[10] invested with emotional associations and evaluative judgments, deployed as resources in specific interactional contexts, and activated by situational triggers or cues. A focus on categories, in short, can illuminate the multifarious ways in which ethnicity, race, and nationhood can exist and "work" without the existence of ethnic groups as substantial entities. It can help us envision ethnicity without groups.

Group Making as Project

If we treat groupness as a variable and distinguish between groups and categories, we can attend to the dynamics of *group making* as a social,

9. Ethnomethodology and conversation analysis have not focused on the use of ethnic categories as such, but Sacks, Schegloff, and others have addressed the problem of situated categorization in general, notably the question of the procedures through which participants in interaction, in deploying categories, choose among alternative sets of categories (since there is always more than one set of categories in terms of which any person can be correctly described). The import of this problem has been formulated as follows by Schegloff: "Given the centrality of . . . categories in organizing vernacular cultural 'knowledge,' this equivocality can be profoundly consequential, for *which* category is employed will carry with it the invocation of common-sense knowledge about *that* category of person and bring it to bear on the person referred to on some occasion, rather than bringing to bear the knowledge implicated with *another* category of which the person being referred to is equally a member" (2001: 309; emphasis added). See also Sacks (1995, vol. 1: 40–48, 333–340, 396–403, 578–596; vol. 2: 184–187).

10. The language of "stereotypes" is, of course, that of cognitive social psychology (for a review of work in this tradition, see D. L. Hamilton and Sherman 1994). But the general ethnomethodological emphasis on the crucial importance of the rich though tacit background knowledge that participants bring to interaction and—more specifically—Harvey Sacks's (1995, vol. 1: 40ff. and passim) discussion of the "inference-rich" categories in terms of which much everyday social knowledge is stored and of the way in which the knowledge thus organized is "protected against induction" (pp. 336ff.) suggest a domain of potentially converging concern between cognitive work, on the one hand, and ethnomethodological and conversation-analytic work, on the other—however different their analytic stances and methodologies (cf. Schegloff 2001: 308ff.).

cultural, and political project aimed at transforming categories into groups or increasing levels of groupness (Bourdieu 1991a, 1991c). Sometimes this is done in quite a cynical fashion. Ethnic and other insurgencies, for example, often adopt what is called in French a *politique du pire,* a politics of seeking the worst outcome in the short run so as to bolster their legitimacy or improve their prospects in the longer run. When the small, ill-equipped, ragtag Kosovo Liberation Army (KLA) stepped up its attacks on Serb policemen and other targets in early 1998, for example, this was done as a deliberate—and successful—strategy of provoking massive regime reprisals. As in many such situations, the brunt of the reprisals was borne by civilians. The cycle of attacks and counter-attacks sharply increased groupness among both Kosovo Albanians and Kosovo Serbs, generated greater support for the KLA among both Kosovo and diaspora Albanians, and bolstered KLA recruitment and funding. This enabled the KLA to mount a more serious challenge to the regime, which in turn generated more brutal regime reprisals, and so on. In this sense, group crystallization and polarization were the result of violence, not the cause (Brubaker 1999).

Of course, this group-making strategy employed in the late 1990s did not start from scratch. It had already begun with relatively high levels of groupness, a legacy of earlier phases of conflict. The propitious "raw materials" the KLA had to work with no doubt help explain the success of its strategy. Not all group-making projects succeed, and those that do succeed (more or less) do so in part as a result of the cultural and psychological materials they have to work with. These materials include not only, or especially, "deep," *longue durée* cultural structures such as the *mythomoteurs* highlighted by Armstrong (1982) and Anthony Smith (1986), but also the moderately durable ways of thinking and feeling that represent "middle-range" legacies of historical experience and political action. Yet while such raw materials—themselves the product and precipitate of past struggles and predicaments—constrain and condition the possibilities for group making in the present, there remains considerable scope for deliberate group-making strategies. Certain dramatic events, in particular, can serve to galvanize and crystallize a potential group or to ratchet up pre-existing levels of groupness. This is why deliberate violence, undertaken as a strategy of provocation, often by a very small number of persons, can sometimes be an exceptionally effective strategy of group making.

Groups and Organizations

Although participants' rhetoric and commonsense accounts treat ethnic groups as the protagonists of ethnic conflict, in fact the chief protagonists of most ethnic conflict—and a fortiori of most ethnic violence—are not ethnic groups as such but various kinds of organizations, broadly understood, and their empowered and authorized incumbents. These include states (or more broadly autonomous polities) and their organizational components such as particular ministries, offices, law enforcement agencies, and armed forces units; they include terrorist groups, paramilitary organizations, armed bands, and loosely structured gangs; and they include political parties, ethnic associations, social movement organizations, churches, newspapers, radio and television stations, and so on. Some of these organizations may represent themselves, or may be seen by others, as organizations of and for particular ethnic groups. But even when this is the case, organizations cannot be equated with ethnic groups. It is because and insofar as they are organizations and possess certain material and organizational resources that they (or more precisely their incumbents) are capable of organized action, and thereby of acting as more or less coherent protagonists in ethnic conflict.[11] Although commonsense and participants' rhetoric attribute discrete existence, boundedness, coherence, identity, interest, and agency to ethnic groups, these attributes are in fact characteristic of organizations. The Irish Republican Army, KLA, and Kurdistan Workers' Party (PKK) claim to speak and act in the name of the (Catholic) Irish, the Kosovo Albanians, and the Kurds respectively, but surely analysts must differentiate between such organizations and the putatively homogeneous and bounded groups in whose name they claim to act. The point applies not only to military, paramilitary, and terrorist organizations, of course, but to all organizations that claim to speak and act in the name of ethnic, racial, or national groups (Heisler 1991).

A fuller and more rounded treatment of this theme, to be sure, would require several qualifications at which I can only gesture here. Conflict and violence vary in the degree to which, as well as the manner in which, organizations are involved. What Donald Horowitz (2001) has called the deadly ethnic riot, for example, differs sharply from organized ethnic insurgencies or terrorist campaigns. Although organizations (sometimes ephemeral ones) may play an important role in preparing, provoking, and permitting such riots, much of the actual violence is committed by broader sets of participants acting in relatively spontaneous fashion and in starkly polarized situations characterized by high levels of groupness. Moreover, even where organizations are the core protagonists, they may depend on a penumbra of ancillary or supportive action on the part of sympathetic nonmembers. The "representativeness" of organizations—the degree to which an organization

11. In this respect the resource mobilization perspective on social movements, eclipsed in recent years by identity-oriented new social movement theory, has much to offer students of ethnicity. For an integrated statement, see McCarthy and Zald (1977).

can justifiably claim to represent the will, express the interests, and enjoy the active or passive support of its constituents—is enormously variable, not only among organizations, but also over time and across domains. In addition, while organizations are ordinarily the *protagonists* of conflict and violence, they are not always the *objects* or *targets* of conflict and violence. Entire population categories—or putative groups—can be the objects of organized action, much more easily than they can be the subjects or undertakers of such action. Finally, even apart from situations of violence, ethnic conflict may be at least partly amorphous, carried out not by organizations as such but spontaneously by individuals through such everyday actions as shunning, insults, demands for deference or conformity, or withholdings of routine interactional tokens of acknowledgment or respect (Bailey 1997). Still, despite these qualifications, it is clear that organizations, not ethnic groups as such, are the chief protagonists of ethnic conflict and ethnic violence and that the relationship between organizations and the groups they claim to represent is often deeply ambiguous.

Framing and Coding

If the protagonists of ethnic conflict cannot, in general, be considered ethnic groups, then what makes such conflict count as *ethnic* conflict?[12] And what makes violence count as ethnic violence? Similar questions can be asked about racial and national conflict and violence. The answer cannot be found in the intrinsic properties of behavior. The "ethnic" quality of "ethnic violence," for example, is not intrinsic to violent conduct itself; it is attributed to instances of violent behavior by perpetrators, victims, politicians, officials, journalists, researchers, relief workers, or others. Such acts of framing and narrative encoding do not simply *interpret* the violence; they *constitute* it *as ethnic.*

Framing may be a key mechanism through which groupness is constructed. The metaphor of framing was popularized by Goffman (1974), drawing on Bateson (1985 [1955]). The notion has been elaborated chiefly in the social movement literature (Gamson 1992; Gamson and Modigliani 1989; Snow and Benford 1988; Snow et al. 1986; uniting rational choice and framing approaches, Esser 1999). When ethnic framing is successful, we may "see" conflict and violence not only in ethnic, but also in groupist terms. Although such imputed groupness is the product of prevailing interpretive frames, not necessarily a measure of the groupness felt and experienced by the participants in an event, a compelling ex post interpretive framing or

12. This section draws on Brubaker and Laitin (1998).

encoding may exercise a powerful feedback effect, shaping subsequent experience and increasing levels of groupness. A great deal is at stake, then, in struggles over the interpretive framing and narrative encoding of conflict and violence.

Interpretive framing, of course, is often contested. Violence—and more generally conflict—is regularly accompanied by social struggles to label, interpret, and explain it. Such "metaconflicts" or "conflict[s] over the nature of the conflict," as Donald Horowitz has called them (1991: 2), do not simply shadow conflicts from the outside but are integral and consequential parts of the conflicts. To impose a label or prevailing interpretive frame—to cause an event to be seen as a "pogrom" or a "riot" or a "rebellion"—is no mere matter of external interpretation but a constitutive act of social definition that can have important consequences (Brass 1996). Social struggles over the proper coding and interpretation of conflict and violence are therefore important subjects of study in their own right (Abelmann and Lie 1995; Brass 1997; Brass, ed. 1996).

Coding and framing practices are heavily influenced by prevailing interpretive frames. Today, ethnic and national frames are accessible and legitimate, suggesting themselves to actors and analysts alike. This generates a "coding bias" in the ethnic direction. And this, in turn, may lead us to overestimate the incidence of ethnic conflict and violence by unjustifiably seeing ethnicity everywhere at work (Bowen 1996). Actors may take advantage of this coding bias, and of the generalized legitimacy of ethnic and national frames, by strategically using ethnic framing to mask the pursuit of clan, clique, or class interests. The point here is not to suggest that clans, cliques, or classes are somehow more real then ethnic groups, but simply to note the existence of structural and cultural incentives for strategic framing.

Ethnicity as Cognition

These observations about the constitutive significance of coding and framing suggest a final point about the cognitive dimension of ethnicity.[13] Ethnicity, race, and nationhood exist only in and through our perceptions, interpretations, representations, categorizations, and identifications. They are not things *in* the world, but perspectives *on* the world.[14] These include

---

13. This section draws on Brubaker, Loveman, and Stamatov (2004).

14. As Emanuel Schegloff reminded me in a different context, this formulation is potentially misleading, since perspectives *on* the world—as every Sociology 1 student is taught—are themselves *in* the world and every bit as "real" and consequential as other sorts of things.

ethnicized ways of seeing (and ignoring), of construing (and misconstru-
ing), of inferring (and misinferring), of remembering (and forgetting). They
include ethnically oriented frames, schemas, and narratives, and the situational cues that activate them, such as the ubiquitous televised images that
have played such an important role in the latest *intifada*. They include
systems of classification, categorization, and identification, formal and informal. And they include the tacit, taken-for-granted background knowledge, embodied in persons and embedded in institutionalized routines and
practices, through which people recognize and experience objects, places,
persons, actions, or situations as ethnically, racially, or nationally marked or
meaningful.

Cognitive perspectives, broadly understood, can help advance constructivist research on ethnicity, race, and nationhood, which has stalled in recent
years as it has grown complacent with success.[15] Instead of simply asserting
that ethnicity, race, and nationhood are constructed, they can help specify
how they are constructed. They can help specify how—and when—people
identify themselves, perceive others, experience the world, and interpret
their predicaments in racial, ethnic, or national rather than other terms.
They can help specify how groupness can crystallize in some situations while
remaining latent and merely potential in others. And they can help link
macro-level outcomes with micro-level processes.

Implications

At this point a critic might interject, "What is the point of all this? Even if we
can study 'ethnicity without groups,' why should we? Concepts invariably
simplify the world; that the concept of discrete and bounded ethnic groups
does so, suggesting something more substantial and clear-cut than really
exists, cannot be held against it. The concept of ethnic group may be a blunt
instrument, but it is good enough as a first approximation. This talk about
groupness and framing and practical categories and cognitive schemas is all
well and good, but meanwhile the killing goes on. Does the critique matter
in the real world, or—if at all—only in the ivory tower? What practical
difference does it make?"

I believe the critique of groupism does have implications, albeit rather

15. Cognitive perspectives, in this broad sense, include not only those developed in cognitive psychology and cognitive anthropology, but also those developed in the post- (and anti-) Parsonian "cognitive
turn" in sociological and (more broadly) social theory (DiMaggio and Powell 1991), especially in
response to the influence of phenomenological and ethnomethodological work (Garfinkel 1967;
Heritage 1984; Schutz 1962). Cognitive perspectives are central to the influential syntheses of Bourdieu
and Giddens and—in a very different form—to the enterprise of conversation analysis.

general ones, for the ways in which researchers, journalists, policymakers, nongovernmental organizations, and others come to terms, analytically and practically, with what we ordinarily—though perhaps too readily—call ethnic conflict and ethnic violence. Here I would like to enumerate five of these.

First, sensitivity to framing dynamics, to the generalized coding bias in favor of ethnicity, and to the sometimes strategic or even cynical use of ethnic framing to mask the pursuit of clan, clique, or class interests can alert us to the risk of over-ethnicized or overly groupist interpretations of (and interventions in) situations of conflict and violence (Bowen 1996). One need not subscribe to a reductionist "elite manipulation" view of politicized ethnicity (Brubaker 1998) to acknowledge that the "spin" put on conflicts by participants may conceal as much as it reveals and that the representation of conflicts as conflicts between ethnic or national groups may obscure the interests at stake and the dynamics involved. What is represented as ethnic conflict or ethnic war, such as the violence in the former Yugoslavia, may have as much or more to do with thuggery, warlordship, opportunistic looting, and black-market profiteering than with ethnicity (Mueller 2000; cf. P. Collier 1999).

Second, recognition of the centrality of organizations in ethnic conflict and ethnic violence, of the often equivocal character of their leaders' claims to speak and act in the name of ethnic groups, and of the performative nature of ethno-political rhetoric, enlisted in the service of group-making projects, can remind us not to mistake groupist rhetoric for real groupness, the putative groups of ethno-political rhetoric for substantial things-in-the-world.

Third, awareness of the interest that ethnic and nationalist leaders may have in living *off* politics, as well as *for* politics, to borrow the classic distinction of Max Weber (1946a: 84), and awareness of the possible divergence between the interests of leaders and those of their putative constituents can keep us from accepting at face value leaders' claims about the beliefs, desires, and interests of their constituents.

Fourth, sensitivity to the variable and contingent, waxing and waning nature of groupness and to the fact that high levels of groupness may be more the result of conflict (especially violent conflict) than its underlying cause can focus our analytical attention and policy interventions on the processes through which groupness tends to develop and crystallize and those through which it may subside. Some attention has been given recently to the former, including tipping and cascade mechanisms (Kuran 1998; Laitin 1995) and mechanisms governing the activation and diffusion of schemas and the "epidemiology of representations" (Sperber 1985). But declining curves of groupness have not been studied systematically, although they are just as important, theoretically and practically. Once ratcheted up to a high level, groupness does not remain there out of inertia. If not sustained at high levels through specific social and cognitive mechanisms, it will tend to decline, as everyday interests reassert themselves, through a process of what Max Weber (in a different but apposite context [1978 (1922): 246–254]) called "routiniza- tion" (*Veralltäglichung;* literally, "toward everydayness").

Last, a disaggregating, nongroupist approach can bring into analytical and policy focus the critical importance of intra-ethnic mechanisms in generat- ing and sustaining putatively inter-ethnic conflict (Brubaker and Laitin 1998: 433). These include in-group "policing," monitoring, or sanctioning pro- cesses (Laitin 1995); "ethnic outbidding," through which electoral competi- tion can foster extreme ethnicization (Horowitz 1985; Rothschild 1981); the calculated instigation or provocation of conflict with outsiders by vulner- able incumbents seeking to deflect in-group challenges to their positions; and in-group processes bearing on the dynamics of recruitment into gangs, militias, terrorist groups, or guerrilla armies, including honoring, shaming, and shunning practices, rituals of manhood, inter-generational tensions, and the promising and provision of material and symbolic rewards for martyrs.

Ethnicity at Work in a Transylvanian Town

At this point, I would like to add some flesh to the bare-bones analytical argument sketched above. It is tempting to comment on the United States. It would be easy to score rhetorical points by emphasizing that the "groups" taken to constitute the canonical "ethnoracial pentagon" (D. A. Hollinger 1995)—African Americans, Asian Americans, Whites, Native Americans, and Latinos—are (with the partial exception of African Americans) not groups at all but categories, backed by political entrepreneurs and en- trenched in governmental and other organizational routines of social count- ing and accounting (Office of Management and Budget 1994). It would be easy to highlight the enormous cultural heterogeneity within these and other putative "groups" and the minimal degree of groupness associated with many ethnic categories in the United States (Gans 1979; Heisler 1991).

But rather than take this tack, I will try to address a more difficult case, drawn from a region historically characterized by much higher degrees of ethnic and national groupness. I want to consider briefly how ethnicity works in an East Central European context characterized by continuous and often intense elite-level ethno-national conflict since the fall of communism (and, of course, by a much longer history of ethno-national tension). Here too, I want to suggest, we can fruitfully analyze ethnicity without groups.

The setting, familiar to me from field research conducted in the second half of the 1990s, is the city of Cluj, the main administrative, economic, and cultural center of the Transylvanian region of Romania. Of the approximately 330,000 residents, a substantial minority—somewhere between 14 and 23 percent—identify themselves as Hungarian by ethno-cultural nationality.[16] The city has been the site of protracted and seemingly intractable ethno-national conflict since the collapse of the Ceauşescu regime in December 1989. But this is not, I will argue, best understood as a conflict between ethnic or national groups. To think of it as a conflict between groups is to conflate categories ("Hungarian" and "Romanian") with groups ("the Hungarians," "the Romanians"); to obscure the generally low, although fluctuating, degree of groupness in this setting; to mistake the putative groups invoked by ethno-national rhetoric for substantial things-in-the-world; to accept, at least tacitly, the claims of nationalist organizations to speak for the "groups" they claim to represent; and to neglect the everyday contexts in which ethnic and national categories take on meaning and the processes through which ethnicity actually "works" in everyday life.

Here, as elsewhere, the protagonists of the conflict have been organizations, not groups. The conflict has pitted the town's three-term mayor—the flamboyant Romanian nationalist Gheorghe Funar—and the statewide Romanian nationalist parties against the Cluj-based Democratic Association of Hungarians of Romania (DAHR), at once a statewide political party with its electoral base in Transylvania and an organization claiming to represent and further the interests of the Hungarian minority in Romania. Rhetoric has been heated on both sides. Mayor Funar has accused Hungary of harboring irredentist designs on Transylvania;[17] he has called the DAHR a "terrorist organization"; and he has accused Transylvanian Hungarians of secretly

16. In the United States and much of Northern and Western Europe, "nationality" ordinarily means "citizenship"—that is, membership of the state—and "nation" and "state" are often used interchangeably. In Central and Eastern Europe, by contrast, "nation" and "nationality" do not refer in the first instance to the state but ordinarily invoke an ethno-cultural frame of reference independent of—and often cutting across the boundaries of—statehood and citizenship. To identify oneself as Hungarian by nationality in Transylvania is to invoke a state-transcending Hungarian ethno-cultural "nation." In the text, following the usage in this setting, I use "ethnic" and "national" interchangeably.

At the last census, conducted in 1992, 23 percent of the population of Cluj identified as Hungarian. More recent statistics, however, suggest a smaller population identifying as Hungarian, at least among younger age cohorts. Of persons getting married in 1999, 14.4 percent identified their nationality as Hungarian. Of primary, middle school, and secondary school students in 1999–2000, 15.1, 14.3, and 14.8 percent respectively identified as Hungarian. Contextual differences in identification may account for part of the difference, as might different age structures of Romanian and Hungarian populations and differential emigration rates during the 1990s.

17. Transylvania had belonged to Hungary for half a century before World War I and again for four years during World War II.

collecting weapons, forming paramilitary detachments, and planning an attack on Romanians. Funar has ordered bilingual signs removed from the few buildings that had them; banned proposed celebrations of the Hungarian national holiday; called for the suspension of Hungarian-language broadcasts on Romanian state television; called for punishment of citizens for displaying the Hungarian flag or singing the Hungarian anthem; and proposed to rename after Romanian personages the few Cluj streets that bear the names of Hungarians.

The DAHR, for its part, is committed to a number of goals that outrage Romanian nationalists.[18] It characterizes Hungarians in Romania as an "indigenous community" entitled to an equal partnership with the Romanian nation as a constituent element of the Romanian state—thereby directly challenging the prevailing (and constitutionally enshrined) Romanian understanding of the state as a unitary nation-state such as France. At the same time, it characterizes Transylvanian Hungarians as an "organic part of the Hungarian nation," and as such claims the right to cultivate relations with the "mother country" across the border, which leads Romanian nationalists to call into question their loyalty to the Romanian state. It demands collective rights for Hungarians as a national minority, and it demands autonomy, including territorial autonomy, for areas in which Hungarians live as a local majority, thereby raising the specter of separatism in the minds of Romanian nationalists. It demands that Hungarians have their own institutional system in the domain of education and culture—yet that this institutional system be financed by the Romanian state. It demands the right to public, state-funded education in Hungarian at every level and in every branch of the educational system, including vocational education. It demands that entrance exams to every school and university be offered in Hungarian, even if the school or department to which a student is applying carries out instruction in Romanian. And it demands the re-establishment of an independent Hungarian university in Cluj and the establishment of publicly funded but independent Hungarian-language radio and television studios.

Like ethnic and nationalist organizations everywhere, the DAHR claims to speak for the Hungarian minority in Romania, often characterizing it as a singular entity, "the Hungariandom of Romania" (*a romániai magyarság*). But no such entity exists.[19] The many Cluj residents who self-identify as

18. The DAHR program can be found in English at *http://www.rmdsz.ro/angol/aboutus/prog.htm*.

19. Of course this point holds not only, or especially, for the Hungarian minority or for minorities generally. In Romania, as elsewhere, those who claim to speak for dominant nations—nations that are closely identified with the states that bear their names, referred to in German as *Staatsvölker* or "state peoples"—also routinely reify those "nations" and characterize them as singular entities with a common will and common interests where in fact no such entity exists.

Hungarian are often sharply critical of the DAHR, and there is no evidence that the demands of the DAHR are the demands of "the Hungarians." On the question of a Hungarian university—the most contentious political issue of the last few years—a survey conducted by a Hungarian sociologist found that a plurality of Hungarian university students in Cluj preferred an autonomous system of Hungarian-language education within the existing university to the DAHR goal of re-establishment of a separate Hungarian university (Magyari-Nándor and Péter 1997). Most Hungarians, like most Romanians, are largely indifferent to politics and preoccupied with problems of everyday life—problems that are not interpreted in ethnic terms. Although survey data and election results suggest that they appear to vote en bloc for the DAHR, most Hungarians are familiar only in a vague way with the DAHR program. Similarly, there is no evidence that Mayor Funar's anti-Hungarian views are widely shared by the town's Romanian residents. When Funar is praised, it is typically as a "good housekeeper" (*bun gospodar*); he is given credit for sprucing up the town's appearance and for providing comparatively good municipal services. Almost everyone—Romanian and Hungarian alike—talks about ethnic conflict as something that "comes from above" and is stirred up by politicians pursuing their own interests. The near-universal refrain is that ethnicity is "not a problem." To be sure, a similar idiom—or perhaps ideology—of everyday inter-ethnic harmony can be found in many other settings, including some deeply divided, violence-plagued ones. So the idiom cannot be taken as evidence of the irrelevance of ethnicity. The point here is simply to underscore the gap between nationalist organizations and the putative "groups" in whose names they claim to speak.

Despite the continuous elite-level ethno-political conflict in Cluj since the fall of Ceauşescu, "groupness" has generally remained low. At no time did Hungarians and Romanians crystallize as distinct, solidary, bounded groups; in this sense groupness failed to "happen." The contrast with Târgu Mureş, another Transylvania city where groups did crystallize in 1990, is instructive. In Târgu Mureş, ethnically framed conflict over the control of a high school and over the control of local government in the immediate aftermath of the fall of Ceauşescu intensified and broadened into a generalized conflict over the "ownership" and control of the ethno-demographically evenly divided city. The conflict culminated in mass assemblies and two days of street fighting that left at least six dead and two hundred injured. In the days leading up to the violent denouement, categories had become palpable, sharply bounded groups united by intensely felt collective solidarity and animated by a single overriding distinction between "us" and "them." The violence itself reinforced this sense of groupness, which then subsided gradually as life returned to normal, and no further Hungarian-Romanian violence occurred, here or elsewhere in Transylvania.

No such crystallization occurred in Cluj. There were, to be sure, a few moments of moderately heightened groupness. One such moment—among Hungarians—occurred when Mayor Funar ordered a new plaque installed on the base of a monumental equestrian statue of Matthias Corvinus, celebrated king of Hungary during the late fifteenth century, in the town's main square. The statue, erected at the turn of the last century at a moment of, and as a monument to, triumphant Hungarian nationalism, is perceived by many Hungarians as "their own," and the new plaque deliberately affronted Hungarian national sensibilities by emphasizing the (partly) Romanian origin of Matthias Corvinus and representing him—contrary to the triumphalist image projected by the statue—as having been defeated in battle by "his own nation," Moldavia (Feischmidt 2001). Another moment occurred when archeological excavations were begun in front of the statue, again in a manner calculated to affront Hungarian national sensibilities by highlighting the earlier Roman—and by extension, Romanian—presence on the site. A third moment occurred in March 1998, when Mayor Funar tried to bar Hungarians from carrying out their annual March 15 celebration commemorating the revolution of 1848, the 1998 celebration, in the sesquicentennial year, having special significance (Brubaker and Feischmidt 2002).[20] A final moment occurred in June 1999, at the time of a much-hyped soccer match in Bucharest between the national teams of Romania and Hungary. In Cluj, the match was televised on a huge outdoor screen in the main square; some fans chanted, "*Afară, afară, cu Ungurii din țară!*" (Out, out, the Hungarians out of the country!) and vandalized cars with Hungarian license plates (*Adevărul de Cluj* 1999).

In each of these cases, groupness—especially among Hungarians, although in the final case among Romanians as well—was heightened, but only to a modest degree and only for a passing moment. The first event occasioned a substantial but isolated Hungarian protest, the second a smaller protest, the third some concern that the commemoration might be broken up (in the event, it proceeded without serious incident), and the last some moments of concern for those who happened to be in the town center during and immediately after the soccer match. But even at these maximally group-like moments, there was no overriding sense of bounded and solidary

20. To Romanian nationalists, the Hungarians' commemoration of 1848 is illegitimate, for it celebrates a regime that was as much nationalist as revolutionary, aspiring to—and briefly securing—unitary control over Transylvania. Romanian nationalist mythology commemorates not the revolution but the guerrilla struggle against the Hungarian revolutionary regime, led by Avram Iancu, to whom a colossal monument was erected under Funar's sponsorship in 1993.

groupness for those not immediately involved in the events.[21] In short, when one shifts one's focus from presupposed groups to variable groupness and treats high levels of groupness as a contingent event, a crystallization, something that happens, then what is striking about Cluj in the 1990s is that groupness remained low and groups failed to happen, to crystallize.

To note the relatively low degree of groupness in Cluj and the gap between organizations and the putative groups they claim to represent is not to suggest that ethnicity is somehow not "real" in this setting or that it is purely an elite phenomenon. Yet to understand how ethnicity works, it may help to begin not with "the Romanians" and "the Hungarians" as groups, but with "Romanian" and "Hungarian" as categories. Doing so suggests a different set of questions than those that come to mind when we begin with "groups." Starting with groups, one is led to ask what groups want, demand, or aspire toward; how they think of themselves and others; and how they act in relation to other groups. One is led almost automatically by the substantialist language to attribute identity, agency, interests, and will to groups. Starting with categories, by contrast, invites us to focus on processes and relations rather than substances. It invites us to specify how people and organizations do things with and to ethnic and national categories; how such categories are used to channel and organize processes and relations; and how categories get institutionalized and with what consequences. It invites us to ask how, why, and in what contexts ethnic categories are used—or not used—to make sense of problems and predicaments, to articulate affinities and affiliations, to identify commonalities and connections, and to frame stories and self-understandings.

Consider here just two of the many ways of pursuing a category-centered rather than a group-centered approach to ethnicity in Cluj. First, a good deal

---

21. Even for those who were involved in the events, one should be cautious about inferring an overriding sense of groupness. I was in Cluj in the summer of 1994, when excavations in the main "Hungarian" square were about to begin. I was staying with the family of a leading figure of the DAHR, albeit one of the more liberal figures. At one point, he proposed, "*Menjünk ásni*" (Shall we go dig)? At a moment of overriding groupness, such a joke would be unthinkable; here, the nationalist projects of Mayor Funar were—at least for some—a joking matter. One further incident is worth mentioning in this connection. In 1997, a long-closed Hungarian consulate reopened in Cluj, reflecting a warming of relations between Budapest and the newly elected pro-Western government in Bucharest. Funar protested—in vain—against its opening, and when it opened, he tried to fine it for flying the Hungarian flag. A few weeks after its opening, five men pulled up in a pickup truck, placed an extendable ladder against the side of the building, and removed the flag, in broad daylight, as a small crowd looked on. The next day, they were apprehended by the police; Funar characterized them as "Romanian heroes." Elsewhere, this sort of incident—which could easily be construed as involving the desecration of a sacred national symbol—has been enough to trigger a riot. Here, nobody paid much attention; the incident was coded as farce, not as sacred drama.

of commonsense cultural knowledge about the social world and one's place in it, here as in other settings, is organized around ethno-national categories.[22] This includes knowledge of one's own and others' ethno-cultural nationality and the ability to assign unknown others to ethno-national categories on the basis of cues such as language, accent, name, sometimes dress, hairstyle, and even phenotype. It includes knowledge of what incumbents of such categories are like, how they typically behave, and how ethno-national category membership matters in various spheres of life.[23] Such commonsense, category-based knowledge shapes everyday interaction, figures in stories people tell about themselves and others, and provides ready-made explanations for certain events or states of affairs. For Hungarians, for example, categorizing an unknown person as Hungarian or Romanian may govern how one interacts with him or her, determining not only the language but also the manner in which one will speak, a more personal and confidential (*bizalmas*) style often being employed with fellow Hungarians. Or for Romanians, categorizing two persons speaking Hungarian in a mixed-language setting as Hungarian (rather than, for example, as friends who happen to be speaking Hungarian) provides a ready-made explanation for their conduct, it being commonsense knowledge about Hungarians that they will form a *bisericuţa* (clique; literally, small church) with others of their kind, excluding co-present Romanians, whenever they have the chance. Or again for Hungarians, categorically organized commonsense knowledge provides a ready-made framework for perceiving differential educational and economic opportunities as structured along ethnic lines, explaining such differentials in terms of what they know about the bearing of ethnic nationality on grading, admissions, hiring, promotion, and firing decisions and justifying the commonly voiced opinion that "we [Hungarians] have to work twice as hard" to get ahead (Feischmidt 2001; Fox 2001). These and many other examples suggest that ethnicity is, in large part, a cognitive phenomenon, a way of seeing and interpreting the world, and that, as such, it works in and through categories and category-based commonsense knowledge.

22. On categories as "repositor[ies] for common sense knowledge" generally (Schegloff 2001: 308), see Sacks (1995, vol. 1: 40–48, 333–340). For cognitive perspectives on social categories as structures of knowledge, with special regard to ethnic, racial, and other "natural kind"–categories, see Hamilton and Sherman (1994); Hirschfeld (1996); Rothbart and Taylor (1992).

23. Even when such commonsense, category-based stereotypical knowledge is overridden, the very manner of overriding may testify to the existence (and the content) of the category-based knowledge that is being overridden. On the general phenomenon of "modifiers" that work by asserting that what is generally known about members of a category is not applicable to some particular member, see Sacks (1995, vol. 1: 44–45). Among Hungarians—even liberal, cosmopolitan Hungarians—I have on several occasions heard someone referred to as "*Román, de rendes*" (Romanian, but quite all right) or something to that effect.

Ethnic categories shape institutional as well as informal cognition and recognition. They not only structure perception and interpretation in the ebb and flow of everyday interaction, but also channel conduct through official classifications and organizational routines. Thus ethnic (and other) categories may be used to allocate rights, regulate actions, distribute benefits and burdens, construct category-specific institutions, identify particular persons as bearers of categorical attributes, "cultivate" populations, or, at the extreme, "eradicate" unwanted "elements."[24]

In Cluj—as in Romania generally—ethnic categories are not institutionalized in dramatic ways. Yet there is one important set of institutions built, in part, around ethnic categories. This is the school system.[25] In Cluj, as in other Transylvanian cities, there is a separate Hungarian-language school system paralleling the mainstream system and running from pre-school through high school. These are not private schools but part of the state school system. Not all persons identifying themselves as Hungarian attend Hungarian schools, but most do (85–90 percent in grades 1–4, smaller proportions, though still substantial majorities, in later grades).[26] In Cluj, moreover, there are also parallel tracks at the university level in many fields of study.

Categories need ecological niches in which to survive and flourish; the parallel school system provides such a niche for "Hungarian" as an ethnonational category. It is a strategically positioned niche. Hungarian schools not only provide a legitimate institutional home and a protected public space for the category, but they also generate the social-structural foundations for a small Hungarian world within the larger Romanian one (Fei-schmidt 2001). Since the schools shape opportunity structures and contact probabilities and thereby influence friendship patterns (and, at the high school and university levels, marriage patterns as well), this world is to a certain extent self-reproducing. Note that the (partial) reproduction of this social world—this interlocking set of social relationships linking school, friendship circles, and family—does not require strong nationalist commitments or group loyalties. Ethnic networks can be reproduced without high

24. On "population politics" and the metaphor of the gardening state, see Bauman (2000 [1989]); Holquist (1997: 131); Weiner (2001). Genocide, as Bauman observes, "differs from other murders in having a *category* for its object" (2000 [1989]: 227; emphasis in original).

25. Traditional churches, too, are built around ethnic categories, with two "Hungarian" churches (Roman Catholic and Calvinist) and two "Romanian" churches (Orthodox and Greek Catholic or Uniate). With aging congregations, dwindling influence, and increased competition from less ethnically marked neo-Protestant denominations, the traditional churches are less significant than schools as institutional loci of ethnic categories.

26. Data are drawn from figures provided by the School Inspectorate of Cluj County.

degrees of groupness, largely through the logic of contact probabilities and opportunity structures and the resulting moderately high degrees of ethnic endogamy.[27]

This brief case study has sought to suggest that even in a setting of intense elite-level ethnic conflict and (by comparison to the United States) deeply rooted and stable ethnic identifications, one can analyze the workings of ethnicity without employing the language of bounded groups.

Conclusion

What are we studying when we study ethnicity and ethnic conflict? This chapter has suggested that we need not frame our analyses in terms of ethnic groups and that it may be more productive to focus on practical categories, cultural idioms, cognitive schemas, commonsense knowledge, organizational routines and resources, discursive frames, institutionalized forms, political projects, contingent events, and variable groupness. It should be noted in conclusion, however, that by framing our inquiry in this way and by bringing to bear a set of analytical perspectives not ordinarily associated with the study of ethnicity—cognitive theory, ethnomethodology, conversation analysis, network analysis, organizational analysis, and institutional theory, for example—we may end up not studying ethnicity at all. It may be that "ethnicity" is simply a convenient—although in certain respects misleading—rubric under which to group phenomena that, on the one hand, are highly disparate, and, on the other, have a great deal in common with phenomena that are not ordinarily subsumed under the rubric of ethnicity.[28] In other words, by raising questions about the *unit* of analysis—the ethnic group—we may end up questioning the *domain* of analysis: ethnicity itself. But that is an argument for another occasion.

27. Of the Hungarians who married in Cluj in 1999, nearly 75 percent married other Hungarians, while about 25 percent married Romanians. This suggests a moderately high degree of ethnic endogamy— but only moderately high, for about 40 percent of all marriages involving Hungarians were mixed marriages. Data were compiled from forms filled out by couples consulted at the Cluj branch of the National Commission for Statistics.

28. As Weber put it nearly a century ago, a precise and differentiated analysis would "surely throw out the umbrella term 'ethnic' altogether," for it is "entirely unusable" for any "truly rigorous investigation" (1964: 313; cf. 1978 [1922]: 394–395).

ELISABETH S. CLEMENS

Afterword: Logics of History? Agency, Multiplicity, and
Incoherence in the Explanation of Change

Faced with the extraordinary variety and detail of history, the sociologist's
first challenge is to find patterns, to detect a contrast or change or sequence
of events to be explained. The initial definition of a pattern has profound
consequences for everything that follows. If a scholar begins by identifying
"important" individuals, those individuals will tend to figure as protagonists
in a historical narrative. If the starting point is a master trend—the progress
of equality or reason—a host of other historical happenings is relegated to
the back stage. This initial finding of form organizes history by establishing a
basic sense of figure and ground.

In art history, periods have been distinguished by shifts in the dominant
methods of finding or portraying form. Contrasting the Italian Renaissance
and the baroque, Heinrich Wölfflin argued that "The baroque uses the same
system of forms, but in place of the perfect, the completed, gives the restless,
the becoming, in place of the limited, the conceivable, gives the limitless, the
colossal. The ideal of beautiful proportion vanishes, interest concentrates
not on being, but on happening" (1950: 10). The prevailing methods or styles
of finding form also structure attention. In the eighteenth century, enthusiasts of the sublime dwelt on stormy oceans and rugged mountains, while
those with a preference for the beautiful depicted ordered gardens. Similarly,
the conventions for finding form in the sequence of events shape the questions that we ask of history. In scholarship, as in art, the prevailing styles of

I am deeply grateful to all the contributors to this volume for their insightful surveys of diverse
literatures. Without their efforts, it would have been impossible to attempt to discern patterns in
contemporary historical sociology. For their generosity with conversation and constructive criticism,
my thanks also go to Julia Adams and Ann Orloff.

finding form change with time—ebbing, flowing, leaving deposits, revealing anomalies and inspirations.

This shared sense of form—what constitutes an important or interesting question as opposed to a subject worth painting—is the basis of scholarly debate. Any theory contest, after all, presumes that two or more theories define the same question as worth our asking and attempting to answer. Although sociologists label areas of specialization with adjectives such as "economic" or "political," these areas are vibrant to the extent that work is organized around a recognized set of substantive questions rather than constituting simply an aggregation of effort around a topic (Fligstein 2001: 10). But these organizing questions themselves are informed and animated by theoretical commitments, whether or not explicitly recognized.

Whereas much of the meta-discussion around historical sociology has concerned issues of epistemology and method, it is worth pondering seemingly simpler questions such as "what questions are asked?" As the editors have argued in the introduction, the second wave of historical sociology was shaped by a particularly powerful imagery of history, grounded in structural versions of Marxism and leavened by Weberian concerns for formal organization. This imagery structured attention within the histories of nations or societies—however problematic these concepts (see Brubaker; Spillman and Faeges; and Steinmetz, all in this volume)—highlighting puzzles about class formation and political mobilization. But a distinctive understanding of temporal patterning was often smuggled in with this theoretical imagery.

The continuing influence of this temporal imagery is easily obscured as successive cohorts of historical sociologists define new topics and seek to make a distinctive theoretical contribution. Cumulatively, these efforts have begun to converge on a new style of finding form in history, a new style of explaining social change.[1] The distinctive features of this new sensibility include appreciations of multiplicity and agency that contrast with the combination of structural coherence and individual rationality that powered the resurgence of historical sociology in past decades (see the introduction). In place of a stark opposition between causal explanation and interpretation, culture is increasingly harnessed to the task of explanation. Yet as historical sociologists learn to see differently, they also see different things.[2] New topics

---

1. At the risk of pushing the parallels to art history too far, let me offer one more example. In major retrospectives, the first rooms of exhibits typically trace young artists experimenting with a variety of available styles in the process of discovering the distinctive style that would become linked with their name. The cumulative force of the contributions to this volume, I would argue, is that they document parallel moves of theoretical innovations (or, less charitably, reinventions of the wheel) across a variety of literatures.

2. As Jack Goldstone has argued, "we are missing a word for the opposite of 'crisis.' The trends that we

and questions are generated by a new theoretical imagery of social change; the results are likely to be more compelling as the principles of this new style are articulated.

The Classical Style in Historical Sociology

Many nineteenth-century theorists had envisioned history as punctuated, an alternating sequence of coherent societal types and periods of transition between types. Two "historical logics" informed such imagery. First, human history as a whole was perceived as possessing a *telos*—universal opulence, the progress of reason, equality, or liberty[3]—or as defined by a master trend.[4] Second, stages within this overall history could be characterized by their own distinctive logics—systems of meaning or interlocked institutions— which might encompass characteristic contradictions whose full develop- ment would provoke the shift to a new social configuration. Philosophical debates pitted the ancients against the moderns. Toennies described how *Gemeinschaft* gave way to *Gesellschaft*; Sumner perceived a move from status to contrast; Durkheim offered the transition from mechanical to organic solidarity. Moving beyond paired ideal types, Comte identified a trilogy of stages: theological, metaphysical, and scientific. Marx traced a sequence of social formations: feudalism, capitalism, socialism and, in due time, com- munism. Although some theorists resisted this typological instinct, the dominant imagery bequeathed by classical social theory is of history as a sequence of stages, each relatively distinct and internally coherent.

This linking of master trend to sequence of stages is a consequential, but not inevitable, step in the finding of form in history.[5] For if history is a sequence of social types, then the central question of social change involves

commonly encounter in comparative and global histories are: growth, stagnation, stability, and crisis. Yet this vocabulary is stunted, and biased in a way that has made it difficult to recognize the dynamics of premodern societies" (2002: 323).

3. A great deal of contemporary macro-sociological inquiry—historical or otherwise—can be charac- terized as the analysis of the progress of one of three equalities: political (e.g., revolution, democratiza- tion, welfare state); economic (e.g., formal equalities of markets); and categorical (e.g., rationalization and commensuration, as addressed by Weber, Meyer, and others).

4. For example, division of labor (Smith, Marx, Durkheim); increasing material production (Smith, Marx); solidarity (Durkheim, Toennies); rationalization (Hegel, Comte, Weber); equality (Tocqueville).

5. By way of comparison, Tocqueville proposed a master trend—the multiplication of "roads to power"—without an accompanying sequence of societal types (1969: 10–11). Indeed, his assessment that the French Revolution changed far less than was commonly thought subverted the clean catego- ries of the "logics-and-transitions" imagery. Yet, as Furet (1981) argued, the conventional use of 1789 as a sharp boundary in French history has organized—and divided—historical inquiry and debate.

the transition between types.[6] Discontinuities with respect to the master trend are foregrounded for explanation, while both continuities and discontinuities along other dimensions are relegated to the background. Viewed through this organizing framework, not all history is of equal theoretical import.[7] Revolutions, the emergence of new institutional forms such as constitutional states, transitions between regimes of rule as well as of social provision, and the emergence of markets are among the substantive topics delineated by this organizing imagery of history as a sequence of societal types.

This organizing imagery of logics and transitions also generated a characteristic set of questions about mechanisms of social change. If the basic units of history are relatively coherent societal types, then historical change can be understood as a product of the limits of coherence, the presence of contradictions or the generation of strain, which drive differentiation and social evolution. Informed by dialectical philosophy, Marx grappled directly with this puzzle in his efforts to trace how systems embodied contradictions that generated their own "gravediggers" and laid the foundations of new modes of production. Without invoking abrupt transitions, Durkheim located the engine of social change in endogenous processes: advances in the division of labor lead to increases in population; increases in density fuel competition and specialization.

This imagery underlies some of the enduring debates within these theoretical traditions. Among Marxists, arguments over the relative autonomy of the state or the superstructure can be read as contentions about coherence. For structural Marxists, "determination in the last instance" is the final line of defense of an ideal-typical image of societies as defined by modes of production. Durkheim also inspired a lasting concern for coherence, although here the conceptual vocabulary featured adjustment, equilibrium, and the normal or abnormal division of labor. The theoretical focus was on the mutual adjustment or interrelationship of parts within a "social whole."

This theoretical imagery of systems and transitions has organized inquiry in at least three distinct ways. By conceptualizing history as progressive in some sense, such theories identified the outcomes that made some of the infinite variety of past happenings significant for inquiry. Patterns of residence or sociability among industrial workers were made relevant by posing

6. Tellingly, Marx's imagery of coherent stages punctuated by transitions has fueled historical inquiry to a degree unmatched by Durkheim's vision of a master trend—differentiation and integration—anchored at either end of human history by a pure societal type.

7. Discussions of "sociology and history" often link the former to systems, the latter to events (e.g., Habermas 1979). But in the underlying logics-and-transitions imagery, the systemic properties of a societal type identify the eventful transitions.

questions of why revolutions did or did not happen. In this sense, philosophies of history answered the question of "what makes events matter?" for historical researchers (Habermas 1979: 10). The imagery of alternating logics and transitions also provided substantive answers to the question of "which events matter?" The answer was those events linked to the establishment or rupture of societal order, characteristically state formation and revolution. Finally, this imagery served as a brief for comparativists, as the assumption of coherent societal types informed taxonomic approaches to variations in social organization over time and space.[8]

Although elements of this imagery—particularly the overarching assumption of the progressive nature of human history—have been explicitly rejected by more recent scholarship, the underlying theoretical framework continues to inform research, serving as a palimpsest for contemporary scholarship. The imagery of logics and transitions guides the choice of questions to be explained. As recent champions of comparative-historical inquiry have claimed, this line of research pursues " 'big questions'—that is, questions about large-scale outcomes that are regarded as substantively and normatively important by both specialists and nonspecialists" (Mahoney and Rueschemeyer 2003: 7). But what defines questions as big, important, and interesting? No explicit answer is given, but Mahoney and Rueschemeyer (2003) offer revolution, state formation, welfare state developments, and transitions from authoritarian to democratic regimes as exemplars of "big questions." A complementary, and similarly restricted, agenda for empirical analysis is evident in the major sociological journals.[9] Thus inherited theories of history—particularly the tendentially Marxist baseline that organized the second wave (see the introduction)—continue to shape the selec-

---

8. Ironically, the imagery of logics and transitions facilitated the dishistoricizing of American sociology during the twentieth century. Although a debate over transitions to capitalism continued among Marxist scholars (Emigh, this volume)—and informed the vision of iconoclastic thinkers such as Polanyi—in general sociological theory developed through efforts to understand the distinctively *modern* type of society. With the important exceptions of research on development and dependency, sociology rarely grappled with the contrasts or sequences of societal types that had so animated classical theorists. This relegation of historical process, of the origins of institutions, to the background could also follow from more classically Marxist conceptions of the transition to capitalism. As Michael Burawoy has argued in a review of recent, more path-dependent arguments about the aftermath of state socialism, "While modern capitalism may have multiple origins . . . once established capitalism constitutes its own system of class reproduction and dynamic accumulation. This systemic logic effectively wipes out origins" (2001: 1114). Here, then, is a powerful case for system over sequence.

9. In the area of social movements, almost three-quarters of the historical research literature (which we defined as anything up to World War II) published in AJS and ASR over the past two decades addressed either the United States (especially the period between the Civil War and the New Deal) or France between the revolution of 1789 and World War I (Clemens and Hughes 2002). As topic sets, these represent exemplary cases of state formation and revolution.

tion of questions, even as their explanatory role is usurped by arguments grounded in the construction of identities, networks, and institutions. This imagery also tends to divide research on "big questions" from other domains of historically informed sociology that address continuities, gradual processes, and "small" topics such as the family and fertility.[10]

The convention of treating societies as coherent societal types also informs contemporary scholarship, particularly in its comparative variant, which justifies treating nations—and spans of time (for a critique, see Haydu 1998)—as independent cases for the purpose of research design. As Steinmetz (this volume) has argued, this assumption of the unity of the nation-state was given plausibility by systems of economic development that homogenized social life within these territorial boundaries (Watkins 1991).[11] Yet the conventions of comparative case design simultaneously erode the imagery of coherent societal types, conceptualizing different aspects of societies as varying independently.[12] As the penetration of national societies by transnational relations becomes increasingly visible, assumptions of social coherence become still less defensible (see Magubane, Sohrabi, this volume). More explicit rejections of this imagery flow from analyses that treat social coherence as an accomplishment, as the product of projects of rationalization and state formation.

From nineteenth-century social theory, contemporary historical sociologists have inherited a legacy that is fragmented and eroded. Although grand progressive narratives have not fared well in contemporary historical research, other key features of the legacy of classical theory are perpetuated through the routine practices of academic research.[13] The existing literature frames puzzles for new research; published studies provide templates for new research designs. Given this situation, the moment may be ripe for a

---

10. For relevant discussions, see Roth (1979) on the contrast between Braudel and Weber, as well as Abbott (2001b) on the two historical sociologies.

11. Here, the substantive silences—specifically attention to the nationalisms of peripheral areas (Hechter 1999; see Spillman and Faeges, this volume)—contributed to the suppression of material that might challenge some of these organizing assumptions.

12. On "experimental time" in historical sociology, see Mahoney (1999).

13. Events have further eroded this legacy of grand narrative. Writing over a decade before the events of 1989, François Furet argued that events—specifically those that generated pressures for leftist critiques of the Soviet Union—were eroding the narrative of progress that had framed inquiry into the French Revolution: "What does matter is that a left-wing culture, once it has made up its mind to think about the facts—namely, the disastrous experience of twentieth-century communism—in terms of its own values, has come to take a critical view of its own ideology, interpretations, hopes and rationalisations. It is in the left-wing culture that the sense of distance between history and the Revolution is taking root, precisely because it was the Left that believed that all of history was contained in the promise of the Revolution" (1981: 11).

project of reconstruction. Indeed debates over transformations in post-socialist nations have inspired a claim to *neo-classical sociology*, understood as a return to "classical sociology's central concern with the historical process of transition to capitalism" (Eyal, Szelényi, and Townsley 2001). Yet such a return will be problematic in the absence of a recognition of how these classical questions sharply defined figure and ground, divorcing some topics of sociological inquiry from analyses of large-scale social change while obscuring other topics almost altogether (in this volume, see Kestnbaum on war, Somers on citizenship, Spillman and Faeges on nationalism). By searching for emergent styles of finding form in historical practice, such a review also begins to highlight the blank spaces on the map and to suggest new questions and comparisons. Taken together, the contributions to this volume begin to chart a distinctive terrain for historical sociology after the second wave.

Topic and Texture in Contemporary Historical Sociology

The second wave of historical sociology was characterized by clear criteria of relevance. The convergence of theoretical engagements and political commitments powerfully illuminated some questions—notably revolution and state formation—while casting other aspects of macro-historical duration and change into shadow. Some of these excluded topics continued to receive considerable attention, organizing sociological literatures divorced from the renewed interest in historical sociology: sociologists of religion continued to explore patterns and mechanisms of secularization, inspired by questions central to the legacies of Weber and Durkheim (Gorski, this volume); following the example of Charles Tilly, research on collective action reconstructed the shifting proportions of distinctive models and targets of collective action (Gould, this volume); the sociology of the professions was transformed in the 1970s by a trio of works that foregrounded issues of power and addressed questions of historical change (Freidson 1970; Johnson 1972; Larson 1977; Lo, this volume). The silences when noted are quite stunning—the lack of attention to war (Kestnbaum, this volume), the forgetting of religion by historical sociology (Gorski, this volume)—testifying to the power of theoretical imagery to both frame questions and suppress topics. And, as Roger Gould observed (this volume), aspects of the past that appear more ephemeral and less linked to durable institutional change—the recurring turbulence of riots and protests and *charivaris*—have been marginalized in the official canon of "big questions." Still other substantive topics that had been central to classical sociological theory were exiled from the discipline almost entirely, most notably economic sociology—an ironic outcome given the centrality of capitalism to the founding inquiries of the discipline (Carruthers, this volume).

The terrain for current work in historical sociology was established by this mapping of topics onto distinct subfields and disciplines, a set of literatures that understood their topics as relatively discrete domains of social life changing in accordance with endogenous processes. Given this organizing imagery, more expansive arguments about social change could be understood as convergences of, or linkages across, different institutionalized logics. Career strategies turned on the combination or addition of categories: approaching the state using theories of gender, understanding markets in terms of kinship, turning the lens of culture or discourse on almost every imaginable topic. Thus Gorski underscores "the possibility—the certainty, really—that secularization was (also) a political program" (this volume: 322), a program whose analysis requires an analytic lens that encompasses formal politics as well as religious organizations, practices, and beliefs. Lo (this volume) contends that analyses of the professions should attend to how they are structured by gender, race, ethnicity, and colonial relationships. Given the recognition of multiple domains rather than one overarching systemic logic, social change could be characterized as "recomposition" rather than development or transition, as "the adjustment and interpenetration of disparate and causally independent phenomena" (Emigh, this volume: 363; D. Stark and Bruszt, 2001). In a world constituted of diverse elements, lineages, and institutions, *bricolage*—or transposition or recomposition— becomes central to the theoretical imagery of social change.

This underlying imagery is also present in the literatures emerging around topics largely obscured by the powerfully theory-driven program of the second wave yet lacking a home in some other speciality within the discipline. Highlighting the importance of linkages among "people," state institutions, and military organization, Kestnbaum (this volume) establishes the relational quality that characterizes the emerging sociology of war. Similarly, Spillman and Faeges (this volume) argue that "nation" and "nationalism" should be theorized not as entities but as a relation between political action or claims-making and some relevant population that is distinguished from other populations. Exploring the central but taken-for-granted concept of "groups," Brubaker arrives at a similar conclusion; rather than being assumed as "discrete, sharply differentiated, internally homogeneous, and externally bounded" entities (this volume: 471), groups are constituted or performed through the relating of categories of identity to relations among actors. The centrality of politics, understood as a distinctively cultural or meaning-making enterprise, follows from the rejections of both modernization theory and structural Marxisms. In turn, this conception of politics requires what Gorski has termed "eschatological agnosticism," a conception of history as shaped by contingent conjunctures, by projects of annealing and linkage.

This agnosticism and appreciation of contingency could not be built on a theoretical foundation infused with progressive or deterministic understandings of societal change. Consequently, recent work in historical sociology appeals to a theoretical imagery that differs sharply from the repeated elaborations and modifications of structural determinism characteristic of the historical political economy of the 1970s and 1980s. The current attention to contingency is grounded in an imagery of multiple domains or orders or institutions that cannot be reduced—in "the last instance" or otherwise—to some master logic. A full embrace of multiplicity displaces structuralism tempered by attention to culture, what might be dubbed "Marx plus meaning." Pierre Bourdieu has been a touchstone for this theoretical move. At the heart of Bourdieu's (1977, 1984) project is a conception of diverse types of capital, anchored in different social fields, which may be partially transformed into one another. Under the rubric of "structuration," Anthony Giddens (1979) and Philip Abrams (1982) have been additional anchors for this reorientation. This theoretical framework delineates puzzles of historical change in new ways. William Sewell (1992), for example, decomposed structure into schemas and resources in order to argue that one form of agency entails the *transposition* of schemas across institutional domains. In the place of systems and transitions, contemporary historical sociology has foregrounded multiplicity and agency, specifically the translation of a cultural component—a schema—into new contexts of action and interpretation.

The extent of this theoretical shift is evident in recent treatments of one of the core topics of the second wave: class formation. Anchored by classics such as E. P. Thompson's (1963) *The Making of the English Working Class*, the emergence of classes as political actors was central to the expansive literatures on revolution, democratization, and state building. While grounded in assumptions about the determining role of economic relations, this line of work increasingly attended to the roles of culture and agency (Calhoun 1982; Katznelson and Zolberg, eds. 1986). But as inquiry into collective identity increasingly turned to gender, race, and nationalism (see Brubaker, Lo, and Spillman and Faeges, this volume), interest in class formation waned among historical sociologists only to reemerge in a much more explicitly combinatorial mode. In a study of the movement to suppress vice in the late nineteenth-century United States, Beisel (1997) drew on Bourdieu to explain elite mobilization as a response to threats to the circuits of conversion between economic wealth and family status. Informed by Sewell and institutional theory, Haydu (2002) and Isaac (2002) present the formation of elites in nineteenth-century American cities as a process that crossed and recrossed domains of economic activity, political citizenship, residence, and cultural refinement.[14] The central tendency of this new work is captured by a phrase from Haydu's subtitle, "Cultural Transposition and Class Formation."

Just as multiplicity is the precondition for transposition as a mode of social action, this imagery of a differentiated, even fragmented, social world complicates questions of meaning and the enchainment of actions. For example, John Padgett and Christopher Ansell grounded their account of "robust action" and the rise of the Medici in an appreciation of the *multivocality* of action: "the fact that single actions can be interpreted coherently from multiple perspectives simultaneously, the fact that single actions can be moves in many games at once, and the fact that public and private motivations cannot be parsed" (1993: 1263). Thus the politics of perception, interpretation, and collective memory (B. Anderson 1983; Olick and Levy 1997) are foregrounded in addition to the strategic moves of particularly "robust" actors.

Taken together, these theoretical turns profoundly destabilized the familiar combination of structural constraint and instrumental action that had allowed historical sociology to engage questions of process more deeply while maintaining some stable ground for framing comparisons and advancing generalizable claims (Kiser and Hechter 1991; see also Kiser and Baer, this volume). Absent these foundations, inquiry increasingly turned to the actors and actions embedded in sequences of events (Abbott 2001b) or to the robust pairings of cause and consequence that have received attention under the banner of "mechanisms" (Hedström and Swedberg, eds. 1998; for a critique, see Steinmetz, this volume). The whole is displaced by an aggregate of parts. In contrast to the social systems or societal types that figured in classical theory, contemporary theorizing centers on components.

Agency and Recomposition

Heightened attention to multiplicity and the consequent under-determination of social change has led, with a most unfashionable inevitability, to a

---

14. Note that this theoretical move is often, but not necessarily, associated with a turn away from the working class and renewed attention to elites (or "to the most advantaged of the disadvantaged"; Clemens 1997: 12). For Gorski, the differentiation of religion from other domains results from "worldly elites . . . defending the autonomy of their own spheres of action, not only from religion, but also from other spheres" (this volume: 332). This shift of emphasis is also evident and has been criticized in analyses of the ongoing transformations in formerly state socialist societies (Burawoy 2001: 1101).

renewed concern with the nature of agency. Despite their many differences, even the oft-opposed "culturally oriented narrativists and rational choice theorists argued that structuralists paid too little attention to human agency" (Kiser and Baer, this volume: 227; see also introduction). Multiplicity begat complexity begat agency. In her review of work on professions, Lo neatly captures this sequence:

> The sociological discussions of professions in the past two decades have, therefore, carefully depicted a picture of the intersections of the professions, the market, and the state. These diligent efforts to detect order therein, as we have seen, eventually led these authors—and us—to consider the messiness of modernity. Having situated professions in this extended web of institutional relationships, sociologists recognized the field of professions as complexly and quite diversely "structurated" not only through its own increasing organizational elaboration, but also through its deep embeddedness in the fields of the state and the market. . . . more specifically, while professionals have thus far largely been assumed to be the unproblematic agents of professions, toward the end of the second wave they were beginning to be positioned in a more ambiguous, and therefore less predictable, structural location and recognized as potential agents of multiple institutions (this volume: 390–391).

Contrast this development with the combination of structural constraints and rational action that characterizes many institutional arguments (see the introduction). Rather than agency understood simply as the absence of constraint, this line of theorizing appreciates agency as constituted through institutional embeddings. Following Weber's insights in *The Protestant Ethic*, it appreciates that the " 'modern subject' qua 'rational actor' . . . is not an ontological universal but a 'historical individual' " (Gorski, this volume: 183). If economic systems and markets are understood as institutional frameworks that sustain distinctive substantive styles of rationality (Emigh, Carruthers, this volume), then it is possible to address the varying conditions under which this model of agency is viable. Kiser and Baer (this volume) offer just such an analysis, arguing—contrary to expectation—that whereas military operations could once be organized through appeals to instrumental motives by way of promises of bounty, the imposition of "rationalized organization" and restriction of predation required that the modern military be infused with appeals to emotion and value. Yet the distinctions among these types of action—instrumental, value-rational, traditional, and habitual, according to Weber—cannot be taken as given. Ends, means, and motivations are not easily disentangled (Biernacki, this volume), and, as

Sohrabi (this volume) demonstrates in the case of Turkish revolutionaries at the turn of the last century, emotion can deeply infuse a commitment to rationalism understood as a rejection of the existing organization of rule.

There is also a dark side to this renewed appreciation of the historical constitution of actors, an awareness of how systems of regulation and surveillance shape subjects and even disciplines. Steinmetz (this volume) portrays American social science as shaped by its implication in successive regulatory formations that, as much as any heritage from Marx and Weber, informed both the questions asked and the answers given. But the home ground of this critique lies in the analysis of the categories of social subordination: gender, race, ethnicity, and sexuality (among others). Feminist scholarship on the systems of social provision has excavated how politics and policies constitute dependency and identity; such arguments illuminate "the continuing deficiencies of institutionalism, even at its historicized, processual best: utilitarian assumptions about interests and identities; a focus on the political economy . . . a thin understanding of how culture shapes politics" (Orloff, this volume: 201). In a similar vein, Lo criticizes the voluntarist or tool-kit reading of social multiplicity, arguing that "instead of asking how professionals 'choose' from their multiple allegiances, each assumed to imply a ready-made identity, we are compelled to study professions as sites of identity formation, where professionals come to terms with the meaning of their racial, ethnic, or gender identities in the context of their professional institution" (this volume: 392).

These problems and complexities have inspired thorough rethinkings of agency. As Biernacki (this volume) argues, the problem with a "goals model" of action—the classic pairing of ends and means familiar from disciplines such as neo-classical economics—is that the deed depends on its context and its relevance to many possible explanatory orders. Thus, the multiplicity of social order infuses action with contingency, both in sequences of causation—a single act may set off diverse sequences in different domains—and with respect to the interpretation of that event. Consequently, Biernacki contends, we should focus on the schemas of action or the conventional recipes for problem solving, placing greater weight on their conventional status than on some carefully calculated relationship of means to ends. This critique, however, should be balanced by the appreciation that one of the central elements in the construction of modern societies has involved establishing domains in which actions are understood to have determinate meanings and predictable outcomes. As Carruthers (this volume) emphasizes in his review of the historical sociology of markets, the creation of a durable infrastructure for predictable, instrumental action was a major social accomplishment.

This line of argument frames a set of research questions: How does the available repertoire of practices or schemas shape the space of possible actions? How are distinctive cultural schemas combined? How are existing schemas linked to new projects or available categories embedded in systems of social relations and practice? What unifies these questions is an imagery of history as constructed but not as an endlessly malleable work in progress; moments of reconfiguration are less than routine yet enduringly signifi-cant.[15] The centrality of this imagery to the current state of historical sociol-ogy is evidenced by the essays in this volume. Biernacki, for example, follows Parsons as far as the *desiderata* of a theory of action, a recognition of both the creative activity of agents in juxtaposing signs or recombining schema and the obdurate character of the world. Rather than calculating the optimal instrumental strategy in a world where all things are possible, actors work with existing templates of action or cultural elements. Moments of appar-ently dramatic change or innovation are then attributable to the recombina-tion or recomposition of these elements. Biblical narratives of Moses and the chosen people are combined with classical accounts of local resistance to the Roman Empire to constitute a grounding for a distinctively new discourse of nationalism (Gorski 2000b; Schama 1987). In the heated events surrounding the storming of the Bastille, concepts of collective violence and the people are annealed in a model of revolution (Sewell 1996a). Lo understands profes-sions through the concept of "hybridization," "the encounter, conflict, and/ or blending of two ethnic or cultural categories that, while by no means pure and distinct in nature, tend to be understood and experienced as meaningful identity labels by members of these categories" (this volume: 396). As Sohrabi explains with respect to the form of revolutions, discussions of different modes of action can produce a "clash of rather coherent sign systems that may generate a new and unexpected system of signs and mean-ings" (this volume: 305).[16]

This line of argument foregrounds the entrepreneur—individual or col-lective—as a central actor in social change. Even the most basic concepts of social science should be recognized as accomplishments: "groups" are the

---

15. Among historical social scientists, there is considerable variation in the extent to which societal arrangements are imagined as mostly very stable and disorganized only by "exogenous shocks" or "critical conjunctures." An alternative view conceptualizes change as more frequent yet still far from incremental or routine. For a review of these debates, see Thelen (2003).

16. This imagery of historical innovation is not restricted to the most theoretical accounts but is evident in popular history as well. Thus, Ellis's (2000) recent account of the innovative quality of the American Revolution rested on the conceit of a small group of "founding brothers," each committed to distinctive understandings of their political endeavor but linked by strong personal ties that con-tained these differences and produced novel recombinations rather than factional dispersal.

product of "group-making projects," "interests" the result of the transposition of social models of identity to political competition (Clemens 1997).
Although this line of argument invites a potentially excessive celebration of
voluntarism and the creativity of agents, this tendency is curbed by appreciation of how such projects necessarily unfold in particular contexts (Thelen
2003). In contrast to the combination of structural constraints and individual rational action that has characterized many institutional analyses (see
the introduction), this theoretical move heightens attention to the embeddedness of social actors rather than the external constraints of social structure (Lo, this volume).

If we judge from these trends in historical sociology, especially the increased attention to forms of agency, questions of contentious—as well as
constitutive or project-oriented—collective action should come front and
center. How are durable configurations of resources, power, and opportunity
constructed? Rather than being explained as functional responses to the
growing complexity of capitalist economies, for example, political institutions come to be understood as the accomplishments of bureaucratic
entrepreneurs enmeshed in particular systems of careers and ideological
commitments (e.g., Carpenter 2001; P. B. Evans 1995).[17] Similarly, the form of
revolutions and their outcomes is traced to the projects of would-be as well as
unintended revolutionaries located in a particular national context but oriented to models of revolution and reform available in broader, even global,
political discourses (see Sohrabi, this volume). Economic development may
be similarly reconfigured as an "efflorescence . . . a relatively sharp, often
unexpected upturn in significant demographic and economic indices, usually accompanied by political expansion and institution building and cultural synthesis and consolidation" (Goldstone 2002: 333). Here again, the
reconfiguration of the whole—at times championed by particularly creative
economic or political leaders—leads to increases in total social production.

From the vantage point of the strong claims of political economy, however, this move may appear to embrace voluntarism with too much enthusiasm. Reviewing scholarship on a more recent wave of macro-social changes,
the transformation of formerly state socialist societies, Burawoy argued that
an undue optimism followed from "an overestimation of the importance of
elites, patterns of privatization, and political democracy, and on an underestimation of the importance of capital accumulation, class relations, and

17. For political historians of the United States, Stephen Skowronek's extremely influential *Building a
New American State* (1982) represented a halfway point in this theoretical shift. For Skowronek, the
transformation of political institutions was provoked by pressure from industrialization and the
expansion of markets but only—and not necessarily—accomplished through the agency of bureaucratic reformers.

global forces" (2001: 1101). Having documented the apparent openness and contingency of social transformations, contemporary historical sociology must meet the charge that deeper, more systemic constraints are being overlooked, obscured by a new theoretical imagery that highlights indeterminacy and agency. One response has been to reject the reimposition of an imagery of hard structural constraints—even in combination with institutionalism's limited space for individual agency—in favor of the challenge of mapping the social world at any given time and place as a space of possibilities or distribution of probabilities.[18] In the words of Roger Gould, "Recognizing that more than one outcome is in principle possible, in other words, does not require one to accept that all outcomes are *equally* possible or that the outcome that ensues is purely a matter of chance or free will" (this volume: 299). Thus the foregrounding of agency also entails a reconsideration of the limits—albeit sometimes soft or indeterminate—of the possible.

Multiplicity and Path Dependence

What changes when we start by looking for multiplicity in social settings? In combination with the foregrounding of a historically constituted agency, processes of social reproduction and change appear as chains of probabilities. From this society at this point in time, not all things are possible, but more than one trajectory of change is conceivable. Thus questions about the transition to capitalism are supplanted by inquiries into transitions to capitalisms; the welfare state is decomposed into distinctive regime types; plurals dominate (see Emigh, Orloff, this volume). A similar focus on explaining variation within a related set of transformations is evident across many specialties within historical sociology. Revisiting a core question of classical theory, the origin of the modern state, Thomas Ertman focused on fragmentation along single dimensions (in this case, political organization) and incoherence across dimensions (political organization and ideology). Seeking to explain the distribution of "estate-type" or tripartite assemblies in early modern Europe, Ertman pointed to a conjuncture of institutional fragmentation and alternative models in the mid-1200s:

> Given the lack of territorially integrated local communities like the Roman *civitas* or the Carolingian county in either Latin Europe or Germany, it must have seemed an easier proposition to create functionally rather than territorially based assemblies. . . . [The] tripartite

18. Kiser and Baer reinforce this point, asserting that "The key question raised but not answered in Weber's model" (this volume: 441) is under what conditions these different micro-foundations (instrumental rationality, values, emotions, or habits) will be important.

vision [of nobles, clergy, and third estate] provided the perfect ideological blueprint for such an assembly since it explicitly encouraged the
solidaristic self-organization of three groups—the clergy, the nobles,
and the burghers—whose privileges were under threat from royal attempts at centralization (1997: 69).

In the place of an ideal-typical representation of medieval states as em-
bodiments of a coherent social model, Ertman sketched how political entrepreneurs engaged in a sort of bricolage, rummaging through the available
tool kit (Swidler 1986) of political theory, in a setting of fragmented institutional legacies. Components may be welded together into more or less durable configurations, but these configurations are like planets crossing an
endless asteroid belt of alternative models of organization and uncontained
forces of opposition. The detritus of history—competing cultural models,
political legacies, and economic formations—both threatens existing configurations and provides the materials for constructing novel institutional arrangements (Clemens and Cook 1999).

The project of mapping multiplicity has been advanced by debates within
organizational sociology, particularly the "new institutionalisms" with their
attention to the concept of the organizational or institutional field. Rather
than being conceived as an integrated system, contemporary capitalism is
portrayed as an aggregate of distinct institutions—market, state, family, policy, religion—that "shape individual preferences and organizational interests
as well as the repertoire of behaviors by which they may attain them. These
institutions are potentially contradictory and hence make multiple logics
available to individuals and organizations. Individuals and organizations
transform the institutional relations of society by exploiting these contradictions" (Friedland and Alford 1991: 232). The mapping of elements from one
domain into another helps to explain why agency can have durable consequences, shaping, constraining, and enabling future possibilities (Sewell
1992). At the intersection of religion and politics, for example, "Cleric, rabbi,
sadhu and mullah mount the rostrum, occupy the public place, seeking to
ordinate society according to a text originating outside of it. The territoriality and the historicity of the nation-state are being transformed into
vessels of divine purpose" (Friedland 1999: 301–302; see also Gorski, Spillman and Faeges, this volume).

In recognizing all this particularism, such analyses risk entering the territory of sociological history as simply one damn thing after another. To avoid
this fate, scholars have begun to ask different questions. What shapes the
perception of components, the archiving of alternatives? Under what conditions and through what mechanisms is bricolage effected and made dura-

ble?[19] By attending to the intentions of agents—but also recognizing when intentions were and were not realized—studies are informed by a more nuanced sense of the interplay of structure and action: "In the realm of social movements . . . mobilizing appeals compete with one another precisely because there are many ways in which people can view their social position relative to others. This is true not only because people linked by a particular set of social relations can be divided into subgroups in a variety of ways that satisfy the equivalence criterion equally well; it is also true because different kinds of social ties are accorded dramatically different amounts of salience from different ideological standpoints" (R.V. Gould 1995: 16–17). Thus attention to the multiplicity of social relations or identities provides leverage on the puzzle of why events of a certain character mobilize or energize some patterns of collective action and not others. Such an enterprise should also provide more precise identification of the sources of contradiction, the moments of rupture (Sewell 1996b), and the character of discontinuities and incoherences (Clemens 1999a). This imagery does not necessarily dissolve into an endless discovery of differences but can be grounded in very basic, old-fashioned theoretical insights: human beings occupy multiple social roles; their lives are woven across multiple social domains.

From this theoretical perspective, durable and relatively coherent sociopolitical formations should be understood as important accomplishments rather than assumed as forms of social order. Capitalism, for example, is not a given system but a political and cultural creation (Emigh, this volume). Actors seeking to secure their political dominance work to eliminate alternatives, to minimize incoherence that can generate challenge. In an elegant study of the development of the state in Japan, Eiko Ikegami (1995) traced how the elaboration of samurai culture was both a mechanism for containing violence and a resource for nonconformism. Relations of dependence build on themselves, cementing durable relationships between networks of social actors and political regimes (Carruthers 1996). In other settings, state efforts at consolidation may provide the seeds for subsequent fragmentation. In the former Soviet Union, Rogers Brubaker (1996) argued, the introduction of an internal passport system for controlling mobility in a heterogeneous society helped to construct and crystallize "national identities," which subsequently fueled secession movements. Projects and processes of social closure (Brubaker, this volume) thus restrict possibilities and shape the distribution of probable trajectories of social change and reproduction.

---

19. In effect, the institutional turn in much historical explanation suggests conscious attention to the structure of "deep analogies" (Stinchcombe 1978) across cases both temporal and spatial. Charles Tilly's recent *Durable Inequality* (1998a) may serve as an example.

To capture the processes by which action at one moment constrains or structures possibilities in the future, theorists have developed a rich vocabulary: lock-in, crystallization, stickiness, feedback processes, and path dependence. The last of these is perhaps the most theoretically developed (Haydu 1998; Pierson 2000), drawing on economic models in which individual behavior—particularly logics of increasing returns and sunk costs—generates a social inertia along a particular path of development. Other analyses focus not on individual instrumental action but the dynamics of mobilization, network development, and the constitution of collective identities. In elaborating a "polity-centered model," Skocpol (1992) illuminated how processes of policy contestation and implementation reinforced particular patterns of group mobilization, thereby shaping the distribution of effective political power for decades to come (see also Hacker 2002; Orloff, this volume; Rothstein 1992).

If these arguments are taken seriously, then it becomes difficult to retain the imagery of discrete social systems and abrupt transitions that is shared by both classical theory and, rather oddly, current discussions of path dependence among institutionally inclined political scientists. Insofar as theories of path dependency emphasize the under-determined and contingent events—"critical conjunctures" (Hacker 2002)—that establish an initial path, all that is prior to this moment is rendered inconsequential to explanations of subsequent developments (Pierson 2000; for critiques, see Katznelson 2003 and Steinmetz, this volume). A relevant touchstone becomes Tocqueville's (1955) analysis of the French Revolution not as an overwhelming discontinuity but as a disorganization that was followed by a recomposition of a new French regime out of the components of the old, a similar institutional regime only more so. Thus the new economic sociology does not sharply differentiate modern from pre-modern (Goldstone 2002) but recognizes the presence of nonmarket forms and relationships of exchange even in the heart of capitalist economies (Carruthers, this volume), and the presence of and the stamp of socialist states on the new capitalisms of Eastern Europe (Eyal, Szelényi, and Townsley 2001; Emigh, this volume). In a quite literal sense, for these arguments the past is what agents make of it, not only through interpretive reconstructions, but also through the recombination of institutional legacies, network structures, and already available cultural schemas.

The Uneasy Alliance of Comparative and Historical

The shift of focus from system to process and multiplicity clearly requires new theories of societal change and reproduction, but it has also undermined the methods centrally deployed in and identified with historical sociology. If the imagery of change as contingency and recomposition could be contained within clearly bounded social units such as nation-states, then it might still be possible to imagine a field of *comparative-historical* sociology that juxtaposed complex sequences or narratives of events from diverse settings. Were this possible, comparative methods—a central element of the identity of this subfield (Skocpol and Somers 1980; C. Tilly 1984)—might be retained as an organizing template for research, albeit in modified form.[20] But just as the imagery of internally coherent social systems has been challenged by a vision of multiple, overlapping, colliding social domains (Magubane, this volume), the clarity of social boundaries has been eroded by other shifts in the practice of historical sociology.

With its sharp focus on capitalism, state building, and revolution, the theoretical framework of the second wave forcefully directed scholarly attention to a limited set of cases, usually nations. For all three topics, Western Europe was given pride of place. Historical sociology is one of the relatively rare specialties in American sociology where the United States is not the taken-for-granted center of gravity. This geographically focused—or restricted—field of inquiry has been transformed by two developments. First, the quest for distinction within scholarship has fueled research on new cases, expanding the evidentiary base far beyond the cases that were central to the elaboration of classical—as well as other—sociological theory. The "named debates" over the transition to capitalism have expanded across both additional early modern cases, such as the "failure" of Tuscany, and later economic transformations across the globe (Emigh, this volume). Building on a wealth of new scholarship on the major social revolutions, attention turned to other cases: Turkey, Iran, and Japan, among others (Sohrabi, this volume). A rapidly growing literature on the historical de-

20. When sociologists of the 1970s and 1980s renewed a sustained, collective engagement with historical research, they had few tools for reconstructing theories of major social or institutional transformations. One initial response was to pursue a "holding constant" approach, which focused on relations among factors within a particular society at a particular time. As Biernacki (this volume) explains, the definition of historical epochs was a strategy for preserving "the identity of action." But this approach leads away from an understanding of transitions between social types and assumes away the *accomplishment* of social integration or religious unification (Gorski, this volume) as a political project. As William Roy has argued, "one cannot construct an explanation without variation in the dependent variable. If large-scale processes are held constant within a period, they have no variation and cannot be fully explained" (1987: 56). Alternatively, there have been heated debates over the merits of pursuing "covering laws" that would apply across settings or periods (Kiser and Hechter 1991; Somers 1998). As Jeffrey Haydu observed, this approach treats "periods" as "cases" that are independent of one another rather than grappling with how to "rethink 'cases' when one case becomes another over time" (1998: 349). Such a rethinking is made more difficult when we start with an imagery of two coherent ideal-types and then challenge ourselves to theorize the transformation of one into the other.

velopment of social provision inspired research on nations beyond Western Europe and Scandinavia (Orloff, this volume). Even the relatively new literature on the sociology of war rapidly moved beyond Europe and, in the process, documented important differences in the relationship of war making and state making (Centeno 2002; Kestnbaum, this volume). In all these instances—and more could be offered—strong, determinate claims about historical relationships and processes were undermined by the addition of cases from different times and places.

Moreover, a second line of critique and contribution erodes the very concept of independent cases. The elision of Africa from historical sociology was not simply a loss of cases (Magubane, this volume), but a misrepresentation of Europe and the Americas, both of which were entwined—politically, economically, militarily, and culturally—with the rarely mentioned continent. Colonies and former colonies could not simply be added to the roster of "cases" without a recognition of their mutual constitution with the metropole and the failure of either colony or metropole to conform to the model of an autonomous, well-bounded social system (Lo, this volume). Even within Western Europe, core topics such as state building and revolution were reinterpreted in light of the interactional process of war making and inter-state competition (Kestnbaum, this volume; Skocpol 1979).[21] Relations across national boundaries or social differences took many forms—domination, exchange, observation—but recognition of the interpenetration of national societies, indeed that societies and nations were not necessarily coterminous (Magubane, this volume), undermined conceptions of societies as closed social systems. In addition to transgressing the thick lines on a map, social processes understood in this fashion linked what were once understood to be distinct levels of analysis: local, national, and global (Böröcz 2001; Lo, this volume). Long twinned with a particular understanding of comparative methodology (e.g., Skocpol and Somers 1980; Smelser 1976), historical sociology has steadily weakened and abraded this tie to this identifying method.

Yet the cumulative shifts in the theoretical foundations of historical sociology may not require an abandonment of systematic comparisons so much as shifts in how those comparisons are structured. For all the lan-

---

21. Outside the core of historical sociologists and before the more constructivist style of the linguistic, cultural, and other turns had taken hold across the social sciences, scholars linked these relational understandings of state building to the transposition of models. Published in 1983, Harold Berman's *Law and Revolution* anticipated this shift, portraying the development of bureaucratic states through a process of inter-state (as well as state-church) competition and imitation. Another prescient analysis was Westney (1987).

guage of linkage and bricolage, for example, we have relatively few studies of when attempts at recombination hold and when they do not. This suggests a distinct comparative strategy focused not on societal wholes but on campaigns or attempts, as exemplified by Brubaker's call (this volume) for analyses of effective and ineffective efforts to activate ethnic cleavages or to define interests or identities in order to "make groups" (Clemens 1997; Steinberg 1999b). Alternatively, the interplay of disruptive events and pre-existing institutional arrangements can exploit the "found experiments" provided by history: the impact of a single colonial power across multiple indigenous social orders (Steinmetz 2003a); the efforts at postwar reconstruction across multiple European nation-states (Djelic 1998); and the near-simultaneous transitions from state socialism across the globe (Luong 2002; D. Stark and Bruszt 1998). To date, a long list of vibrant verbs and nouns—crystallize, bricolage, entrepreneur (among many others)—have stood in the place of careful analysis of how durable configurations are or are not constructed through collective action; are or are not disrupted by major events or critical conjunctures; or arc or are not reproduced over time. Given the current commitments of historical sociology, these are surely critical questions.

Finding Form in History

Michael Mann provided one rallying cry for the rejection of the typological or systemic imagery of classical social theory: "Societies are not unitary. They are not social systems (closed or open); they are not totalities. We can never find a single bounded society in geographical or social space" (1986: 1). This rejection, however, was far from total. Rather than contending that there is absolutely no coherence to be found, Mann's imagery of social life as organized through *overlapping* networks of power exemplified the directive to turn competing assumptions into variables (Stinchcombe 1990: 214). As Lo asserts in her essay on professionalism, analysis must recognize the "messiness of modernity" as the "key question becomes one about the interpenetration of the professions, bureaucracy, and the market," as well as "social categories located on the other side of the modernity/tradition divide, such as race, ethnicity, and gender" (this volume: 386, 390, 392). Rather than assuming social types, we can inquire into the varying coherence or closure of overlapping and intersecting networks. But if there are regularities across multiple "capitalisms" or "revolutions," this becomes a puzzle to be explained by reference to either processes of diffusion (as in the work of John Meyer and his many colleagues) or some systemic logic that effectively overrides the diverse and uneven terrain provided by legacies of the past (Burawoy 2001).[22]

Thus the current challenge for historical sociology is to define or discover patterns of regularity and difference that are surprising in light of a theoretical framework substantially altered from the Marxist political economy that informed the resurgence of historical sociology in the 1970s and 1980s. This will involve constructing the "deep analogies" that Stinchcombe (1978) has long argued are central to the finest works in the field, the "theorizable elements [that] can be extracted from the unique ones" (Emigh, this volume: 355–356). These efforts will inevitably reflect the tendency to redefine the past in terms of the present.[23] But the relevance of such efforts does not negate their importance. Writing in the spring of 2001, the late Roger Gould characterized the "historical sociology of social movements" as something of an anachronism, rather like finding a book on the Crusades in the international relations section of a bookstore (this volume: 286).[24] A few years later, this second pairing seems much less odd, underlining the heightened salience—both historical and utterly immediate—of the interlinkages of politics and religion (Friedland 1999; Gorski, this volume), as well as the more complex sense of "international relations" in a world where well-defined nations (mapping on to clearly bounded societies) can no longer be assumed to be the most relevant actors. The construction of relatively integrated social orders, capable of limiting variation within some territory or across some population, has been a distinctive sort of historical accomplishment. But rather than assuming such orders as the basis for our current theorizing of social change, we need to understand not only their construction, but also their unraveling.

22. Sohrabi's analysis of the interplay of local and global in constitutional revolutions rests on strong claims for diffusion: "Contrary to our sociological intuition, I suggest that revolutionaries choose their paths *irrespective* of local conflicts" (this volume: 303). Rather than stopping with evidence of the diffusion of form, however, he integrates this insight into the combination of agency and multiplicity characteristic of contemporary historical sociology: "Agency was the link between the global ideology of constitutionalism and its local metamorphosis, and in the Ottoman Empire it also connected a clandestine movement with a global wave of constitutional revolutions. With the coming of the wave, the movement's rhetoric and organization underwent transformations that made it populist and revolutionary. Agency did not create revolutionary organizations without pre-existing potentialities, but it recognized the domestic possibilities after receiving clues from the international context. Departing from its previous conservatism, the movement brought together disparate, disorganized elements under one cohesive whole to stage a revolution that could be characterized as organized, planned, and executed from above and assisted with energetic mass action from below" (this volume: 319).

23. Thanks to Tessie Liu for reminding the editors of this point.

24. The chapter by Gould included here is basically the same paper he delivered at the conference that generated this volume.

   Whereas the historical imagery of classical sociology began with the delineation of coherent societal types and then posed puzzles about transformation, evolution, and revolution, contemporary historical sociologists seem more puzzled by the accomplishment of coherence or the creation of relatively durable institutional configurations. These accomplishments are understood in terms of the contextually shaped lines of action that are culturally available to actors who are themselves culturally constituted. As many works converge on this style of explanation, however, we should begin to take the style seriously and consider how its implicit theoretical commitments might generate future research. Rather than tracing ever more episodes of institution building to the transposition of cultural models by creative actors, we need to develop new strategies of "casing," structuring new comparisons that illuminate the conditions and processes by which institutional rearrangements do or do not cohere and endure. In this way, style may shape the substance of inquiry and, in turn, inform new theories of social reproduction and change.

References

Abbas, Ihsan, ed. 1969. *'Ahd-i Ardashir*. Tehran: Silsilah-'i Intisharat-i Anjuman-i Asar-i Milli.

Abbott, Andrew. 1983. "Sequences of Social Events." *Historical Methods* 16:129–147.

———. 1988. *The System of Professions: An Essay on the Division of Expert Labor*. Chicago: University of Chicago Press.

———. 1992. "From Causes to Events: Notes on Narrative Positivism." *Sociological Methods and Research* 20.

———. 1993. "The Sociology of Work and Occupations." *Annual Review of Sociology* 19:187–209.

———. 1994. "History and Sociology: The Lost Synthesis." Pp. 77–112 in *Engaging the Past: The Uses of History across the Social Sciences*. Ed. Eric H. Monkkonen. Durham, N.C.: Duke University Press.

———. 1998. "Transcending General Linear Reality." *Sociological Theory* 6:169–186.

———. 1999. *Department and Discipline*. Chicago: University of Chicago Press.

———. 2001a. *Chaos of Disciplines*. Chicago: University of Chicago Press.

———. 2001b. *Time Matters: On Theory and Method*. Chicago: University of Chicago Press.

Abbott, Andrew, and A. Tsay. 2000. "Sequence Analysis and Optimal Matching Methods in Sociology: Review and Prospect." *Sociological Methods and Research* 29:3–33.

Abelmann, Nancy, and John Lie. 1995. *Blue Dreams: Korean Americans and the Los Angeles Riots*. Cambridge, Mass.: Harvard University Press.

Abraham, David. 1981. *The Collapse of the Weimar Republic: Political Economy and Crisis*. Princeton, N.J.: Princeton University Press.

Abrams, Philip. 1972. "The Sense of the Past and the Origins of Sociology." *Past and Present* 55:18–32.

———. 1980. "History, Sociology, Historical Sociology." *Past and Present* 87:3–16.

———. 1982. *Historical Sociology*. Ithaca, N.Y.: Cornell University Press.

Abu-Lughod, Janet. 1989. *Before European Hegemony: The World-System A.D. 1250–1350*. New York: Oxford University Press.

———, ed. 1999. *Sociology for the Twenty-first Century: Continuities and Cutting Edges*. Chicago: University of Chicago Press.

Adamiyat, Faridun. 1972. *Andishah-'i Taraqqi va Hukumat-i Qanun: 'Asr-iSipahsalar*. Tehran: Khvarazmi.

Adamiyat, Faridun, and Huma Natiq. 1977. *Afkar-i Ijtima'i va Siyasi va Iqtisadi dar Asar-i Muntashir'nashudah-'i Dawran-i Qajar*. Tehran: Intisharat-i Agah.

Adams, Julia. 1994. "The Familial State: Elite Family Practices and State-Making in the Early Modern Netherlands." *Theory and Society* 23 (4): 505–539.

——. 1996. "Principals and Agents, Colonialists and Company Men: The Decay of Colonial Control in the Dutch East Indies." *American Sociological Review* 61 (1): 12–28.

——. 1998. "Feminist Theory as Fifth Columnist or Discursive Vanguard: Some Contested Uses of Gender Analysis in Historical Sociology." *Social Politics* 5 (1): 1–16.

——. 1999. "Culture in Rational-Choice Theories of State-Formation." Pp. 98–122 in *State/Culture: State Formation after the Cultural Turn*. Ed. George Steinmetz. Ithaca, N.Y.: Cornell University Press. Wilder House Series in Culture, Power, and History.

——. 2002. "Signs and Regimes Revisited." *Social Politics* 9:187–202.

——. 2004. "The Rule of the Father: Patriarchy and Patrimonialism in Early Modern Europe." In *Max Weber at the Millennium: Economy and Society in the Twenty-first Century*. Ed. Charles Camic, Philip Gorski, and David Trubek. Stanford, Calif.: Stanford University Press.

——. Forthcoming. *The Familial State: Ruling Families and Merchant Capitalism in Early Modern Europe*. Ithaca: N.Y.: Cornell University Press.

Adams, Julia, and Tasleem J. Padamsee. 2001. "Signs and Regimes: Rereading Feminist Work on Welfare States." *Social Politics* 8 (spring): 1–23.

Adevărul de Cluj. 1999. "Confruntarea dintre România și Ungaria a continuat și după meci" [The confrontation between Romania and Hungary continued also after the match]. June 7.

Adorno, Theodor, and Max Horkheimer. 1986 [1944]. *The Dialectic of the Enlightenment*. New York: Continuum.

Adorno, Theodor W., et al. 1976. *The Positivist Dispute in German Sociology*. Trans. Glyn Adey and David Frisby. London: Heinemann.

Aglietta, Michel. 1987. *A Theory of Capitalist Regulation: The U.S. Experience*. London: Verso.

Ahmad, Salma. 1991. "American Foundations and the Development of the Social Sciences between the Wars: Comment on the Debate between Martin Bulmer and Donald Fisher." *Sociology* 25 (August): 511–520.

Alchian, Armen A., and Harold Demsetz. 1972. "Production, Information Costs, and Economic Organization." *American Economic Review* 62:777–795.

Alexander, Amir. 2002. *Geometrical Landscapes: The Voyages of Discovery and the Transformation of Mathematical Practice*. Stanford, Calif.: Stanford University Press.

Alexander, Gregory S. 1997. *Commodity and Propriety: Competing Visions of Property in American Legal Thought, 1776–1970*. Chicago: University of Chicago Press.

Alexander, Jeffrey C. 1982. *Positivism, Presuppositions, and Current Controversies*. Vol. 1 of *Theoretical Logic in Sociology*. Berkeley: University of California Press.

——. 1993. "The Return of Civil Society." *Contemporary Sociology* 22 (6): 797–803.

——. 1995a [1994]. "Modern, Anti, Post, and Neo: How Intellectuals Have Coded, Narrated, and Explained the 'New World of Our Time.'" Pp. 6–64 in *Fin de Siècle Social Theory: Relativism, Reduction, and the Problem of Reason*. New York: Verso.

——. 1995b. "The Reality of Reduction: The Failed Synthesis of Pierre Bourdieu." Pp. 128–217 in *Fin de Siècle Social Theory: Relativism, Reduction, and the Problem of Reason*. New York: Verso.

Alexander, Jeffrey, and Giuseppe Sciortino. 1996. "On Choosing One's Intellectual Predecessors: The Reduction of Camic's Treatment of Parsons and the Institutionalists." *Sociological Theory* 14 (2): 154–171.

Alexander, Jeffrey, and Philip Smith. 1993. "The Discourse of American Civil Society: A New Proposal for Cultural Studies." *Theory and Society* 22:151–207.

Alford, William P. 1995. *To Steal a Book Is an Elegant Offense: Intellectual Property Law in Chinese Civilization*. Stanford, Calif.: Stanford University Press.

Alinsky, Saul. 1971. *Rules for Radicals: A Practical Primer for Realistic Radicals*. New York: Random House.

Allen, Douglas W. 1998. "Compatible Incentives and the Purchase of Military Commissions." *Journal of Legal Studies* 27:45–66.

Allen, Robert C. 1982. "The Efficiency and Distributional Consequences of Eighteenth-Century Enclosures." *Economic Journal* 92:937–953.

——. 1992. *Enclosures and the Yeoman*. Oxford: Oxford University Press.

Allen, Tim, and Jean Seaton. eds. 1999. *The Media of Conflict: War Reporting and Representations of Ethnic Violence*. London: Zed.

Almond, Gabriel, and Sidney Verba. 1963. *The Civic Culture*. Princeton, N.J.: Princeton University Press.

al-Mulk, Nizam. 1993. *Siyasatnamah*. Ed Abbas Iqbal. Tehran: Intisharat-i Asatir.

Alpert, Harry. 1954. "The National Science Foundation and Social Science Research." *American Sociological Review* 19 (April): 208–211.

——. 1955a. "The Social Sciences and the National Science Foundation." *American Sociological Review* 20 (December): 653–661.

——. 1955b. "The Social Sciences and the National Science Foundation." *Proceedings of the American Philosophical Society* 99 (October 15): 332–333.

——. 1957. "The Social Science Research Program of the National Science Foundation." *American Sociological Review* 22 (October): 582–585.

Althusser, Louis. 1969. "Contradiction and Overdetermination." Pp. 117–128 in *For Marx*. New York: Pantheon Books.

——. 1972. "Ideology and Ideological State Apparatuses." *Lenin and Philosophy, and Other Essays*. New York: Monthly Review Press.

——. 1990 [1969]. "On the Materialist Dialectic." Pp. 161–218 in *For Marx*. London: Verso.

——. 1994. "Philosophie et marxisme: Entretiens avec Fernanda Navarro (1984–1987)." Pp. 17–79 in *Sur la philosophie*. Paris: Gallimard.

Althusser, Louis, and Etienne Balibar. 1970. *Reading "Capital."* London: Verso.

Amenta, Edwin. 1998. *Bold Relief: Institutional Politics and the Origins of Modern American Social Policy*. Princeton, N.J.: Princeton University Press.

Amenta, Edwin, and Jane D. Poulsen. 1994. "Where to Begin: A Survey of Five Approaches to Selecting Independent Measures for Qualitative Comparative Analysis." *Sociological Methods and Research* 23:21–52.

——. 1996. "Social Politics in Context: The Institutional Politics Theory and State-Level U.S. Social Spending Policies at the End of the New Deal." *Social Forces* 75:33–60.

Amenta, Edwin, Chris Bonastia, and Neal Caren. 2001. "U.S. Social Policy in Comparative and Historical Perspective: Concepts, Images, Arguments and Research Strategies." *Annual Review of Sociology* 27:213–234.

Amenta, Edwin, Bruce G. Carruthers, and Yvonne Zylan. 1992. "A Hero for the Aged? The Townsend Movement, the Political Mediation Model, and U.S. Old-Age Policy, 1934–1950." *American Journal of Sociology* 98:308–339.

Amin, Ash, ed. 1994. *Post-Fordism: A Reader*. Oxford: Blackwell.

Amin, Samir. 1976. *Unequal Development: Essay on the Social Formation of Peripheral Capitalism*. New York: Monthly Review Press.

Aminzade, Ronald. 1981. *Class, Politics, and Early Industrial Capitalism: A Study of Mid-Nineteenth-Century Toulouse, France*. Albany: State University of New York Press.

——. 1992. "Historical Sociology and Time." *Sociological Methods and Research* 20 (4): 465–480.

——. 1993. *Ballots and Barricades: Class Formation and Republican Politics in France, 1830–1871*. Princeton, N.J.: Princeton University Press.

——. 2003. "From Race to Citizenship: The Indigenization Debate in Post-Socialist Tanzania." *Studies in Comparative International Development* 38 (1): 43–63.

Aminzade, R., J. Goldstone, D. McAdam, E. J. Perry, W. H. Sewell Jr., S. Tarrow, and C. Tilly.

2001. *Silence and Voice in the Study of Contentious Politics*. Cambridge: Cambridge University Press.

Amsden, Alice. 1989. *Asia's Next Giant: South Korea and Late Industrialization*. Oxford: Oxford University Press.

Anderson, Benedict. 1983. *Imagined Communities: Reflections on the Origin and Spread of Nationalism*. London: Verso.

——. 1991. *Imagined Communities: Reflections on the Origin and Spread of Nationalism*. 2nd ed. London: Verso.

Anderson, Elizabeth. 1993. *Value in Ethics and Economics*. Cambridge, Mass.: Harvard University Press.

Anderson, Michael. 1971. *Family Structure in Nineteenth-Century Lancashire*. Cambridge: Cambridge University Press.

Anderson, Perry. 1974a. *Lineages of the Absolutist State*. London: Verso.

——. 1974b. *Passages from Antiquity to Feudalism*. London: New Left Books.

——. 1998. *The Origins of Postmodernity*. London: Verso.

Andreski, Stanislav. 1971. *Military Organization and Society*, 2nd ed. Berkeley: University of California Press.

Antonen, Anneli, and Jorma Sipila. 1996. "European Social Care Services: Is It Possible to Identify Models?" *Journal of European Social Policy* 5 (2): 87–100.

Appadurai, Arjun. 1996. *Modernity at Large: Cultural Dimensions of Globalization*. Minneapolis: University of Minnesota Press.

Apter, David E. 1968. *Some Conceptual Approaches to the Study of Modernization*. Englewood Cliffs, N.J.: Prentice-Hall.

——. 1987. *Rethinking Development: Modernization, Dependency, and Postmodern Politics*. Newbury Park, Calif.: Sage.

Archer, Margaret. 1995. *Realist Social Theory: The Morphogenetic Approach*. Cambridge: Cambridge University Press.

Archibugi, D., and D. Held. 1995. *Cosmopolitan Democracy: An Agenda for a New World Order*. Cambridge: Polity Press.

Archibugi, D., et al. 1998. *Re-imagining Political Community: Studies in Cosmopolitan Democracy*. Cambridge: Polity Press.

Arendt, Hannah. 1951. *The Origins of Totalitarianism*. New York: Harcourt Brace.

——. 1965. *Eichmann in Jerusalem: A Report on the Banality of Evil*. New York: Viking.

Arhin, K. 1976. "The Pressure of Cash and Its Political Consequences in Asante in the Colonial Period, 1900–1940." *Journal of African Studies* 3:453–468.

Arjomand, Said Amir. 1984. *The Shadow of God and the Hidden Imam: Religion, Political Order, and Societal Change in Shi'ite Iran from the Beginning to 1890*. Chicago: University of Chicago Press.

——. 1988. *The Turban for the Crown: The Islamic Revolution in Iran*. New York: Oxford University Press.

——. 2001. "Perso-Indian Statecraft, Greek Political Science and the Muslim Idea of Government." *International Sociology* 16 (3): 455–473.

Armstrong, John A. 1982. *Nations before Nationalism*. Chapel Hill: University of North Carolina Press.

Arnason, Johann P. 2002. *The Peripheral Centre: Essays on Japanese History and Civilization*. Melbourne: Trans Pacific Press.

Arnold, David. 1993. *Colonizing the Body: State Medicine and Epidemic Disease in Nineteenth-Century India*. Berkeley: University of California Press.

Aron, Raymond. 1966. *Peace and War: A Theory of International Relations*. Trans. Richard Howard and Annette Baker Fox. New York: Frederick A. Praeger.

Arrighi, Giovanni. 1994. *The Long Twentieth Century: Money, Power, and the Origins of Our Times*. London: Verso.

——. 1999. "Globalization and Historical Macrosociology." Pp. 117–133 in *Sociology for the Twenty-first Century*. Ed. Janet Abu-Lughod. Chicago: University of Chicago Press.

Arrighi, Giovanni, and Beverly J. Silver. 1999. *Chaos and Governance in the Modern World System*. Minneapolis: University of Minnesota Press.

Arthur, W. Brian. 1989. "Competing Technologies, Increasing Returns, and Lock-In by Historical Events." *Economic Journal* 99:116–131.

Ascher, Abraham. 1988. *The Revolution of 1905: Russia in Disarray*. Stanford, Calif.: Stanford University Press.

Ashcroft, Bill, Gareth Griffiths, and Helen Tiffin, eds. 1995. *The Post-Colonial Studies Reader*. New York: Routledge.

Ashton, T. S. 1997 [1948]. *The Industrial Revolution, 1760–1830*. Oxford: Oxford University Press.

Asian Development Bank. 1998. *Annual Report*. Manila: ADB.

Åslund, Anders. 1995. *How Russia Became a Market Economy*. Washington, D.C.: Brookings Institution.

Aston, T. H., and C. H. E. Philpin, eds. 1988. *The Brenner Debate: Agrarian Class Structure and Economic Development in Pre-Industrial Europe*. New York: Cambridge University Press.

Avant, Deborah. 2000. "From Mercenaries to Citizen Armies: Explaining Change in the Practice of War." *International Organization* 54:41–72.

Axel, Brian Keith, ed. 2002. *From the Margins: Historical Anthropology and Its Futures*. Durham, N.C.: Duke University Press.

Axelrod, Robert. 1981. "The Emergence of Cooperation among Egoists." *American Political Science Review* (June): 306–318.

——. 1984. *The Evolution of Cooperation*. New York: Basic Books.

Aymard, Maurice. 1982. "From Feudalism to Capitalism in Italy: The Case That Doesn't Fit." *Review* 6:131–208.

Baechler, Jean. 1988. "The Origins of Modernity: Caste and Feudality (India, Europe and Japan)." Pp. 39–65 in *Europe and the Rise of Capitalism*. Ed. Jean Baechler, John A. Hall, and Michael Mann. Oxford: Basil Blackwell.

Baehr, Peter. 2002. "Identifying the Unprecedented: Hannah Arendt, Totalitarianism, and the Critique of Sociology." *American Sociological Review* 67:804–831.

Bailey, Benjamin. 1997. "Communication of Respect in Interethnic Service Encounters." *Language in Society* 26:327–356.

Bain, R. 1933. "Scientist as Citizen." *Social Forces* 11 (3):412–415.

Baker, Keith Michael. 1990. *Inventing the French Revolution*. Cambridge: Cambridge University Press.

Baker, Paula. 1984. "The Domestication of Politics: Women and American Political Society, 1780–1920." *American Historical Review* 89:620–647.

Balakrishnan, Gopal, ed. 1996. *Mapping the Nation*. London: Verso.

Balbo, Laura. 1982. "The Servicing Work of Women and the Capitalist State." *Political Power and Social Theory* 3:251–270.

Baldwin, Carliss, and Kim Clark. 1994. "Capital-Budgeting Systems and Capabilities Investments in U.S. Companies after the Second World War." *Business History Review* 68:73–109.

Baldwin, Peter. 1990. *The Politics of Social Solidarity: Class Bases of the European Welfare State 1875–1975*. New York: Cambridge University Press.

Balibar, Etienne. 1994. *Masses, Classes, Ideas: Studies on Politics and Philosophy Before and After Marx*. New York: Routledge.

Balzer, Harley D. 1996. "Introduction." Pp. 3–38 in *Russia's Missing Middle Class: The Professions in Russian History*. Ed. Harley D. Balzer. London: M. E. Sharpe.

Bannister, Robert C. 1987. *Sociology and Scientism: The American Quest for Objectivity, 1880–1940*. Chapel Hill: University of North Carolina Press.

Barbalet, J. M. 1994. *Citizenship: Rights, Struggle, and Class Inequality*. Minneapolis: University of Minnesota Press.

Barber, Bennett. 1962. "Resistance by Scientists to Scientific Discovery." Pp. 539–556 in *The Sociology of Science*. Ed. Bennett Barber and Walter Hirsch. New York: Free Press.

Barker, David C., and Christopher Jan Carman. 2000. "The Spirit of Capitalism? Religious Doctrine, Values, and Economic Attitude Constructs." *Political Behavior* 22:1–27.

Barkey, Karen. 1991. "Rebellious Alliances: The State and Peasant Unrest in Early Seventeenth-Century France and the Ottoman Empire." *American Sociological Review* 56 (6): 699–715.

——. 1994. *Bandits and Bureaucrats: The Ottoman Route to State Centralization*. Ithaca, N.Y.: Cornell University Press.

Barkey, Karen, and Ronan Van Rossem. 1997. "Networks of Contention: Villages and Regional Structure in the Seventeenth-Century Ottoman Empire." *American Journal of Sociology* 102 (5): 1345–1382.

Baron, Ava. 1998. "Romancing the Field: The Marriage of Feminism and Historical Sociology." *Social Politics* 5:17–37.

——, ed. 1991. *Work Engendered: Toward a New History of American Labor*. Ithaca, N.Y.: Cornell University Press.

Baron, James N., Frank R. Dobbin, and P. Devereaux Jennings. 1986. "War and Peace: The Evolution of Modern Personnel Administration in U.S. Industry." *American Journal of Sociology* 92:350–383.

Baron, James N., P. Devereaux Jennings, and Frank R. Dobbin. 1988. "Mission Control? The Development of Personnel Systems in U.S. Industry." *American Sociological Review* 53:497–514.

Barrett, Richard, and Martin Whyte. 1982. "Dependency Theory and Taiwan: A Deviant Case Analysis." *American Journal of Sociology* 87:1064–1089.

Barth, Fredrik. 1969. "Introduction." Pp. 9–38 in *Ethnic Groups and Boundaries: The Social Organization of Culture Difference*. Ed. Fredrik Barth. London: George Allen and Unwin.

Bartov, Omer. 1992. "The Conduct of War: Soldiers and the Barbarization of Warfare." *Journal of Modern History* 64, supplement S32–S45.

——. 1994. " 'The Nation in Arms': Germany and France, 1789–1939." *History Today* 44:27–33.

——. 1996a. "The European Imagination in the Age of Total War." In *Murder in Our Midst: The Holocaust, Industrial Killing and Representation*. Oxford: Oxford University Press.

——. 1996b. *Murder in Our Midst: The Holocaust, Industrial Killing and Representation*. Oxford: Oxford University Press.

——. 2000. *Mirrors of Destruction: War, Genocide and Modern Identity*. Oxford: Oxford University Press.

——. N.d. "Industrial Killing, World War I, the Holocaust, and Representation." Unpublished manuscript.

Baskin, Jonathan Barron, and Paul J. Miranti Jr. 1997. *A History of Corporate Finance*. Cambridge: Cambridge University Press.

Bates, Robert H. 2001. *Prosperity and Violence: The Political Economy of Development*. New York: W. W. Norton.

Bates, Robert H., Avner Greif, Margaret Levi, Jean-Laurent Rosenthal, and Barry R. Weingast. 1998. *Analytic Narratives*. Princeton, N.J.: Princeton University Press.

Bateson, Gregory. 1985 [1955]. "A Theory of Play and Fantasy." Pp. 131–144 in *Semiotics: An Introductory Anthology*. Ed. Robert E. Innis. Bloomington: Indiana University Press.

Bauböck, R. 1991. *Immigration and the Boundaries of Citizenship*. Vienna: Institut für Höhere Studien.

——. 1994. *From Aliens to Citizens: Redefining the Status of Immigrants in Europe*. Aldershot, Hants, U.K.: Avebury.

Bauböck, R., et al. 1998. *Blurred Boundaries: Migration, Ethnicity, Citizenship*. Aldershot, Hants, U.K.: Ashgate.

Baudrillard, Jean. 1981. *For a Critique of the Political Economy of the Sign*. St. Louis: Telos Press.

Bauman, Zygmunt. 2000 [1989]. *Modernity and the Holocaust*. Ithaca, N.Y.: Cornell University Press.

Baxandall, Michael. 1985. *Patterns of Intention: On the Historical Explanation of Pictures*. New Haven, Conn.: Yale University Press.

——. 1988. *Painting and Experience in Fifteenth-Century Italy*, 2nd ed. New York: Oxford University Press.

Bearman, Peter S. 1991. "Desertion as Localism: Army Unit Solidarity and Group Norms in the U.S. Civil War." *Social Forces* 70 (2): 321–342.

——. 1993. *Relations into Rhetorics: Local Elite Structure in Norfolk, England, 1540–1640*. New Brunswick, N.J.: Rutgers University Press.

Beck, E. M., and Stuart Tolnay. 1990. "The Killing Fields of the Deep South: The Market for Cotton and the Lynching of Blacks, 1882–1930." *American Sociological Review* 55 (4): 526–539.

Beck, Ulrich. 1992. *The Risk Society*. London: Sage.

Beck, Ulrich, Anthony Giddens, and Scott Lash. 1994. *Reflexive Modernization*. Stanford, Calif.: Stanford University Press.

Becker, Gary S. 1976. *The Economic Approach to Human Behavior*. Chicago: University of Chicago Press.

——. 1996. *Accounting for Tastes*. Cambridge, Mass: Harvard Univerity Press.

Becker, Gary, and George Stigler. 1974. "Law Enforcement, Malfeasance, and Compensation of Enforcers." *Journal of Legal Studies* 3:1–18.

Beetham, David. 1974. *Max Weber and the Theory of Modern Politics*. London: George Allen and Unwin.

Beiner, R. 1995. *Theorizing Citizenship*. Albany: State University of New York Press.

Beisel, Nicola. 1997. *Imperiled Innocents: Anthony Comstock and Family Reproduction in Victorian America*. Princeton, N.J.: Princeton University Press.

Bell, Daniel. 1980. *The Winding Passage: Essays and Sociological Journeys, 1960–1980*. Cambridge: Abt Books.

Bellah, Robert N. 1957a. *Tokugawa Religion: Cultural Roots of Modern Japan*. Glencoe, Ill.: Free Press.

——. 1957b. *Tokugawa Religion: The Values of Pre-Industrial Japan*. Glencoe, Ill.: Free Press.

Bellamy, R., and A. Warleigh. 2001. *Citizenship and Governance in the European Union*. London: Continuum.

Bellingham, Bruce, and Mary Pugh Mathis. 1994. "Race, Citizenship and the Bio-Politics of the Maternalist Welfare State: 'Traditional' Midwifery in the American South under the Sheppard-Towner Act, 1921–29." *Social Politics* 1:157–189.

Ben-David, Joseph. 1960a. "Roles and Innovations in Medicine." *American Journal of Sociology* 65 (May): 557–568.

——. 1960b. "Scientific Productivity and Academic Organization in Nineteenth-Century Medicine." *American Sociological Review* 25 (December): 828–843.

——. 1971. *The Scientist's Role in Society: A Comparative Study*. Englewood Cliffs, N.J.: Prentice-Hall.

Ben-David, Joseph, and Randall Collins. 1966. "Social Factors in the Origins of a New Science: The Case of Psychology." *American Sociological Review* 31 (August): 451–465.

Bendix, Reinhard. 1956. *Work and Authority in Industry: Ideologies of Management in the Course of Industrialization*. New York: Wiley.

——. 1960. *Max Weber: An Intellectual Portrait*. Garden City, N.Y.: Doubleday.

——. 1964. *Nation-Building and Citizenship: Studies of Our Changing Social Order*. New York: Wiley.

——. 1967. "Tradition and Modernity Reconsidered." *Comparative Studies in Society and History* 9:292–346.

———. 1977 [1964]. *Nation-Building and Citizenship: Studies of Our Changing Social Order*, enlarged ed. Berkeley: University of California Press.

———. 1978. *Kings or People: Power and the Mandate to Rule*. Berkeley: University of California Press.

———, ed. 1973 [1968]. *State and Society*. Edited in collaboration with Coenraad Brand, Randall Collins, Robert G. Michels, Hans-Eberhard Mueller, Gail Omvedt, Eliezer Rosenstein, Jean-Guy Vaillancourt, and R. Stephen Warner. Berkeley: University of California Press.

Benhabib, Seyla. 1990. "Hannah Arendt and the Redemptive Power of Narrative." *Social Research* 57:167–196.

———. 1995. *Feminist Contentions: A Philosophical Exchange*. New York: Routledge.

———. 1996. *Democracy and Difference: Contesting the Boundaries of the Political*. Princeton, N.J.: Princeton University Press.

———. 2001. *Transformations of Citizenship: Dilemmas of the Nation State in the Era of Globalization: Two Lectures*. Assen: Koninklijke Van Gorcum.

———. 2002. *The Claims of Culture: Equality and Diversity in the Global Era*. Princeton, N.J.: Princeton University Press.

Bensel, Richard Franklin. 1990. *Yankee Leviathan: The Origins of Central State Authority in America 1859–1877*. Cambridge: Cambridge University Press.

Bentley, Arthur F. 1908. *The Process of Government: A Study of Social Pressures*. Chicago: University of Chicago Press.

Berezin, Mabel. 1997. *Making the Fascist Self: The Political Culture of Interwar Italy*. Ithaca, N.Y.: Cornell University Press.

———. 1999. "State, Nation, and Identity in Fascist Italy." In *State/Culture: State Formation after the Cultural Turn*. Ed. George Steinmetz. Ithaca, N.Y.: Cornell University Press. Wilder House Series in Culture, Power, and History.

Berger, Peter. 1990 [1967]. *The Sacred Canopy*. Garden City, N.Y.: Anchor Doubleday.

Bergesen, Albert, and Ronald Schoenberg. 1980. "Long Waves of Colonial Expansion and Contraction, 1415–1969." In *Studies of the Modern World System*. Ed. Albert Bergesen. New York: Academic Press.

Bergqvist, Christina, Anette Borchorst, Ann-Dorte Christensen, Viveca Ramstedt-Silen, Nina Raaum, and Auour Styrkarsdottir, eds. 2000. *Equal Democracies? Gender and Politics in the Nordic Countries*. Oslo: Scandinavian University Press.

Berkovitch, Nitza. 1999. *From Motherhood to Citizenship: Women's Rights and International Organizations*. Baltimore: Johns Hopkins University Press.

Berlant, Lauren Gail. 1997. "The Theory of Infantile Citizenship." Pp. 25–33 in *The Queen of America Goes to Washington City: Essays on Sex and Citizenship*. Durham, N.C.: Duke University Press.

Berlin, Ira, et al. 1979. *The Black Military Experience in the Civil War*, vol. 4. New York: Cambridge University Press.

Berman, Harold J. 1983. *Law and Revolution: The Formation of the Western Legal Tradition*. Cambridge, Mass.: Harvard University Press.

Berman, Marshall. 1976. *All That Is Solid Melts into Air: The Experience of Modernity*. New York: Viking Penguin.

Bernstein, Henry. 1994. "Agrarian Classes in Capitalist Development." Pp. 40–71 in *Capitalism and Development*. Ed. Leslie Sklair. London: Routledge.

Best, Geoffrey. 1980. *Humanity in Warfare*. New York: Columbia University Press.

———. 1982. *War and Society in Revolutionary Europe, 1770–1870*. London: Fontana.

———. 1997. *War and Law since 1945*. Oxford: Clarendon Press.

Beveridge, Andrew A. 1985. "Local Lending Practice: Borrowers in a Small Northeastern Industrial City, 1832–1915." *Journal of Economic History* 45:393–403.

Bhabha, Homi K. 1985. "Signs Taken for Wonders: Questions of Ambivalence and Authority under a Tree outside Delhi, May 1817." *Critical Inquiry* 12 (1): 144–165.

——. 1994. "Of Mimicry and Man: The Ambivalence of Colonial Discourse." Pp. 85–92 in *The Location of Culture*. New York: Routledge.

Bhaskar, Roy. 1979. *The Possibility of Naturalism: A Philosophical Critique of the Contemporary Human Sciences*. New York: Humanities Press.

——. 1986. *Scientific Realism and Human Emancipation*. London: Verso.

——. 1989. *Reclaiming Reality: A Critical Introduction to Contemporary Philosophy*. London: Verso.

——. 1991. *Philosophy and the Idea of Freedom*. Oxford: Basil Blackwell.

——. 1994. *Plato Etcetera: The Problems of Philosophy and Their Resolution*. New York: Verso.

——. 1997 [1975]. *A Realist Theory of Science*. New York: Verso.

——. 1998. "General Introduction." Pp. ix–xxiv in *Critical Realism, Essential Readings*. Ed. Margaret Archer, Tony Lawson, and Roy Bhaskar. London: Routledge.

Bhavnani, Kum-Kum, ed. 2001. *Feminism and "Race."* New York: Oxford University Press.

Biernacki, Richard. 1995. *The Fabrication of Labor: Germany and Britain, 1640–1914*. Berkeley: University of California Press.

Bierstedt, Robert. 1949. "A Critique of Empiricism in Sociology." *American Sociological Review* 14 (October): 584–592.

Biggs, Michael. 1999. "Putting the State on the Map: Cartography, Territory, and European State Formation." *Comparative Studies in Society and History* 41 (2): 374–411.

Billig, Michael. 1995. *Banal Nationalism*. Thousand Oaks, Calif.: Sage.

Billings, Dwight B., and Kathleen M. Blee. 2000. *The Road to Poverty: The Making of Wealth and Hardship in Appalachia*. Cambridge: Cambridge University Press.

Binder, Leonard. 1986. "The Natural History of Development Theory." *Comparative Studies in Society and History* 28:3–33.

Black, Jeremy. 1991. *A Military Revolution? Military Change and European Society, 1550–1800*. New York: St. Martin's Press.

——. 1994. *European Warfare, 1660–1815*. New Haven, Conn.: Yale University Press.

——. 2001. *Western Warfare, 1775–1882*. Bloomington: Indiana University Press.

Blackbourn, David, and Geoff Eley. 1985. *The Peculiarities of German History*. New York: Oxford University Press.

Blair, T. 1996. *New Britain: My Vision of a Young Country*. London: 4th Estate.

——. 1998. *The Third Way: New Politics for a New Century*. London: Fabian Society.

Blalock, Hubert M., Jr. 1964. *Causal Inferences in Nonexperimental Research*. Chapel Hill: University of North Carolina Press.

Blanchard, Olivier Jean, Kenneth A. Froot, and Jeffrey D. Sachs. 1994. "Introduction." Pp. 1–18 in *The Transition in Eastern Europe*, vol. 1: *Country Studies*. Ed. Olivier Jean Blanchard, Kenneth A. Froot, and Jeffrey D. Sachs. Chicago: University of Chicago Press.

Blaut, James M. 1993. *The Colonizer's Model of the World: Geographical Diffusionism and Eurocentric History*. New York: Guilford Press.

Blee, Kathleen. 1991. *Women of the Klan: Racism and Gender in the 1920s*. Berkeley: University of California Press.

Blim, Michael. 2000. "Capitalisms in Late Modernity." *Annual Review of Anthropology* 29: 25–38.

Bloch, Marc. 1953. *The Historian's Craft*. New York: Vintage.

Block, Fred. 1977. *The Origins of International Economic Disorder: A Study of United States International Monetary Policy from World War II to the Present*. Berkeley: University of California Press.

——. 1981. "The Fiscal Crisis of the Capitalist State." *Annual Review of Sociology* 7:1–27.

——. 1986. "Political Choice and the Multiple 'Logics' of Capital." *Theory and Society* 15 (1/2): 175–192.

——. 1987. *Revising State Theory: Essays in Politics and Postindustrialism*. Philadelphia: Temple University Press.

Block, Fred, and Margaret Somers. 1984. "Beyond the Economistic Fallacy: The Holistic Social Science of Karl Polanyi." Pp. 47–84 in *Vision and Method in Historical Sociology*. Ed. Theda Skocpol. New York: Cambridge University Press.

Bloom, Harold. 1997 [1973]. *The Anxiety of Influence: A Theory of Poetry*. New York: Oxford University Press.

Bloom, William. 1990. *Personal Identity, National Identity, and International Relations*. Cambridge: Cambridge University Press.

Blumer, Herbert. 1956. "Sociological Analysis and the 'Variable.'" *American Sociological Review* 21 (December): 683–690.

Bobbio, N. 1992. *Democracy and Dictatorship: The Nature and Limits of State Power*. Minneapolis: University of Minnesota Press.

———. 1996. *The Age of Rights*. Cambridge: Polity Press.

Bock, Gisela. 1991. "Antinatalism, Maternity and Paternity in National Socialist Racism." Pp. 233–255 in *Maternity and Gender Politics: Women and the Rise of the European Welfare States, 1880s—1950s*. Ed. Gisela Bock and Pat Thane. New York: Routledge.

Bock, Gisela, and Pat Thane, eds. 1991. *Maternity and Gender Politics: Women and the Rise of the European Welfare States, 1880s–1950s*. New York: Routledge.

Bodenhorn, Howard. 2000. *A History of Banking in Antebellum America: Financial Markets and Economic Development in an Era of Nation-Building*. Cambridge: Cambridge University Press.

Bohannan, Paul. 1955. "Some Principles of Exchange and Investment among the Tiv." *American Anthropologist* 57:60–67.

Bohstedt, John. 1983. *Riots and Community Politics in England and Wales, 1790–1810*. Cambridge, Mass.: Harvard University Press.

Boli, John. 1987. "World Polity Sources of Expanding State Authority in National Constitutions, 1870–1970." Pp. 71–91 in *Institutional Structure: Constituting State, Society, and the Individual*. Ed. G. Thomas. Beverly Hills, Calif.: Sage.

Boli, John, and George M. Thomas. 1997. "World Culture in the World Polity: A Century of International Non-Governmental Organization." *American Sociological Review* 62:171–190.

Boli-Bennett, John. 1979. "The Ideology of Expanding State Authority in National Constitutions, 1870–1970." In *National Development and the World System: Educational, Economic, and Political Change, 1950–1970*. Ed. J. W. Meyer and M. T. Hannan. Chicago: University of Chicago Press.

Bonnell, Victoria. 1980. "The Uses of Theory, Concepts and Comparison in Historical Sociology." *Comparative Studies in Society and History* 22:156–173.

———. 1983. *Roots of Rebellion: Workers' Politics and Organizations in St. Petersburg and Moscow, 1900–1914*. Berkeley: University of California Press.

Bonner, Thomas Neville. 1992. *To the Ends of the Earth: Women's Search for Education in Medicine*. Cambridge, Mass.: Harvard University Press.

Borchorst, Anette. 1994. "The Scandinavian Welfare States: Patriarchal, Gender Neutral or Woman-Friendly?" *International Journal of Contemporary Sociology* 31:1–23.

Boris, Eileen. 1995. "The Racialized Gendered State: Constructions of Citizenship in the United States." *Social Politics* 2:160–180.

Böröcz, József. 2001. "Change Rules." *American Journal of Sociology* 106 (4): 1152–1168.

Bosher, J. F. 1995. "Huguenot Merchants and the Protestant International in the Seventeenth Century." *William and Mary Quarterly* 52:77–102.

Boswell, Terry. 1989. "Colonial Empires and the Capitalist World-System: A Time-Series Analysis of Colonization, 1640–1960." *American Sociological Review* 54:180–196.

Bourdieu, Pierre. 1977. *Outline of a Theory of Practice*. Trans. Richard Nice. Cambridge: Cambridge University Press.

———. 1981. "The Specificity of the Scientific Field." Pp. 257–292 in *French Sociology: Rupture and Renewal since 1968*. Ed. Charles C. Lemert. New York: Columbia University Press.

———. 1984. *Distinction: A Social Critique of the Judgment of Taste.* Cambridge, Mass.: Harvard University Press.

———. 1985. "The Genesis of the Concepts of *Habitus* and Field." *Sociocriticism* 2 (2): 11–24.

———. 1986. "The Forms of Capital." Pp. 241–260 in *Handbook of Theory and Research for the Sociology of Education.* Ed. J. G. Richardson. New York: Greenwood Press.

———. 1987. "Legitimation and Structured Interests in Weber's Sociology of Religion." Pp. 119–136 in *Max Weber, Rationality and Modernity.* Ed. Scott Lash and Sam Whimster. London: Allen and Unwin.

———. 1988. *Homo Academicus.* Stanford, Calif.: Stanford University Press.

———. 1990. "The Scholastic Point of View." *Cultural Anthropology* 5:380–391.

———. 1991a. "Identity and Representation: Elements for a Critical Reflection on the Idea of Region." Pp. 220–228 in *Language and Symbolic Power.* Cambridge, Mass.: Harvard University Press.

———. 1991b. *Language and Symbolic Power.* Cambridge, Mass.: Harvard University Press.

———. 1991c. "Social Space and the Genesis of 'Classes.'" Pp. 229–251 in *Language and Symbolic Power.* Cambridge, Mass.: Harvard University Press.

———. 1993. "Concluding Remarks: For a Sociogenetic Understanding of Intellectual Works." In *Bourdieu: Critical Perspectives.* Ed. Craig Calhoun et al. Chicago: University of Chicago Press.

———. 2001. *Science de la science et réflexivité.* Paris: Editions Raisons d'Agir.

Bourdieu, Pierre, and Loïc J. D. Wacquant. 1992. *An Invitation to Reflexive Sociology.* Chicago: University of Chicago Press.

Bowen, John R. 1996. "The Myth of Global Ethnic Conflict." *Journal of Democracy* 7 (4): 3–14.

Bowker, Geoffrey C., and Susan Leigh Star. 1999. *Sorting Things Out: Classification and Its Consequences.* Cambridge, Mass.: MIT Press.

Boyce, M., ed. 1968. *The Letter of Tansar.* Rome: Instituto Italiano per il Medio Ed Estremo Oriente.

Boyer, Robert. 1990. *The Regulation School: A Critical Introduction.* New York: Columbia University Press.

Brada, Josef C. 1996. "Privatization Is Transition—Or Is It?" *Journal of Economic Perspectives* 10:67–86.

Braddick, Michael J. 2000. *State Formation in Early Modern England, c. 1550–1700.* Cambridge: Cambridge University Press.

Branford, V. V. 1906. "Science and Citizenship." *American Journal of Sociology* 11 (6): 721–762.

Brass, Paul R. 1996. "Introduction: Discourse of Ethnicity, Communalism, and Violence." Pp. 1–55 in *Riots and Pogroms.* Ed. Paul R. Brass. New York: New York University Press.

———. 1997. *Theft of an Idol: Text and Context in the Representation of Collective Violence.* Princeton, N.J.: Princeton University Press.

———, ed. 1996. *Riots and Pogroms.* New York: New York University Press.

Braudel, Fernand. 1949. *The Mediterranean and the Mediterranean World in the Age of Philip II.* New York: Harper and Row.

———. 1980. "History and the Social Sciences: The *Longue Durée.*" In *On History.* Trans. Sarah Matthews. Chicago: University of Chicago Press.

Brechin, Steve. 1999. "Objective Problems, Subjective Values and Global Environmentalism: Evaluating the Postmaterialist Argument and Challenging a New Explanation." *Social Science Quarterly* 80 (4): 793–809.

Breen, T. H. 1985. *Tobacco Culture: The Mentality of the Great Tidewater Planters on the Eve of Revolution.* Princeton, N.J.: Princeton University Press.

Brenner, Erica. 1995. *Really Existing Nationalisms: A Post-Communist View from Marx and Engels.* Oxford: Clarendon Press.

Brenner, Johanna, and Maria Ramos. 1984. "Rethinking Women's Oppression." *New Left Review* 144:33–71.

Brenner, Neil. 1998. "Between Fixity and Motion: Accumulation, Territorial Organization and the Historical Geography of Spatial Scales." *Environment and Planning D: Society and Space* 16:459–481.

———. 1999. *Global Cities, Glocal States: State-Scaling and the Making of Urban Governance in the European Union.* Ph.D. dissertation, University of Chicago, Department of Political Science.

Brenner, Robert. 1977. "The Origins of Capitalist Development: A Critique of Neo-Smithian Marxism." *New Left Review* 104:25–92.

———. 1985a. "Agrarian Class Structure and Economic Development in Pre-Industrial Europe." Pp. 10–63 in *The Brenner Debate: Agrarian Class Structure and Economic Development in Pre-Industrial Europe.* Ed. T. H. Aston and C. H. E. Philpin. Cambridge: Cambridge University Press.

———. 1985b. "The Agrarian Roots of European Capitalism." Pp. 213–327 in *The Brenner Debate: Agrarian Class Structure and Economic Development in Pre-Industrial Europe.* Ed. T. H. Aston and C. H. E. Philpin. Cambridge: Cambridge University Press.

———. 1993. *Merchants and Revolution: Commercial Change, Political Conflict, and London's Overseas Traders, 1550–1653.* Princeton, N.J.: Princeton University Press.

Breslau, Daniel. 1998. *In Search of the Unequivocal: The Political Economy of Measurement in U.S. Labor Market Policy.* Westport, Conn.: Praeger.

———. 2003. "Economies Invents the Economy: Mathematics, Statistics, and Models in the Work of Irving Fisher and Wesley Mitchell. *Theory & Society* 32: 379–411.

Breuer, Joseph, and Sigmund Freud. 1937. *Studies in Hysteria.* Trans. A. A. Brill. New York: Nervous and Mental Disease Monographs.

Breuilly, John. 1982. *Nationalism and the State.* Chicago: University of Chicago Press.

———. 1993 [1982]. *Nationalism and the State,* 2nd ed. Manchester: Manchester University Press.

Brewer, John. 1988. *The Sinews of Power: War, Money, and the English State, 1688–1783.* New York: Knopf.

Brint, Steven. 1993. "Eliot Freidson's Contribution to the Sociology of Professions." *Work and Occupations* 20 (3): 259–278.

———. 1994. *In the Age of Experts: The Changing Role of Professionals in Politics and Public Life.* Princeton, N.J.: Princeton University Press.

Brinton, Crane. 1952. *The Anatomy of Revolution.* New York: Prentice-Hall.

Brinton, Mary. 1988. "The Social-Institutional Bases of Gender Stratification: Japan as an Illustrative Case." *American Journal of Sociology* 94 (2): 300–334.

Brockway, Lucile H. 1979. *Science and Colonial Expansion: The Role of the British Royal Botanic Gardens.* New York: Academic Press.

Brown, Michael. 1999. *Race, Money, and the American Welfare State.* Ithaca, N.Y.: Cornell University Press.

Brown, William Wells. 1863. *The Black Man: His Antecedents, His Genius, and His Achievements.* Boston: R. F. Wallcut.

Brubaker, Rogers. 1992. *Citizenship and Nationhood in France and Germany.* Cambridge, Mass.: Harvard University Press.

———. 1994. "Nationhood and the National Question in the Soviet Union and Post-Soviet Eurasia." *Theory and Society* 23 (1): 47–78.

———. 1996. *Nationalism Reframed: Nationhood and the National Question in the New Europe.* Cambridge: Cambridge University Press.

———. 1998. "Myths and Misconceptions in the Study of Nationalism." Pp. 272–306 in *The State of the Nation: Ernest Gellner and the Theory of Nationalism.* Ed. John A. Hall. New York: Cambridge University Press.

———. 1999. "A Shameful Debacle." *UCLA Magazine,* summer: 15–16.

Brubaker, Rogers, and Margit Feischmidt. 2002. "1848 in 1998: The Politics of Commemoration in Hungary, Romania, and Slovakia." *Comparative Studies in Society and History* 44 (4): 700–744.

Brubaker, Rogers, and David D. Laitin. 1998. "Ethnic and Nationalist Violence." *Annual Review of Sociology* 24:423–452.

Brubaker, Rogers, Mara Loveman, and Peter Stamatov. 2004. "Ethnicity as Cognition." *Theory and Society*.

Bruce, Steve. 1996. *Religion in the Modern World: From Cathedrals to Cults*. Oxford: Basil Blackwell.

———. 1999. *Choice and Religion: A Critique of Rational Choice Theory*. New York: Oxford University Press.

———, ed. 1995. *The Sociology of Religion*. Brookfield, Vt.: E. Elgar.

Brush, Lisa D. 2002. "Changing the Subject: Gender and Welfare Regime Studies." *Social Politics* 9:161–186.

Brustein, William. 1996. *Logic of Evil: The Social Origins of the Nazi Party, 1925–1933*. New Haven, Conn.: Yale University Press.

Bruun, Ole. 1993. *Business and Bureaucracy in a Chinese City: An Ethnography of Private Business Households in Contemporary China*. Berkeley: Institute of East Asian Studies.

Bryant, Christopher. 1985. *Positivism in Social Theory and Research*. New York: Macmillan.

Bryant, Joseph. 1992. "Positivism Redivivus? A Critique of Recent Uncritical Proposals for Reforming Sociological Theory (and Related Foibles)." *Canadian Journal of Sociology* 17 (winter): 29–53.

Buckley, Kerry W. 1989. *Mechanical Man: John Broadus Watson and the Beginnings of Behaviorism*. New York: Guilford Press.

Bulmer, Martin. 1982. "Support for Sociology in the 1920s: The Laura Spelman Rockefeller Memorial and the Beginnings of Modern, Large-Scale, Sociological Research in the University." *American Sociologist* 17 (November): 185–192.

———. 1984. "Philanthropic Foundations and the Development of the Social Sciences in the Early Twentieth Century: A Reply to Donald Fisher." *Sociology* 18 (November): 572–579.

Bulmer, M., and A. M. Rees. 1996. *Citizenship Today: The Contemporary Relevance of T. H. Marshall*. London: UCL Press.

Burawoy, Michael. 1972. *The Colour of Class on the Copper Mines: From African Advancement to Zambianization*. Manchester: Manchester University Press.

———. 1989. "Two Methods in Search of Science: Skocpol versus Trotsky." *Theory and Society* 18 (November): 759–805.

———. 1996. "The Power of Feminism." *Perspectives: The ASA Theory Section Newsletter* 18 (3): 3–8.

———. 1997. "Review Essay: The Soviet Descent into Capitalism." *American Journal of Sociology* 102:1430–1444.

———. 2001. "Neoclassical Sociology: From the End of Communism to the End of Classes." *American Journal of Sociology* 106 (4): 1099–1120.

Burawoy, Michael, and Pavel Krotov. 1992. "The Soviet Transition from Socialism to Capitalism: Worker Control and Economic Bargaining in the Wood Industry." *American Sociological Review* 57:16–36.

Burawoy, Michael, and János Lukács. 1992. *The Radiant Past: Ideology and Reality in Hungary's Road to Capitalism*. Chicago: University of Chicago Press.

Burawoy, Michael, and Katherine Verdery. 1999. "Introduction." In *Uncertain Transition: Ethnographies of Change in the Postsocialist World*. Ed. Michael Burawoy and Katherine Verdery. Lanham, Md.: Rowman and Littlefield.

Burawoy, Michael, William Gamson, Charlotte Ryan, Stephen Pfohl, Diane Vaughan, Charles Derber, and Juliet Schor. N.d. "Public Sociologies: A Symposium at Boston College." Unpublished manuscript.

Burawoy, Michael, ed. 1991. *Ethnography Unbound: Power and Resistance in the Modern Metropolis*. Berkeley: University of California Press.

———. 2000. *Global Ethnography: Forces, Connections, and Imaginations in a Postmodern World*. Berkeley: University of California Press.

Burchell, Graham, Colin Gordon, and Peter Miller, eds. 1991. *The Foucault Effect: Studies in Governmentality*. Chicago: University of Chicago Press.

Burk, James. 1992. "The Decline of Mass Armed Forces and Compulsory Military Service." *Defense Analysis* 8 (1): 45–59.

———. 1995. "Citizenship Status and Military Service: The Quest for Inclusion." *Armed Forces and Society* 21:503–529.

———. 2001. "The Military Obligations of Citizens since Vietnam." *Parameters* 31: 48–60.

———. Forthcoming. "Military Mobilization in Western Societies." In *The Handbook of Military Sociology*. Ed. Vincent Caforio.

———, ed. 1994. *The Military in New Times*. Boulder, Colo.: Westview Press.

Burke, Peter. 1980. *Sociology and History*. Boston: Allen and Unwin.

———. 1987. *The Historical Anthropology of Early Modern Italy: Essays on Perception and Communication*. Cambridge: Cambridge University Press.

Burrage, Michael. 1990. "Introduction: The Professions in Sociology and History." Pp. 1–23 in *Professions in Theory and History*. Ed. Michael Burrage and Rolf Torstendahl. London: Sage.

Burton, Antoinette. 2000. "States of Injury: Josephine Butler on Slavery, Citizenship and the Boer War." Pp. 18–32 in *Women's Suffrage in the British Empire: Citizenship, Nation and Race*. Ed. Ian Christopher Fletcher, Laura E. Nym Mayhall, and Phillippa Levine. London: Routledge.

Butler, Judith. 1990. *Gender Trouble*. New York: Routledge.

Buttrick, John. 1952. "The Inside Contract System." *Journal of Economic History* 12:205–221.

Byres, T. J. 1991. "The Agrarian Question and Differing Forms of Capitalist Agrarian Transition: An Essay with Reference to Asia." Pp. 3–76 in *Rural Transformation in Asia*. Ed. J. Breman and S. Mundle. Delhi: Oxford University Press.

Calhoun, Craig J. 1982. *The Question of Class Stuggle: Social Foundations of Popular Radicalism during the Industrial Revolution*. Chicago: University of Chicago Press.

———. 1993a. "Civil Society and the Public Sphere." *Public Culture* 5 (2): 267–280.

———. 1993b. "Nationalism and Civil Society: Democracy, Diversity and Self-Determination." *International Sociology* 8:387–411.

———. 1993c. "Nationalism and Ethnicity." *Annual Review of Sociology* 19:211–239.

———. 1995. *Critical Social Theory: Culture, History and the Challenge of Difference*. Cambridge, Mass.: Blackwell.

———. 1996. "The Rise and Domestication of Historical Sociology." Pp. 305–338 in *The Historic Turn in the Human Sciences*. Ed. Terrence J. McDonald. Ann Arbor: University of Michigan Press.

———. 1997. *Nationalism*. Minneapolis: University of Minnesota Press.

———. 1998. "Explanation in Historical Sociology: Narrative, General Theory, and Historically Specific Theory." *American Journal of Sociology* 104:846–871.

———. 1999. "Symposium on Religion." *Sociological Theory* 17 (3): 237–239.

———. 1993. *Habermas and the Public Sphere*. Boston: MIT Press.

Calhoun, Craig J., Paul Price, and Ashley Timmer, eds. 2002. *Understanding September 11*. New York: New Press.

Cameron, Rondo. 1993. *A Concise Economic History of the World from Paleolithic Times to the Present*. Oxford: Oxford University Press.

Camic, Charles. 1983. *Experience and Enlightenment: Socialization for Cultural Change in Eighteenth-Century Scotland*. Chicago: University of Chicago Press.

———. 1992. "Reputation and Predecessor Selection: Parsons and the Institutionalists." *American Sociological Review* 57 (4): 421–445.

Camic, Charles, and Neil Gross. 1998. "Contemporary Developments in Sociological Theory: Current Projects and Conditions of Possibility." *Annual Review of Sociology* 24:453–476.

Camic, Charles, and Yu Xie. 1994. "The Statistical Turn in American Social Science: Columbia University, 1890 to 1915." *American Sociological Review* 59 (October): 773–805.

Campbell, D'Ann. 1984. *Women at War with America: Private Lives in a Patriotic Era*. Cambridge, Mass.: Harvard University Press.

Campbell, John L. 1993. "The State and Fiscal Sociology." *Annual Review of Sociology* 19:163–185.

Campbell, John L., and Leon N. Lindberg. 1990. "Property Rights and the Organization of Economic Activity by the State." *American Sociological Review* 55:634–647.

Caplow, Theodore. 1984. "Rule Enforcement without Visible Means: Christmas Gift Giving in Middletown." *American Journal of Sociology* 89:1306–1323.

Caplow, Theodore, and Louis Hicks. 2002. *Systems of War and Peace*, 2nd ed. New York: University Press of America.

Cardoso, Fernando Henrique, and Enzo Faletto. 1979 [1971]. *Dependency and Development in Latin America*. Trans. Marjory M. Urquidi. Berkeley: University of California Press.

Carlos, Ann M., and Frank D. Lewis. 1995. "Foreign Financing of Canadian Railroads: The Role of Information." Pp. 383–413 in *Anglo-American Financial Systems: Institutions and Markets in the Twentieth Century*. Ed. Michael D. Bordo and Richard Sylla. New York: Irwin.

Carpenter, Daniel P. 2000. "State Building through Reputation Building: Coalitions of Esteem and Program Innovation in the National Postal System, 1883–1913." *Studies in American Political Development* 14 (2): 121–155.

———. 2001. *The Forging of Bureaucratic Autonomy: Reputations, Networks, and Policy Innovation in Executive Agencies, 1862–1928*. Princeton, N.J.: Princeton University Press.

Carroll, Eero. 1999. *Emergence and Structuring of Social Insurance Institutions: Comparative Studies on Social Policy and Unemployment Insurance*. Stockholm: Swedish Institute for Social Research. Dissertation Series 38.

Carroll, Glenn R., and Michael T. Hannan. 1989. "Density Dependence in the Evolution of Populations of Newspaper Organizations." *American Sociological Review* 54:524–541.

Carruthers, Bruce G. 1996. *City of Capital: Politics and Markets in the English Financial Revolution*. Princeton, N.J.: Princeton University Press.

Carruthers, Bruce G., and Sarah L. Babb. 1996. "The Color of Money and the Nature of Value: Greenbacks and Gold in Postbellum America." *American Journal of Sociology* 101:1556–1591.

Carruthers, Bruce G., and Wendy Nelson Espeland. 1991. "Accounting for Rationality: Double-Entry Bookkeeping and the Rhetoric of Economic Rationality." *American Journal of Sociology* 97 (1): 31–69.

Carruthers, Bruce G., and Arthur L. Stinchcombe. 1999. "The Social Structure of Liquidity: Flexibility, Markets, and States." *Theory and Society* 28:353–382.

Carver, Terrell. 1996. *Gender Is Not a Synonym for Women*. Boulder, Colo.: Lynne Reiner.

Centeno, Miguel Angel. 1997. "Blood and Debt: War and Taxation in Nineteenth-Century Latin America." *American Journal of Sociology* 102:1565–1605.

———. 2002. *Blood and Debt: War and the Nation-State in Latin America*. University Park: Pennsylvania State University Press.

Centeno, Miguel Angel, and Fernando Lopez-Alves. 2002. "Introduction." Pp. 3–23 in *The Other Mirror: Grand Theory through the Lens of Latin America*. Ed. Migel Angel Centeno and Fernando Lopez-Alves. Princeton, N.J.: Princeton University Press.

Césaire, Aimé. 1972 [1955]. *Discourse on Colonialism*. New York: Monthly Review Press.

Chabot, Sean, and Jan Willem Duyvendak. 2002. "Globalization and Transnational Diffusion between Social Movements: Reconceptualizing the Dissemination of the Gandhian Repertoire and the 'Coming Out' Routine." *Theory and Society* 31:697–740.

Chakrabarty, Dipesh. 2000. *Provincializing Europe*. Princeton, N.J.: Princeton University Press.

Chandler, Alfred D., Jr. 1962. *Strategy and Structure: Chapters in the History of the American Industrial Enterprise*. Cambridge, Mass.: MIT Press.

———. 1977. *The Visible Hand: The Managerial Revolution in American Business*. Cambridge, Mass.: Harvard University Press.

Charles, Gerard Pierre. 1980. "Racialism and Sociological Theories." Pp. 69–83 in *Sociological Theories: Race and Colonialism*. Paris: UNESCO.

Charrad, Mounira M. 2001. *States and Women's Rights: The Making of Postcolonial Tunisia, Algeria, and Morocco*. Berkeley: University of California Press.

Charron, William C. 2000. "Greeks and Games: The Ancient Forerunners of Mathematical Game Theory." *Forum for Social Economics* 29 (2): 1–32.

Chatterjee, Partha. 1999. *The Partha Chatterjee Omnibus*. New Delhi: Oxford University Press.

Chaves, Mark, and Philip S. Gorski. 2001. "Religious Pluralism and Religious Participation." *Annual Review of Sociology* 27:261–281.

Chibber, Vivek. 1998. "Breaching the Nadu: Lordship and Economic Development in Pre-Colonial South India." *Journal of Peasant Studies* 26 (1): 1–42.

———. 1999. "Building a Developmental State: The Korean Case Reconsidered." *Politics and Society* 27 (3): 309–346.

Chirot, Daniel. 1976. *Social Change in a Peripheral Society: The Creation of a Balkan Colony*. New York: Academic Press.

———. 1985. "The Rise of the West." *American Sociological Review* 50:181–195.

Ciepley, D. 2000. "Why the State Was Dropped in the First Place." *Critical Review* 14 (2–3): 157–213.

Clark, Christopher. 1990. *The Roots of Rural Capitalism: Western Massachusetts, 1780–1860*. Ithaca, N.Y.: Cornell University Press.

Clark, Geoffrey. 1999. *Betting on Lives: The Culture of Life Insurance in England, 1695–1775*. Manchester: Manchester University Press.

Clark, Samuel. 1995. *State and Status: The Rise of the State and Aristocratic Power in Western Europe*. Montreal: McGill-Queen's University Press.

Clarke, Simon. 1993a. "The Crisis of the Soviet System." Pp. 30–55 in *What about the Workers? Workers and the Transition to Capitalism in Russia*. Ed. Simon Clarke, Peter Fairbrother, Michael Burawoy, and Pavel Krotov. London: Verso.

———. 1993b. "Privatisation and the Development of Capitalism in Russia." In *What about the Workers? Workers and the Transition to Capitalism in Russia*. Ed. Simon Clarke, Peter Fairbrother, Michael Burawoy, and Pavel Krotov. London: Verso.

Clausewitz, Carl von. 1976 [1832]. *On War*. Ed. and trans. Michael Howard and Peter Paret. Princeton, N.J.: Princeton University Press.

———. 1992. *Historical and Political Writings*. Ed. and trans. Peter Paret and Daniel Moran. Princeton, N.J.: Princeton University Press.

Clawson, Dan. 1980. *Bureaucracy and the Labor Process: The Transformation of U.S. Industry, 1860–1920*. New York: Monthly Review Press.

Clawson, Mary Ann. 1989. *Constructing Brotherhood: Class, Gender, and Fraternalism*. Princeton, N.J.: Princeton University Press.

Clemens, Elisabeth S. 1993. "Organizational Repertoires and Institutional Change: Women's Groups and the Transformation of U.S. Politics, 1890–1920." *American Journal of Sociology* 98:755–798.

———. 1997. *The People's Lobby: Organizational Innovation and the Rise of Interest Group Politics in the United States, 1890–1925*. Chicago: University of Chicago Press.

———. 1999a. "Continuity and Coherence: Periodization and the Problem of Institutional Change." Pp. 62–83 in *Social Time and Social Change: Perspectives on Sociology and History*. Ed. Fredrik Engelstad and Ragnvald Kalleberg. Oslo: Scandinavian University Press.

———. 1999b. "Securing Political Returns to Social Capital: Women's Associations in the United States, 1880s–1920s." *Journal of Interdisciplinary History* 29:613–638.

Clemens, Elisabeth S., and James Cook. 1999. "Politics and Institutionalism: Explaining Durability and Change." *Annual Review of Sociology* 25:441–466.

Clemens, Elisabeth S., and Martin D. Hughes. 2002. "Recovering Past Protest: Archival Research on Social Movements." In *Methods of Social Movement Research*. Ed. Suzanne Staggenborg and Bert Klandermans. Minneapolis: University of Minnesota Press.

Clemens, Elisabeth S., Walter W. Powell, Kris McIlwaine, and Dina Okamoto. 1997. "Careers in Print: Books, Journals, and Scholarly Reputations." *American Journal of Sociology* 101:433–494.

Coase, R. H. 1937. "The Nature of the Firm." *Economica* 4:386–405.

Cohen, Jean L. 1982. *Class and Civil Society: The Limits of Marxian Critical Theory*. Amherst: University of Massachusetts Press.

Cohen, Jean L., and A. Arato. 1992. *Civil Society and Political Theory*. Cambridge, Mass.: MIT Press.

Cohen, Jere. 1980. "Rational Capitalism in Renaissance Italy." *American Journal of Sociology* 85:1340–1355.

———. 1983. "Reply to Holton." *American Journal of Sociology* 89:181–187.

———. 2002. *Protestantism and Capitalism: The Mechanisms of Influence*. New York: Aldine de Gruyter.

Cohen, Patricia Cline. 1982. *A Calculating People: The Spread of Numeracy in Early America*. Chicago: University of Chicago Press.

Cohn, Samuel. 1985. *The Process of Occupational Sex-Typing: The Feminization of Clerical Labor in Great Britain*. Philadelphia: Temple University Press.

Cole, Michael, Yrjö Engeström, and Olga Vasquez, eds. 1997. *Mind, Culture, and Activity*. Cambridge: Cambridge University Press.

Cole, Stephen. 1983. "The Hierarchy of the Sciences?" *American Journal of Sociology* 89 (July): 111–139.

Coleman, James S. 1974. *Power and the Structure of Society*. New York: W. W. Norton.

———. 1990. *Foundations of Social Theory*. Cambridge, Mass.: Harvard University Press.

———. 1992. "The Power of Social Norms." *Duke Dialogue: Faculty Newsletter* 3 (April): 1–8.

———. 2000 [1988]. "Social Capital in the Creation of Human Capital." Pp. 17–42 in *Knowledge and Social Capital*. Ed. E. L. Lesser. Woburn, Mass.: Butterworth-Heinemann.

Collier, Andrew. 1994. *Critical Realism: An Introduction to Roy Bhaskar's Philosophy*. New York: Verso.

———. 2005. "Critical Realism." In *The Politics of Method in the Human Sciences: Positivism and Its Epistemological Others*. Ed. George Steinmetz. Durham, N.C.: Duke University Press.

Collier, Paul. 1999. "Doing Well Out of War." *http:/www.worldbank.org/research/conflict/papers/econ agenda.htm*.

Collins, Patricia Hill. 1990. *Black Feminist Thought*. Boston: Unwin, Hyman.

Collins, Randall. 1973 [1968]. "A Comparative Approach to Political Sociology." Pp. 42–67 in *State and Society*. Ed. Reinhard Bendix, in collaboration with Coenraad Brand, Randall Collins, Robert G. Michels, Hans-Eberhard Mueller, Gail Omvedt, Eliezer Rosenstein, Jean-Guy Vaillancour, and R. Stephen Warner. Berkeley: University of California Press.

———. 1979. *The Credential Society: An Historical Sociology of Education and Stratification*. New York: Academic Press.

———. 1980. "Weber's Last Theory of Capitalism: A Systematization." *American Sociological Review* 45:925–942.

———. 1986. *Weberian Sociological Theory*. New York: Cambridge University Press.

———1989. "Sociological Theory, Disaster Research, and War." Pp. 365–385 in *Social Structure and Disaster*. Ed. Gary A. Kreps. Newark: University of Delaware Press.

———. 1997a. "An Asian Route to Capitalism: Religious Economy and the Origins of Self-Transforming Growth in Japan." *American Sociological Review* 62:843–865.

———. 1997b. "A Sociological Guilt Trip: Comment on Connell." *American Journal of Sociology* 102 (6): 1558–1564.

———. 1999. *Macrohistory: Essays in the Sociology of the Long Run*. Stanford, Calif.: Stanford University Press.

Coltrane, Scott, and Justin Galt. 2000. "The History of Men's Caring." Pp. 15–36 in *Care Work: Gender, Labor, and the Welfare State*. Ed. Madonna Harrington Meyer. New York: Routledge.

Comaroff, Jean, and John Comaroff. 1992. *Ethnography and the Historical Imagination*. Boulder, Colo.: Westview Press.

Comaroff, John, and Paul Stern. 1994. "New Perspectives on Nationalism and War." *Theory and Society* 33:35–45.

Commission of the European Communities. 1997. *Citizenship of the Union: Second Report from the Commission.* Luxembourg: Office for Official Publications of the EC.

Comte, Auguste. 1975 [1830–1842]. *Auguste Comte and Positivism: The Essential Writings.* Ed. and with an introduction by Gertrud Lenzer. New York: Harper and Row.

Connell, R. W. 1987. *Gender and Power: Society, the Person, and Sexual Politics.* Stanford, Calif.: Stanford University Press.

———. 1995. *Masculinities.* Berkeley: University of California Press.

———. 1997. "Why Is Classical Theory Classical?" *American Journal of Sociology* 102:1511–1557.

Connor, Walker. 1994. *Ethno-Nationalism.* Princeton, N.J.: Princeton University Press.

Cooke, C. A. 1951. *Corporation Trust and Company: An Essay in Legal History.* Cambridge, Mass.: Harvard University Press.

Cooley, Charles H. 1962 [1909]. *Social Organization.* New York: Schocken Books.

Corrigan, Philip, and Derek Sayer. 1985. *The Great Arch: English State Formation as Cultural Revolution.* New York: Blackwell.

Corviser, André. 1979. *Armies and Societies in Europe, 1494–1789.* Trans. Abigail T. Siddall. Bloomington: Indiana University Press.

Cowan, Robin. 1990. "Nuclear Power Reactors: A Study in Technological Lock-in." *Journal of Economic History* 50:541–567.

Cowan, Robin, and Dominique Foray. 1997. "The Economics of Codification and the Diffusion of Knowledge." *Industrial and Corporate Change* 6:595–622.

Crafts, N. F. R., and C. Knick Harley. 1992. "Ouput Growth and the Industrial Revolution: A Restatement of the Crafts-Harley View." *Economic History Review* 45:703–730.

Crafts, N. F. R., and Terence C. Mills. 1997. "Endogenous Innovation, Trend Growth, and the British Industrial Revolution: Reply to Greasley and Oxley." *Journal of Economic History* 57 (4): 950–956.

Creed, Gerald W. 2000. "'Family Values' and Domestic Economies." *Annual Review of Anthropology* 29:329–355.

Crosby, Alfred W. 1997. *The Measure of Reality: Quantification and Western Society, 1250–1600.* Cambridge: Cambridge University Press.

Crouch, C. 2001. "Citizenship and Markets in Recent British Education Policy." Pp. 111–133 in *Citizenship, Markets and the State.* Ed. K. Eder, C. Crouch, and D. Tambini. Oxford: Oxford University Press.

Crummell, Alexander. 1891. *Africa and America: Addresses and Discourses.* Springfield, Mass.: Wiley.

Cummins, Ian. 1980. *Marx, Engels and National Movements.* London: Croom Helm.

Cyert, Richard M., and James G. March. 1963. *A Behavioral Theory of the Firm.* Englewood Cliffs, N.J.: Prentice-Hall.

Dahrendorf, R. 1996. "Citizenship and Social Class." In *Citizenship Today: The Contemporary Relevance of T. H. Marshall.* Ed. M. Bulmer and A. M. Rees. London: UCL Press.

Daly, Mary, and Jane Lewis. 2000. "The Concept of Social Care and the Analysis of Contemporary Welfare States." *British Journal of Sociology* 51 (2): 281–298.

Damghani, Muhammad Taqi, ed. 1978. *Avvalin Qavanin-i Iran Qabl az Mashrutiyat.* Tehran: Markaz-i Pakhsh-i Intisharat-i Bihzad.

Daston, Lorraine J. 1987. "The Domestication of Risk: Mathematical Probability and Insurance 1650–1830." Pp. 237–260 in *The Probabilistic Revolution*, vol. 1. Ed. Lorenz Kruger, Lorraine Daston, and Michael Heidelberger. Cambridge, Mass.: MIT Press.

David, Paul A. 1985. "Clio and the Economics of QWERTY." *American Economic Review* 75 (2): 332–337.

Davies, Celia. 1995. *Gender and the Professional Predicament in Nursing.* Philadelphia: Open University Press.

———. 1996. "The Sociology of Professions and the Profession of Gender." *Sociology* 30 (4): 661–678.

Davies, James C. 1962. "Toward a Theory of Revolution." *American Sociological Review* 27:5–19.

Davis, Diane. 1994. *Urban Leviathan: Mexico City in the Twentieth Century*. Philadelphia: Temple University Press.

Davis, Gerald F., and Michael Useem. 2002. "Top Management, Company Directors and Corporate Control." Pp. 233–259 in *Handbook of Strategy and Management*. Ed. Andrew Pettigrew, Howard Thomas, and Richard Whittington. London: Sage.

Davis, Natalie Zemon. 1983. *The Return of Martin Guerre*. Cambridge, Mass.: Harvard University Press.

———. 1999. "Religion and Capitalism Once Again? Jewish Merchant Culture in the Seventeenth Century." In *The Fate of "Culture": Geertz and Beyond*. Ed. Sherry B. Ortner. Berkeley: University of California Press.

Dawlatabadi, Yahya. 1983. *Hayat-i Yahya*, vol. 2. Tehran: Intisharat-i 'Attar, Intisharat-i Firdawsi. New York: Oxford University Press.

Deacon, Desley. 1989. *Managing Gender: The State, the New Middle Class and Women Workers, 1830–1930*. Melbourne: Oxford University Press.

Deflem, Mathieu. 2002. *Policing World Society: Historical Foundations of International Police Cooperation*. New York: Oxford University Press.

Delacroix, J., and F. Nielsen. 2001. "The Beloved Myth: Protestantism and the Rise of Industrial Capitalism in Nineteenth-Century Europe." *Social Forces* 80 (2): 509–553.

Demerath, N. J., III. 2001. *Crossing the Gods: World Religions and Worldly Politics*. New Brunswick, N.J.: Rutgers University Press.

De Pauw, Linda Grant. 1998. *Battle Cries and Lullabies: Women in War from Prehistory to the Present*. Norman: University of Oklahoma Press.

Derluguian, Georgi M. 2000. "The Russian Neo-Cossacks: Militant Provincials in the Geoculture of Clashing Civilizations." Pp. 288–314 in *Globalization and Social Movements*. Ed. John Guidry, Michael Kennedy, and Mayer Zald. Ann Arbor: University of Michigan Press.

———. 2001. "Recasting Russia." *New Left Review* 12:5–31.

———. Forthcoming. *Bourdieu's Secret Admirer in the Caucusus*. Chicago: University of Chicago Press.

Derrida, Jacques. 1976. *Of Grammatology*. Trans. Gayatri Chakravorty Spivak. Baltimore: Johns Hopkins University Press.

———. 1982. *Margins of Philosophy*. Trans. Alan Bass. Chicago: University of Chicago Press.

———. 1987. *The Truth in Painting*. Trans. Geoff Bennington and Ian McLeod. Chicago: University of Chicago Press.

———. 1996. *Archive Fever: A Freudian Impression*. Trans. Eric Prenowitz. Chicago: University of Chicago Press.

Despy-Meyer, Andrée, and Didier Devriese, eds. 1999. *Positivismes: Philosophie, sociologie, histoire, sciences*. Brussels: Brepols.

De Swaan, Abram. 1988. *In Care of the State: Health Care, Education and Welfare in Europe and the USA in the Modern Era*. Cambridge: Polity Press.

Deutsch, Karl. 1966 [1953]. *Nationalism and Social Communication: An Inquiry into the Foundations of Nationality*. 2nd ed. Cambridge, Mass.: MIT Press.

Devereux, Robert. 1963. *The First Ottoman Constitutional Period: A Study of the Midhat Constitution and Parliament*. Baltimore: Johns Hopkins University Press.

Devine, Joel. 1983. "State and Social Expenditure: Determinants of Social Investment and Social Consumption Spending in the Postwar United States." *American Sociological Review* 50:150–165.

De Vries, Jan, and Ad van der Woude. 1997. *The First Modern Economy: Success, Failure and Perseverance of the Dutch Economy, 1500–1815*. Cambridge: Cambridge University Press.

Dewey, John. 1929. *The Quest for Certainty: A Study of the Relation of Knowledge and Action*. New York: Minton, Balch.

Deyo, Frederic, ed. 1987. *The Political Economy of the New Asian Industrialism*. Ithaca, N.Y.: Cornell University Press.

Dibble, Vernon K. 1975. *The Legacy of Albion Small*. Chicago: University of Chicago Press.

Dilthey, Wilhelm. 1910. *Der Aufbau der geschichtlichen Welt in den Geisteswissenschaften*. Berlin: Verlag der Königlichen Akademie der Wissenschaften, in Commission bei Georg Reimer.

DiMaggio, Paul J., and Walter W. Powell. 1983. "The Iron Cage Revisited: Institutional Isomorphism and Collective Rationality in Organizational Fields." *American Sociological Review* 48 (2): 147–160.

———. 1991. "Introduction." Pp. 1–38 in *The New Institutionalism in Organizational Analysis*. Ed. Walter W. Powell and Paul J. DiMaggio. Chicago: University of Chicago Press.

Dirlik, Arif. 1997. "The Postcolonial Aura: Third World Criticism in the Age of Global Capitalism." *Critical Inquiry* 20:328–356.

Dixit, Avinash K., and Susan Skeath. 1999. *Games of Strategy*. New York: W. W. Norton.

Djelic, Marie-Laure. 1998. *Exporting the American Model: The Postwar Reconstruction of European Business*. New York: Oxford University Press.

Dobb, Maurice. 1947. *Studies in the Development of Capitalism*. London: Routledge.

———. 1963. *Studies in the Development of Capitalism*, rev. ed. New York: International Publishers.

Dobbin, Frank. 1994. *Forging Industrial Policy: The United States, Britain and France in the Railway Age*. Cambridge: Cambridge University Press.

Dobbin, Frank, and Timothy J. Dowd. 1997. "How Policy Shapes Competition: Early Railroad Foundings in Massachusetts." *Administrative Science Quarterly* 42:501–529.

———. 2000. "The Market That Antitrust Built: Public Policy, Private Coercion, and Railroad Acquisitions, 1825 to 1922." *American Sociological Review* 65:631–657.

Domar, E. 1947. "Expansion and Employment." *American Economic Review* 37:343–355.

Domhoff, G. William. 1996. *State Autonomy or Class Dominance? Case Studies on Policy Making in America*. New York: Aldine de Gruyter.

Domínguez, Virginia R. 1986. *White by Definition: Social Classification in Creole Louisiana*. New Brunswick, N.J.: Rutgers University Press.

Dosse, François. 1997 [1991]. *History of Structuralism*, vol. 1: *The Rising Sign, 1945–1966*. Trans. Deborah Glassman. Minneapolis: University of Minnesota Press.

Douglas, Mary. 1986. *How Institutions Think*. Syracuse: Syracuse University Press.

Dower, John W. 1986. *War without Mercy: Race and Power in the Pacific War*. New York: Pantheon Books.

Downing, Brian M. 1992. *The Military Revolution and Political Change: Origins of Democracy and Autocracy in Early Modern Europe*. Princeton, N.J.: Princeton University Press.

DuBois, W. E. B. 1964 [1935]. *Black Reconstruction in America*. New York: Meridian Books.

———. 1965 [1946]. *The World and Africa: An Inquiry into the Part Which Africa Has Played in World History*. New York: International Publishers.

———. 1969 [1896]. *The Suppression of the African Slave-Trade to the United States of America, 1638–1870*. New York: Schocken Press.

———. 1977 [1938]. *Black Reconstruction in America*. New York: Atheneum.

Duby, Georges. 1968. *Rural Economy and Country Life in the Medieval West*. Columbia: University of South Carolina Press.

Duffy, Christopher. 1987. *The Military Experience in the Age of Reason*. London: Routledge and Kegan Paul.

Duffy, Elizabeth A., and Idana Goldberg. 1998. *Crafting a Class: College Admissions and Financial Aid, 1955–1994*. Princeton, N.J.: Princeton University Press.

Duncan, Simon, and Rosalind Edwards. 1999. *Lone Mothers, Paid Work, and Gendered Moral Rationalities*. New York: St. Martin's Press.

———, eds. 1997. *Single Mothers in an International Context: Mothers or Workers?* London: UCL Press.

Duplessis, Robert S. 1997. *Transitions to Capitalism in Early Modern Europe*. Cambridge: Cambridge University Press.

Durkheim, Emile. 1915. *The Elementary Forms of the Religious Life*. New York: Free Press.

———. 1951. *Suicide: A Study in Sociology*. Trans. John Spaulding. Ed. George Simpson. New York: Free Press.

———. 1961. *Moral Education: A Study in the Theory and Application of the Sociology of Education*. New York: Free Press.

———. 1965 [1915]. *The Elementary Forms of the Religious Life*. New York: Free Press.

———. 1982 [1907]. *The Rules of Sociological Method*. Trans. W. D. Halls. Ed. Steven Lukes. New York: Free Press.

———. 1984. *The Division of Labor in Society*. Trans. W. D. Halls. New York: Free Press.

———. 1995 [1915]. *The Elementary Forms of the Religious Life*. Trans. Karen E. Fields. New York: Free Press.

Durkheim, Emile, and Marcel Mauss. 1963. *Primitive Classification*. Chicago: University of Chicago Press.

Dutton, Michael. 2002. "Lead Us Not Into Translation: Notes Toward a Theoretical Foundation for Asian Studies." *Nepantla: Views from South* 3 (3): 495–537.

Eardley, Tony, Jonathan Bradshaw, John Ditch, Ian Gough, and Peter Whiteford. 1996a. *Social Assistance in OECD Countries: Country Reports*. London: HMSO. Department of Social Security Research Report 47.

———. 1996b. *Social Assistance in OECD Countries: Synthesis Report*. London: HMSO. Department of Social Security Research Report 46.

Earle, Peter. 1989. *The Making of the English Middle Class: Business, Society, and Family Life in London 1660–1730*. Berkeley: University of California Press.

Eder, K., and B. Giesen. 2001. *European Citizenship: Between National Legacies and Postnational Projects*. Oxford: Oxford University Press.

Eder, K., C. Crouch, and D. Tambini, eds. 2001. *Citizenship, Markets and the State*. Oxford: Oxford University Press.

Edwards, Lyford. 1970. *The Natural History of Revolution*. Chicago: University of Chicago Press.

Eggertsson, Thráinn. 1990. *Economic Behavior and Institutions*. Cambridge: Cambridge University Press.

Eisenstadt, S. N. 1963. *The Political Systems of Empires*. New York: Free Press.

———. 1964. "Modernization and Conditions of Sustained Growth." *World Politics* 16:576–594.

———. 1966. *Modernization: Protest and Change*. Englewood Cliffs, N.J.: Prentice-Hall.

———. 1978a. *Revolution and the Transformation of Societies: A Comparative Study of Civilization*. New York: Free Press.

———. 1978b. "The Social Framework and Conditions of Revolution." *Research in Social Movements, Conflicts and Change* 1:85–104.

———. 1995. *Japanese Civilization*. Chicago: University of Chicago Press.

———. 2000. "The Civilizational Dimension in Sociological Analysis." *Thesis Eleven* 62 (August): 1–21.

———. 2002. "The Civilizations of the Americas: The Crystallization of Distinct Modernities." *Comparative Sociology* 1 (1): 43–62.

———, ed. 1986. *The Origins and Diversity of Axial Age Civilizations*. Albany: State University of New York Press.

Eisner, Marc Allen. 2000. *From Warfare State to Welfare State: World War I, Compensatory State Building, and the Limits of the Modern Order*. University Park: Pennsylvania State University Press.

Elder, Glenn H., Jr. 1998 [1974]. *Children of the Great Depression*. Boulder, Colo.: Westview Press.

Eldridge, S. 1928. "Community Organization and Citizenship." *Social Forces* 7 (1): 132–140.

Eley, Geoff. 1996. "Is All the World a Text? From Social History to the History of Society Two Decades

Later." Pp. 193–243 in *The Historical Turn in the Human Sciences*. Ed. Terrence J. McDonald. Ann Arbor: University of Michigan Press.

——. 2002. *Forging Democracy: The History of the Left in Europe, 1850–2000*. Oxford: Oxford University Press.

Elias, Norbert. 1978. *What Is Sociology?* London: Hutchinson.

——. 1982 [1939]. *The Civilizing Process*. Trans. Edmund Jephcott. New York: Pantheon Books.

——. 1994 [1939]. *The Civilizing Process*. Oxford: Blackwell.

Eliot, George. 1994. *Middlemarch*. New York: Penguin.

Ellingson, Stephen. 1995. "Understanding the Dialectic of Discourse and Collective Action: Public Debate and Rioting in Antebellum Cincinnati." *American Journal of Sociology* 101 (1): 100–144.

Ellis, Joseph J. 2000. *Founding Brothers: The Revolutionary Generation*. New York: Knopf.

Elman, Colin, and Miriam Fendius Elman, eds. 2001. *Bridges and Boundaries: Historians, Political Scientists, and the Study of International Relations*. Cambridge, Mass.: MIT Press.

Elshtain, Jean Bethke. 1987. *Women and War*. Chicago: University of Chicago Press.

Elster, Jon. 1985. *Making Sense of Marx*. Cambridge: Cambridge University Press.

——. 1998. "A Plea for Mechanisms." Pp. 45–73 in *Social Mechanisms*. Ed. Peter Hedström and Richard Swedborg. Cambridge: Cambridge University Press.

——. 1999. *Alchemies of the Mind: Rationality and the Emotions*. Cambridge: Cambridge University Press.

Ely, James W., Jr. 1992. *The Guardian of Every Other Right: A Constitutional History of Property Rights*. New York: Oxford University Press.

Emigh, Rebecca Jean. 1997a. "The Power of Negative Thinking: The Use of Negative Case Methodology in the Development of Sociological Theory." *Theory and Society* 26:649–684.

——. 1997b. "The Spread of Sharecropping in Tuscany: The Political Economy of Transaction Costs." *American Sociological Review* 62:423–442.

——. 1998. "The Mystery of the Missing Middle-Tenants: The 'Negative' Case of Fixed-Term Leasing and Agricultural Investment in Fifteenth-Century Tuscany." *Theory and Society* 27 (3): 351–375.

——. 1999. "Means and Measures: Productive Comparisons of Agricultural Output of Sharecropping and Smallholding in Fifteenth-Century Tuscany." *Social Forces* 78 (2): 461–491.

——. 2000. "Economic Outcomes: Forms of Property Rights or Class Capacities? The Example of Tuscan Sharecropping." *European Journal of Sociology* 41 (1): 22–52.

——. 2002. "Numeracy or Enumeration? The Uses of Numbers by States and Societies." *Social Science History* 26 (4): 653–698.

——. 2003. "Economic Interests and Sectoral Relations: The Undevelopment of Capitalism in Fifteenth-Century Tuscany." *American Journal of Sociology* 108 (5): 1075–1113.

Emigh, Rebecca Jean, and Iván Szelényi, eds. 2001. *Poverty, Ethnicity, and Gender in Eastern Europe during the Market Transition*. Westport, Conn.: Praeger.

Emirbayer, Mustafa. 1992. "Beyond Structuralism and Voluntarism: The Politics and Discourse of Progressive School Reform, 1890–1930." *Theory and Society* 21 (5): 621–664.

——. 1997. "Manifesto for a Relational Sociology." *American Journal of Sociology* 103:281–317.

——. Forthcoming. "Beyond Weberian Action Theory." In *Max Weber at the Millennium*. Ed. Charles Camic, David Trubek, and Philip Gorski. Stanford, Calif.: Stanford University Press.

Emirbayer, Mustafa, and Jeff Goodwin. 1994. "Network Analysis, Culture, and the Problem of Agency." *American Journal of Sociology* 99 (6): 1411–1454.

Emirbayer, Mustafa, and Ann Mische. 1998. "What Is Agency?" *American Journal of Sociology* 103 (4): 962–1023.

Emmanuel, Arghiri. 1972. *Unequal Exchange: An Essay on the Imperialism of Trade*. New York: Monthly Review Press.

England, Paula, and Nancy Folbre. 1999. "The Costs of Caring." *Annals of the American Academy of Political and Social Sciences* 561:39–51.

Enloe, Cynthia. 1990. "Nationalism and Masculinity." Pp. 42–64 in *Bananas, Beaches, and Bases: Making Feminist Sense of International Politics*. Berkeley: University of California Press.

Enver, Paşa. 1991. *Enver Paşa'nın Anıları (1881–1908)*. Ed. Halil Erdoğan Cengiz. Istanbul: İletişim Yayınları.

Epstein, Steven. 1996. *Impure Science: AIDS, Activism, and the Politics of Knowledge*. Berkeley: University of California Press.

Ermakoff, Ivan. 1997. "Prelates and Princes: Aristocratic Marriages, Canon Law Prohibitions, and Shifts in the Norms and Patterns of Domination in the Central Middle Ages." *American Sociological Review* 62:405–422.

———. 2001. "Strukturelle Zwange und Zufallige Geschehnisse." *Geschichte und Gesellschaft* 19 (March): 224–256.

Ertman, Thomas. 1997. *Birth of the Leviathan: Building States and Regimes in Medieval and Early Modern Europe*. Cambridge: Cambridge University Press.

Espeland, Wendy Nelson. 1998. *The Struggle for Water: Politics, Rationality, and Identity in the American Southwest*. Chicago: University of Chicago Press.

Espeland, Wendy Nelson, and Mitchell Stevens. 1998. "Commensuration as a Social Process." *Annual Review of Sociology* 23:313–343.

Esping-Andersen, Gøsta. 1985. *Politics against Markets*. Princeton, N.J.: Princeton University Press.

———. 1990. *The Three Worlds of Welfare Capitalism*. Princeton, N.J.: Princeton University Press.

———. 1999. *Social Foundations of Postindustrial Society*. New York: Oxford University Press.

———. ed. 1996. *Welfare States in Transition: National Adaptations in Global Economies*. Thousand Oaks, Calif.: Sage.

Esping-Andersen, Gøsta, Duncan Gallie, Anton Hemerijk, and John Myles. 2002. *Why We Need a New Welfare State*. New York: Oxford University Press.

Esser, Hartmut. 1999. "Die Situationslogik ethnischer Konflikte: Auch eine Anmerkung zum Beitrag 'Ethnische Mobilisierung und die Logik von Identitätskämpfen' von Klaus Eder und Oliver Schmidtke." *Zeitschrift für Soziologie* 28 (4): 245–262.

Ettehadieh (Nezam-Mafi), Mansoureh. 1989. "The Council for the Investigation of Grievances: A Case Study of Nineteenth-Century Iranian Social History." *Iranian Studies* 22 (1): 51–61.

Etzioni, A. 1997. *The New Golden Rule: Community and Morality in a Democratic Society*. London: Profile.

Evans, Ivan. 1997. *Bureaucracy and Race: Native Administration in South Africa*. Berkeley: University of California Press.

———. N.d. "Racial Violence and State Formation in Two Radical Orders: South Africa and the United States." Unpublished manuscript.

Evans, Peter B. 1979. *Dependent Development: The Alliance of Multinational, State, and Local Capital in Brazil*. Princeton, N.J.: Princeton University Press.

———. 1995. *Embedded Autonomy: States and Industrial Transformation*. Princeton, N.J.: Princeton University Press.

Evans, R. J. W., and T. V. Thomas, eds. 1991. *Crown, Church, and Estates: Central European Politics in the Sixteenth and Seventeenth Centuries*. New York: St. Martin's Press.

Ewald, François. 1986. *L'Etat Providence*. Paris: Grasset.

———. 1991. "Insurance and Risk." Pp. 197–210 in *The Foucault Effect: Studies in Governmentality*. Ed. Graham Burchell, Colin Gordon, and Peter Miller. Chicago: University of Chicago Press.

Eyal, Gil. 2000. "Anti-Politics and the Spirit of Capitalism: Dissidents, Monetarists, and the Czech Transition to Capitalism." *Theory and Society* 29:49–92.

Eyal, Gil, Iván Szelényi, and Eleanor Townsley. 1998. *Making Capitalism without Capitalists: Class Formation and Elite Struggles in Post-Communist Europe.* London: Verso.

——. 2001. "The Utopia of Postsocialist Theory and the Ironic View of History in Neoclassical Sociology." *American Journal of Sociology* 106 (4): 1121–1128.

Faeges, Russell. 1999. "Theory-Driven Concept Definition: The Challenge of Perverse Cases." Paper presented at the annual meeting of the American Political Science Association, Atlanta, September 2–5.

——. 2001a. "Contending Conceptions of Nationalism, or the Bases of Political Community." Paper presented at the annual meeting of the American Political Science Association, San Francisco, August 29–September 2.

——. 2001b. "Durkheim." In *Encyclopedia of Nationalism*, vol. 2. Ed. Alexander Motyl. San Diego: Academic Press.

——. 2001c. "Weber." In *Encyclopedia of Nationalism*, vol. 2. Ed. Alexander Motyl. San Diego: Academic Press.

——. N.d. "Why Definitions Multiply." Unpublished manuscript.

Fairbank, J. K. 1986. *The Great Chinese Revolution, 1800–1985.* New York: Harper and Row.

Falasca-Zamponi, Simonetta. 1997. *Fascist Spectacle: The Aesthetics of Power in Mussolini's Italy.* Berkeley: University of California Press.

Fanon, Frantz. 1967. *Black Skin, White Masks.* New York: Grove Weidenfeld.

——. 1991. *Black Skin, White Masks.* New York: Grove Weidenfeld.

Farquhar, J. 1994. "Market Magic: Getting Rich and Getting Personal Medicine after Mao." *American Ethnologist* 23:239–257.

Fauconnier, Gilles, and Mark Turner. 2002. *The Way We Think: Conceptual Blending and the Mind's Hidden Complexities.* New York: Basic Books.

Faue, Elizabeth. 1991. *Community of Suffering and Struggle: Women, Men, and the Labor Movement in Minneapolis, 1915–1945.* Chapel Hill: University of North Carolina Press.

Faulhaber, Gerald R., and William J. Baumol. 1988. "Economists as Innovators: Practical Products of Theoretical Research." *Journal of Economic Literature* 26:577–600.

Fearon, James, and David D. Laitin. 1996. "Explaining Interethnic Cooperation." *American Political Science Review* 90 (4): 715–735.

Featherman, David L., and Maris A. Vinovskis. 2001. "Growth and Use of Social and Behavioral Science in the Federal Government since World War II." Pp. 40–82 in *Social Science and Policy-Making: A Search for Relevance in the Twentieth Century.* Ed. David L. Featherman and Maris A. Vinovskis. Ann Arbor: University of Michigan Press.

Feischmidt, Margit. 2001. "Zwischen Abgrenzung und Vermischung: Ethnizität in der siebenbürgischen Stadt Cluj (Kolozsvár, Klausenburg)." Ph.D. dissertation, Humboldt University, Berlin.

Felski, Rita. 2000. *Doing Time: Feminist Theory and Postmodern Culture.* New York: New York University Press.

Fenn, Richard K., ed. 2001. *The Blackwell Companion to Sociology of Religion.* Oxford: Blackwell.

Fenton, C. Stephen. 1980. "Race, Class, and Politics in the Work of Emile Durkheim." Pp. 143–181 in *Sociological Theories: Race and Colonialism.* Paris: UNESCO.

Fernandez, Roberto M., and Doug McAdam. 1988. "Social Networks and Social Movements: Multiorganizational Fields and Recruitment to Mississippi Freedom Summer." *Sociological Forum* 3: 357–382.

Ferree, Myra Marx, and Beth B. Hess. 1985. *Controversy and Coalition: The New Feminist Movement.* Boston: Twayne Publishers.

Ferrera, Maurizio, and Martin Rhodes, eds. 2000. *Recasting European Welfare States.* London: Frank Cass.

Field, Daniel. 1989. *Rebels in the Name of the Tsar.* Boston: Unwin, Hyman.

Fierlbeck, K. 1991. "Redefining Responsibility: The Politics of Citizenship in the United Kingdom." *Canadian Journal of Political Science—Revue Canadienne de Science Politique* 24 (3): 575–593.

Finch, Janet, and Dulcie Groves, eds. 1983. *A Labour of Love: Women, Work and Caring*. London: Routledge and Kegan Paul.

Findley, Carter V. 1980. *Bureaucratic Reform in the Ottoman Empire: The Sublime Porte, 1789–1922*. Princeton, N.J.: Princeton University Press.

——. 1989. *Ottoman Civil Officialdom: A Social History*. Princeton, N.J.: Princeton University Press.

Finegold, Kenneth, and Theda Skocpol. 1995. *State and Party in America's New Deal*. Madison: University of Wisconsin Press.

Fineman, Martha. 1995. *The Neutered Mother, the Sexual Family, and Other Twentieth-Century Tragedies*. New York: Routledge.

Finke, Roger, and Rodney Stark. 1988. "Religious Economies and Sacred Canopies: Religious Mobilization in American Cities, 1906." *American Sociological Review* 53: 41–49.

——. 1992. *The Churching of America, 1776–1990: Winners and Losers in Our Religious Economy*. New Brunswick, N.J.: Rutgers University Press.

Finke, Roger, Avery M. Guest, and Rodney Stark. 1996. "Mobilizing Local Religious Markets: Religious Pluralism in the Empire State, 1855–1865." *American Sociological Review* 61:203–218.

Firmin-Sellers, Kathryn. 1995. "The Politics of Property Rights." *American Political Science Review* 89:867–881.

Fischer, David Hackett. 1970. *Historians' Fallacies*. New York: Harper and Row.

Fisher, Donald. 1993. *Fundamental Development of the Social Sciences: Rockefeller Philanthropy and the United States Social Science Research Council*. Ann Arbor: University of Michigan Press.

Fitzgerald, Thomas. 2002. "Public Opinion Sampling." *Society* 39 (September/October): 53–59.

Flacks, Richard. 1989. "Gouldner's Prophetic Voice." *American Sociologist* 20 (winter): 353–356.

Fligstein, Neil. 1990. *The Transformation of Corporate Control*. Cambridge, Mass.: Harvard University Press.

——. 2001. *The Architecture of Markets: An Economic Sociology of Twenty-first-Century Capitalist Societies*. Princeton, N.J.: Princeton University Press.

Fodor, Eva. 2003. *Working Difference: Women's Working Lives in Hungary and Austria, 1945–1995*. Durham, N.C.: Duke University Press.

Foran, John. 1992. "An Historical-Sociological Framework for the Study of Long-Term Transformations in the Third World." *Humanity and Society* 16 (3): 330–349.

——. 1993a. *Fragile Resistance: Social Transformation in Iran from 1500 to the Revolution*. Boulder, Colo.: Westview Press.

——. 1993b. "Theories of Revolution Revisited: Toward a Fourth Generation?" *Sociological Theory* 11 (1): 1–20.

Förster, Stig, and Jörg Nagler, eds. 1997. *On the Road to Total War: The American Civil War and the German Wars of Unification, 1861–1871*. Cambridge: Cambridge University Press.

Foucault, Michel. 1972. *The Archaeology of Knowledge*. New York: Pantheon.

——. 1978. *The History of Sexuality*, vol. 1. New York: Pantheon.

——. 1979. *Discipline and Punish: The Birth of the Prison*. New York: Vintage.

——. 1990. *The History of Sexuality*, vol. 2: *The Use of Pleasure*. Trans. Robert Hurley. New York: Vintage.

Fourcade-Gourinchas, Marion. 2001. "Politics, Institutional Structures, and the Rise of Economics: A Comparative Study." *Theory and Society* 30:397–447.

Fox, Jon E. 2001. "Nationness and Everyday Life: Romanian and Hungarian University Students in Transylvania." Paper presented to the Center for Comparative Social Analysis Workshop, Department of Sociology, UCLA.

Frank, Andre Gunder. 1966a. "The Development of Underdevelopment." *Monthly Review* 18:17–31.

——. 1966b. *The Underdevelopment of Development*. Boston, Mass.: New England Free Press.

——. 1971. *The Sociology of Underdevelopment and the Underdevelopment of Sociology*. London: Pluto Press.

——. 1998. *Reorient: Global Economy in the Asian Age*. Berkeley: University of California Press.

Frank, Stephen P., and Mark D. Steinberg, eds. 1994. *Cultures in Flux: Lower-class Values, Practices, and Resistance in Late Imperial Russia*. Princeton, N.J.: Princeton University Press.

Frantilla, Anne. 1998. *Social Science in the Public Interest: A Fiftieth-Year History of the Institute for Social Research*. Bulletin 45 (September). Ann Arbor: Bentley Historical Library.

Franzosi, Roberto. 1998. "Narrative Analysis: Why (and How) Sociologists Should Be Interested in Narrative." *Annual Review of Sociology* 24:517–554.

Franzosi, Roberto, and John Morh. 1997. "New Directions in Formalization and Historical Analysis." *Theory and Society* 26 (2/3): 133–160.

Fraser, Nancy. 1989. *Unruly Practices: Power, Discourse, and Gender in Contemporary Social Theory*. Minneapolis: University of Minnesota Press.

——. 1997. *Justice Interruptus: Critical Reflections on the "Postsocialist" Condition*. New York: Routledge.

Fraser, Nancy, and Linda Gordon. 1992. "Contract versus Charity: Why Is There No Social Citizenship in the United States? *Socialist Review* 22 (3): 45–68.

——. 1994a. " 'Dependency' Demystified: Inscriptions of Power in a Keyword of the Welfare State." *Social Politics* 1:4–31.

——. 1994b. " 'A Genealogy of 'Dependency': Tracing a Keyword of the U.S. Welfare State." *Signs* 19:309–336.

Fredrickson, George. 1981. *White Supremacy: A Comparative Study in American and South African History*. New York: Oxford.

Freedland, M. 2001. "The Marketization of Public Services." Pp. 91–110 in *Citizenship, Markets and the State*. Ed. K. Eder, C. Crouch, and D. Tambini. Oxford: Oxford University Press.

Freeland, Robert F. 1996. "The Myth of the M-Form? Governance, Consent, and Organizational Change." *American Journal of Sociology* 102: 483–526.

Freeman, Jo. 1975. *The Politics of Women's Liberation: A Case Study of an Emerging Social Movement and Its Relation to the Policy Process*. New York: McKay.

Freidson, Eliot. 1970a. *Profession of Medicine: A Study of the Sociology of Applied Knowledge*. New York: Harper and Row.

——. 1970b. *Professional Dominance: The Social Structure of Medical Care*. New York: Atherton Press.

——. 1983. "The Theory of the Professions: The State of the Art." Pp. 19–37 in *The Sociology of Professions: Lawyers, Doctors, and Others*. Ed. R. Dingwall and P. Lews. New York: St. Martin's Press.

——. 1984. "The Changing Nature of Professional Control." *Annual Review of Sociology* 10:1–20.

——. 1986. *Professional Powers*. Chicago: University of Chicago Press.

——. 1994. *Professionalism Reborn: Theory, Prophecy, and Policy*. Chicago: University of Chicago Press.

——. 2001. *Professionalism: The Third Logic of the Practice of Knowledge*. Chicago: University of Chicago Press.

Freud, Sigmund. 1963 [1927]. "Fetishism." Pp. 149–157 in *The Standard Edition of the Complete Psychological Works of Sigmund Freud*, vol. 21. Ed. James Strachey. London: Hogarth Press.

——. 1975. *The Future of an Illusion*. Trans. James Strachey. New York: W. W. Norton.

Frieden, Jeffry A. 1994. "International Investment and Colonial Control: A New Interpretation." *International Organization* 48 (4): 559–593.

Friedland, Roger. 1999. "When God Walks in History: The Institutional Politics of Religious Nationalism." *International Sociology* 14 (3): 301–319.

——. 2001. "Religious Nationalism and the Problem of Collective Representation." *Annual Review of Sociology* 27:125–152.

Friedland, Roger, and Robert R. Alford. 1991. "Bringing Society Back In: Symbols, Practices, and

Institutional Contradiction." Pp. 232–263 in *The New Institutionalism in Organizational Analysis*. Ed. Walter W. Powell and Paul J. DiMaggio. Chicago: University of Chicago Press.

Friedman, Milton. 1953. *Essays in Positive Economics*. Chicago: University of Chicago Press.

Friedmann, Harriet. 1982. "The Political Economy of Food: The Rise and Fall of the Postwar International Food Order." *American Journal of Sociology* 88:S248–S286 (Supplement: Marxist Inquiries: Studies of Labor, Class, and States).

Froese, Paul, and Steven Pfaff. 2001. "Replete and Desolate Markets: Poland, East Germany and the New Religious Paradigm." *Social Forces* 80 (2): 481–507.

Fukuyama, Francis. 1993. *The End of History and the Last Man*. New York: Avon.

Furet, François. 1981. *Interpreting the French Revolution*. New York: Cambridge University Press.

Gadamer, Hans-Georg. 1975. *Truth and Method*. New York: Seabury Press.

Gal, Susan, and Gail Kligman. 2000. *The Politics of Gender after Socialism: A Comparative-Historical Essay*. Princeton, N.J.: Princeton University Press.

——, eds. 2000. *Reproducing Gender: Politics, Publics, and Everyday Life after Socialism*. Princeton, N.J.: Princeton University Press.

Gamson, William A. 1992. *Talking Politics*. New York: Cambridge University Press.

Gamson, William A., and Andre Modigliani. 1989. "Media Discourse and Public Opinion on Nuclear Power: A Constructionist Approach." *American Journal of Sociology* 95:1–37.

Gans, Herbert J. 1979. "Symbolic Ethnicity: The Future of Ethnic Groups and Cultures in America." *Ethnic and Racial Studies* 2:1–20.

Gaonkar, Dilip Parameshwar, ed. 2001. *Alternative Modernities*. Durham, N.C.: Duke University Press.

Garber, Peter M. 2000. *Famous First Bubbles: The Fundamentals of Early Manias*. Cambridge, Mass.: MIT Press.

Garfinkel, Harold. 1967. *Studies in Ethnomethodology*. Englewood Cliffs, N.J.: Prentice-Hall.

Garland, David. 1985. *Punishment and Welfare: A History of Penal Strategies*. Brookfield, Vt.: Gower.

Gartrell, C. David, and John W. Gartrell. 1996. "Positivism in Sociological Practice: 1967–1990." *Canadian Journal of Sociology and Anthropology* 33 (May): 143–158.

Geary, Patrick. 1986. "Sacred Commodities: The Circulation of Medieval Relics." Pp. 169–191 in *The Social Life of Things*. Ed. Arjun Appadurai. Cambridge: Cambridge University Press.

Geertz, Clifford. 1973. "Thick Description: Toward an Interpretive Theory of Culture." Pp. 3–30 in *The Interpretation of Cultures*. New York: Basic Books.

——, ed. 1963. *Old Societies and New States: The Quest for Modernity in Asia and Africa*. New York: Free Press.

Geiger, Reed. 1994. *Planning the French Canals*. Newark: University of Delaware Press.

Gelber, Steven M., and Martin L. Cook. 1990. *Saving the Earth: The History of a Middle-Class Millenarian Movement*. Berkeley: University of California Press.

Gellner, Ernest. 1983. *Nations and Nationalism*. Oxford: Blackwell.

——. 1997. *Nationalism*. London: Wiedenfeld and Nicolson.

Gerber, Theodore P. 2002. "Structural Change and Post-Socialist Stratification: Labor Market Transitions in Contemporary Russia." *American Sociological Review* 67:629–659.

Gerber, Theodore P., and Michael Hout. 1998. "More Shock than Therapy: Market Transition, Employment, and Income in Russia, 1991–1995." *American Journal of Sociology* 104:1–50.

Gerriets, Marilyn. 1981. "The Organization of Exchange in Early Christian Ireland." *Journal of Economic History* 41:171–176.

Gerschenkron, Alexander. 1962. *Economic Backwardness in Historical Perspective*. Cambridge, Mass.: Belknap Press.

Gerteis, Joseph. 2002. "The Possession of Civic Virtue: Movement Narratives of Race and Class in the Knights of Labor." *American Journal of Sociology* 108 (3): 580–615.

Gerth, Hans H., and C. Wright Mills, eds. 1946. *From Max Weber*. New York: Oxford University Press.

Ghazzali Tusi, Muhammad. 1938. *Nasihat al-Muluk*. Ed. J. Huma'i. Tehran: Chapkhanah-'i Majlis.

Giddens, Anthony. 1971. *Capitalism and Modern Social Thought*. Cambridge: Cambridge University Press.

———. 1979. *Central Problems in Social Theory: Action, Structure and Contradiction in Social Analysis*. Berkeley: University of California Press.

———. 1982. "Class Division, Class Conflict, and Citizenship Rights." In *Profiles and Critiques in Social Theory*. Ed. A. Giddens and F. Dallmayr. Berkeley: University of California Press.

———. 1984. *The Constitution of Society: Outline of the Theory of Structuration*. Berkeley: University of California Press.

———. 1985. *The Nation-State and Violence*. Berkeley: University of California Press.

Giddens, Anthony, and Christopher Pierson. 1998. *Conversations with Anthony Giddens: Making Sense of Modernity*. Stanford, Calif.: Stanford University Press.

Giere, Ronald N., and Alan W. Richardson, eds. 1996. *Origins of Logical Empiricism*. Minneapolis: University of Minnesota Press.

Gieryn, Thomas F. 1999. *Cultural Boundaries of Science: Credibility on the Line*. Chicago: University of Chicago Press.

Giesey, Ralph E. 1983. "State-Building in Early Modern France: The Role of Royal Officialdom." *Journal of Modern History* 55:191–207.

Gilbert, Jess, and Carolyn Howe. 1991. "Beyond 'State vs. Society': Theories of the State and New Deal Agricultural Policies." *American Sociological Review* 56 (2): 204–220.

Gille, Zsuzsa. 1999. "Wastelands in Transition: Forms and Concepts of Waste in Hungary since 1948." Pp. 165–185 in *Ecology and the World-System*. Ed. W. Goldfrank, D. Goodman, and A. Szasz. Westport, Conn.: Greenwood Press.

———. 2000. "Legacy of Waste or Wasted Legacy? The End of Industrial Ecology in Hungary." *Environmental Politics* 9(1): 203–234.

Gillis, M. 1989. *Tax Reform in Developing Countries*. Durham, N.C.: Duke University Press.

Gilroy, Paul. 1993. *The Black Atlantic: Modernity and Double Consciousness*. Cambridge, Mass.: Harvard University Press.

Gil-White, Francisco. 1999. "How Thick Is Blood? The Plot Thickens . . . : If Ethnic Actors Are Primordialists, What Remains of the Circumstantialist/Primordialist Controversy?" *Ethnic and Racial Studies* 22 (5): 789–820.

Ginzburg, Carlo. 1980. *The Cheese and the Worms: The Cosmos of a Sixteenth-Century Miller*. Trans. John and Anne Tedeschi. Baltimore: Johns Hopkins University Press.

———. 1989. *Clues, Myths, and the Historical Method*. Baltimore: Johns Hopkins University Press.

Gitlin, T. 1995. *The Twilight of Common Dreams: Why America Is Wracked by Culture Wars*. New York: Metropolitan Books.

Glenn, Evelyn Nakano. 1992. "From Servitude to Service Work: Historical Continuities in the Racial Division of Reproductive Labor." *Signs* 18:1–43.

———. 2002. *Unequal Freedom: How Race and Gender Shaped American Citizenship and Labor*. Cambridge, Mass.: Harvard University Press.

Gluckman, Max. 1963. "Rituals of Rebellion in South-East Africa." In *Order and Rebellion in Tribal Africa*. London: Cohen and West.

Go, Julian. 2000. "Chains of Empire, Projects of State: Political Education and U.S. Colonial Rule in Puerto Rico and the Philippines." *Comparative Studies in Society and History* 42 (2): 333–362.

Gocek, Fatma Muge. 1996. *Rise of the Bourgeoisie, Demise of Empire: Ottoman Westernization and Social Change*. New York: Oxford University Press.

Godechot, Jacques. 1983 [1956]. *La Grande Nation*, 2nd ed. Paris: Aubier.

Goffman, Erving. 1974. *Frame Analysis*. Cambridge, Mass.: Harvard University Press.

Goldberg, David Theo. 2002. *The Racial State*. London: Basil Blackwell.

Goldman, Michael. Forthcoming. *The Birth of a Discipline: The New Politics and Science of the World Bank*. New Haven: Yale University Press.

Goldstein, Joshua S. 2001. *War and Gender: How Gender Shapes the War System and Vice Versa.* Cambridge: Cambridge University Press.

Goldstone, Jack A. 1991. *Revolution and Rebellion in the Early Modern World.* Berkeley: University of California Press.

———. 1996. "Gender, Work, and Culture: Why the Industrial Revolution Came Early to England but Late to China." *Sociological Perspectives* 39:1–21.

———. 2000. "The Rise of the West—Or Not? A Revision to Socio-Economic History." *Sociological Theory* 18 (2): 175–194.

———. 2001a. "Population and Progress in the Middle Ages: A Review Essay." *Population and Development Review* 27:585–595.

———. 2001b. "Toward a Fourth Generation of Revolutionary Theory." *Annual Review of Political Science* 4:139–187.

———. 2002. "Efflorescences and Economic Growth in World History: Rethinking the 'Rise of the West' and the Industrial Revolution." *Journal of World History* 13 (2): 323–389.

———. 2003. "Comparative Historical Analysis and Knowledge Accumulation in the Study of Revolutions." Pp. 41–90 in *Comparative Historical Analysis in the Social Sciences.* Ed. James Mahoney and Dietrich Rueschemeyer. Cambridge: Cambridge University Press.

Goldthorpe, John. 1991. "The Uses of History in Sociology: Reflections on Some Recent Tendencies." *British Journal of Sociology* 42 (2): 211–230.

———. 1997. "Current Issues in Comparative Macrosociology: A Debate on Methodological Issues." *Social Research* 16:1–26.

Gole, Nilufer. 1997. "Global Expectations, Local Experiences: Non-Western Modernities." In *Through a Glass, Darkly: The Blurred Images of Cultural Tradition and Modernity over Distance and Time.* Ed. Wil Arts. Leiden: Brill.

Goodwin, Jeff. 1997. "The Libidinal Constitution of a High-Risk Social Movement: Affectual Ties and Solidarity in the Huk Rebellion, 1946 to 1954." *American Sociological Review* 62 (1): 53–69.

———. 2001. *No Other Way Out: States and Revolutionary Movements, 1945–1991.* Cambridge: Cambridge University Press.

Goody, Jack. 1983. *The Development of the Family and Marriage in Europe.* Cambridge: Cambridge University Press.

———. 1996a. "Comparing Family Systems in Europe and Asia: Are There Different Sets of Rules?" *Population and Development Review* 22:1–20.

———. 1996b. *The East in the West.* Cambridge: Cambridge University Press.

Gordon, Colin. 1991. "Governmental Rationality: An Introduction." Pp. 1–52 in *The Foucault Effect: Studies in Governmentality.* Ed. Graham Burchell, Colin Gordon, and Peter Miller. Chicago: University of Chicago Press.

Gordon, Linda. 1990. *Women, the State, and Welfare.* Madison: University of Wisconsin Press.

———. 1994. *Pitied but Not Entitled: Single Mothers and the History of Welfare, 1890–1935.* New York: Free Press.

Gordon, Robert. 1995. "Paradoxical Property." Pp. 95–110 in *Early Modern Conceptions of Property.* Ed. John Brewer and Susan Staves. London: Routledge.

Gorski, Philip S. 1993. "The Protestant Ethic Revisited: Disciplinary Revolution and State Formation in Holland and Prussia." *American Journal of Sociology* 99 (2): 265–316.

———. 1995. "The Protestant Ethic and the Spirit of Bureaucracy." *American Sociological Review* 60 (5): 783–787.

———. 2000a. "Historicizing the Secularization Debate: Church, State and Society in Late Medieval and Early Modern Europe." *American Sociological Review* 65 (1): 138–167.

———. 2000b. "The Mosaic Moment: An Early Modernist Critique of the Modernist Theory of Nationalism." *American Journal of Sociology* 105 (5): 1428–1468.

———. 2001. "Calvinism and Revolution: The Walzer Thesis Re-Considered." Pp. 78–104 in *Meaning and Modernity: Religion, Polity, and Self.* Ed. Richard Madsen, Ann Swidler, and Steven Tipton. Berkeley: University of California Press.

———. 2003. *The Disciplinary Revolution: Calvinism, Confessionalism and the Growth of State Power in Early Modern Europe.* Chicago: University of Chicago Press.

———. Forthcoming a. "The Protestant Ethic and the Spirit of Bureaucracy: Ascetic Protestantism and Political Rationalism in Early Modern Europe." In *Max Weber at the Millennium.* Ed. Charles Camic, Philip Gorski, and David Trubek. Stanford, Calif.: Stanford University Press.

———. Forthcoming b. "Historicizing the Secularization Debate: An Agenda for Research." In *The Cambridge Handbook of the Sociology of Religion.* Ed. Michelle Dillon. Cambridge: Cambridge University Press.

Gossez, Rémi. 1956. "Diversité des antagonismes sociaux vers le milieu du XIXè siècle." *Revue Economique.*

Goudsblom, Johan. 1992. *Fire and Civilization.* New York: Penguin.

———. 1996. *The Course of Human History: Economic Growth, Social Process and Civilization.* Armonk, N.Y.: M. E. Sharpe.

Gough, Ian. 1979. *The Political Economy of the Welfare State.* London: Macmillan.

———. 1999. "Welfare Regimes: On Adapting the Framework to Developing Countries." *Discourse: A Journal of Policy Studies* 3(1): 1–18.

Gould, Mark. 1987. *Revolution in the Development of Capitalism: The Coming of the English Revolution.* Berkeley: University of California Press.

Gould, Roger. 1991. "Multiple Networks and Mobilization in the Paris Commune, 1871." *American Sociological Review* 56(6): 716–29.

———. 1995. *Insurgent Identities: Class, Community, and Protest in Paris from 1848 to the Commune.* Chicago: University of Chicago Press.

———. 1999. "Collective Violence and Group Solidarity: Evidence from a Feuding Society." *American Sociological Review* 64(3): 356–380.

———, ed. 2001. *The Rational Choice Controversy in Historical Sociology.* Chicago: University of Chicago Press.

Gouldner, Alvin W. 1954. *Patterns of Industrial Bureaucracy: A Case Study of Modern Factory Administration.* New York: Free Press.

———. 1970. *The Coming Crisis of Western Sociology.* London: Heinemann.

Graham, Hilary. 1983. "Caring: A Labour of Love." Pp. 13–30 in *A Labour of Love: Women, Work and Caring.* Ed. Janet Finch and Dulcie Groves. London: Routledge and Kegan Paul.

Graham, Stephen, and Simon Marvin. 2001. *Splintering Urbanism: Networked Infrastructures, Technological Mobilities and the Urban Condition.* London: Routledge.

Gramsci, Antonio. 1971. "Americanism and Fordism." Pp. 277–320 in *Selections from the Prison Notebooks.* Ed. Quintin Hoare and Geoffrey Nowell Smith. New York: International Publishers.

Grandy, Christopher. 1989. "New Jersey Chartermongering, 1875–1929." *Journal of Economic History* 49:677–692.

Granovetter, Mark. 1985. "Economic Action and Social Structure: The Problem of Embeddedness." *American Journal of Sociology* 91:481–510.

Granovetter, Mark, and Patrick McGuire. 1998. "The Making of an Industry: Electricity in the United States." Pp. 147–173 in *The Laws of Markets.* Ed. Michel Callon. Oxford: Blackwell.

Grassby, Richard. 1995. *The Business Community of Seventeenth-Century England.* Cambridge: Cambridge University Press.

———. 1999. *The Idea of Capitalism before the Industrial Revolution.* Lanham, Md.: Rowman and Littlefield.

———. 2001. *Kinship and Capitalism: Marriage, Family and Business in the English-Speaking World, 1580–1740.* Cambridge: Cambridge University Press.

Greasley, David, and Les Oxley. 1997a. "Endogenous Growth or 'Big Bang': Two Views of the First Industrial Revolution." *Journal of Economic History* 57 (4): 935–949.

——. 1997b. "Endogenous Growth, Trend Output, and the Industrial Revolution: Reply to Crafts and Mills." *Journal of Economic History* 57 (4): 957–960.

Greenblatt, Stephen, and Catherine Gallagher. 2000. *Practicing the New Historicism*. Chicago: University of Chicago Press.

Greenfeld, Liah. 1990. "The Formation of the Russian National Identity: The Role of Status Insecurity and *Ressentiment*." *Comparative Studies in Society and History* 32:549–591.

——. 1992. *Nationalism: Five Roads to Modernity*. Cambridge, Mass.: Harvard University Press.

——. 2001. *The Spirit of Capitalism: Nationalism and Economic Growth*. Cambridge, Mass.: Harvard University Press.

Gregerson, Linda. 1995. "Native Tongues: Effeminization, Miscegenation and the Construct of Tudor Nationalism." *Mitteilungen des Zentrums zur Erforschung der Fruhen Neuzeit* 3, pp. 18–38. Frankfurt: Renaissance Institute, Johan Wolfgang Goethe Universitat.

Greif, Avner. 1999. "Reputation and Coalitions in Medieval Trade: Evidence on the Maghribi Traders." *Journal of Economic History* 49:857–882.

——. 1991. "Institutions and International Trade: Lessons from the Commercial Revolution." *American Economic Review* 82:128–133.

——. 1994. "Cultural Beliefs and the Organization of Society: A Historical and Theoretical Reflection on Collectivist and Individualist Societies." *Journal of Political Economy* 102:912–950.

Grell, Ole Peter, and Andrew Cunningham, eds. 1997. *Health Care and Poor Relief in Protestant Europe, 1500–1700*. London: Routledge.

Grell, Ole Peter, and Andrew Cunningham, with Jon Arrizabalaga, eds. 1999. *Health Care and Poor Relief in Counter-Reformation Europe*. London: Routledge.

Grew, Raymond. 1980. "The Case for Comparing Histories." *American Historical Review* 85 (4): 763–778.

——. 1985. "The Comparative Weakness of American History." *Journal of Interdisciplinary History* 16 (1): 87–103.

Grierson, Philip. 1959. "Commerce in the Dark Ages: A Critique of the Evidence." *Transactions of the Royal Historical Society*, sixth series, 9:123–140.

Griffin, Larry J. 1992. "Temporality, Events, and Explanation in Historical Sociology." *Sociological Methods and Research* 20 (4): 403–427.

——. 1993. "Narrative, Event-Structure Analysis, and Causal Interpretation in Historical Sociology." *American Journal of Sociology* 98 (5): 1094–1133.

Griswold, Wendy. 1986. *Renaissance Revivals: City Comedy and Revenge Tragedy in the London Theatre, 1576–1980*. Berkeley: University of California Press.

——. 1987. "A Methodological Framework for the Sociology of Culture." *Sociological Methodology* 17:1–35.

——. 1990. "Provisional, Provincial Positivism: Reply to Denzin." *American Journal of Sociology* 95 (May): 1580–1583.

Guha, Ranajit. 1982. *Subaltern Studies*, vol. 1. Delhi: Oxford University Press.

——. 2002. *History at the Limit of World History*. New York: Columbia University Press.

Guinnane, Timothy W. 1994. "A Failed Institutional Transplant: Raiffeisen's Credit Cooperatives in Ireland, 1894–1914." *Explorations in Economic History* 31:38–61.

Gundersen, Joan R., and Gwen Victor Gampel. 1982. "Married Women's Legal Status in Eighteenth-Century New York and Virginia." *William and Mary Quarterly* 39:114–134.

Gurr, Ted Robert. 1969. *Why Men Rebel*. Princeton, N.J.: Princeton University Press.

Guseva, Alya, and Ákos Róna-Tas. 2001. "Uncertainty, Risk and Trust: Russian and American Credit Card Markets Compared." *American Sociological Review* 66:623–646.

Gutek, Barbara. 1989. "Sexuality in the Workplace: Key Issues in Social Research and Organization." Pp. 56–70 in *The Sexuality of Organization*. Ed. Jeff Hearn et al. London: Sage.

Haag-Higuchi, Roxane. 1996. "A Topos and Its Dissolution: Japan in Some 20th-Century Iranian Texts." *Iranian Studies* 29 (1–2): 71–83.

Haas, Ernst. 1997. *Nationalism, Liberalism, and Progress*. Ithaca, N.Y.: Cornell University Press.

Haas, Linda. 1992. *Equal Parenthood and Social Policy: A Study of Parental Leave in Sweden*. Albany: State University of New York Press.

Habakkuk, H. J. 1958. "The Economic History of Modern Britain." *Journal of Economic History* 18:486–501.

Habermas, Jürgen. 1971. *Knowledge and Human Interests*. Trans. Jeremy J. Shapiro. Boston: Beacon Press.

——. 1979. *Communication and the Evolution of Society*. Trans. Thomas McCarthy. Boston: Beacon Press.

——. 1987. *The Philosophical Discourse of Modernity: Twelve Lectures*. Trans. Frederick Lawrence. Cambridge, Mass.: MIT Press.

——. 1989. *The Structural Transformation of the Public Sphere: An Inquiry into a Category of Bourgeois Society*. Cambridge, Mass.: MIT Press.

——. 2001. *The Postnational Constellation: Political Essays*. Cambridge: Polity Press.

Hachen, David, and Joey Sprague. 1982. "The American Class Structure." *American Sociological Review* 47:709–726.

Hacker, Jacob S. 2002. *The Divided Welfare State: The Battle over Public and Private Social Benefits in the United States*. New York: Cambridge University Press.

Hacking, Ian. 1990. *The Taming of Chance*. Cambridge: Cambridge University Press.

——. 1995. "The Looping Effects of Human Kinds." Pp. 351–394 in *Causal Cognition: A Multidisciplinary Debate*. Ed. David Premack, Dan Sperber, and Ann J. Premack. Oxford: Oxford University Press.

——. 1999. *The Social Construction of What?* Cambridge, Mass.: Harvard University Press.

Hafferty, Frederic W., and John B. McKinlay. 1993. "Conclusion: Cross-Cultural Perspectives on the Dynamics of Medicine as a Profession." Pp. 210–226 in *The Changing Medical Profession: An International Perspective*. Ed. Frederic W. Hafferty and John B. McKinlay. New York: Oxford University Press.

Hajnal, John. 1965. "European Marriage Patterns in Perspective." Pp. 101–143 in *Population in History: Essays in Historical Demography*. Ed. D. V. Glass and D. E. C. Eversley. Chicago: Aldine.

——. 1982. "Two Kinds of Preindustrial Household Formation Systems." *Population and Development Review* 8 (3) 449–494.

Halfpenny, Peter. 1982. *Positivism and Sociology: Explaining Social Life*. London: George Allen and Unwin.

Hall, Catherine. 1992. *White, Male and Middle Class: Explorations in Feminism and History*. London: Routledge.

——. 1996. "Histories, Empires, and the Post-Colonial Moment." Pp. 65–77 in *The Post-Colonial Question: Common Skies, Divided Horizons*. Ed. Iain Chambers and Lidia Curti. New York: Routledge.

Hall, John A. 1986. *Powers and Liberties*. London: Penguin.

——. 1989. "They Do Things Differently There, or, the Contribution of British Historical Sociology." *British Journal of Sociology* 40 (4): 544–564.

Hall, John R. 1988. "States and Societies: The Miracle in Comparative Perspective." Pp. 20–38 in *Europe and the Rise of Capitalism*. Ed. Jean Baechler, John A. Hall, and Michael Mann. Oxford: Basil Blackwell.

——. 1990. "Epistemology and Sociohistorical Inquiry." *Annual Review of Sociology* 16:329–351.

——. 1992. "Where History and Sociology Meet: Forms of Discourse and Socio-Historical Inquiry." *Sociological Theory* 10.

——. 1999a. *Cultures of Inquiry: From Epistemology to Discourse in Sociohistorical Research*. Cambridge: Cambridge University Press.

——. 1999b. "The Transition to New Thinking about the Emergence of Capitalism." Paper presented at "On the Origins of the Modern World," All-University of California Group in Economic History, October 15–17.

——, ed. 1997. *Reworking Class*. Ithaca, N.Y.: Cornell University Press.

Hall, Peter A., and Rosemary C. R. Taylor. 1996. "Political Science and the Three New Institutionalisms." *Political Studies* 44:936–957.

Hall, Peter A., and David Soskice, eds. 2001. *Varieties of Capitalism: The Institutional Foundations of Comparative Advantage*. New York: Oxford University Press.

Hall, Rupert A. 1963. "Merton Revisited: Science and Society in the Seventeenth Century." *History of Science* 2:1–16.

Hall, Stuart. 1977. "Rethinking the 'Base-Superstructure' Metaphor." Pp. 43–72 in *Class, Hegemony and Party*. Ed. Jon Bloomfield. London: Lawrence and Wishart.

——. 1983. "The Problem of Ideology: Marxism without Guarantees." Pp. 56–85 in *Marx 100 Years On*. Ed. B. Matthews. London: Lawrence and Wishart.

——. 1992. "The West and the Rest: Discourse and Power." In *Formations of Modernity*. Ed. Stuart Hall and Adam Gieben. Cambridge: Open University Press.

——. 1996. "When Was the Post-Colonial: Thinking at the Limit." Pp. 240–260 in *The Post-Colonial Question: Common Skies, Divided Horizons*. Ed. Iain Chambers and Lidia Curti. New York: Routledge.

Halliday, Terence C. 1987. *Beyond Monopoly: Lawyers, State Crises, and Professional Empowerment*. Chicago: University of Chicago Press.

Halpern, Sydney A. 1988. *American Pediatrics: The Social Dynamics of Professionalism, 1880–1980*. Berkeley: University of California Press.

Halsey, A. H. 1982. "Provincials and Professionals: The British Post-War Sociologists." *Archives Européennes de Sociologie* 23 (1): 150–175.

Hamilton, David L., and Jeffrey W. Sherman. 1994. "Stereotypes." Pp. 1–68 in *Handbook of Social Cognition*, 2nd ed. Ed. Robert S. Wyer and Thomas K. Srull. Mahwah, N.J.: Lawrence Erlbaum Associates.

Hamilton, David L., Steven J. Sherman, and Brian Lickel. 1998. "Perceiving Social Groups: The Importance of the Entitativity Continuum." Pp. 47–74 in *Intergroup Cognition and Intergroup Behavior*. Ed. Constantine Sedikides, John Schopler, and Chester A. Insko. Mahwah, N.J.: Lawrence Erlbaum Associates.

Hamilton, Gary G. 1984. "Patriarchalism in Imperial China and Western Europe." *Theory and Society* 13 (3): 393–426.

——. 1989. "The Problem of Control in the Weak State: Domination in the United States, 1880–1920." *Theory and Society* 18:1–46.

——. 1990. "Patriarchy, Patrimonialism and Filial Piety: A Comparison of China and Western Europe." *British Journal of Sociology* 41 (1): 77–104.

——. 1994. "Civilizations and the Organization of Economies." Pp. 183–205 in *The Handbook of Economic Sociology*. Ed. Neil J. Smelser and Richard Swedberg. New York: Russell Sage Foundation, and Princeton, N.J.: Princeton University Press.

Hamilton, Gary, and Nicole Woolsey Biggart. 1980. "Making the Dilettante an Expert: Personal Staffs in Public Bureaucracies." *Journal of Applied Behavioral Science* 16:192–210.

——. 1984. *Governor Reagan, Governor Brown*. New York: Columbia University Press.

Hamilton, Malcolm. 1995. *The Sociology of Religion: Theoretical and Comparative Perspectives*. New York: Routledge.

Hanagan, Michael. 1997. "Introduction to the Special Issue on Recasting Citizenship." *Theory and Society* 26 (4): 397–402.

Hancock, David. 1995. *Citizens of the World: London Merchants and the Integration of the British Atlantic Community, 1735–1785.* Cambridge: Cambridge University Press.

Handelman, Don. 1977. "The Organization of Ethnicity." *Ethnic Groups* 1:187–200.

Haney, Lynne A. 1996. "Homeboys, Babies, and Men in Suits: The State and the Reproduction of Male Dominance." *American Sociological Review* 61:759–778.

———. 2002. *Inventing the Needy: Gender and the Politics of Welfare in Hungary.* Berkeley: University of California Press.

Haney, Lynne, and Lisa Pollard, eds. 2003. *Families of a New World: Gender, Politics, and State Development in a Global Context.* New York: Routledge.

Hanioğlu, M. Şükrü. 1986. *Bir Siyasal Örgüt Olarak Osmanlı İttihad ve Terakki Cemiyeti ve Jön Türklük, Cilt I (1889–1902).* Istanbul ¥letiim Yaynlar.

———. 1995. *The Young Turks in Opposition.* New York: Oxford University Press.

———. 2001. *Preparation for a Revolution: The Young Turks 1902–1908.* New York: Oxford University Press.

Hanley, Susan B., and Arthur P. Wolf, eds. 1985. *Family and Population in East Asian History.* Stanford, Calif.: Stanford University Press.

Hannan, Michael T., and John Freeman. 1988. "The Ecology of Organizational Mortality: American Labor Unions, 1836–1985." *American Journal of Sociology* 94:25–52.

Hansen, Thomas Blom, and Finn Stepputat. 2001. "Introduction: States of Imagination." In *States of Imagination: Ethnographic Explorations of the Postcolonial State.* Ed. Thomas Blom Hansen and Finn Stepputat. Durham, N.C.: Duke University Press.

Hanson, Victor Davis. 1989. *The Western Way of War: Infantry Battle in Classical Greece.* New York: Oxford University Press.

———. 1999. *The Soul of Battle: From Ancient Times to the Present Day, How Three Great Liberators Vanquished Tyranny.* New York: Anchor Books.

———. 2001. *Carnage and Culture.* New York: Doubleday.

Hanushek, Erik A., and John E. Jackson. 1977. *Statistical Methods for Social Scientists.* New York: Academic Press.

Harding, Sandra. 1991. *Whose Science? Whose Knowledge?* Ithaca, N.Y.: Cornell University Press.

———. 1999. "The Case for Strategic Realism: A Response to Lawson." *Feminist Economics* 5 (3): 127–133.

Hardt, Michael, and Antonio Negri. 2000. *Empire.* Cambridge, Mass.: Harvard University Press.

Hargrove, Barbara. 1979. *The Sociology of Religion: Classical and Contemporary Approaches.* Arlington Heights, Ill.: Harlan Davidson.

Harley, C. Knick. 1999. "Reassessing the Industrial Revolution: A Macro View." Pp. 160–205 in *The British Industrial Revolution: An Economic Perspective*, 2nd ed. Ed. Joel Mokyr. Boulder, Colo.: Westview Press.

Harley, C. Knick, and N. F. R. Crafts. 2000. "Simulating the Two Views of the British Industrial Revolution." *Journal of Economic History* 60:819–841.

Harrod, R. F. 1948. *Towards a Dynamic Economics.* London: Macmillan.

Hartmann, Heidi. 1981. "The Unhappy Marriage of Marxism and Feminism: Toward a More Progressive Union." Pp. 1–42 in *Women and Revolution.* Ed. Lydia Sargent. Boston: South End Press.

Harvey, David. 1989. *The Condition of Postmodernity: An Enquiry into the Origins of Cultural Change.* Cambridge, Mass.: Blackwell.

Haskell, Thomas L. 1984. "Introduction." Pp. ix–xxxix in *The Authority of Experts: Studies in History and Theory.* Ed. Thomas L. Haskell. Bloomington: Indiana University Press.

Hauser, Philip M. 1946. "Are the Social Sciences Ready?" *American Sociological Review* 11 (August): 379–384.

Hausman, William J., and John L. Neufeld. 1991. "Property Rights versus Public Spirit: Ownership and

Efficiency of U.S. Electric Utilities Prior to Rate-of-Return Regulation." *Review of Economics and Statistics* 73:414–423.

Haydu, Jeffrey. 1998. "Making Use of the Past: Time Periods as Cases to Compare and as Sequences of Problem Solving." *American Journal of Sociology* 104 (2): 339–371.

——. 2002. "Business Citizenship at Work: Cultural Transposition and Class Formation in Cincinnati, 1870–1910." *American Journal of Sociology* 107 (6): 1424–1468.

Heater, D. B. 1996. *World Citizenship and Government: Cosmopolitan Ideas in the History of Western Political Thought*. Basingstoke: Macmillan.

Hebdige, Dick. 1979. *Subculture: The Meaning of Style*. London: Methuen.

Hechter, Michael. 1975. *Internal Colonialism: The Celtic Fringe in British National Development, 1536–1966*. London: Routledge and Kegan Paul.

——. 1978. "Group Formation and the Cultural Division of Labor." *American Journal of Sociology* 84:293–318.

——. 1987. *Principles of Group Solidarity*. Berkeley: University of California Press.

——. 1999 [1975]. *Internal Colonialism: The Celtic Fringe in British Development*, 2nd ed. New Brunswick, N.J.: Transaction Publishers.

——. 2000. *Containing Nationalism*. Oxford: Oxford University Press.

Hechter, Michael, and Satoshi Kanazawa. 1997. "Sociological Rational Choice Theory." *Annual Review of Sociology* 23:191–214.

Hedström, Peter, and Richard Swedberg, eds. 1998. *Social Mechanisms: An Analytical Approach to Social Theory*. New York: Cambridge University Press.

Hegel, G. W. F. 1975 [1822]. *Lectures on the Philosophy of World History*. Trans. H. B. Nisbet. New York: Oxford University Press.

Heisler, Martin. 1991. "Ethnicity and Ethnic Relations in the Modern West." Pp. 21–51 in *Conflict and Peacemaking in Multiethnic Societies*. Ed. Joseph Montville. Lexington, Ky.: Lexington Books.

Held, D. 1995. *Democracy and the Global Order: From the Modern State to Cosmopolitan Governance*. Stanford, Calif.: Stanford University Press.

——. 1999. *Global Transformations: Politics, Economics and Culture*. Stanford, Calif.: Stanford University Press.

Held, D., and A. G. McGrew. 2002. *Governing Globalization: Power, Authority and Global Governance*. Cambridge: Polity Press.

Hemerijk, Anton. 2002. "The Self-Transformation of the European Social Model." Pp. 173–213 in *Why We Need a New Welfare State*, by Gøsta Esping-Andersen, with Duncan Gallie, Anton Hemerijk, and John Myles. New York: Oxford University Press.

Hempel, Carl Gustav. 1966. "Explanation in Science and History." Pp. 95–126 in *Philosophical Analysis and History*. Ed. William H. Dray. New York: Harper and Row.

Hempel, Carl Gustav, and Paul Oppenheimer. 1948. *Studies in the Logic of Explanation*. Indianapolis, Ind.: Bobbs-Merrill.

Herbst, Jeffrey. 2000. *States and Power in Africa: Comparative Lessons in Authority and Control*. Princeton, N.J.: Princeton University Press.

Heritage, John. 1983. "Accounts in Action." Pp. 117–131 in *Accounts and Action: Surrey Conferences on Sociological Theory and Method*. Ed. G. Nigel Gilbert and Peter Abell. Aldershot: Gower.

——. 1984. *Garfinkel and Ethnomethodology*. Cambridge: Polity Press.

Herman, Ellen. 1996. *The Romance of American Psychology: Political Culture in the Age of Experts*. Berkeley: University of California Press.

Hernes, Helga. 1987. *Welfare State and Woman Power*. Oslo: Norwegian University Press.

Herr, Richard. 1962. *Tocqueville and the Old Regime*. Princeton, N.J.: Princeton University Press.

Herrnstein, Richard. 1997. *The Matching Law: Papers in Psychology and Economics*. Cambridge, Mass.: Harvard University Press.

Hertz, F. 1941. "The Nature of Nationalism." *Social Forces* 19 (3): 409–415.

Hesse, Barnor. 2001. *Un/Settled Multiculturalisms: Diasporas, Entanglements, Transruptions*. London: Zed.

Hexter, J. H. 1979. *On Historians: Reappraisals of Some of the Makers of Modern History*. Cambridge, Mass.: Harvard University Press.

Hicks, Alexander. 1999. *Social Democracy and Welfare Capitalism: A Century of Income Security Politics*. Ithaca, N.Y.: Cornell University Press.

Hicks, Alexander, and Joya Misra. 1993. "Political Resources and the Growth of Welfare in Affluent Capitalist Democracies, 1960–1982." *American Journal of Sociology* 99:668–710.

Hill, Christopher. 1958. *Puritanism and Revolution: Studies in Interpretation of the English Revolution of the Seventeenth Century*. London: Secker and Warburg.

Hintze, Otto. 1975 [1902]. *The Historical Essays of Otto Hintze*. Ed. Felix Gilbert. New York: Oxford University Press.

Hirdman, Yvonne. 1991. "The Gender System." Pp. 187–207 in *Moving On: New Perspectives on the Women's Movement*. Ed. T. Andreasen et al. Aarhus, Denmark: Aarhus University Press.

Hirsch, Joachim, and Roland Roth. 1986. *Das neue Gesicht des Kapitalismus*. Hamburg: VSA-Verlag.

Hirschfeld, Lawrence A. 1996. *Race in the Making: Cognition, Culture and the Child's Construction of Human Kinds*. Cambridge, Mass.: MIT Press.

Hirschman, Albert O. 1968. "The Political Economy of Import-Substituting Industrialization in Latin America." *Quarterly Journal of Economics* 82:1–32.

——. 1990. *Rhetoric of Reaction: Perversity, Futility, Jeopardy*. Cambridge, Mass.: Harvard University Press.

HM Government 1991a. *The Citizen's Charter: A Guide*. London: HMSO.

——. 1991b. *The Citizen's Charter: Raising the Standard*. London: HMSO.

——. 1991c. *Competing for Quality*. London: HMSO.

Hobbes, T. 1968. *Leviathan*. Harmondsworth: Penguin Books.

Hobhouse, L. T. 1964 [1911]. *Liberalism*. New York: Oxford University Press.

Hobsbawm, Eric J. 1975. *The Age of Capital, 1848–1875*. New York: Scribner.

——. 1990. *Nations and Nationalism since 1780: Programme, Myth, Reality*, 2nd ed. Cambridge: Cambridge University Press.

——. 1994. *Age of Extremes: A History of the World, 1914–1991*. New York: Pantheon Books.

Hobsbawm, E. J., and Terence Ranger, eds. 1983. *The Invention of Tradition*. Cambridge: Cambridge University Press.

Hobson, Barbara. 1990. "No Exit, No Voice: Women's Economic Dependency and the Welfare State." *Acta Sociologica* 33:235–250.

Hobson, Barbara, and Marika Lindholm. 1997. "Collective Identities, Power Resources, and the Making of Welfare States." *Theory and Society* 26:1–34.

Hobson, Barbara. ed. 2002. *Making Men into Fathers*. Cambridge: Cambridge University Press.

Hoffman, Philip T. 1996. *Growth in a Traditional Society: The French Countryside, 1450–1815*. Princeton, N.J.: Princeton University Press.

Hoffman, Philip T., Gilles Postel-Vinay, and Jean-Laurent Rosenthal. 2000. *Priceless Markets: The Political Economy of Credit in Paris 1660–1870*. Chicago: University of Chicago Press.

Holifield, E. Brooks. 1994. "Toward a History of American Congregations." Pp. 23–53 in *American Congregations*, vol. 2: *New Perspectives in the Study of Congregations*. Ed. J. P. Wind and J. W. Lewis. Chicago: University of Chicago Press.

Hollinger, David A. 1995. *Postethnic America: Beyond Multiculturalism*. New York: Basic Books.

Höllinger, Franz. 1996. *Volksreligion und Herrschaftskirche: Die Würzeln religiösen Verhaltens in westlichen Gesellschaften*. Oplanden: Leske und Budrich.

Holquist, Peter. 1997. " 'Conduct Merciless Mass Terror': Decossackization on the Don, 1919." *Cahiers du Monde Russe* 38 (1–2): 127–162.

Holton, R. J. 1983. "Max Weber, 'Rational Capitalism,' and Renaissance Italy: A Critique of Cohen." *American Journal of Sociology* 89:66–187.

———. 1985. *The Transition from Feudalism to Capitalism*. New York: St. Martin's Press.

Homans, George C. 1950. *The Human Group*. New York: Harcourt, Brace and World.

Hooks, Gregory. 1990a. "From an Autonomous to a Captured State Agency: The Decline of the New Deal in Agriculture." *American Sociological Review* 55:29–43.

———. 1990b. "The Rise of the Pentagon and U.S. State Building: The Defense Program as Industrial Policy." *American Journal of Sociology* 96:358–404.

Hopcroft, Rosemary L. 1994. "The Social Origins of Agrarian Change in Late Medieval England." *American Journal of Sociology* 99:1559–1595.

———. 1999. *Regions, Institutions, and Agrarian Change in European History*. Ann Arbor: University of Michigan Press.

Hopkins, Keith. 1999. *A World Full of Gods: The Strange Triumph of Christianity*. New York: Free Press.

Horn, David. 1994. *Social Bodies: Science, Reproduction, and Italian Modernity*. Princeton, N.J.: Princeton University Press.

Horne, John. 1989. " 'L'Impôt du sang': Republican Rhetoric and Industrial Warfare in France, 1914–1918." *Social History* 14:201–223.

———. 1994. *Labour at War: France and Britain, 1914–1918*. Oxford: Clarendon Press.

———. 2000. "Labor and Labor Movements in World War I." In *The Great War and the Twentieth Century*. Ed. Jay Winter, Geoffrey Parker, and Mary R. Habeck. New Haven, Conn.: Yale University Press.

———, ed. 1997. *State, Society and Mobilization in Europe during the First World War*. Cambridge: Cambridge University Press.

Horowitz, Donald L. 1985. *Ethnic Groups in Conflict*. Berkeley: University of California Press.

———. 1991. *A Democratic South Africa? Constitutional Engineering in a Divided Society*. Berkeley: University of California Press.

———. 2001. *The Deadly Ethnic Riot*. Berkeley: University of California Press.

Horwitz, Morton J. 1977. *The Transformation of American Law, 1780–1860*. Cambridge, Mass.: Harvard University Press.

Hoselitz, Bert F. 1960. "Theories of Stages of Economic Growth." Pp. 193–238 in *Theories of Economic Growth*. Ed. Bert F. Hoselitz, Joseph J. Spengler, J. M. Letiche, Erskine McKinley, John Buttrick, and Henry J. Bruton. Glencoe, Ill.: Free Press.

———. 1963. "Levels of Economic Performance and Bureaucratic Structures." Pp. 168–198 in *Bureaucracy and Political Development*. Ed. Joseph La Palombara. Princeton, N.J.: Princeton University Press.

Hoult, Thomas Ford. 1958. *The Sociology of Religion*. New York: Dryden Press.

Hout, Michael, and Claude S. Fischer. 2002. "Why More Americans Have No Religious Preference: Politics and Generations." *American Sociological Review* 67 (2): 165–190.

Hover, E. J. 1932. "Citizenship of Women in the United States." *American Journal of International Law* 26 (4): 700–719.

Howard, Christopher. 1997. *The Hidden Welfare State: Tax Expenditures and Social Policy in the United States*. Princeton, N.J.: Princeton University Press.

Howard, Michael. 1976. *War in European History*. New York: Cambridge University Press.

Howard, Michael, George J. Andreopoulos, and Mark R. Shulman, eds. 1994. *The Laws of War: Constraints on Warfare in the Western World*. New Haven, Conn.: Yale University Press.

Howkins, Alun. 1994. "Peasants, Servants, and Laborers: The Marginal Workforce in British Agriculture, c. 1870–1914." *Agricultural History Review* 42:49–62.

Huang, Chien-Ju, and Heidi Gottfried. 1997. "The 'Making' of State Policy: The Case of the National Industrial Recovery Act." *Critical Sociology* 23 (1): 25–52.

Huang, Philip C. C. 1993. " 'Public Sphere'/'Civil Society' in China?" *Modern China* 19 (2): 216 –240.

——. 1998. "Theory and the Study of Modern Chinese History." *Modern China* 24 (2): 183–208.

Huang, R. 1974. *Taxation and Government Finance in Sixteenth-Century Ming China*. Cambridge: Cambridge University Press.

Huber, Evelyne, and John Stephens. 2000. "Partisan Governance, Women's Employment, and the Social Democratic Service State." *American Sociological Review* 65:323–343.

——. 2001. *Development and Crisis of the Welfare State: Parties and Policies in Global Markets*. Chicago: University of Chicago Press.

Huber, Evelyne, Charles Ragin, and John Stephens. 1993. "Social Democracy, Christian Democracy, Constitutional Structure, and the Welfare State." *American Journal of Sociology* 99:711–749.

Hume, David. 1975 [1748]. *An Enquiry Concerning Human Understanding*. Oxford: Clarendon Press.

Humphries, Jane. 1990. "Enclosures, Common Rights, and Women: The Proletarianization of Families in the Late Eighteenth and Early Nineteenth Centuries." *Journal of Economic History* 50:17–42.

Hunt, Lynn. 1984. *Politics, Culture, and Class in the French Revolution*. Berkeley: University of California Press.

——. 1992. *The Family Romance of the French Revolution*. Berkeley: University of California Press.

——. 1996. *The French Revolution and Human Rights: A Brief Documentary History*. Boston: Bedford Books.

Hunt, Margaret R. 1996. *The Middling Sort: Commerce, Gender, and the Family in England 1680–1780*. Berkeley: University of California Press.

Huntington, Samuel P. 1957. *The Soldier and the State: The Theory and the Politics of Civil-Military Relations*. Cambridge, Mass.: Belknap Press.

——. 1968. *Political Order in Changing Societies*. New Haven, Conn.: Yale University Press.

——. 1973 [1968]. "Political Modernization: America vs. Europe." Pp. 170–200 in *State and Society*. Ed. Reinhard Bendix, in collaboration with Coenraad Brand, Randall Collins, Robert G. Michels, Hans-Eberhard Mueller, Gail Omvedt, Eliezer Rosenstein, Jean-Guy Vaillancourt, and R. Stephen Warner. Berkeley: University of California Press.

——. 1991. *The Third Wave: Democratization in the Late Twentieth Century*. Norman: University of Oklahoma Press.

——. 1996. *The Clash of Civilizations and the Remaking of World Order*. New York: Simon and Schuster.

Hurst, J. Willard. 1974. *A Legal History of Money in the United States, 1774–1970*. Lincoln: University of Nebraska Press.

Hutchings, K., and R. Dannreuther. 1999. *Cosmopolitan Citizenship*. Houndmills, Basingstoke, Hampshire: Macmillan.

Hutchinson, John, and Anthony Smith, eds. 1994. *Nationalism*. Oxford: Oxford University Press.

Ignacio, Emily. 2004. *Building Diaspora: Forming a Filipino Community on the Internet*. New Brunswick, N.J.: Rutgers University Press.

Ikegami, Eiko. 1995. *The Taming of the Samurai: Honorific Individualism and the Making of Modern Japan*. Cambridge, Mass.: Harvard University Press.

Ikenberry, G. John. 2001. *After Victory: Institutions, Strategic Restraint, and the Rebuilding of Order after Major Wars*. Princeton, N.J.: Princeton University Press.

Immergut, Ellen. 1998. "The Theoretical Core of the New Institutionalism." *Politics and Society* 26:5–34.

Ingham, Geoffrey. 1999. "Capitalism, Money and Banking: A Critique of Recent Historical Sociology." *British Journal of Sociology* 50:76–96.

Inglehart, Ronald, and Wayne E. Baker. 2000. "Modernization, Cultural Change, and the Persistence of Traditional Values." *American Sociological Review* 65 (1): 19–51.

Inkeles, Alex. 1997. *National Character: A Psycho-Social Perspective*. New Brunswick, N.J.: Transaction Publishers.

Inkeles, Alex, and David H. Smith. 1974. *Becoming Modern: Individual Change in Six Developing Countries*. Cambridge: Cambridge University Press.

Innes, Stephen. 1995. *Creating the Commonwealth: The Economic Culture of Puritan New England*. New York: W. W. Norton.

International Monetary Fund. 1999. *Orderly and Effective Insolvency Procedures: Key Issues*. Washington, D.C.: Legal Department, IMF.

International Police Cooperation. New York: Oxford University Press.

Irvine, Leslie. 1999. *Codependent Forevermore: The Invention of Self in a Twelve Step Group*. Chicago: University of Chicago Press.

Isaac, Larry. 2002. "To Counter 'The Very Devil' and More: The Making of an Independent Capitalist Militia in the Gilded Age." *American Journal of Sociology* 108 (2): 353–405.

Isin, E. F. 1992. *Cities without Citizens*. Montreal: Black Rose Books.

———. 2002. *Being Political: Genealogies of Citizenship*. Minneapolis: University of Minnesota Press.

Isin, E. F., and B. S. Turner. 2002. *Handbook of Citizenship Studies*. London: Sage.

Isin, E. F., and P. K. Wood. 1999. *Citizenship and Identity*. Thousand Oaks, Calif.: Sage.

I'timad al-Saltanah, Muhammad Hasan Khan. 1969. *Khalsah*. Ed. M. Katira'i. Tehran: Intisharat-i Tuka.

Itzkowitz, Gary. 1996. *Contingency Theory: Rethinking the Boundaries of Social Thought*. Lanham, Md.: University Press of America.

Jackson, Robert Max. 1998. *Destined for Equality: The Inevitable Rise of Women's Status*. Cambridge, Mass.: Harvard University Press.

Jacoby, Sanford M. 1985. *Employing Bureaucracy: Managers, Unions, and the Transformation of Work in American Industry, 1900–1945*. New York: Columbia University Press.

James, C. L. R. 1989 [1963]. *The Black Jacobins*. New York: Vintage.

James, David R. 1988. "The Transformation of the Southern Racial State: Class and Race Determinants of Local-State Structures." *American Sociological Review* 53 (2): 191–208.

James, Paul. 1996. *Nation Formation: Toward a Theory of Abstract Community*. Thousand Oaks, Calif.: Sage.

Jameson, Fredric. 1981. *The Political Unconscious: Narrative as a Socially Symbolic Act*. Ithaca, N.Y.: Cornell University Press.

———. 1984. "Postmodernism, or, the Cultural Logic of Late Capitalism." *New Left Review* (146): 52–92.

———. 1991. *Postmodernism, or, the Cultural Logic of Late Capitalism*. Durham, N.C.: Duke University Press.

———. 1998. "Globalization as a Philosophic Issue." Pp. 54–77 in *The Cultures of Globalization*. Ed. Fredric Jameson and Masao Miyoshi. Durham, N.C.: Duke University Press.

Janoski, Thomas. 1998. *Citizenship and Civil Society: A Framework of Rights and Obligations in Liberal, Traditional, and Social Democratic Regimes*. Cambridge: Cambridge University Press.

Janoski, Thomas, and Alexander Hicks, eds. 1994. *The Comparative Political Economy of the Welfare State*. Cambridge: Cambridge University Press.

Janowitz, Morris. 1971 [1960]. *The Professional Soldier: A Social and Political Portrait*. New York: Free Press.

Jarausch, Konrad H. 1990. *The Unfree Professions: German Lawyers, Teachers, and Engineers, 1900–1950*. New York: Cambridge University Press.

Jaspers, Karl. 1949. *Vom Ursprung und Ziel der Geschichte*. Munich: Piper.

Jay, Martin. 1993. *Downcast Eyes: The Denigration of Vision in Twentieth-Century French Thought*. Berkeley: University of California Press.

Jayawardena, Kumari. 1986. *Feminism and Nationalism in the Third World*. London: Zed.

Jenkins, Craig J., and Barbara G. Brents. 1989. "Social Protest, Hegemonic Competition, and Social Reform: A Political Struggle Interpretation of the Origins of the American Welfare State." *American Sociological Review* 54:891–909.

Jenkins, Richard. 1997. *Rethinking Ethnicity*. London: Sage.

Jensen, Michael C., and William H. Meckling. 1976. "Theory of the Firm: Managerial Behavior, Agency Costs, and Ownership Structure." *Journal of Financial Economics* 3:305–360.

Jenson, Jane. 1986. "Gender and Reproduction: Or, Babies and the State." *Studies in Political Economy* 20:9–45.

———. 1997. "Who Cares? Gender and Welfare Regimes." *Social Politics* 4:182–187.

Jenson, Jane, and Rianne Mahon. 1993. "Representing Solidarity: Class, Gender and the Crisis in Social-Democratic Sweden." *New Left Review* 201 (1993): 76–100.

Jessop, Bob. 1999. "Narrating the Future of the National Economy and the National State: Remarks on Remapping Regulation and Reinventing Governance." In *State/Culture: State Formation after the Cultural Turn*. Ed. George Steinmetz. Ithaca, N.Y.: Cornell University Press. Wilder House Series in Culture, Power, and History.

———. 2000. "The Temporal Fix and the Tendential Ecological Dominance of Globalizing Capitalism." *International Journal of Urban and Regional Research* 24 (1): 231–233.

———. 2001. *Developments and Extensions*. Vol. 5 of *Regulation Theory and the Crisis of Capitalism*. Cheltenham, U.K.: Edward Elgar.

Joas, Hans. 1996. *The Creativity of Action*. Chicago: University of Chicago Press.

Johnson, Terence J. 1972. *Professions and Power*. London: Macmillan.

———. 1993. "Expertise and the State." In *Foucault's New Domains*. Ed. Mike Gane and Terry Johnson. London: Routledge.

———. 1995. "Governmentality and the Institutionalization of Expertise." Pp. 7–24 in *Health Professions and the State in Europe*. Ed. Terry Johnson, Gerry Larkin, and Mike Saks. New York: Routledge.

Jones, Colin. 1995 [1980]. "The Military Revolution and the Professionalization of the French Army under the Ancien Régime." Pp. 149–167 in *The Military Revolution Debate: Readings on the Military Transformation of Early Modern Europe*. Ed. Clifford J. Rogers. Boulder, Colo.: Westview Press.

Jones, Eric L. 1994. "Patterns of Growth in History." Pp. 15–28 in *Capitalism in Context: Essays on Economic Development and Cultural Change in Honor of R. M. Hartwell*. Ed. John A. James and Mark Thomas. Chicago: University of Chicago Press.

———. 2000 [1988]. *Growth Recurring: Economic Change in World History*. Ann Arbor: University of Michigan Press.

Jones, Gareth S. 1976. "From Historical Sociology to Theoretical History." *British Journal of Sociology* 27 (3): 295–304.

———. 1983. *Languages of Class: Studies in English Working Class History, 1832–1982*. Cambridge: Cambridge University Press.

Joppke, Christian. 1998. *Challenge to the Nation-State: Immigration in Western Europe and the United States*. Oxford: Oxford University Press.

———. 1999. *Immigration and the Nation-State: The United States, Germany and Great Britain*. Oxford: Oxford University Press.

Joshi, Heather. 1990. "The Cash Opportunity Costs of Childbearing: An Approach to Estimation Using British Data." *Population Studies* 44 (1): 41–60.

Jucius, Michael J. 1943. "Historical Development of Uniform Accounting." *Journal of Business of the University of Chicago* 16: 219–229.

Juergensmeyer, Mark. 2000. *Terror in the Mind of God: The Global Rise of Religious Violence*. Berkeley: University of California Press.

Jung, Moon-kie. 1999. "No Whites, No Asians: Race, Marxism, and Hawaii's Preemergent Working Class." *Social Science History* 23 (3): 357–393.

Kagan, Donald. 1995. *On the Origins of War and the Preservation of Peace*. New York: Anchor Doubleday.

Kalb, Don. 1998. *Expanding Class: Power and Everyday Politics in Communities, the Netherlands, 1850–1950*. Durham, N.C.: Duke University Press.

Kaldor, Nicholas. 1960. *Essays on Economic Stability and Growth*. London: Duckworth.

Kandiyoti, Deniz, ed. 2000. "Gender and Nationalism." Special issue of *Nations and Nationalism* 6 (4).

Kane, Anne. 1997. "Theorizing Meaning Construction in Social Movements: Interpretation and Symbolic Meaning during the Irish Land War, 1879–1882." *Sociological Theory* 3:249–276.

——. 2000. "Narratives of Nationalism: Constructing Irish National Identity during the Land War, 1879–1882." *National Identities* 2 (3): 245–264.

Kansu, Aykut. 1997. *The Revolution of 1908 in Turkey*. Leiden: E. J. Brill.

Kant, Immanuel. 1960. *Religion within the Limits of Reason Alone*. Trans. Theodore M. Greene. New York: Harper and Row.

Kanter, Rosabeth Moss. 1977. *Men and Women of the Corporation*. New York: Basic Books.

Kantorowicz, Ernst H. 1957. *The King's Two Bodies: A Study in Medieval Political Theology*. Princeton, N.J.: Princeton University Press.

Karabekir, Kazım. 1995. *İttihat ve Terakki Cemiyeti, 1896–1909*. Istanbul: Emre Yayınları.

Kasakoff, Alice Bee. 1999. "Is There a Place for Anthropology in Social Science History?" *Social Science History* 23 (4): 535–559.

Katz, Jack. 1999. *How Emotions Work*. Chicago: University of Chicago Press.

Katznelson, Ira. 1981. *City Trenches: Urban Politics and the Patterning of Class in the United States*. Chicago: University of Chicago Press.

——. 2003. "Periodization and Preferences: Reflections on Purposive Action in Comparative Historical Social Science." In *Comparative Historical Analysis in the Social Sciences*. Ed. James Mahoney and Dietrich Rueschemeyer. Cambridge: Cambridge University Press.

Katznelson, Ira, and Aristide R. Zolberg, eds. 1986. *Working-Class Formation: Nineteenth-Century Patterns in Western Europe and the United States*. Princeton, N.J.: Princeton University Press.

Kaufman, Jason. 1999. "Three Views of Associationalism in 19th Century America: An Empirical Examination." *American Journal of Sociology* 104 (3): 1296–1345.

Kaye, Harvey J. 1986. "From Feudalism to Capitalism: The Debate Goes On." *Peasant Studies* 13 (3): 171–180.

Keane, Webb. 2005. "Estrangement, Intimacy, and the Object of Anthropology." In *The Politics of Method in the Human Sciences: Positivism and Its Epistemological Others*. Ed. George Steinmetz. Durham, N.C.: Duke University Press.

Keat, Russell, and John Urry. 1975. *Social Theory as Science*. London: Routledge and Kegan Paul.

Keegan, John. 1976. *The Face of Battle*. London: Harmondsworth.

Keller, Morton. 1977. *Affairs of State: Public Life in Late Nineteenth-Century America*. Cambridge, Mass.: Belknap Press.

Kelley, Robin. 1996. "The World of Diaspora Made: C. L. R. James and the Politics of History." Pp. 103–130 in *Rethinking C. L. R. James*. Ed. Grant Farred. Cambridge: Blackwell.

Kennedy, Michael D. 1990a. "The Constitution of Critical Intellectuals: Polish Physicians, Peace Activists and Democratic Civil Society." *Studies in Comparative Communism* 23 (3/4): 281–304.

——. 1990b. *The Intelligentsia in the Constitution of Civil Societies and Post Communist Regimes in Hungary and Poland*. Ann Arbor: University of Michigan Press.

——. 1991. *Professionals, Power and Solidarity in Poland: A Critical Sociology of Soviet-Type Society*. Cambridge: Cambridge University Press.

——. 1994. "Introduction." Pp. 1–45 in *Envisioning Eastern Europe: Postcommunist Cultural Studies*. Ed. Michael D. Kennedy. Ann Arbor: University of Michigan Press.

——. 2001. "Postcommunist Capitalism, Culture, and History." *American Journal of Sociology* 106 (4): 1138–1151.

——. 2002. *Cultural Formations of Postcommunism: Emancipation, Transition, Nation, and War*. Minneapolis: University of Minnesota Press.

Kennedy, Michael, and Ronald Grigor Suny, eds. 1999. *Intellectuals and the Articulation of the Nation.* Ann Arbor: University of Michigan Press.

Kerber, Linda. 1980. *Women of the Republic: Intellect and Ideology in Revolutionary America.* Chapel Hill: University of North Carolina Press.

Kersbergen, Kees van. 1995. *Social Capitalism: A Study of Christian Democracy and the Welfare State.* London: Routledge.

Kestnbaum, Meyer. 2000. "Citizenship and Compulsory Military Service: The Revolutionary Origins of Conscription in the United States." *Armed Forces and Society* 27:7–36.

———. 2002. "Citizen-Soldiers, National Service and the Mass Army: The Birth of Conscription in Revolutionary Europe and North America." *Comparative Social Research* 20:117–144.

———. N.d.a. "State Building in Revolution: Citizen Conscription and the Politics of Incorporation." Manuscript.

———. N.d.b. "When War Became the People's Business: Citizenship and Military Mobilization in Revolutionary Europe and North America." Manuscript.

Kharkhordin, Oleg. 1999. *The Collective and the Individual in Russia: A Study of Practices.* Berkeley: University of California Press.

Kiewiet, D. Roderick, and Mathew McCubbins. 1991. *The Logic of Delegation.* Chicago: University of Chicago Press.

Kimball, Bruce A. 1992. *The "True Professional Ideal" in America: A History.* Cambridge, Mass.: Blackwell.

Kimeldorf, Howard. 1999. *Battling for American Labor: Wobblies, Craft Workers, and the Making of the Union Movement.* Berkeley: University of California Press.

Kimmel, Michael. 1988. *Absolutism and Its Discontents: State and Society in Seventeenth-Century France and England.* New Brunswick, N.J.: Transaction Publishers.

King, Desmond. 1995. *Actively Seeking Work? The Politics of Unemployment and Welfare Policy in the United States and Great Britain.* Chicago: University of Chicago Press.

King, Gary, Robert O. Keohane, and Sidney Verba. 1994. *Designing Social Inquiry: Scientific Inference in Qualitative Research.* Princeton, N.J.: Princeton University Press.

Kippenberg, Hans G. Forthcoming. "Religious Communities as Vehicles of Meaning in Social Interaction: The 'Sociology of Religion' Section of *Economy and Society*." Ch. 7 in *Max Weber at the Millennium.* Ed. Charles Camic, Philip Gorski, and David Trubek. Stanford, Calif.: Stanford University Press.

Kirmani, Ahmad Majd al-Islam. 1968. *Tarikh-i Inqilab-i Mashrutiyat-i Iran: Safarnamah-i Kalat.* Ed. M. Khalilpur. Isfahan: Intisharat-i Danishgah-i Isfahan.

Kirmani, Muhammad Nazim al-Islam. 1983. *Tarikh-i Bidari-i Iraniyan,* 2 vols. Ed. S. Sirjani. Tehran: Intisharat-i Agah, Intisharat-i Nuvin.

Kiser, Edgar. 1989. "A Principal-Agent Analysis of the Initiation of War in Absolutist States." Pp. 65–82 in *War and the World System.* Ed. Robert Schaeffer. New York: Greenwood Press.

———. 1994. "Markets and Hierarchies in Early Modern Fiscal Systems: A Principal-Agent Analysis." *Politics and Society* 22 (3): 284–315.

———. 1996. "The Revival of Narrative in Historical Sociology: What Rational Choice Theory Can Contribute." *Politics and Society* 24 (3): 249–271.

———. 1999. "Comparing Varieties of Agency Theory in Economics, Political Science, and Sociology: An Illustration from State Policy Implementation." *Sociological Theory* 7 (2): 146–170.

Kiser, Edgar, and Kathryn Baker. 1994. "Could Privatization Increase the Efficiency of Tax Collection in Less Developed Countries?" *Policy Studies Journal* 22 (3): 489–500.

Kiser, Edgar, and Yong Cai. 2003. "War and Bureaucratization in Qin China: Exploring the Anomalous Case." *American Sociological Review* 68: 511–539.

Kiser, Edgar, and Michael Hechter. 1991. "The Role of General Theory in Comparative-Historical Sociology." *American Journal of Sociology* 97 (1): 1–30.

——. 1998. "The Debate on Historical Sociology: Rational Choice Theory and Its Critics." *American Journal of Sociology* 104 (3): 785–816.

Kiser, Edgar, and Joshua Kane. 2001. "Revolution and State Structure: The Bureaucratization of Tax Administration in Early Modern England and France." *American Journal of Sociology* 107 (1): 183–223.

Kiser, Edgar, and April Linton. 2002. "The Hinges of History: State-Making and Revolt in Early Modern France." *American Sociological Review* 67:889–910.

Kiser, Edgar, and Joachim Schneider. 1994. "Bureaucracy and Efficiency: An Analysis of Taxation in Early Modern Prussia." *American Sociological Review* 59 (April): 187–204.

——. 1995. "Rational Choice versus Cultural Explanations of the Efficiency of the Prussian Tax System." *American Sociological Review* 60 (5): 787–791.

Kiser, Edgar, and Xiaoxi Tong. 1992. "Determinants of the Amount and Type of Corruption in State Fiscal Bureaucracies: An Analysis of Late Imperial China." *Comparative Political Studies* 25:300–331.

Kittay, Eva. 1999. *Love's Labor: Essays on Women, Equality, and Dependency.* New York: Routledge.

Klausner, Samuel Z. 1986. "The Bid to Nationalize American Social Science." Pp. 3–40 in *The Nationalization of the Social Sciences.* Ed. Samuel Z. Klausner and Victor D. Lidz. Philadelphia: University of Pennsylvania Press.

Klausner, Samuel Z., and Victor D. Lidz, eds. 1986. *The Nationalization of the Social Sciences.* Philadelphia: University of Pennsylvania Press.

Kleinman, Daniel Lee. 1995. *Politics on the Endless Frontier: Postwar Research Policy in the United States.* Durham, N.C.: Duke University Press.

——. 2003. *Impure Cultures: University Biology and the Commercial World.* Madison: University of Wisconsin Press.

Kligman, Gail. 1998. *The Politics of Duplicity: Controlling Reproduction in Ceausescu's Romania.* Berkeley: University of California Press.

Knight, Alan. 2002. "Subalterns, Signifiers, and Statistics: Perspectives on Mexican Historiography." *Latin American Research Review* 37 (2): 136–158.

Knijn, Trudie, and Monique Kremer. 1997. "Gender and the Caring Dimension of Welfare States: Toward Inclusive Citizenship." *Social Politics* 4:328–361.

Kogut, Bruce, and Udo Zander. 2000. "Did Socialism Fail to Innovate? A Natural Experiment of the Two Zeiss Companies." *American Sociological Review* 65:169–190.

Kohn, Hans. 1955. *Nationalism: Its Meaning and History.* Princeton, N.J.: D. Van Nostrand.

——. 1961 [1944]. *The Idea of Nationalism: A Study in Its Origins and Background.* New York: Macmillan.

Kohn, Melvin. 1987. "Cross-National Research as an Analytic Strategy." *American Sociological Review* 52:713–731.

Kolakowski, Leszek. 1968. *The Alienation of Reason: A History of Positivist Thought.* Garden City, N.Y.: Doubleday.

Konrád, George, and Iván Szelényi. 1979. *The Intellectuals on the Road to Class Power.* Trans. Andrew Arato and Richard E. Allen. New York: Harcourt Brace Jovanovich.

Koonz, Claudia. 1987. *Mothers in the Fatherland: Women, the Family, and Nazi Politics.* New York: St. Martin's Press.

Korpi, Walter. 1978. *The Working Class in Welfare Capitalism: Work, Unions, and Politics in Sweden.* Boston: Routledge and Kegan Paul.

——. 1983. *The Democratic Class Struggle.* Boston: Routledge and Kegan Paul.

——. 1989. "Power, Politics, and State Autonomy in the Development of Social Citizenship: Social Rights during Sickness in Eighteen OECD Countries since 1930." *American Sociological Review* 54:309–328.

——. 2000. "Faces of Inequality: Gender, Class and Patterns of Inequalities in Different Types of

Welfare States." *Social Politics* 7:127–191.

Korpi, Walter, and Joakim Palme. 1998. "The Paradox of Redistribution and Strategies of Equality: Welfare State Institutions, Inequality, and Poverty in the Western Countries." *American Sociological Review* 63:661–687.

Kovács, János Mátyás. 1994. "Introduction: Official and Alternative Legacies." Pp. xi–xxiii in *Transition to Capitalism? The Communist Legacy in Eastern Europe*. Ed. János Mátyás Kovács. New Brunswick, N.J.: Transaction Publishers.

Koven, Seth, and Sonya Michel. 1990. "Womanly Duties: Materialist Politics and the Origins of Welfare States in France, Germany, Great Britain, and the United States, 1800–1920." *American Historical Review* 95 (4): 1076–1108.

——, eds. 1993. *Mothers of a New World: Maternalist Politics and the Origins of Welfare States*. New York: Routledge.

Krantz, Frederick, and Paul M. Hohenberg. 1975. *Failed Transitions to Modern Industrial Society: Renaissance Italy and Seventeenth-Century Holland*. Montreal: Interuniversity Centre for European Studies.

Krause, Elliott. 1996. *Death of the Guilds: Professions, States, and the Advance of Capitalism, 1930 to the Present*. New Haven, Conn.: Yale University Press.

Kriedte, Peter, Hans Medick, and Jurgen Schlumbohm. 1981. *Industrialization before Industrialization: Rural Industry in the Genesis of Capitalism*. Trans. Beate Schempp. Cambridge: Cambridge University Press.

Kuboniwa, Masaaki, and Evgeny Gavrilenkov. 1997. *Development of Capitalism in Russia: The Second Challenge*. Tokyo: Maruzen.

Kuhn, Thomas S. 1970. *The Structure of Scientific Revolutions*. Chicago: University of Chicago Press.

Kuhnle, Stein, ed. 2000. *Survival of the European Welfare State*. London: Routledge.

Kula, Witold. 1986. *Measures and Men*. Princeton, N.J.: Princeton University Press.

Kuran, Timur. 1998. "Ethnic Norms and Their Transformation through Reputational Cascades." *Journal of Legal Studies* 27:623–659.

Kymlicka, W. 1995. *Multicultural Citizenship: A Liberal Theory of Minority Rights*. Oxford: Clarendon Press.

——. 1997. *State, Nations and Cultures*. Assen: Van Gorcum.

——. 1998. "American Multiculturalism in the International Arena." *Dissent* (fall): 73–79.

Kymlicka, W., and W. Norman. 1995. "Return of the Citizen: A Survey of Recent Work on Citizenship Theory." Pp. 283–322 in *Theorizing Citizenship*. Ed. R. Beiner. Albany: State University of New York Press.

Lucan, Jacques. 1991. *The Seminar of Jacques Lacan, Book 1: Freud's Papers on Technique 1953–1954*. New York: W. W. Norton.

Lachmann, Richard. 1987. *From Manor to Market: Structural Change in England, 1536–1640*. Madison: University of Wisconsin Press.

——. 1989. "Origins of Capitalism in Western Europe: Economic and Political Aspects." *Annual Review of Sociology* 15:47–52.

——. 2000. *Capitalists in Spite of Themselves: Elite Conflict and Economic Transitions in Early Modern Europe*. New York: Oxford University Press.

Laclau, Ernesto. 1971. "Feudalism and Capitalism in Latin America." *New Left Review* 67:19–38.

Laclau, Ernesto, and Chantal Mouffe. 1985. *Hegemony and Socialist Strategy: Towards a Radical Democratic Politics*. London: Verso.

Laitin, David D. 1986. *Hegemony and Culture: Politics and Religious Change among the Yoruba*. Chicago: University of Chicago Press.

——. 1995. "National Revivals and Violence." *Archives Européennes de Sociologie* 35 (1): 3–43.

——. 1998. *Identity in Formation: The Russian-Speaking Populations in the Near Abroad.* Ithaca, N.Y.: Cornell University Press.

——. 1999. "The Cultural Elements of Ethnically Mixed States: Nationality Re-Formation in the Soviet Successor States." In *State/Culture: State Formation after the Cultural Turn.* Ed. George Steinmetz. Ithaca, N.Y.: Cornell University Press. Wilder House Series in Culture, Power, and History.

Lambek, Michael. 1991. "Tryin' to Make It Real, but Compared to What?" *Culture* 11:43–51.

Lamont, Michele. 1987. "How to Become a Dominant French Philosopher: The Case of Jacques Derrida." *American Journal of Sociology* 93 (3): 584–622.

——. 1992. *Money, Morals, and Manners: The Culture of the French and American Upper-Middle Class.* Chicago: University of Chicago Press.

——. 2000. *The Dignity of Working Men: Morality and the Boundaries of Race, Class, and Immigration.* New York: Russell Sage Foundation.

Lamoreaux, Naomi R. 1994. *Insider Lending: Banks, Personal Connections and Economic Development in Industrial New England.* Cambridge: Cambridge University Press.

Lancaster, L. W. 1930. "Possibilities in the Study of 'Neighborhood' Politics." *Social Forces* 8 (3): 429–432.

Land, Hilary. 1978. "Who Cares for the Family?" *Journal of Social Policy* 7:257–284.

Landa, Janet T. 1981. "A Theory of the Ethnically Homogeneous Middleman Group: An Institutional Alternative to Contract Law." *Journal of Legal Studies* 10:349–362.

Landes, David S. 1969. *Prometheus Unbound: Technological Change and Industrial Development in Western Europe from 1750 to the Present.* Cambridge: Cambridge University Press.

——. 1998. *The Wealth and Poverty of Nations: Why Some Are So Rich and Some So Poor.* New York: W. W. Norton.

——. 1999. "The Fable of the Dead Horse; or, the Industrial Revolution Revisited." Pp. 128–159 in *The British Industrial Revolution: An Economic Perspective.* 2d ed. Ed. Joel Mokyr. Boulder, Colo.: Westview Press.

Landes, Joan. 1988. *Women and the Public Sphere in the Age of the French Revolution.* Ithaca, N.Y.: Cornell University Press.

Langan, Mary, and Ilona Ostner. 1991. "Gender and Welfare." Pp. 127–150 in *Towards a European Welfare State?* Ed. G. Room. Bristol: School for Advanced Urban Studies.

La Palombara, Joseph. 1963. "Bureaucracy and Political Development: Notes, Queries, and Dilemmas." Pp. 34–61 in *Bureaucracy and Political Development.* Ed. Joseph La Palombara. Princeton, N.J.: Princeton University Press.

Laplanche, J., and J.-B. Pontalis. 1973 [1967]. *The Language of Psycho-Analysis.* New York: W. W. Norton.

Larsen, Otto N. 1992. *Millstones and Milestones: Social Science at the National Science Foundation.* New Brunswick, N.J.: Transaction Publishers.

Larson, Magali S. 1977. *The Rise of Professionalism: A Sociological Analysis.* Berkeley: University of California Press.

——. 1984. "The Production of Expertise and the Constitution of Expert Power." Pp. 28–80 in *The Authority of Experts: Studies in History and Theory.* Ed. Thomas L. Haskell. Bloomington: Indiana University Press.

——. 1990. "In the Matter of Experts and Professionals, or How Impossible It Is to Leave Nothing Unsaid." Pp. 24–50 in *The Formation of Professions.* Ed. Rolf Torstendahl and Michael Burrage. London: Sage.

Lash, Scott. 1985. "Postmodernity and Desire." *Theory and Society* 14 (1): 1–33.

Lash, Scott, and John Urry. 1987. *The End of Organized Capitalism.* Madison: University of Wisconsin Press.

——. 1994. *Economies of Signs and Space.* London: Sage.

Laslett, Barbara. 1991. "Biography as Historical Sociology: The Case of William Fielding Ogburn." *Theory and Society* 20 (4): 511–538.

Laslett, Barbara, and Johanna Brenner. 1989. "Gender and Social Reproduction: Historical Perspectives." *Annual Review of Sociology* 15:381–404.

Laslett, Barbara, Johanna Brenner, and Yesim Arat, eds. 1995. *Rethinking the Political: Gender, Resistance, and the State.* Chicago: University of Chicago Press.

Laslett, Peter. 1988. "The European Family and Early Modernization." Pp. 234–241 in *Europe and the Rise of Capitalism.* Ed. Jean Baechler, John A. Hall, and Michael Mann. Oxford: Basil Blackwell.

Latour, Bruno. 1987. *Science in Action: How to Follow Scientists and Engineers through Society.* Cambridge, Mass.: Harvard University Press.

———. 1999. *Pandora's Hope: Essays on the Reality of Science Studies.* Cambridge, Mass.: Harvard University Press.

Latour, Bruno, and Steve Woolgar. 1986 [1979]. *Laboratory Life.* Princeton, N.J.: Princeton University Press.

Lawson, Tony. 1997. *Economics and Reality.* London: Routledge.

Layder, Derek. 1988. "The Relation of Theory and Method: Causal Relatedness, Historical Contingency, and Beyond." *Sociological Review* 36 (August): 441–463.

Lazerson, Marvin. 1998. "The Disappointments of Success: Higher Education after World War II." *Annals of the American Academy of Political and Social Science* 559:64–76.

Lebsock, Suzanne D. 1977. "Radical Reconstruction and the Property Rights of Southern Women." *Journal of Southern History* 43:195–216.

Ledeneva, Alena V. 1998. *Russia's Economy of Favors: Blat, Networking and Informal Exchange.* Cambridge: Cambridge University Press.

Lefebvre, Georges. 1947. *The Coming of the French Revolution.* Princeton, N.J.: Princeton University Press.

Leibfried, S., and P. Pierson. 1995. *European Social Policy: Between Fragmentation and Integration.* Washington, D.C.: Brookings Institution.

Leira, Arnlaug. 1992. *Welfare States and Working Mothers: The Scandinavian Experience.* New York: Cambridge University Press.

———. 2002. *Working Parents and the Welfare State: Family Change and Policy Reform in Scandinavia.* Cambridge: Cambridge University Press.

Lenin, V. I. 1926. *What Is to Be Done? Burning Questions of Our Movement.* New York: International Publishers.

———. 1964. "Statistics and Sociology." Pp. 271–277 in *Collected Works,* vol. 23. Trans. M. S. Levin and Joe Fineberg. Ed. M. S. Levin. Moscow: Progress Publishers.

———. 1975. "Imperialism, the Highest Stage of Capitalism: A Popular Outline." Pp. 204–274 in *The Lenin Anthology.* Ed. Robert Tucker. New York: W. W. Norton.

———. 1980. "The Collapse of the Second International." Pp. 205–259 in *Collected Works,* vol. 21. Trans. Julius Katzer. Moscow: Progress Publishers.

———. 1992. *The State and Revolution.* London: Penguin.

Lenski, Gerhard. 1988. "Rethinking Macrosociological Theory." *American Sociological Review* 53 (April): 163–171.

Lepenies, Wolf. 1988. *Between Literature and Science: The Rise of Sociology.* Cambridge: Cambridge University Press.

Lerner, Daniel. 1958. *The Passing of Traditional Society: Modernizing the Middle East.* New York: Free Press.

Le Roy Ladurie, Emmanuel. 1974. *The Peasants of Languedoc.* Urbana: University of Illinois Press.

———. 1985. "A Reply to Robert Brenner." Pp. 101–106 in *The Brenner Debate: Agrarian Class Structure and Economic Development in Pre-Industrial Europe.* Ed. T. H. Aston and C. H. E. Philpin. Cambridge: Cambridge University Press.

Lessnoff, Michael H. 1994. *The Spirit of Capitalism and the Protestant Ethic.* Brookfield, Vt.: Edward Elgar.

Levi, Margaret. 1988. *Of Rule and Revenue.* Berkeley: University of California Press.

———. 1997. *Consent, Dissent and Patriotism.* Cambridge: Cambridge University Press.

Levine, David. 2001. *At the Dawn of Modernity: Biology, Culture, and Material Life in Europe after the Year 1000.* Berkeley: University of California Press.

Levine, George. 1996. "Science and Citizenship: Karl Pearson and the Ethics of Epistemology." *Modernism/Modernity* 3 (3): 137–143.

Levine, Hal B. 1999. "Reconstructing Ethnicity." *Journal of the Royal Anthropological Institute,* new series, 5:165–180.

Lévi-Strauss, Claude. 1966. *The Savage Mind.* Chicago: University of Chicago Press.

Lewis, C. S. 1987. *Studies in Words.* Cambridge: Cambridge University Press.

Lewis, Gail. 2000. *"Race," Gender, Social Welfare: Encounters in a Postcolonial Society.* Cambridge: Polity Press.

Lewis, Jane. 1992. "Gender and the Development of Welfare Regimes." *Journal of European Social Policy* 3:159–173.

———. 1997. "Gender and Welfare Regimes: Further Thoughts." *Social Politics* 4:160–177.

Lewis, Jane, ed. 1997. *Lone Mothers in European Welfare Regimes.* London: Jessica Kingsley.

Lewis, Jane, and Gertrude Åstrom. 1992. "Equality, Difference, and State Welfare: Labor Market and Family Policies in Sweden." *Feminist Studies* 18:59–86.

Lewis, N. 1993. "The Citizen's Charter and Next Steps: A New Way of Governing?" *Political Quarterly* 64:316–326.

Lewis, Robert Benjamin. 1844. *Light and Truth: Collected from the Bible and Ancient and Modern History, Containing the Universal History of the Colored and Indian Race, from the Creation of the World to the Present Time.* Boston: Benjamin E. Roberts.

Lewis, W. Arthur. 1955. *The Theory of Economic Growth.* London: Allen and Unwin.

Libecap, Gary D. 1978. "Economic Variables and the Development of the Law: The Case of Western Mineral Rights." *Journal of Economic History* 38:338–362.

———. 1981. "Bureaucratic Opposition to the Assignment of Property Rights: Overgrazing on the Western Range." *Journal of Economic History* 41:151–158.

Lie, John. 2001. *Multiethnic Japan.* Cambridge, Mass.: Harvard University Press.

Lieberman, Robert. 1998. *Shifting the Color Line: Race and the American Welfare State.* Cambridge, Mass.: Harvard University Press.

Lieberson, Stanley. 1991. "Small N's and Big Conclusions: An Examination of the Reasoning in Comparative Studies Based on a Small Number of Cases." *Social Forces* 70 (December): 307–320.

———. 1992. "Einstein, Renoir, and Greeley: Some Thoughts about Evidence in Sociology: 1991 Presidential Address." *American Sociological Review* 57 (1): 1–15.

Linklater, A. 1990. *Men and Citizens in the Theory of International Relations.* London: Macmillan.

———. 2000. *International Relations: Critical Concepts in Political Science.* London: Routledge.

Lipartito, Kenneth. 1989. *The Bell System and Regional Business: The Telephone in the South, 1877–1920.* Baltimore: Johns Hopkins University Press.

Lipietz, Alain. 1987. *Mirages and Miracles: The Crisis of Global Fordism.* London: Verso.

———. 1992. *Towards a New Economic Order: Postfordism, Ecology and Democracy.* Cambridge: Polity Press.

Lipset, Seymour Martin. 1950. *Agrarian Socialism: The Cooperative Commonwealth Federation in Saskatchewan.* Berkeley: University of California Press.

———. 1963. *The First New Nation: The United States in Historical and Comparative Perspective.* New York: Basic Books.

———. 1964. "Introduction." Pp. vi–vii in *Class, Citizenship, and Social Development.* Ed. S. M. Lipset. Garden City, N.Y.: Doubleday.

———. 1968. "History and Sociology: Some Methodological Considerations." Pp. 20–58 in *Sociology and History: Methods*. Ed. Seymour Martin Lipset and Richard Hofstadter. New York: Basic Books.

———. 1990. *Continental Divide: The Values and Institutions of the United States and Canada.* New York: Routledge.

———. 1996. *American Exceptionalism: A Double-Edged Sword.* New York: W. W. Norton.

Lipset, Seymour Martin, and Stein Rokkan, eds. 1967. *Party Systems and Voter Alignments: Cross-National Perspectives.* New York: Free Press.

Lipton, David, and Jeffrey D. Sachs. 1992. "Prospects for Russia's Economic Reforms." *Brookings Papers on Economic Activity* 2:213–265.

Lister, Ruth. 1997. *Citizenship: Feminist Perspectives.* New York: New York University Press.

Liu, J. T. C. 1967. "Sung Roots of Chinese Political Conservatism: The Administrative Problems." *Journal of Asian Studies* 26:457–463.

Liu, Tessie. 1991. "Teaching the Differences among Women from a Historical Perspective: Rethinking Race and Gender as Social Categories." *Women's Studies International Forum* 14:265–276.

Lloyd, Christopher. 1986. *Explanation in Social History.* Oxford: Basil Blackwell.

Lo, Ming-cheng M. 2002. *Doctors within Borders: Profession, Ethnicity, and Modernity in Colonial Taiwan.* Berkeley: University of California Press.

Locke, John. 1947 [1690]. *Of Civil Government.* London: J. M. Dent and Sons, Ltd.

Locke, Richard M., and Kathleen Thelen. 1995. "Apples and Oranges Revisited: Contextualized Comparisons and the Study of Comparative Local Politics." *Politics and Society* 23 (September): 337–367.

Logan, Enid. 2000. "Conspirators, Pawns, Patriots and Brothers: Race and Politics in Western Cuba, 1906–1909." Pp. 3–51 in *Political Power and Social Theory.* Ed. Diane Davis. Amsterdam: JAI Press.

Loveman, Mara. 2001. "Nation-State Building, 'Race,' and the Production of Official Statistics: Brazil in Comparative Perspective." Ph.D. dissertation, Department of Sociology, University of California, Los Angeles.

Löwy, Michael, and Robert Sayre. 2001. *Romanticism against the Tide of Modernity.* Trans. Catherine Porter. Durham, N.C.: Duke University Press.

Luckmann, Thomas 1990. "Shrinking Transcendence, Expanding Religion?" *Sociological Analysis* 50 (2): 127–138.

Lukács, Georg. 1968. "Reification and the Consciousness of the Proletariat." Pp. 83–222 in *History and Class Consciousness.* Cambridge, Mass.: MIT Press.

Lukes, S. 1973. *Emile Durkheim: His Life and Work.* London: Allen Lane.

Lundberg, George A. 1947. "The Senate Ponders Social Science." *Scientific Monthly* 44 (May): 397–411.

Lundberg, George A., Clarence C. Schrag, and Otto N. Larsen. 1954. *Sociology.* New York: Haroer and Brothers.

Luong, Pauline Jones. 2002. *Institutional Change and Political Continuity in Post-Soviet Central Asia: Power, Perception, and Pacts.* New York: Cambridge University Press.

Lupher, Mark. 1996. *Power Restructuring in China and Russia.* Boulder, Colo.: Westview Press.

Lynn, John A. 1996. "The Evolution of Army Style in the Modern West, 800–2000." *International History Review* 18 (3): 505–545.

Lyotard, Jean-François. 1984 [1979]. *The Postmodern Condition: A Report on Knowledge.* Trans. Geoff Bennington and Brian Massumi. Minneapolis: University of Minnesota Press.

Macdonald, Keith M. 1995. *The Sociology of the Professions.* London: Sage.

Macfarlane, Alan. 1978. *The Origins of English Individualism: The Family, Property and Social Transition.* Oxford: Blackwell.

Mach, Ernst. 1886. *Beiträge zur Analyse der Empfindungen.* Jena: G. Fischer.

MacIntyre, A. C. 1984. *After Virtue: A Study in Moral Theory.* Notre Dame, Ind.: University of Notre Dame Press.

MacKinnon, Catharine A. 1989. *Toward a Feminist Theory of the State.* Cambridge, Mass.: Harvard University Press.

Maddison, Angus. 2001. *The World Economy: A Millennial Perspective.* Paris: OECD.

Magubane, Zine. 2003. *Bringing the Empire Home: Imagining Race, Class, and Gender in Great Britain and Colonial South Africa.* Chicago: University of Chicago Press.

Magyari-Nándor, László, and László Péter. 1997. "Az egytemről magyar diákszemmel" [Hungarian students' views on the university]. *Korunk* 4:112–119.

Mahoney, James. 1999. "Nominal, Ordinal, and Narrative Appraisal in Macrocausal Analysis." *American Journal of Sociology* 104 (4): 1154–1196.

——. 2000. "Path Dependence in Historical Sociology." *Theory and Society* 29:507–548.

——. 2001a. "Beyond Correlational Analysis: Recent Innovations in Theory and Method." *Sociological Forum* 16 (3): 575–593.

——. 2001b. *Legacies of Liberalism: Path Dependence and Political Regimes in Central America.* Baltimore: Johns Hopkins University Press.

Mahoney, James, and Dietrich Rueschemeyer. 2003. "Comparative Historical Analysis: Achievements and Agendas." Pp. 3–38 in *Comparative Historical Analysis in the Social Sciences.* Ed. James Mahoney and Dietrich Rueschemeyer. Cambridge: Cambridge University Press.

——, eds. 2003. *Comparative Historical Analysis in the Social Sciences.* Cambridge: Cambridge University Press.

Maier, Pauline. 1993. "The Revolutionary Origins of the American Corporation." *William and Mary Quarterly* 50:51–84.

Majd al-Mulk (Sinaki), Muhammad Khan. 1979. *Risalah-'i Majdiyah.* Ed. Fazl Allah Gurkani. Tehran: Iqbal.

Malik, Kenan. 1996. *The Meaning of Race.* New York: New York University Press.

Mamdani, Mahmood. 1996. *Citizen and Subject: Contemporary Africa and the Legacy of Late Colonialism.* Princeton, N.J.: Princeton University Press.

Mandelbaum, Maurice. 1961. "Historical Explanation: The Problem of Covering Laws." *History and Theory* 1 (3): 229–242.

Manderson, Lenore. 1996. *Sickness and the State: Health and Illness in Colonial Malaya, 1870–1940.* Cambridge: Cambridge University Press.

Mann, Michael. 1986. *The Sources of Social Power,* vol. 1. Cambridge: Cambridge University Press.

——. 1987a. "The Roots and Contradictions of Modern Militarism." Pp. 166–187 in *States, War and Capitalism.* Reprinted from *New Left Review* 162 (March–April).

——. 1987b. "Ruling Class Strategies and Citizenship." *Sociology* 21 (3): 339–354.

——. 1993. *The Sources of Social Power.* vol. 2: *The Rise of Classes and Nation-States, 1760–1914.* Cambridge: Cambridge University Press.

——. 1998. *States, War and Capitalism: Studies in Political Sociology.* Oxford: Basil Blackwell.

Mannheim, Karl. 1929. *Ideologie und Utopie.* Bonn: Verlag Friedrich Cohen.

Manza, Jeff. 2000. "Political Sociological Models of the U.S. New Deal." *Annual Review of Sociology* 26:297–322.

Manza, Jeff, and Clem Brooks. 1997. "The Religious Factor in U.S. Presidential Elections, 1960–1992." *American Journal of Sociology* 103 (1): 38–81.

Marcella, R., and G. Baxter. 1999. "The Information Needs and the Information Seeking Behaviour of a National Sample of the Population in the United Kingdom, with Special Reference to Needs Related to Citizenship." *Journal of Documentation* 55 (2): 159–183.

March, James G. 1994. *A Primer on Decision Making: How Decisions Happen.* New York: Free Press.

Marcuse, Herbert. 1964. *One Dimensional Man: Studies in the Ideology of Advanced Industrial Society.* Boston: Beacon Press.

Mardin, Şerif. 1962. *The Genesis of Young Ottoman Thought: A Study in the Modernization of Turkish Political Ideas.* Princeton, N.J.: Princeton University Press.

Markoff, John. 1994. "The Great Wave of Democracy in Historical Perspective." Ithaca, N.Y.: Cornell University. Western Societies Occasional Paper 34.

——. 1996a. *The Abolition of Feudalism: Peasants, Lords, and Legislators in the French Revolution.* University Park: Pennsylvania State University Press.

——. 1996b. *Waves of Democracy: Social Movements and Political Change.* Thousand Oaks, Calif.: Pine Forge Press.

——. 1999. "From Center to Periphery and Back Again: Reflections on the Geography of Democratic Innovation." Pp. 229–246 in *Extending Citizenship, Reconfiguring States.* Ed. Michael Hanagan and Charles Tilly. Lanham, Md.: Rowman and Littlefield.

Marlow, Louise. 1997. *Hierarchy and Egalitarianism in Islamic Thought.* Cambridge: Cambridge University Press.

Marriott, McKim. 1990. "Constructing an Indian Ethnosociology." Pp. 1–39 in *India through Hindu Categories.* Ed. McKim Marriott. New Delhi: Sage.

Marshall, Barbara L. 1994. *Engendering Modernity: Feminism, Social Theory and Social Change.* Boston: Northeastern University Press.

——. 2000. *Configuring Gender: Explorations in Theory and Politics.* Peterborough, Ontario: Broadview Press.

Marshall, Gordon. 1982. *In Search of the Spirit of Capitalism.* New York: Columbia University Press.

Marshall, T. H. 1950. *Citizenship and Social Class, and Other Essays.* Cambridge: Cambridge University Press.

——. 1963. *Sociology at the Crossroads, and Other Essays.* London: Heinemann.

——. 1964. *Class, Citizenship, and Social Development.* Garden City, N.Y.: Doubleday.

——. 1981. *The Right to Welfare and Other Essays.* New York: Free Press.

Marshall, T. H., and T. B. Bottomore. 1992. *Citizenship and Social Class.* London: Pluto Press.

Martin, David. 1979. *A General Theory of Secularization.* New York: Harper.

Martin, John Frederick. 1991. *Profits in the Wilderness: Entrepreneurship and the Founding of New England Towns in the Seventeenth Century.* Chapel Hill: University of North Carolina Press.

Martin, Terry. 2001. *The Affirmative Action Empire.* Ithaca, N.Y.: Cornell University Press.

Marwick, Arthur. 1974. *War and Social Change in the Twentieth Century: A Comparative Study of Britain, France, Germany, Russia and the United States.* London: Macmillan.

Marx, Anthony W. 1998. *Making Race and Nation: A Comparison of South Africa, the United States and Brazil.* Cambridge: Cambridge University Press.

——. 2003. *Faith in Nation: Exclusionary Origins of Nationalism.* New York: Oxford University Press.

Marx, Karl. 1963 [1852]. *The Eighteenth Brumaire of Louis Bonaparte.* New York: International Publishers.

——. 1964. *Pre-Capitalist Economic Formations.* Trans. Jack Cohen. Ed. E. J. Hobsbawm. New York: International Publishers.

——. 1967 [1867]. *Capital,* vol. 1. New York: International Publishers.

——. 1976 [1852]. *Le 18. Brumaire de Louis Bonaparte.* Paris: Editions sociales.

——. 1977 [1894]. *Capital,* vol. 1. Trans. Ben Fowkes. New York: Vintage.

Marx, Karl, and Friedrich Engels. 1970. *The German Ideology.* Ed. C. J. Arthur. New York: International Publishers.

——. 1972 [1845–1846]. "The German Ideology." Pp. 146–200 in *The Marx-Engels Reader.* Ed. Robert C. Tucker. New York: W. W. Norton.

——. 1978. "Manifesto of the Communist Party." Pp. 469–500 in *The Marx-Engels Reader,* 2nd ed. Ed. Robert C. Tucker. New York: W. W. Norton.

——. 1998 [1848]. *The Communist Manifesto.* Oxford: Oxford University Press.

Mastboom, Joyce M. 1996. "Protoindustrialization and Agriculture in the Eastern Netherlands." *Social Science History* 20 (2): 235–258.

Matson, Cathy. 1994. "'Damned Scoundrels' and 'Libertisme of Trade': Freedom and Regulation in Colonial New York's Fur and Grain Trades." *William and Mary Quarterly* 51:389–418.

Maza, Sara. 1993. *Private Lives and Public Affairs: The Causes Célèbres of Prerevolutionary France.* Berkeley: University of California Press.

Mazlish, Bruce, and Ralph Buultjens. 1993. *Conceptualizing Global History.* Boulder, Colo.: Westview Press.

McAdam, Doug. 1982. *Political Process and the Development of Black Insurgency.* Chicago: University of Chicago Press.

———. 1988. *Freedom Summer.* New York: Oxford University Press.

McAdam, Doug, and William H. Sewell Jr. 2001. "It's about Time: Temporality in the Study of Social Movements and Revolutions." In *Silence and Voice in the Study of Contentious Politics.* Ed. Ronald Aminzade, et al. Cambridge: Cambridge University Press.

McAdam, Doug, Sidney Tarrow, and Charles Tilly. 2001. *Dynamics of Contention.* Cambridge: Cambridge University Press.

McCall, Leslie. 2001. *Complex Inequality: Gender, Class, and Race in the New Economy.* New York: Routledge.

McCarthy, John D., and Mayer N. Zald. 1977. "Resource Mobilization and Social Movements: A Partial Theory." *American Journal of Sociology* 82 (6): 1212–1241.

McCartney, James L. 1971. "The Financing of Sociological Research: Trends and Consequences." Pp. 372–397 in *The Phenomenon of Sociology: A Reader in the Sociology of Sociology.* Ed. Edward A. Tiryakian. New York: Appleton-Century-Crofts.

McClelland, Charles E. 1991. *The German Experience of Professionalization: Modern Learned Professions and Their Organizations from the Early Nineteenth Century to the Hitler Era.* New York: Cambridge University Press.

McClintock, Anne. 1995. *Imperial Leather: Race, Gender and Sexuality in the Colonial Contest.* London: Routledge.

McCurdy, Charles W. 1978. "American Law and the Marketing Structure of the Large Corporation, 1875–1890." *Journal of Economic History* 38:631–649.

McCusker, John J. 1973. "Weights and Measures in the Colonial Sugar Trade: The Gallon and the Pound and Their International Equivalents." *William and Mary Quarterly* 30:599–624.

McDonald, Terrence J., ed. 1996. *The Historic Turn in the Human Sciences.* Ann Arbor: University of Michigan Press.

McGranahan, Leslie Moscow. 2000. "Charity and the Bequest Motive: Evidence from Seventeenth-Century Wills." *Journal of Political Economy* 108:1270–1291.

McGrath, Joseph E. 1984. *Groups: Interaction and Performance.* Englewood Cliffs, N.J.: Prentice-Hall.

McIlwee, Judith, and J. Gregg Robinson. 1992. *Women in Engineering: Gender, Power, and Workplace Culture.* Albany: State University of New York Press.

McIntosh, Mary. 1978. "The State and the Oppression of Women." Pp. 254–289 in *Feminism and Materialism.* Ed. A. Kuhn and A. Wolpe. London: Routledge and Kegan Paul.

McKay, James, and Frank Lewins. 1978. "Ethnicity and the Ethnic Group: A Conceptual Analysis and Reformulation." *Ethnic and Racial Studies* 1 (4): 412–427.

McKendrick, Neil, John Brewer, and J. H. Plumb. 1982. *The Birth of a Consumer Society: The Commercialization of Eighteenth-Century England.* Bloomington: Indiana University Press.

McLean, Paul D. 1998. "A Frame Analysis of Favor Seeking in the Renaissance: Agency, Networks, and Political Culture." *American Journal of Sociology* 104 (1): 51–91.

McLean, Paul D., and John F. Padgett. 1997. "Was Florence a Perfectly Competitive Market? Transactional Evidence from the Renaissance." *Theory and Society* 26:209–244.

McLeod, Hugh. 2000. *Secularisation in Western Europe, 1848–1914.* New York: St. Martin's Press.

———, ed. 1995. *European Religion in the Age of the Great Cities, 1830–1930.* New York: Routledge.

McMichael, Philip. 1990. "Incorporating Comparison within a World-Historical Perspective." *American Sociological Review* 55:385–397.

McNeely, Connie. 1995. *Constructing the Nation-State: International Organization and Prescriptive Action*. Westport, Conn.: Greenwood Press.

McNeill, William H. 1971. *A World History*. Oxford: Oxford University Press.

———. 1982. *The Pursuit of Power: Technology, Armed Force, and Society since A.D. 1000*. Chicago: University of Chicago Press.

———. 1989. *The Age of Gunpowder Empires, 1450–1800*. Washington, D.C.: American Historical Association.

———. 1995. *Keeping Together in Time: Dance and Drill in Human History*. Cambridge, Mass.: Harvard University Press.

McPherson, James. 1997. "From Limited to Total War in America." In *On the Road to Total War*. Ed. Stig Förster and Jörg Nagler. Cambridge: Cambridge University Press.

Mead, George Herbert. 1964. "National-Mindedness and International-Mindedness." Pp. 355–370 in *Selected Writings*. Ed. Andrew Reck. Indianapolis, Ind.: Bobbs-Merrill.

Mead, L. M. 1997. "Citizenship and Social Policy: T. H. Marshall and Poverty." *Social Philosophy and Policy* 14 (2): 197–230.

Medin, Douglas L. 1989. "Concepts and Conceptual Structure." *American Psychologist* 44:1469–1481.

Megill, Allan. 1985. *Prophets of Extremity: Nietzsche, Heidigger, Foucault, Derrida*. Berkeley: University of California Press.

Mekeel, S. 1944. "Citizenship, Education, and Culture." *American Journal of Sociology* 50 (3): 208–213.

Menand, Louis. 2001a. *The Marketplace of Ideas*. New York: American Council of Learned Societies. ACLS Occasional Paper 49.

———. 2001b. *The Metaphysical Club*. New York: Farrar, Straus and Giroux.

Mendels, Franklin. 1972. "Proto-Industrialization: The First Phase of the Industrialization Process." *Journal of Economic History* 32:241–261.

Merton, Robert K. 1936. "Puritanism, Pietism, and Science." *Sociological Review* 28.

———. 1965. *On the Shoulders of Giants: A Shandean Postscript*. New York: Free Press.

———. 1970 [1938]. *Science, Technology, and Society in Seventeenth-Century England*. New York: H. Fertig.

Mettler, Suzanne. 1998. *Dividing Citizens: Gender and Federalism in New Deal Public Policy*. Ithaca, N.Y.: Cornell University Press.

Meyer, John W. 1999. "The Changing Cultural Content of the Nation-State: A World Society Perspective." Pp. 123–143 in *State/Culture: State Formation after the Cultural Turn*. Ed. George Steinmetz. Ithaca, N.Y.: Cornell University Press. Wilder House Series in Culture, Power, and History.

Meyer, John W., and Ronald Jepperson. 2000. "The 'Actors' of Modern Society: The Cultural Construction of Social Agency." *Sociological Theory* 18 (1): 100–120.

Meyer, John W., John Boli, George Thomas, and Francisco Ramirez. 1997. "World Society and the Nation-State." *American Journal of Sociology* 103 (1): 144–181.

Meyer, John W., and Michael T. Hannan, eds. 1970. *National Development and the World System*. Chicago: University of Chicago Press.

Meyer, Madonna Harrington, ed. 2000. *Care Work: Gender, Labor, and the Welfare State*. New York: Routledge.

Michel, Sonya. 1999. *Children's Interests/Mothers' Rights: The Shaping of America's Child Care Policy*. New Haven, Conn.: Yale University Press.

Michel, Sonya, and Rianne Mahon, eds. 2002. *Child Care Policy at the Crossroads: Gender and Welfare State Restructuring*. New York: Routledge.

Mihic, Sophia, Stephen Engelmann, and Elisabeth Wingrove. 1995. "Transcending the Fact/Value Dichotomy in Political Science: Making Sense in and of Political Science." In *The Politics of Method in the Human Sciences: Positivism and its Epistemological Others*. Ed. George Steinmetz. Durham, N.C.: Duke University Press.

Milkman, Ruth. 1987. *Gender and Work: The Dynamic of Job Segregation by Sex during World War II.* Urbana: University of Illinois Press.

Mill, John Stuart. 1875. *A System of Logic, Ratiocinative and Inductive, Being a Connected View of the Principles of Evidence, and the Methods of Scientific Investigation,* 9th ed. London: Longmans, Green, Reader, and Dyer.

Miller, Pavla. 1998. *Transformations of Patriarchy in the West, 1500–1900.* Bloomington: Indiana University Press.

Miller, Richard W. 1987. *Fact and Method: Explanation, Confirmation and Reality in the Natural and Social Sciences.* Princeton, N.J.: Princeton University Press.

Miller, William Ian. 1986. "Gift, Sale, Payment, Raid: Case Studies in the Negotiation and Classification of Exchange in Medieval Iceland." *Speculum* 61:18–50.

Mills, C. Wright. 1940. "Situated Actions and Vocabularies of Motive." *American Sociological Review* 5:904–913.

———. 1959. *The Sociological Imagination.* New York: Oxford University Press.

Mink, Gwendolyn. 1998. *Welfare's End.* Ithaca, N.Y.: Cornell University Press.

Mink, Louis O. 1987. *Historical Understanding.* Ed. Eugene O. Golob, Brian Fay, and Richard T. Vann. Ithaca, N.Y.: Cornell University Press.

Mintz, Beth, and Michael Schwartz. 1985. *The Power Structure of American Business.* Chicago: University of Chicago Press.

Mintz, Sidney W. 1985. *Sweetness and Power: The Place of Sugar in Modern History.* New York: Penguin Books.

Mishra, Ramesh. 1999. *Globalization and the Welfare State.* Cheltenham, U.K.: Edward Elgar.

Misra, Joya. 2002. "Class, Race, and Gender and Theorizing Welfare States." *Theoretical Directions in Political Sociology for the Twenty-first Century* 11:19–52.

Mitchell, M. Marion. 1931. "Emile Durkheim and the Philosophy of Nationalism." *Political Science Quarterly* 46:87–106.

Mitchell, Timothy. 1991. "The Limits of the State: Beyond Statist Approaches and Their Critics." *American Political Science Review* 85:77–96.

Mizruchi, Mark S. 1996. "What Do Interlocks Do? An Analysis, Critique, and Assessment of Research on Interlocking Directorates." *Annual Review of Sociology* 22:271–298.

Moaddel, Mansoor. 1992. *Class, Politics, and Ideology in the Iranian Revolution.* New York: Columbia University Press.

Moerman, Michael. 1968. "Being Lue: Uses and Abuses of Ethnic Identification." Pp. 153–169 in *Essays on the Problem of Tribe.* Ed. June Helm. Seattle: University of Washington Press.

Mohanty, Chandra Talpade. 1991. "Under Western Eyes: Feminist Scholarship and Colonial Discourses." Pp. 51–80 in *Third World Women and the Politics of Feminism.* Ed. Chandra Mohanty, Ann Russo, and Lourdes Torres. Bloomington: Indiana University Press.

Mohr, John. 1994. "Soldiers, Mothers, Tramps and Others: Discourse Roles in the 1907 New York City Charity Directory." *Poetics* 22:327–357.

———. 1998. "Measuring Meaning Structures." *Annual Review of Sociology* 24:345–370.

Mohr, John, and Vincent Duquenne. 1997. "The Duality of Culture and Practice: Poverty Relief in New York City, 1888–1917." *Theory and Society* 26 (2–3): 305–356.

Mohr, Reinhard. 1992. *Zaungäste: Die Generation, die nach der Revolte kam.* Frankfurt am Main: S. Fischer.

Mokyr, Joel. 1990. *The Lever of Riches: Technological Creativity and Economic Progress.* New York: Oxford University Press.

———. 1992. "Technological Inertia in Economic History." *Journal of Economic History* 52:325–338.

———. 1994. "Savings, Investment, and Economic Growth." Pp. 230–254 in *Capitalism in Context: Essays on Economic Development and Cultural Change in Honor of R. M. Hartwell.* Ed. John A. James and Mark Thomas. Chicago: University of Chicago Press.

———. 1999. "Editor's Introduction: The New Economic History and the Industrial Revolution." Pp. 1–127 in *The British Industrial Revolution: An Economic Perspective*, 2nd ed. Ed. Joel Mokyr. Boulder, Colo.: Westview Press.

Montgomery, James D. 1992. "Job Search and Network Composition: Implications of the Strength-of-Weak-Ties Hypothesis." *American Sociological Review* 57:586–596.

Mooers, Colin. 1991. *The Making of Bourgeois Europe*. London: Verso.

Moore, Barrington. 1965. *Soviet Politics—The Dilemma of Power: The Role of Ideas in Social Change*. New York: Harper and Row.

———. 1966. *Social Origins of Dictatorship and Democracy: Lord and Peasant in the Making of the Modern World*. Boston: Beacon Press.

———. 1969. *Social Origins of Dictatorship and Democracy: Lord and Peasant in the Making of the Modern World*. Harmondsworth: Penguin.

Morawska, Ewa. 1998. "A Historical Turn in Feminism and Historical Sociology." *Social Politics* 5:38–47.

Morley, D., and K. Robins. 1995. *Spaces of Identity: Global Media, Electronic Landscapes and Cultural Boundaries*. London: Routledge.

Morris, Aldon. 1984. *The Origins of the Civil Rights Movement: Black Communities Organizing for Change*. New York: Free Press.

Morris, Cynthia Taft. 1995. "How Fast and Why Did Early Capitalism Benefit the Majority?" *Journal of Economic History* 55:211–226.

Morris, Ian. 1986. "Gift and Commodity in Archaic Greece." *Man* 21:1–17.

Moskos, Charles. 1970. *The American Enlisted Man*. New York: Russell Sage Foundation.

Moskos, Charles, and Frank R. Wood. 1989. *The Military: More Than Just a Job?* Washington, D.C.: Pergammon-Brasseys.

Moss, Peter. 1978. *Modern World History*. St. Albans: Hart-Davis Educational.

Mosse, George. 1990. *Fallen Soldiers: Reshaping the Memory of World Wars*. Oxford: Oxford University Press.

Mouffe, C. 1995. "Democratic Politics and the Question of Identity." In *The Identity in Question*. Ed. J. Rajchman. New York: Routledge.

Mueller, John. 2000. "The Banality of 'Ethnic War.'" *International Security* 25:42–70.

Muldrew, Craig. 1998. *The Economy of Obligation: The Culture of Credit and Social Relations in Early Modern England*. New York: St. Martin's Press.

Mullins, Nicholas C., with the assistance of Carolyn J. Mullins. 1973. *Theories and Theory Groups in Contemporary American Sociology*. New York: Harper and Row.

Murad, Mehmet. 1891. *Turfanda Mı Yoksa Turfa Mı, Milli Roman*. Istanbul: Mahmud Bey.

Murray, C. A. 1984. *Losing Ground: American Social Policy, 1950–1980*. New York: Basic Books.

Mustashar al-Dawlah, Mirza Yusuf Khan. 1985. *Yak Kalamah*. Ed. Sadiq Sajjadi. Tehran: Nashr-i Tarikh-i Iran.

Mustawfi, 'Abdullah. 1945. *Sharh-i Zindagani-i Man ya Tarikh-i Ijtima'i va Idari-i Dawrah-'i Qajariyah*, vol. 1. Tehran: 'Ilmi.

Myles, John. 1984. *Old Age in the Welfare State: The Political Economy of Public Pensions*. Boston: Little, Brown.

Myles, John, and Jill Quadagno. 2002. "Political Theories of the Welfare State." *Social Service Review* 76:34–57.

Nabokov, Vladimir. 1967. *Speak Memory: An Autobiography Revisited*. New York: Vintage Books.

Nadel, S. F. 1957. *A Theory of Social Structure*. London: Cohen and West.

Nagel, Ernest. 1979 [1961]. *The Structure of Scientific Explantion*. Indianapolis, Ind.: Hackett.

Nairn, Tom. 1977. *The Break-Up of Britain: Crisis and Neo-Nationalism*. London: New Left Books.

Nancy, Jean-Luc. 2000. *Being Singular Plural*. Stanford, Calif.: Stanford University Press.

Naples, Nancy. 1997. "The 'New Consensus' on the Gendered 'Social Contract': The 1987–1988 U.S. Congressional Hearings on Welfare Reform." *Signs* 22 (4): 907–945.

Neal, Larry. 1990. *The Rise of Financial Capitalism: International Capital Markets in the Age of Reason*. Cambridge: Cambridge University Press.

Nee, Victor. 2000. "The Role of the State in Making a Market Economy." *Journal of Institutional and Theoretical Economics* 156:64–88.

Nee, Victor, and Yang Cao. 1999. "Path Dependent Societal Transformation: Stratification in Hybrid Mixed Economies." *Theory and Society* 28:799–834.

Neeson, J. M. 1993. *Commoners: Common Right, Enclosure and Social Change in England, 1700–1820*. Cambridge: Cambridge University Press.

Nef, John U. 1950. *War and Human Progress: An Essay on the Rise of Industrial Civilization*. Cambridge, Mass.: Harvard University Press.

Nelson, Barbara. 1990. "The Origins of the Two-Channel Welfare State: Workmen's Compensation and Mothers' Aid." Pp. 123–151 in *Women, the State, and Welfare*. Ed. Linda Gordon. Madison: University of Wisconsin Press.

Neuhouser, Kevin. 1989. "The Radicalization of the Brazilian Catholic Church in Comparative Perspective." *American Sociological Review* 54 (2): 233–244.

Neumann, Franz L. 1944. *Behemoth: The Structure and Practice of National Socialism, 1933–1944*. Oxford: Oxford University Press.

Nevins, Allan. 1954–1963. *Ford*. New York: Charles Scribner's Sons.

Newell, Margaret Ellen. 1998. *From Dependency to Independence: Economic Revolution in Colonial New England*. Ithaca, N.Y.: Cornell University Press.

Nichols, Elizabeth. 1986. "Skocpol and Revolution: Comparative Analysis vs. Historical Conjuncture." *Comparative Social Research* 9:163–186.

Nimni, Ephraim. 1991. *Marxism and Nationalism: Theoretical Origins of a Political Crisis*. London: Pluto Press.

Niyazi, Ahmed. 1908. *Hatırat-i Niyazi Yahud Tarihçe-i İnkılab-ı Kebir-i Osmaniden Bir Sahife*. Istanbul: Sabah Matbassı.

Noddings, Nel. 2002. *Starting at Home: Caring and Social Policy*. Berkeley: University of California Press.

Noiriel, Gérard. 1991. *La Tyrannie du national: Le Droit d'asile en Europe 1793–1993*. Paris: Calmann-Lévy.

Norkus, Zenonas. 2001. *Max Weber and Rational Choice*. Marburg: Metropolis-Verlag.

North, Douglass C. 1981. *Structure and Change in Economic History*. New York: W. W. Norton.

——. 1990. *Institutions, Institutional Change and Economic Performance*. Cambridge: Cambridge University Press.

North, Douglass C., and Robert Paul Thomas. 1973. *The Rise of the Western World: A New Economic History*. Cambridge: Cambridge University Press.

North, Douglass C., and Barry R. Weingast. 1989. "Constitutions and Commitment: The Evolution of Institutions Governing Public Choice in Seventeenth-Century England." *Journal of Economic History* 49:803–832.

Novak, William J. 1996. *The People's Welfare: Law and Regulation in Nineteenth-Century America*. Chapel Hill: University of North Carolina Press.

Nuri, Osman. 1911. *Abdülhamid-i Sani ve Devr-i Saltanatı: Hayat-i Hususiye ve Siyasiyesi*, 3 volumes in 1. Dersaadet: Matbaa-i Osmaniye.

Nussbaum, M. C. 2000. *Women and Human Development: The Capabilities Approach*. Cambridge: Cambridge University Press.

Nussbaum, M. C., and J. Cohen. 1996. *For Love of Country: Debating the Limits of Patriotism*. Boston: Beacon Press.

Oakes, Guy. 1993. "The Thing That Would Not Die: Notes on Refutation." In *Weber's Protestant Ethic:*

Origins, Evidence, Contexts. Ed. Hartmut Lehmann and Guenther Roth. Cambridge: Cambridge University Press.

Oberschall, Anthony. 1996. "The Great Transition: China, Hungary, and Sociology Exit Socialism into the Market." *American Journal of Sociology* 101: 1028–1041.

O'Brien, Conor Cruise. 1988. *God Land: Reflections on Religion and Nationalism.* Cambridge, Mass.: Harvard University Press.

O'Brien, P. K., and D. Heath. 1994. "English and French Landowners, 1688–1789." Pp. 23–62 in *Landowners, Capitalists and Entrepreneurs: Essays for Sir John Habakkuk.* Ed. F. M. L. Thompson. Oxford: Clarendon Press.

O'Connor, Alice. 2001. *Poverty Knowledge: Social Science, Social Policy, and the Poor in Twentieth-Century U.S. History.* Princeton, N.J.: Princeton University Press.

O'Connor, James. 1973. *The Fiscal Crisis of the State.* New York: St. Martin's Press.

O'Connor, Julia S. 1993. "Gender, Class and Citizenship in the Comparative Analysis of Welfare State Regimes: Theoretical and Methodological Issues." *British Journal of Sociology* 44:501–518.

O'Connor, Julia S., Ann Shola Orloff, and Sheila Shaver. 1999. *States, Markets, Families: Gender, Liberalism and Social Policy in Australia, Canada, Great Britain and the United States.* Cambridge: Cambridge University Press.

O'Connor, Julia S., and Gregg Olsen, eds. 1998. *Power Resources Theory and the Welfare State.* Toronto: University of Toronto Press.

O'Connor, William Thomas. 1942. *Naturalism and the Pioneers of American Sociology.* Washington, D.C.: Catholic University of America Press.

O'Dea, Thomas F. 1966. *The Sociology of Religion.* Englewood Cliffs, N.J.: Prentice-Hall.

O'Donnell, Guillermo. 1978. "Reflections on the Patterns of Change in the Bureaucratic-Authoritarian State." *Latin American Research Review* 13:3–37.

Offe, Claus. 1984. *The Contradictions of the Welfare State.* Cambridge, Mass.: MIT Press.

Offer, Avner. 1997. "Between the Gift and the Market: The Economy of Regard." *Economic History Review* 50:450–476.

Office of Management and Budget. 1994. "Standards for the Classification of Federal Data on Race and Ethnicity." *http://www.whitehouse.gov/omb/fedreg/notice_15.html.*

Okin, S. M., et al. 1999. *Is Multiculturalism Bad for Women?* Princeton, N.J.: Princeton University Press.

Olasky, M. N. 1992. *The Tragedy of American Compassion.* Washington, D.C.: Regnery Gateway.

Oldfield, A. 1990. *Citizenship and Community: Civic Republicanism and the Modern World.* London: Routledge.

Olick, Jeffrey K., and Daniel Levy. 1997. "Collective Memory and Cultural Constraint: Holocaust Myth and Rationality in German Politics." *American Sociological Review* 62 (6): 921–936.

Olick, Jeffrey K., ed. 2003. *States of Memory: Continuities, Conflicts, and Transformations in National Retrospection.* Durham, N.C.: Duke University Press.

Olson, Daniel V. 1999. "Religious Pluralism and Affiliation among Canadian Counties and Cities." *Journal for the Scientific Study of Religion* 38:490–508.

Olson, Mancur. 1965. *The Logic of Collective Action: Public Goods and the Theory of Groups.* Cambridge, Mass.: Harvard University Press.

———. 1982. *The Rise and Decline of Nations: Economic Growth, Stagflation, and Social Rigidities.* New Haven, Conn.: Yale University Press.

Ong, Aihwa. 1999. *Flexible Citizenship: The Cultural Logics of Transnationality.* Durham, N.C.: Duke University Press.

Oommen, T. K. 1997a. *Citizenship and National Identity: From Colonialism to Globalism.* Thousand Oaks, Calif.: Sage.

———. 1997b. *Citizenship, Nationality, and Ethnicity: Reconciling Competing Identities.* Oxford: Blackwell.

Orloff, Ann Shola. 1991. "Gender in Early U.S. Social Policy." *Journal of Policy History* 3:249–281.

——. 1993a. "Gender and the Social Rights of Citizenship: The Comparative Analysis of Gender Relations and Welfare States." *American Sociological Review* 58 (3): 303–328.

——. 1993b. *The Politics of Pensions: A Comparative Analysis of Britain, Canada and the United States, 1880s–1940.* Madison: University of Wisconsin Press.

——. 1996. "Gender in the Welfare State." *Annual Review of Sociology* 22: 51–78.

——. 1997. "On Jane Lewis's Male Breadwinner Regime Typology." *Social Politics* 4 (2): 188–202.

——. 2000. "Farewell to Maternalism: Welfare Reform, Liberalism, and the End of Mothers' Right to Choose between Employment and Full-Time Care." Evanston, Ill.: Institute for Policy Research, Northwestern University.

——. Forthcoming. *Farewell to Maternalism: U.S. Welfare Reform, Care, Employment, and Shifting Citizenship Claims.* Durham, N.C.: Duke University Press.

Orloff, Ann Shola, and Renee Monson. 2002. "Citizens, Workers or Fathers? Men in the History of U.S. Social Policy." Pp. 61–91 in *Making Men into Fathers.* Ed. Barbara Hobson. Cambridge: Cambridge University Press.

Orloff, Ann Shola, and Theda Skocpol. 1984. "Why Not Equal Protection? Explaining the Politics of Public Social Spending in Britain, 1900–1911, and the United States, 1880s–1920." *American Sociological Review* 49:726–750.

Ortner, Sherry B. 1984. "Theory in Anthropology since the Sixties." *Comparative Studies in Society and History* 26 (1): 126–166.

Oxford English Dictionary. 1971. Vol. 1, compact edition. New York: Oxford University Press.

Pack, Howard. 1994. "Endogenous Growth Theory: Intellectual Appeal and Empirical Shortcomings." *Journal of Economic Perspectives* 8:55–72.

Padamsee, Tasleem J., and Julia Adams. 2002. "Signs and Regimes Revisited." *Social Politics* 9(2): 187–202.

Padgett, John F., and Christopher K. Ansell. 1993. "Robust Action and the Rise of the Medici, 1400–1434." *American Journal of Sociology* 98 (6): 1259–1319.

Paige, Jeffrey M. 1975. *Agrarian Revolution: Social Movements and Export Agriculture in the Underdeveloped World.* New York: Free Press.

——. 1997. *Coffee and Power: Revolution and the Rise of Democracy in Central America.* Cambridge, Mass.: Harvard University Press.

Palmer, R. R. 1959–1964. *The Age of the Democratic Revolutions,* 2 vols. Princeton, N.J.: Princeton University Press.

Paret, Peter. 1986. "Napoleon and the Revolution in War." Pp. 123–142 in *The Makers of Modern Strategy.* Ed. Peter Paret. Princeton, N.J.: Princeton University Press.

——. 1992. *Understanding War: Essays on Clausewitz and the History of Military Power.* Princeton, N.J.: Princeton University Press.

Parker, Geoffrey. 1976. "The 'Military Revolution,' 1560–1660: A Myth?" *Journal of Modern History* 48:195–224.

——. 1988. *The Military Revolution: Military Innovation and the Rise of the West, 1500–1800.* Cambridge: Cambridge University Press.

——. 1994. "Early Modern Europe." Pp. 40–58 in *The Laws of War: Constraints on Warfare in the Western World.* Ed. Michael Howard, George J. Andreopoulos, and Mark R. Shulman. New Haven, Conn.: Yale University Press.

——. 1995 [1976]. "The 'Military Revolution': A Myth?" Pp. 37–54 in *The Military Revolution Debate: Readings on the Military Transformation of Early Modern Europe.* Ed. Clifford J. Rogers. Boulder, Colo.: Westview Press.

Parker, Stephen, Gavin Tritt, and Wing Thye Woo. 1997. "Some Lessons Learned from the Comparison of Transitions in Asia and Eastern Europe." Pp. 3–16 in *Economies in Transition: Comparing Asia and Eastern Europe.* Ed. Wing Thye Woo, Stephen Parker, and Jeffrey D. Sachs. Cambridge, Mass.: MIT Press.

Parker, William N. 1984. *Europe, America, and the Wider World: Essays on the Economic History of Western Capitalism*, vol. 1: *Europe and the World Economy*. Cambridge: Cambridge University Press.

Parlin, Bradley W. 1976. *Immigrant Professionals in the United States: Discrimination in the Scientific Labor Market*. New York: Praeger.

Parry, Jonathan. 1989. "On the Moral Perils of Exchange." Pp. 64–93 in *Money and the Morality of Exchange*. Ed. Jonathan Parry and Maurice Bloch. Cambridge: Cambridge University Press.

Parsa, Misagh. 2000. *States, Ideologies, and Social Revolutions: A Comparative Analysis of Iran, Nicaragua, and the Philippines*. New York: Cambridge University Press.

Parsons, Talcott. 1935. "The Place of Ultimate Values in Sociological Theory." *International Journal of Ethics* 45:282–316.

——. 1937. *The Structure of Social Action*, 2 vols. New York: Free Press.

——. 1949. *The Structure of Social Action*. New York: Free Press.

——. 1966. *Societies: Evolutionary and Comparative Perspectives*. Englewood Cliffs, N.J.: Prentice-Hall.

——. 1971. *The System of Modern Societies*. Englewood Cliffs, N.J.: Prentice-Hall.

——. 1993. *Talcott Parsons on National Socialism*. Ed. Ute Gerhardt. New York: De Gruyter.

Parsons, Talcott, and Neil J. Smelser. 1956. *Economy and Society: A Study in the Integration of Economic and Social Theory*. London: Routledge and Kegan Paul.

Pateman, Carole. 1988a. "The Patriarchal Welfare State." Pp. 231–278 in *Democracy and the Welfare State*. Ed. Amy Gutmann. Princeton, N.J.: Princeton University Press.

——. 1988b. *The Sexual Contract*. Stanford, Calif.: Stanford University Press.

——. 1989. *The Disorder of Women: Democracy, Feminism, and Political Theory*. Stanford, Calif.: Stanford University Press.

Patterson, Orlando. 1990. *Slavery and Social Death: A Comparative Study*. Cambridge, Mass.: Harvard University Press.

Pearson, Karl. 1892. *The Grammar of Science*. London: Walter Scott.

Pedersen, Susan. 1993. *Family, Dependence, and the Origins of the Welfare State: Britain and France, 1914–1945*. New York: Cambridge University Press.

Peirce, Charles S. 1931–1932. *Collected Papers*. Cambridge, Mass.: Harvard University Press.

——. 1955. *Philosophical Writings of Peirce*. Ed. Justus Buchler. New York: Dover Publishers.

Pendergast, Tom. 1998. "Consuming Questions: Scholarship on Consumerism in America to 1940." *American Studies International* 36:23–43.

Peng, Ito. 2002. "Social Care in Crisis: Gender, Demography, and Welfare State Restructuring in Japan." *Social Politics* 9:411–443.

Perelman, Michael. 2000. *The Invention of Capitalism: Classical Political Economy and the Secret History of Primitive Accumulation*. Durham, N.C.: Duke University Press.

Perrow, Charles. 1990. "Economic Theories of Organization." Pp. 121–152 in *Structures of Capital*. Ed. Sharon Zukin and Paul DiMaggio. Cambridge: Cambridge University Press.

Petersen, Mitchell A., and Raghuram G. Rajan. 1994. "The Benefits of Lending Relationships: Evidence from Small Business Data." *Journal of Finance* 49:3–37.

Petersen, William. 1987. "Politics and the Measurement of Ethnicity." Pp. 187–233 in *The Politics of Numbers*. Ed. William Alonso and Paul Starr. New York: Russell Sage Foundation.

Petersen, Claes. 1979. *Peter the Great's Administrative and Judicial Reforms*. Lund, Sweden: Bloms Boktryckeri AB.

Pettee, George S. 1938. *The Process of Revolution*. New York: Harper and Brothers.

Pickering, Andrew. 1995. *The Mangle of Practice*. Chicago: University of Chicago Press.

Pickles, John, and Adrian Smith. 1998. "Preface." P. xvii in *Theorising Transition: The Political Economy of Post-Communist Transformations*. Ed. John Pickles and Adrian Smith. London: Routledge.

Pierson, Paul. 1994. *Dismantling the Welfare State? Reagan, Thatcher and the Politics of Retrenchment*. Cambridge: Cambridge University Press.

———. 2000. "Increasing Returns, Path Dependence, and the Study of Politics." *American Political Science Review* 94 (2): 251–267.

———. 2001. "Post-Industrial Pressures on the Mature Welfare States." Pp. 80–104 in *The New Politics of the Welfare State*. Ed. Paul Pierson. New York: Oxford University Press.

———, ed. 2001. *The New Politics of the Welfare State*. New York: Oxford University Press.

Pieterse, Jan. 2001. *Development Theory: Deconstructions/Reconstructions*. London: Sage.

Pirenne, Henri. 1914. "The Stages in the Social History of Capitalism." *American Historical Review* 19:494–515.

———. 1952 [1925]. *Medieval Cities: Their Origins and the Revival of Trade*. Princeton, N.J.: Princeton University Press.

Pistor-Hatam, Anja. 1996. "Progress and Civilization in Nineteenth Century Japan: The Far Eastern State as a Model for Modernization." *Iranian Studies* 29 (1–2): 111–126.

Piven, Frances Fox, and Richard Cloward. 1971. *Regulating the Poor: The Functions of Public Welfare*. New York: Vintage.

———. 1977. *Poor People's Movements: Why They Succeed, How They Fail*. New York: Random House.

Podolny, Joel M., and Fiona M. Scott Morton. 1999. "Social Status, Entry and Predation: The Case of British Shipping Cartels 1879–1929." *Journal of Industrial Economics* 47: 41–67.

Poggi, Gianfranco. 1978. *The Development of the Modern State: A Sociological Introduction*. Stanford, Calif.: Stanford University Press.

Polanyi, Karl. 1957a. "Aristotle Discovers the Economy." Pp. 64–94 in *Trade and Market in the Early Empires*. Ed. Karl Polanyi, Conrad M. Arensberg, and Harry W. Pearson. Chicago: Regnery.

———. 1957b. "The Economy as Instituted Process." In *Trade and Market in the Early Empires*. Ed. Karl Polanyi, Conrad M. Arensberg, and Harry W. Pearson. Chicago: Regnery.

———. 1957c [1944]. *The Great Transformation: The Political and Economic Origins of Our Time*. Boston: Beacon Press.

———. 2000 [1944]. *The Great Transformation: The Political and Economic Origins of Our Time*. Boston: Beacon Press.

Pomeranz, Kenneth. 2000. *The Great Divergence: Europe, China, and the Making of the Modern World Economy*. Princeton, N.J.: Princeton University Press.

Popper, Karl R. 1992 [1934]. *The Logic of Scientific Discovery*. London: Routledge.

Porter, Theodore M. 1955. *Trust in Numbers: The Pursuit of Objectivity in Science and Public Life*. Princeton, N.J.: Princeton University Press.

Posen, Barry R. 1993. "Nationalism, the Mass Army and Military Power." *International Security* 18 (2): 80–124.

Postan, M. M. 1937. "The Chronology of Labor Services." *Transactions of the Royal Historical Society*, fourth series, 20:169–193.

———. 1966. "Medieval Agrarian Society in Its Prime: England." Pp. 549–632 in *The Cambridge Economic History of Europe*, vol. 1: *The Agrarian Life of the Middle Ages*. Ed. M. M. Postan and H. J. Habakkuk. Cambridge: Cambridge University Press.

Poster, Winnifred. 1998. "Globalization, Gender, and the Workplace: Women and Men in an American Multinational Corporation in India." *Journal of Developing Societies* 14 (1): 40–65.

———. 2001. "Dangerous Places and Nimble Fingers: Discourses of Gender Discrimination and Rights in Global Organizations." *International Journal of Politics, Culture, and Society* 15 (1): 77–105.

———. 2002. "Racialism, Sexuality, and Masculinity: Gendering the Global Ethnography of the Workplace." *Social Politics: International Studies in Gender, State, and Society* 9 (1): 126–158.

Postone, Moishe. 1993. *Time, Labor, and Social Domination: A Reinterpretation of Marx's Critical Theory*. New York: Cambridge University Press.

Poulantzas, Nicos. 1973. *Political Power and Social Classes*. London: Verso.

Povinelli, Elisabeth. 2001. "Radical Worlds: The Anthropology of Incommensurability and Inconceivability." *Annual Review of Anthropology* 30:319–334.

Powell, Walter W. 1990. "Neither Market nor Hierarchy: Network Forms of Organization." *Research in Organizational Behavior* 12:295–336.

Pred, Allan. 2000. *Even in Sweden: Racisms, Racialized Spaces, and the Popular Geographical Imagination.* Berkeley: University of California Press.

Pred, Allan, and Michael John Watts. 1992. *Reworking Modernity: Capitalisms and Symbolic Discontent.* New Brunswick, N.J.: Rutgers University Press.

Prelec, Drazen, Birger Wernerfelt, and Florian Zettelmeyer. 1997. "The Role of Inference in Context Effects: Inferring What You Want from What Is Available." *Journal of Consumer Research* 24 (June): 118–125.

Prest, Wilfird R. 1998. *Albion Ascendant: English History, 1660–1815.* Oxford: Oxford University Press.

Preuss, U. 1995. "Citizenship and Identity: Aspects of a Theory of Citizenship." In *Democracy and Constitutional Culture in the Union of Europe.* Ed. Richard Bellamy, V. Buffachi, and Dario Castiglione. London: Lothian Foundation Press.

Procacci, G. 2001. "Poor Citizens." Pp. 49–68 in *Citizenship, Markets and the State.* Ed. K. Eder, C. Crouch, and D. Tambini. Oxford: Oxford University Press.

Procacci, G., and N. Salamone. 2000. *Mutamento sociale e identità: La sociologia di fronte alla contemporaneità.* Milan: Guerini Studio.

Prochaska, David. 1990. *Making Algeria French: Colonialism in Bône, 1870–1920.* Cambridge: Cambridge University Press.

Prothero, Iowerth. 1997. *Radical Artisans in England and France, 1830–1870.* Cambridge: Cambridge University Press.

Pryor, John H. 1977. "The Origins of the Commenda Contract." *Speculum* 52:5–37.

Putnam, R. D. 2000. *Bowling Alone: The Collapse and Revival of American Community.* New York: Simon and Schuster.

Putnam, R. D., et al. 1993. *Making Democracy Work: Civic Traditions in Modern Italy.* Princeton, N.J.: Princeton University Press.

Pye, Lucian W. 1991. "Political Culture Revisited." *Political Psychology* 12:487–508.

Quadagno, Jill. 1988. *The Transformation of Old Age Security: Class and Politics in the American Welfare State.* Chicago: University of Chicago Press.

———. 1994. *The Color of Welfare: How Racism Undermined the War on Poverty.* New York: Oxford University Press.

———. 2000. "Another Face of Inequality: Racial and Ethnic Exclusion in the Welfare State." *Social Politics* 7:227–237.

Quine, W. V. 1960. *Word and Object.* Cambridge, Mass.: MIT Press.

———. 1987. "Indeterminacy of Translation Again." *Journal of Philosophy* 84 (1): 5–10.

Radice, Hugo. 2000. "Globalization and National Capitalisms: Theorizing Convergence and Differentiation." *Review of International Political Economy* 7:719–742.

Raffin, Anne. 2002a. "Easternization Meets Westernization: Patriotic Youth Organizations in French Indochina during World War II." *French Politics, Culture and Society* 20 (2): 121–140.

———. 2002b. "The Integration of Difference in French Indochina during World War II: Organizations and Ideology Concerning Youth." *Theory and Society* 31 (3): 365–390.

Ragin, Charles. 1987. *The Comparative Method: Moving beyond Qualitative and Quantitative Strategies.* Berkeley: University of California Press.

———. 2000. *Fuzzy-Set Social Science.* Chicago: University of Chicago Press.

Ragin, Charles, and Daniel Chirot. 1984. "The World System of Immanuel Wallerstein: Sociology and Politics as History." Pp. 276–312 in *Vision and Method in Historical Sociology.* Ed. Theda Skocpol. New York: Cambridge University Press.

Rajchman, J. 1995. *The Identity in Question.* New York: Routledge.

Rajogopal, Arvind. 2001. *Politics after Television: Hindu Nationalism and the Reshaping of the Public in India.* Cambridge: Cambridge University Press.

Ralston, David B. 1990. *Importing the European Army: The Introduction of European Military Techniques and Institutions in the Extra-European World, 1600–1914*. Chicago: University of Chicago Press.

Ramirez, Francisco. 1987. "Institutional Analysis." Pp. 316–328 in *Institutional Structure: Constituting State, Society, and the Individual*. Ed. George M. Thomas, John W. Meyer, Francisco O. Ramirez, and John Boli. Newbury Park, Calif.: Sage.

Ramirez, Francisco, Yasemin Soysal, and Suzanne Shanahan. 1997. "The Changing Logic of Political Citizenship: Cross-National Acquisition of Women's Suffrage Rights, 1890–1990." *American Sociological Review* 62:735–745.

Rammstedt, Otthein. 1988. "Wertfreiheit und die Konstitution der Soziologie in Deutschland." *Zeitschrift für Soziologie* 17 (4): 264–271.

Rawls, J. 1971. *A Theory of Justice*. Cambridge, Mass.: Belknap Press.

Ray, Raka. 1999. *Fields of Protest: Women's Movements in India*. Minneapolis: University of Minnesota Press.

Redlich, Fritz. 1964–1965. *The German Military Enterpriser and His Workforce: A Study in Economic History*, 2 vols. Wiesbaden: Franz Steiner.

Reese, Ellen. 2001. "The Politics of Motherhood: The Restriction of Poor Mothers' Welfare Rights in the United States, 1949–1960." *Social Politics* 8:65–112.

Refik, Ahmed. 1908. *İnkılab-i Azim*. Istanbul: Asır Matbassı.

Reiter, Dan, and Allan C. Stam. 2002. *Democracies at War*. Princeton, N.J.: Princeton University Press.

Renan, Ernest. 1994 [1882]. "Qu'est-ce qu'une nation?" Pp. 17–18 in *Nationalism*. Ed. John Hutchinson and Anthony D. Smith. New York: Oxford.

Reverby, Susan. 1987. *Ordered to Care: The Dilemma of American Nursing, 1850–1945*. New York: Cambridge University Press.

Rex, J. 1996. *Ethnic Minorities in the Modern Nation State: Studies in the Theory of Multiculturalism and Political Integration*. Houndmills, Basingstoke: Macmillan, in association with Centre for Research in Ethnic Relations, University of Warwick.

Rex, J., and B. Drury. 1994. *Ethnic Mobilisation in a Multi-Cultural Europe*. Aldershot, Hants, U. K.: Avebury.

Riley, Denise. 1989. *Am I That Name? Feminism and the Category of Women in History*. Minneapolis: University of Minnesota Press.

Rimlinger, Gaston. 1971. *Welfare Policy and Industrialization in Europe, America, and Russia*. New York: Wiley.

Riska, Elianne, and Katarina Weger, eds. 1993. *Gender, Work, and Medicine: Women and the Medical Division of Labour*. London: Sage.

Roberts, Dorothy. 1993. "Racism and Patriarchy in the Meaning of Motherhood." *Journal of Gender and the Law* 1:1–38.

———. 1995. "Race, Gender, and the Value of Mothers' Work." *Social Politics* 2:195–207.

Roberts, Michael. 1995 [1967]. "The Military Revolution, 1560–1660." Pp. 13–36 in *The Military Revolution Debate: Readings on the Military Transformation of Early Modern Europe*. Ed. Clifford J. Rogers. Boulder, Colo.: Westview Press.

Robertson, Roland, comp. 1969. *Sociology of Religion: Selected Readings*. New York: Penguin.

Robinson, Cedric. 1983. *Black Marxism: The Making of the Black Radical Tradition*. London: Zed.

Rodney, Walter. 1981 [1972]. *How Europe Underdeveloped Africa*. Washington, D.C.: Howard University Press.

Roemer, John. 1986. *Analytical Marxism*. Cambridge: Cambridge University Press.

Rogers, Clifford J., ed. 1995. *The Military Revolution Debate: Readings on the Military Transformation of Early Modern Europe*. Boulder, Colo.: Westview Press.

Rokkan, Stein. 1970. *Citizens, Elections, Parties: Approaches to the Comparative Study of the Processes of Development*. New York: David McKay.

Romer, Paul M. 1994. "The Origins of Endogenous Growth." *Journal of Economic Perspectives* 8:3–22.

Róna-Tas, Ákos. 1994. "The First Shall Be Last? Entrepreneurship and Communist Cadres in the Transition from Socialism." *American Journal of Sociology* 100 (1): 40–69.

——. 1997. *The Great Surprise of the Small Transformation: The Demise of Communism and the Rise of the Private Sector in Hungary.* Ann Arbor: University of Michigan Press.

Root, Hilton L. 1987. *Peasants and King in Burgundy: Agrarian Foundations of French Absolutism.* Berkeley: University of California Press.

——. 1994. *The Fountain of Privilege: Political Foundations of Markets in Old Regime France and England.* Berkeley: University of California Press.

Rose, Sonya. 1986. "Gender at Work: Sex, Class and Industrial Capitalism." *History Workshop Journal* 21 (spring).

——. 1988. "Proto-Industry, Women's Work and the Household Economy in the Transition to Industrial Capitalism." *Journal of Family History* 13 (spring): 181–193.

——. 1992. *Limited Livelihoods: Gender and Class in Nineteenth-Century England.* Berkeley: University of California Press.

Ross, Dorothy. 1991. *The Origins of American Social Science.* Cambridge: Cambridge University Press.

Ross, Fiona. 2000. "Interests and Choice in the 'Not Quite So New' Politics of Welfare." *West European Politics* 23:11–34.

Ross, Trevor. 1992. "Copyright and the Invention of Tradition." *Eighteenth-Century Studies* 26:1–27.

Rostow, W. W. 1960. *The Stages of Economic Growth: A Non-Communist Manifesto.* Cambridge: Cambridge University Press.

Roth, Guenther. 1963. *The Social Democrats in Imperial Germany: A Study in Working-Class Isolation and National Integration.* Totowa, N.J.: Bedminister Press.

——. 1979. "Duration and Rationalization: Fernand Braudel and Max Weber." In *Max Weber's Vision and History: Ethics and Methods.* Ed. Guenther Roth and Wolfgang Schluchter. Berkeley: University of California Press.

Rothbart, Myron, and Marjorie Taylor. 1992. "Category Labels and Social Reality: Do We View Social Categories as Natural Kinds?" In *Language, Interaction and Social Cognition.* Ed. Gün R. Semin and Klaus Fiedler. London: Sage.

Rothschild, Joseph. 1981. *Ethnopolitics: A Conceptual Framework.* New York: Columbia University Press.

Rothstein, Bo. 1992. "Labor-Market Institutions and Working-Class Strength." In *Structuring Politics: Historical Institutionalism in Comparative Politics.* Ed. Sven Steinmo, Kathleen Thelen, and Frank Longstreth. New York: Cambridge University Press.

Roudinesco, Elisabeth. 2001. *Why Psychoanalysis?* New York: Columbia University Press.

Roudometof, Victor. 2002. *Collective Memory, National Identity, and Ethnic Conflict.* Westport, Conn.: Praeger.

Rowbotham, Sheila. 1972. *Women, Resistance, and Revolution: A History of Women and Revolution in the Modern World.* New York: Pantheon Books.

Roxborough, Ian. 1979. *Theories of Underdevelopment.* London: Macmillan.

——. 1988. "Modernization Theory Revisited: A Review Article." *Comparative Studies in Society and History* 1 (30): 753–761.

——. 1994. "Clausewitz and the Sociology of War." *British Journal of Sociology* 45:619–636.

Roy, William G. 1983. "The Unfolding of the Interlocking Directorate Structure of the United States." *American Sociological Review* 48:248–257.

——. 1987. "Time, Place, and People in History and Sociology: Boundary Definitions and the Logic of Inquiry in Social Science History." *Social Science History* 11 (2): 53–62.

——. 1997. *Socializing Capital: The Rise of the Large Industrial Corporation in America.* Princeton, N.J.: Princeton University Press.

Roy, William G., and Philip Bonacich. 1988. "Interlocking Directorates and Communities of Interest among American Railroad Companies, 1905." *American Sociological Review* 53:368–379.

Royal Institute of International Affairs. 1939. *Nationalism*. London: Oxford University Press.

Royster, Charles. 1991. *The Destructive War: William Tecumseh Sherman, Stonewall Jackson, and the Americans*. New York: Vintage.

Ruane, Christine. 1995. "Clothes Shopping in Imperial Russia: The Development of Consumer Culture." *Journal of Social History* 28:765–782.

Rubinow, Isaac Max. 1913. *Social Insurance: With Special Reference to American Conditions*. New York: Henry Holt.

Rubinson, Richard. 1986. "Class Formation, Politics, and Institutions: Schooling in the United States." *American Journal of Sociology* 92 (3): 519–548.

Rudé, George. 1964. *The Crowd in History, 1730–1848*. New York: Wiley.

Rueschemeyer, Dietrich. 1973. *Lawyers and Their Society: A Comparative Study of the Legal Profession in Germany and in the United States*. Cambridge, Mass.: Harvard University Press.

Rueschemeyer, Dietrich, Evelyne Huber Stephens, and John D. Stephens. 1992. *Capitalist Development and Democracy*. Chicago: University of Chicago Press.

Rueschemeyer, Dietrich, and Theda Skocpol, eds. 1996. *States, Social Knowledge, and the Origins of Modern Social Policies*. Princeton, N.J.: Princeton University Press, and New York: Russell Sage Foundation.

Ruggie, Mary. 1984. *The State and Working Women: A Comparative Study of Britain and Sweden*. Princeton, N.J.: Princeton University Press.

Rustin, Michael. 1991. *The Good Society and Inner World*. London: Verso.

———. 1999. "Psychoanalysis: The Last Modernism?" Pp. 105–121 in *Psychoanalysis and Culture: A Kleinian Perspective*. London: Duckworth.

Sachs, Jeffrey D. 1992. "Privatization in Russia: Some Lessons from Eastern Europe." *American Economic Review* 82:43–48.

Sachs, Jeffrey D., and Katharina Pistor, eds. 1997. *The Rule of Law and Economic Reform in Russia*. Boulder, Colo.: Westview Press.

Sacks, Harvey. 1995. *Lectures on Conversation*. Oxford: Blackwell.

Sahlins, Marshall. 1981. *Historical Metaphors and Mythical Realities: Structure in the Early History of the Sandwich Islands Kingdom*. Ann Arbor: University of Michigan Press.

———. 1985. *Islands of History*. Chicago: University of Chicago Press.

———. 2002. *Waiting for Foucault, Still*. Chicago: Prickly Paradigm Press.

Said, Edward. 1979. *Orientalism*. New York: Vintage.

———. 1994. *Culture and Imperialism*. New York: Vintage.

Sainsbury, Diane, ed. 1994. *Gendering Welfare States*. Thousand Oaks, Calif.: Sage.

Salmon, Marylynn. 1982. "Women and Property in South Carolina: The Evidence from Marriage Settlements, 1730–1830." *William and Mary Quarterly* 39: 655–685.

———. 1986. *Women and the Law of Property in Early America*. Chapel Hill: University of North Carolina Press.

Salmon, Wesley C. 1984. *Scientific Explanation and the Causal Structure of the World*. Princeton, N.J.: Princeton University Press.

Sandel, M. J. 1984. *Liberalism and Its Critics*. Oxford: Blackwell.

———. 1998. *Liberalism and the Limits of Justice*. Cambridge: Cambridge University Press.

Sanderson, Stephen K. 1994. "The Theoretical Significance of the Japanese Case." *Review* 17:15–55.

Sargent, Lydia, ed. 1981. *Women and Revolution*. Boston: South End Press.

Sasaki, Masamichi, ed. 1998. *Values and Attitudes across Nations and Time*. Leiden: Brill.

Sassen, Saskia. 1991. *The Global City: New York, London, Tokyo*. Princeton, N.J.: Princeton University Press.

———. 1996. *Losing Control? Sovereignty in an Age of Globalization*. New York: Columbia University Press.

——. 1998. *Globalization and Its Discontents [Essays on the New Mobility of People and Money]*. New York: New Press.

——. 2001. *The Global City: New York, London, Tokyo*. Princeton, N.J.: Princeton University Press.

Sassoon, Anne Showstack, ed. 1987. *Women and the State: The Shifting Boundaries of Public and Private*. London: Hutchinson.

Saussure, Ferdinand de. 1959. *Course in General Linguistics*. New York: Philosophical Library.

Sayer, Andrew. 1992. *Method in Social Sciences: A Realist Approach*. London: Routledge.

Sayer, Derek. 1987. *The Violence of Abstraction: The Analytic Foundations of Historical Materialism*. Oxford: Blackwell.

——. 1992. "A Notable Administration: English State Formation and the Rise of Capitalism." *American Journal of Sociology* 97 (5): 1382–1415.

Scarry, Elaine. 1985. *The Body in Pain: The Making and Unmaking of the World*. New York: Oxford University Press.

——. 1990. "War and the Social Contract: The Right to Bear Arms." *Yale Journal of Law and the Humanities* 2:119–127.

——. 1991. "War and the Social Contract: Nuclear Policy, Distribution and the Right to Bear Arms." *University of Pennsylvania Law Review* 139:1257–1316.

——. 1996. "The Difficulty in Imagining Other People." Pp. 98–110 in *For Love of Country: Debating the Limits of Patriotism*. By Martha C. Nussbaum with Respondents. Ed. Joshua Cohen. Boston: Beacon Press.

Schama, Simon. 1987. *The Embarrassment of Riches: An Interpretation of Dutch Culture in the Golden Age*. New York: Knopf.

Scharff, Robert C. 1995. *Comte after Positivism*. Cambridge: Cambridge University Press.

Scharpf, Fritz, and Vivien Schmidt, eds. 2000. *Welfare and Work in the Open Economy*. New York: Oxford University Press.

Schegloff, Emanuel A. 2001. "Accounts of Conduct in Interaction: Interruption, Overlap, and Turn-Taking." Pp. 287–321 in *Handbook of Sociological Theory*. Ed. J. H. Turner. New York: Plenum.

Schlesinger, A. M. 1992. *The Disuniting of America*. New York: W. W. Norton.

——. 1998. *The Disuniting of America: Reflections on a Multicultural Society*. New York: W. W. Norton.

Schluchter, Wolfgang. 1989. *Rationalism, Religion, and Domination: A Weberian Perspective*. Trans. Neil Solomon. Berkeley: University of California Press.

——. 1996. *Paradoxes of Modernity: Culture and Conduct in the Theory of Max Weber*. Trans. Neil Solomon. Stanford, Calif.: Stanford University Press.

Schmidt, Leigh Eric. 1995. *Consumer Rites: The Buying and Selling of American Holidays*. Princeton, N.J.: Princeton University Press.

Schmitt, Carl. 1976 [1927]. *The Concept of the Political*. Trans. George Schwab. New Brunswick, N.J.: Rutgers University Press.

Schneiberg, Marc. 1999. "Political and Institutional Conditions for Governance by Association: Private Order and Price Controls in American Fire Insurance." *Politics and Society* 27:67–103.

Schooler, Carmi. 1996. "Cultural and Social-Structural Explanations of Cross-National Psychological Differences." *Annual Review of Sociology* 22:323–349.

Schroeder, Paul W. 1994. *The Transformation of European Politics 1763–1848*. Oxford: Clarendon Press.

Schutz, Alfred. 1962. *Collected Papers I: The Problem of Social Reality*. Ed. Maurice Natanson. The Hague: Marinus Nijhoff.

Schwartz, Michael. 1976. *Radical Protest and Social Structure: The Southern Farmers' Alliance and Cotton Tenancy, 1880–1890*. New York: Academic Press.

Schweber, Libby. 2001. "Manipulation and Articulation: Population Statistics in Nineteenth-Century France and England." *Social Research* 68(2): 547–582.

Schwendinger, Herman, and Julia R. Schwendinger. 1974. *The Sociologists of the Chair*. New York: Basic Books.

Scott, James C. 1985. *Weapons of the Weak: Everyday Forms of Peasant Resistance*. New Haven, Conn.: Yale University Press.

———. 1990. *Domination and the Arts of Resistance: Hidden Transcripts*. New Haven, Conn.: Yale University Press.

Scott, Joan W. 1986. "Gender: A Useful Category of Historical Analysis." *American Historical Review* 91:1053–1075.

———. 1988. *Gender and the Politics of History*. New York: Columbia University Press.

———. 1992. "Experience." Pp. 22–40 in *Feminists Theorize the Political*. Ed. Judith Butler and Joan W. Scott. New York: Routledge.

Scott, Samuel F. 1984. "Foreign Mercenaries, Revolutionary War, and Citizen-Soldiers in the Late Eighteenth Century." *War and Society* 2 (2): 41–58.

———. 1986. "Military Nationalism in Europe in the Aftermath of the American Revolution." Pp. 160–189 in *Peace and the Peacemakers: The Treaty of 1783*. Ed. Ronald Hoffman and Peter Albert. Charlottesville: University Press of Virginia.

Scott, W. Richard. 1998. *Organizations: Rational, Natural, and Open Systems*, 4th ed. Upper Saddle River, N.J.: Prentice-Hall.

Scruggs, W. L. 1886. "Ambiguous Citizenship." *Political Science Quarterly* 1 (2): 199–205.

Seaton, Jean. 1999. "Why Do We Think the Serbs Do It? The New 'Ethnic' Wars and the Media." *Political Quarterly* 70 (3): 254–270.

Segal, David R. 1989. *Recruiting for Uncle Sam: Citizenship and Military Manpower Policy*. Lawrence: University Press of Kansas.

Segal, David R., and Mady Weschler Segal. 1993. *Peacekeepers and Their Wives: American Military Participation in the Multinational Force of Observers*. Westport, Conn.: Greenwood Press.

Segal, Mady Weschler. 1995. "Women's Military Roles Cross-Nationally: Past, Present, and Future." *Gender and Society* 9:757–775.

Seidman, Gay. 1993. " 'No Freedom without the Women': Mobilization and Gender in South Africa, 1970–1992." *Signs* 18:291–320.

———. 1994. *Manufacturing Militance: Workers' Movements in Brazil and South Africa, 1970–1985*. Berkeley: University of California Press.

Seligman, A. B. 1992. *The Idea of Civil Society*. New York: Maxwell Macmillan International.

Sell, Susan K. 1995. "Intellectual Property Protection and Antitrust in the Developing World: Crisis, Coercion, and Choice." *International Organization* 49:315–349.

Sellars, Roy Wood. 1916. *Critical Realism*. Chicago: Rand McNally.

———. 1939. "Positivism in Contemporary Philosophic Thought." *American Sociological Review* 4 (February): 26–42.

Sevenhuijsen, Selma. 1998. *Citizenship and the Ethics of Care*. New York: Routledge.

Sewell, William H., Jr. 1967. "Marc Bloch and the Logic of Comparative History." *History and Theory* 6 (2): 208–218.

———. 1980. *Work and Revolution in France: The Language of Labor from the Old Regime to 1848*. New York: Cambridge University Press.

———. 1985. "Ideologies and Social Revolutions: Reflections on the French Case." *Journal of Modern History* 57 (1): 57–85.

———. 1990. "Collective Violence and Collective Loyalties in France: Why the French Revolution Made a Difference." *Politics and Society* 18:527–552.

———. 1992. "A Theory of Structure: Duality, Agency and Transformation." *American Journal of Sociology* 98 (1): 1–29.

———. 1994. *A Rhetoric of Bourgeois Revolution*. Durham, N.C.: Duke University Press.

———. 1996a. "Historical Events as Transformations of Structures: Inventing Revolution at the Bastille." *Theory and Society* 25 (6): 841–881.

———. 1996b. "Three Temporalities: Toward an Eventful Sociology." Pp. 245–280 in *The Historic Turn in the Human Sciences*. Ed. Terrence J. McDonald. Ann Arbor: University of Michigan Press.

———. 2005. "The Political Unconscious of Social and Cultural History, or, Confessions of a Former Quantitative Historian." In *The Politics of Method in the Human Sciences: Positivism and Its Epistemological Others*. Ed. George Steinmetz. Durham, N.C.: Duke University Press.

Shafir, Gershon. 1995. *Immigrants and Nationalists: Ethnic Conflict and Accommodation in Catalonia, the Basque Country, Latvia, and Estonia*. Albany: State University of New York Press.

———, ed. 1998. *The Citizenship Debates: A Reader*. Minneapolis: University of Minnesota Press.

Shapin, Steven. 1994. *A Social History of Truth: Civility and Science in Seventeenth-Century England*. Chicago: University of Chicago Press.

———. 1995. "Here and Everywhere: Sociology of Scientific Knowledge." *Annual Review of Sociology* 21:289–321.

Sharif Kashani, Muhammad Mahdi. 1983. *Vaqi'at-i Ittifaqiyah dar Ruzgar*. Ed. M. Ettehadieh Nezam-Mafi and S. Sa'dvandiyan. Tehran: Nashr-i Tarikh-i Iran.

Shaver, Sheila. 2002. "Gender, Welfare, Regimes, and Agency." *Social Politics* 9:203–211.

Shaw, G. 1981. "Leading Issues of Tax Policy in Developing Countries: The Economic Problems." Pp. 148–162 in *The Political Economy of Taxation*. Ed. A. Peacock and F. Forte. Oxford: Blackwell.

Shaw, Martin. 1998. "The Historical Sociology of the Future." Review of International Political Economy 5(2): 321–326.

Shaw, Stephanie J. 1996. *What a Woman Ought to Be and to Do*. Chicago: University of Chicago Press.

Sheppard, Deborah. 1989. "Organizations, Power and Sexuality: The Image and Self-Image of Women Managers." Pp. 139–157 in *The Sexuality of Organization*. Ed. Jeff Hearn et al. London: Sage.

Sherratt, Andrew. 1995. "Reviving the Grand Narrative: Archaeology and Long-Term Change." *Journal of European Archaeology* 3.

Sherwood, H. N. 1923. "Problems of Citizenship." *Journal of Negro History* 8 (2): 162–166.

Shin, Gi-Wook. 1998. "Agrarian Conflict and the Origins of Korean Capitalism." *American Journal of Sociology* 103:1309–1351.

Shipton, Parker. 1989. *Bitter Money: Cultural Economy and Some African Meanings of Forbidden Commodities*. Washington, D.C.: American Anthropological Association.

Shorter, Edward, and Charles Tilly, eds. 1974. *Strikes in France, 1830–1968*. London: Cambridge University Press.

Shy, John. 1973. "The American Revolution: The Military Conflict Considered as a Revolutionary War." In *Essays on the American Revolution*. Ed. Stephen G. Kurtz and James H. Hutson. New York: W. W. Norton.

Silver, Allan. 1989. "Friendship and Trust as Moral Ideals: An Historical Approach." *Archives Européennes de Sociologie* 30:274–297.

Silverberg, Helene, ed. 1998. *Gender and American Social Science: The Formative Years*. Princeton, N.J.: Princeton University Press.

Simmel, Georg. 1978. *The Philosophy of Money*. Trans. Tom Bottomore and David Frisby. Boston: Routledge.

Simpson, A. W. B. 1986. *A History of the Land Law*, 2nd ed. Oxford: Oxford University Press.

Skinner, Quentin. 1989. "Language and Political Change." Pp. 6–23 in *Political Innovation and Conceptual Change*. Ed. Terence Ball, James Farr, and Russell L. Hanson. Cambridge: Cambridge University Press.

Skocpol, Theda. 1979. *States and Social Revolutions: A Comparative Analysis of France, Russia, and China*. New York: Cambridge University Press.

———. 1980. "Political Response to Capitalist Crisis: Neo-Marxist Theories of the State and the Case of the New Deal." *Politics and Society* 10 (2): 155–201.

———. 1984a. "Emerging Agendas and Recurrent Strategies in Historical Sociology." Pp. 356–391 in

Vision and Method in Historical Sociology. Ed. Theda Skocpol. New York: Cambridge University Press.

——. 1984b. "Sociology's Historical Imagination." Pp. 1–21 in *Vision and Method in Historical Sociology.* Ed. Theda Skocpol. New York: Cambridge University Press.

——. 1985a. "Bringing the State Back In: Strategies of Analysis in Current Research." Pp. 3–43 in *Bringing the State Back In.* Ed. Peter B. Evans, Dietrich Rueschemeyer, and Theda Skocpol. New York: Cambridge University Press.

——. 1985b. "Cultural Idioms and Political Ideologies in Revolutionary Reconstruction of State Power: A Rejoinder to Sewell." *Journal of Modern History* 57:86–96.

——. 1988a. "The Limits of the New Deal System and the Roots of Contemporary Welfare Dilemmas." Pp. 293–312 in *The Politics of Social Policy in the United States.* Ed. Margaret Weir, Ann Shola Orloff, and Theda Skocpol. Princeton, N.J.: Princeton University Press.

——. 1988b. "An 'Uppity Generation' and the Revitalization of Macroscopic Sociology: Reflections at Mid-Career by a Woman from the Sixties." *Theory and Society* 17:627–643.

——. 1992. *Protecting Soldiers and Mothers: The Political Origins of Social Policy in the United States.* Cambridge, Mass.: Harvard University Press.

——. 1994. "Social Revolutions and Mass Military Mobilization." Pp. 279–298 in *Social Revolutions in the Modern World.* Cambridge: Cambridge University Press. Reprinted from *World Politics* 40 (January 1988): 147–168.

——. 1997. "The G.I. Bill and U.S. Social Policy, Past and Future." *Social Philosophy and Policy* 14 (summer): 95–115.

——. 2003. "Doubly Engaged Social Science: The Promise of Comparative-Historical Analysis." *Comparative Historical Analysis in the Social Sciences.* Ed. James Mahoney and Dietrich Rueschemeyer. Cambridge: Cambridge University Press.

——, ed. 1984. *Vision and Method in Historical Sociology.* New York: Cambridge University Press.

Skocpol, Theda, and Edwin Amenta. 1985. "Did Capitalists Shape Social Security?" *American Sociological Review* 50 (4): 572–575.

——. 1986. "States and Social Policies." *Annual Review of Sociology* 12:131–157.

Skocpol, Theda, and John Ikenberry. 1983. "The Political Formation of the American Welfare State in Historical and Comparative Perspective." *Comparative Social Research* 6:87–148.

Skocpol, Theda, and Margaret Somers. 1980. "The Uses of Comparative History in Macrosocial Inquiry." *Comparative Studies in Society and History* 22 (2): 174–197.

Skocpol, Theda, Ziad Munson, Andrew Karch, and Bayliss Camp. 2002. "Patriotic Partnerships: Why Great Wars Nourished American Civic Voluntarism." Pp. 134–180 in *Shaped by War and Trade: International Influences on American Political Development.* Ed. Ira Katznelson and Martin Shefter. Princeton, N.J.: Princeton University Press.

Skocpol, Theda, Ziad Munson, Meyer Kestnbaum, and Andrew Karch. 2000. "Mars and Tocqueville: War and Civic Voluntarism in the United States." Paper presented in the session on "The State and the Emergence of Voluntary Associations," annual meeting of the American Political Science Association, Washington, D.C., September 1, 2000.

Skowronek, Stephen. 1982. *Building a New American State: The Expansion of National Administrative Capacities, 1877–1920.* New York: Cambridge University Press.

Slezkine, Yuri. 1994. "The USSR as a Communal Apartment, or How a Socialist State Promoted Ethnic Particularism." *Slavic Review* 53 (4): 414–452.

Smelser, Neil J. 1959a. *Social Change in the Industrial Revolution: An Application of Theory to the British Cotton Industry.* Chicago: University of Chicago Press.

——. 1959b. *Social Change in the Industrial Revolution: An Application of Theory to the Lancashire Cotton Industry, 1770–1840.* London: Routledge.

——. 1963. *The Sociology of Economic Life.* Englewood Cliffs, N.J.: Prentice-Hall.

——. 1976. *Comparative Methods in the Social Sciences.* Englewood Cliffs, N.J.: Prentice-Hall.

——. 1986. "Die Beharrlichkeit des Positivismus in der amerikanischen Soziologie." *Kölner Zeitschrift für Soziologie und Sozialpsychologie* 38 (March): 133–150.

Smith, Adam. 1961 [1776]. *The Wealth of Nations*. Ed. Bruce Mazlish. Indianapolis, Ind.: Bobbs-Merrill.

Smith, Adrian, and John Pickles. 1998. "Introduction: Theorising the Transition and the Political Economy of Transformation." Pp. 1–22 in *Theorising Transition: The Political Economy of Post-Communist Transformations*. Ed. John Pickles and Adrian Smith. London: Routledge.

Smith, Adrian, and Adam Swain. 1998. "Regulating and Institutionalising Capitalisms: The Macro-Foundations of Transformation in Eastern and Central Europe." Pp. 25–53 in *Theorising Transition: The Political Economy of Post-Communist Transformations*. Ed. John Pickles and Adrian Smith. London: Routledge.

Smith, Alan K. 1991. *Creating a World Economy: Merchant Capital, Colonialism, and World Trade, 1400–1825*. Boulder, Colo.: Westview Press.

Smith, Anthony D. 1983 [1971]. *Theories of Nationalism*, 2nd ed. New York: Holmes and Meier.

——. 1986. *The Ethnic Origins of Nations*. Oxford: Blackwell.

——. 1998. *Nationalism and Modernism: A Critical Survey of Recent Theories of Nations and Nationalism*. London: Routledge.

Smith, Christian. 1991. *The Emergence of Liberation Theology: Radical Religion and Social Movement Theory*. Chicago: University of Chicago Press.

——, ed. 2003. *The Secular Revolution: Power, Interest, and Conflict in the Secularization of American Public Life*. Berkeley: University of California Press.

Smith, Dennis. 1991. *The Rise of Historical Sociology*. Philadelphia: Temple University Press.

Smith, James Ward. 1952. "Pragmatism, Realism and Positivism in the United States." *Mind*, new series, 61 (April): 190–208.

Snooks, Graeme Donald. 1994a. "Great Waves of Economic Change: The Industrial Revolution in Historical Perspective, 1000 to 2000." Pp. 43–78 in *Was the Industrial Revolution Necessary?* Ed. Graeme Donald Snooks. London: Routledge.

——. 1994b. "New Perspectives on the Industrial Revolution." Pp. 1–26 in *Was the Industrial Revolution Necessary?* Ed. Graeme Donald Snooks. London: Routledge.

Snow, David A., and Robert D. Benford. 1988. "Ideology, Frame Resonance, and Participant Mobilization." *International Social Movement Research* 1:197–217.

——. 1992. "Master Frames and Cycles of Protest." Pp. 133–155 in *Frontiers in Social Movement Theory*. Ed. Aldon D. Morris and Carol McClurg Meuller. New Haven, Conn.: Yale University Press.

Snow, David A., E. Burke Rochford Jr., Steven K. Worden, and Robert D. Benford. 1986. "Frame Alignment Processes, Micromobilization, and Movement Participation." *American Sociological Review* 51 (4): 464–481.

Soboul, Albert, and Walter M. Markov. 1957. *Die Sansculotten von Paris; Dokumente zur Geschichte der Volksbewegung 1793–1794*. Berlin: Akademie-Verlag.

Sohrabi, Nader. 1995. "Historicizing Revolutions: Constitutional Revolutions in the Ottoman Empire, Iran, and Russia, 1905–1908." *American Journal of Sociology* 100 (6): 1383–1447.

——. 1999. "Revolution and State Culture: The Circle of Justice and Constitutionalism in 1906 Iran." Pp. 253–288 in *State/Culture: State-Formation after the Cultural Turn*. Ed. George Steinmetz. Ithaca, N.Y.: Cornell University Press. Wilder House Series in Culture, Power, and History.

——. 2002. "Global Waves, Local Actors: What the Young Turks Knew about Other Revolutions and Why It Mattered." *Comparative Studies in Society and History* 44 (1): 45–79.

Solow, Robert. 1956. "A Contribution to the Theory of Economic Growth." *Quarterly Journal of Economics* 70:65–94.

——. 1994. "Perspectives on Growth Theory." *Journal of Economic Perspectives* 8:45–54.

Sombart, Werner. 1967. *The Quintessence of Capitalism*. Trans. M. Epstein. New York: Howard Fertig.

Somers, Margaret R. 1989. "Workers of the World, Compare!" *Contemporary Sociology* 18 (3).

——. 1993. "Citizenship and the Place of the Public Sphere: Law, Community, and Political-Culture in the Transition to Democracy." *American Sociological Review* 58 (5): 587–620.

——. 1994. "Rights, Relationality, and Membership: Rethinking the Making and Meaning of Citizenship." *Law and Social Inquiry* 19 (1): 63–112.

——. 1995a. "Narrating and Naturalizing Civil Society and Citizenship Theory: The Place of Political Culture and the Public Sphere." *Sociological Theory* 13 (3): 229–274.

——. 1995b. "What's Political or Cultural about the Political Culture Concept? Toward an Historical Sociology of Concept Formation." *Sociological Theory* 13 (2): 113–144.

——. 1996a. "Class Formation and Capitalism: A Second Look at a Classic (Katznelson and Zolberg's *Working Class Formation*)." *Archives de Sociologie Européenne* 37 (1): 180–202.

——. 1996b. "Narrativity, Narrative Identity, and Social Action: Rethinking English Working Class Formation." *Social Science History* 16 (4): 591–630.

——. 1996c. "Where Is Sociology after the Historic Turn? Knowledge Cultures, Narrativity, and Historical Epistemologies." Pp. 53–90 in *The Historic Turn in the Human Sciences*. Ed. Terrence J. McDonald. Ann Arbor: University of Michigan Press.

——. 1998. " 'We're No Angels': Realism, Rational Choice, and Relationality in Social Science." *American Journal of Sociology* 104 (3): 722–784.

——. 1999. "The Privatization of Citizenship: How to Unthink a Knowledge Culture." Pp. 121–161 in *Beyond the Cultural Turn: New Directions in the Study of Society and Culture*. Ed. Victoria E. Bonnell and Lynn Hunt. Berkeley: University of California Press.

——. 2001. "Romancing the Market, Reviling the State: Historicizing Liberalism, Privatization, and the Competing Claims to Civil Society." Pp. 23–48 in *Citizenship, Markets, and the State*. Ed. K. Eder, C. Crouch, and D. Tambini. Oxford: Oxford University Press.

Soule, Sarah, and Yvonne Zylan. 1997. "Runaway Train? The Diffusion of State-Level Reform in ADC/AFDC Eligibility Requirements, 1950–1967." *American Journal of Sociology* 103 (3): 733–762.

Soysal, Yasemin. 1994. *Limits of Citizenship: Migrants and Postnational Membership in Europe*. Berkeley: University of California Press.

Spencer, Herbert. 1972. *On Social Evolution*. Ed. J. D. Y. Peel. Chicago: University of Chicago Press.

Sperber, Dan. 1985. "Anthropology and Psychology: Towards an Epidemiology of Representations." *Man* 20:73–89.

Spillman, Lyn. 1995. "Culture, Social Structure, and Discursive Fields." *Current Perspectives in Social Theory* 15:129–145.

——. 1997. *Nation and Commemoration: Creating National Identities in the United States and Australia*. Cambridge: Cambridge University Press.

——. 1998. "When Do Collective Memories Last? Founding Moments in the United States and Australia." *Social Science History* 22:445–477.

——. 2002a. "Causal Reasoning, Historical Logic, and Sociological Explanation." In *Self, Social Structure, and Beliefs: Explorations in the Sociological Thought of Neil J. Smelser*. Ed. Jeffrey Alexander, Gary Marx, and Christine Williams. Berkeley: University of California Press.

——. 2002b. "Culture and Cultural Sociology." Pp. 1–15 in *Cultural Sociology*. Ed. Lyn Spillman. Oxford: Blackwell.

Spivak, Gayatri Chakravorty. 1987. *In Other Worlds: Essays in Cultural Politics*. New York: Methuen.

Spruyt, Hendrik. 1994. *The Sovereign State and Its Competitors*. Princeton, N.J.: Princeton University Press.

——. N.d. "Rebellion in the Ranks: Oversight, Control and Resistance in Translocal Organizations." Working draft (available from the author).

Spufford, Peter. 1988. *Money and Its Use in Medieval Europe*. Cambridge: Cambridge University Press.

Stacey, Judith. 1983. *Patriarchies and Socialist Revolution in China*. Berkeley: University of California Press.

Stacey, Judith, and Barrie Thorne. 1985. "The Missing Feminist Revolution in Sociology." *Social Problems* 32:301–315.

——. 1996. "Is Sociology Still Missing Its Feminist Revolution?" *Perspectives: The ASA Theory Section Newsletter* 18:1–3.

Stage, Sarah, and Virginia B. Vincenti, eds. 1997. *Rethinking Home Economics: Women and the History of a Profession*. Ithaca, N.Y.: Cornell University Press.

Staniszkis, Jadwiga. 1991. "Political Capitalism in Poland." *East European Politics and Societies* 5:127–141.

Stark, David. 1994. "Path Dependence and Privatization Strategies in East Central Europe." Pp. 63–100 in *Transition to Capitalism? The Communist Legacy in Eastern Europe*. Ed. János Mátyás Kovács. New Brunswick, N.J.: Transaction Publishers.

——. 1996. "Recombinant Property in East European Capitalism." *American Journal of Sociology* 101 (4): 993–1027.

Stark, David, and László Bruszt. 1998. *Postsocialist Pathways: Transforming Politics and Property in East Central Europe*. New York: Cambridge University Press.

——. 2001. "One Way or Multiple Paths: For a Comparative Sociology of East European Capitalism." *American Journal of Sociology* 106 (4): 1129–1137.

Stark, Rodney. 1996. *The Rise of Christianity: A Sociologist Re-Considers History*. Princeton, N.J.: Princeton University Press.

Stark, Rodney, and William S. Bainbridge. 1985. *The Future of Religion*. Berkeley: University of California Press.

Stark, Rodney, and Laurence Iannaccone. 1994. "A Supply-Side Reinterpretation of the 'Secularization' of Europe." *Journal for the Scientific Study of Religion* 33:230–252.

Starr, Paul. 1982. *The Social Transformation of American Medicine*. New York: Basic Books.

——. 1987. "The Sociology of Official Statistics." Pp. 7–57 in *The Politics of Numbers*. Ed. William Alonso and Paul Starr. New York: Russell Sage Foundation.

Staves, Susan. 1990. *Married Women's Separate Property in England, 1660–1833*. Cambridge, Mass.: Harvard University Press.

Steedman, Carolyn. 1986. *Landscape for a Good Woman: A Story of Two Lives*. New Brunswick, N.J.: Rutgers University Press.

——. 2002. *Dust: The Archives and Cultural History*. New Brunswick, N.J.: Rutgers University Press.

Steinberg, Marc W. 1999a. *Fighting Words: Working-Class Formation, Collective Action, and Discourse in Early Nineteenth-Century England*. Ithaca, N.Y.: Cornell University Press.

——. 1999b. "The Talk and Back Talk of Collective Action: A Dialogic Analysis of Discourse among Nineteenth-Century English Cotton Spinners." *American Journal of Sociology* 105 (3): 736–780.

Steinberg, Mark D. 2001. *Voices of Revolution*. Trans. by Marian Schwartz. New Haven, Conn.: Yale University Press.

Steinmetz, George. 1993. *Regulating the Social: The Welfare State and Local Politics in Imperial Germany*. Princeton, N.J.: Princeton University Press.

——. 1994a. "Regulation Theory, Post-Marxism, and the New Social Movements." *Comparative Studies in Society and History* 36 (1): 176–212.

——. 1994b. "Die (un)moralische Ökonomie rechtsextremer Gewalt im Übergang zum Postfordismus." *Das Argument* 23 (January/February): 23–40.

——. 1997a. "German Exceptionalism and the Origins of Nazism: The Career of a Concept." Pp. 251–284 in *Stalinism and Nazism: Dictatorship in Comparison*. Ed. Ian Kershaw and Moshe Lewin. Cambridge: Cambridge University Press.

——. 1997b. "Social Class and the Reemergence of the Radical Right in Contemporary Germany." Pp. 335–368 in *Reworking Class: Cultures and Institutions of Economic Stratification and Agency*. Ed. John R. Hall. Ithaca, N.Y.: Cornell University Press.

——. 1998. "Critical Realism and Historical Sociology." *Comparative Studies in Society and History* 39 (4): 170–186.

——. 1999. "Culture and the State." Pp. 1–49 in *State/Culture: State Formation after the Cultural Turn.* Ed. George Steinmetz. Ithaca, N.Y.: Cornell University Press.

——. 2002. "Precoloniality and Colonial Subjectivity: Ethnographic Discourse and Native Policy in German Overseas Imperialism, 1780s–1914." *Political Power and Social Theory* 15:135–228.

——. 2003a. " 'The Devil's Handwriting': Precolonial Discourse, Ethnographic Acuity, and Cross-Identification in German Colonialism." *Comparative Studies in Society and History* 45 (1): 41–95.

——. 2003b. "The State of Emergency and the Revival of American Imperialism: Toward an Authoritarian Post-Fordism." *Public Culture* 15 (2): 323–346.

——. 2004. "Odious Comparisons: Incommensurability, the Case Study, and 'Small N's' " *Sociological Theory* 22 (3): 371–400.

——. Forthcoming a. *The Devil's Handwriting: Precoloniality, Ethnography, and Native Policy in the German Overseas Empire (Samoa, Qingdao/China, and Southwest Africa).* Durham, N.C.: Duke University Press.

——. "Scientific Authority and the Transition to Post-Fordism: The Plausibility of Positivism in U.S. Sociology since 1945." In *The Politics of Method in the Human Sciences: Positivism and Its Epistemological Others.* Ed. George Steinmetz. Durham, N.C.: Duke University Press.

——. Forthcoming b. "Odious Comparisons: Incommensurability, the Case Study, and 'Small N's' " *Sociological Theory* 22(3).

Steinmetz, George, and Ou-Byung Chae. 2002. "Sociology in an Era of Fragmentation: From the Sociology of Knowledge to the Philosophy of Science, and Back Again." *Sociological Quarterly* 43 (winter): 111–137.

Steinmetz, George, ed. 1999. *State/Culture: State Formation after the Cultural Turn.* Ithaca, N.Y.: Cornell University Press.

Stephens, John. 1979. *The Transition from Capitalism to Socialism.* London: Macmillan.

Stiglitz, Joseph E. 1994. *Whither Socialism?* Cambridge, Mass.: MIT Press.

——. 2000. "The Contributions of the Economics of Information to Twentieth Century Economics." *Quarterly Journal of Economics* 115:1441–1478.

Stinchcombe, Arthur L. 1978. *Theoretical Methods in Social History.* New York: Academic Press.

——. 1990. "Comment." *Rationality and Society* 2 (2): 214–223.

——. 1991. "The Conditions of Fruitfulness of Theorizing about Mechanisms in Social Science." *Philosophy of the Social Sciences* 21 (3): 367–387.

——. 1995. *Sugar Island Slavery in the Age of Enlightenment: The Political Economy of the Caribbean World.* Princeton, N.J.: Princeton University Press.

——. 2002a. *When Formality Works: Authority and Abstraction in Law and Organizations.* Chicago: University of Chicago Press.

——. 2002b. "Epistemology as an Optimizing Discipline." Paper presented at Department of Sociology, University of Michigan.

Stoler, Ann Laura. 1989. "Rethinking Colonial Categories: European Communities and the Boundaries of Rule." *Comparative Studies in Society and History* 31:134–161.

——. 1995. *Race and the Education of Desire: Foucault's History of Sexuality and the Colonial Order of Things.* Durham, N.C.: Duke University Press.

——. 2002a. *Carnal Knowledge and Imperial Power.* Berkeley: University of California Press.

——. 2002b. "Developing Historical Negatives: Race and the (Modernist) Visions of a Colonial State." Pp. 156–185 in *From the Margins: Historical Anthropology and Its Futures.* Ed. Brian Keith Axel. Durham, N.C.: Duke University Press.

Stone, Lawrence. 1992. "The Revolution over the Revolution." Review of *Revolution and Rebellion in the Early Modern World,* by Jack Goldstone. *New York Review of Books,* June 11.

Stovel, Katherine, Michael Savage, and Peter Bearman. 1996. "Ascription into Achievement: Models of Career Systems at Lloyds Bank, 1890–1970." *American Journal of Sociology* 102:358–399.

Strang, David. 1996. "From Dependency to Sovereignty: An Event History Analysis of Decolonization, 1870–1987." *American Sociological Review* 53 (6): 846–860.

Strassberger, Elfriede. 1969. *The Rhenish Mission Society in South Africa 1830–1950.* Cape Town: C. Struik.

Straw, J. 1998. "Building Social Cohesion, Order and Inclusion in a Market Economy [Online]." Paper presented to the Nexus Conference on Mapping Out the Third Way. Available at *http://www .netnexus.org/.*

Stryker, Robin. 1989. "Limits on Technocratization of the Law: The Elimination of the National Labor Relations Board's Division of Economic Research." *American Sociological Review* 54 (3): 341–358.

———. 1990. "Science, Class, and the Welfare State: A Class-Centered Functional Account." *American Journal of Sociology* 96 (3): 684–726.

Stukuls, Daina. 1999. "Body of the Nation: Mothering, Prostitution, and Women's Place in Post-Communist Latvia." *Slavic Review* 58 (3): 537–558.

Sunstein, Cass R. 2003. "The Right-Wing Assault: What's at Stake, What's Already Happened and What Could Yet Occur." *The American Prospect* 14(3), March 1.

Suny, Ronald Grigor. 2002. "Back and Beyond: Reversing the Cultural Turn?" *American Historical Review* (December): 1476–1499.

Sutton, John. 1988. *Stubborn Children: Controlling Delinquency in the United States, 1640–1981.* Berkeley: University of California Press.

Swank, Duane. 2002. *Global Capital, Political Institutions, and Policy Change in Developed Welfare States.* New York: Cambridge University Press.

Swanson, Guy A. 1960. *The Birth of the Gods: The Origin of Primitive Beliefs.* Ann Arbor: University of Michigan Press.

———. 1967. *Religion and Regime: A Sociological Account for the Reformation.* Ann Arbor: University of Michigan Press.

Swart, K. W. 1949. *Sale of Offices in the Seventeenth Century.* The Hague: M. Nijhoff.

Swartz, David. 1988. "Introduction." *Theory and Society* 17:615 -625.

Swedberg, Richard. 1991. "Major Traditions of Economic Sociology." *Annual Review of Sociology* 17:251–276.

———. 1998. *Max Weber and the Idea of Economic Sociology.* Princeton, N.J.: Princeton University Press.

Sweezy, Paul. 1976. *The Transition from Feudalism to Capitalism.* London: New Left Books.

Swenson, Peter. 2002. *Capitalists against Markets: The Making of Labor Markets and Welfare States in the United States and Sweden.* New York: Oxford University Press.

Swidler, Ann. 1986. "Culture in Action: Symbols and Strategies." *American Sociological Review* 51:273–286.

———. 1992. "Inequality and American Culture: The Persistence of Voluntarism." Pp. 294–314 in *Reexamining Democracy: Essays in Honor of Seymour Martin Lipset.* Ed. Gary Marks and Larry Diamond. Newbury Park, Calif.: Sage.

———. 2001. *Talk of Love.* Chicago: University of Chicago Press.

Sykes, Robert, Bruno Palier, and Pauline Prior, eds. 2001. *Globalization and European Welfare States: Challenges and Changes.* Basingstoke, U.K.: Palgrave.

Szelényi, Iván, and Eric Kostello. 1996. "The Market Transition Debate: Toward a Synthesis?" *American Journal of Sociology* 101:1082–1096.

Szelényi, Iván, and Szonja Szelényi. 1995. "Circulation and Reproduction of Elites in Post-Communist Transformation." *Theory and Society* 24 (5): 615–638.

Szostak, Richard. 1991. *The Role of Transportation in the Industrial Revolution: A Comparison of England and France.* Montreal: McGill-Queen's University.

Tahsin Paşa. 1931. *Abdülhamit Yıldız Hatıraları.* Istanbul: Muallim Ahmet Halit Kitaphanesi.

Takahashi, Kohachiro. 1976. "A Contribution to the Discussion." Pp. 68–97 in *The Transition from Feudalism to Capitalism*. Ed. Paul Sweezy. London: New Left Books.

Tarrow, Sidney. 1992. "Mentalities, Political Cultures, and Collective Action Frames." Pp. 174–202 in *Frontiers in Social Movement Theory*. Ed. Aldon D. Morris and Carol McClurg Mueller. New Haven, Conn.: Yale University Press.

——. 1994. *Power in Movement: Social Movements, Collective Action and Politics*. Cambridge: Cambridge University Press.

Taylor, Charles. 1975. *Hegel*. Cambridge: Cambridge University Press.

——. 1979. "Interpretation and the Sciences of Man." Pp. 25–72 in *Interpretive Social Science: A Reader*. Ed. Paul Rabinow and William M. Sullivan. Berkeley: University of California Press.

——. 1985a. *Human Agency and Language: Philosophical Papers I*. New York: Cambridge University Press.

——. 1985b. *Philosophy and the Human Sciences*. New York: Cambridge University Press.

——. 1989. *Sources of the Self: The Making of the Modern Identity*. Cambridge, Mass.: Harvard University Press.

——. 1990. "Modes of Civil Society." *Public Culture* 3 (1): 95–118.

——. 1999. "Two Theories of Modernity?" *Public Culture* 11 (1): 153–174.

Taylor, Peter J. 2003. "The State as Container: Territoriality in the Modern World System." Pp. 101–113 in *State/Space: A Reader*. Ed. Bob Jessop, Martin Jones, Neil Brenner, and Gordon Macleod. London: Blackwell.

Taylor, Verta. 1989. "Social Movement Continuity: The Women's Movement in Abeyance." *American Sociological Review* 54 (5):761–775.

te Brake, Wayne. 1998. *Shaping History: Ordinary People in European Politics, 1500–1700*. Berkeley: University of California Press.

Temin, Peter. 1997. "Two Views of the British Industrial Revolution." *Journal of Economic History* 57:63–82.

——. 2000. "A Response to Harley and Crafts." *Journal of Economic History* 60:842–845.

Thapar, Romila. 1980. "Durkheim and Weber on Theories of Society and Race Relating to Pre-Colonial India." Pp. 93–116 in *Sociological Theories: Race and Colonialism*. Paris: UNESCO.

't Hart, Marjolein C. 1993. *The Making of a Bourgeois State: War, Politics and Finance during the Dutch Revolt*. Manchester: Manchester University Press.

Thelen, Kathleen. 1999. "Historical Institutionalism in Comparative Politics." *Annual Review of Political Science* 2:369–404.

——. 2003. "How Institutions Evolve: Insights from Comparative Historical Analysis." In *Comparative Historical Analysis in the Social Sciences*. Ed. James Mahoney and Dietrich Rueschemeyer. Cambridge: Cambridge University Press.

Thelen, Kathleen, and Sven Steinmo. 1992. "Historical Institutionalism in Comparative Politics." In *Structuring Politics: Historical Institutionalism in Comparative Perspective*. Ed. Sven Steinmo, Kathleen Thelen, and Frank Longstreth. New York: Cambridge University Press.

Therborn, Goran. 1980. *The Ideology of Power and the Power of Ideology*. London: New Left Books.

Thomas, George, and John Meyer. 1984. "The Expansion of the State." *Annual Review of Sociology* 10:461–482.

Thomas, George, John W. Meyer, Francisco O. Ramirez, and John Boli. 1987. *Institutional Structure: Constituting State, Society, and the Individual*. Newbury Park, Calif.: Sage.

Thompson, E. P. 1963, 1966. *The Making of the English Working Class*. New York: Vintage.

——. 1967. "The Moral Economy of the English Crowd in the Eighteenth Century." *Past and Present* 50:76–136.

Thomson, Janice E. 1994. *Mercenaries, Pirates, and Sovereigns: State-Building and Extraterritorial Violence in Early Modern Europe*. Princeton, N.J.: Princeton University Press.

Thorne, Susan. 1999. *Congregational Missions and the Making of an Imperial Culture in Nineteenth-Century England*. Stanford, Calif.: Stanford University Press.

Thornton, Arland. 2001. "The Developmental Paradigm, Reading History Sideways, and Family Change." *Demography* 38 (4): 449–465.

Tigar, Michael E., and Madelaine R. Levy. 1977. *Law and the Rise of Capitalism*. New York: Monthly Review Press.

Tilly, Charles. 1963. "The Analysis of a Counter-Revolution." *History and Theory* 3(1):30–58.

———. 1964. *The Vendée*. Cambridge, Mass.: Harvard University Press.

———. 1978. *From Mobilization To Revolution*. Reading, Mass.: Addison-Wesley.

———. 1981. *As Sociology Meets History*. New York: Academic Press.

———. 1984. *Big Structures, Large Processes, Huge Comparisons*. New York: Russell Sage Foundation.

———. 1985. "War-Making and State-Making as Organized Crime." In *Bringing the State Back In*. Ed. Peter B. Evans, Dietrich Rueschemeyer, and Theda Skocpol. New York: Cambridge University Press.

———. 1990. *Coercion, Capital and European States, A.D. 990–1990*. Oxford: Basil Blackwell.

———. 1993a. "Contentious Repertoires in Britain, 1758–1834." *Social Science History* 17 (2): 253–280.

———. 1993b. *European Revolutions, 1492–1992*. Oxford: Blackwell.

———. 1994. "States and Nationalism in Europe 1492–1992." *Theory and Society* 23:131–146.

———. 1998a. *Durable Inequality*. Berkeley: University of California Press.

———. 1998b. "Social Movements and (All Sorts of) Other Political Interactions—Local, National, and International—Including Identities." *Theory and Society* 27:453–480.

———. 1998c. "Where Do Rights Come From?" Pp. 55–72 in *Democracy, Revolution, and History*. Ed. Theda Skocpol. Ithaca, N.Y.: Cornell University Press.

———. 1999. "Epilogue: Now Where?" Pp. 407–419 in *State/Culture: State-Formation after the Cultural Turn*. Ed. George Steinmetz. Ithaca, N.Y.: Cornell University Press. Wilder House Series in Culture, Power, and History.

———. 2002. *Stories, Identities, and Political Change*. Lanham, Md.: Rowman and Littlefield.

———. Forthcoming. "Historical Analysis of Political Processes." In *Handbook of Sociological Theory*. Ed. Jonathan H. Turner. New York: Plenum.

Tilly, Charles, Louise Tilly, and Richard Tilly. 1975. *The Rebellious Century, 1830–1930*. Cambridge, Mass.: Harvard University Press.

Tilly, Charles, ed. 1975. *The Formation of National States in Western Europe*. Princeton, N.J.: Princeton University Press.

———. 1995. *International Review of Social History Special Issue: Citizenship Identity and Social History*. Amsterdam: Cambridge University Press.

Tilly, Louise A., and Joan W. Scott. 1978. *Women, Work, and Family*. New York: Holt, Rinehart and Winston.

Tilly, Louise A., and Patricia Gurin, eds. 1990. *Women, Politics, and Change*. New York: Russell Sage Foundation.

Tiryakian, Edward. 1997. "The Wildcards of Modernity." *Daedalus* 126:147–181.

Tiryakian, Edward, and Ronald Rogowski, eds. 1985. *New Nationalisms of the Developed West*. Boston: Allen and Unwin.

Tittler, Robert. 1994. "Money-Lending in the West Midlands: The Activities of Joyce Jefferies, 1638–49." *Historical Research* 67:249–263.

Tocqueville, Alexis de. 1955. *The Old Regime and the French Revolution*. Trans. Stuart Gilbert. Garden City, N.Y.: Doubleday.

———. 1969. *Democracy in America*. Trans. George Lawrence. Ed. J. P. Mayer. New York: Anchor Books.

Tolnay, Stuart. 1998. "Educational Selection in the Migration of Southern Blacks, 1880–1990." *Social Forces* 77 (2):487–514.

Torpey, John. 2000. *The Invention of the Passport: Surveillance, Citizenship and the State*. Cambridge: Cambridge University Press.

Toulmin, Stephen E. 1969. "From Logical Analysis to Conceptual History." Pp. 25–53 in *The Legacy of Logical Positivism*. Ed. Peter Achinstein and Stephen F. Barker. Baltimore: Johns Hopkins University Press.

Trattner, Walter. 1999 [1974]. *From Poor Law to Welfare State*, 6th ed. New York: Free Press.

Traugott, Mark. 1980. "Determinants of Political Orientation: Class and Organization in the Parisian Insurrection of June 1848." *American Journal of Sociology* 86 (1): 32–49.

———. 1985. *Armies of the Poor: Determinants of Working-Class Participation in the Parisian Insurrection of June 1848*. Princeton, N.J.: Princeton University Press.

———. 1993. "Barricades as Repertoire: Continuities and Discontinuities in the History of French Contention." *Social Science History* 17 (2): 309–323.

Trend, D. 1996. *Radical Democracy: Identity, Citizenship, and the State*. New York: Routledge.

Trimberger, Ellen Kay. 1978. *Revolution from Above: Military Bureaucrats and Development in Japan, Turkey, Egypt, and Peru*. New Brunswick, N.J.: Transaction Books.

Tritter, J. 1994. "The Citizen's Charter: Opportunities for Users' Perspectives?" *Political Quarterly* 65:397–414.

Tronto, Joan. 1993. *Moral Boundaries: A Political Argument for an Ethic of Care*. New York: Routledge.

Truman, David B. 1951. *The Governmental Process: Political Interests and Public Opinion*. 2nd ed. New York: Knopf.

Tschannen, Olivier. 1992. *Les Théories de la sécularisation*. Geneva: Droz.

Tuchman, Barbara W. 1978. *A Distant Mirror: The Calamitous 14th Century*. New York: Ballantine.

Turbin, Carole. 1992. *Working Women of Collar City: Gender, Class and Community in Troy, New York, 1864–1886*. Urbana: University of Illinois Press.

Turner, B. S. 1986. *Citizenship and Capitalism: The Debate over Reformism*. London: Allen and Unwin.

———. 1990. *Theories of Modernity and Postmodernity*. London: Sage.

Turner, Jonathan H. 1993. *Classical Sociological Theory: A Positivist's Perspective*. Chicago: Nelson-Hall.

Turner, Mark. 2001. *Cognitive Dimensions of Social Science*. Oxford: Oxford University Press.

Turner, Stephen Park, and Jonathan H. Turner. 1990. *The Impossible Science: An Institutional Analysis of American Sociology*. Newbury Park, Calif.: Sage.

Tusi, Nasir al-Din. 1964. *The Nasirean Ethics*. Trans. G. M. Wickens. London: Allen and Unwin.

Tyler, Stephen. 1986. "Post-Modern Ethnography: From Document of the Occult to Occult Document." In *Writing Culture: The Poetics and Politics of Ethnography*. Ed. James Clifford and George E. Marcus. Berkeley: University of California Press.

Udovitch, Abraham L. 1962. "At the Origins of the Western Commenda: Islam, Israel, Byzantium?" *Speculum* 37:198–207.

Ungerson, Clare. 1997. "Social Politics and the Commodification of Care." *Social Politics* 4:362–391.

United Kingdom, Commission on Citizenship. 1990. *Encouraging Citizenship: Report of the Commission on Citizenship*. London: HMSO.

United Nations Development Programme. 2000. *Human Development Report 2000*. New York: Oxford University Press.

U.S. Social Security Administration, Office of Policy. 1999. *Social Security Programs Throughout the World, 1999*. http://www.ssa.gov/policy/docs/progdesc/ssptw/1999/index.html#toc.

Uzzi, Brian. 1996. "The Sources and Consequences of Embeddedness for the Economic Performance of Organizations: The Network Effect." *American Sociological Review* 61:674–698.

Valelly, Richard M. 1993. "Party, Coercion, and Inclusion: The Two Reconstructions of the South's Electoral Politics." *Politics and Society* 21 (March): 37–67.

Verdery, Katherine. 1996. *What Was Socialism, and What Comes Next?* Princeton, N.J.: Princeton University Press.

——. 1999. *The Political Lives of Dead Bodies: Reburial and Postsocialist Change*. New York: Columbia University Press.

Vernon, Glenn M. 1962. *Sociology of Religion*. New York: McGraw-Hill.

Vidich, Arthur. 1985. *American Sociology: Worldly Rejections of Religion and Their Directions*. New Haven, Conn.: Yale University Press.

Voet, R. 1998. *Feminism and Citizenship*. London: Sage.

Volosinov, V. N. 1973. *Marxism and the Philosophy of Language*. Cambridge, Mass.: Harvard University Press.

Voss, Kim. 1993. *The Making of American Exceptionalism: The Knights of Labor and Class Formation in the Nineteenth Century*. Ithaca, N.Y.: Cornell University Press.

Vries, P. H. H. 2002. "Governing Growth: A Comparative Analysis of the Role of the State in the Rise of the West." *Journal of World History* 13:67–138.

Wachter, J. 1987. *The Roman Empire*. London: Dent and Sons.

Wacquant, Loïc. 2002. "Scrutinizing the Street: Poverty, Morality, and the Pitfalls of Urban Ethnography." *American Journal of Sociology* 107 (6): 1468–1532.

Waerness, Kari. 1984. "Caregiving as Women's Work in the Welfare State." Pp. 67–87 in *Patriarchy in a Welfare Society*. Ed. Harriet Holter. Oslo: Universitetsforlaget.

Waetjen, Thembisa. 2001. "The Limits of Gender Rhetoric for Nationalism: A Case Study of Southern Africa." *Theory and Society* 30:121–152.

Walby, Sylvia. 1986. *Patriarchy at Work: Patriarchal and Capitalist Relations in Employment*. Minneapolis: University of Minnesota Press.

Walker, Henry A., and Bernard P. Cohen. 1985. "Scope Statements: Imperatives for Evaluating Theory." *American Sociological Review* 50 (June): 288–301.

Wallerstein, Immanuel. 1974. *The Modern World-System*, vol. 1: *Capitalist Agriculture and the Origins of the European World Economy in the Sixteenth Century*. New York: Academic Press.

——. 1974–1989. *The Modern World-System*, 3 vols. San Diego: Academic Press.

——. 1976. "Modernization: Requiescat in Pace." In *The Uses of Controversy in Sociology*. Ed. Lewis A. Coser and Otto N. Larsen. New York: Free Press.

——. 1979. *The Capitalist World-Economy*. Cambridge: Cambridge University Press.

——. 1991. *Unthinking Social Science: The Limits of Nineteenth-Century Paradigms*. London; Polity Press.

——. 1999. *The End of the World as We Know It: Social Science for the Twenty-first Century*. Minneapolis: University of Minnesota Press.

Wallerstein, Immanuel, et al. 1996. *Open the Social Sciences: Report of the Gulbenkian Commission on the Restructuring of the Social Sciences*. Stanford, Calif.: Stanford University Press.

Wallerstein, Immanuel, ed. 1966. *Social Change: The Colonial Situation*. New York: John Wiley and Sons.

Walt, Stephen M. 1996. *Revolution and War*. Ithaca, N.Y.: Cornell University Press.

Walters, Pamela Barnhouse, and Philip J. O'Connell. 1988. "The Family Economy, Work, and Educational Participation in the United States, 1890–1940." *American Journal of Sociology* 93 (5): 1116–1152.

Walters, Pamela Barnhouse, David R. James, and Holly J. McCammon. 1997. "Citizenship and Public Schools: Accounting for Racial Inequality in Education in the Pre- and Post-Disfranchisement South." *American Sociological Review* 62 (1): 34–52.

Walzer, Michael. 1965. *The Revolution of the Saints: A Study in the Origins of Radical Politics*. Cambridge, Mass.: Harvard University Press.

——. 1970. *Obligations: Essays on Disobedience, War, and Citizenship*. Cambridge, Mass.: Harvard University Press.

——. 1977. *Just and Unjust Wars: A Moral Argument with Historical Illustrations*. New York: Basic Books.

———. 1983. *Spheres of Justice: A Defense of Pluralism and Equality*. New York: Basic Books.

———. 1985. *Exodus and Revolution*. New York: Basic Books.

———. 1988. *The Company of Critics: Social Criticism and Political Commitment in the Twentieth Century*. New York: Basic Books.

———. 1995. "The Civil Society Argument." Pp. 153–175 in *Theorizing Citizenship*. Ed. R. Beiner. Albany: State University of New York Press.

———. 1997. *On Toleration*. New Haven, Conn.: Yale University Press.

Wank, David L. 1999. "Producing Property Rights: Strategies, Networks, and Efficiency in Urban China's Nonstate Firms." Pp. 248–272 in *Property Rights and Economic Reform in China*. Ed. Jean C. Oi and Andrew G. Walder. Stanford, Calif.: Stanford University Press.

Ware, Vron. 1992. *Beyond the Pale: Explorations in Feminism and History*. London: Verso.

Warner, R. Stephen. 1978. "Toward a Redefinition of Action Theory: Paying the Cognitive Element Its Due." *American Journal of Sociology* 83:1317–1349.

Warren, Mark R. 2001. *Dry Bones Rattling: Community Building to Revitalize American Democracy*. Princeton, N.J.: Princeton University Press.

Wasserman, Stanley, and Katherine Faust. 1994. *Social Network Analysis: Methods and Applications*. Cambridge: Cambridge University Press.

Watkins, Susan Cotts. 1991. *From Provinces into Nations: Demographic Integration in Western Europe, 1870–1960*. Princeton, N.J.: Princeton University Press.

Weber, Eugen. 1976. *Peasants into Frenchmen: The Modernization of Rural France, 1870–1914*. Stanford, Calif.: Stanford University Press.

Weber, Max. 1920. "Die protestantischen Sekten und der Geist der Kapitalismus." In *Gesammelte Aufsätze zur Religionssoziologi*, 1. Tubingen: Mohr.

———. 1930. *The Protestant Ethic and the Spirit of Capitalism*. Trans. Talcott Parsons. New York: Harper Collins.

———. 1946a. *From Max Weber: Essays in Sociology*. Ed. Hans H. Gerth and C. Wright Mills. New York: Oxford University Press.

———. 1946b. "Religious Rejections of the World and Their Directions." Pp. 323–359 in *From Max Weber: Essays in Sociology*. Ed. Hans H. Gerth and C. Wright Mills. New York: Oxford University Press.

———. 1946c. "Science as a Vocation." Pp. 129–158 in *From Max Weber: Essays in Sociology*. Ed. Hans H. Gerth and C. Wright Mills. New York: Oxford University Press.

———. 1946d. "The Social Psychology of the World Religions." Pp. 267–301 in *From Max Weber: Essays in Sociology*. Ed. Hans H. Gerth and C. Wright Mills. New York: Oxford University Press.

———. 1949. " 'Objectivity' in Social Science and Social Policy." In *The Methodology of the Social Sciences*. Ed. Edward A. Shils and Henry A. Finch. New York: Free Press.

———. 1958. *The Protestant Ethic and the Spirit of Capitalism*. New York: Charles Scribner's Sons.

———. 1963. *Sociology of Religion*. Boston: Beacon Press.

———. 1964. *Wirtschaft und Gesellschaft*, 4th ed. Cologne: Kiepenheurer and Witsch.

———. 1976. *The Protestant Ethic and the Spirit of Capitalism*. Trans. R. I. Frank. London: Verso.

———. 1978 [1922]. *Economy and Society*, 2 vols. Ed. Guenther Roth and Claus Wittich. Berkeley: University of California Press.

———. 1981. *General Economic History*. Trans. Frank Knight. New Brunswick, N.J.: Transaction Books.

———. 1982. *Die protestantische Ethik II*. Gütersloh: Gerd Mohn.

———. 1988. *The Agrarian Sociology of Ancient Civilizations*. Trans. R. I. Frank. London and New York: Verso.

———. 1998 [1920]. *The Protestant Ethic and the Spirit of Capitalism*. Los Angeles: Roxbury.

———. 2002a. *The Protestant Ethic and the Spirit of Capitalism*. Trans. Stephen Kalberg. Los Angeles: Roxbury.

——. 2002b. *The Protestant Ethic and the "Spirit" of Capitalism and Other Writings*. Trans. Peter Baehr and Gordon C. Wells. London: Penguin.

Webley, Paul, and R. Wilson. 1989. "Social Relationships and the Unacceptability of Money as a Gift." *Journal of Social Psychology* 129:85–91.

Weiman, David F., and Richard C. Levin. 1994. "Preying for Monopoly? The Case of Southern Bell Telephone Company, 1894–1912." *Journal of Political Economy* 102:103–126.

Weiner, Amir. 2001. *Making Sense of War: The Second World War and the Fate of the Bolshevik Revolution*. Princeton, N.J.: Princeton University Press.

Weingast, Barry. 1983. "The Congressional-Bureaucratic System: A Principal-Agent Perspective." *Public Choice* 44:147–192.

Weir, Margaret. 1992. *Politics and Jobs: The Boundaries of Employment Policy in the United States*. Princeton, N.J.: Princeton University Press.

Weir, Margaret, and Theda Skocpol. 1985. "State Structures and the Possibilities for 'Keynesian' Responses to the Great Depression in Sweden, Britain, and the United States." Pp. 107–168 in *Bringing the State Back In*. Ed. Peter B. Evans, Dietrich Rueschemeyer, and Theda Skocpol. New York: Cambridge University Press.

Weir, Margaret, Ann Shola Orloff, and Theda Skocpol, eds. 1988. *The Politics of Social Policy in the United States*. Princeton, N.J.: Princeton University Press.

Weller, Robert P. 1994. "Cultural Legacies and Development: A View from East Asia." Pp. 309–317 in *Transition to Capitalism? The Communist Legacy in Eastern Europe*. Ed. János Mátyás Kovács. New Brunswick, N.J.: Transaction Publishers.

Wellman, Barry. 1988. "Structural Analysis: From Method and Metaphor to Theory and Substance." Pp. 19–61 in *Social Structures: A Network Approach*. Ed. Barry Wellman and S. D. Berkowitz. Cambridge: Cambridge University Press.

Wennemo, Irene. 1994. *Sharing the Costs of Children: Studies on the Development of Family Support in the OECD Countries*. Stockholm: Swedish Institute for Social Research. Dissertation Series 25.

Wernick, Andrew. 1991. *Promotional Culture: Advertising, Ideology, and Symbolic Expression*. London: Sage.

West, Lois, ed. 1997. *Feminist Nationalism*. New York: Routledge.

Westney, D. Eleanor. 1987. *Imitation and Innovation: The Transfer of Western Organizational Patterns to Meiji Japan*. Cambridge, Mass.: Harvard University Press.

White, Harrison C. 1963. *An Anatomy of Kinship: Mathematical Models for Structures of Cumulated Roles*. Englewood Cliffs, N.J.: Prentice Hall.

——. 1992. *Identity and Control: A Structural Theory of Social Action*. Princeton, N.J.: Princeton University Press.

White, Harrison C., Scott A. Boorman, and Ronald L. Breiger. 1976. "Social Structure from Multiple Networks. I. Blockmodels of Roles and Positions." *American Journal of Sociology* 81:730–780.

White, Hayden. 1973. *Metahistory: The Historical Imagination in Nineteenth-Century Europe*. Baltimore: Johns Hopkins University Press.

——. 1987. *The Content of the Form*. Baltimore: Johns Hopkins University Press.

Whyte, M. K. 1996. "The Chinese Family and Economic Development: Obstacle or Engine?" *Economic Development and Cultural Change* 45:1–30.

Wickham-Crowley, Timothy P. 1992. *Guerrillas and Revolution in Latin America: A Comparative Study of Insurgents and Regimes since 1956*. Princeton, N.J.: Princeton University Press.

Wilensky, Harold L. 1964. "The Professionalization of Everyone?" *American Journal of Sociology* 70:137–158.

——. 2002. *Rich Democracies: Political Economy, Public Policy, and Performance*. Berkeley: University of California Press.

Williams, Eric. 1964. *Capitalism and Slavery*. London: Andre Deutsch.

Williams, Fiona. 1995. "Race/Ethnicity, Gender and Class in Welfare States: A Framework for Comparative Analysis." *Social Politics* 2:27–59.

Williams, George Washington. 1882. *A History of the Negro Race in America from 1619–1880*. New York: Ayer.

Williams, Raymond. 1975. *The Country and the City*. New York: Oxford University Press.

———. 1976. *Keywords: A Vocabulary of Culture and Society*. New York: Oxford University Press.

Williams, Rosalind H. 1982. *Dream Worlds: Mass Consumption in Late Nineteenth-Century France*. Berkeley: University of California Press.

Williamson, John B., and Fred Pampel. 1993. *Old-Age Security in Comparative Perspective*. New York: Oxford University Press.

Williamson, Oliver E. 1985. *The Economic Institutions of Capitalism*. New York: Free Press.

Willis, Paul. 1977. *Learning to Labor*. New York: Columbia University Press.

Wilson, A. N. 1999. *God's Funeral*. New York: Ballantine.

Wilson, Bryan. 1967. *Religion in Secular Society: A Sociological Comment*. London: Heinemann.

Wilson, John T. 1983. *Academic Science, Higher Education, and the Federal Government, 1950–1983*. Chicago: University of Chicago Press.

Winant, Howard. 2002. *The World Is a Ghetto*. New York: Routledge.

Winter, Jay. 1995. *Sites of Memory, Sites of Mourning: The Great War in European Cultural History*. Cambridge: Cambridge University Press.

Winter, Jay, and Emmanuel Sivan, eds. 1999. *War and Remembrance in the Twentieth Century*. Cambridge: Cambridge University Press.

Witz, Anne. 1992. *Professions and Patriarchy*. New York: Routledge.

Wolf, Eric. 1982. *Europe and the People without History*. Berkeley: University of California Press.

Wolfe, A. 1989. *Whose Keeper? Social Science and Moral Obligation*. Berkeley: University of California Press.

Wölfflin, Heinrich. 1950. *Principles of Art History: The Problem of the Development of Style in Later Art*. New York: Dover.

Wolin, S. S. 1960. *Politics and Vision: Continuity and Innovation in Western Political Thought*. Boston: Little Brown.

Wong, R. Bin. 1997. *China Transformed: Historical Change and the Limits of European Experience*. Ithaca, N.Y.: Cornell University Press.

Woo, Jung-En. 1991. *Race to the Swift: State and Finance in Korean Industrialization*. New York: Columbia University Press.

Woo, Wing Thye, Stephen Parker, and Jeffrey D. Sachs, eds. 1997. *Economies in Transition: Comparing Asia and Eastern Europe*. Cambridge, Mass.: MIT Press.

Wood, Ellen Meiksins. 1991. *The Pristine Culture of Capitalism: A Historical Essay on Old Regimes and Modern States*. London: Verso.

———. 1999. *The Origin of Capitalism*. New York: Monthly Review Press.

Wood, Richard L. 2002. *Faith in Action: Religion, Race, and Democratic Organizing in America*. Chicago: University of Chicago Press.

Woodiwiss, Anthony. 2001. *The Visual in Social Theory*. London: Athlone Press.

Woodruff, David. 1999. "Barter of the Bankrupt: The Politics of Demonetization in Russia's Federal State." Pp. 83–124 in *Uncertain Transition: Ethnographies of Change in the Postsocialist World*. Ed. Michael Burawoy and Katherine Verdery. Lanham, Md.: Rowman and Littlefield.

Woods, James D. 1993. *The Corporate Closet: The Professional Lives of Gay Men in America*. New York: Free Press.

World Bank. 2000. *East Asia: Recovery and Beyond*. Washington, D.C.: World Bank.

Wright, Erik Olin. 1994. *Interrogating Inequality*. London: Verso.

Wright, Erik Olin, and Luca Perrone. 1977. "Marxist Class Categories and Income Inequality." *American Sociological Review* 42:32–55.

Wright, Erik Olin, Cynthia Costello, David Hachen, and Joey Sprague. 1982. "The American Class Structure." *American Sociological Review* 47:709–726.

Wu, Lawrence. 2000. "Some Comments on Sequence Analysis and Optimal Matching Methods in Sociology: Review and Prospect." *Sociological Methods and Research* 29:41–64.

Wuthnow, Robert. 1988. *The Restructuring of American Religion: Society and Faith since World War II.* Princeton, N.J.: Princeton University Press.

——. 1989. *Communities of Discourse: Ideology and Social Structure in the Reformation, the Enlightenment, and European Socialism.* Cambridge, Mass.: Harvard University Press.

Yakubovich, Valery, Mark Granovetter, and Patrick McGuire. 2000. "Electrical Charges: The Social Construction of Rate Systems." Unpublished manuscript.

Yates, JoAnne. 1989. *Control through Communication: The Rise of System in American Management.* Baltimore: Johns Hopkins University Press.

Yengoyan, Aram A. Forthcoming. "Comparison and Its Discontents." In *Festschrift for Raymond Grew.* Ed. Aram Yengoyan. Ann Arbor: University of Michigan Press.

Yinger, Milton J. 1957. *Religion, Society, and the Individual.* New York: Macmillan.

Young, I. M. 1990. *Justice and the Politics of Difference.* Princeton, N.J.: Princeton University Press.

——. 2000. *Inclusion and Democracy.* Oxford: Oxford University Press.

Young, Michael. 2002. "Confessional Protest: The Religious Birth of U.S. National Social Movements." *American Sociological Review* 67 (October): 660–688.

Young, Robert J. C. 1990. *White Mythologies: Writing History and the West.* London: Routledge.

——. 1995. *Colonial Desire: Hybridity in Theory, Culture and Race.* London: Routledge.

——. 2001. *Postcolonialism: An Historical Introduction.* Cambridge, Mass.: Blackwell.

Yuval-Davis, Nira. 1997. *Gender and Nation.* London: Sage.

Zakaria, Fareed. 1998. *From Wealth to Power: The Unusual Origins of America's World Role.* Princeton, N.J.: Princeton University Press.

Zald, Mayer N. 1996. "More Fragmentation? Unfinished Business in Linking the Social Sciences and the Humanities." *Administrative Science Quarterly* 41 (2): 251–261.

Zanden, Jan Luiten van. 2000. "The Great Convergence from a West-European Perspective." *Itinerario* 24 (3/4): 9–28.

Zaret, David. 1980a. "From Max Weber to Parsons and Schutz: The Eclipse of History in Modern Social Theory." *American Journal of Sociology* 85:1180–1201.

——. 1980b. "Ideology and Organization in Puritanism." *Archives Europeenes de Sociologie* 21 (1):83–115.

——. 1985. *The Heavenly Contract: Ideology and Organization in Pre-Revolutionary Puritanism.* Chicago: University of Chicago Press.

Zeitlin, Jonathan, and Charles F. Sabel. 1985. "Historical Alternatives to Mass Production." *Past and Present* 108:133–176.

Zeitlin, Maurice. 1984. *The Civil Wars in Chile, or, the Bourgeois Revolutions That Never Were.* Princeton, N.J.: Princeton University Press.

Zelizer, Viviana A. 1979. *Morals and Markets: The Development of Life Insurance in the United States.* New York: Columbia University Press.

——. 1985. *Pricing the Priceless Child: The Changing Social Value of Children.* New York: Basic Books.

——. 1994. *The Social Meaning of Money: Pin Money, Paychecks, Poor Relief, and Other Currencies.* New York: Basic Books.

Zerilli, Linda. 1994. *Signifying Woman: Culture and Chaos in Rousseau, Burke, and Mill.* Ithaca, N.Y.: Cornell University Press.

Zerubavel, Eviatar. 1982. "The Standardization of Time: A Sociohistorical Perspective." *American Journal of Sociology* 88:1–23.

——. 2003. *Time Maps, Collective Memory and the Social Shape of the Past.* Chicago: University of Chicago Press.

Žižek, Slavoj. 1989. *The Sublime Object of Ideology*. New York: Verso.

Znaniecki, Florian. 1952. *Modern Nationalities*. Urbana: University of Illinois Press.

Zubrzycki, Geneviève. 2001. " 'We the Polish Nation': Ethnic and Civic Visions of Nationhood." *Theory and Society* 30 (5): 629–668.

Zuckerman, Ezra W. 1999. "The Categorical Imperative: Securities Analysts and the Illegitimacy Discount." *American Journal of Sociology* 104:1398–1438.

Zuckerman, Harriet A., and Robert K. Merton. 1973. "Age, Aging, and Age Structure in Science." In *The Sociology of Science*. Ed. Robert K. Merton. Chicago: University of Chicago Press.

Zürcher, Erik. 1993. *Turkey: A Modern History*. London: I. B. Tauris.

Contributors

JULIA ADAMS is Professor in Sociology at Yale University. Her principal scholarly interests revolve around the formation of states and nations, colonialism and empire, gender and sexuality, family, and early modern European politics. Her new book, *The Familial State: Ruling Families and Merchant Capitalism in Early Modern Europe*, is forthcoming in 2005.

JUSTIN BAER is Research Analyst at the American Institutes for Research in Washington, D.C. He has investigated the structure of networks among technology organizations, and his research currently focuses on issues related to education and transportation policy.

RICHARD BIERNACKI is Associate Professor of Sociology at the University of California, San Diego. In *The Fabrication of Labor: Germany and Britain, 1640–1914* (1995), he compares the influence of culture on the execution of factory manufacture. His interests are theory, comparative method, and the historical invention of key forms of cultural practice in Europe.

ROGERS BRUBAKER is Professor of Sociology at the University of California, Los Angeles. His books include *Citizenship and Nationhood in France and Germany* (1992), *Nationalism Reframed* (1996), and *Ethnicity without Groups* (2004). He is currently completing a book on the relationship between nationalist politics and the everyday experience of ethnicity in a Transylvanian town.

BRUCE G. CARRUTHERS is Professor of Sociology at Northwestern University. His research in the areas of historical sociology, economic sociology, political sociology, and the sociology of law has generated many publications, including *City of Capital: Politics and Markets in the English Financial Revolution* (1996), *Rescuing Business: The Making of Corporate Bankruptcy Law in England and the United States* (1998), and *Economy/Society: Markets, Meanings and Social Structure* (2000).

ELISABETH S. CLEMENS is Associate Professor of Sociology at the University of Chicago. Building on organizational theory and political sociology, her research has addressed the role of social movements and voluntary organizations in processes of institutional change. Her publications include *The People's Lobby: Organizational Innovation and the Rise of Interest Group Politics in the United States, 1890–1925* (1997) and a co-edited volume, *Private Action and the Public Good* (with Walter W. Powell, 1998).

REBECCA JEAN EMIGH is Associate Professor of Sociology at the University of California, Los Angeles. She has published numerous articles from a long-standing project on agriculture and the origins of capitalism in Tuscany during the fifteenth century. She has also collaborated on a major study of the transition from socialism in contemporary Eastern Europe.

RUSSELL FAEGES teaches social theory, nationalism, and the sociology of time at the University of Notre Dame. Trained in political science, he has written on the methodology of definition, nationalism, and social theory in both political science and sociology.

PHILIP S. GORSKI is Professor of Sociology and Director of the Max and Marianne Weber Center at the University of Wisconsin and Adjunct Professor of Sociology and Director of the Center for Comparative Social Analysis at Yale University. His research focuses on the relationship between religion and politics, particularly in early modern Europe. His most recent book, *The Disciplinary Revolution* (2003), looks at the relationship among confessionalization, social disciplining, and the growth of state power in seventeenth- and eighteenth-century Europe. He has also developed a strong interest in contemporary religion.

ROGER V. GOULD was Professor of Sociology at Yale University at the time of his death. He had published important studies in historical sociology and social theory, including *Insurgent Identities: Class, Community, and Protest in Paris from 1848 to the Commune* (1995) and *Collision of Wills: How Ambiguity about Social Rank Breeds Conflict* (2003).

MEYER KESTNBAUM is Associate Professor of Sociology at the University of Maryland. His interests span the sociological study of the military, history, and technology. His recent work has been on the sociology of war, military conscription, citizenship and military mobilization, and the social impact of the Internet.

EDGAR KISER is Professor of Sociology at the University of Washington. He has published widely in comparative-historical sociology, with particular attention to bureaucratization and war making. He is also the author of major theoretical arguments that explore the contributions of rational choice theory to historical explanation, including "The Role of General Theory in Comparative-Historical Sociology" (*American Journal of Sociology*, 1991).

MING-CHENG M. LO is Associate Professor of Sociology at the University of California, Davis. Working in the areas of professions, social movements, and political and comparative historical sociology, she has recently published *Doctors within Borders: Profession, Ethnicity, and Modernity in Colonial Taiwan* (2002).

ZINE MAGUBANE is Associate Professor of Sociology at the University of Illinois and specializes in historical sociology and African studies. Her recent book, *Bringing the Empire Home: Race, Class, and Gender in Britain and Colonial South Africa* (2003), traces colonial images of blackness from South Africa to England and back again to explore how stereotypes were used to justify both new capitalist class and gender hierarchies in England and the subhuman treatment of Blacks in South Africa.

ANN SHOLA ORLOFF is Professor of Sociology at Northwestern University. Her research has focused on states, politics, and gender, particularly in the social policies of the developed world. She is the author of *States, Markets, Families: Gender, Liberalism and Social Policy in Australia, Canada, Great Britain and the United States* (with Julia O'Connor and Sheila Shaver; 1999) and *The Politics of Pensions: A Comparative Analysis of Canada, Great Britain and the United States* (1993). She is co-editor and founder of *Social Politics: International Studies in Gender, State and Society*.

NADER SOHRABI is Assistant Professor in the Department of Middle East and Asian Languages and Cultures at Columbia University. Trained in sociology, his research interests include the comparative study of state formation, nationalism, and revolution in the Middle East, with emphasis on the Ottoman Empire and Iran. He has published various articles on the constitutional revolutions of the early 20th century that emphasize their similarity by highlighting their distinctive temporality, and explore differences by emphasizing their unique political cultures and modes of operation of agency.

MARGARET R. SOMERS is Associate Professor in Sociology at the University of Michigan, with research interests in political sociology, law, citizenship, economic sociology, and social and political theory. Her articles on the sociology of knowledge and historical sociology, including "We're No

Angels" (*American Journal of Sociology*, 1998), have been influential contributions to debates over historical inquiry in the social sciences.

LYN SPILLMAN is Associate Professor of Sociology at the University of Notre Dame. Her research interests are grounded in cultural and comparative-historical sociology and extend to political and economic sociology and social therapy. She is the author of *Nation and Commemoration: Creating National Identities in the United States and Australia* (1997) and a number of articles on cultural theory and national identity, as well as editor of *Cultural Sociology* (2002). Her current project examines culture in economic action.

GEORGE STEINMETZ is Professor of Sociology and Germanic Languages and Literatures at the University of Michigan. Following his study of the welfare state in *Regulating the Social: The Welfare State and Local Politics in Imperial Germany* (1993), he edited *State/Culture: State Formation after the Cultural Turn* (1999). His forthcoming books are *The Politics of Method in the Human Sciences: Positivism and Its Epistemological Others* (Duke University Press) and *The Devil's Handwriting: Precoloniality, Ethnography, and Native Policy in the German Overseas Empire* (Duke University Press).

Index

Abbott, Andrew, 19 n.40

Absolutism, 18

Action, 28, 31, 37–38, 70, 75, 77–78, 80–81, 85, 87–88, 90, 156, 227, 476, 502–504, 509–510

Actor, 3, 32, 53, 69, 215, 230, 322, 335, 340, 351, 430, 472, 502, 505–506, 515. *See also* Market actors; Rational action; Utilitarian: model of action

Africa, 92–93, 97–103, 108, 512

Agency, 32, 62, 66, 69, 81, 227, 230, 236, 238, 297, 301, 307–308, 319, 321, 327, 329, 386–387, 391, 401–402, 406, 444, 448, 463, 494, 501–509, 514 n.22

Agency theory, 64, 226, 228, 234 n.12, 245; and second-wave scholarship, 22, 46, 48

Agriculture, 368, 370, 372

AIDS activists, 400, 402

American Journal of Sociology, 20 n.41, 30, 120, 126, 166

American Sociological Association, 19 n.40, 30, 149

American Sociological Review, 20 n.41, 30, 118, 120, 126, 137, 166

American Sociological Society, 121

Anderson, Perry, 18, 163–164, 185

Annales School, 6, 19

Anthropology, 7, 11–12, 39, 122, 143, 147, 161, 249, 334, 357, 410, 415–416, 472

Anti-essentialism, 49

Anti-statism, 456, 461

Area studies, 130, 131, 416

Army. *See* Military

Art, 249, 493–494

Asia, 93–94, 103, 108, 201

Associations, 281–282, 468, 479

Authority, 122, 229, 261, 422–425, 435, 455; political, 411, 423, 436, 445; professional, 399–401

Autonomy, 17, 47, 84, 486; of professionals, 383, 389–390; of the state, 17, 206, 208, 414–415, 496

Behavior, 148, 156, 353

Behaviorist psychology, 76, 122 n.15, 129, 134. *See also* Psychology

Belgium, 307

Bendix, Reinhard, 422–424, 442, 460

Bookkeeping, 41, 350

Boundaries, 41, 45, 399, 471, 511

Bourdieu, Pierre, 38 n.83, 40, 90, 111 n.1, 122–123, 125, 501

Britain, 95, 99, 108, 178, 196–197, 213 n.16, 233, 239–243, 343, 347–348, 356–358, 363–364, 366, 368–370, 373, 403, 427, 453–455

Brubaker, Rogers, 431–432

Bureaucracy, 22, 194, 225–245, 310–314

Bureaucratization, 36, 52, 70, 108, 338, 360, 386, 390

Calhoun, Craig, 7, 10

Capital, 183, 191, 203, 383, 501; and Max Weber, 94–96, 182–184, 333, 362; and second wave scholarship, 18, 21–22, 46, 66, 153, 155, 209, 500, 508, 511

I know I said I wanted to but what have I done?

Julia Adams is a professor of sociology at Yale University.
Elisabeth S. Clemens is an associate professor of sociology at the
University of Chicago.
Ann Shola Orloff is a professor of sociology at Northwestern
University.

LIBRARY OF CONGRESS CATALOGING-IN-PUBLICATION DATA

Remaking modernity : politics, history, and sociology / Julia Adams,
Elisabeth Clemens, and Ann Shola Orloff, editors.
p. cm. — (Politics, history, and culture)
Includes bibliographical references and index.
ISBN 0-8223-3352-X (cloth : alk. paper) — ISBN 0-8223-3363-5 (pbk. :
alk. paper)
1. Historical sociology. 2. Social change. 3. Poststructuralism.
I. Adams, Julia. II. Clemens, Elisabeth Stephanie. Orloff, Ann Shola.
IV. Series.
HM487.R46 2004
301′.09—dc22   2004011855

Make the state the factor of cohesion in historical sociology

the state is the modern factor of cohesion

this cohesion can be present in a strong society, as in the case of liberalism, in which case the state does not need to actively manage I·E·M power sources.

the state can also be the factor of cohesion in a weak society, as in the case of fascism or state socialism, in which case there are relatively few traditions effectively managing I·E·M power sources. In this case the society has become vulnerable to a strong state. the strong state's innovations will always be more ~~violent~~ violent than those of the weak state. In liberal societies, recognition of the strong state's violence leads to anti-statist ideologies.

this liberal anti-statism ~~~~ has the potential to protect ppl from violence, but it must be expanded to realize its full potential first, anti-statists must ~~~~ consider the ways that civil society can strengthen itself, and by so doing protect society from needing statism so much. second, anti-statists must recognize that ~~~~ instances of weak societies have purely internal causes. nations exist in conditions of economic and geo-political competition. competition produces winners and losers, the winners will tend to win strong societies, and the losers will tend to see their societies laid to waste. adding insult to injury, the winners will preach to

society. The effective autonomy of state elites may indeed be the source of public benefit, but the interstices are the source of innovation. Establish[ed] power tends to ~~also~~ be doctrinaire. The interstices are the realm of common sense and practicality. Interstitial innovations ~~stand~~ stand to empower society, in a particular way. They offer it new forms of infrastructural power.

rise ~~to~~ monopoly ~~and~~ and modernizing authoritarianism
use adams, nasir or fascist

the losers, explaining that they, too, could enjoy the fruits of peace and prosperity if only they cast off their statist interventions and grew strong societies. but many of these weak societies were previously stronger, and their decline was caused by the ascendancy of the victors. the preaching does not win many converts (though it is effective in creating enemies).
when the preaching does not work, strong societies resort to the violence of the victors. in this event, the ~~strong~~ victors promise peace and prosperity to those countries that accept their loaned support. of course, there is interest on the loan. and, of course, the weak societies are allowed no state interventions to nurture home industries until they are ready for int'l competition. without any protections for home grown economic institutions, the inhabitants of weak societies must sell the

only good today possess themselves.

the state is the factor of cohesion in the new his soc
but the state is not the solution to social problems, but rather
their cause.

peace - prosperity - freedom - sustainability

work with the Bourdieusian notion of symbolic violence
how can it be ~~supplemented~~ complemented to account for classist laws,
development policies (instrumental violence), physical
force (physical violence)
violence is often associated with anger and irrationality.
but it is essential to recognize the ~~system~~ of violence.

every political theorist since weber has tried
in vain to divorce the state from violence. they
have failed because the state is violent
in its nature.
it is a source of
confusion that state employees sometimes do use violence
in anger or irrationally. these notable incidents conceal
the ~~system~~ of violence that is in place

critique the preposterous theories of the state that
emerged out of the 1990s globalization fever
but note that in spite of their falsity, the state need
not operate at the level of the nation-state. it
is known by many names: empire, EU, citystate, etc

In contrast, Mann's work at first strikes many readers, who are accustomed to empirical microscopy, as hopelessly overreaching. Like Foucault, however, Mann is hesitant to make sweeping pronouncements summarizing his findings or advocating policy goals. Mann's work first appears to bear the risk of old-fashioned modernist hubris (e.g. ethnocentrism, imperialism), but those who engage with it often find the opposite, finding it to lie in the direction of timidity ~~either ~~ and the commonplace, or else in the defeated ~~~~ obscurantism.

But Mann is neither a hubristic modernist nor a timid / obscure overreacher. Rather, he, like ~~Foucault,~~ communicates much with what goes unsaid. Mann's work is a history of the present. ~~~~

The predicaments of our time cannot be solved with new totalizing utopian ideologies, whether of socialism, the caliphate, Christian conservatism, or laissez-faire. Rather, the biggest thinker in historical sociology sees the beauty of thinking small or in their. If social actors can avoid the hubris that leads to ethnic cleansing, fascism, and imperialism, then genuine progress is possible. This progress will be humble. It will emerge interstitially.

The interstices are the source not only of emergencies that can cause the downfall of regimes, but also the source of new ideas that can improve the lives of people throughout